T0088190

GIANT BOOK OF GAMES AND PUZZLES FOR SMART KIDS

GIANT BOOK OF GAMES AND PUZZLES FOR SMART KIDS

MORE THAN 1000 FUN AND EDUCATIONAL ACTIVITIES

DIEGO JOURDAN PEREIRA

FOR YOUNG READERS

DEDICATED TO THE MEMORY OF JASON SCOTT SCHNEIDER (1975-2019).

COPYRIGHT © 2019 BY DIEGO JOURDAN PEREIRA

ALL RIGHTS RESERVED. NO PART OF THIS BOOK MAY BE REPRODUCED IN ANY MANNER WITHOUT THE EXPRESS WRITTEN CONSENT OF THE PUBLISHER, EXCEPT IN THE CASE OF BRIEF EXCERPTS IN CRITICAL REVIEWS OR ARTICLES. ALL INQUIRIES SHOULD BE ADDRESSED TO RACEHORSE FOR YOUNG READERS, 307 WEST 36TH STREET, 11TH FLOOR, NEW YORK, NY 10018.

RACEHORSE FOR YOUNG READERS BOOKS MAY BE PURCHASED IN BULK AT SPECIAL DISCOUNTS FOR SALES PROMOTION, CORPORATE GIFTS, FUND-RAISING, OR EDUCATIONAL PURPOSES. SPECIAL EDITIONS CAN ALSO BE CREATED TO SPECIFICATIONS. FOR DETAILS, CONTACT THE SPECIAL SALES DEPARTMENT, SKYHORSE PUBLISHING, 307 WEST 36TH STREET, 11TH FLOOR, NEW YORK, NY 10018 OR INFO@SKYHORSEPUBLISHING.COM.

RACEHORSE FOR YOUNG READERS™ IS A PENDING TRADEMARK OF SKYHORSE PUBLISHING, INC.®, A DELAWARE CORPORATION.

VISIT OUR WEBSITE AT WWW.SKYHORSEPUBLISHING.COM.

10 9 8 7 6 5 4 3 2

LIBRARY OF CONGRESS CATALOGING-IN-PUBLICATION DATA IS AVAILABLE ON FILE.

COVER DESIGN BY DIEGO JOURDAN PEREIRA
COVER AND INTERIOR ARTWORK BY DIEGO JOURDAN PEREIRA
"10CENT COMICS" AND "GRAVESIDE" FONTS DESIGNED BY NATE PIEKOS. USED UNDER LICENSE.

ISBN: 978-1-63158-329-2

PRINTED IN CHINA

LEVEL
1

THE POOR ZEBRA GOT SCARED AND LOST HER STRIPES!
CAN YOU DRAW THEM?

WHAT ABOUT THE TIGER'S?

COLOR THEM BOTH!

COLOR THE CUTE CATERPILLAR.
REPEAT THE THREE PATTERNS.
AND FINISH DRAWING HER BODY!

1 = GREEN AND 2 = BLUE

WHAT ANIMAL IS IT?

HOW MANY WATERLILIES DO YOU COUNT?

HOW MANY LEAPS DOES THE FROG NEED TO CATCH THE FLY?

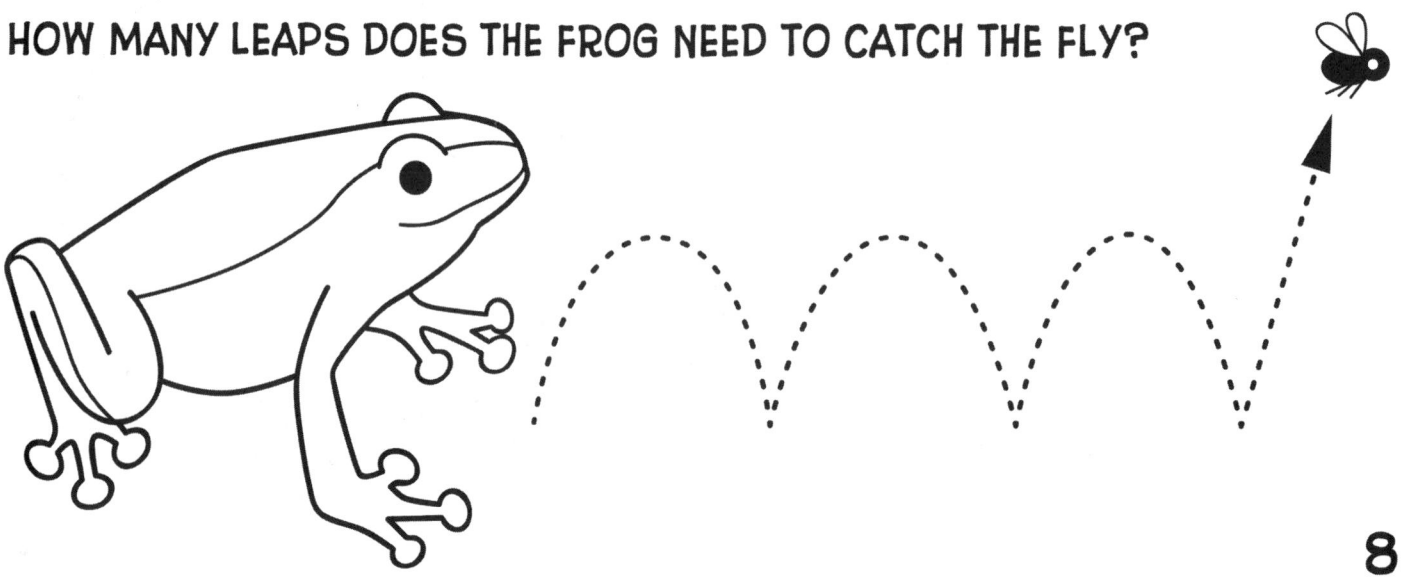

FILL EACH FISH WITH A DIFFERENT PATTERN.

HOW MANY FISH DO YOU COUNT?

DECORATE AND COLOR THE SEASHELLS TOO!

COLOR THE INSECTS IN EACH GROUP.
THEN COUNT THEM, AND COLOR THE RIGHT NUMBER.

HOW MANY ANTS DO YOU COUNT?

1 2 3 4

HOW MANY LADYBUGS?

1 2 3 4

HOW MANY BEES?

1 2 3 4

COLOR THE FOODS YOU HAVE EATEN.

WHICH TEDDY BEAR DOES NOT LOOK LIKE THE OTHERS?

WHAT IS THIS?
WHERE DOES IT LIVE?

COLOR IT!

TURN THESE CIRCLES INTO FUN STUFF AND COLOR THEM ALL!

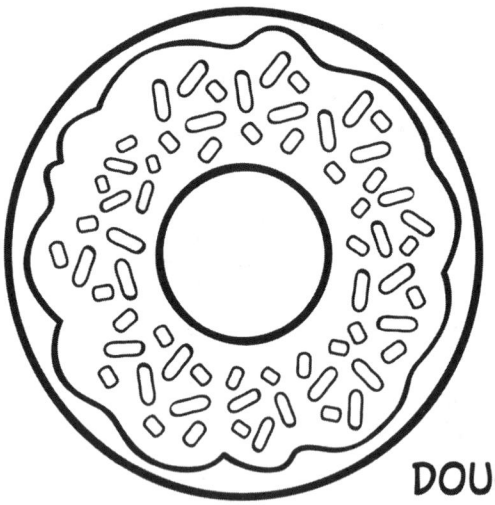

DOUGHNUT.

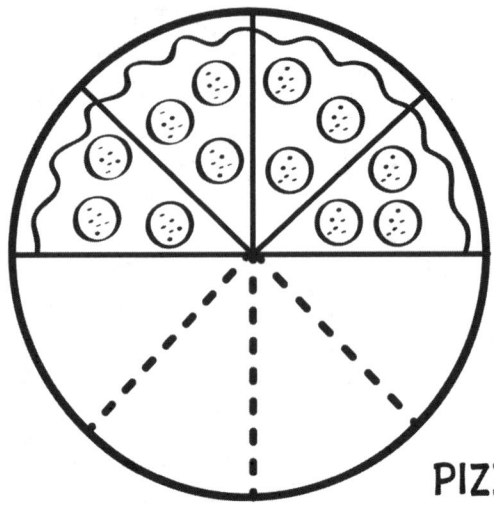

PIZZA.

BASKETBALL.

TIRE.

PUMPKIN.

PLANET.

IF THE CABBAGE IS ALL GREEN, WHAT COLORS IS THE CARROT?

DECORATE THE GHOST'S SHEET TO MAKE HIM HAPPY!

COUNT AND COLOR THE STARS YOU SEE.

TRACE THE DOTS TO DRAW THE WATER THE ELEPHANT IS SPRAYING.

COLOR THIS RUBBER DUCK YELLOW!

CONNECT EACH ANIMAL TO THE NOISE IT MAKES.

DRAW THE MYSTERIOUS TREASURE
HIDDEN UNDERGROUND.
WHAT ELSE CAN BE FOUND BELOW? DRAW IT!

DRAW A TREAT TO FEED THE CAT.

HOW MANY APPLES DO YOU COUNT?

COLOR THE BIG ONES RED, THE SMALL ONES GREEN, AND THE REST YELLOW.

DRAW A HAPPY FACE, A SAD FACE, AND AN ANGRY FACE.

WHICH PUPPY DOES NOT LOOK LIKE THE OTHERS?

DECORATE THE BUTTERFLY WINGS AND COLOR THEM.

CONNECT THE DOTS TO COMPLETE THIS VERY TALL ANIMAL.

WHAT IS IT CALLED?

COLOR HER SPOTS!

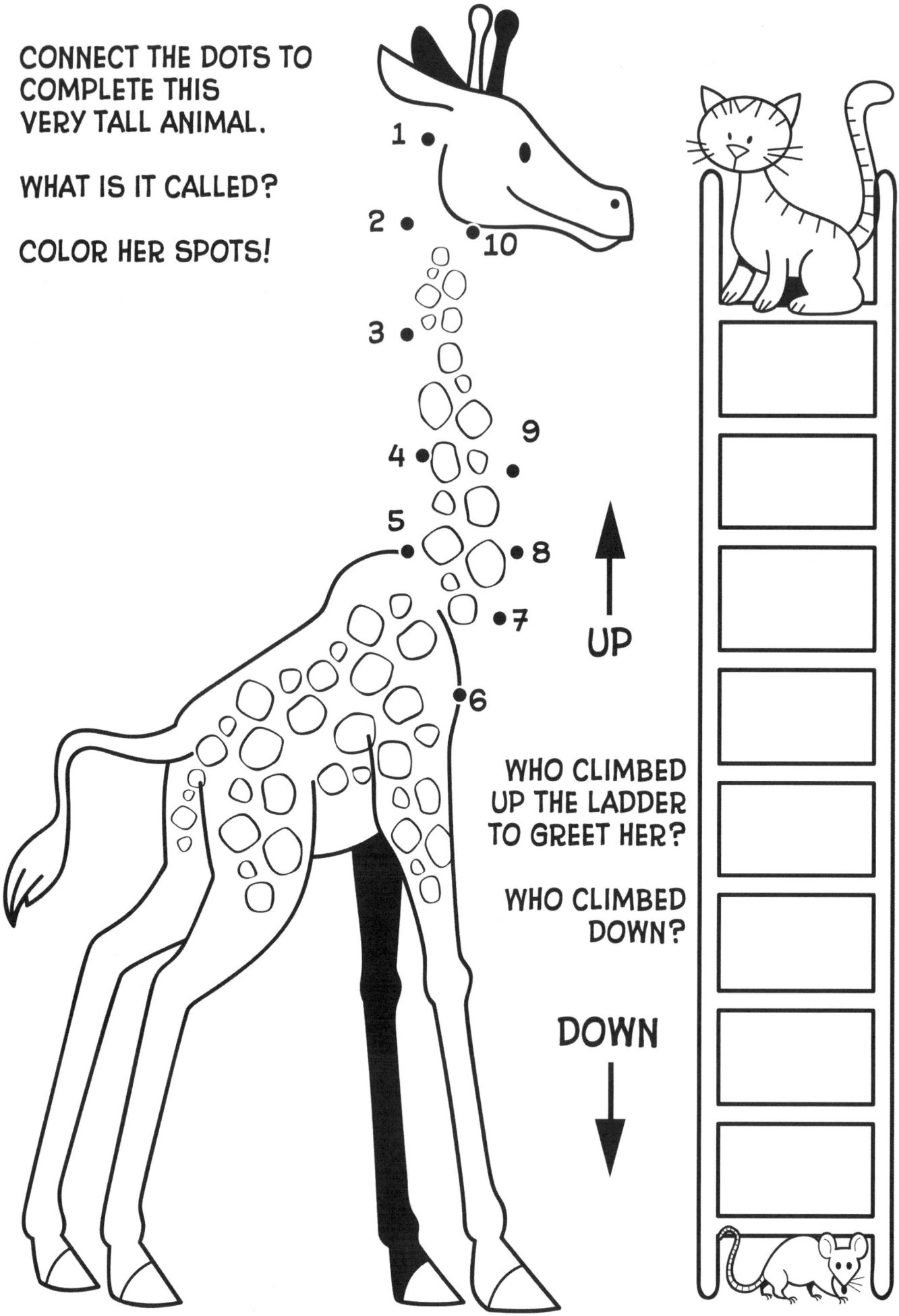

WHO CLIMBED UP THE LADDER TO GREET HER?

WHO CLIMBED DOWN?

DRAW THE LIONS' MANE –
ONE STRAIGHT AND THE OTHER CURLY.

DRAW TWO MORE LIONS
WITH DIFFERENT MANES.

1 = BLUE , 2 = GREEN, AND 3 = BROWN

WHAT IS IT?

WHICH PATH WILL TAKE THE BUNNY TO THE EASTER EGG?

CONNECT THE DOTS TO DRAW THE ROCKET,
THEN DRAW THE ASTRONAUT LOOKING OUT THE WINDOW
AND COLOR EVERYTHING!

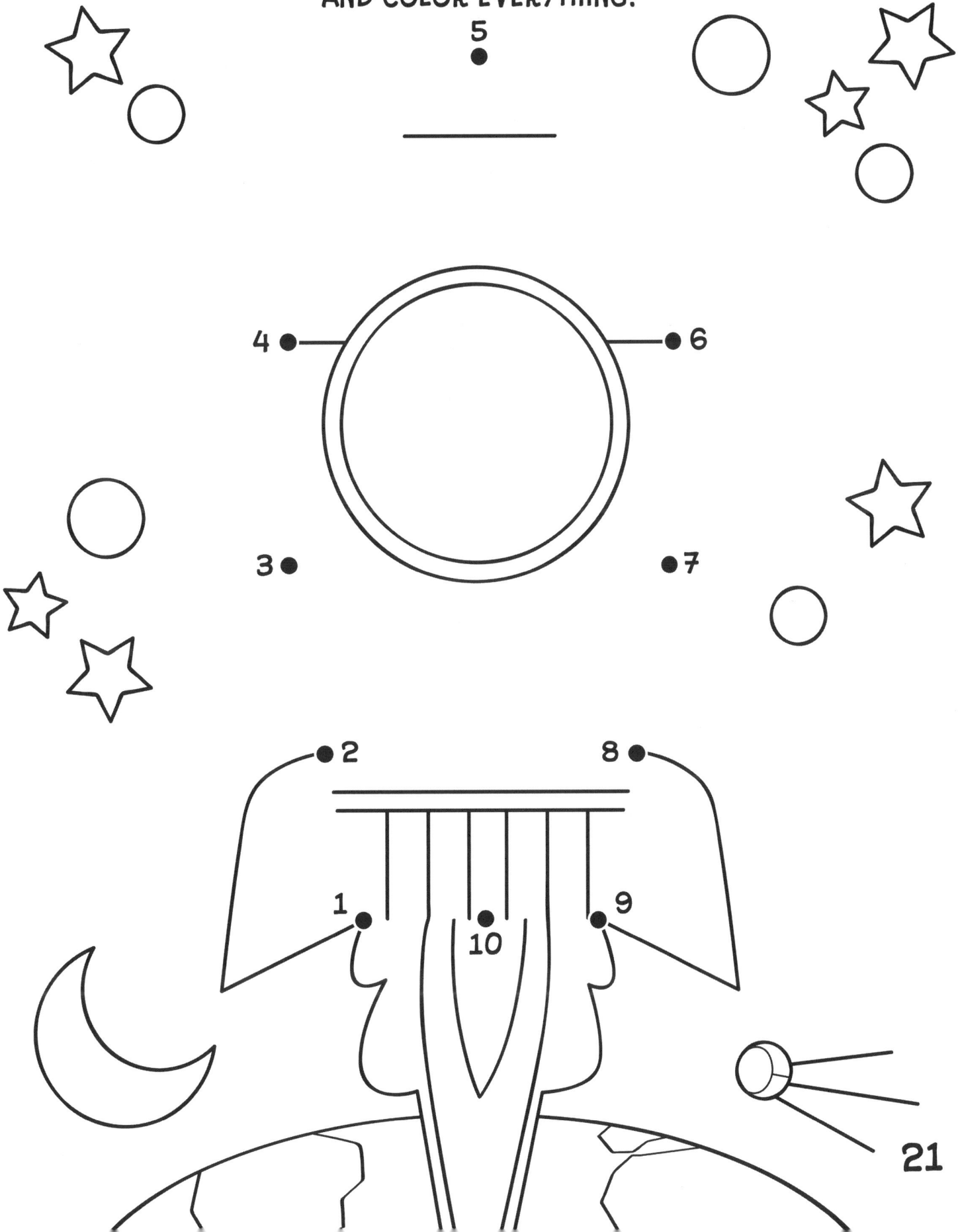

WHAT ANIMAL IS THIS?

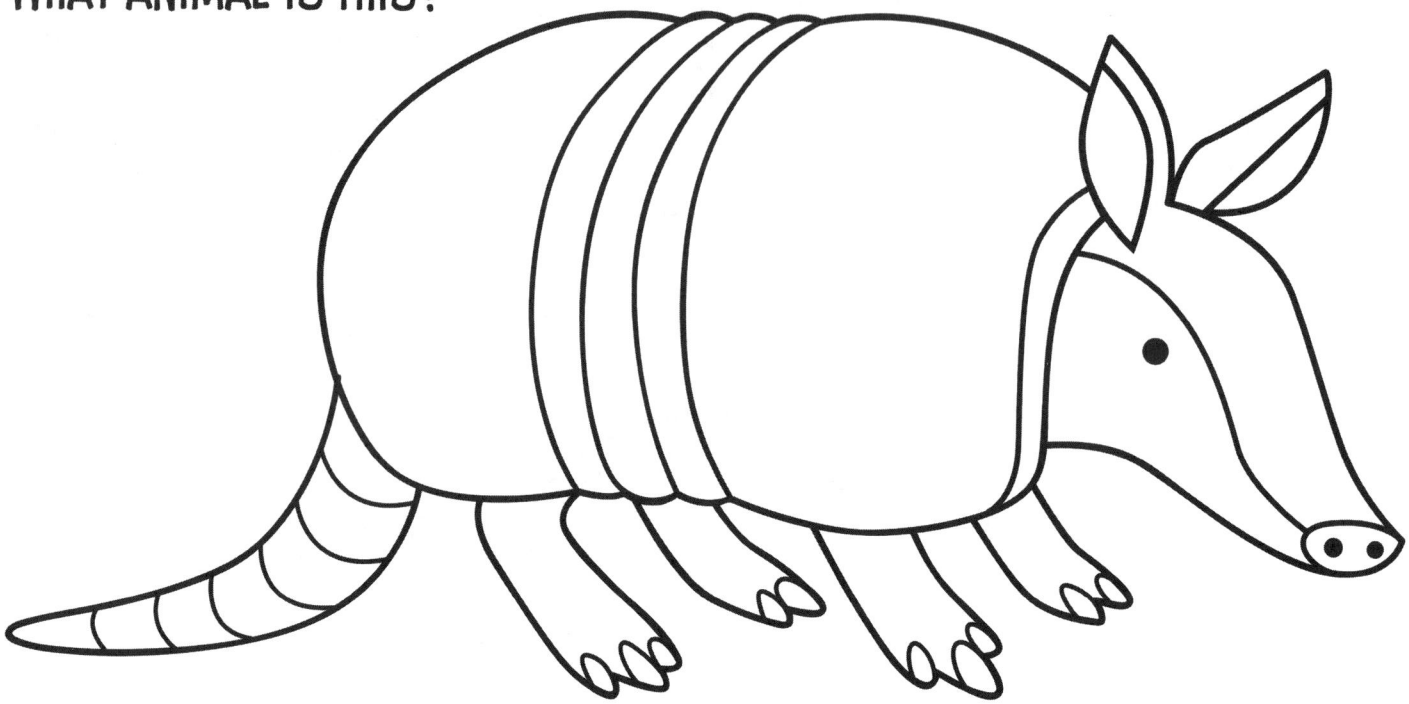

TRACE THE DOTTED LINE TO HELP THE LITTLE HUMMINGBIRD REACH THE FLOWER.

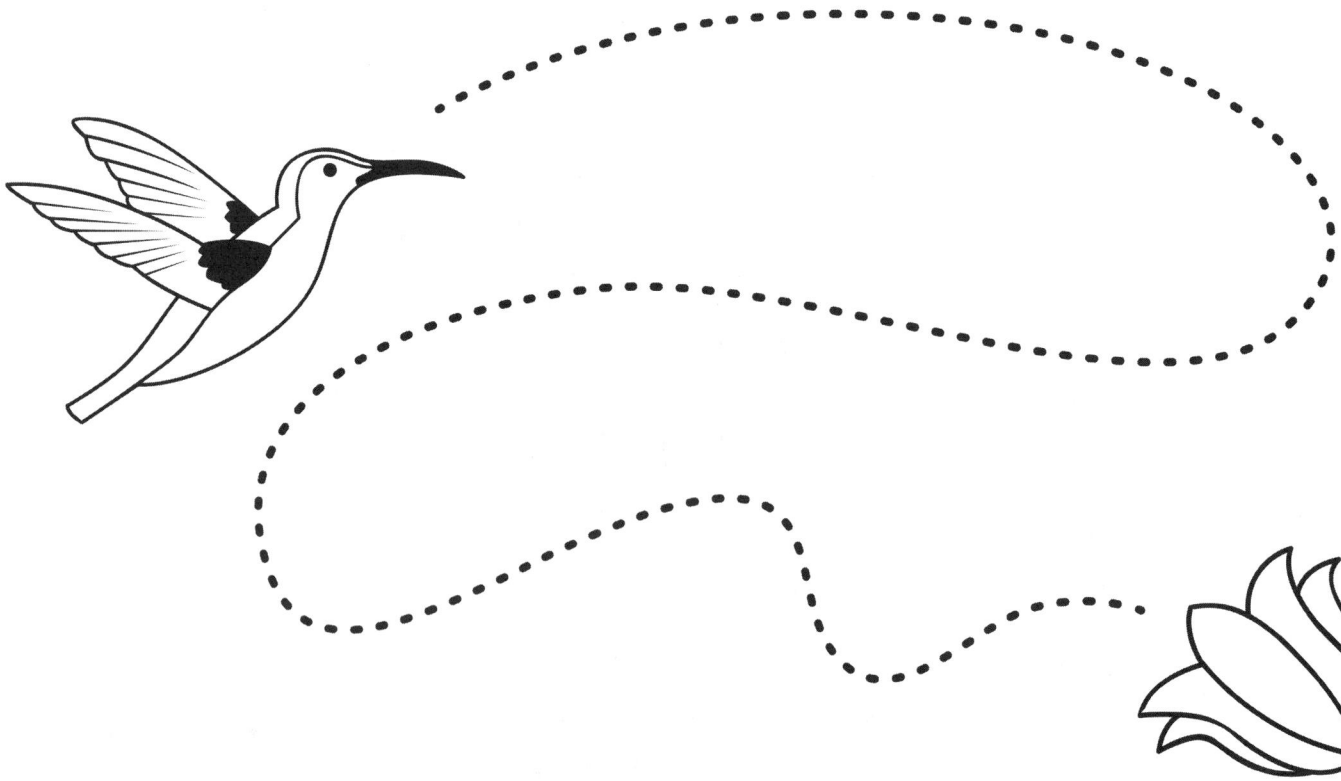

COLOR THE FRUITS IN EACH GROUP.
COUNT THEM AND COLOR THE RIGHT NUMBER.

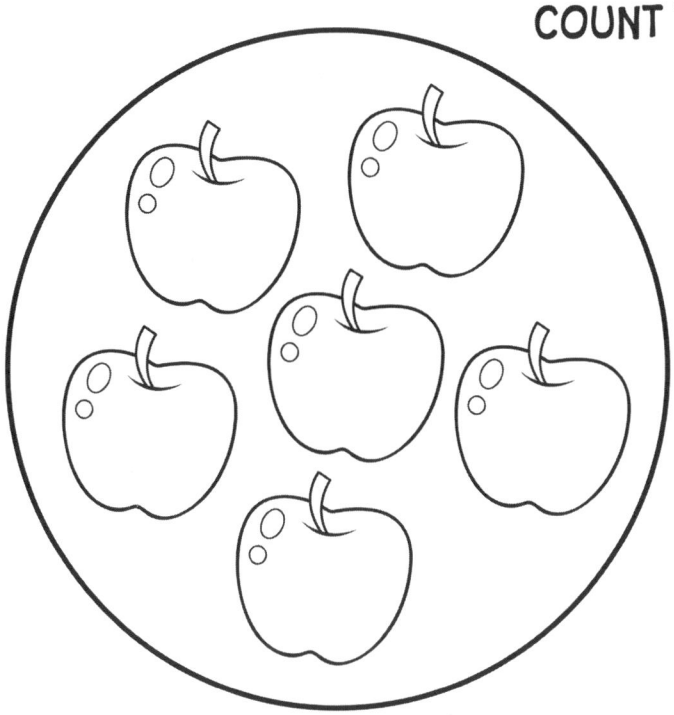

HOW MANY APPLES DO YOU COUNT?

1 2 3 4
5 6 7 8

HOW MANY BANANAS DO YOU COUNT?

1 2 3 4
5 6 7 8

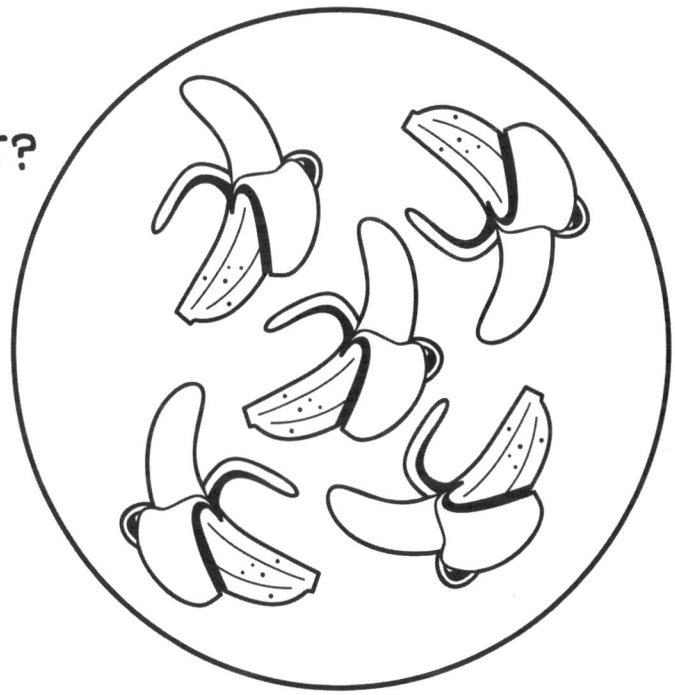

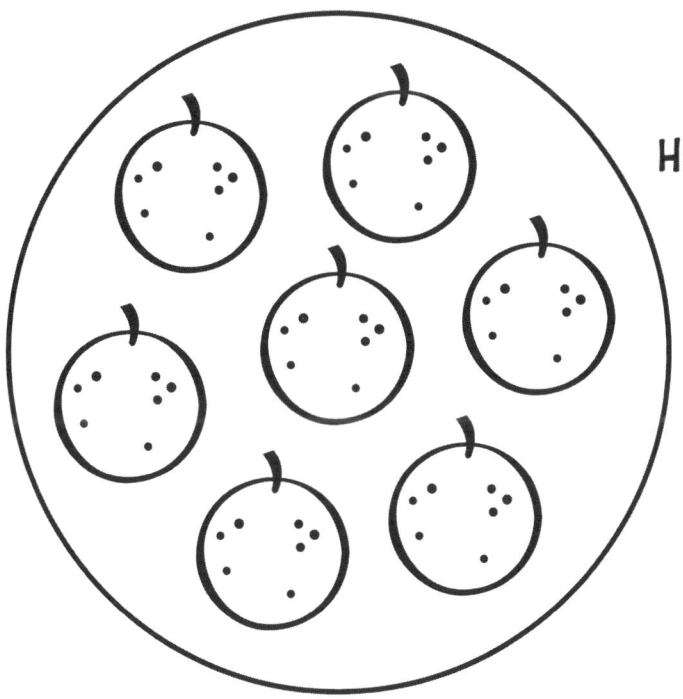

HOW MANY ORANGES DO YOU COUNT?

1 2 3 4
5 6 7 8

COLOR AND NAME EACH FRUIT.

DRAW THE COINS INSIDE THE PURSE.

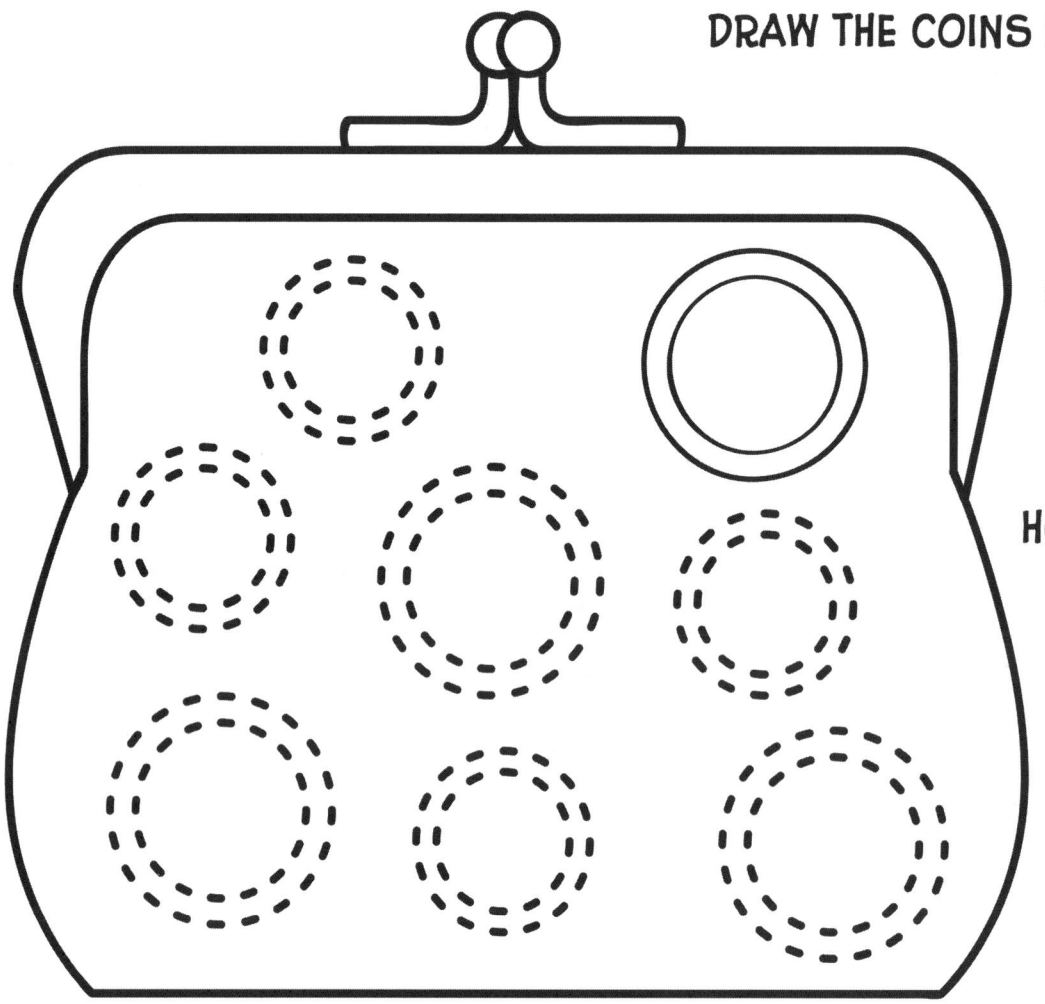

COLOR THE SMALL ONES RED, AND THE BIG ONES YELLOW.

HOW MANY OF EACH DO YOU COUNT? HOW MANY IN TOTAL?

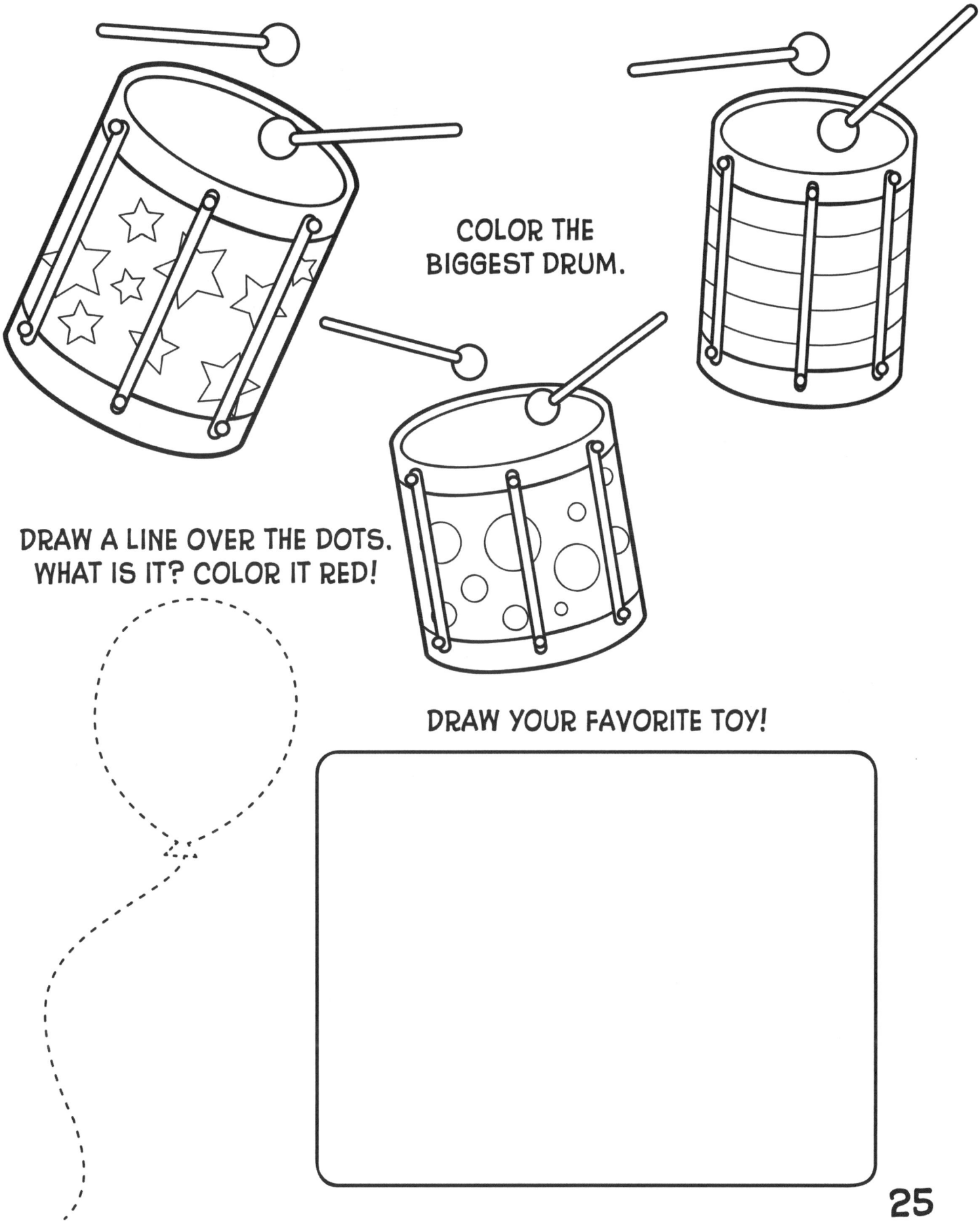

COLOR THE BIGGEST DRUM.

DRAW A LINE OVER THE DOTS. WHAT IS IT? COLOR IT RED!

DRAW YOUR FAVORITE TOY!

WHAT ANIMAL IS THIS?
CAN YOU COLOR IT?

ONE OF THE CREATURES ON THE RIGHT
IS HIDING FROM THE CAT.

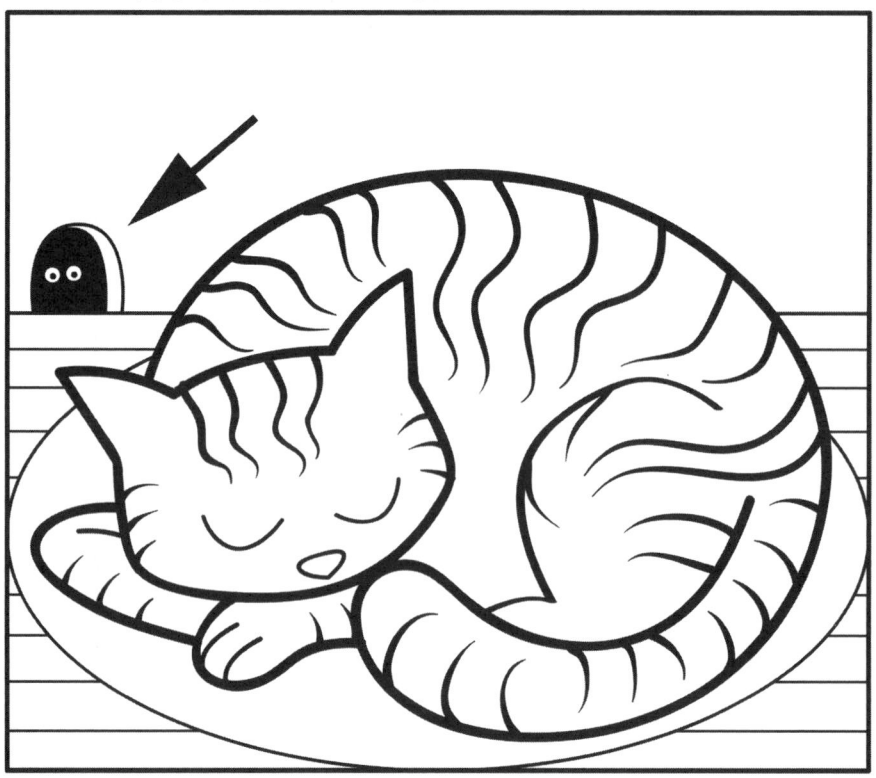

WHICH ONE IS IT?

FILL THIS PAGE WITH THE DOG'S MUD PRINTS!

DRAW FOUR RAISINS ON TOP OF THE ROLL AND THEN COLOR THE CUP.

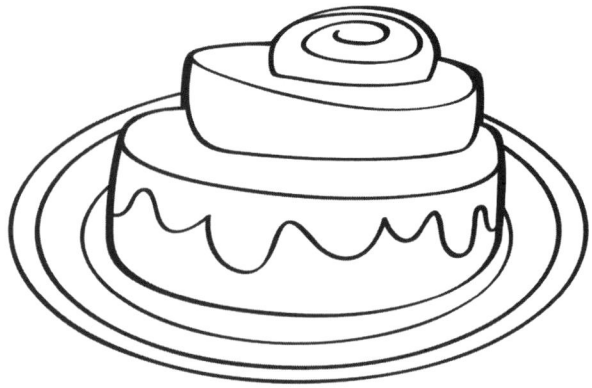

FILL THE HEDGEHOG'S BACK WITH SPINES
AND DRAW ANOTHER ONE JUST LIKE IT.

WHICH PENGUIN DOES NOT LOOK LIKE THE OTHERS?

TRACE THE DOTS TO DRAW THE SAIL AND THE FLAG.
WHAT SHOULD BILLY USE AS BAIT TO CATCH FISH?
DRAW THE MISSING FISHING LINE.
COLOR ALL SIMILAR FISH THE SAME. HOW MANY OF EACH GROUP CAN YOU COUNT?
DRAW THE BAIT!
ONE OF THEM IS MISSING! WHERE IS IT?
WHAT KIND OF FISH IS THIS?

FIND THE MISSING PIECE.

DRAW MOMMA GOOSE AND BABY GEESE OVER THE DOTS WITHOUT LIFTING YOUR HAND.

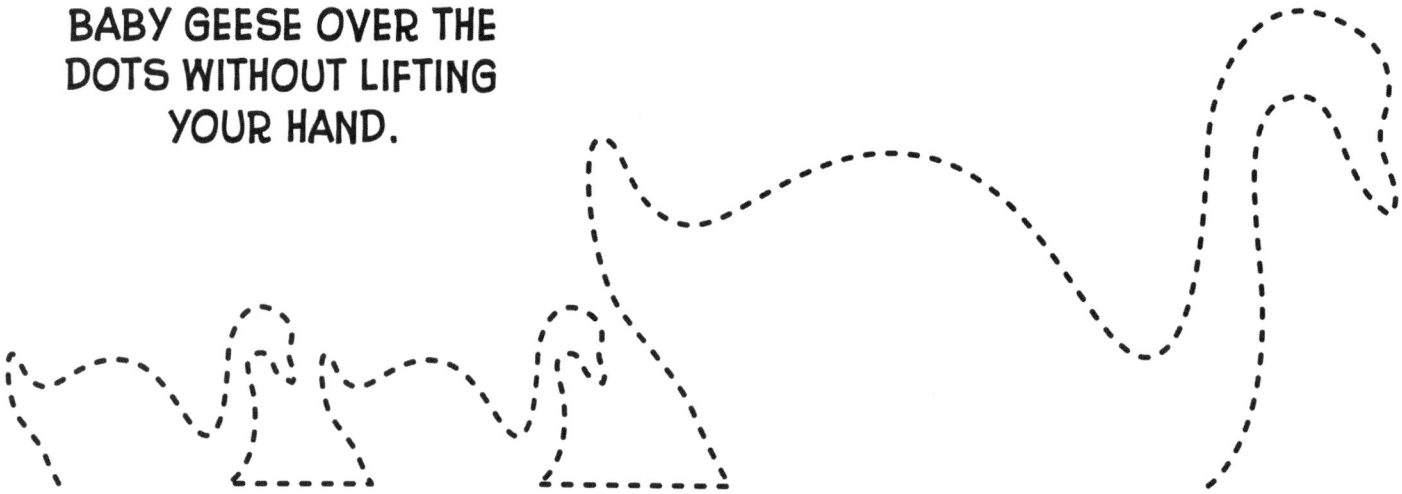

DECORATE AND COLOR THIS SET OF NESTING DOLLS.

A WHOLE LOT OF HATS! CAN YOU GUESS THEIR NAMES?

C F B F T

DRAW THREE SCOOPS OF ICE CREAM ON THE FIRST CONE, TWO ON THE SECOND ONE, AND ONE ON THE THIRD ONE. COLOR EACH LIKE YOUR FAVORITE FLAVORS!

WHICH ONES ARE NOT FRUITS?

WRITE THE NUMBERS MISSING ON THE CARS.
COLOR ONE LOCOMOTIVE RED
AND THE OTHER GREEN.

DRAW THE SPOTS
MISSING FROM THIS COW!

HOW MANY CUBES
CAN YOU COUNT?
WHICH TOWER IS THE TALLEST?

COLOR ALL HEARTS RED,
ALL STARS YELLOW,
ALL WATER DROPS BLUE,
AND ALL LEAVES GREEN.

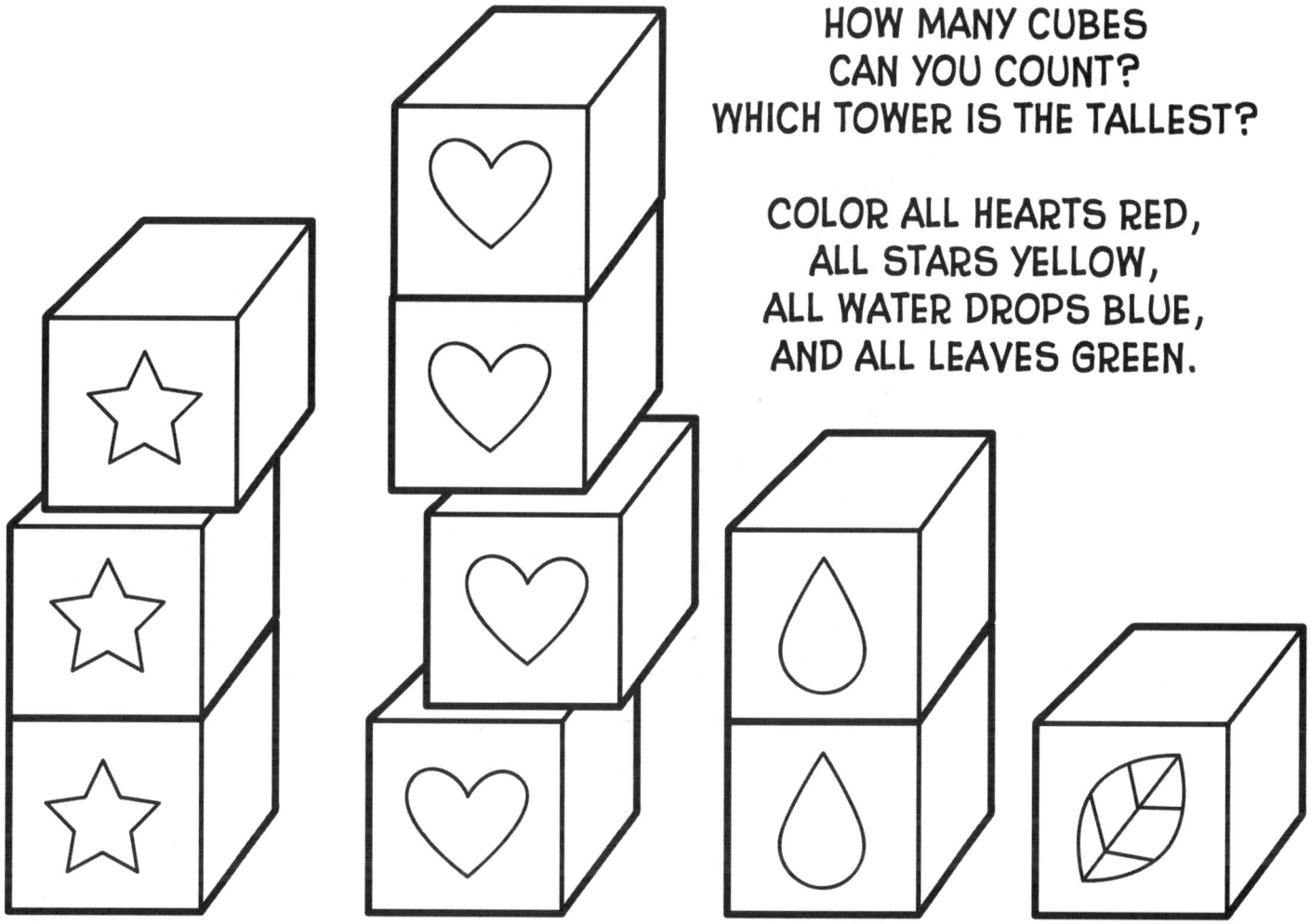

WHICH OF THESE ANIMALS STANDS
ON ONLY TWO LEGS?

WHAT ANIMAL IS THIS?
WHERE DOES IT LIVE?

CAN YOU DRAW THE SPIRAL ON THE LOLLIPOP, TRACING THE DOTS FROM THE STAR AT THE CENTER ALL THE WAY OUT?

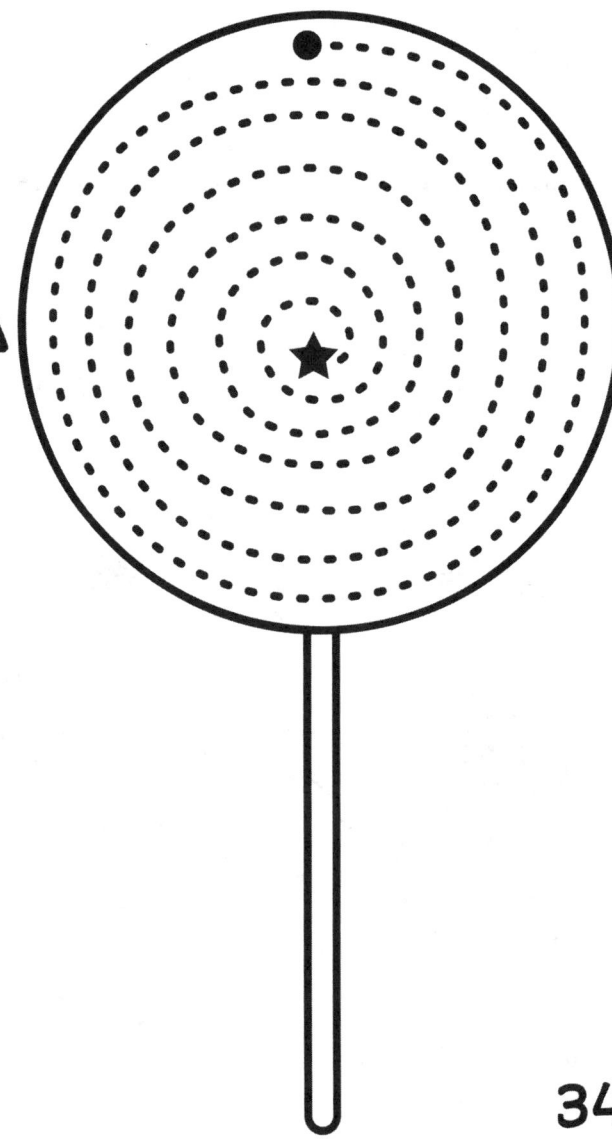

DECORATE AND COLOR THE GIFT WRAPPING!

WHAT DOES THE MOUSE EAT?

DRAW YOUR MOM'S PORTRAIT.

DRAW YOUR DAD'S PORTRAIT.

HOW MANY TIMES DID THE RABBIT LEAP TO GET THE CARROT?

FIND THE MATCHING SAILBOATS AND COLOR THEM ALIKE!

COMPLETE THE PATTERN FROM LEFT TO RIGHT.

COLOR EACH SHAPE A DIFFERENT COLOR.

FIND THE IDENTICAL TWIN BIRDS.

HELP MINDY GET HOME BY TRACING THE SUN'S DOTTED LINES YELLOW, AND THE CAR'S RED. COLOR THE WHOLE SCENE.

HOW MANY BALLOONS DO YOU SEE? COLOR THEM RED!

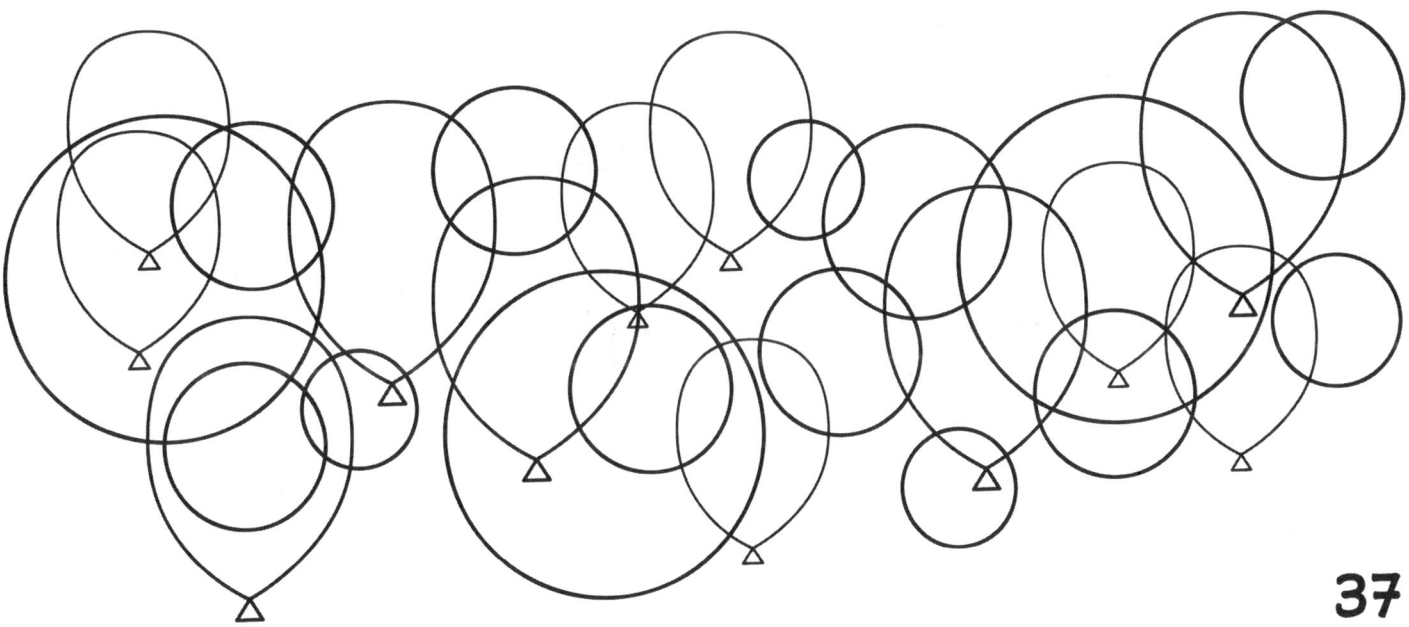

CONNECT THE DOTS TO FIND OUT WHAT CREATURE THIS IS.
WHERE DOES IT LIVE?

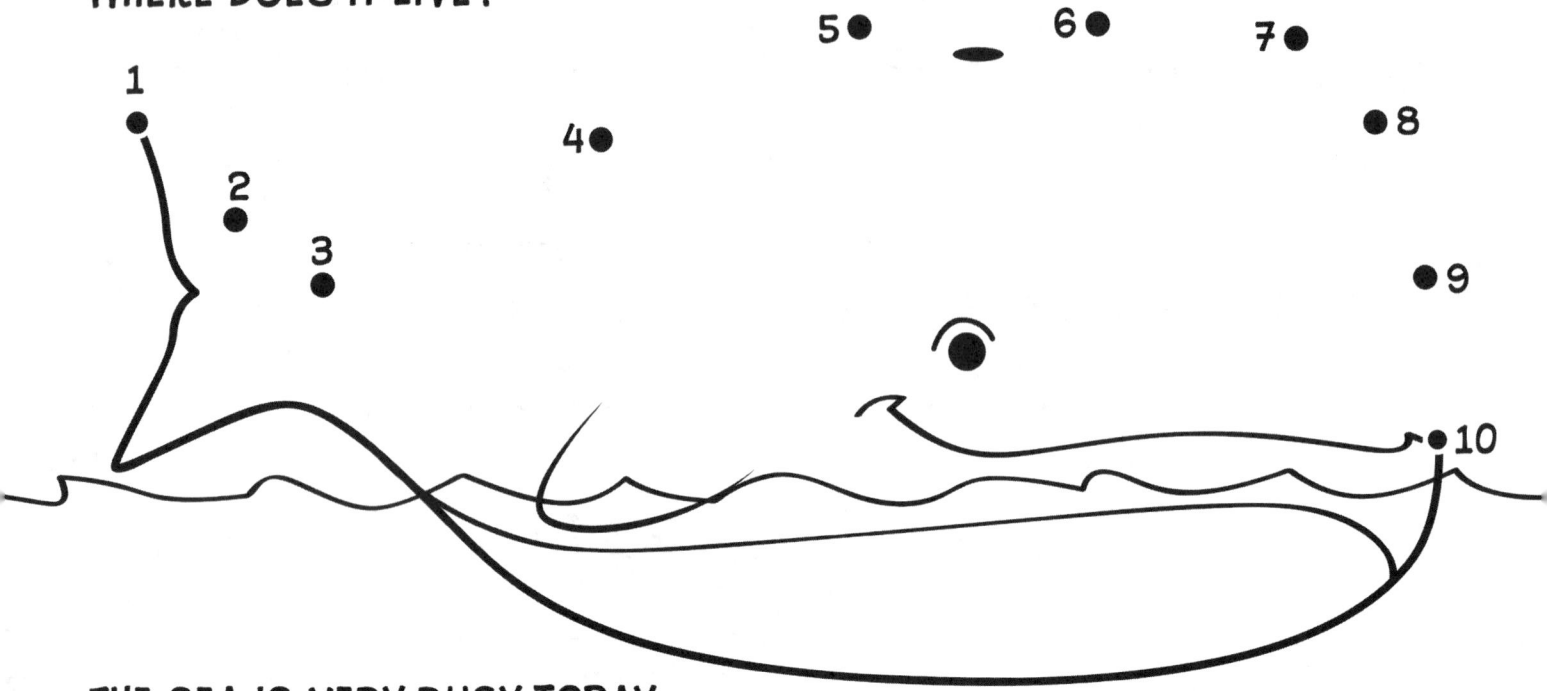

THE SEA IS VERY BUSY TODAY.
DRAW CIRCLES AROUND THE FISH.

WHAT IS NOT POSSIBLE
IN THIS PICTURE?
COLOR EVERYTHING BUT!

THERE'S AN INTRUDER AND THE BEES ARE SLEEPING!
CAN YOU DRAW THE ONES MISSING FROM THE HIVE AND WAKE THEM UP?
CAN YOU COUNT THEM ALL? WHERE IS THE QUEEN?

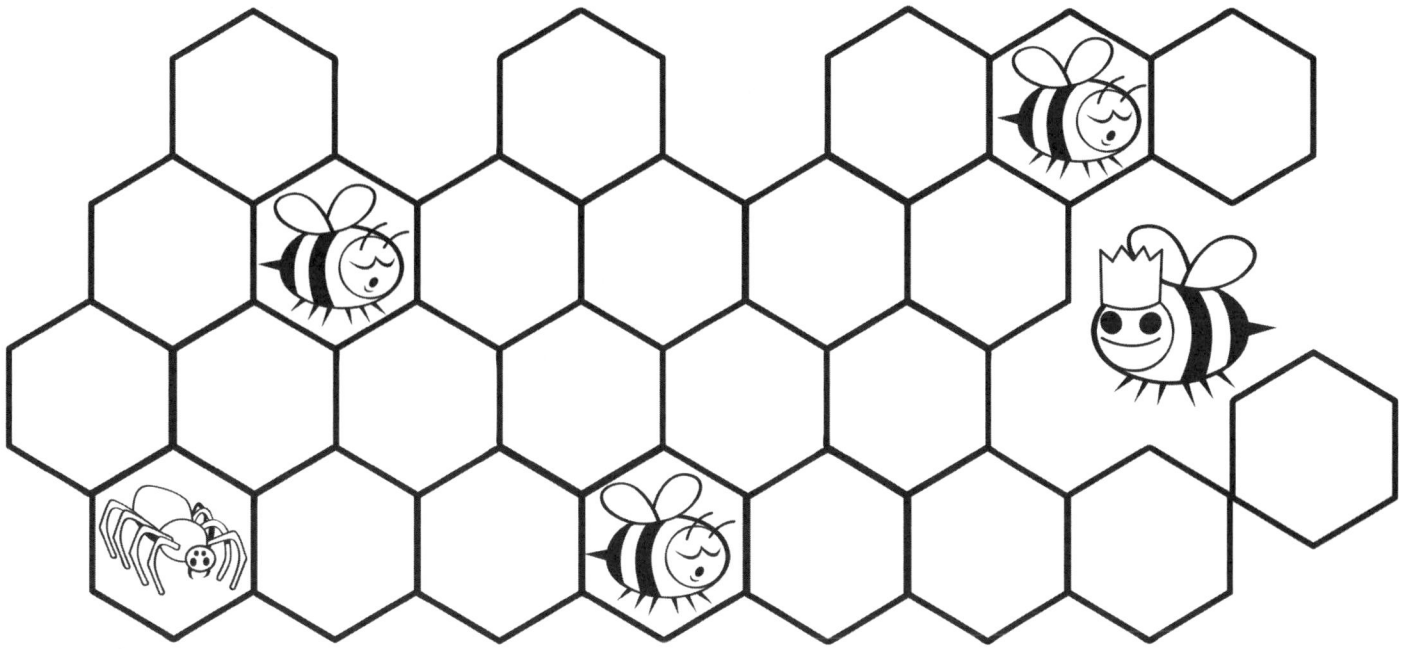

GIVE NUMBERS TO THE BIRDS FROM THE SMALLEST (1)
TO THE BIGGEST (4) IN REAL LIFE.

WHAT IS THE NAME OF THIS ANIMAL?
WHERE DOES IT LIVE?

FILL THIS PAGE WITH BLUE BUBBLES!

WHAT ARE BUBBLES MADE OF?
UNSCRAMBLE THE LETTERS TO FIND OUT!

COLOR THE SQUIRRELS BROWN AND THE HEDGEHOGS GRAY.
HOW MANY OF EACH DO YOU COUNT?

WHAT HUNGRY ANIMAL IS THIS?
CONNECT THE DOTS TO FIND OUT AND COLOR IT.

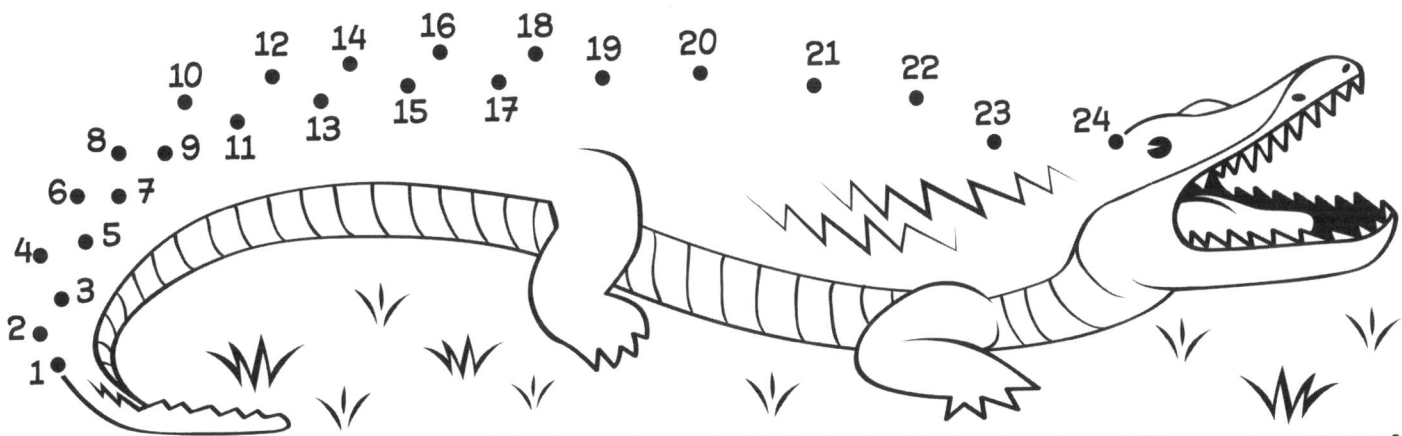

FINISH DRAWING THE SCALES ON ITS BACK TOO!

WHICH BUNNY DOES NOT LOOK LIKE THE OTHERS?

HELP JIMMY FIND HIS SNEAKERS
BY COLORING THEM BLUE!

COLOR THE COWBOY BOOTS BROWN,
THE HIGH HEELS RED,
AND THE REST AS YOU WISH!

DRAW THE GARDEN SNAIL'S SHELL BY TRACING THE DOTTED LINE.
WHAT DOES IT EAT?

GUIDE THE PLANE THROUGH THE CLOUDS
SO IT LANDS SAFELY!

1 = BROWN
2 = BLUE
3 = GREEN
4 = YELLOW

WHAT ANIMAL IS IT?

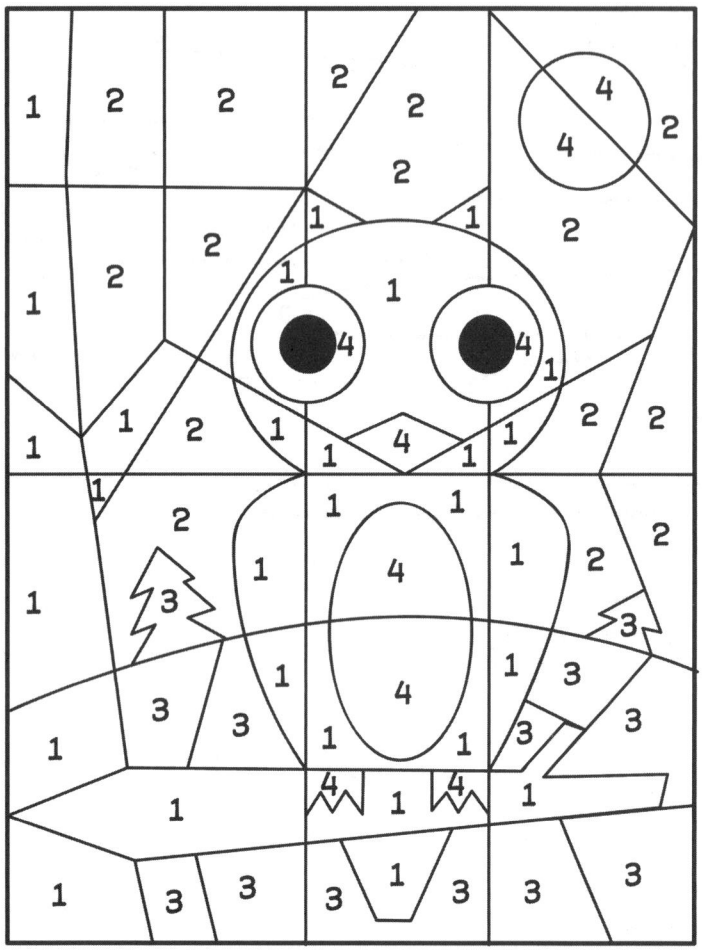

FIND THE EAGLE'S SHADOW.

DRAW A SLEEPY FACE, A SURPRISED FACE, AND A SERIOUS FACE.

FIND THE SEVEN DIFFERENCES.

CAN YOU DRAW A DINOSAUR IN THIS PREHISTORIC LANDSCAPE?

COLOR THE OBJECTS YOU CAN OPEN.

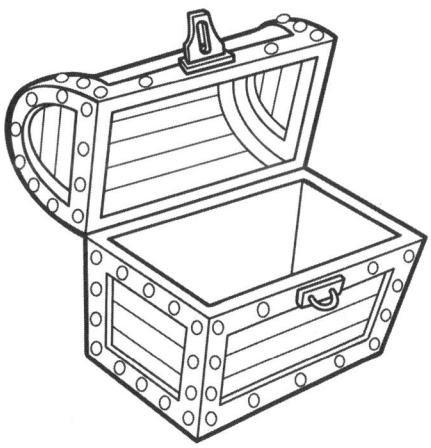

FILL THIS PAGE WITH BLUE RAINDROPS!

COLOR ANNIE'S UMBRELLA RED, HER COAT YELLOW, AND HER BOOTS GREEN.

TRACE THE DOTTED LINES
TO DRAW THE HIVE.

WHAT SWEET TREAT
DO THE BEES MAKE?
NAME IT!

WHAT IS THIS ANIMAL CALLED?

DRAW ANOTHER ONE JUST LIKE IT!

DRAW DIFFERENT HAIRCUTS FOR THE BOY!

DRAW THE LION'S OTHER HALF AND COLOR THE WHOLE PICTURE.

DOES THE SPIDER CATCH THE FLY?

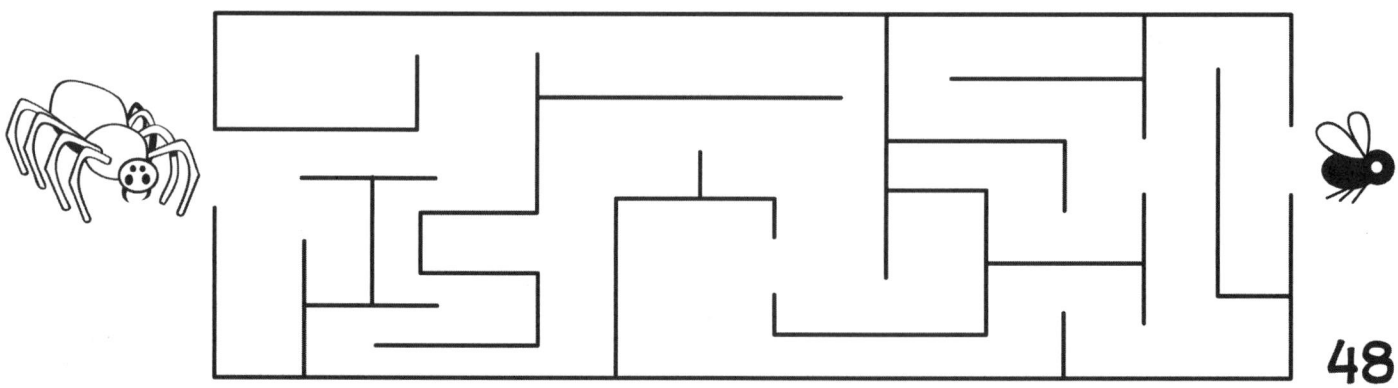

WHAT'S MISSING FROM THIS CAMEL? CAN YOU DRAW IT?

WHICH ONE OF THESE ANIMALS DOES NOT LAY EGGS?

COLOR THE FOODS THAT TASTE SWEET.

COLOR ONLY THE STRIPED T-SHIRTS.

DECORATE THE ONE IN THE MIDDLE ANY WAY YOU LIKE!

COLOR THE BENT WANDS ORANGE AND THE STRAIGHT ONES YELLOW.

DRAW THE RAYS OF SUNSHINE THROUGH THE CLOUDS.

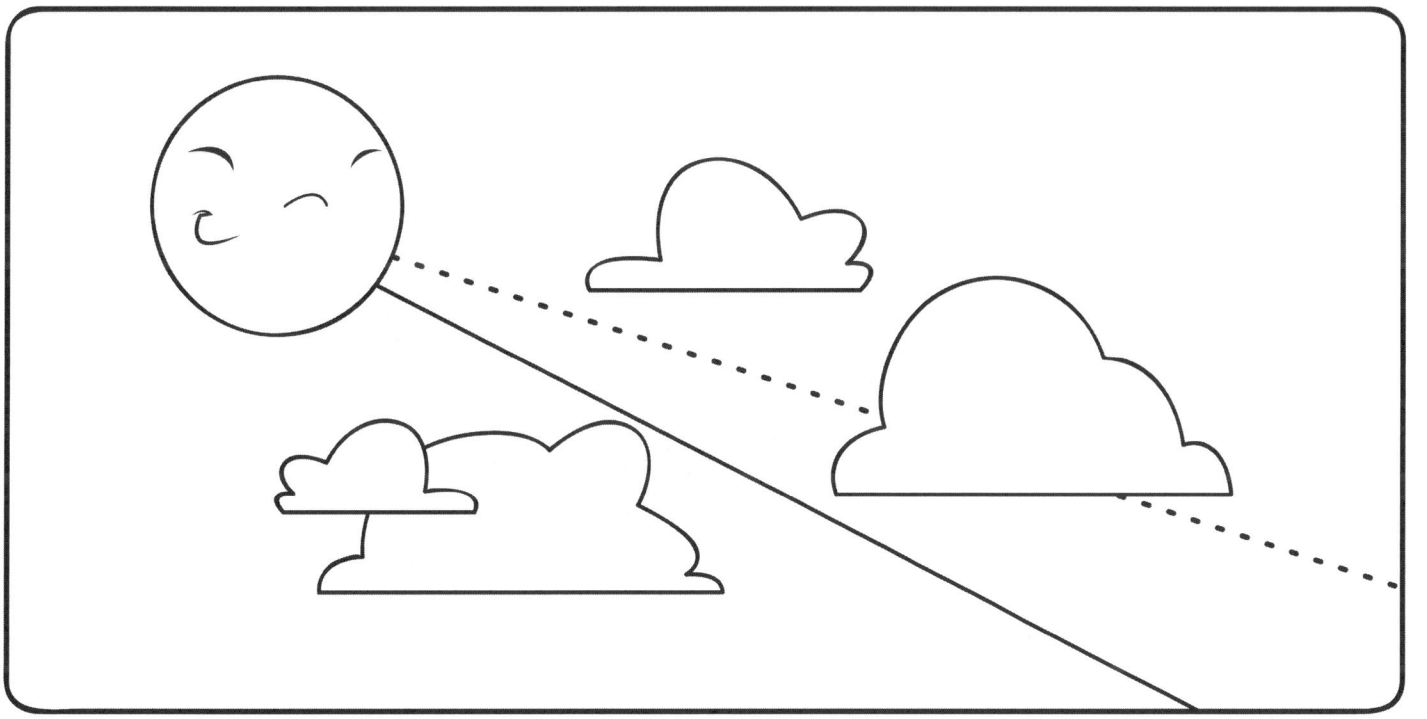

WHAT ANIMAL IS THIS?
WHERE DOES IT LIVE?

TRACE THE FIRST FLOWER AND THEN FOLLOW THE BEE'S FLIGHT PATH TO THE NEXT FLOWER.

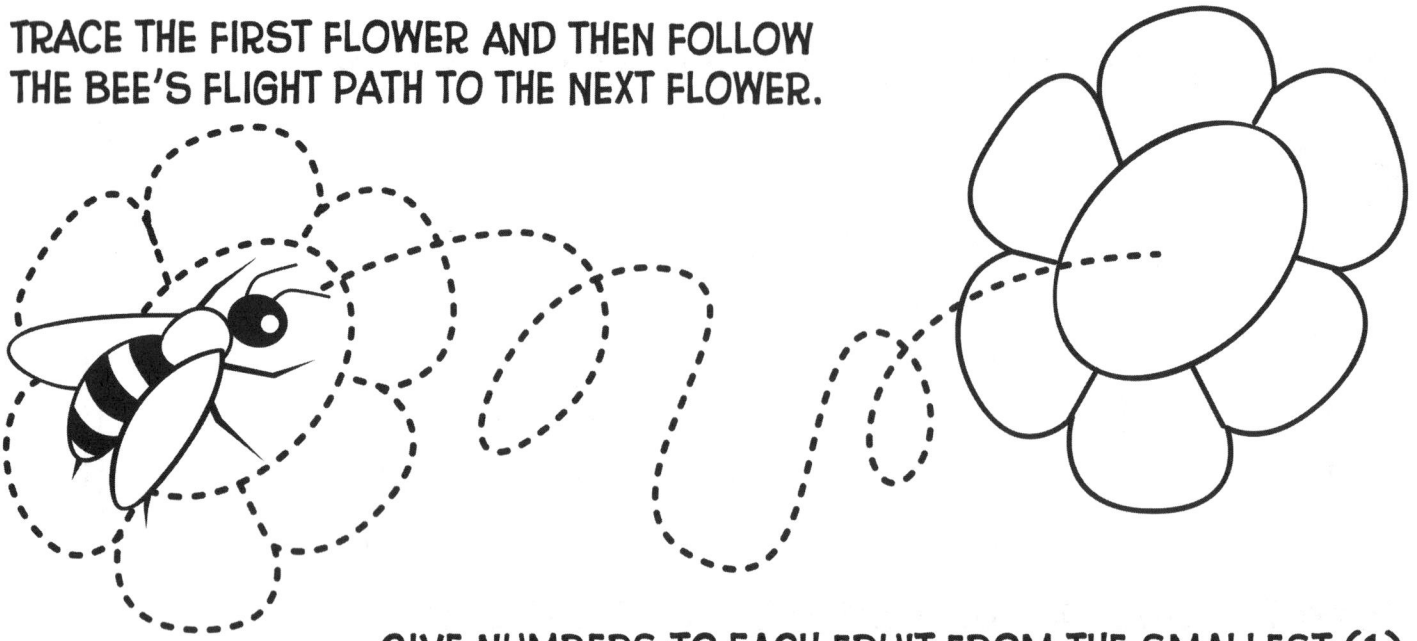

GIVE NUMBERS TO EACH FRUIT FROM THE SMALLEST (1) TO THE BIGGEST (4) IN REAL LIFE.

COLOR THE GRAPES PURPLE, THE BANANA YELLOW, AND THE STRAWBERRY RED. WHAT COLOR IS THE ORANGE?

WHICH ONE IS NOT A VEHICLE?

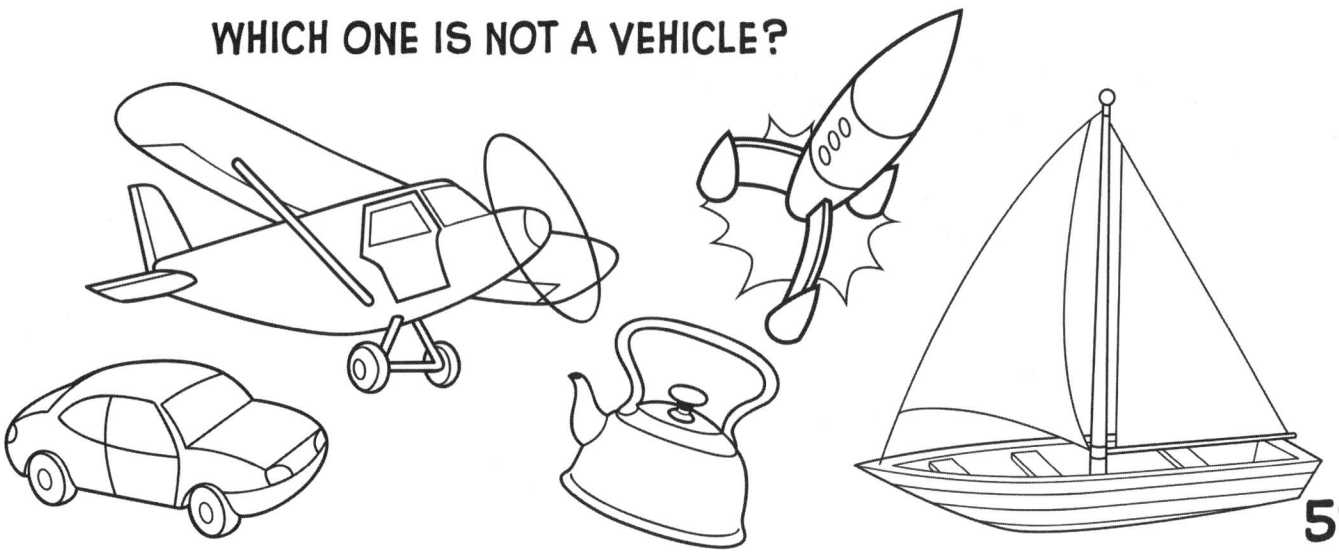

TURN THESE SQUARES INTO FUN STUFF, AND COLOR IT ALL!

TV SET.

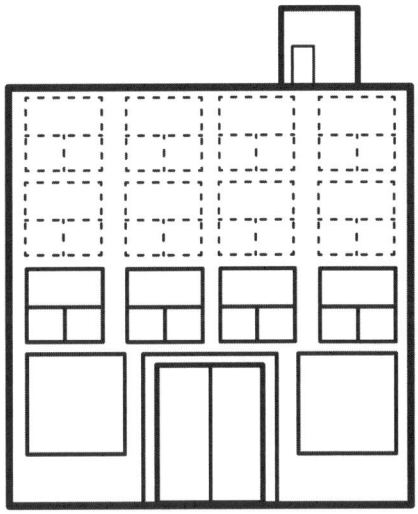

BUILDING.

ENVELOPE.

TABLET.

PRESENT.

BOOK.

COLOR THE SWALLOWS BLUE AND THE BUTTERFLIES PINK!

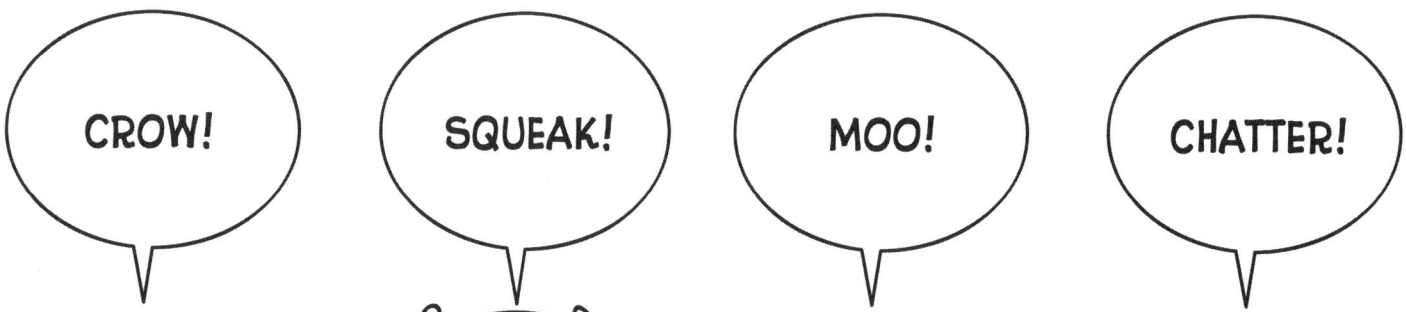

CONNECT EACH ANIMAL
TO THE NOISE IT MAKES.

DRAW THE KITTY'S LONG TAIL, AND THEN COLOR HIM ORANGE.

DO YOU HAVE A PET? DRAW IT HERE.

FILL THE JAR WITH CANDY. COLOR HALF OF THEM RED AND THE REST BLUE.

COUNT THEM ALL.

WHOOPS!
HOW MANY DOUGHNUTS
DID SALLY DROP?

WHICH ONE OF THESE DOES NOT
BELONG IN THE KITCHEN?

DRAW THE SHEEP'S COAT OF WOOL—
ONE WAVY AND THE OTHER CURLY.

DRAW TWO MORE SHEEP
WITH DIFFERENT COATS.

WHAT IS NOT POSSIBLE IN THIS PICTURE? WHY?

1 = GRAY
2 = PINK
3 = WHITE
4 = YELLOW
5 = ORANGE

WHAT ANIMAL IS IT? DRAW A CIRCLE AROUND ITS FAVORITE FOOD BELOW.

ONE OF THESE ANIMALS CAN'T SWIM. CAN YOU GUESS WHICH ONE?

WHAT IS THIS ANIMAL CALLED?

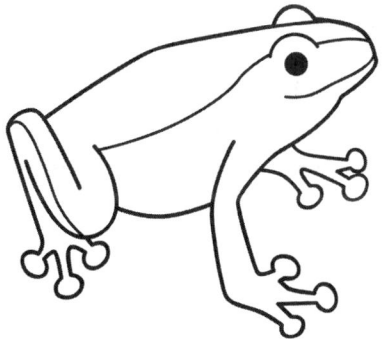

DRAW ANOTHER ONE JUST LIKE IT!

FINISH THIS DRAWING.

WHICH ARMADILLO DOES NOT LOOK LIKE THE OTHERS?

HELP THE ROCKET REACH EARTH!

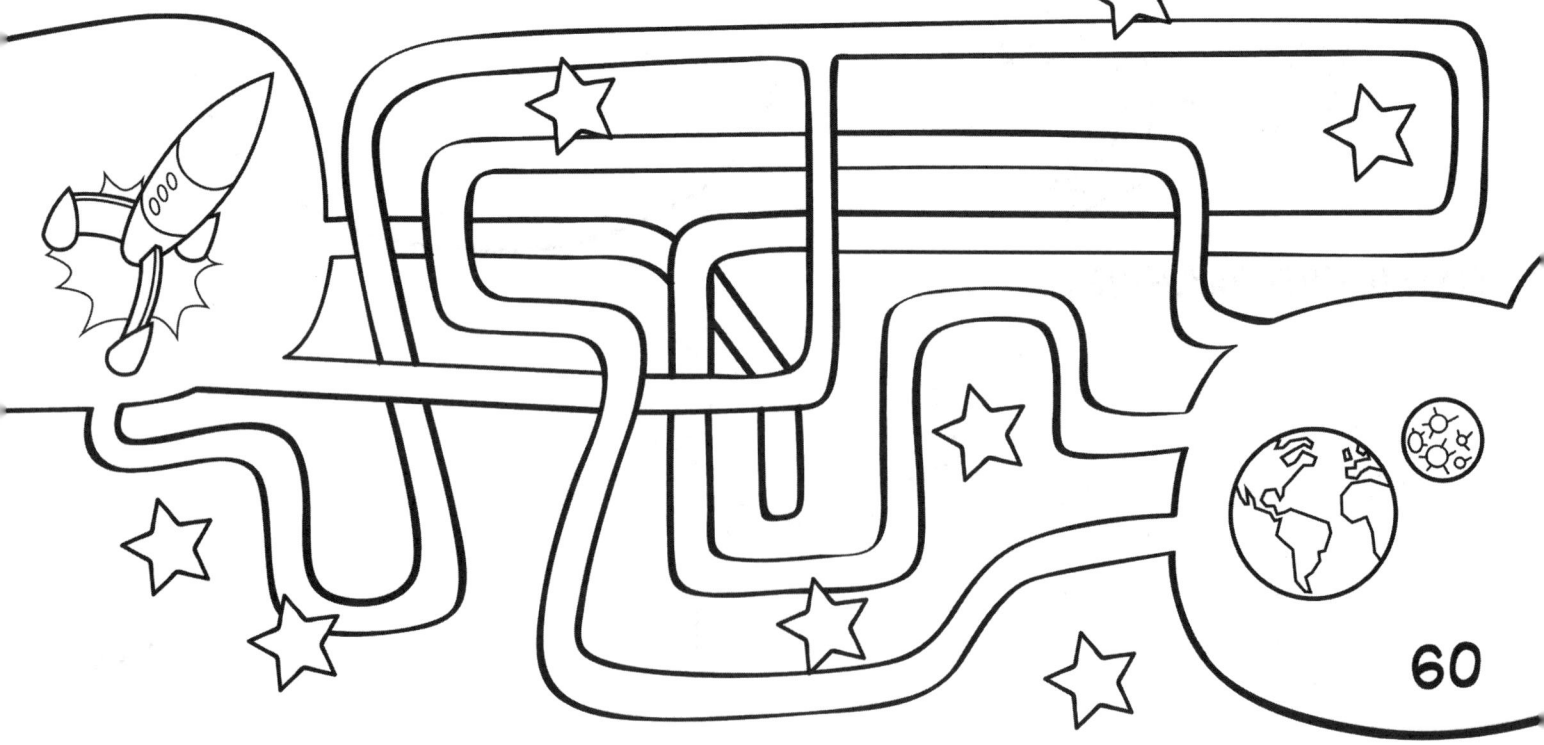

FILL THE SKY WITH FALLING SNOWFLAKES!

COLOR THE CARROT ORANGE AND THE PINE TREES GREEN.

COLOR THE CABIN BROWN AND THE SNOWMAN'S BUTTONS RED.

DRAW A LINE TO MATCH EACH WORD TO DIFFERENT PARTS OF THE TEDDY BEAR.

COMPLETE THE NIGHT VIEW WITH STARS, BATS, AND OWLS!

HELP THE LITTLE MONKEY REACH THE BANANA!

COLOR THE BIG BALLS ORANGE AND THE SMALL ONES PURPLE.

FILL THE OTHER COMPARTMENTS WITH OTHER CREATURES FROM YOUR GARDEN!

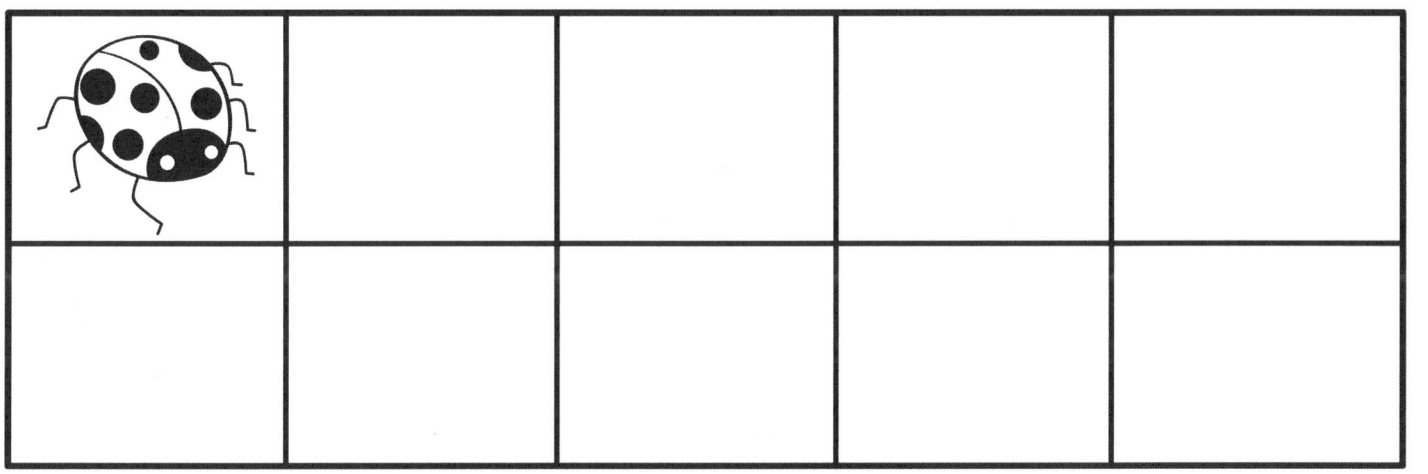

DRAW A CIRCLE AROUND THE TOYS,
AND COLOR THE ANIMALS.

COLOR THE COLD THINGS BLUE
AND THE HOT ONES RED.

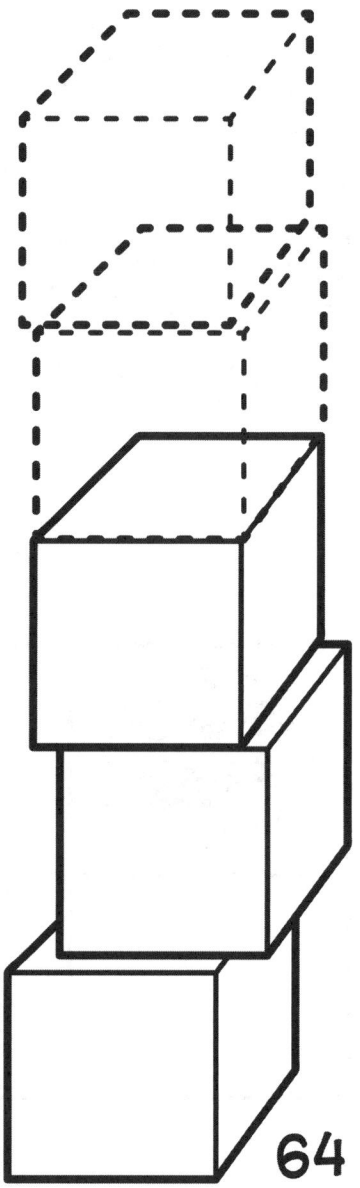

CONTINUE DRAWING UPWARD, AS
MANY BLOCKS AS YOU NEED,
TO REACH THE TOP OF THIS PAGE!

DRAW EIGHT LEGS ON EACH BABY SPIDER, AND THEN COLOR THEM AND THEIR MOM.

HOW MANY SPIDERS DO YOU COUNT?

COLOR THE PIGEONS GREY, BROWN, AND WHITE, AS YOU PLEASE.

COLOR THE TALLEST GNOME HAT RED, THE MIDDLE SIZED HAT YELLOW, AND THE SMALL ONE BLUE.

COLOR THE FIRST GNOME'S JACKET RED, THE SECOND ONE BLUE, AND THE LAST ONE YELLOW.

IF YOU MIX THE COLORS ON EACH GNOME'S HAT AND JACKET AND USE IT TO COLOR THEIR PANTS, WHAT COLOR WOULD EACH GNOME'S PANTS BE?

FIND THE ONE THAT'S DIFFERENT.

WHAT DOES THE ELEPHANT EAT?

MATCH THE ROOSTER TO THE APPROPRIATE OUTLINE.

DRAW THE OTHER HALF.

HOW CAN THIS LITTLE DRAGONFLY ESCAPE THE MOSQUITO NET?

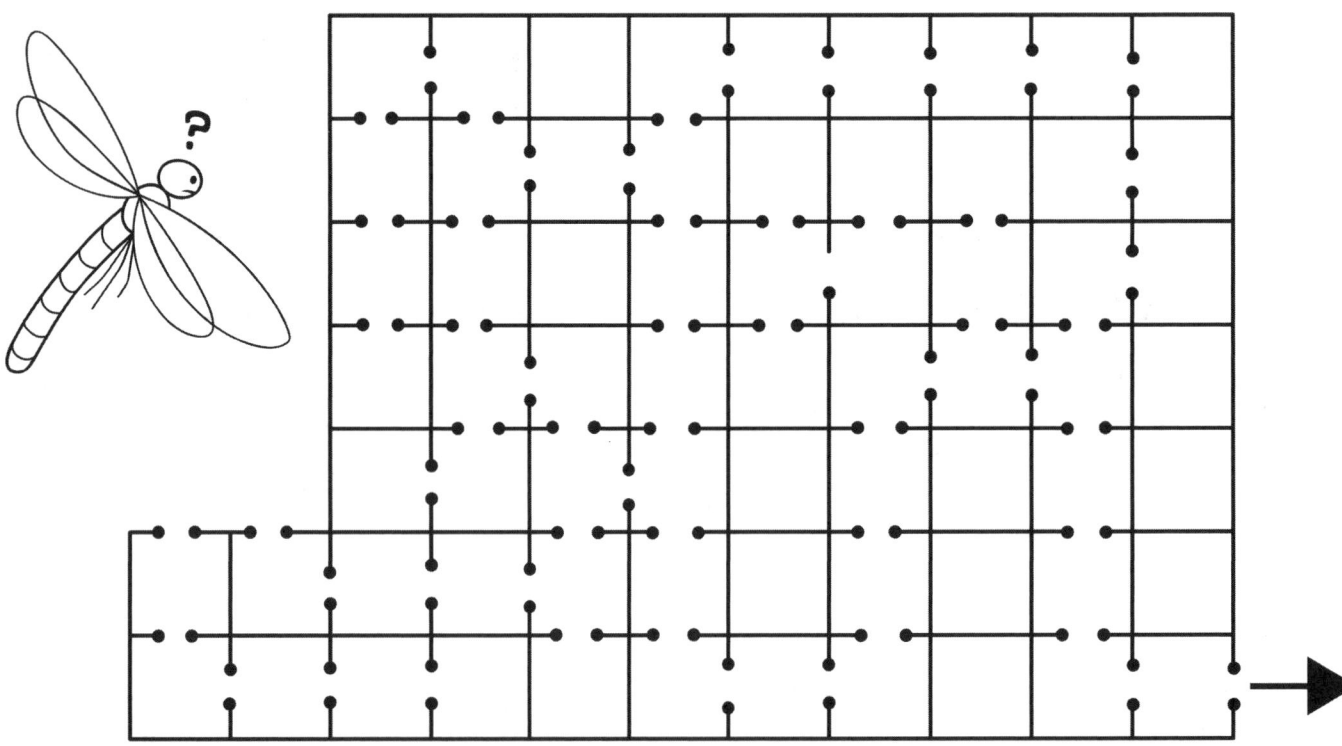

WHICH PINEAPPLE DOES NOT LOOK LIKE THE OTHERS?

WHAT PIECE DOES NOT MATCH THE DRAWING?

TRACE A LINE OVER THE DOTS WITHOUT LIFTING YOUR HAND.

WHAT IS IT?

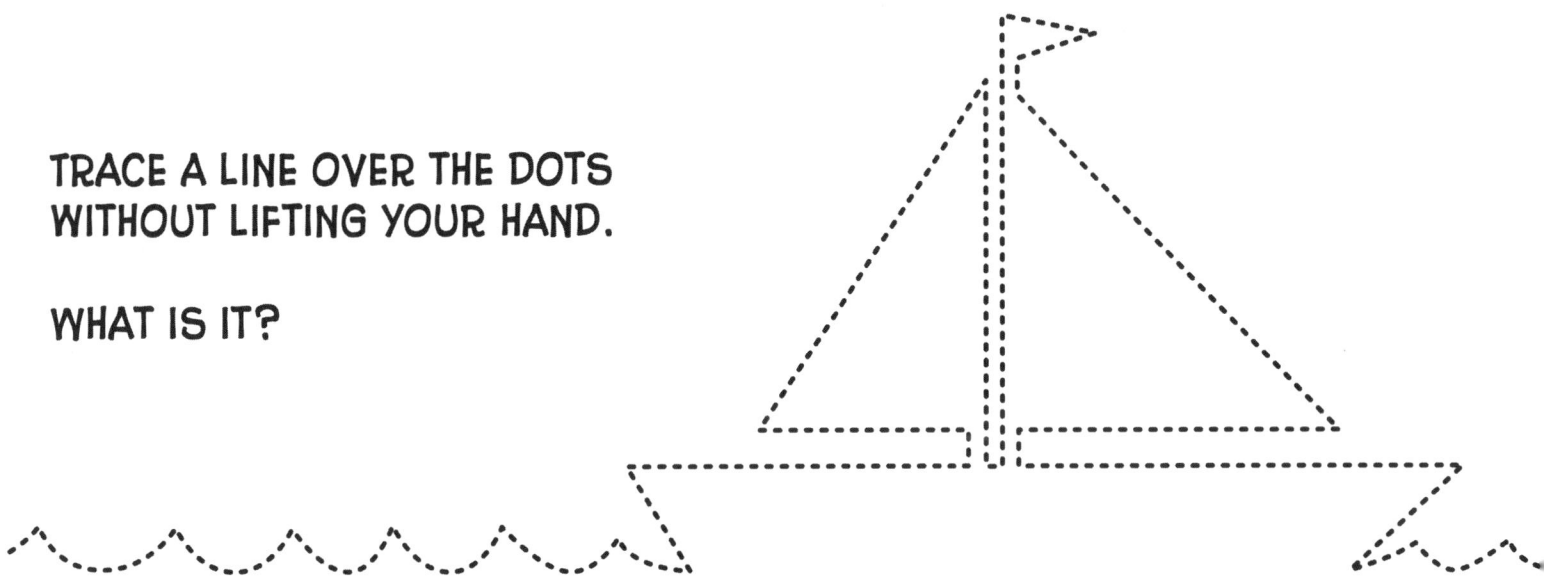

FILL THE JAR WITH LICORICE. COLOR HALF OF THEM RED AND THE REST PURPLE.

COUNT THEM ALL.

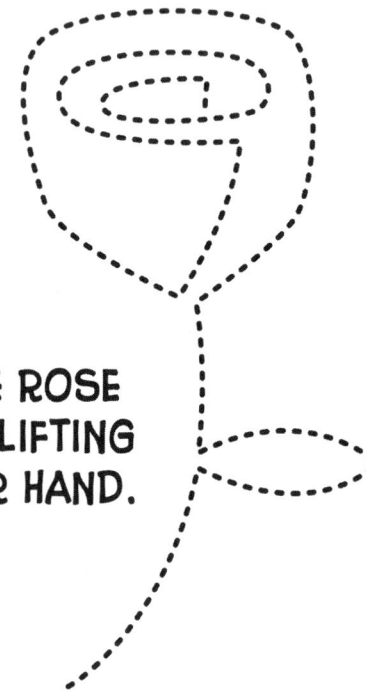

DRAW THE ROSE WITHOUT LIFTING YOUR HAND.

WHICH ONE OF THESE ANIMALS IS NOT A MAMMAL?

WHAT'S MISSING FROM MR. SCARECROW'S HEAD?
WHAT DO WE CALL THE BLACK BIRD PERCHED ON HIS ARM?
C_ _ _
DECORATE THE SHIRT, AND COLOR THE BIB BLUE.
CHOOSE A FACE TO DRAW ON IT'S HEAD.
WHAT ARE THESE CALLED? COLOR THEM!

COLOR THE CAT WITH THE LONGEST TAIL PURPLE
AND THE ONE WITH THE SHORTEST ORANGE.

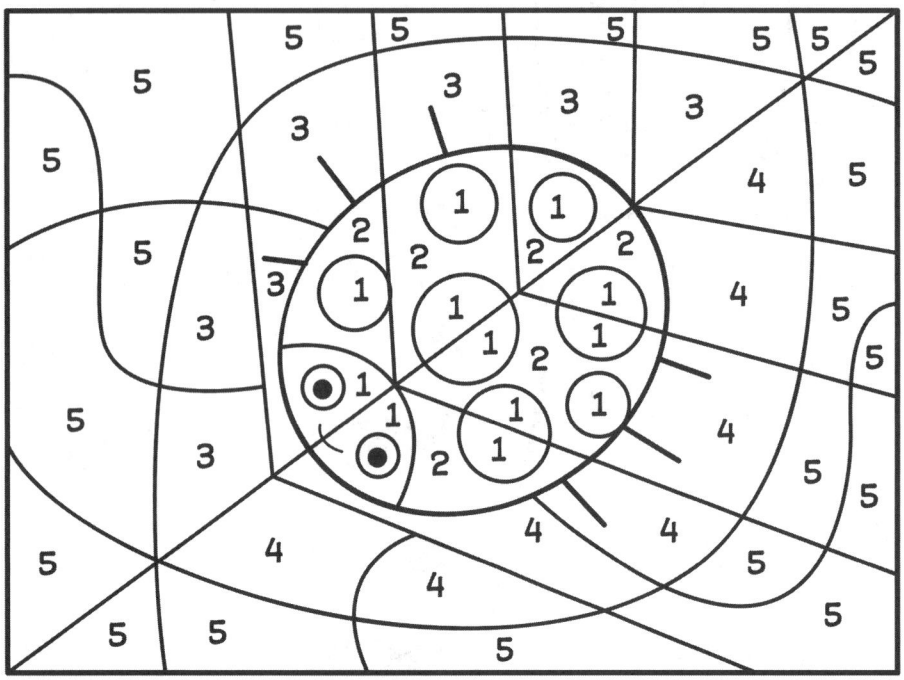

1 = BLACK
2 = RED
3 = DARK GREEN
4 = LIGHT GREEN
5 = BLUE

WHAT ANIMAL IS IT?
WHERE DOES IT LIVE?

COLOR ONLY THE ROUND THINGS.

HOW MANY TRIANGLES DO YOU SEE? COLOR THEM YELLOW.

FIND THE SIX DIFFERENCES.

COLOR THE BROKEN LOLLIPOPS GREEN AND THE STRAIGHT ONES RED. WHICH ONE ISN'T A LOLLIPOP? WHAT IS IT? COLOR IT PINK.

HELP ICHA'S KISS FIND ITS WAY
TO DIEGO'S CHEEK!
FILL THE PAGE WITH HEARTS!

COLOR ONLY THE THINGS PEOPLE WEAR.

COLOR THE BASKET WITH THE MOST APPLES IN IT.

COLOR THE BIG PEARS YELLOW
AND THE SMALL ONES GREEN.
COLOR ALL CHERRIES RED.

FIND THE ONE THAT'S DIFFERENT.

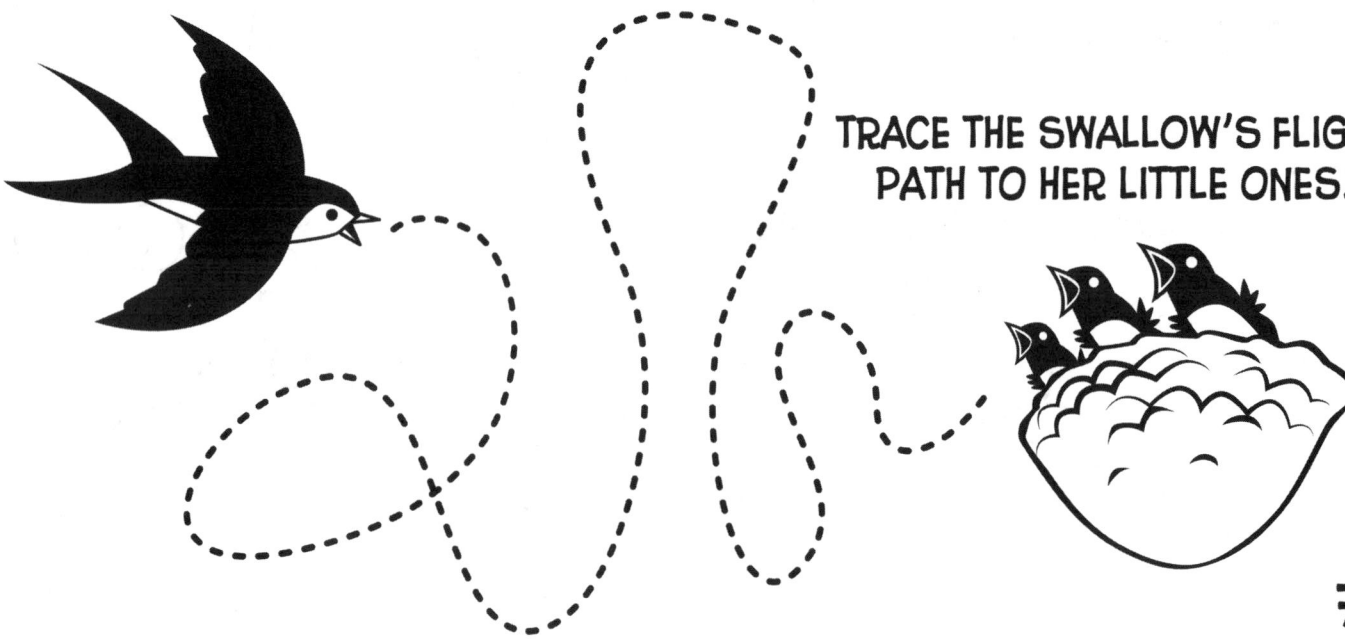

TRACE THE SWALLOW'S FLIGHT PATH TO HER LITTLE ONES.

WHICH ONE DOESN'T BELONG?

WHY?

DRAW THE OTHER HALF, AND PAINT FRECKLES ON HIS FACE.

WHAT IS THE NAME OF THIS TOOL?

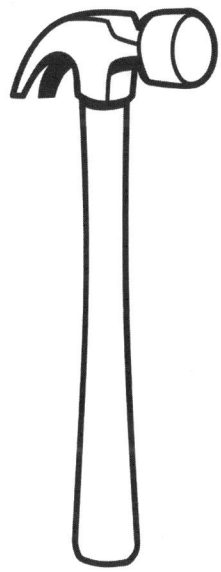

WHAT IS IT FOR?

FINISH DRAWING THE SPAGHETTI ON THE FIRST PLATE,
AND FILL THE SECOND ONE TOO!

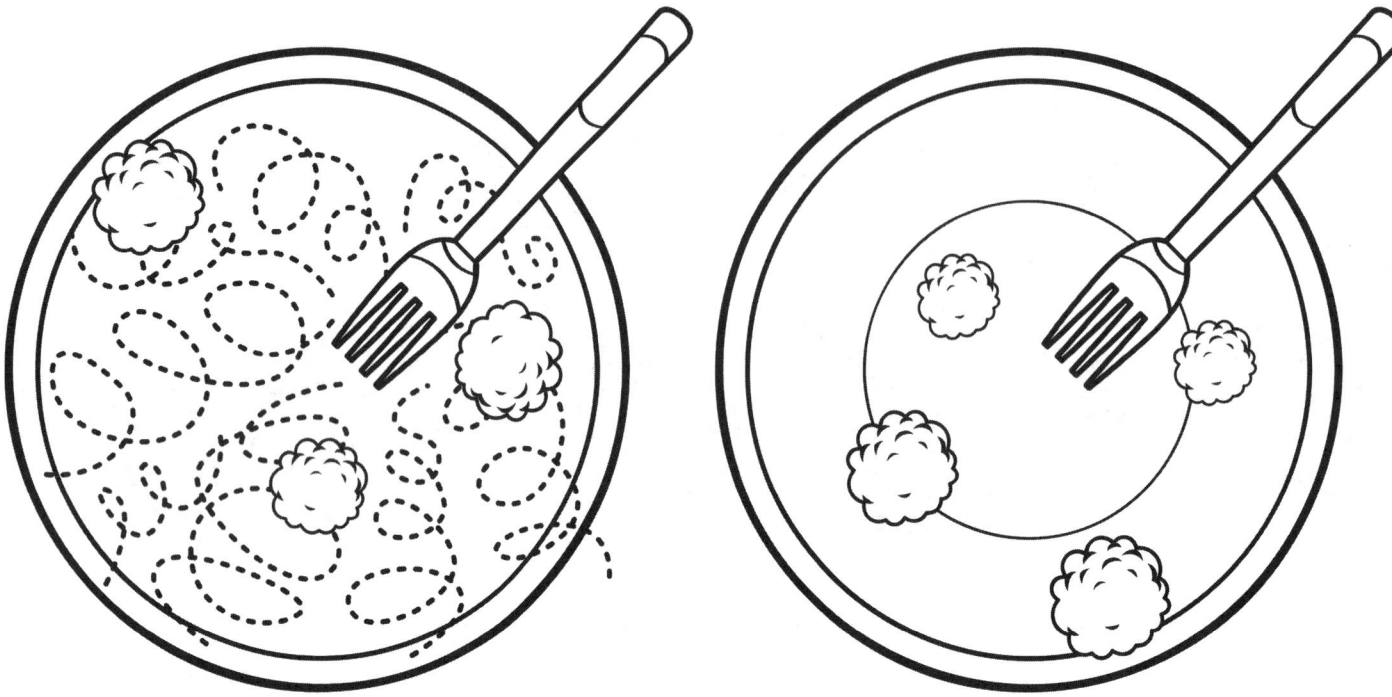

DECORATE EACH TORTOISE SHELL THE WAY SHE WANTS.

WHICH ONE OF THESE BIRDS DOES NOT FLY?

COLOR EACH CIRCLE.

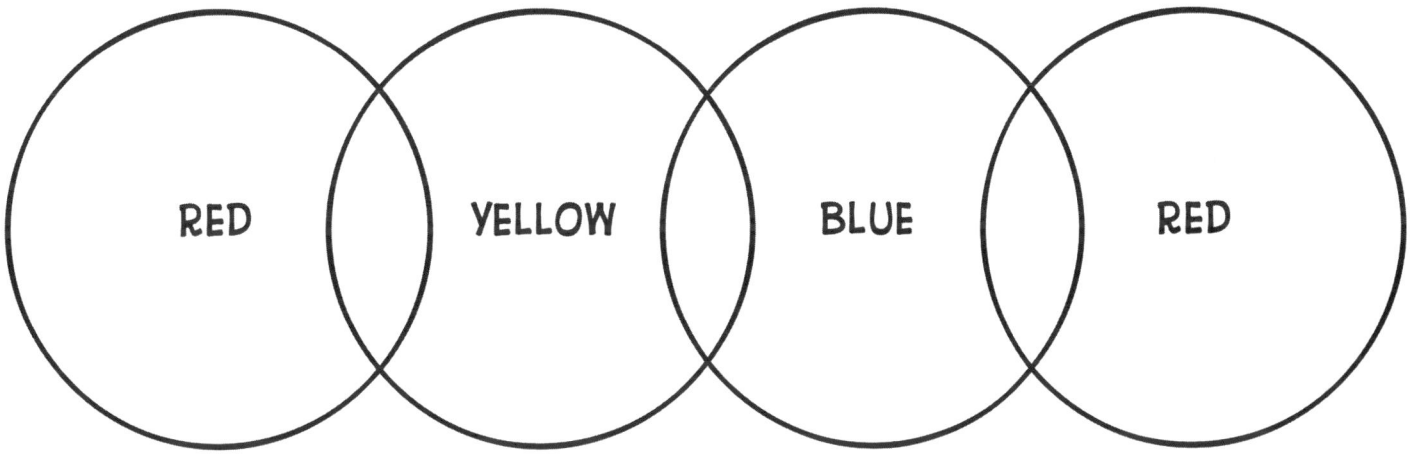

WHAT COLORS DO YOU GET WHERE THE CIRCLES OVERLAP?

HOW MANY HEARTS DO YOU COUNT?

TURN THESE TRIANGLES INTO FUN STUFF, AND COLOR IT ALL!

TEEPEE.

PENCIL TIP.

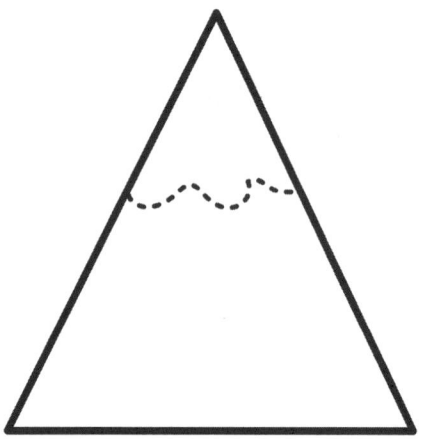

MOUNTAIN.

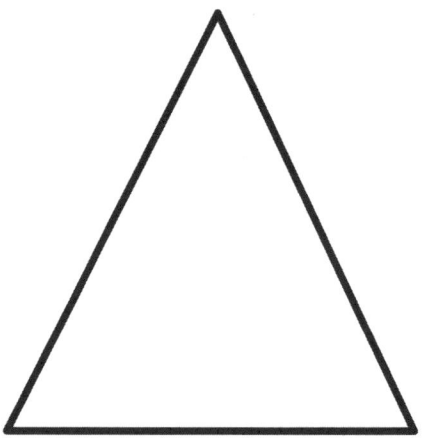

PARTY HAT.

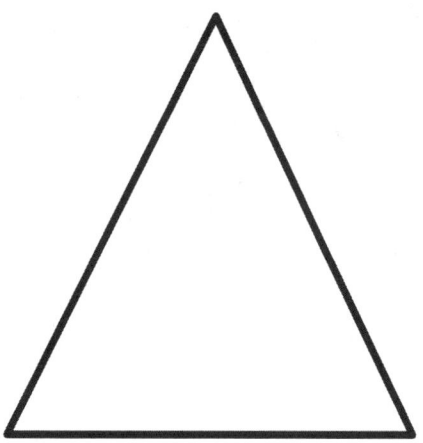

PAPER PLANE.

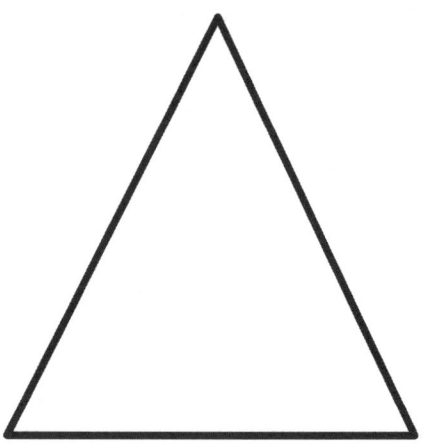

PYRAMID.

HELP THE LITTLE PIRATE FIND THE TREASURE!

COLOR THE DOUBLOONS YELLOW AND THE CHEST BROWN!

HOW MANY ICEBERGS DOES THE PENGUIN HOP ON TO REACH HIS FRIEND?
FIND THE MATCHING KITES AND COLOR THEM ALIKE!

CAN YOU COUNT THE NUMBER OF SPOTS ON THE DALMATIAN ON THE LEFT, AND MIRROR THEM ON THE SPOTLESS ONE?

COLOR THE TALLEST ONE PURPLE AND THE SMALLEST YELLOW.

DO YOU LIKE THIS PUPPY?
DRAW ANOTHER ONE JUST LIKE IT,
AND COLOR THE FRISBEE RED!

FOLLOW EACH THREAD TO FIND OUT
WHICH BALLOON IS SHE HOLDING,
AND COLOR IT BLUE!

FIND THE TRUE SHADOW OF THE HAMBURGER.

WHICH ONE DOESN'T BELONG?

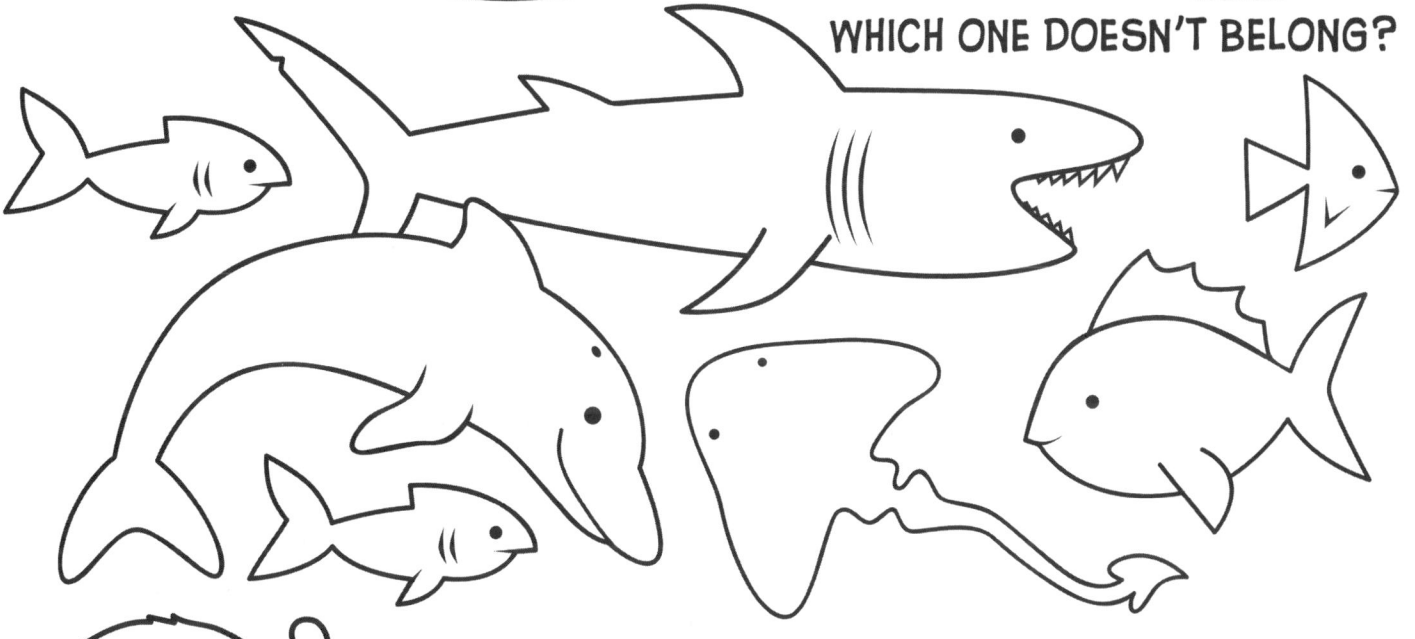

HELP THE MOUSE FIND HER CHEESE!

CAN YOU COUNT ALL THE BUBBLES IN THIS GLASS OF WATER?

COLOR THE RABBIT THAT MADE IT HIGHER UPSTAIRS!

COLOR THE VASE WITH THE MOST FLOWERS.

HOW MANY FLOWERS DO ALL THE VASES HAVE IN TOTAL?

COLOR ONLY THE THINGS THAT FLY.

THE BIRTHDAY CAKE ON THE RIGHT NEEDS FOUR CANDLES LIKE THIS ONE. CAN YOU DRAW THEM?

COLOR THE PRESENT THAT IS NOT LIKE THE OTHERS.

HOW MANY OWLS ARE ASLEEP? HOW MANY AWAKE?
COLOR THE RIGHT NUMBER.

1 2 3 4 5 6 7 8

COLOR AND DECORATE THE EGGS BEFORE THEY HATCH!

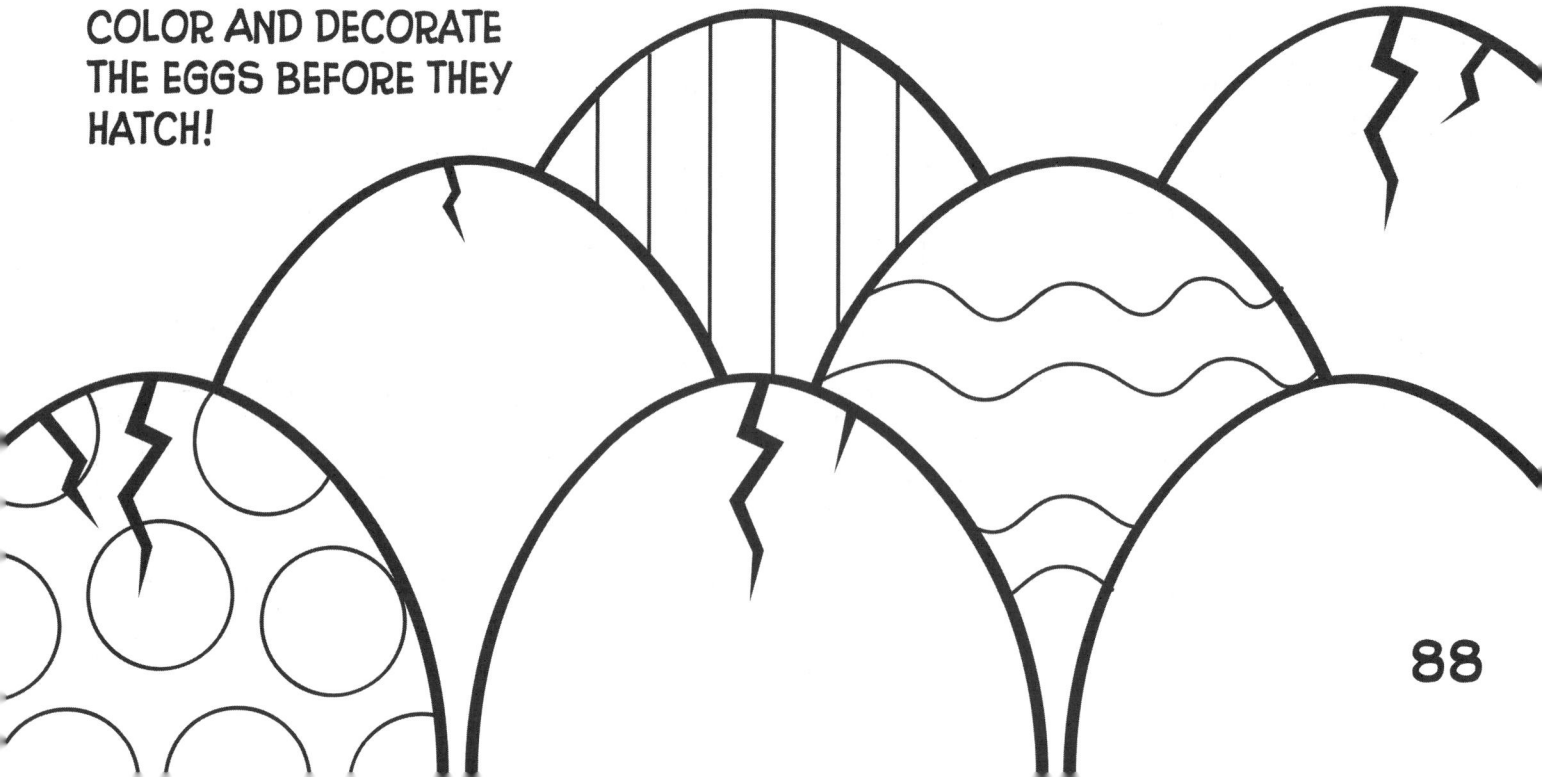

CAN YOU DRAW WHAT'S ON AMY'S MIND?
WHICH TOOL DO PAINTERS NOT USE?
CONNECT THE DOTS TO SEE WHAT SHE'S PAINTING!
1
2
3
4
5
6
7
8
9
10
11
12

HELP MISSY FIND HER LUNCH.

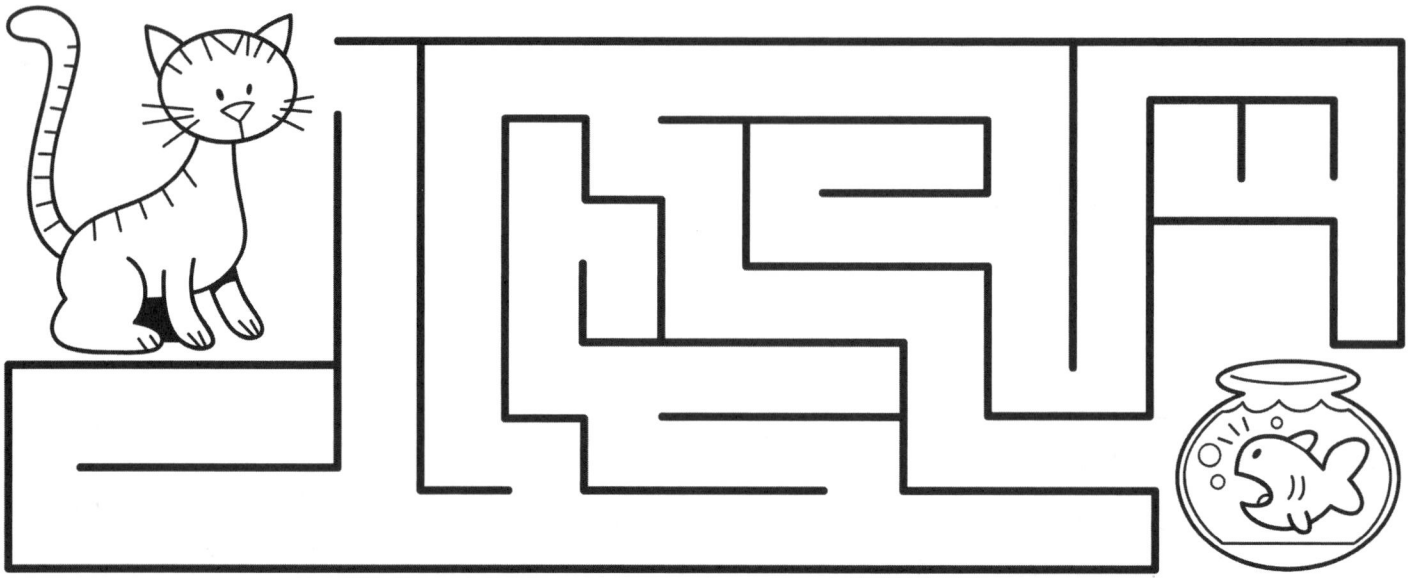

FIND THE TWO LADYBUGS WITH THE SAME SPOTS PATTERN.

HOW MANY CARS DO YOU COUNT?

COLOR THE BIG ONES RED, THE SMALL ONES BLUE, AND THE REST GREEN.

COLOR THE BUTTERFLY ON THE LEFT, AND DRAW ANOTHER JUST LIKE IT.

CAN YOU DRAW THE LOVE LETTER ENVELOPE WITHOUT LIFTING YOUR HAND?

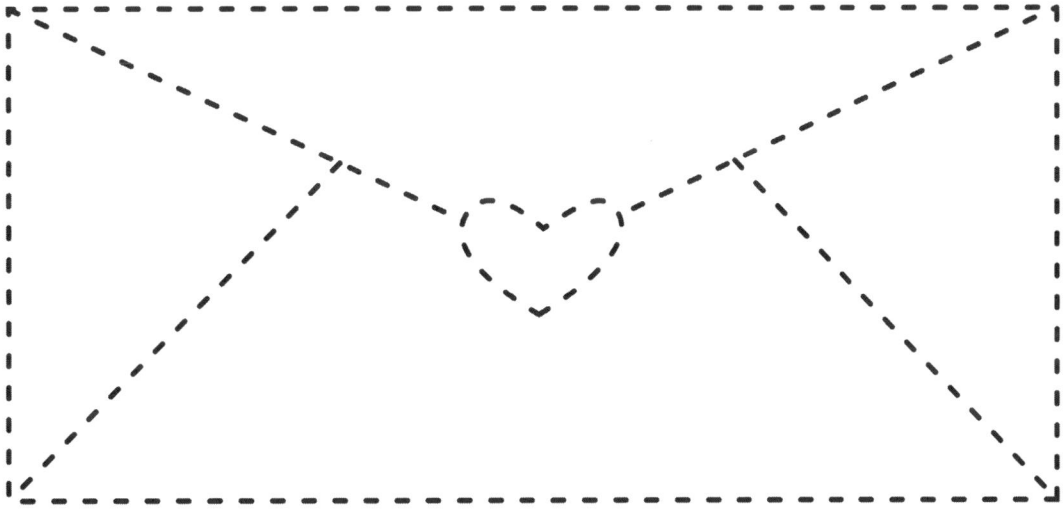

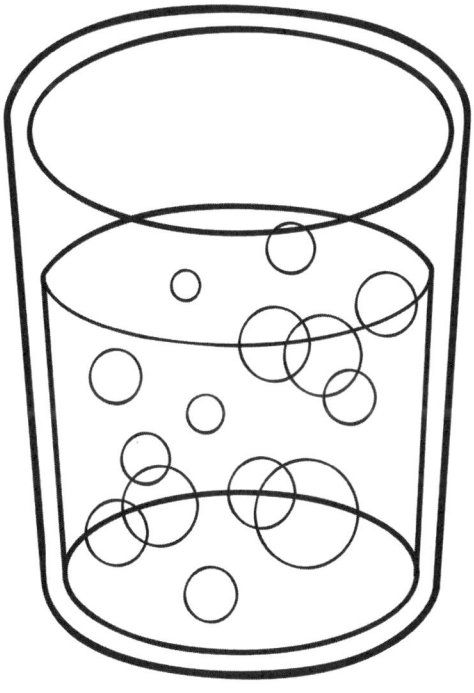

THIS GLASS IS FILLED WITH ORANGE SODA.

AND THIS ONE WITH GRAPE SODA.

COLOR THEM!

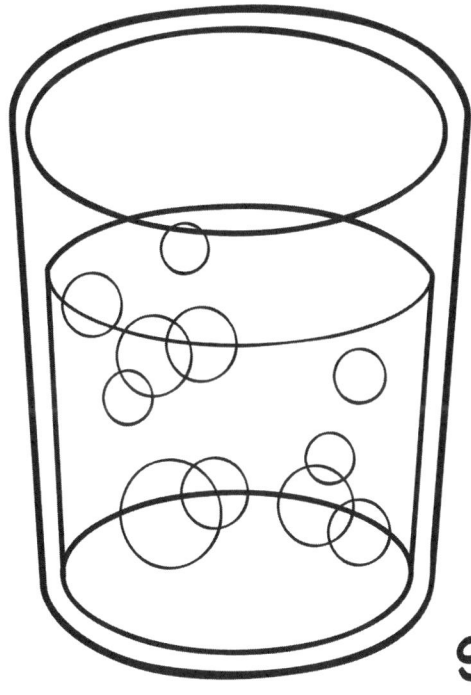

FIND THE DIFFERENCES BETWEEN THESE TWO SCENES...

... AND COLOR THEM ACCORDINGLY!

DO YOU KNOW THIS ANIMAL?

WHERE DOES IT LIVE?

WHAT DOES IT EAT?

1 = LIGHT BROWN
2 = DARK BROWN
3 = YELLOW
4 = GREEN

WHAT IS IT?

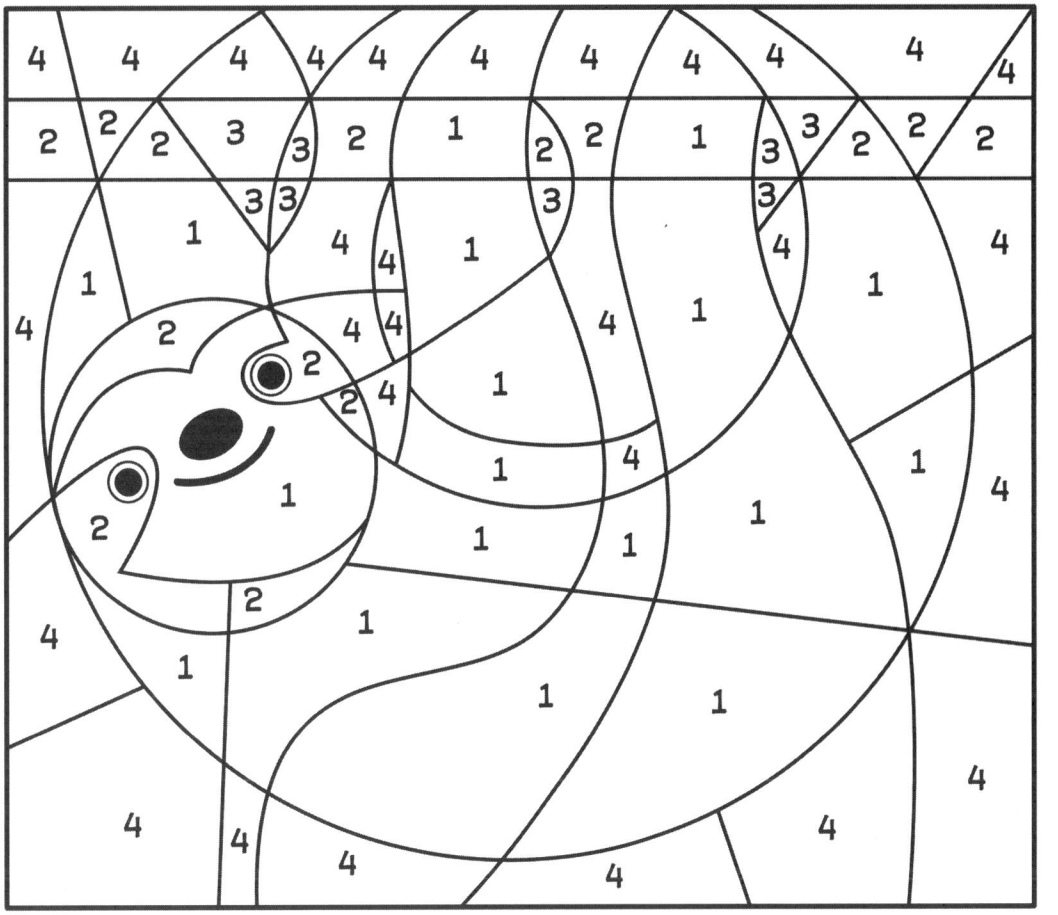

CONNECT EACH ANIMAL TO ITS FAVORITE FOOD.

WHAT IS THE NAME OF THIS TOOL?

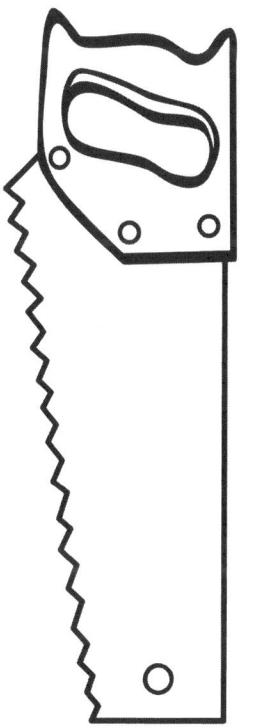

WHAT IS IT FOR?

WHICH FROG DOES NOT LOOK LIKE THE REST?

WHERE DO HUMANS LIVE?

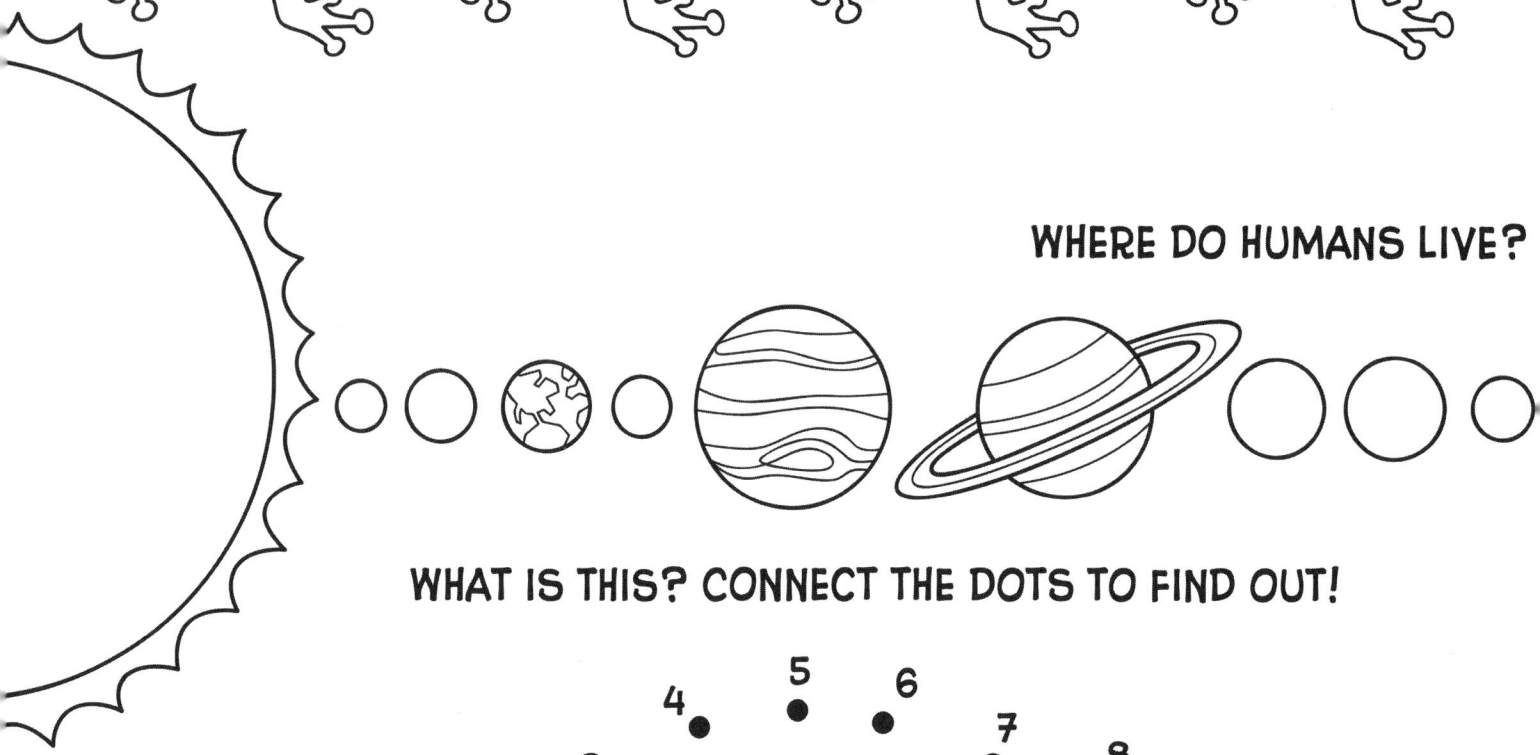

WHAT IS THIS? CONNECT THE DOTS TO FIND OUT!

FIND THE MISSING PIECE.

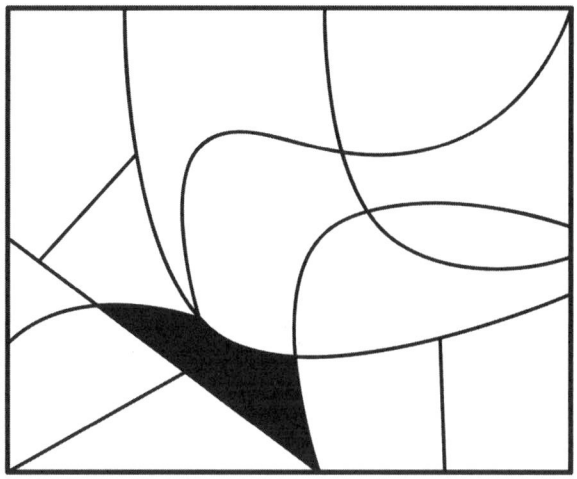

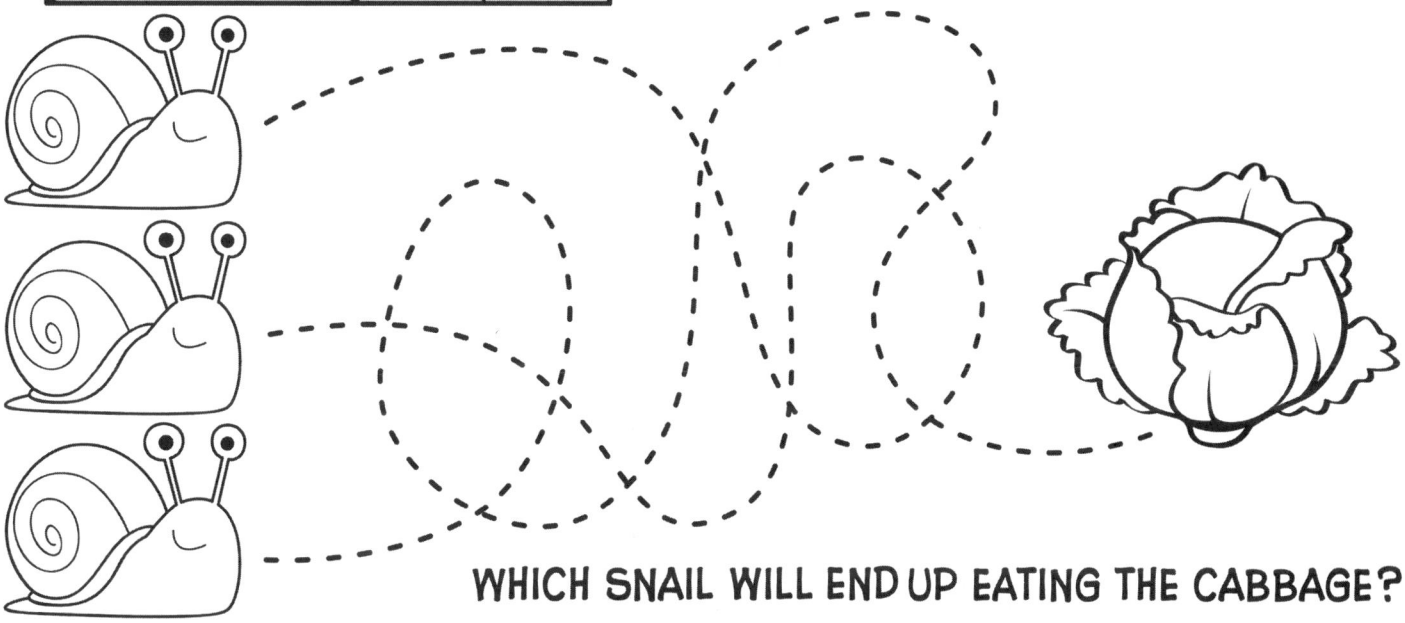

WHICH SNAIL WILL END UP EATING THE CABBAGE?

DO YOU RECOGNIZE THESE OUTLINES?
WHICH ONES CAN FLY?

COLOR EACH CAKE A DIFFERENT FLAVOR.
COUNT AND COLOR THE RIGHT NUMBER OF CANDLES ON EACH.
LIGHT THE ONE WITH THE MOST CANDLES.

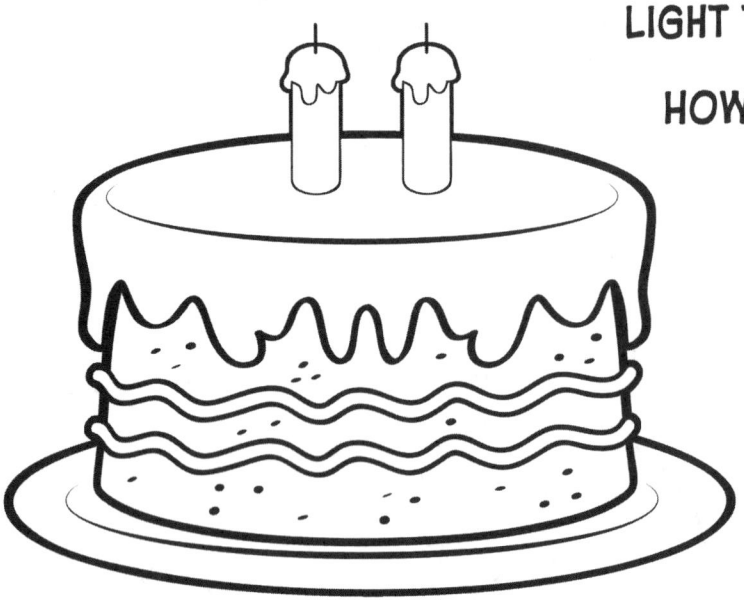

HOW MANY CANDLES DO YOU COUNT?

1 2 3 4
5 6 7 8

HOW MANY CANDLES DO YOU COUNT?

1 2 3 4
5 6 7 8

HOW MANY CANDLES DO YOU COUNT?

1 2 3 4
5 6 7 8

ONE OF THESE OUTLINES DOES NOT MATCH THE ELEPHANT ON THE LEFT.

THIS FISH HAS A THREE LETTER NAME. WHAT IS IT?

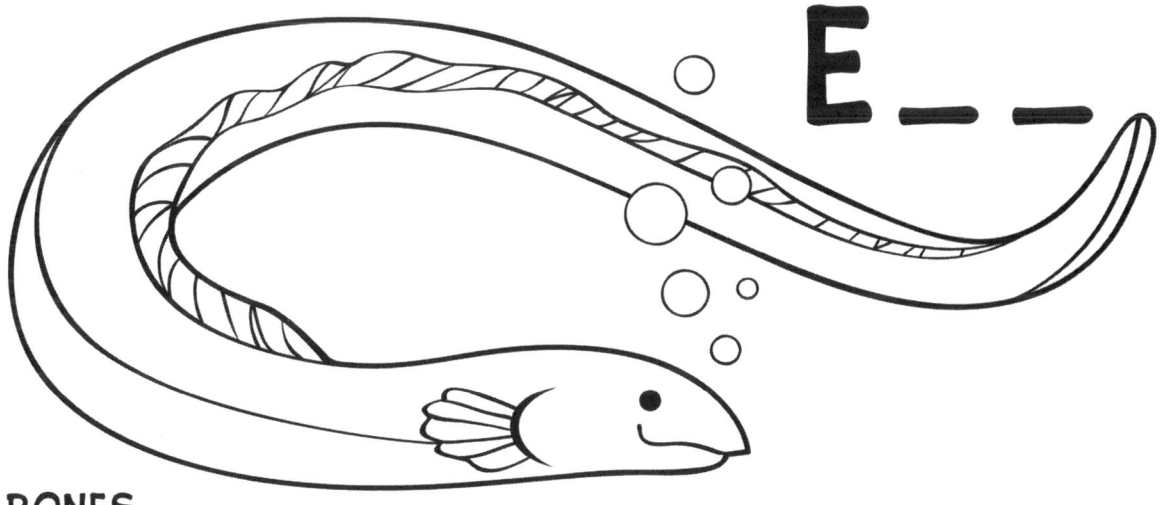

FIDO WANTS BONES. IF HE TAKES TWO, HOW MANY ARE LEFT?

COLOR THE TWO IDENTICAL MICE.

COUNT THE NUMBER OF STARS AND STRIPES, AND THEN COLOR THE FLAG.

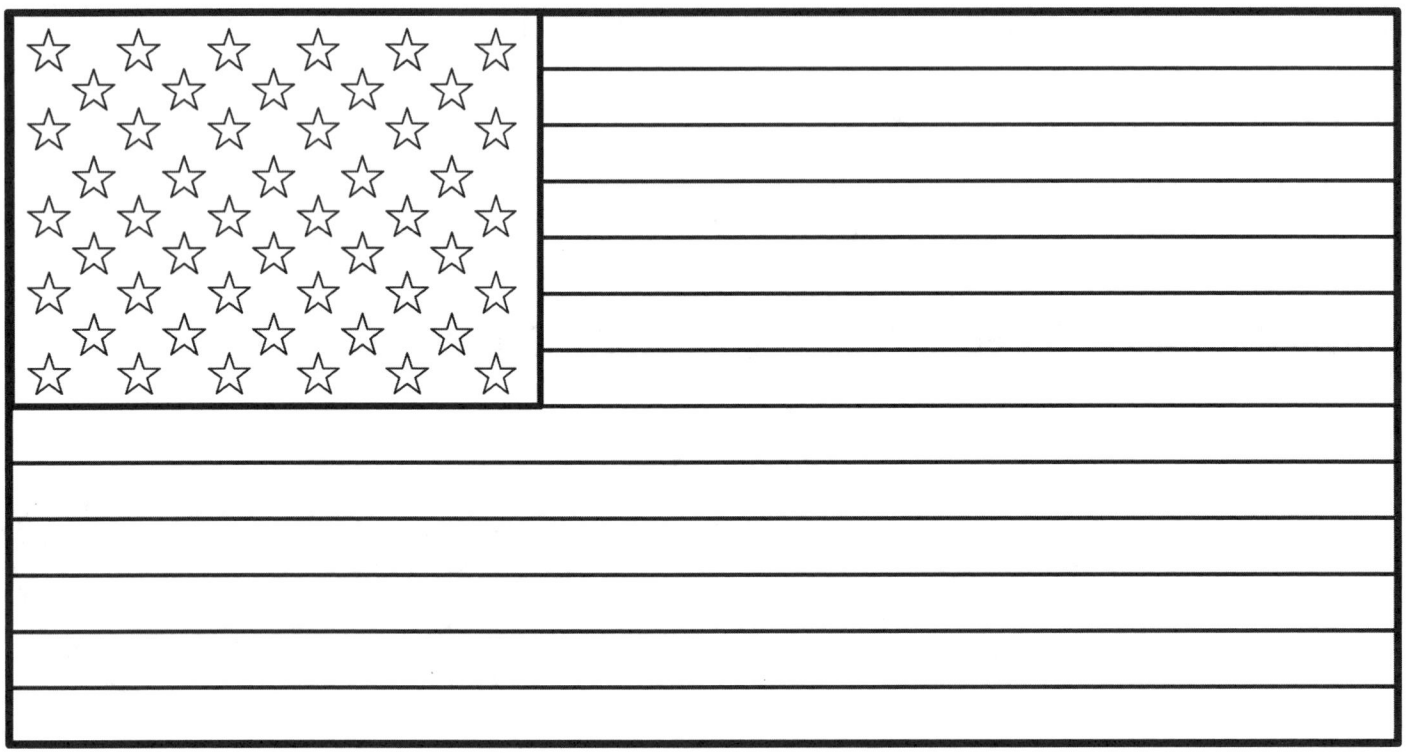

BILLY'S KITE GOT TANGLED WITH OTHERS. HELP HIM FIND IT!

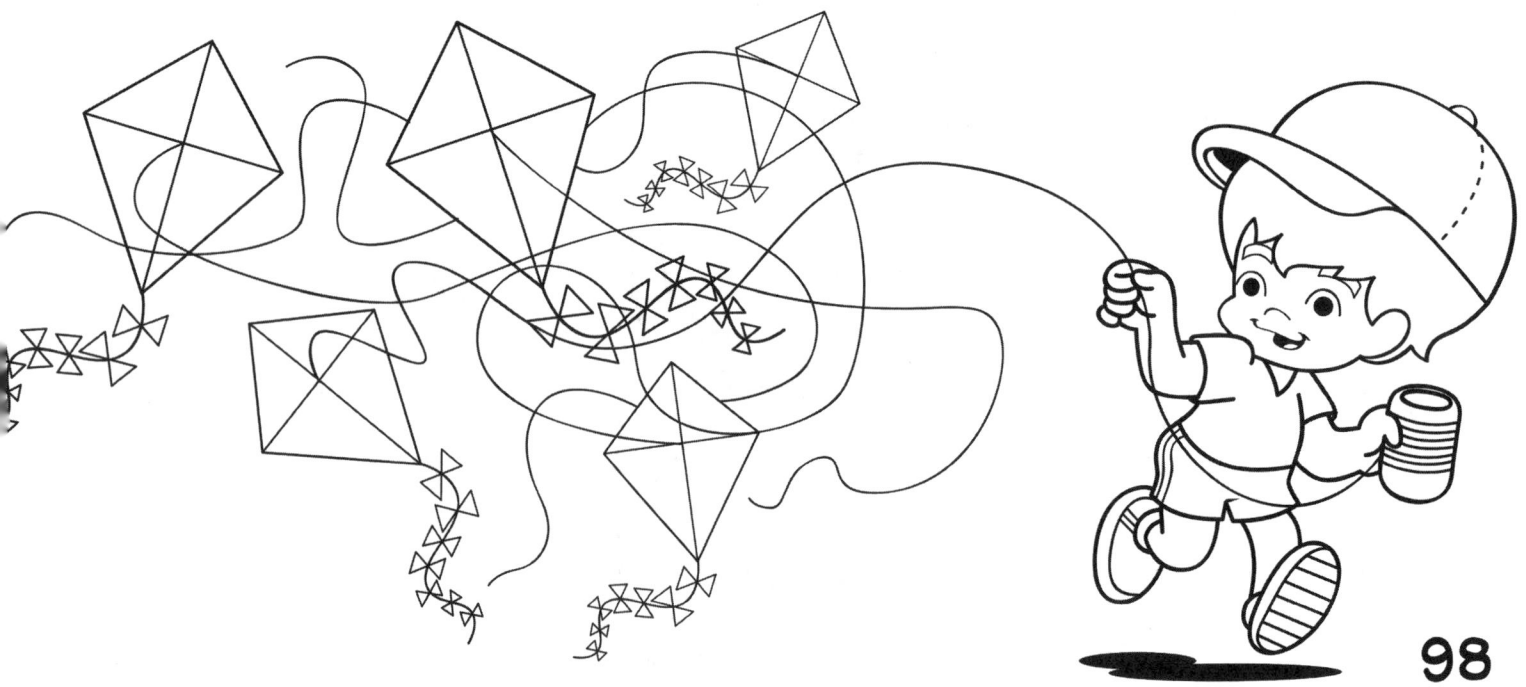

WHAT IS SALLY KNITTING?
FOLLOW THE WOOL THREAD TO THE RIGHT PIECE OF CLOTHING, AND COLOR EACH ACCORDING TO THE LIST BELOW.

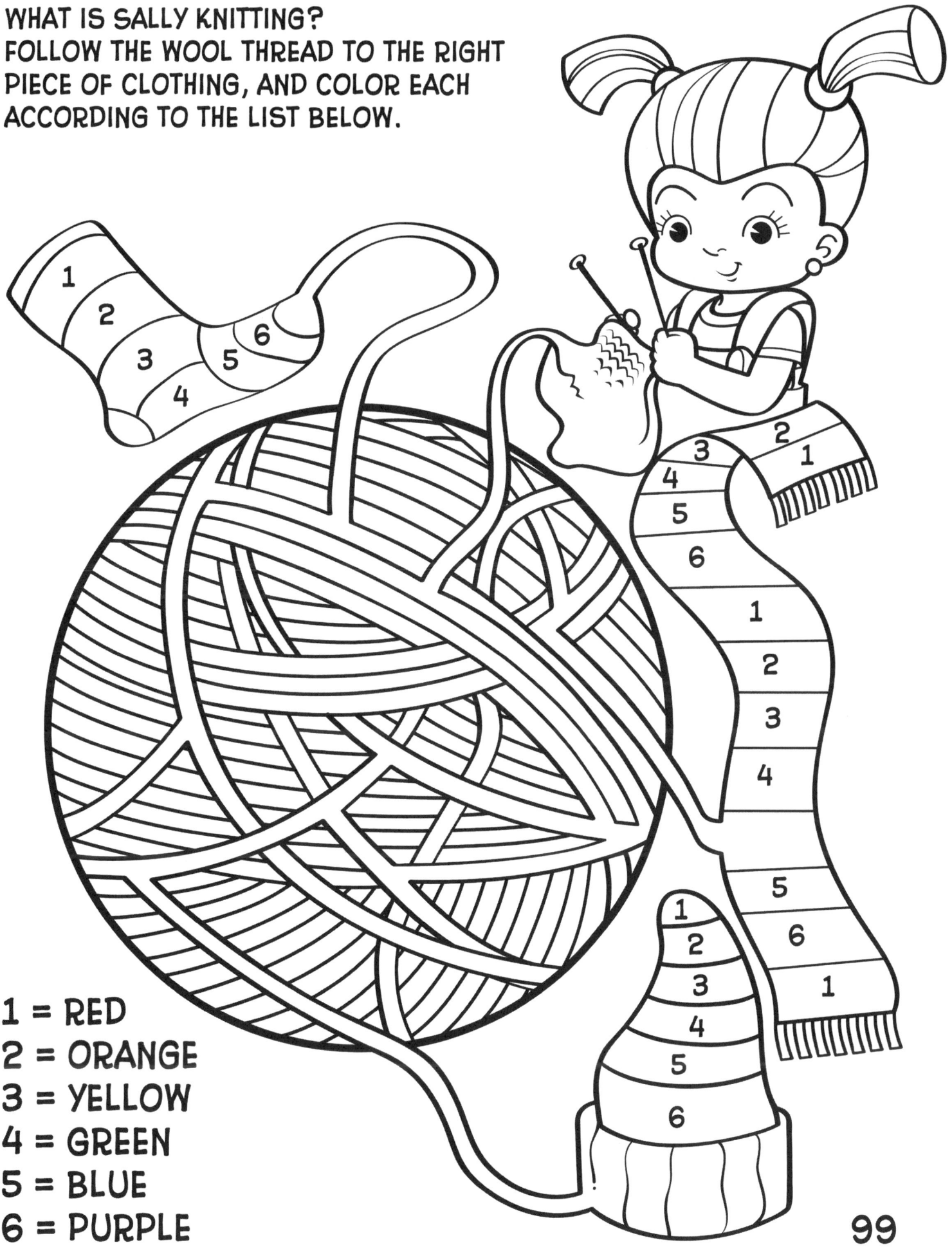

1 = RED
2 = ORANGE
3 = YELLOW
4 = GREEN
5 = BLUE
6 = PURPLE

CONNECT EACH ANIMAL TO ITS PORTRAIT

WHICH ONE OF THESE ANIMALS DOES NOT LIVE IN THE SEA?

LEVEL
2

WRITE THE FIRST LETTER OF YOUR NAME, AND TURN IT INTO A BIRD!

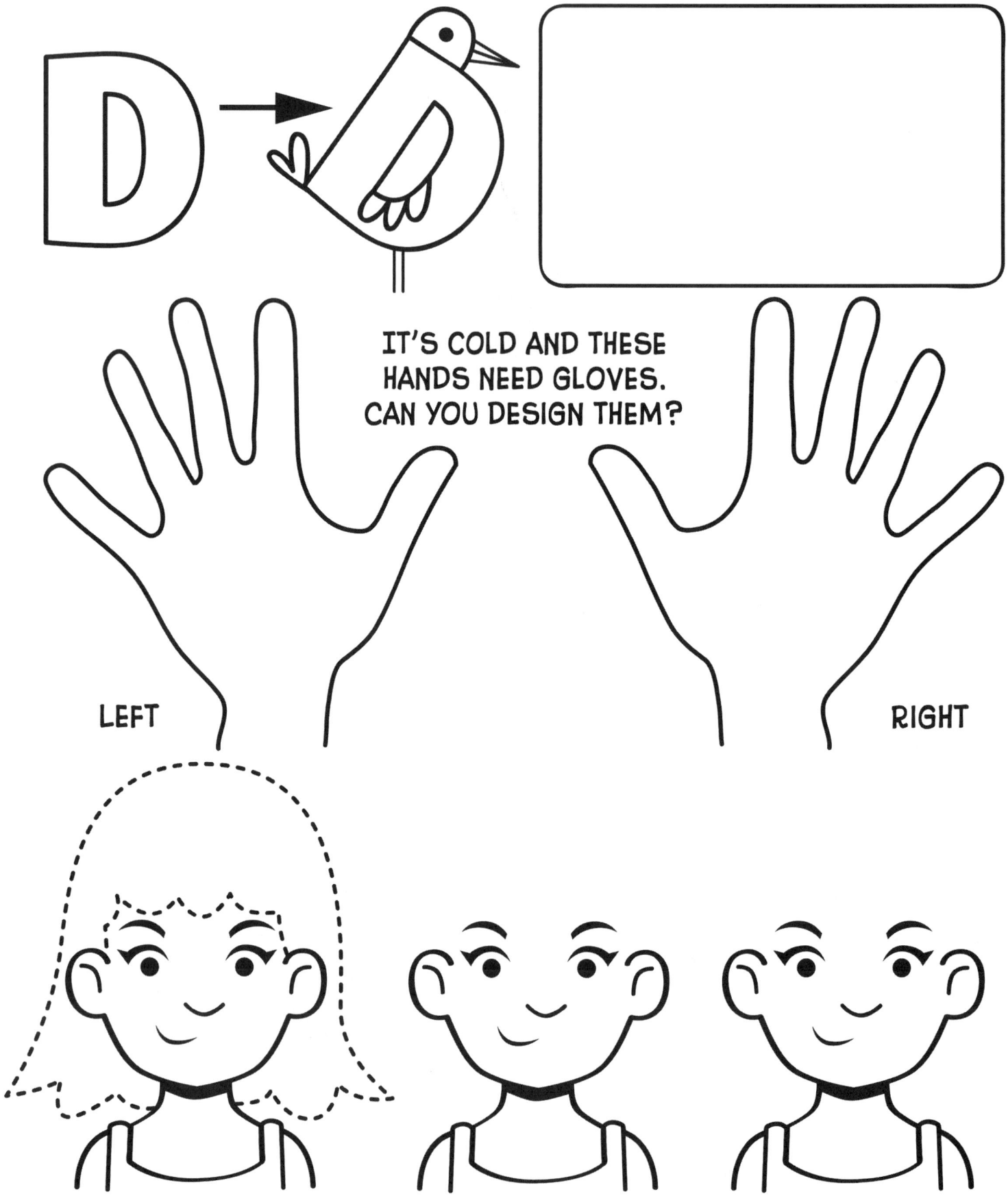

GIVE HER DIFFERENT HAIRCUTS.

DRAW FEATHERS FOR EACH ONE!

WHAT SONG IS THE BIRD SINGING? WRITE IT DOWN.

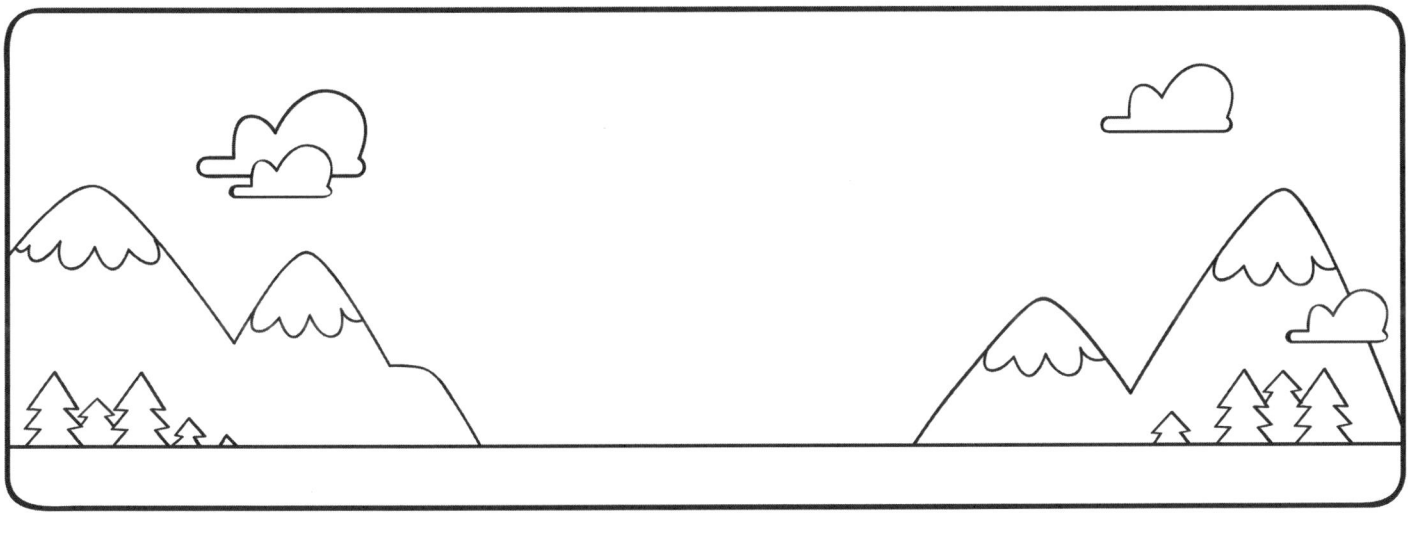

DRAW AND COLOR YOUR OWN SUNSET.

DRAW AND COLOR YOUR OWN SNOWMAN ARMY!

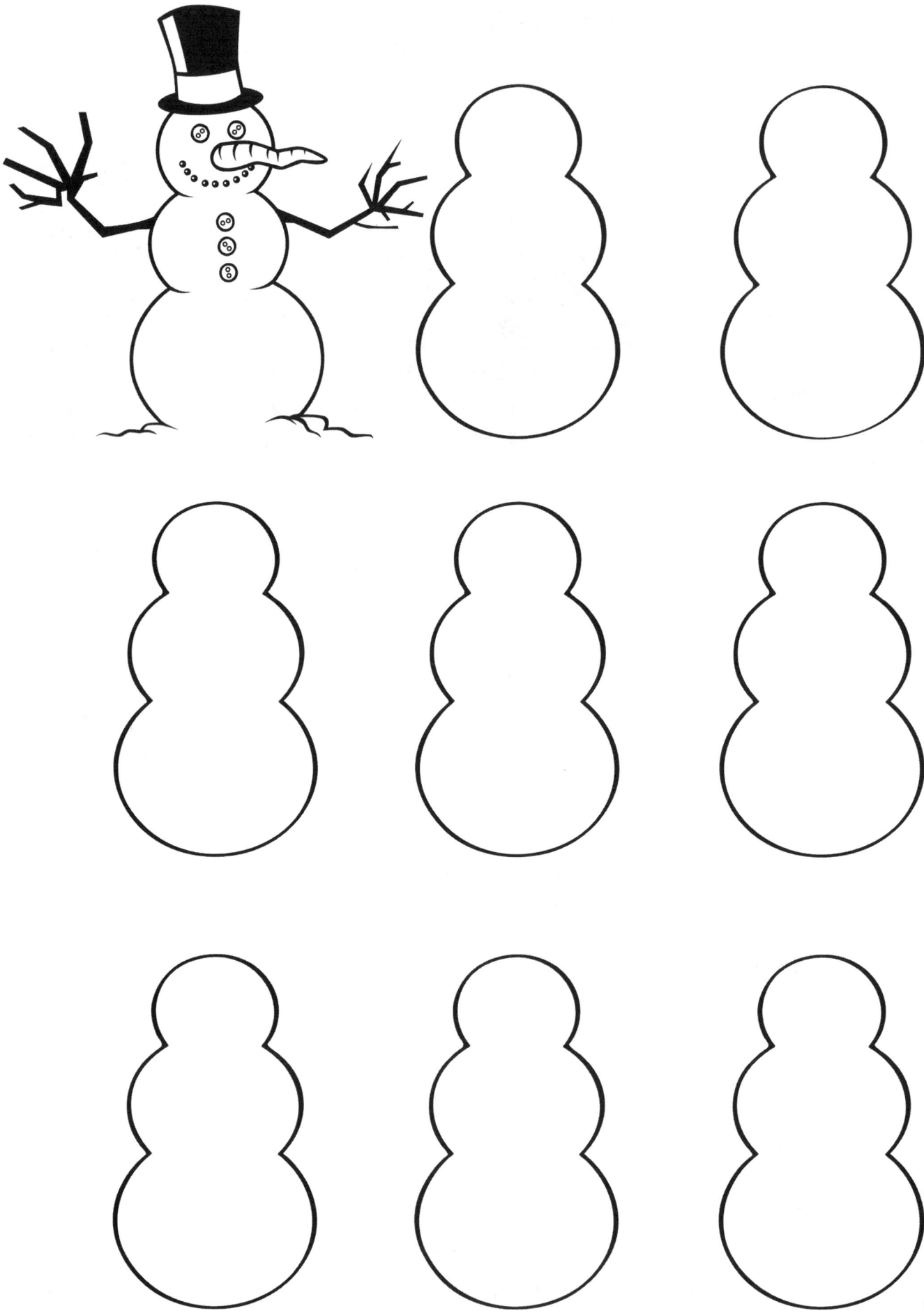

DRAW THE HEADS AND FACES OF THE PEOPLE WEARING THESE HATS.

CONNECT THE DOTS!

WHAT DOES THIS ANIMAL EAT? DRAW IT!

WHICH ITEM DOES A DOCTOR NOT USE?

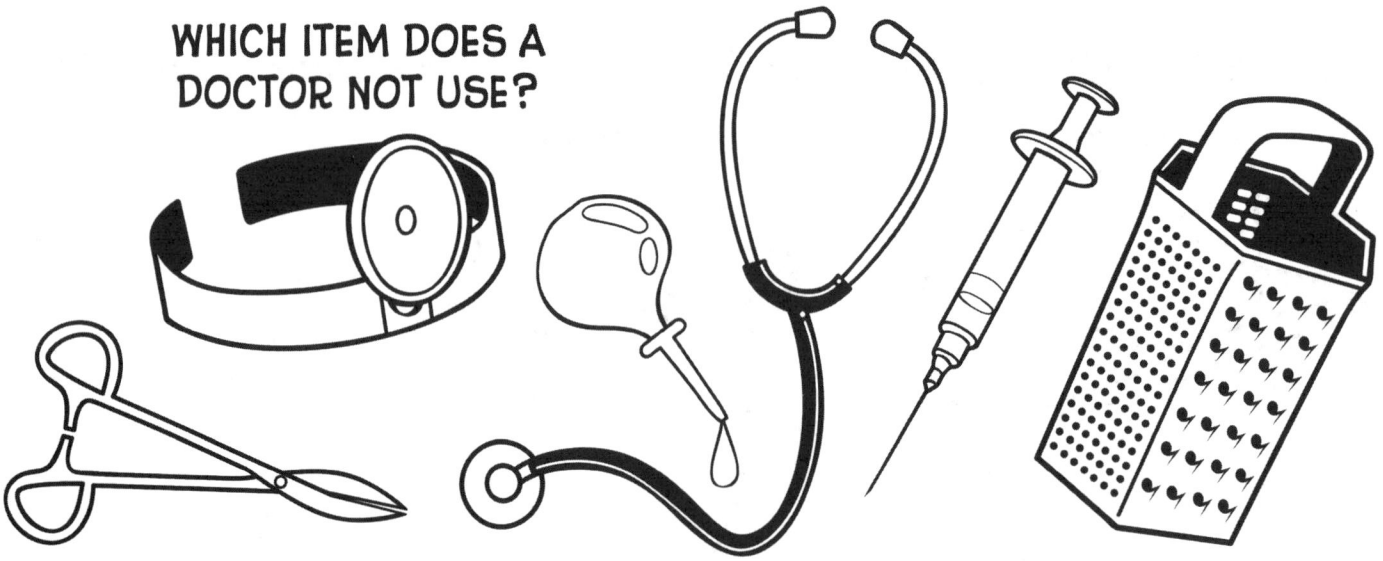

WHAT COUNTRY DOES THE FLAG BELONG TO? COLOR IT!

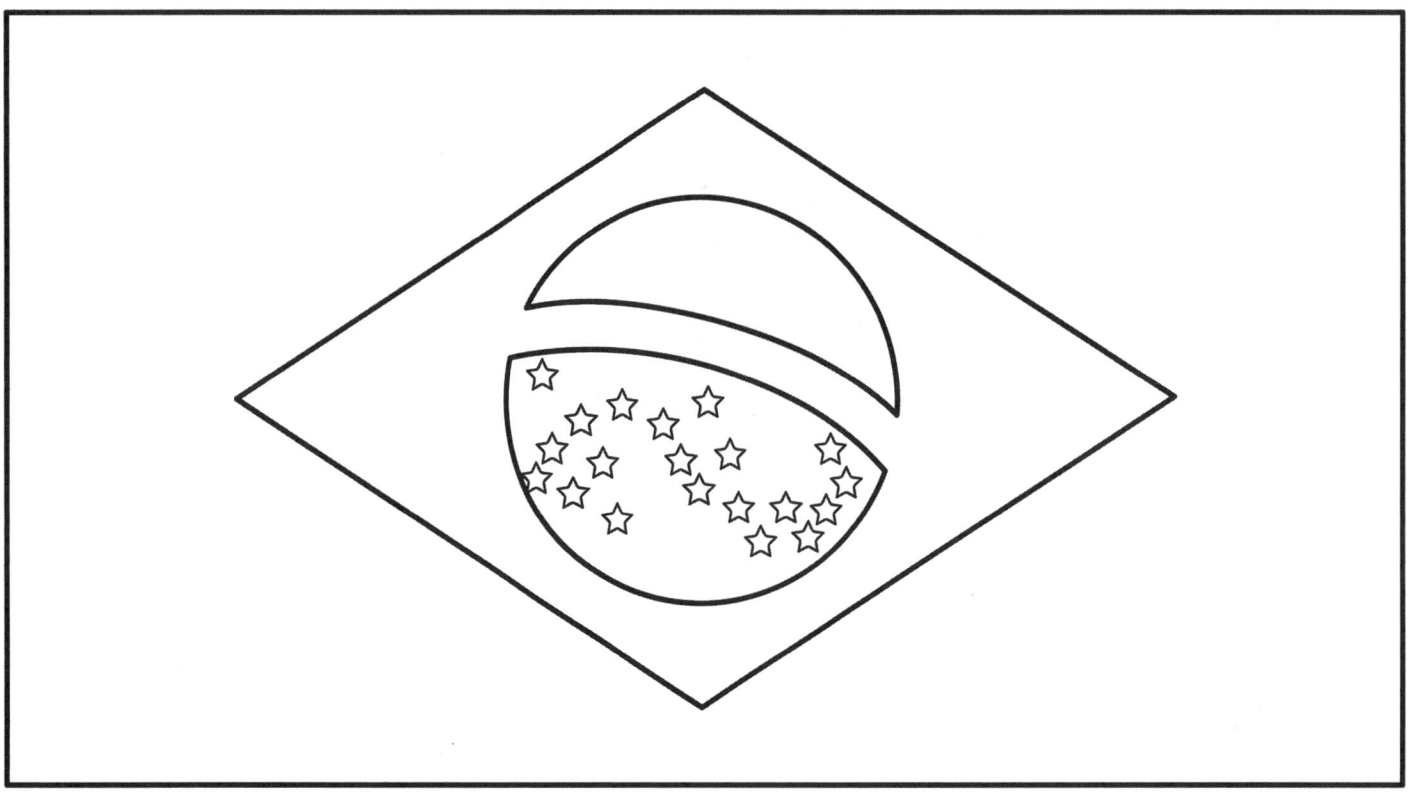

CONNECT THE SQUID TO THE RIGHT SILHOUETTE.

FILL THIS PAGE WITH MUSIC NOTES!

TRACE THE DOTS TO DRAW THE FISH IN A SINGLE STROKE.

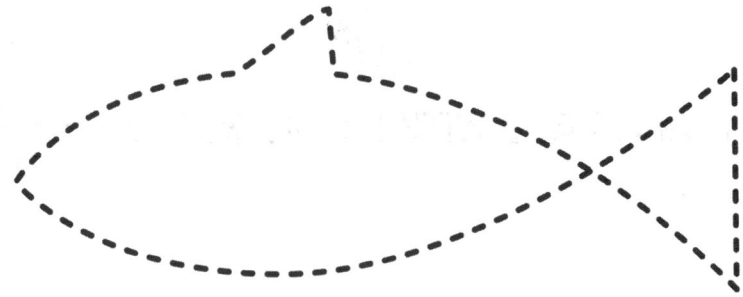

FIND THE SIX DIFFERENCES.

WHAT ANIMALS IS THIS CREATURE MADE OF?

DRAW THE OTHER HALF AND COLOR IT!

ONE OF THESE DOESN'T BELONG IN THE GROUP. WHY?

COLOR AND DECORATE THE ELEPHANTS ANYWAY YOU LIKE!

HOW MANY ARE MARCHING EAST? →

← HOW MANY ARE MARCHING WEST?

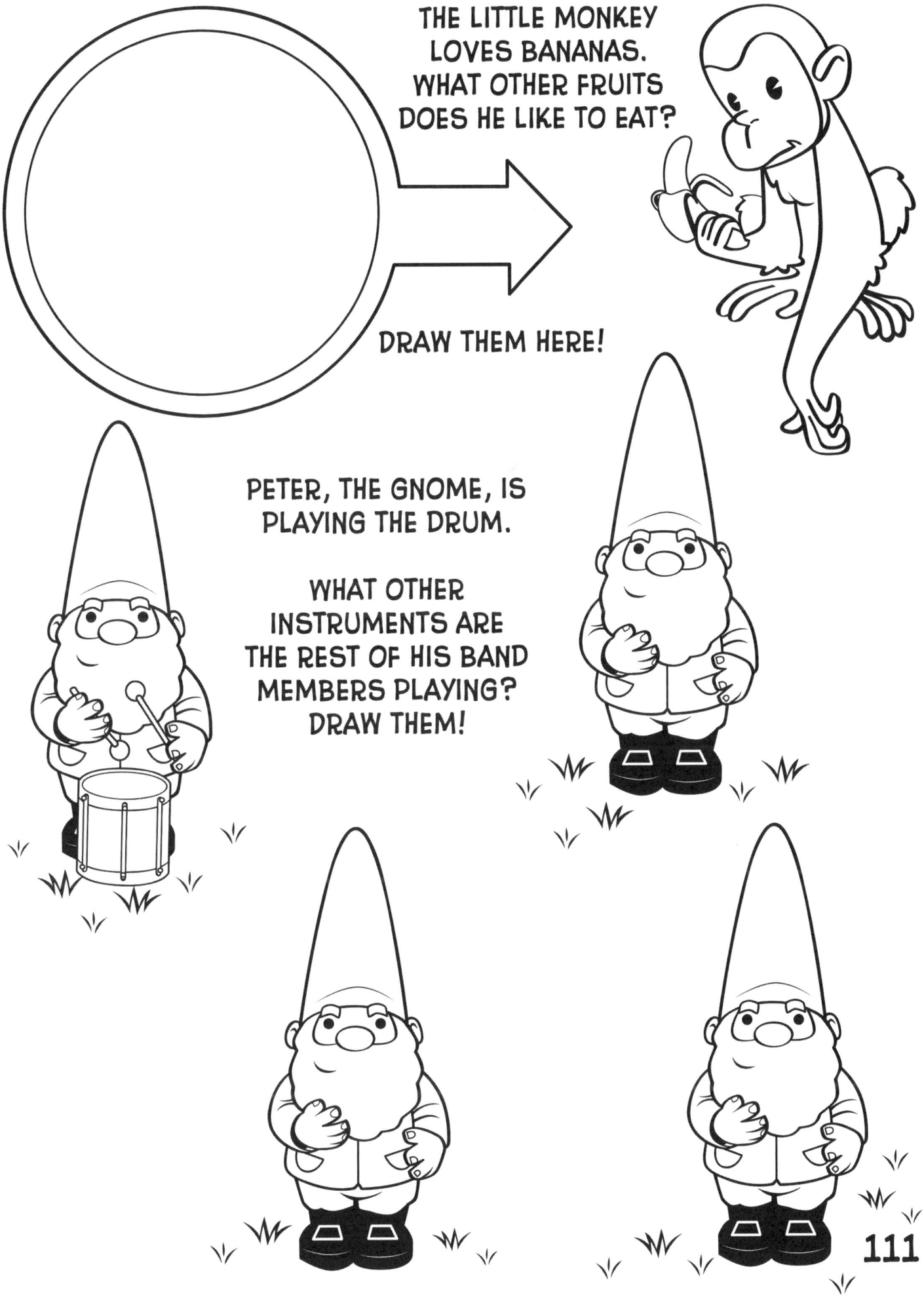
THE LITTLE MONKEY LOVES BANANAS. WHAT OTHER FRUITS DOES HE LIKE TO EAT?
DRAW THEM HERE!
PETER, THE GNOME, IS PLAYING THE DRUM.
WHAT OTHER INSTRUMENTS ARE THE REST OF HIS BAND MEMBERS PLAYING? DRAW THEM!

COLOR THE FIRST MASK BROWN, AND THEN CREATE YOUR OWN MONSTERS FOR HALLOWEEN!

WEREWOLF

VAMPIRE

ZOMBIE

MUTANT

ALIEN

DEVIL

COUNT THE NUMBER OF ORANGES. WHICH TREE HAS MORE OF THEM?
COLOR THE ONES THAT CAN'T FLY.

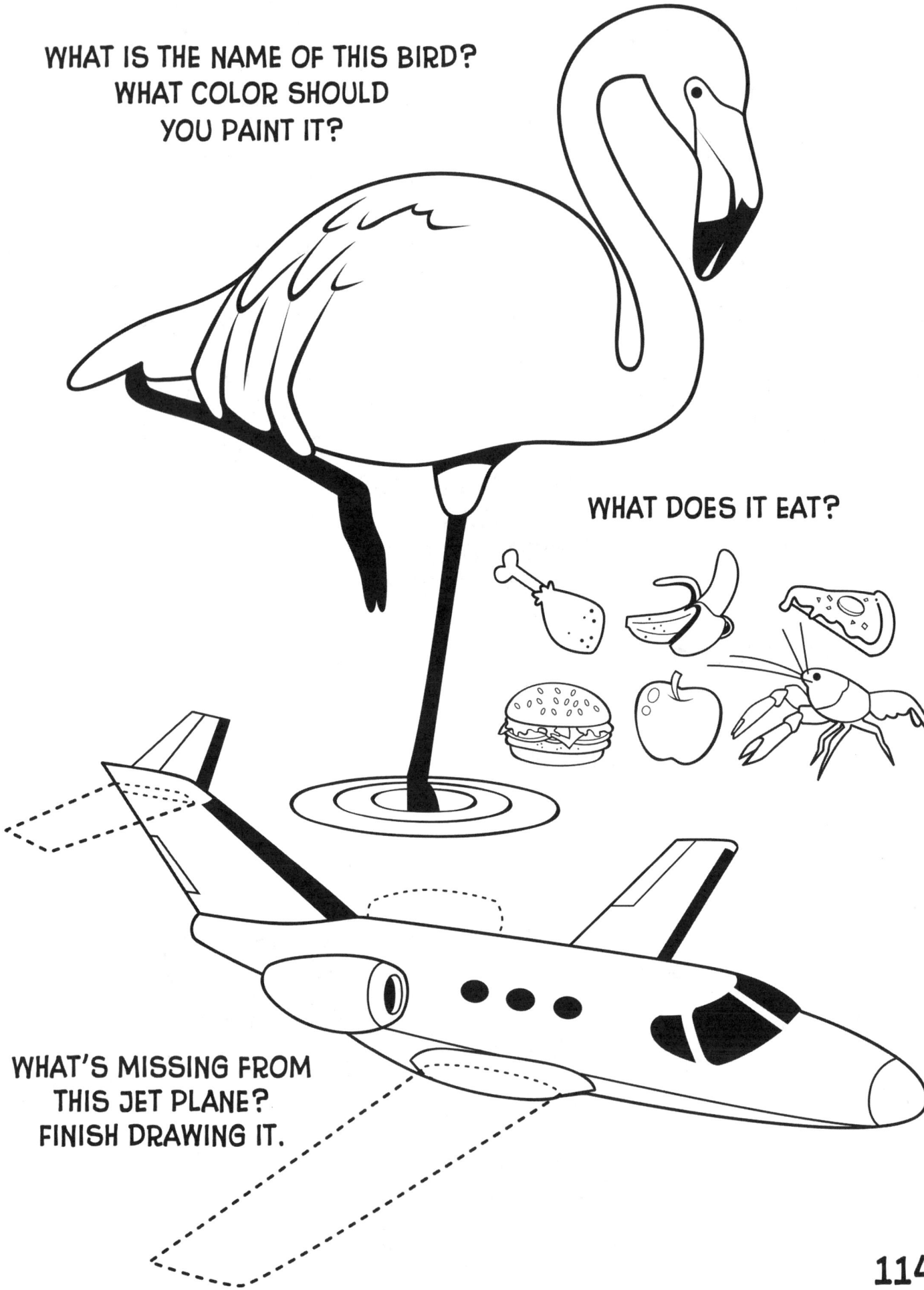
WHAT IS THE NAME OF THIS BIRD?
WHAT COLOR SHOULD
YOU PAINT IT?
WHAT DOES IT EAT?
WHAT'S MISSING FROM
THIS JET PLANE?
FINISH DRAWING IT.

HELP THE ANT FIND ITS LEAF.

COLOR THE TWO IDENTICAL CATS.

DECORATE YOUR DAD'S TIE
ANYWAY YOU LIKE!

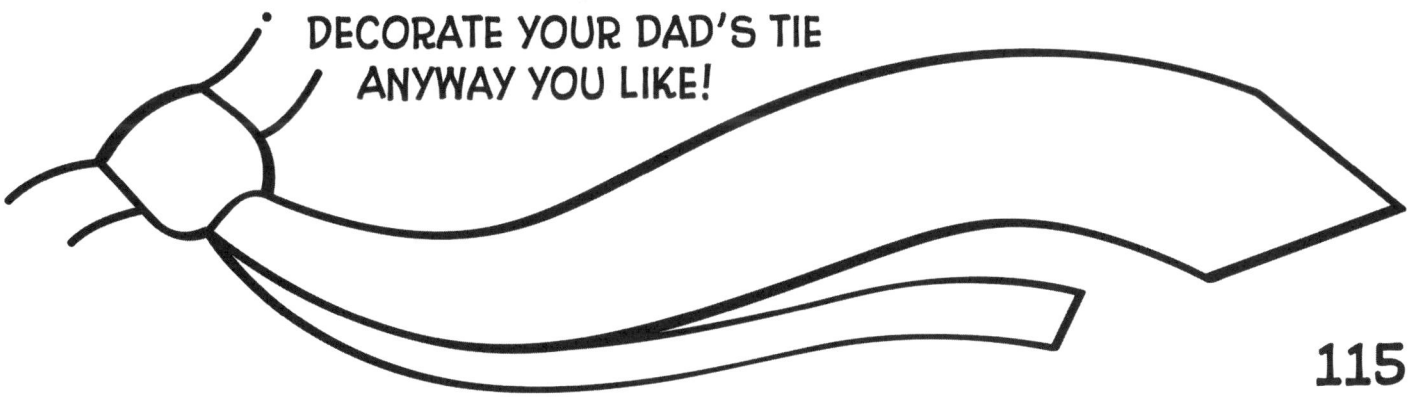

BREAKFAST IS THE MOST IMPORTANT MEAL OF THE DAY.

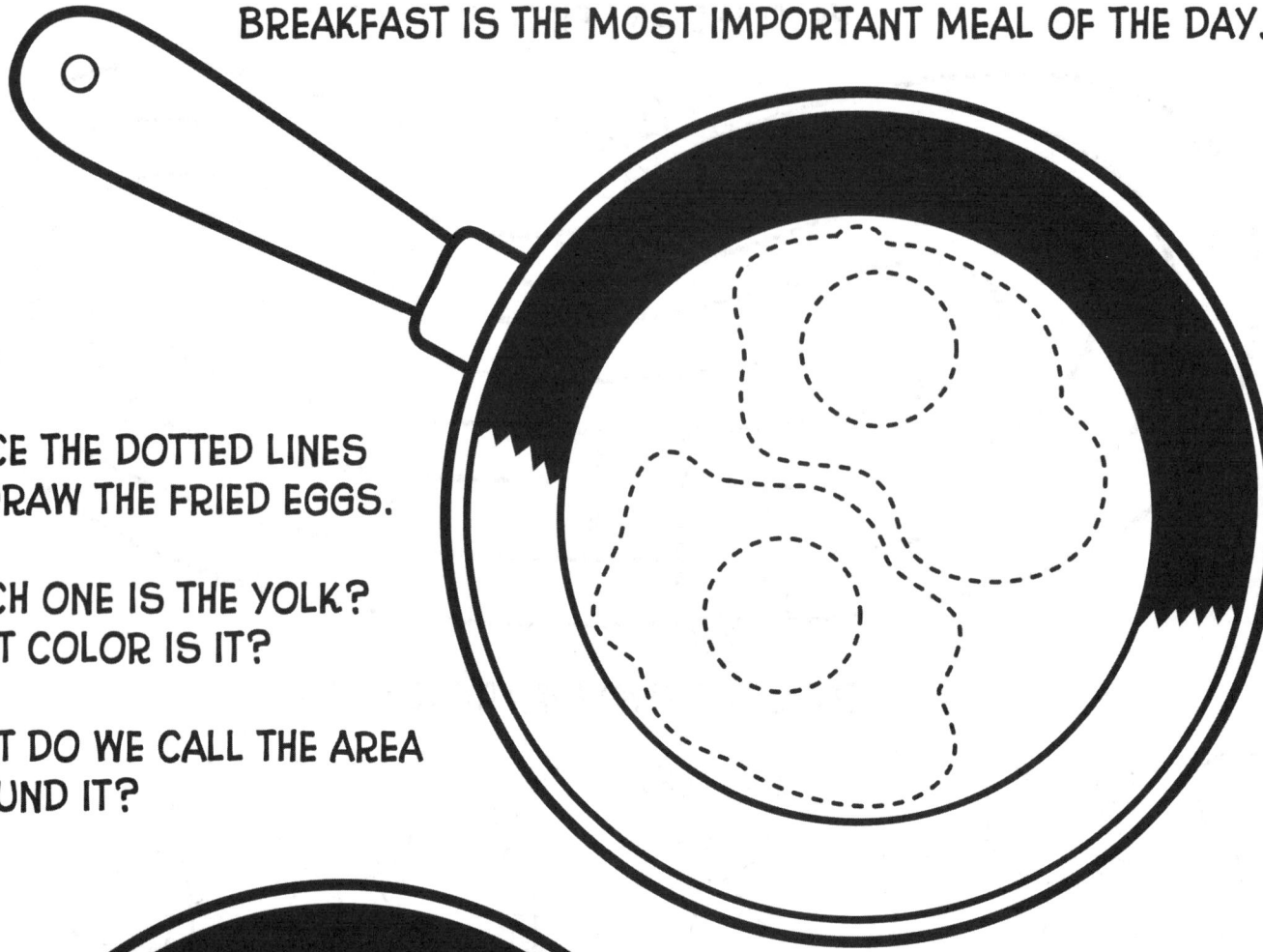

TRACE THE DOTTED LINES TO DRAW THE FRIED EGGS.

WHICH ONE IS THE YOLK? WHAT COLOR IS IT?

WHAT DO WE CALL THE AREA AROUND IT?

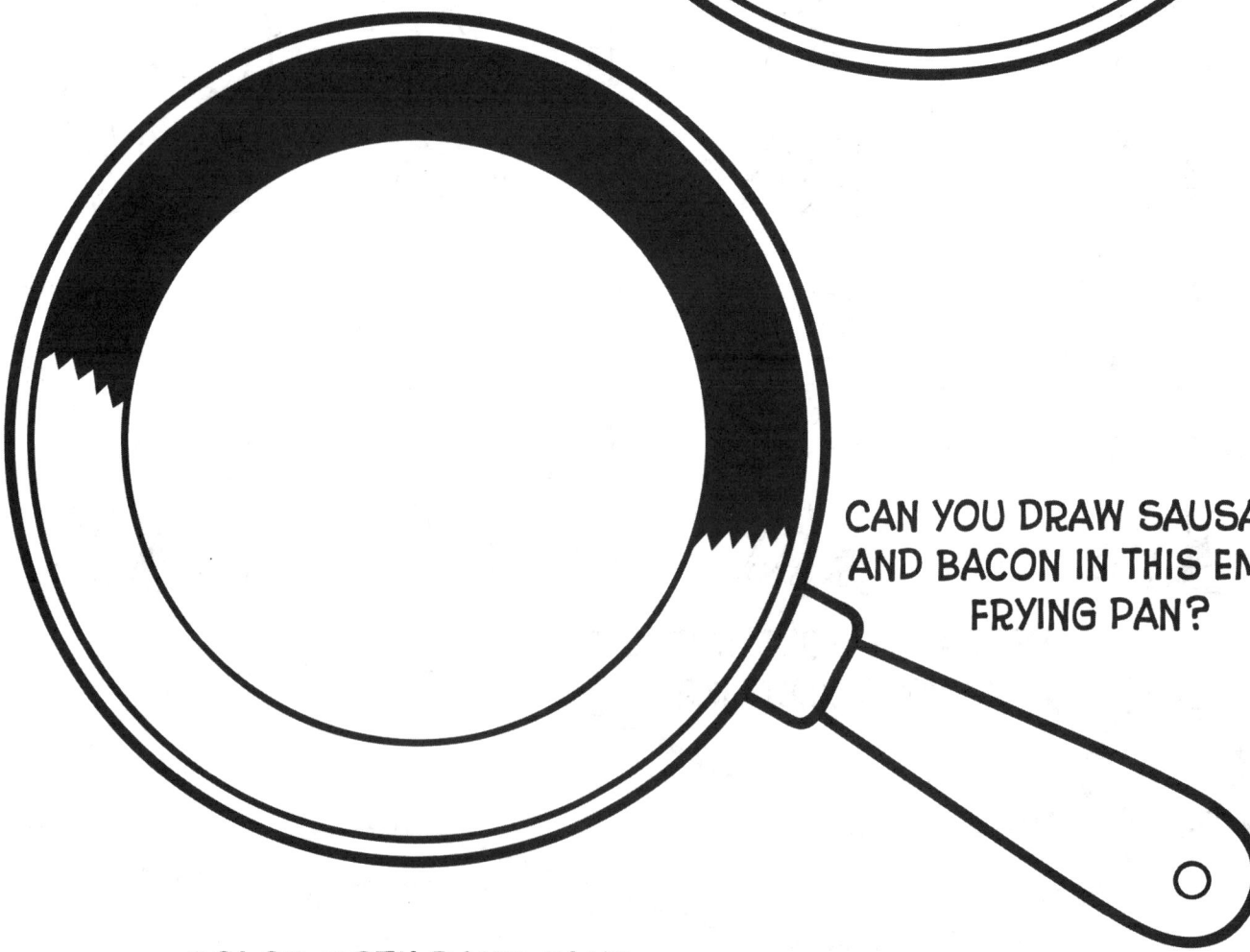

CAN YOU DRAW SAUSAGES AND BACON IN THIS EMPTY FRYING PAN?

COLOR BOTH PANS BLUE.

CONNECT EACH PERSON TO THE RIGHT TOOL.

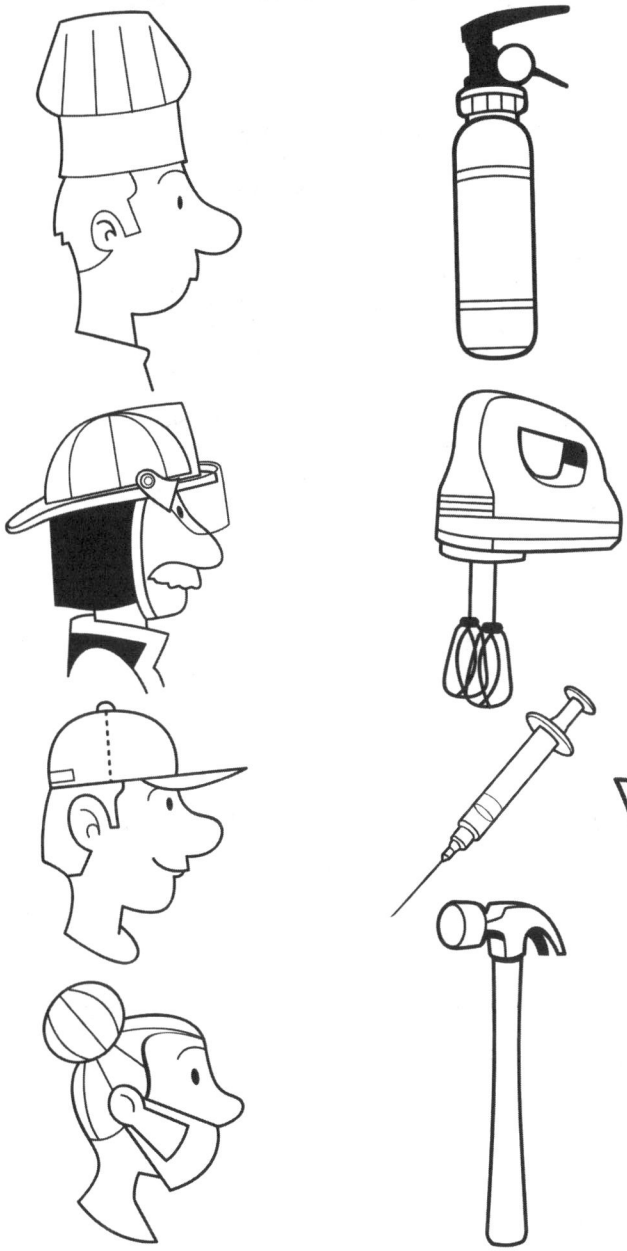

WHAT ANIMALS IS THIS STRANGE CREATURE MADE OF?

WHAT DOES THE SHARK EAT?

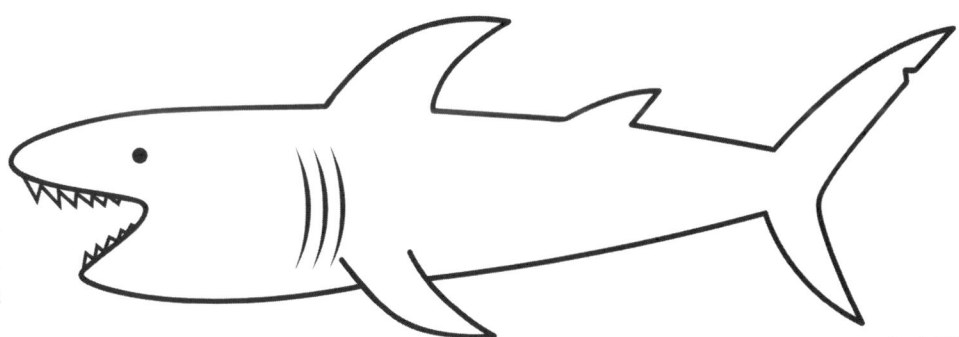

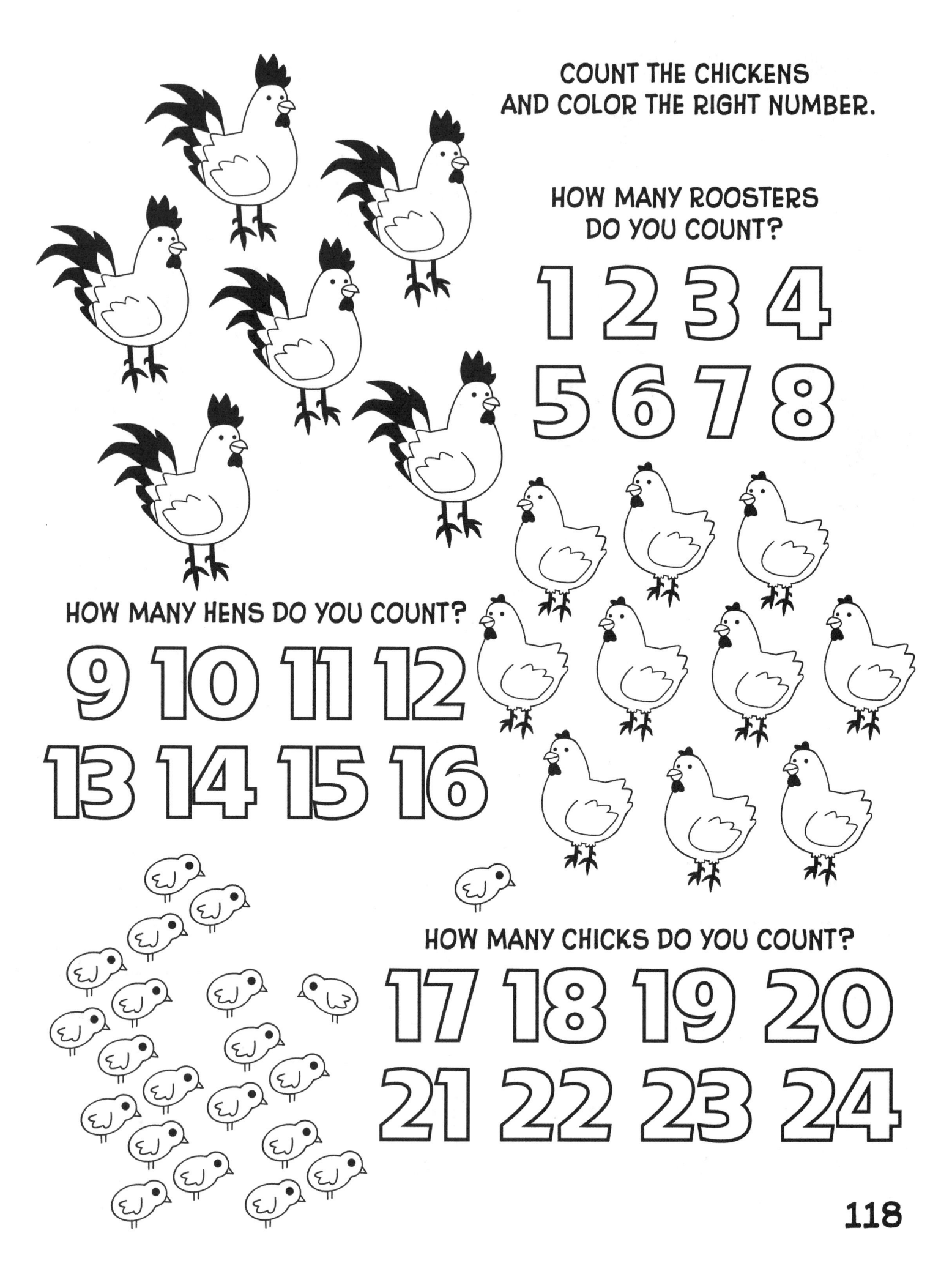

COUNT THE CHICKENS
AND COLOR THE RIGHT NUMBER.

HOW MANY ROOSTERS
DO YOU COUNT?

1 2 3 4
5 6 7 8

HOW MANY HENS DO YOU COUNT?

9 10 11 12
13 14 15 16

HOW MANY CHICKS DO YOU COUNT?

17 18 19 20
21 22 23 24

TRACE THE DOTTED LINES TO FINISH DRAWING THE TRAIN.

FIND THE PIECE OF THE DRAWING ON THE RIGHT
THAT DOESN'T BELONG TO THE ONE ON THE LEFT.

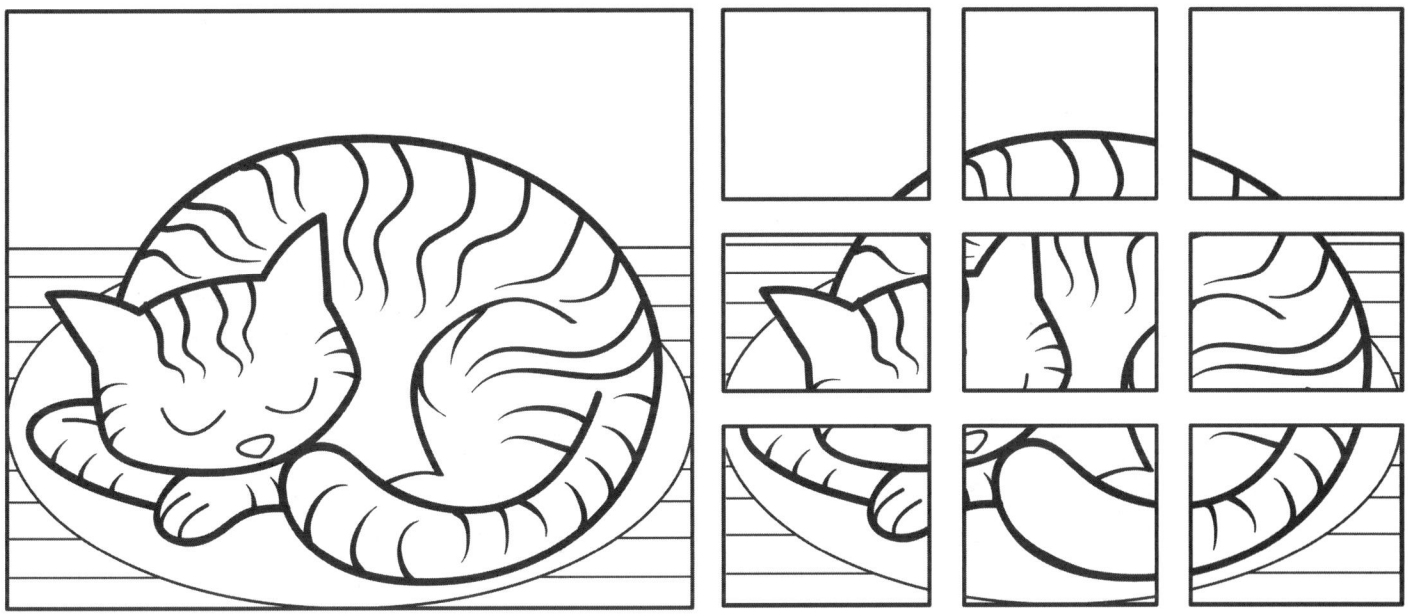

WHICH COW DOES NOT LOOK LIKE THE OTHERS?

CONNECT EACH ANIMAL TO THE GRID IT BELONGS TO, BUT BEWARE, ONLY ONE ANIMAL GOES IN EACH GRID!

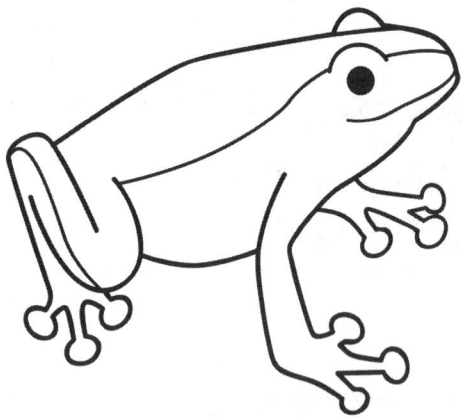

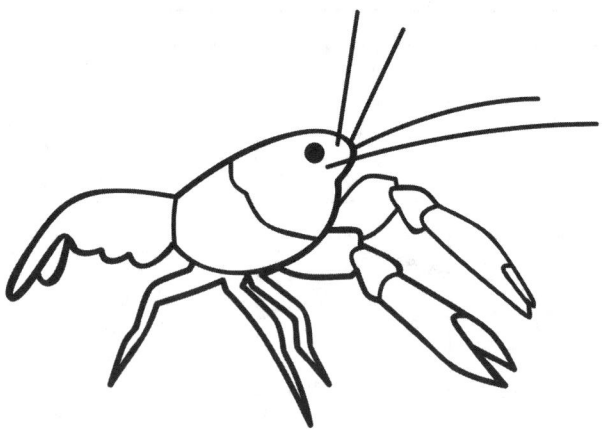

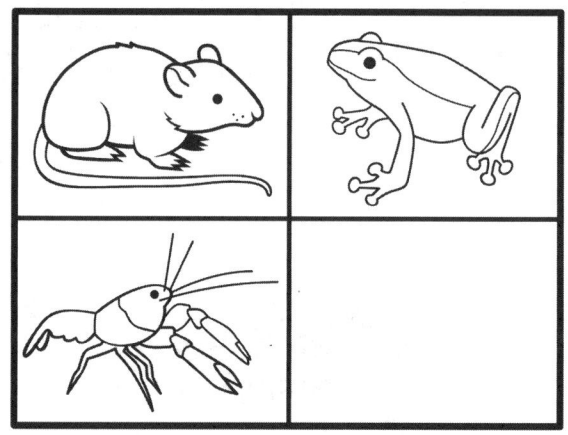

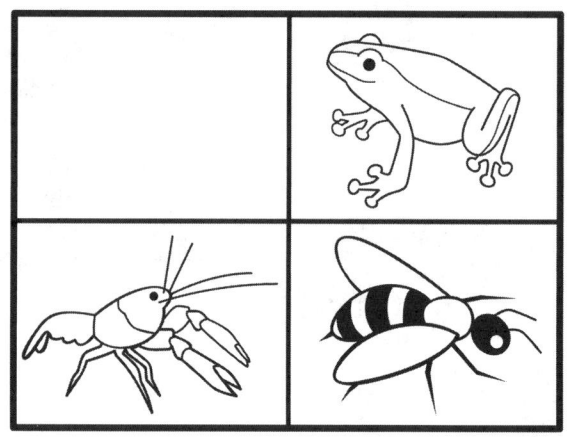

COLOR ONLY THE RED FOODS.

DO YOU LIKE THIS TORTOISE?
DRAW ANOTHER ONE JUST LIKE HER!

WHAT DOES THE PLATYPUS EAT?

DRAW THE SECOND CHERRY AND THE STRAWBERRY.

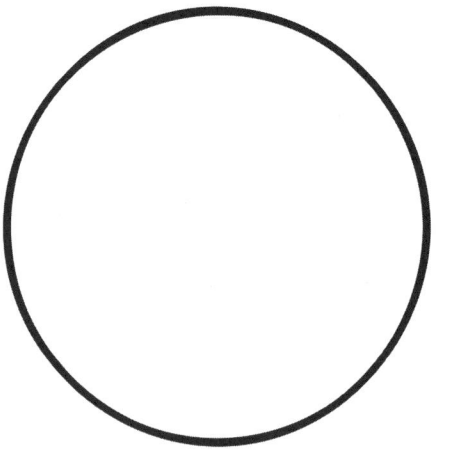

CAN YOU DRAW A RASPBERRY INSIDE THIS CIRCLE?

CRACK THE SUDOKU!
EACH FRUIT CAN ONLY BE PLACED ONCE ON EACH LINE, ONCE ON EACH ROW, AND ONCE IN EACH FOUR CELL GRID.

WHICH RABBIT WILL GET THE CARROT?
FOLLOW THE DOTTED LINES TO FIND OUT.

FIND THE SIX DIFFERENCES.

CAN YOU BEAT DAPHNE AT DOMINOES?
COMPLETE THE SERIES BY DRAWING
THE RIGHT ANIMAL ON EACH END.

IF YOU PUT ALL THESE CHERRIES INSIDE THE JAR, HOW MANY CHERRIES WILL IT CONTAIN IN TOTAL?

THESE DOLLS ARE ALL SCRAMBLED! NUMBER EACH ONE FROM THE SMALLEST TO THE BIGGEST, IN THE ORDER THEY'D BE NESTED INSIDE ONE ANOTHER.

NAME ALL PLANETS. WHICH ONE IS CLOSEST TO THE SUN?

IF THE DOG CHASES THE CAT, THE CAT CHASES THE MOUSE, AND THE MOUSE EATS THE CHEESE, WHICH ONE IS NOT BEING CHASED?
HELP THE DOLPHIN FIND THE TUNA!

CAN YOU FIND THE SMALLER COMBINATIONS IN THE BIG GRID BELOW?
COLOR THEM WHEN YOU DO!

COMPLETE EACH LINE IN THE CORRECT SEQUENCE.

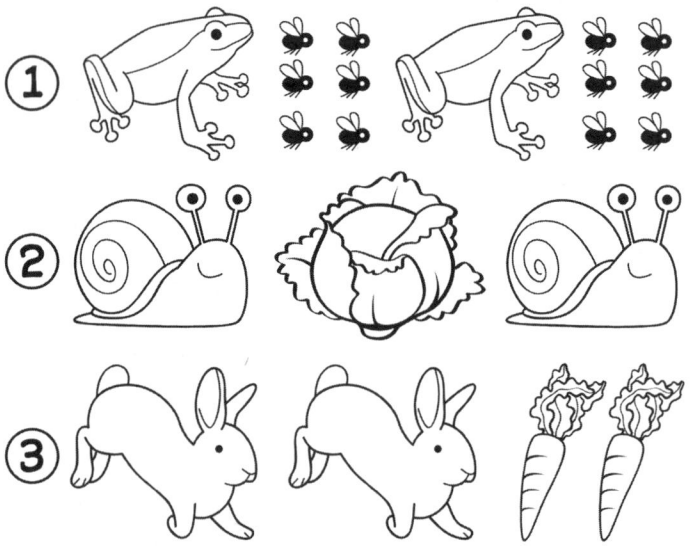

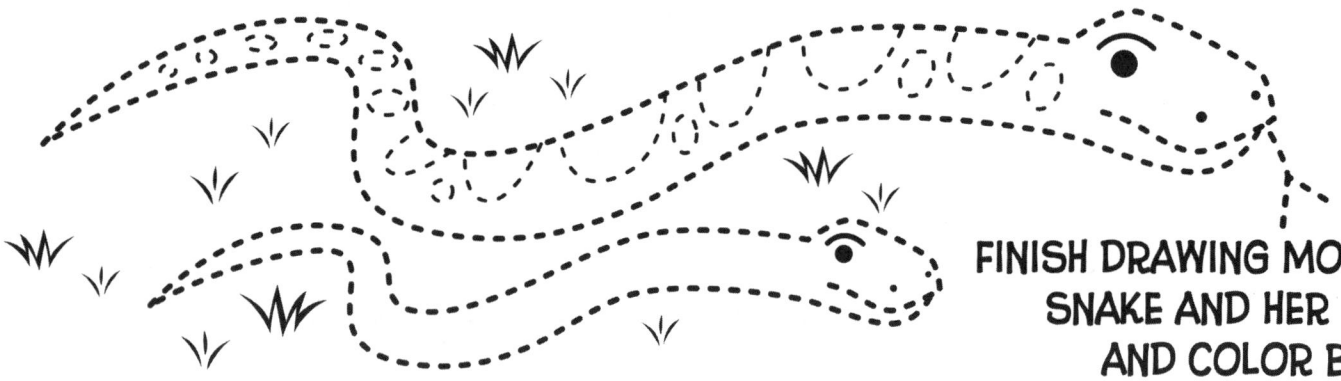

FINISH DRAWING MOMMY SNAKE AND HER SON, AND COLOR BOTH!

WHICH OF THESE BIRDS SHOULDN'T BE HERE? WHY? COLOR THE CHICKS YELLOW.

FILL THIS TREE WITH APPLES AND LEAVES!
HOW MANY DID YOU DRAW?
WHAT'S HIDING BEHIND THE TRUNK?
CARVE YOUR INITIALS INSIDE THE HEART.

1 = YELLOW
2 = BROWN
3 = GREEN
4 = BLUE

WHAT ANIMAL IS IT?

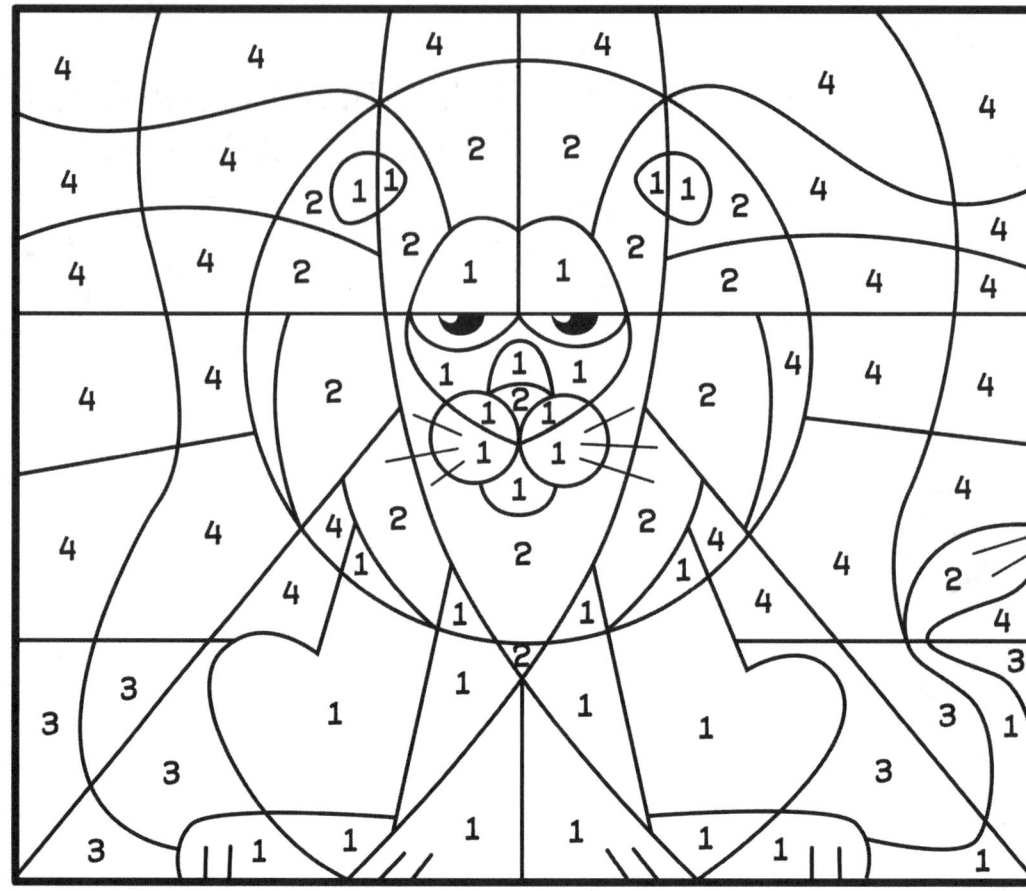

WRITE THE NAME OF THE SPORT YOU PLAY WITH EACH BALL.

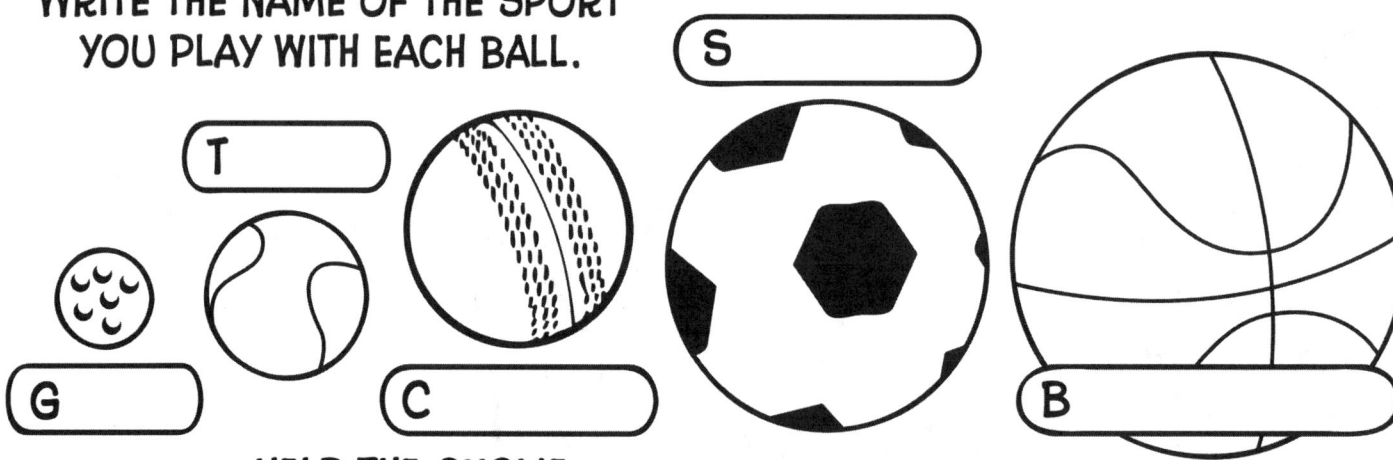

HELP THE GNOME FIND HIS HAT!

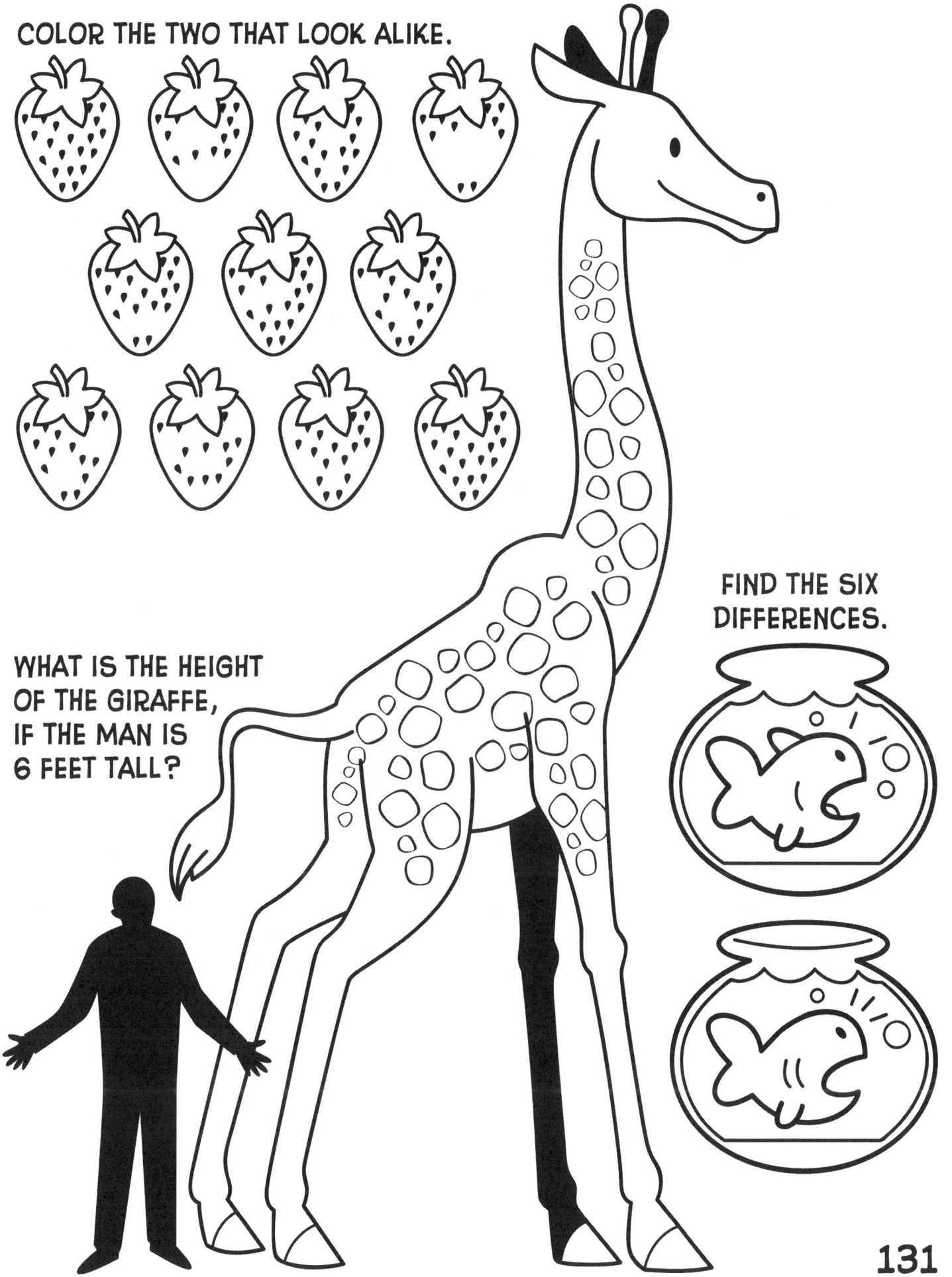
COLOR THE TWO THAT LOOK ALIKE.
WHAT IS THE HEIGHT OF THE GIRAFFE, IF THE MAN IS 6 FEET TALL?
FIND THE SIX DIFFERENCES.

CONNECT THE DOTS!

WHAT IS IT?
WHERE DOES IT LIVE?

WHICH BOWL GIVES THE CORRECT NUMBER OF CANDY IN THE JAR?

HOW MANY CIRCLES ARE IN THIS TABLE?
HOW MANY STARS? AND SQUARES?

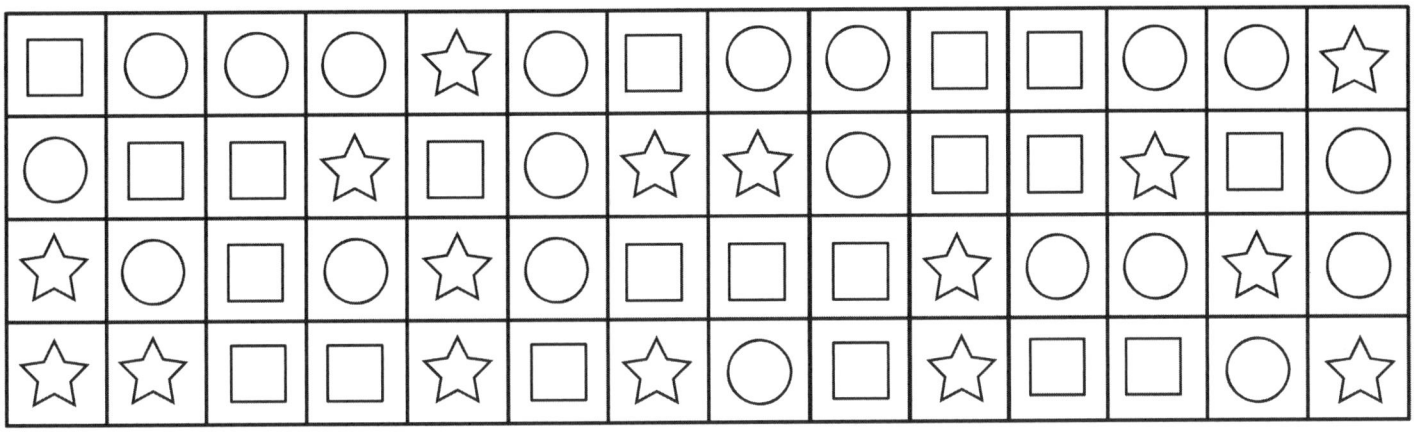

WRITE FOUR ANIMALS THAT START WITH THE LETTER "O".

O
O
O
O

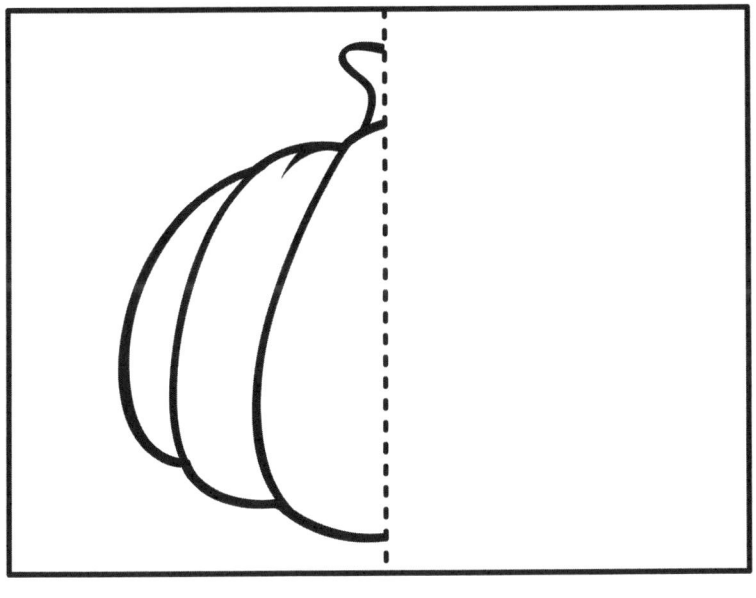

DRAW THE OTHER HALF OF THE PUMPKIN, AND COLOR IT.

DRAW A CIRCLE AROUND THE FOODS THAT AREN'T GOOD FOR YOU, AND COLOR THE HEALTHY ONES.

DRAW YOURSELF A HEALTHY MEAL!

FILL THE PLATE ON THE LEFT WITH THE MAIN COURSE.

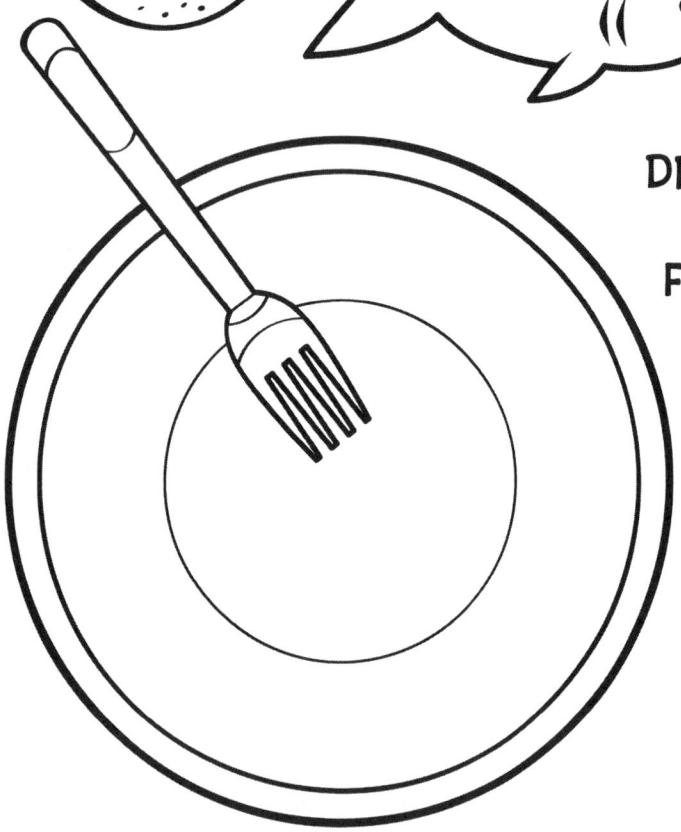

AND THE ONE AT YOUR RIGHT WITH A HEALTHY DESSERT.

ADD THE NUMBERS WRITTEN ON THE SAILS.
WHAT RESULTS DO YOU GET?

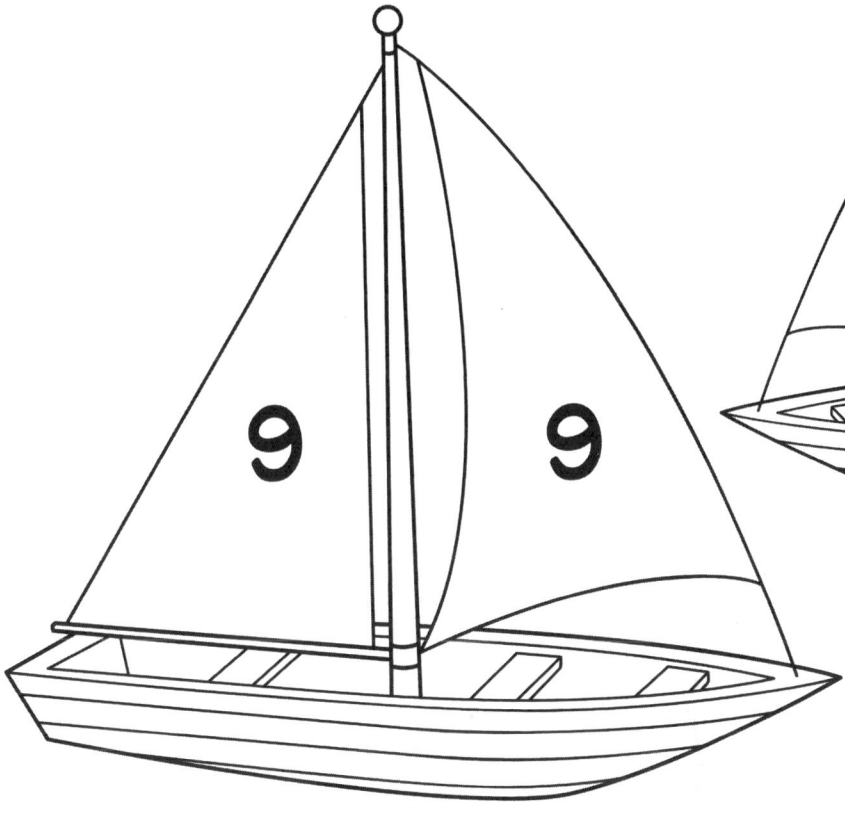

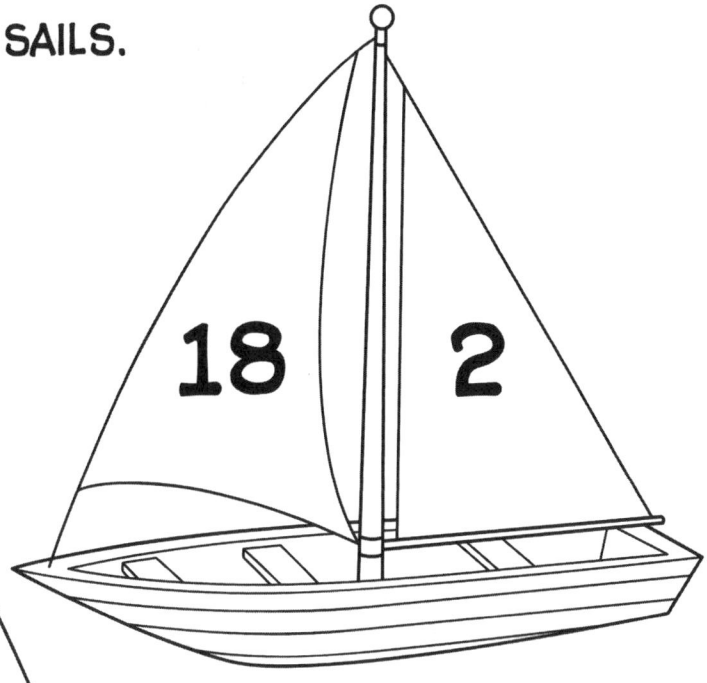

ONLY TWO HENS ARE MOMS. THREE CHICKS BELONG TO ONE, AND ONLY ONE TO THE OTHER. CAN YOU GUESS WHICH CHICKS BELONG TO EACH HEN?

THIS PIG LOVES PLAYING IN THE MUD, SO GRAB A BROWN CRAYON, FILL THIS PAGE WITH MUD SPLATTERS OF EVERY SHAPE AND SIZE, AND THEN COLOR THE PIG PINK!

FIND THE 10 DIFFERENCES.

WHAT IS INSIDE THIS BOTTLE?

IN WHAT BOX WILL CAR #1 AND CAR #2 MEET, KNOWING THAT #2 GOES TWO TIMES FASTER THAN #1? COLOR #1 BLUE AND #2 RED.

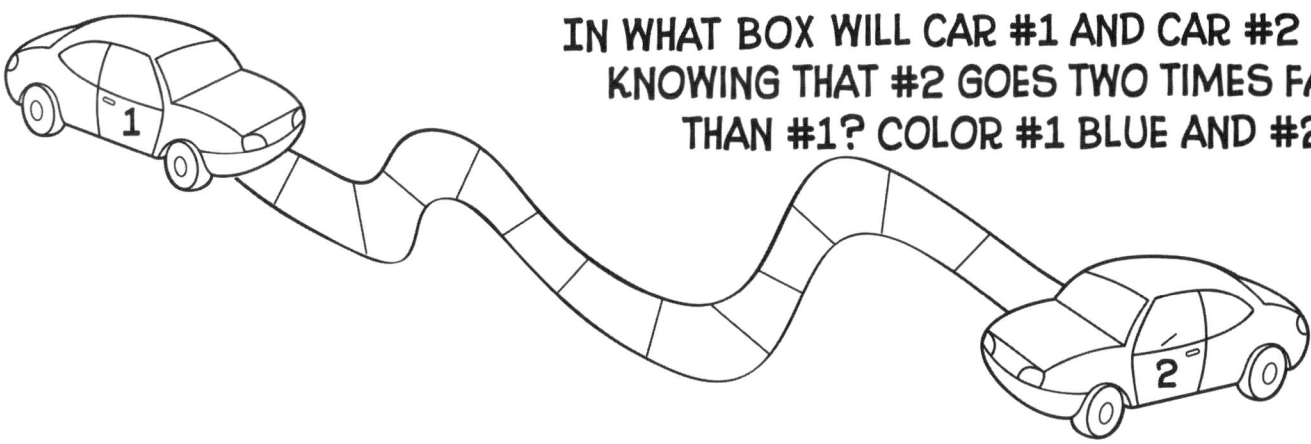

COLOR ONLY THE THINGS THAT GIVE LIGHT.

HELP CRISSY FIND HER PRESENT!

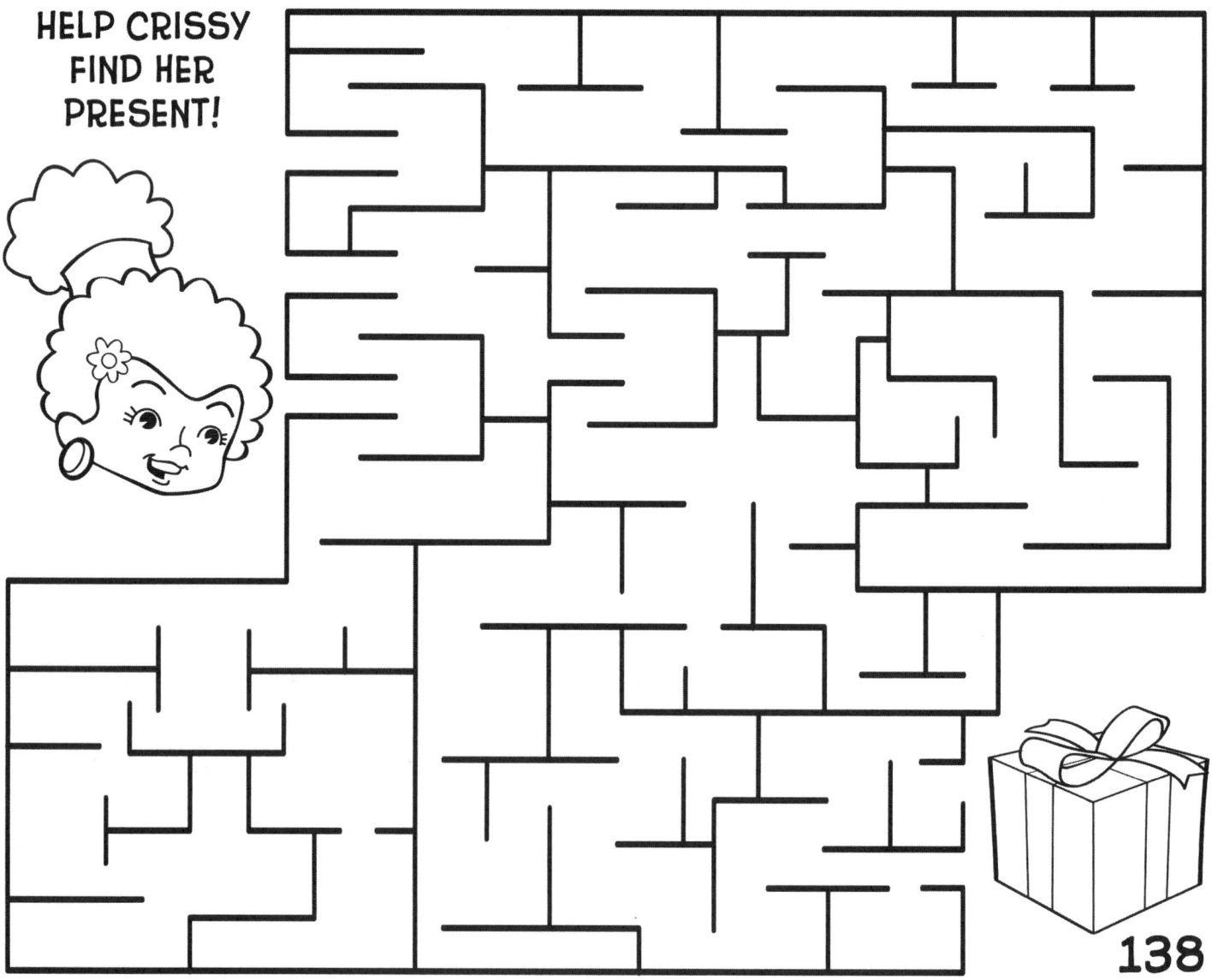

WHICH DRAWING ON THE RIGHT IS IDENTICAL TO THE ONE IN THE LEFT COLUMN?

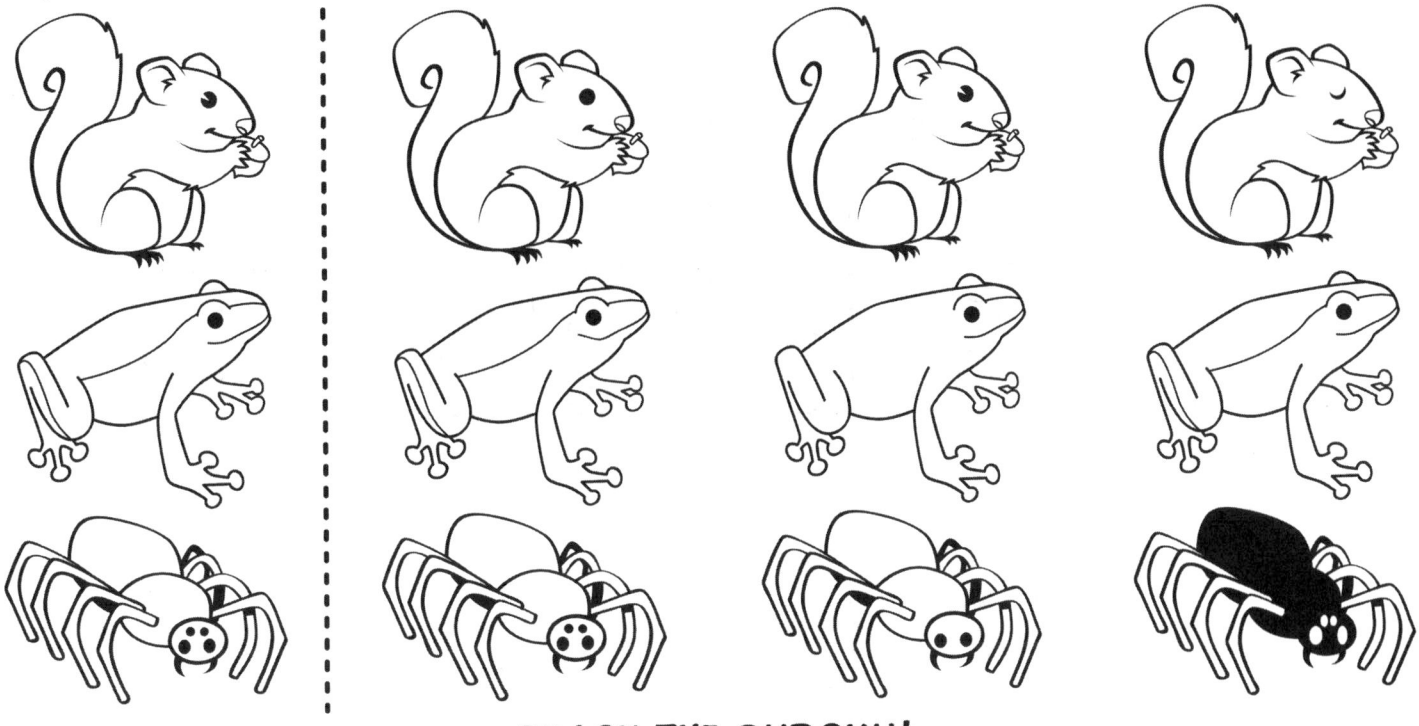

CRACK THE SUDOKU!

EACH ELEMENT CAN ONLY BE PLACED ONCE ON EACH LINE, ONCE ON EACH ROW, AND ONCE IN EACH FOUR CELL GRID.

CAN YOU FIND THE SMALLER COMBINATIONS IN THE BIG GRID BELOW?
COLOR THEM WHEN YOU DO!

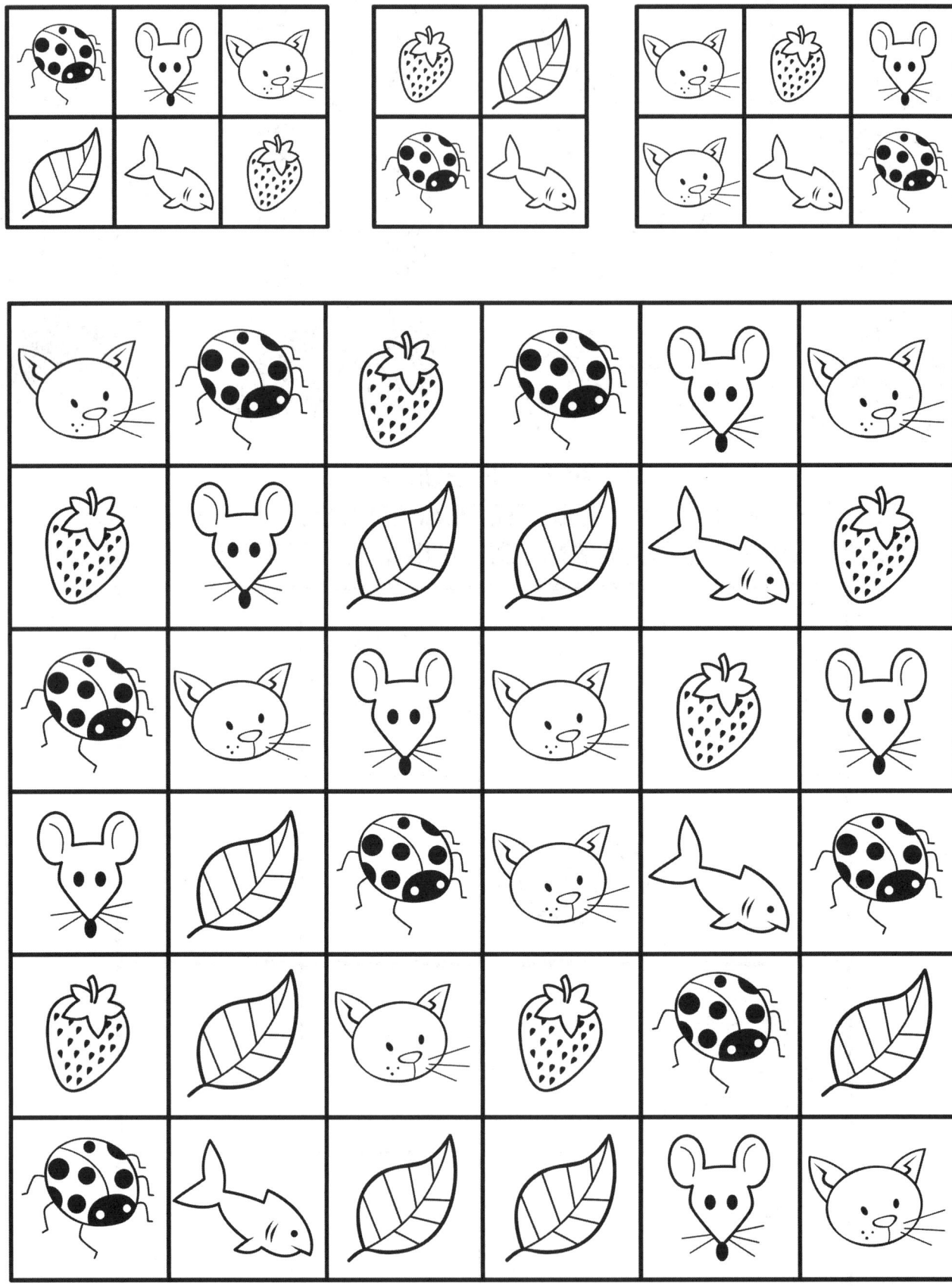

WHICH ELEPHANT WEIGHS MORE?

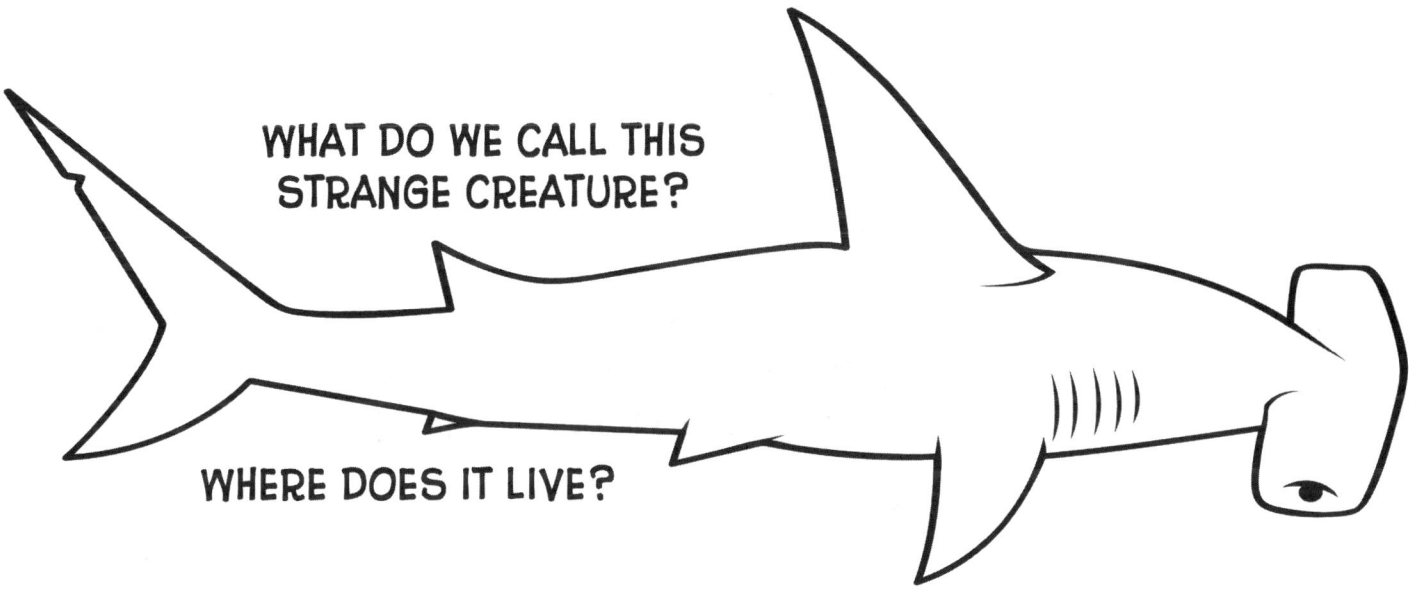

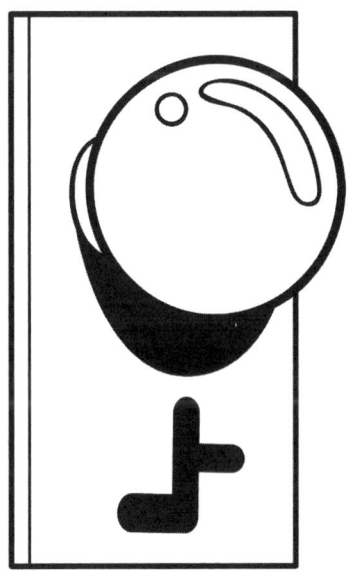

WHICH OF THESE KEYS IS MADE FOR THAT LOCK?

IF THE GORILLA EATS TWO BANANAS PER DAY,
HOW MANY DAYS WILL IT TAKE HIM TO EAT THEM ALL?

HOW MANY WATERLILIES DOES THE
FROG JUMP ON IF IT GOES AROUND
THE POND THREE TIMES?

WHICH ONE IS NOT A TOY?

HOW MANY POUNDS OF COAL DOES THE TRAIN TRANSPORT?

GIVE NUMBERS TO THE ANIMALS FROM THE SMALLEST (1) TO THE BIGGEST (6) IN REAL LIFE.

HOW OLD IS THIS FELLED TREE?
COUNT THE TRUNK RINGS TO FIND OUT!

COLOR THE TWO LOOKALIKE TUNA!

1 APPLE = $2
2 CHERRIES = $3
1 PEAR = $4
HOW MUCH DO THESE COST ALL TOGETHER?

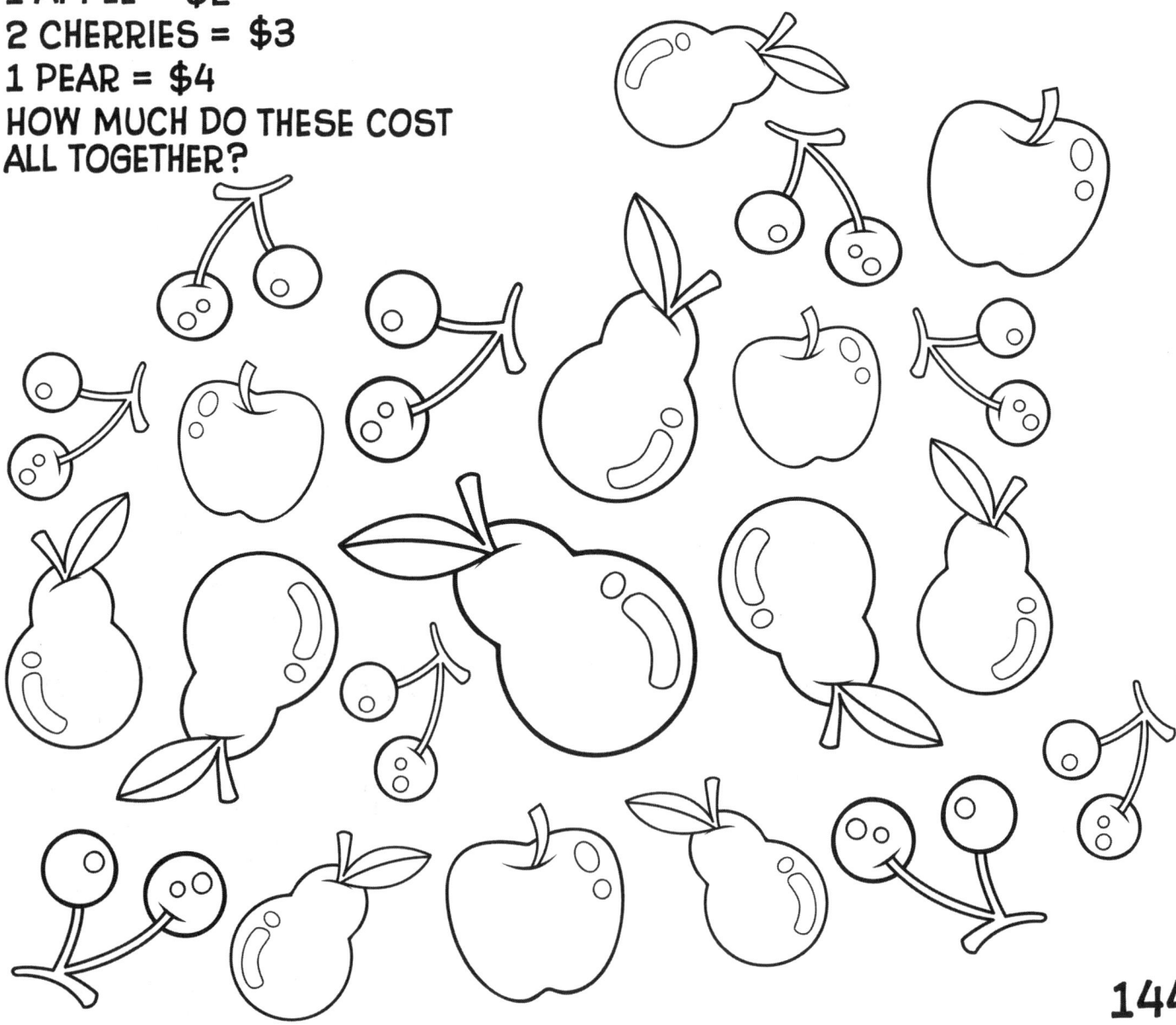

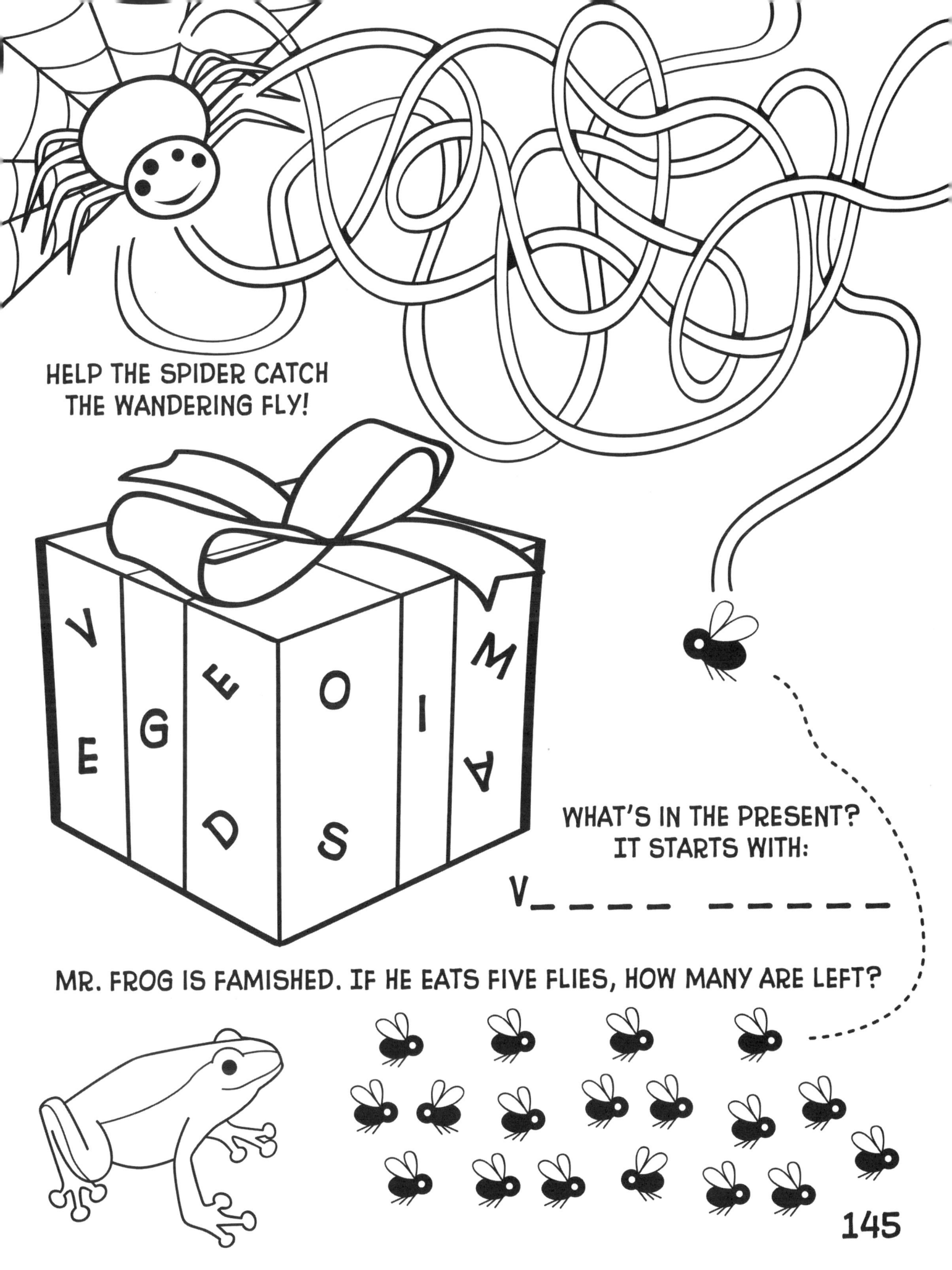
HELP THE SPIDER CATCH
THE WANDERING FLY!
V
E
G
E
D
O
S
I
M
A
WHAT'S IN THE PRESENT?
IT STARTS WITH:
V_ _ _ _ _ _ _ _ _ _
MR. FROG IS FAMISHED. IF HE EATS FIVE FLIES, HOW MANY ARE LEFT?

WHAT ANIMALS IS THIS CREATURE MADE OF?
HOW MANY FLOWERS DO YOU SEE? COLOR THEM!
CROSSWORDS.
1.
A
2.
3.
4.
1.
2.
3.
4.

CREATE YOUR OWN FLAG!
MATCH THESE ANIMALS
TO THEIR PROPER FEET!

ONE OF THESE ANIMALS HAS
HAS NO LUNGS... WHICH ONE?

IF YOU ADD ALL THE NUMBERS IN THE SQUARES AND SUBTRACT
ALL THE NUMBERS IN THE CIRCLES, WHAT WILL THE RESULT BE?

DO YOU KNOW THIS INSECT?

WHERE HAVE YOU SEEN IT?

CAN IT FLY?

COLOR IT BRIGHTLY!

THE KIDS HAVE GONE OUTSIDE TO PLAY!

TRACE THE DOTTED LINE TO FINISH THE SWINGS.

FOLLOW THE THREAD TO FIND OUT WHICH TOP SALLY IS REALLY THROWING FOR A SPIN.

CREATE AN ORIGINAL DESIGN TO DECORATE BILLY'S CAP.

COLOR THE BIG MARBLES GREEN AND THE SMALL ONES BLUE.

CROSSWORDS.

WHICH BOWL GIVES THE CORRECT NUMBER, FOR THE NUMBER OF CHERRIES IN THE JAR?

WHICH ANIMALS HERE EAT THE NECTAR FROM FLOWERS?

WHICH BALL DOES NOT LOOK LIKE THE OTHERS?

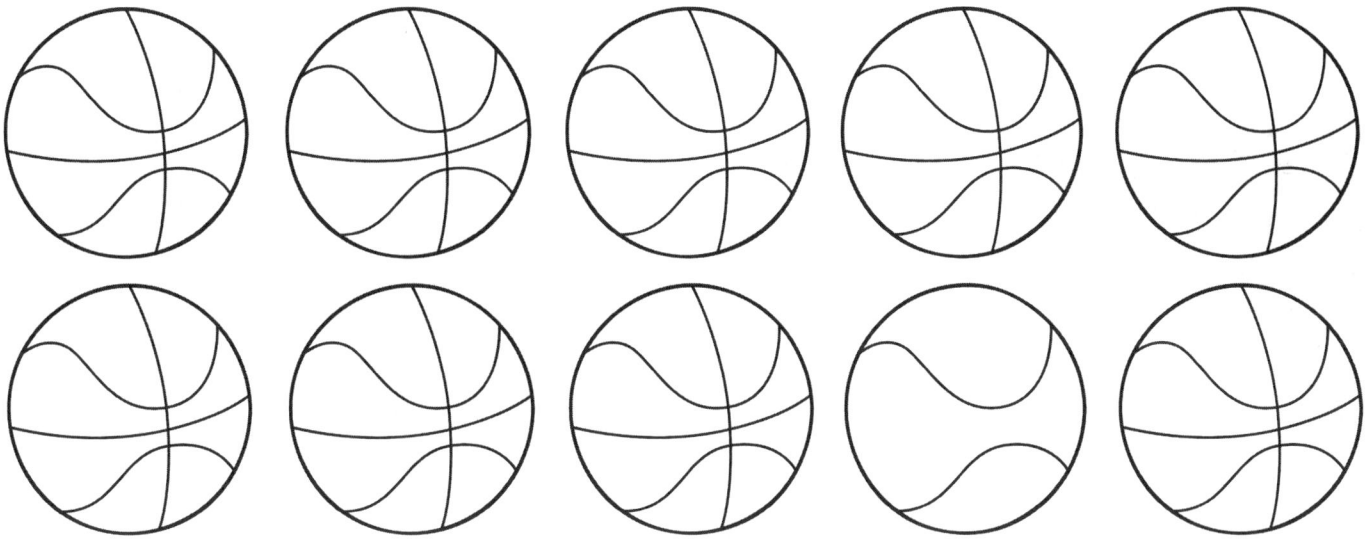

HOW MANY CAN YOU COUNT IN EACH SERIES? COLOR THE RIGHT NUMBER.

1 2 3 4 5 6 7 8

1 2 3 4 5 6 7 8

1 2 3 4 5 6 7 8

FIND THE STALLION'S CORRESPONDING SHADOW.

WHICH RABBIT GOT THE MOST CARROTS? COLOR HIS STASH!

FIDO FORGOT WHERE HE BURIED HIS TREASURE TROVE OF BONES.
CAN YOU HELP HIM FIND IT?

WHICH RUBBER DUCK IS DIFFERENT FROM THE OTHERS?

COLOR THE TREE WITH MORE PEARS.

IF BILLY EATS TWO CHEESEBURGERS PER DAY,
HOW MANY DAYS WILL IT TAKE HIM TO EAT THEM ALL?

CRACK THE SUDOKU!
EACH DRAWING CAN ONLY BE PLACED ONCE ON EACH LINE,
ONCE ON EACH ROW, AND ONCE IN EACH FOUR CELL GRID.

WRITE FOUR ANIMALS THAT START WITH THE LETTER "B" .

B
B
B
B

WHAT COLOR IS THE LIGHT?

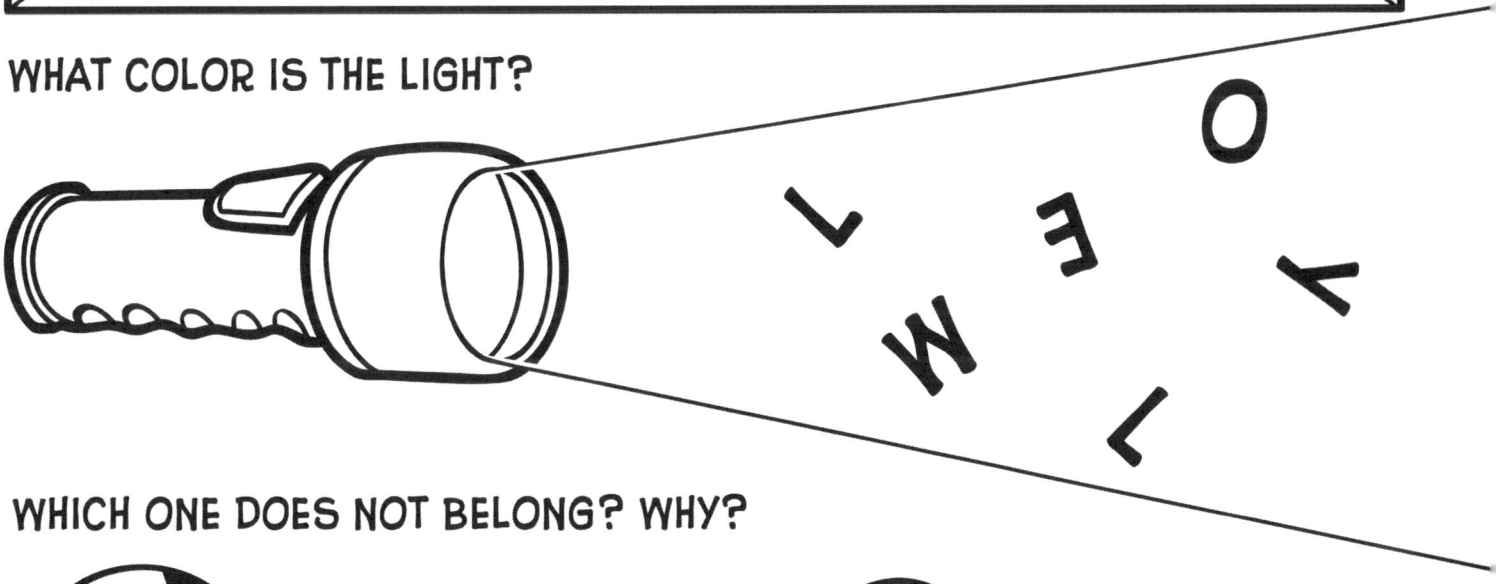

WHICH ONE DOES NOT BELONG? WHY?

LOOK FOR THE DRAWING THAT APPEARS ONLY ONCE IN THE WHOLE GRID AND SURROUND IT WITH A CIRCLE.

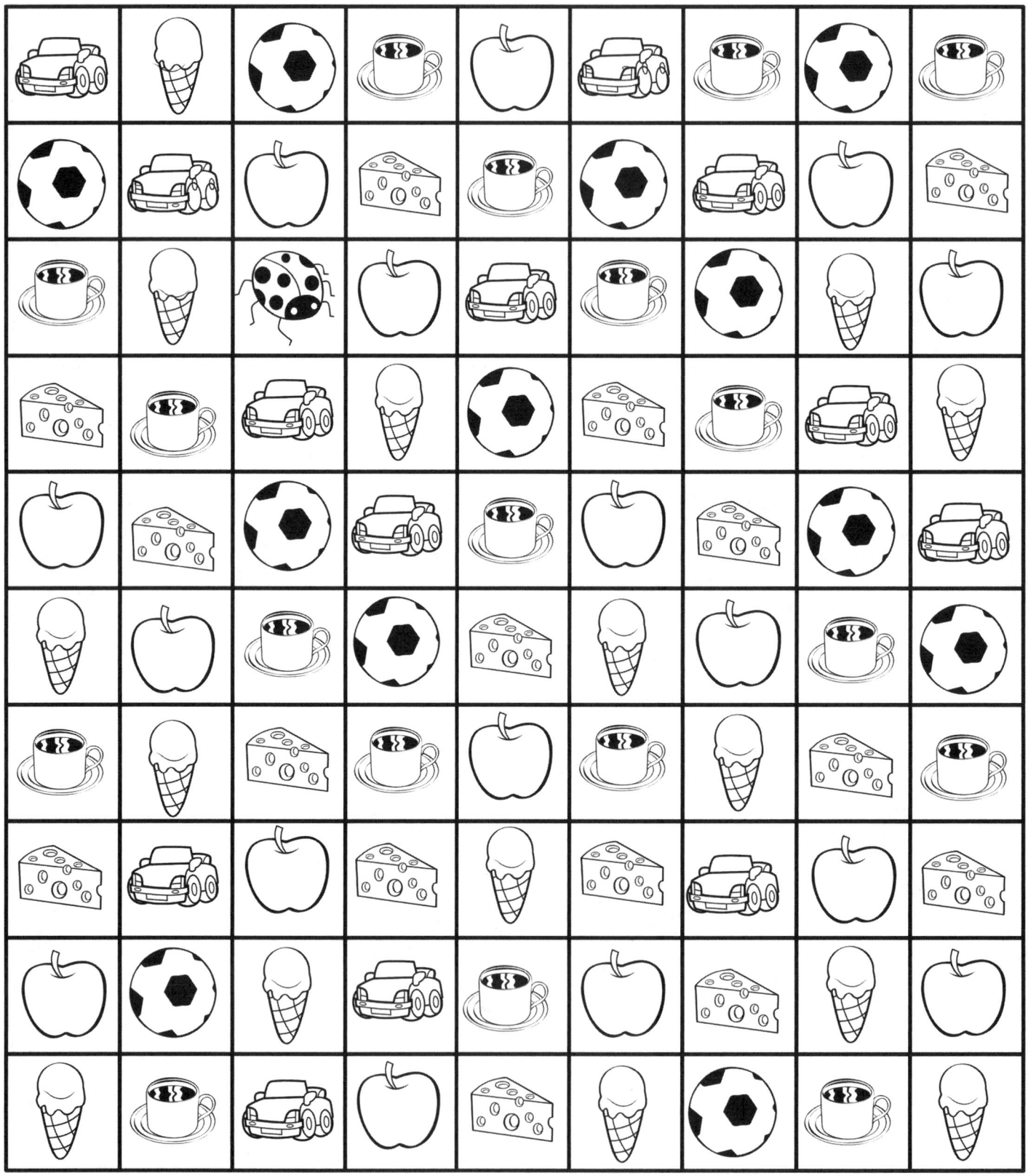

WHICH DRAWING ON EACH LINE LOOKS JUST LIKE THE ONE IN THE LEFT COLUMN?

WHICH ONE IS NOT A FIREFIGHTER TOOL?

WHICH PLANETS ARE SOLID? WHICH ARE MADE OF GAS?

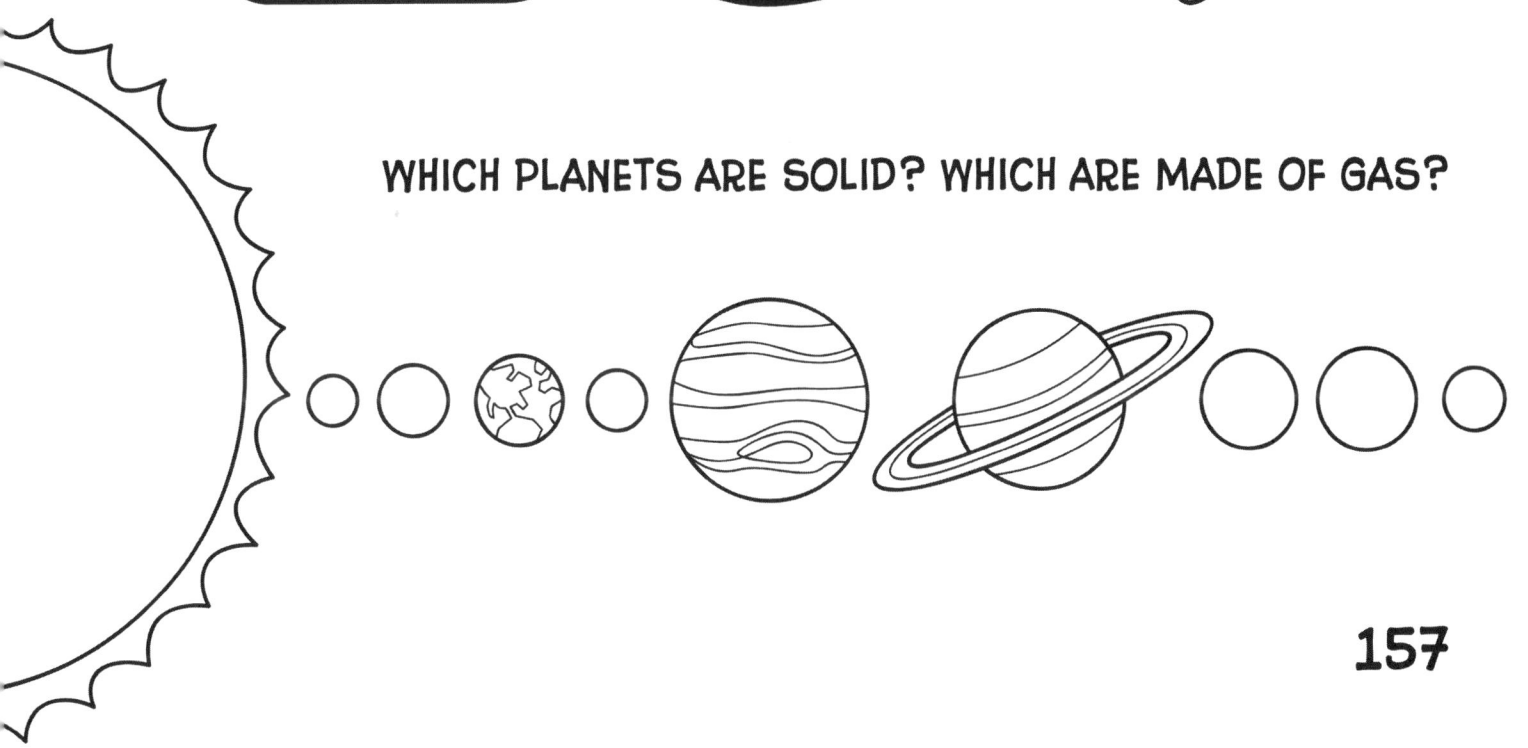

DAPHNE WANTS A DOMINOES REMATCH!
TO WIN, DRAW THE CORRESPONDING
FRUIT ON EACH END.

CROSSWORDS.

IF MIMI EATS THREE TREATS PER DAY,
HOW MANY DAYS WILL IT TAKE HER TO EAT THEM ALL?

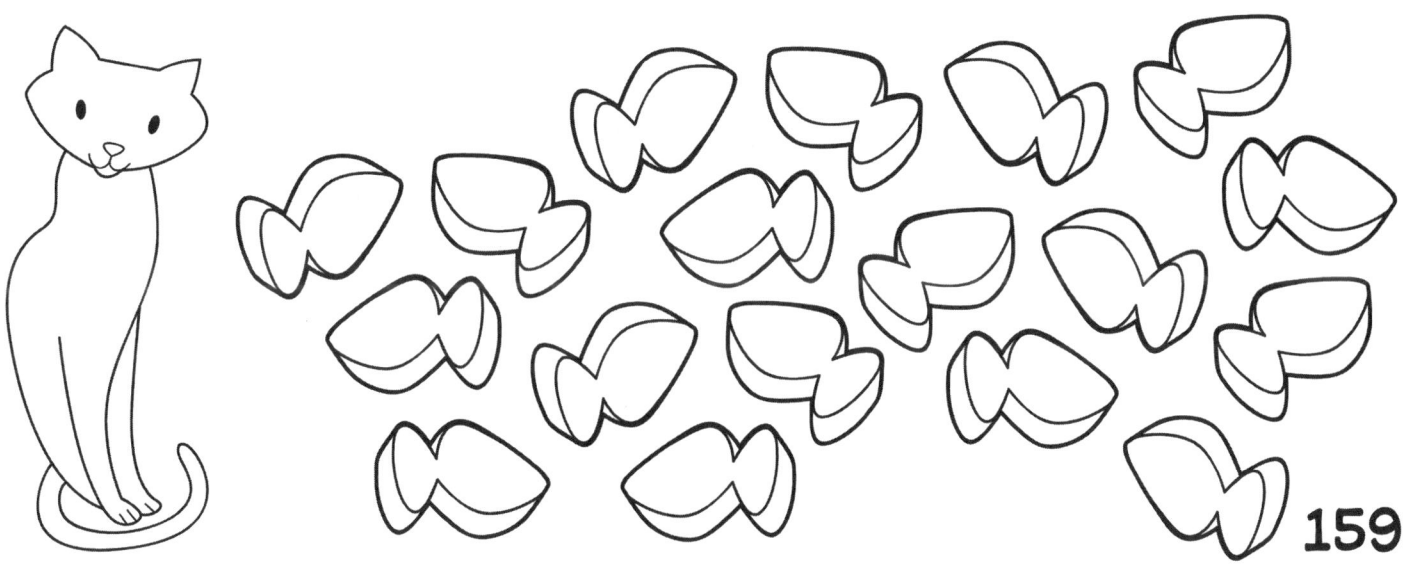

COUNT THE FISH, AND COLOR THE RIGHT TOTAL NUMBER PER SCHOOL.

HOW MANY DO YOU COUNT?

1 2 3 4

5 6 7 8

HOW MANY DO YOU COUNT?

9 10 11 12

13 14 15 16

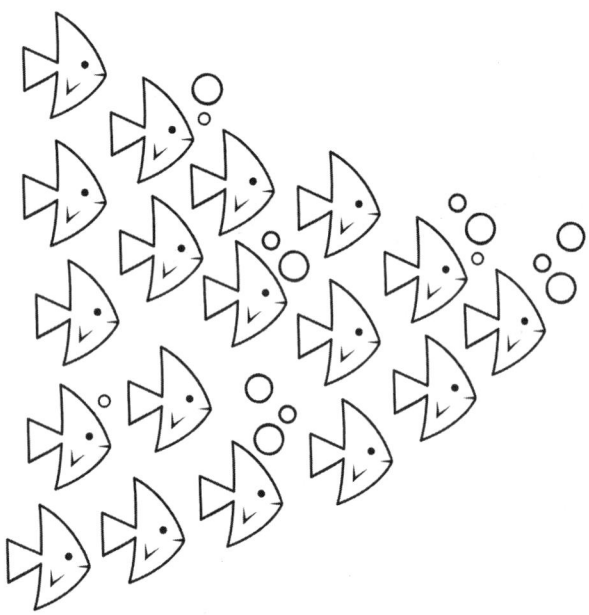

HOW MANY DO YOU COUNT?

17 18 19 20

21 22 23 24

CROSS OUT THE PIG THAT APPEARS IN THE IMAGE ONLY ONCE.

EVERY ANIMAL HAS A SHADOW. WHICH ONE HAS NONE?

CAN YOU FIND THE SMALLER COMBINATIONS IN THE BIG GRID BELOW?
COLOR THEM WHEN YOU DO!

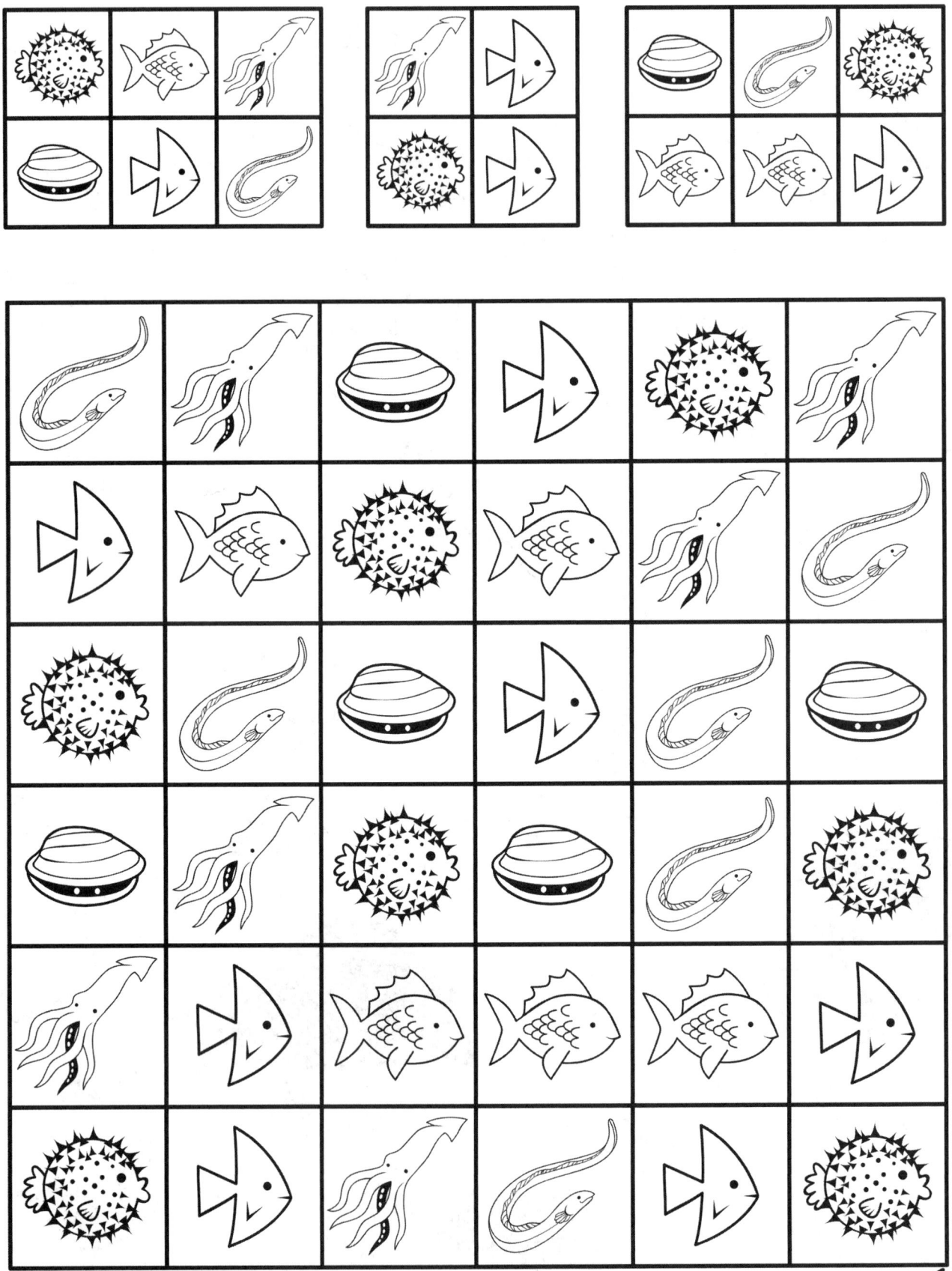

COMPLETE THE UNDERWATER VIEW WITH FISH AND OTHER MARINE LIFE!

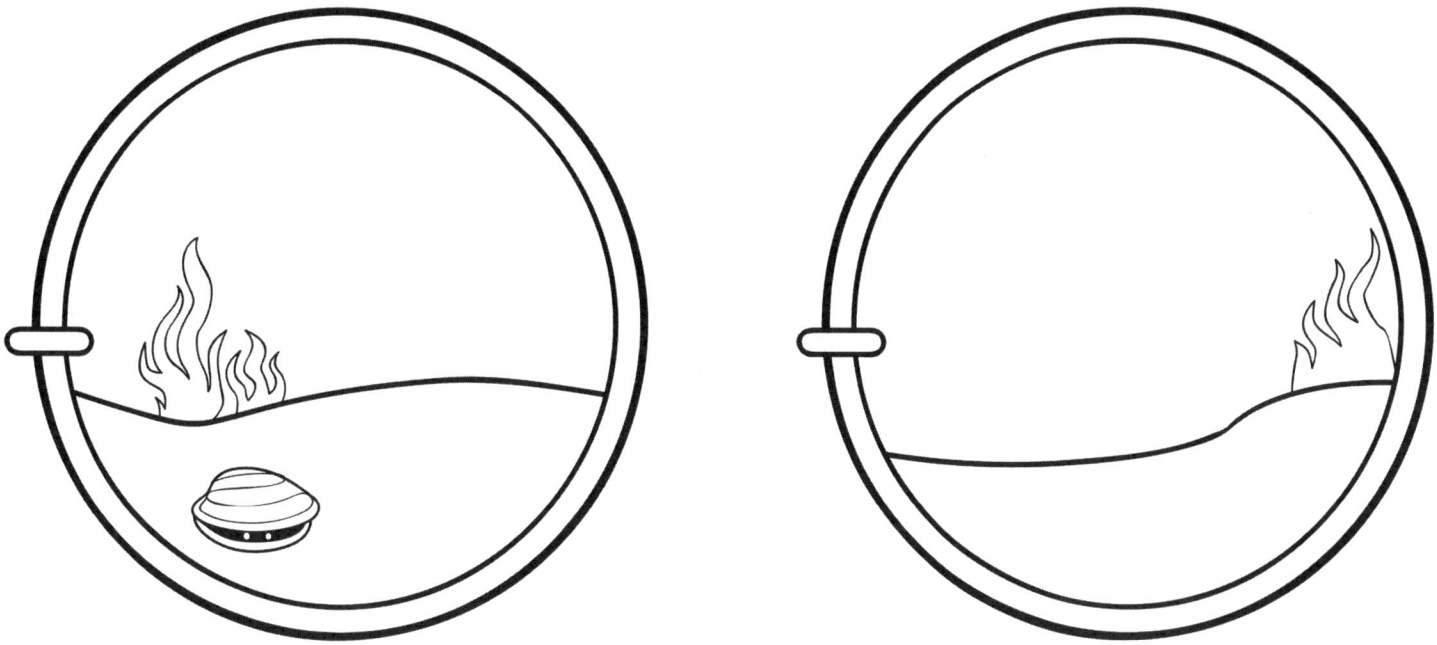

WHICH OUTLINE DOES NOT MATCH THE FROG'S DRAWING?

DRAW DIFFERENT FLOWER BOUQUETS ACCORDING TO THE FLOWERS NAMED ON EACH VASE.

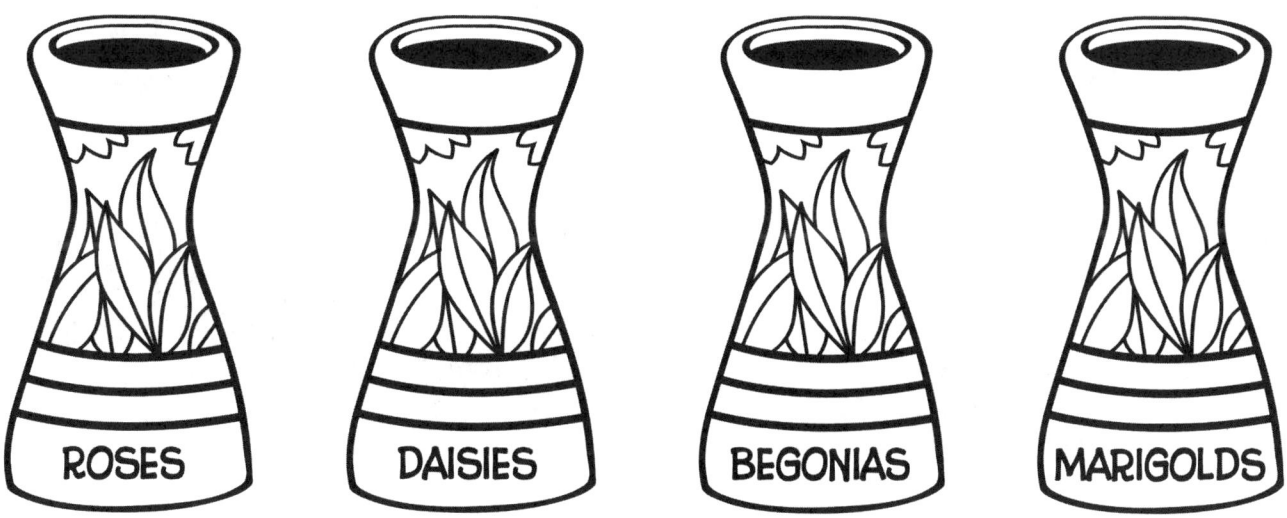

HOW MANY ORANGES DO YOU NEED TO FILL THESE GLASSES IF YOU MUST SQUEEZE ONE ORANGE TO FILL HALF A GLASS?

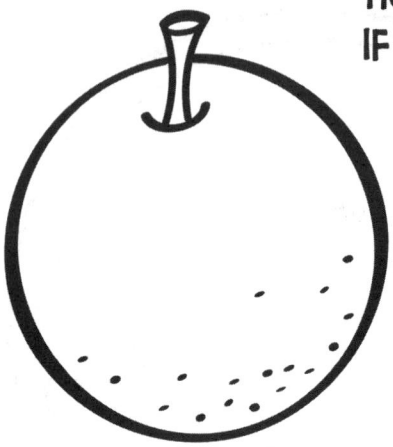

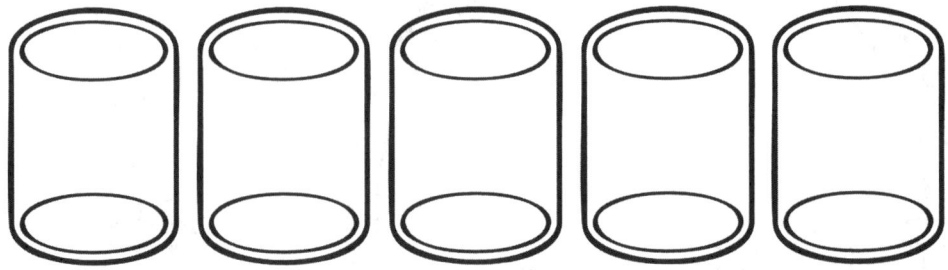

WHAT'S THE NAME OF THIS ANIMAL?
CAN YOU DRAW ITS MISSING TENTACLES?

FIND THE TRUE SHADOW OF THE TORTOISE.

CONNECT EACH FRUIT AND VEGGIE TO THE GRID IT BELONGS TO, BUT BEWARE, ONLY ONE OF EACH BELONGS IN EACH GRID!

FIND THE TEN DIFFERENCES.

WHICH DRAWING ON EACH LINE IS IDENTICAL TO THE ONE IN THE LEFT COLUMN?

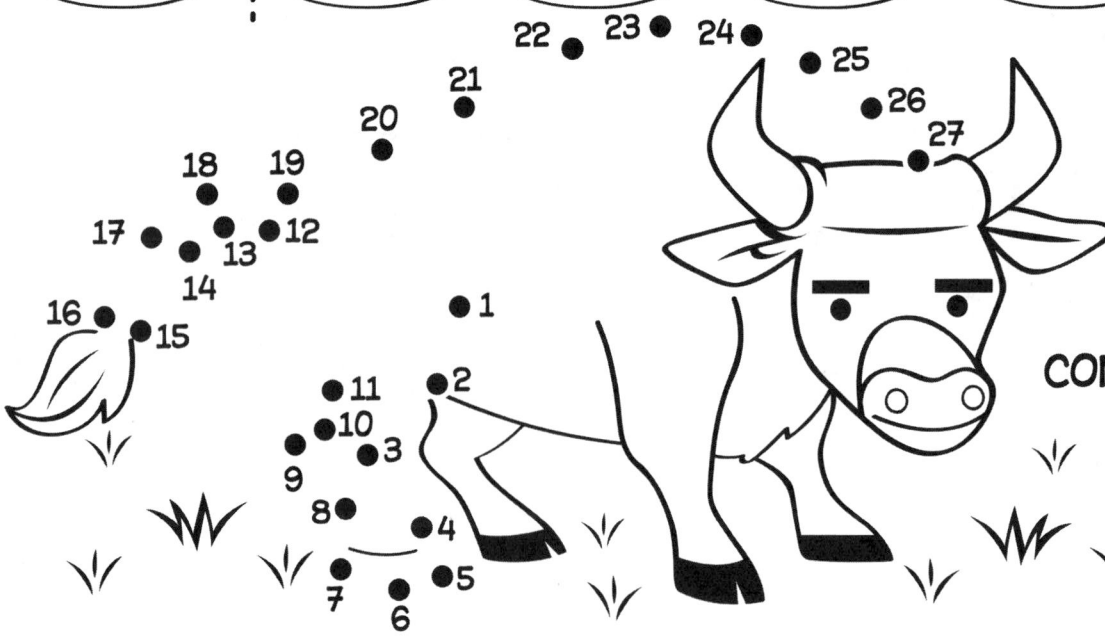

CONNECT THE DOTS!

ALL THESE FLAGS ARE RED, WHITE, AND BLUE.
COLOR THEM ACCORDING TO THEIR COUNTRY.

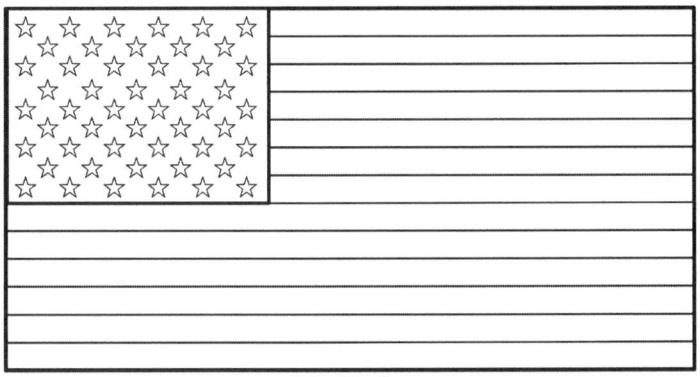

U.S.A.

RUSSIA

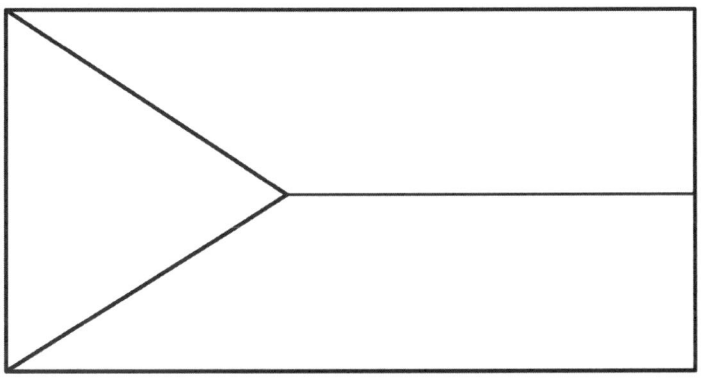

CZECH REPUBLIC

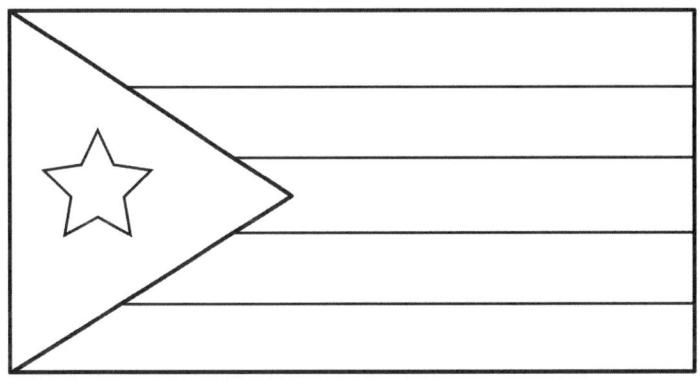

CUBA

NETHERLANDS

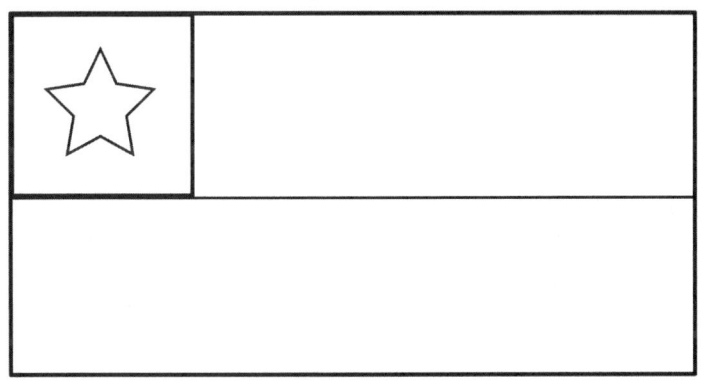

CHILE

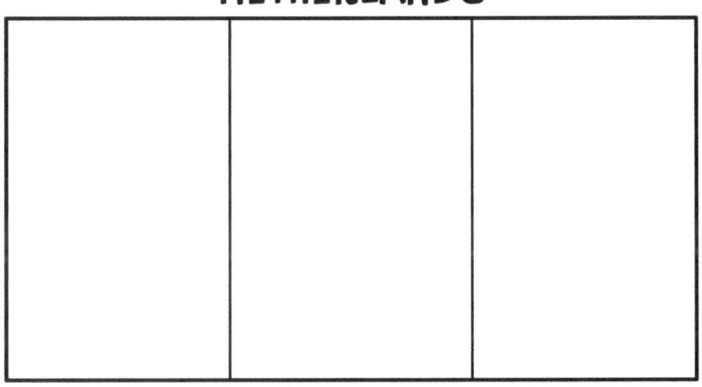

FRANCE

UNITED KINGDOM

FIND THE ONE THAT DOESN'T BELONG.

HELP THE RAT FIND ITS WAY OUT!

COUNT THE HEXAGONS ONLY.

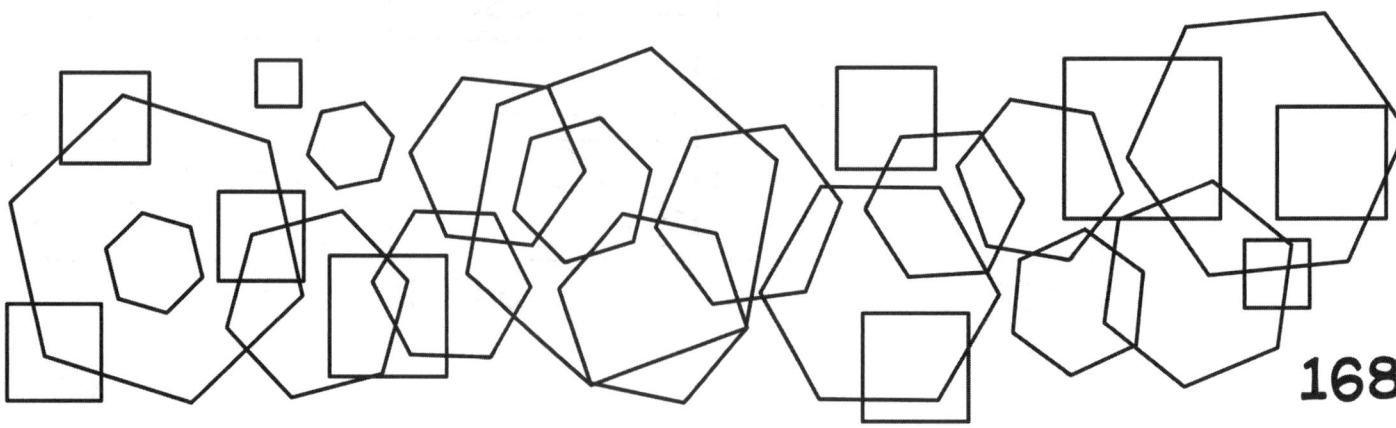

WHAT DOES THE BEE EAT?

FILL THE OTHER COMPARTMENTS WITH MORE TOYS YOU LIKE.

WHICH ONE DOES NOT EAT OTHER ANIMALS?

CAN YOU DRAW THE SAILBOAT IN THE RIGHT PANEL?

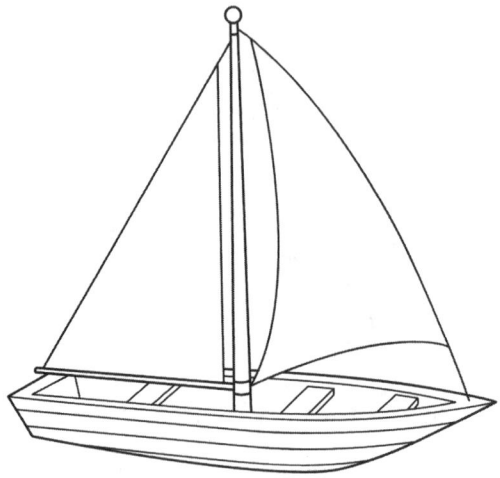

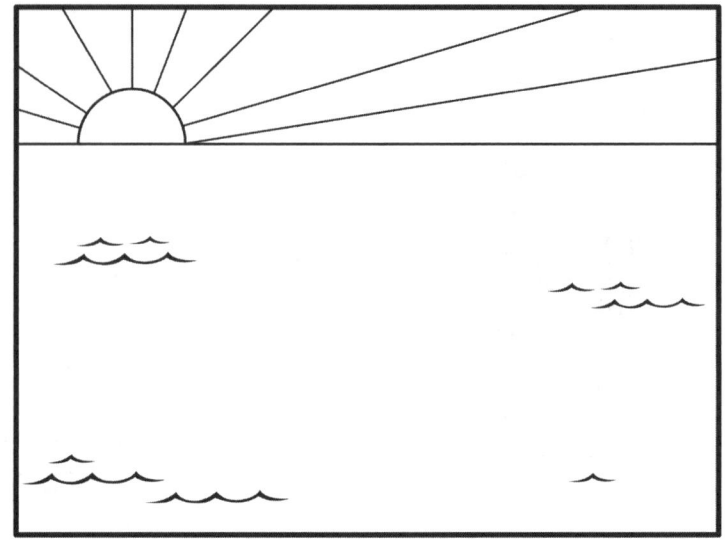

DO YOU RECOGNIZE THE ANIMALS IN THESE INCOMPLETE DRAWINGS?

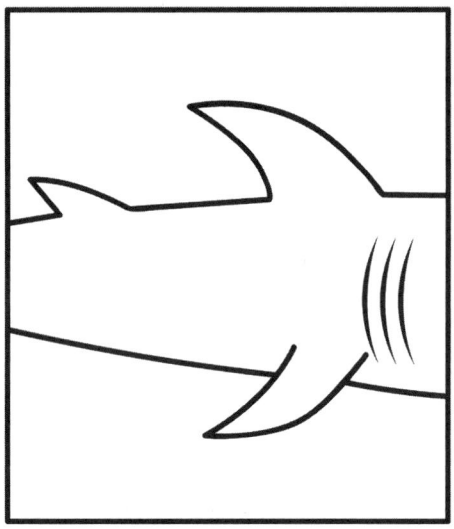

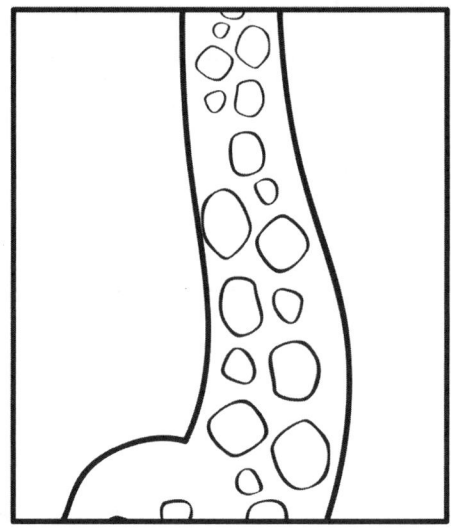

FIND THE MATCHING BUTTERFLIES
AND COLOR THEM ALIKE.

DO YOU RECOGNIZE THESE SILHOUETTES? WHICH ONE DOES NOT BELONG?

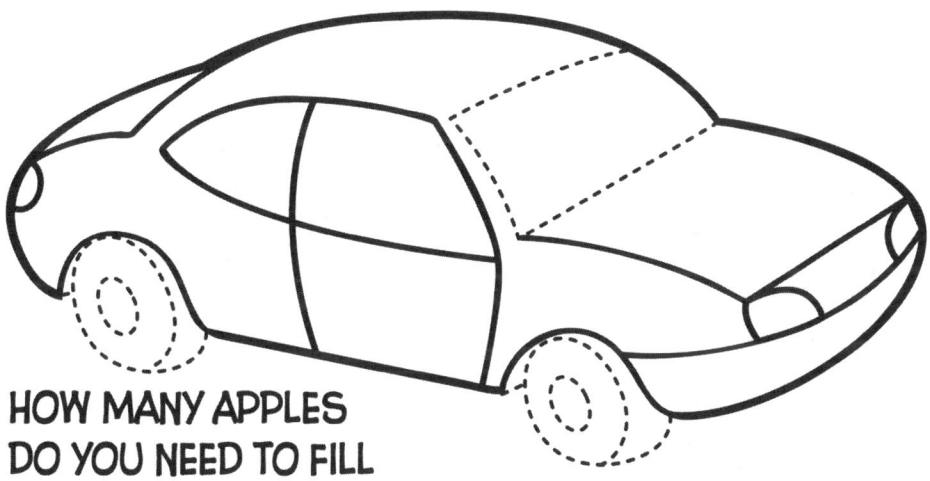

WHAT'S MISSING FROM THIS PICTURE? DRAW IT BY TRACING THE DOTTED LINE.

HOW MANY APPLES DO YOU NEED TO FILL THESE GLASSES IF YOU MUST SQUEEZE TWO APPLES TO FILL A GLASS?

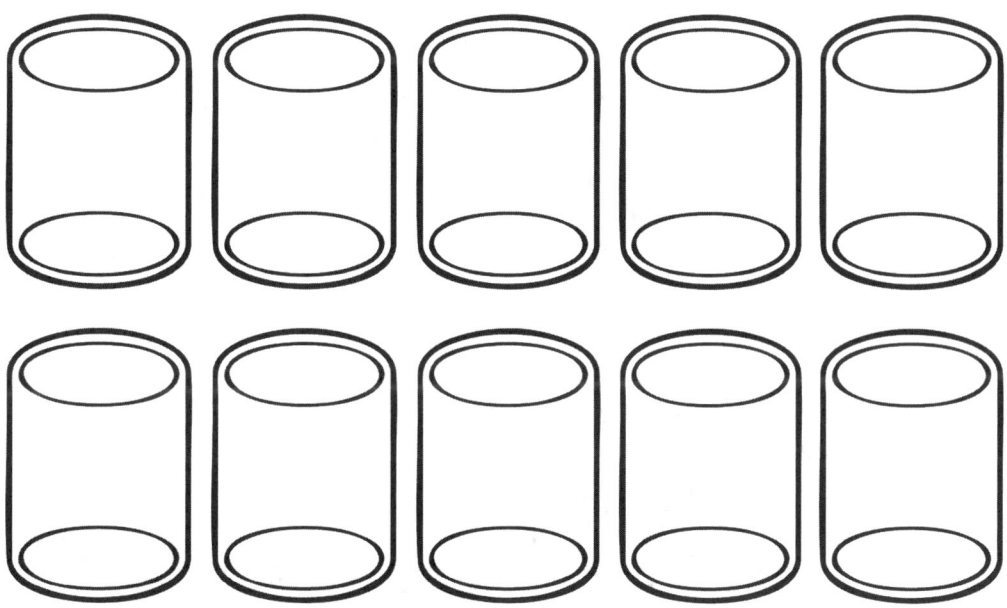

FILL THIS PAGE WITH FALLING LEAVES
FOR SALLY TO RAKE!

IF YOU CONTINUE THE PROGRESSION OF SYMBOLS FROM LEFT TO RIGHT, WHICH ONE WOULD SUBSTITUTE THE QUESTION MARK?

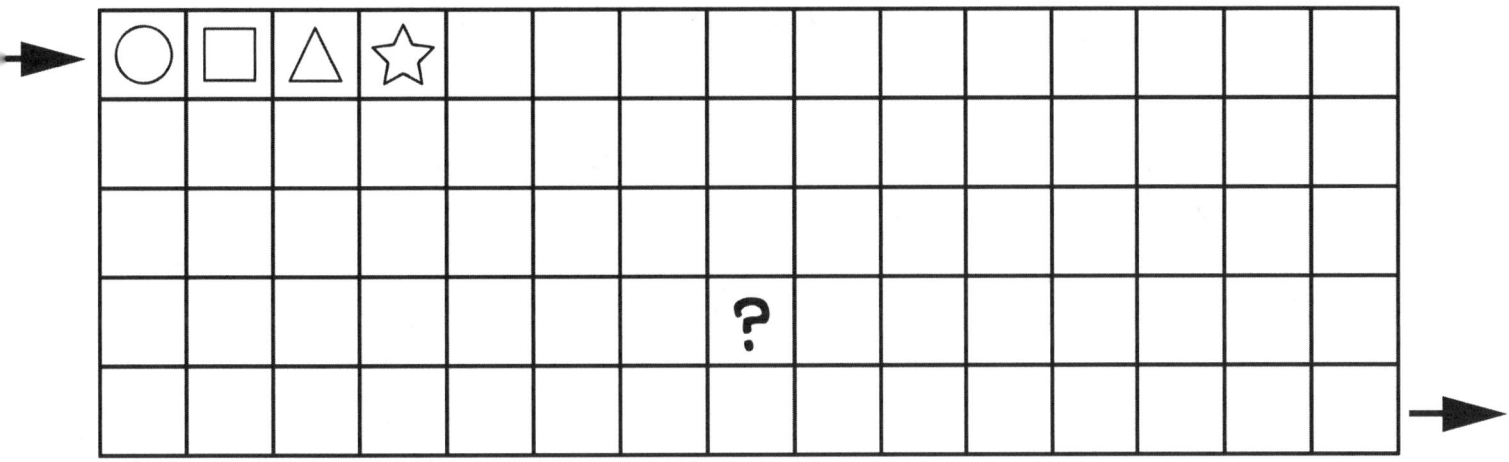

WHAT BIRDS ARE HIDING IN THE TREES?

COLOR ONLY THE ONES THAT ARE MAN-MADE.

EACH RABBIT CAN ONLY TAKE ONE CARROT.
HOW MANY WILL THEY LEAVE BEHIND?

C
C
C
C

WRITE FOUR ANIMALS THAT START WITH THE LETTER "C".

CAN YOU SEE THE TWO IDENTICAL LEAVES?

HOPPING ONLY ON THE WATERLILY PATH,
AND AVOIDING THE INSECTS, HELP THE FROG REACH HIS GIRLFRIEND.
HOW MANY JUMPS WILL IT TAKE?

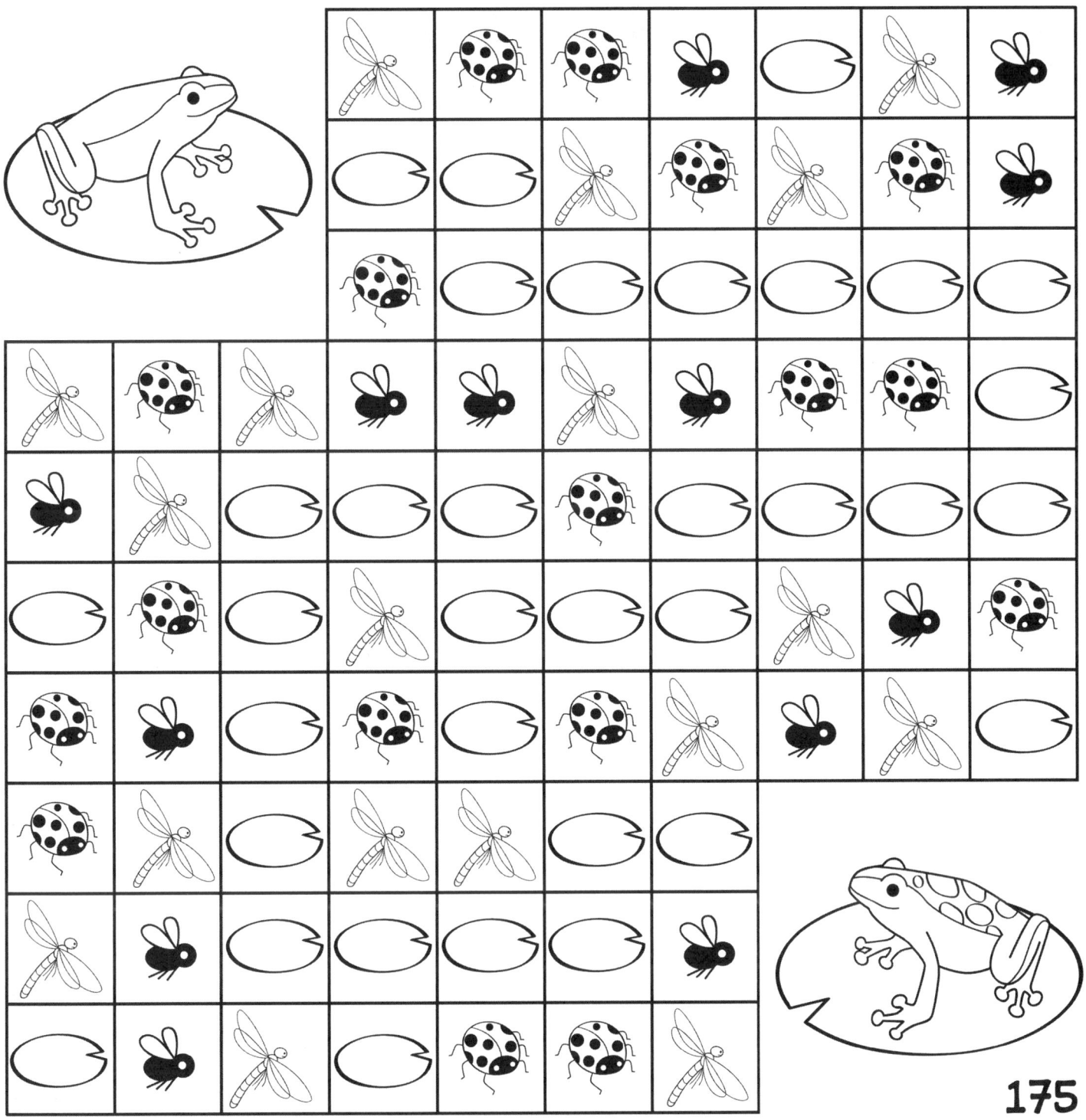

MATCH THE IDENTICALLY SHAPED SPOT.

CROSSWORDS.

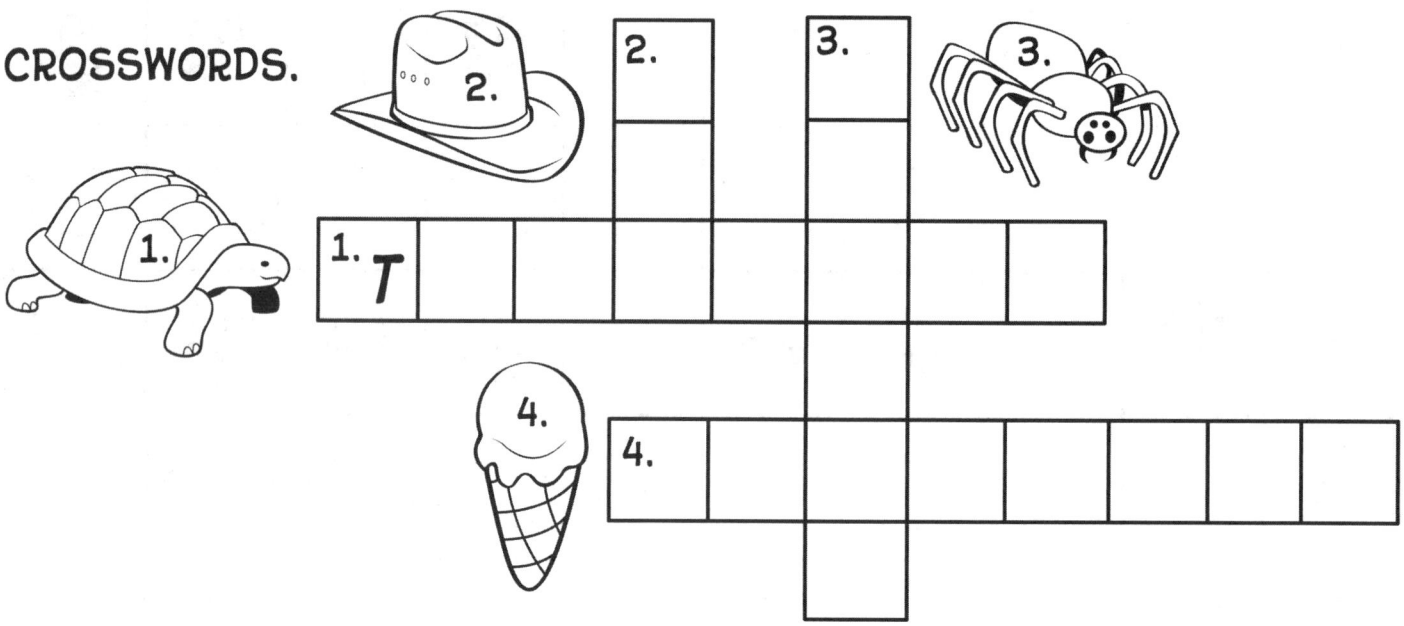

HOW MANY FISH CAN YOU COUNT IN THE AQUARIUM?

MATCH THE ANIMAL TO ITS TAIL.

TO GET TO THE APPLE, YOU CAN GO VERTICALLY OR HORIZONTALLY, BUT CANNOT CROSS OVER THE SAME SYMBOL TWICE!

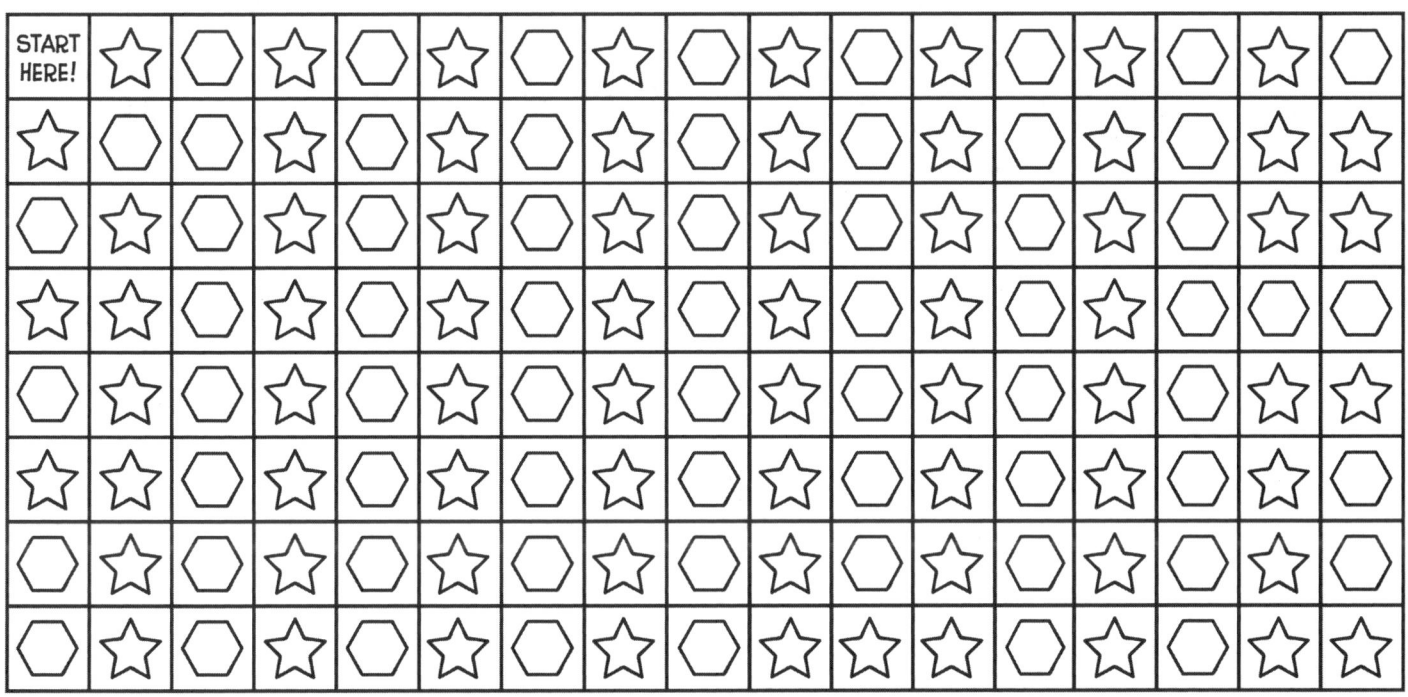

IDENTIFY THE TEEPEE THAT BELONGS TO ANOTHER TRIBE.

WHAT CLASSIC FAIRY TALE DO ALL THESE ELEMENTS BELONG TO?

C _ _ _ _ _ _ _ _ _

WHAT DOES THE ARMADILLO EAT?

DRAW YOUR FAVORITE TV SHOW!

WHAT IS IT CALLED?

IF YOU FOLLOW THE PATTERN, WHAT SYMBOL DOES THE RABBIT ARRIVE AT?

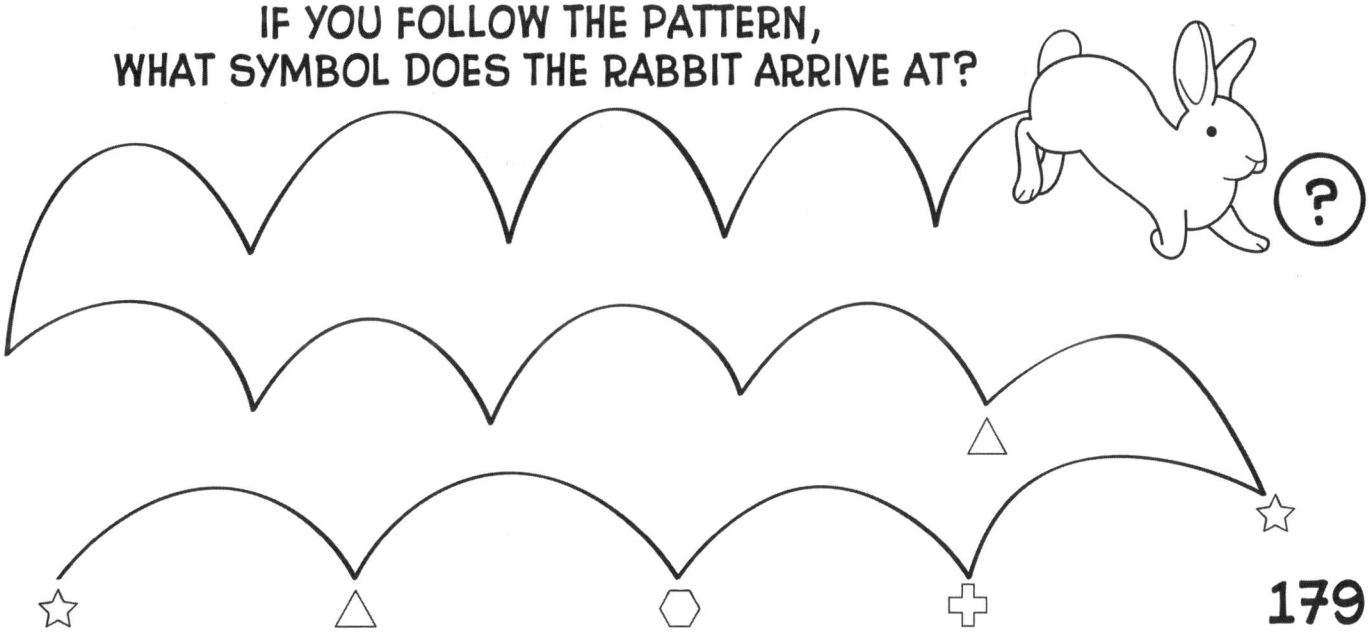

ALL THESE FLAGS ARE RED, GREEN, AND WHITE.
COLOR THEM ACCORDING TO THEIR COUNTRY.

BULGARIA

HUNGARY

ITALY

MEXICO

WHICH DRAWING ON EACH LINE IS IDENTICAL TO THE ONE IN THE LEFT COLUMN?

COLOR THE SKY BLUE, THE SUN YELLOW, AND THE BUILDINGS IN COLORS OTHER THAN BLUE AND YELLOW.

WHICH PAW HAS LEFT THIS PRINT?

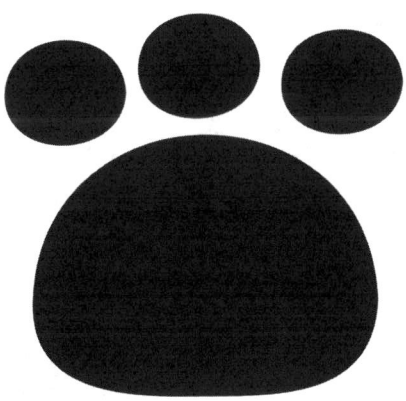

CAN YOU COLOR THIS CITYSCAPE FROM THE PREVIOUS PAGE AS A NIGHT SCENE? WHAT COLOR DOES THE LIGHT FROM BUILDING WINDOWS SHINE AT NIGHT?

ANTS MAY CARRY MANY TIMES THEIR BODY WEIGHT. WHICH ONE WEIGHS MORE?

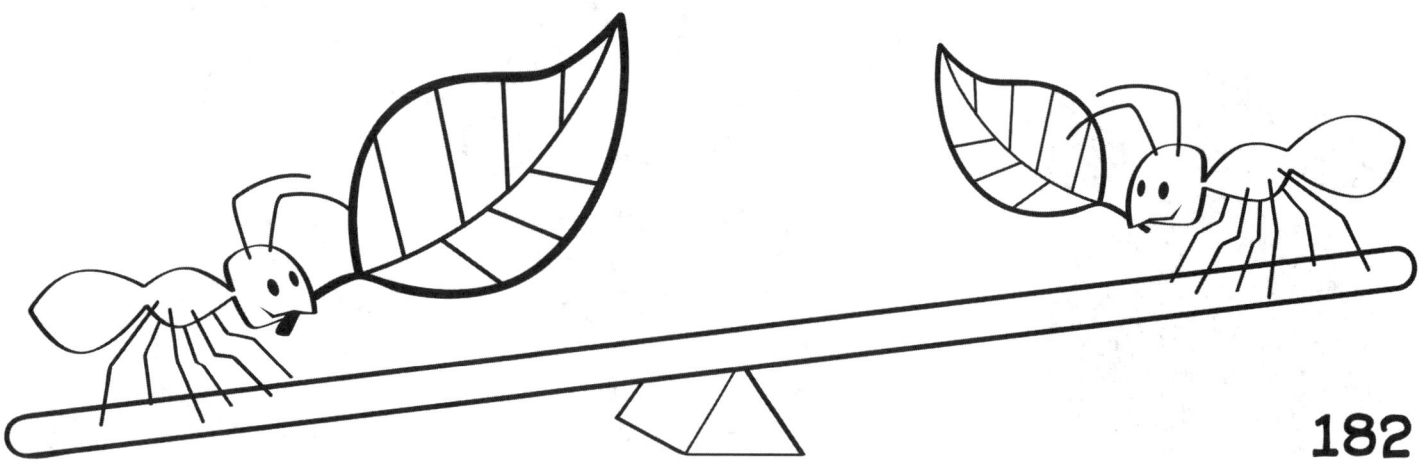

WHICH ONE DOES NOT LOOK LIKE THE REST?

HOW MANY DIFFERENCES CAN YOU FIND?

WHAT ANIMAL LIVES HERE?

SOMETHING IN THIS PICTURE IS IMPOSSIBLE. CAN YOU GUESS WHAT?

IDENTIFY THE MATCHING OWL COUPLES AND COLOR THEM ALIKE.

THESE TWO ARE RELATED. CAN YOU GUESS THE NAME OF THEIR FAMILY?

C_ _ _ _ _ _ _ _ _

WRITE FOUR ANIMALS THAT START WITH THE LETTER "S" .

S
S
S
S

DECORATE AND COLOR THIS CAKE TO MATCH YOUR FAVORITE FLAVORS.

EACH APE CAN ONLY TAKE TWO BANANAS.
HOW MANY WILL THEY LEAVE BEHIND?

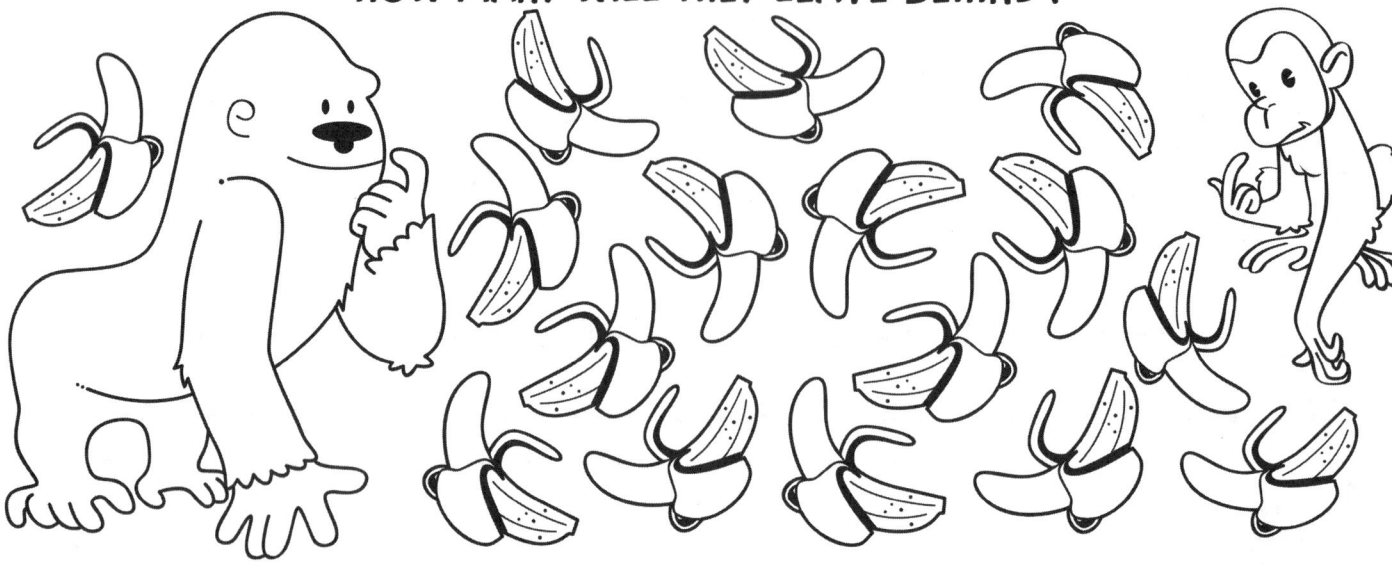

COMPLETE THIS BY CREATING YOUR OWN SYMBOLS MOVING FORWARD.

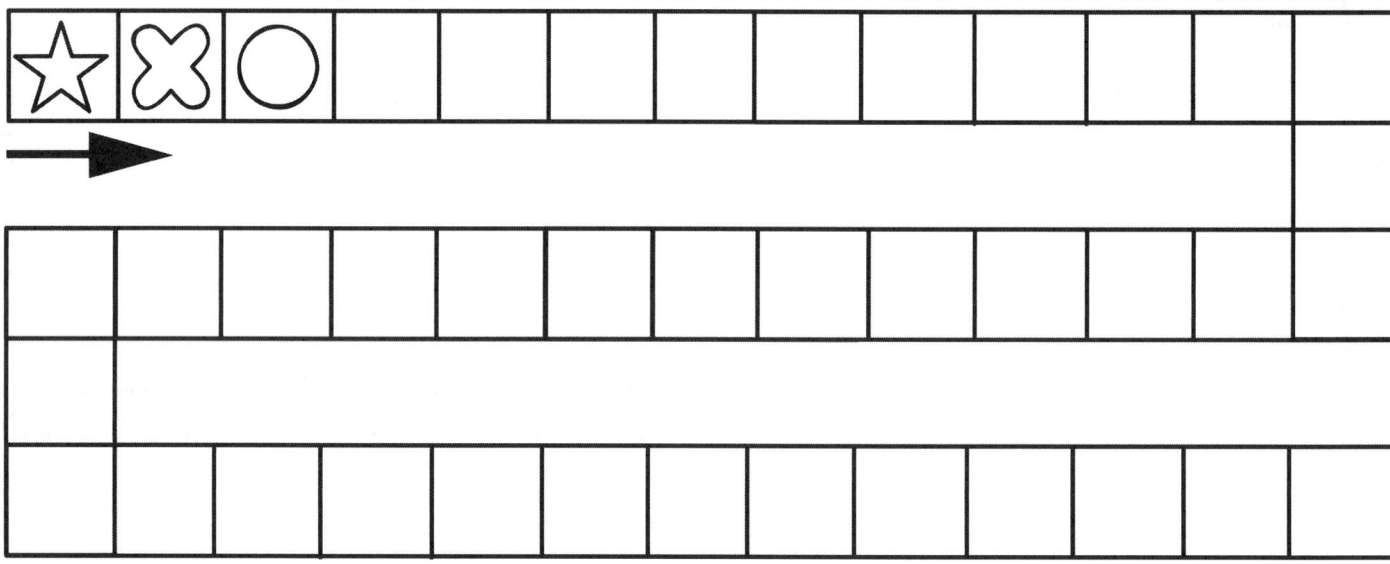

HELP THE SWALLOWS MEET!

CONNECT EACH ANIMAL TO THE GRID IT BELONGS TO, BUT BEWARE, ONLY ONE ANIMAL BELONGS IN EACH GRID!

HOW MANY PLANES DO YOU COUNT?

COLOR THE BIG ONES RED, THE SMALL ONES YELLOW, AND THE REST GREEN.

IF THE BOWLING BALL KNOCKS SEVEN PINS, HOW MANY ARE LEFT STANDING?

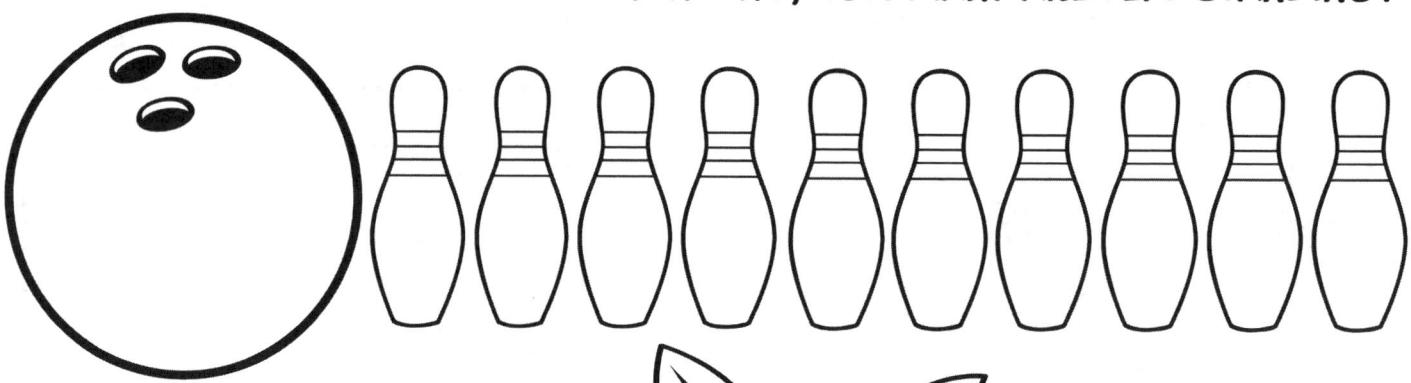

WHAT ANIMALS IS THIS WEIRD CREATURE MADE OF?

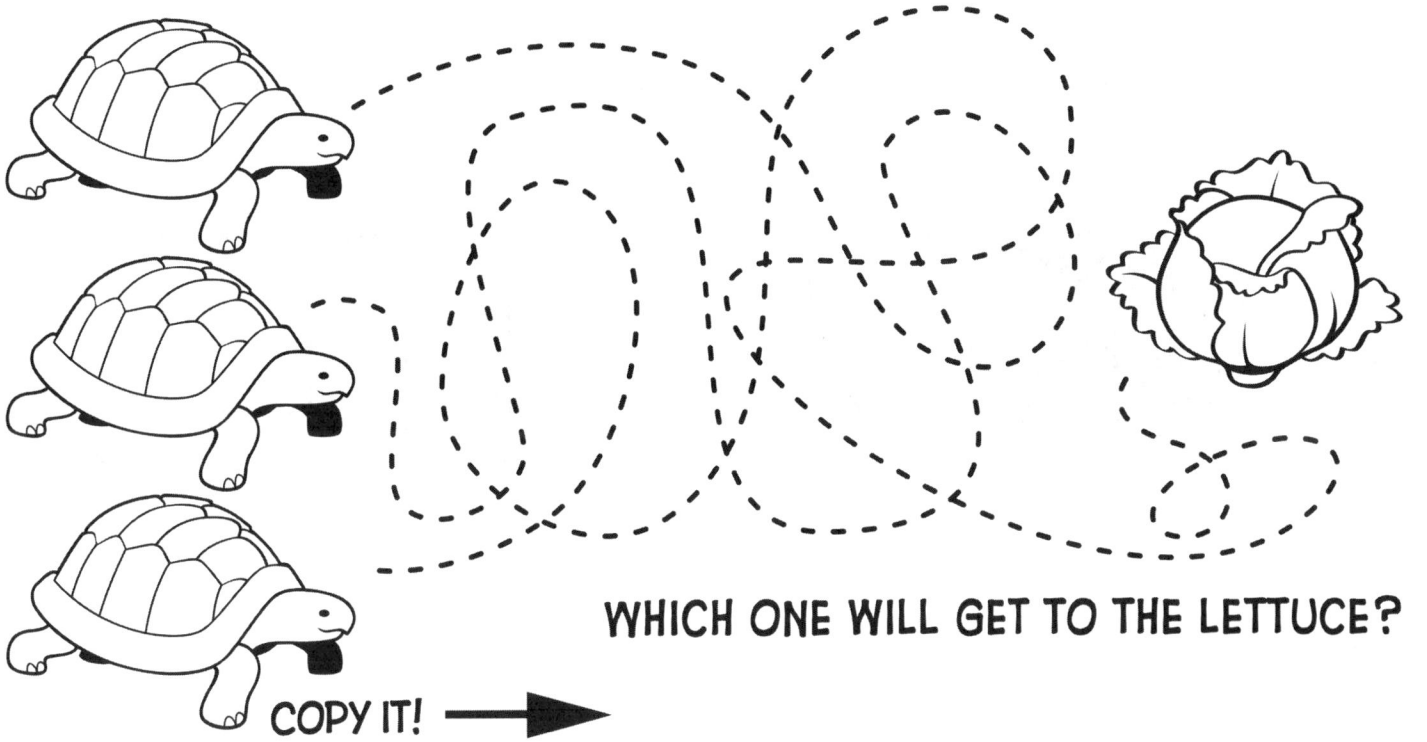

WHICH ONE WILL GET TO THE LETTUCE?

COPY IT!

WHAT DO THESE HAVE IN COMMON?

TURN THESE SEMICIRCLES INTO FUN STUFF, AND COLOR THEM ALL!

EYE.

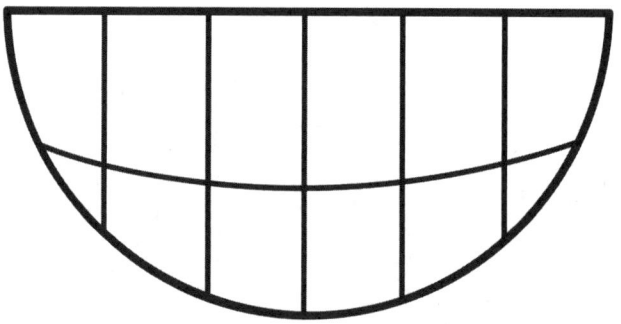

SMILE.

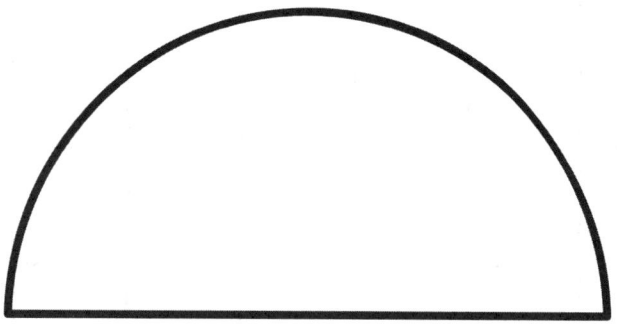

BASEBALL CAP.

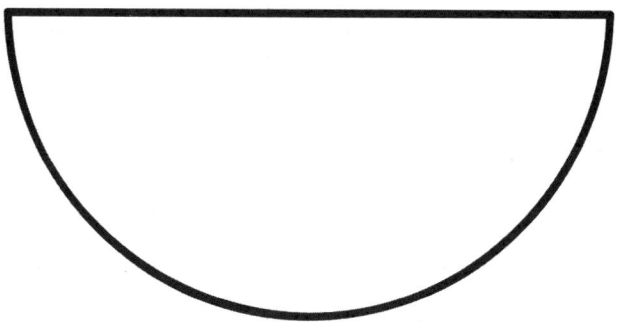

CANOE.

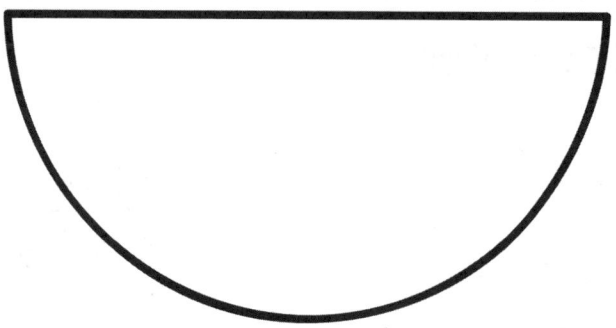

WATERMELON SLICE.

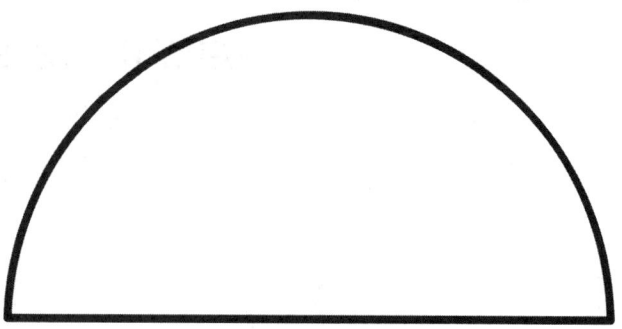

RAINBOW.

DRAW THE OTHER HALF.

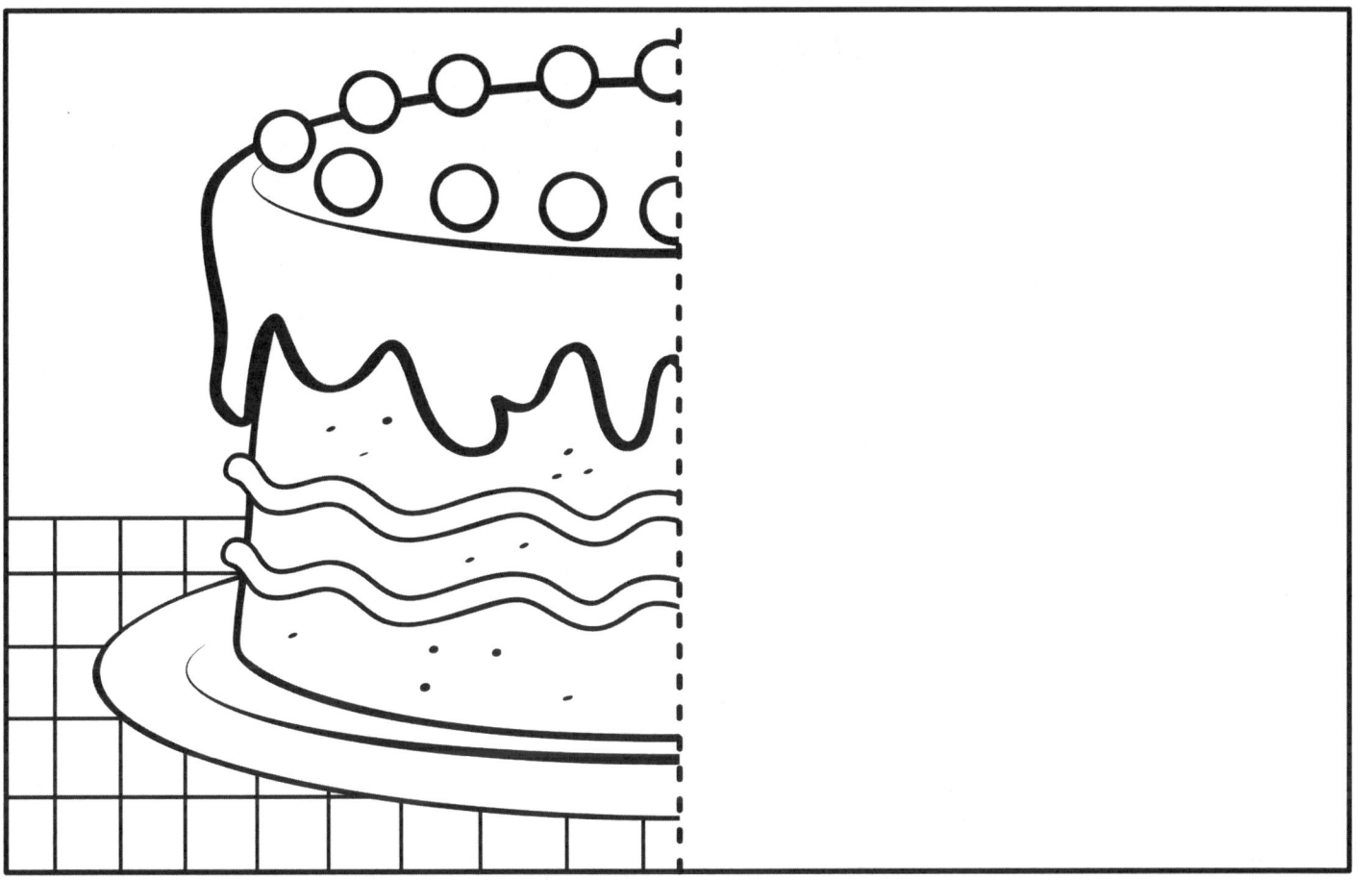

HOW MANY CARROTS DO YOU NEED TO FILL THESE GLASSES IF YOU MUST GRIND THREE TO FILL A GLASS?

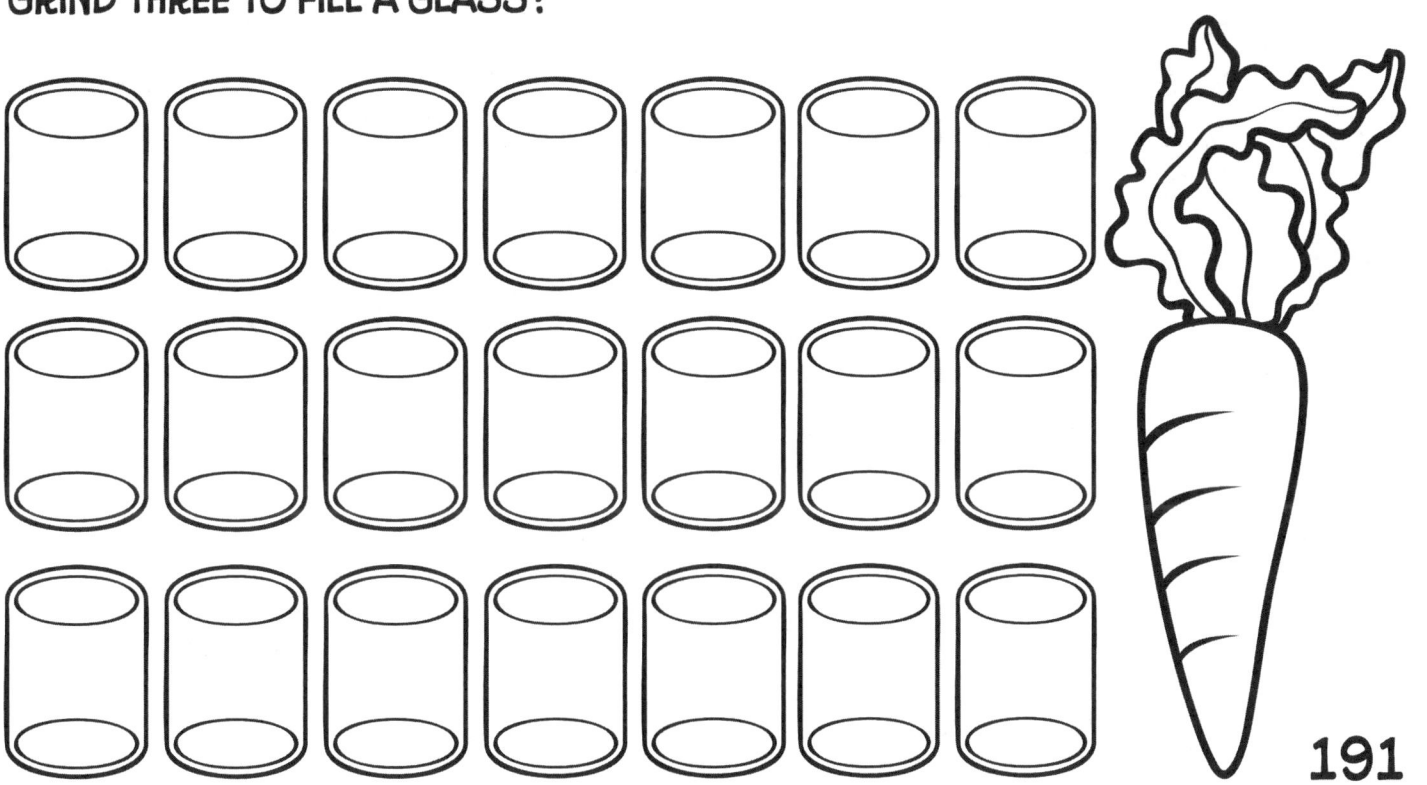

MATCH THE MOUSE TO THE APPROPRIATE SHADOW.

TAKING THE TUNNELS AND AVOIDING DELAYS,
DRIVE THE CAR SAFELY TO MAKE IT HOME ON TIME.

HORSES CAN ONLY WEAR FOUR HORSESHOES EACH.
HOW MANY WILL THEY LEAVE BEHIND?

COMPLETE EACH LOGICAL SEQUENCE.

DRAW A CIRCLE AROUND THE GIRAFFE WITH MOST SPOTS.

FILL THE WATER WITH FRIENDLY FISH,
AND COLOR IT ALL!

WHERE DO YOU FIND THESE PIECES IN THE DRAWING?

WHO LIVES IN HERE?

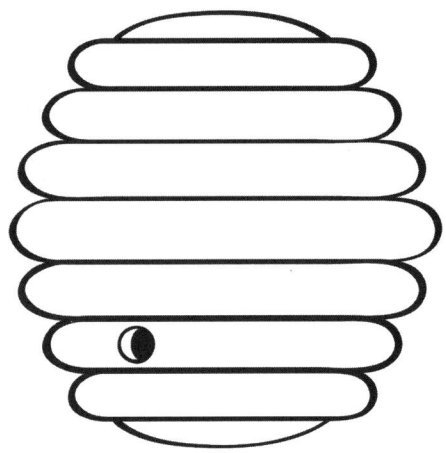

HOW DOES THE FLY GET TO THE ICE CREAM?

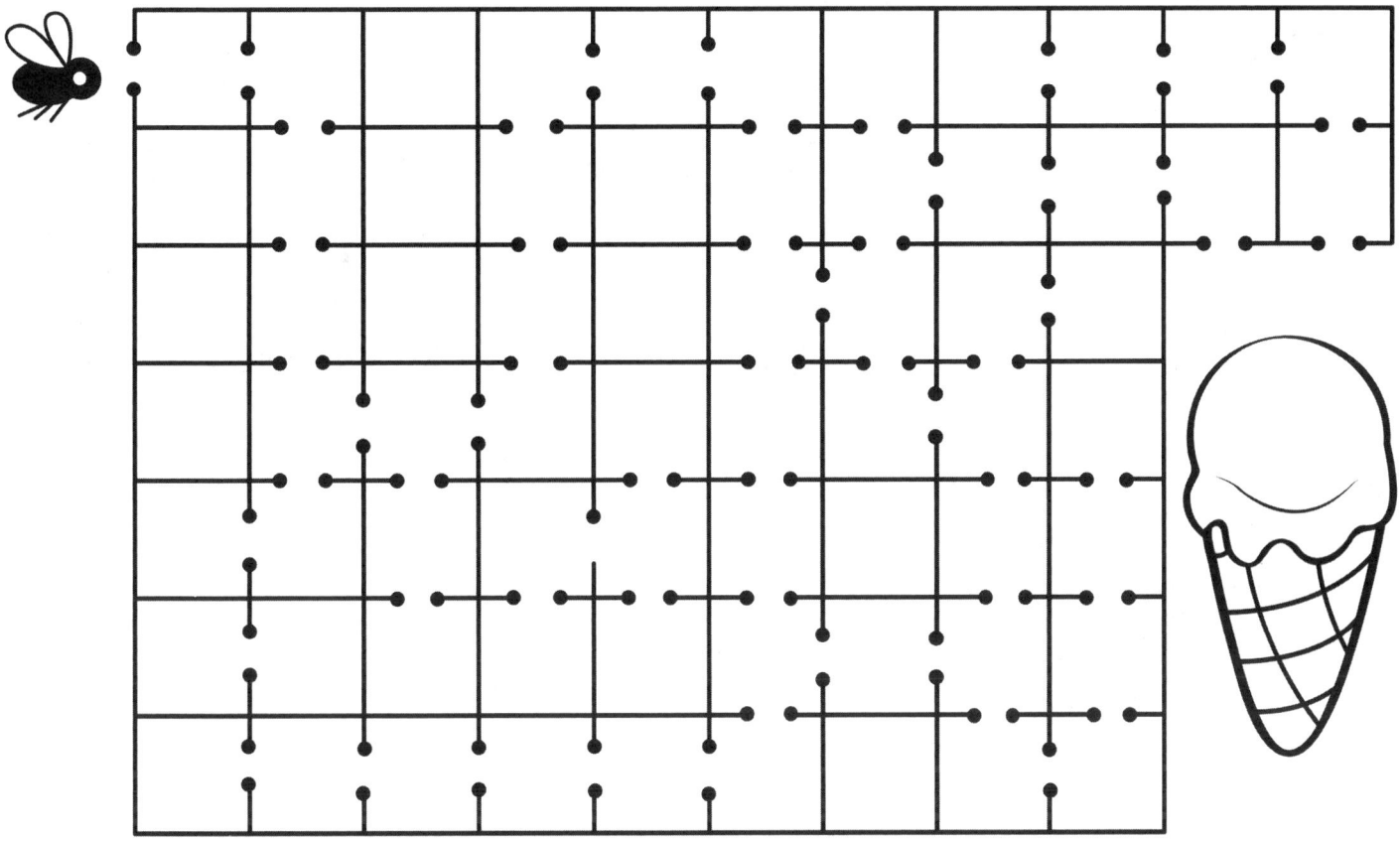

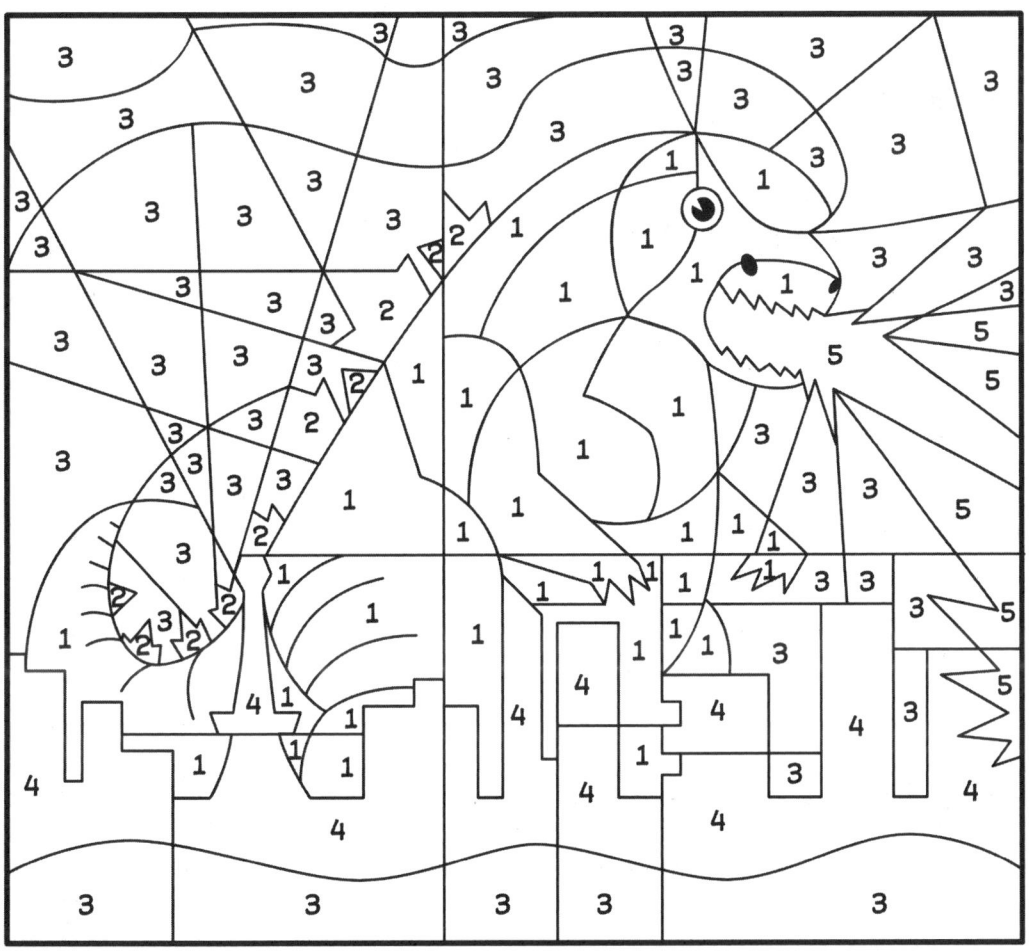

1 = GREEN
2 = PURPLE
3 = BLUE
4 = GRAY
5 = YELLOW

WHAT IS IT?

COLOR THE PAINTING TOOLS RED, THE CARPENTRY TOOLS BLUE, AND THE TOOLS THAT MAY BE USED FOR BOTH CRAFTS PURPLE.

JOIN THE FIGURES FROM 1 TO 24 IN THE CORRECT ORDER.

37	36	35	34	29	33	1	25	26	27
38	39	30	31	32	24	57	2	28	53
40	41	59	58	23	54	55	56	3	60
49	50	42	22	21	20	7	6	5	4
51	46	45	17	18	19	8	9	10	11
52	47	48	44	16	15	14	13	12	43

IF EACH HAMBURGER COSTS TWO DOLLARS,
HOW MUCH DO THEY COST ALL TOGETHER?

WHAT CHANGED IN THE SECOND AND THIRD IMAGES, COMPARED TO THE FIRST?

WHAT COUNTRY IS IT?
DO YOU REMEMBER THE COLORS OF ITS FLAG?
COLOR THE MAP THE SAME WAY.

REMEMBER THESE INSECTS' NAMES?
CAN YOU SPELL THEM?

A _ _

S _ _ _ _ _

B _ _

L _ _ _ _ _ _

G _ _ _ _ _ _ _ _ _ _ _

THE PACK HAS BEEN INFILTRATED! CAN YOU TELL WHO THE OUTSIDER IS?

WHICH ONE WEIGHS MORE?

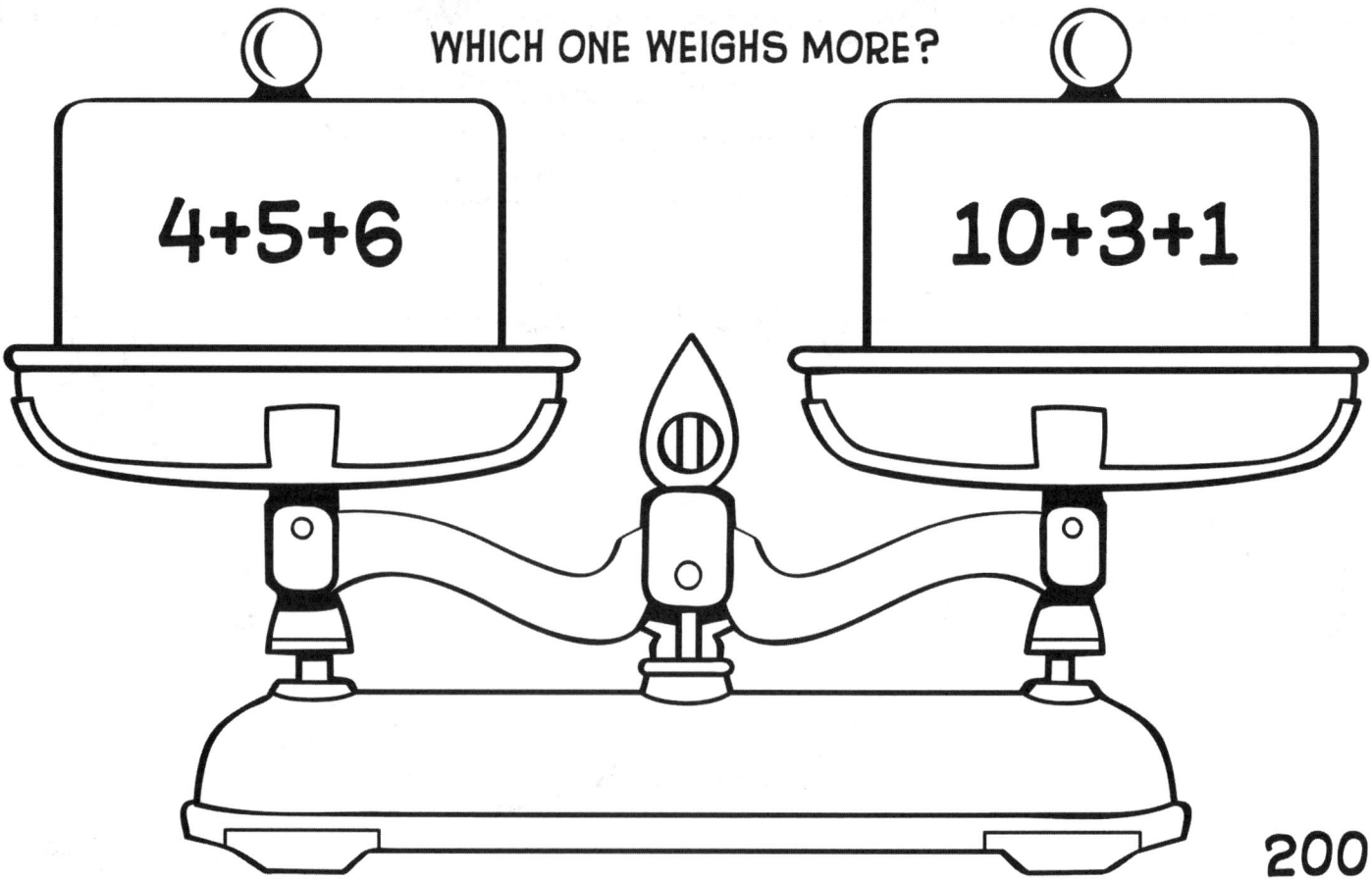

LEVEL
3

IF MAYA EATS FOUR SLICES OF PIZZA PER DAY,
HOW MANY DAYS WILL IT TAKE HER TO EAT THEM ALL?

WHAT IS THE SAXOPHONE PLAYING?

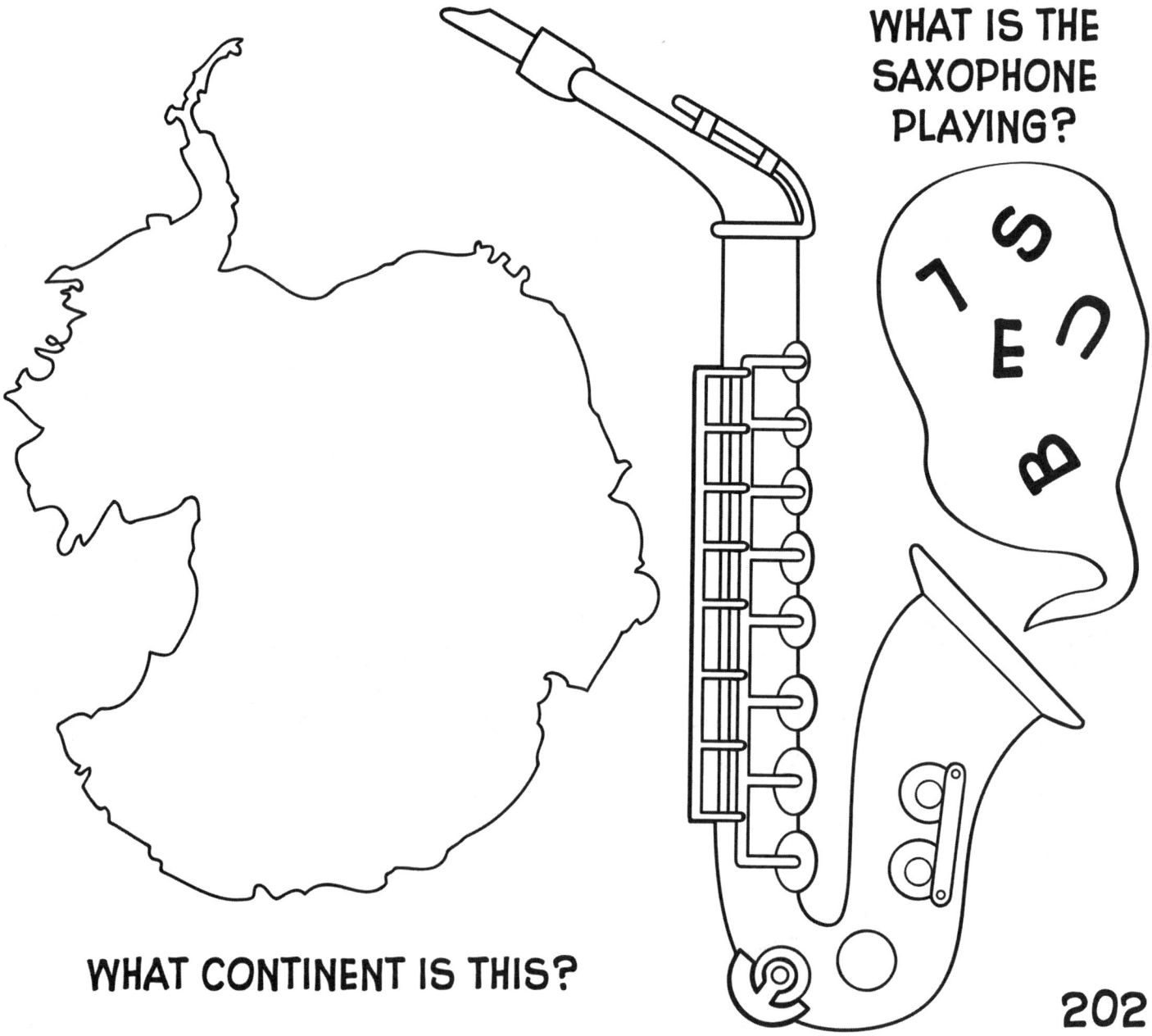

WHAT CONTINENT IS THIS?

WHAT IS THE AVERAGE NUMBER OF APPLES IN THESE BASKETS?

WHICH DRAWING ON EACH LINE IS IDENTICAL TO THE ONE IN THE LEFT COLUMN?

TO CATCH THE MOUSE, THE CAT NEEDS TO GO THROUGH THE ODD NUMBERS.

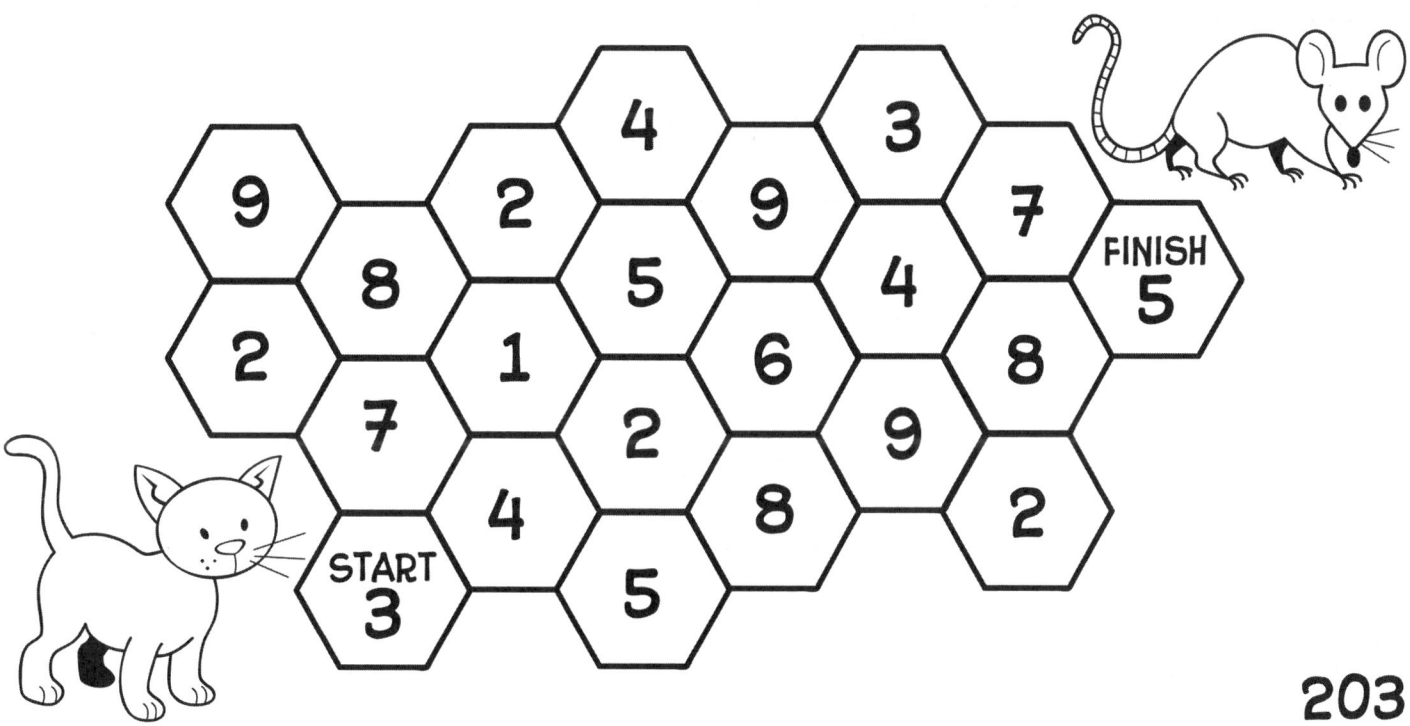

DRAW A CIRCLE AROUND THE ITEMS YOU PUT ON YOUR FEET.
COLOR THE ONES THAT COVER YOUR HEAD.

CAN YOU SPELL THE NAME
OF THIS ANIMAL? C _ _.
WHAT DOES IT EAT? G _ _ _ _.
WHERE DOES IT LIVE? F _ _ _.

COMPLETE EACH LINE IN THE CORRECT SEQUENCE.

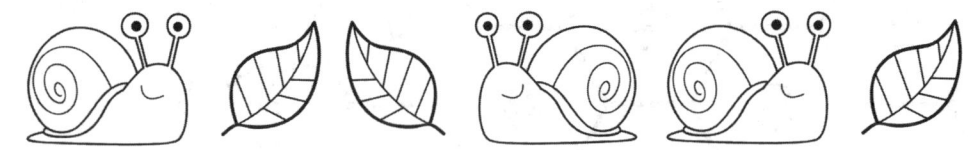

WHICH ONE OF THESE ANIMALS IS BEST CAPABLE OF WITHSTANDING FREEZING TEMPERATURES?

HOW MANY SWALLOWS ARE FLYING EAST? COLOR THEM BLUE.
HOW MANY FLY WEST? COLOR THEM PURPLE.

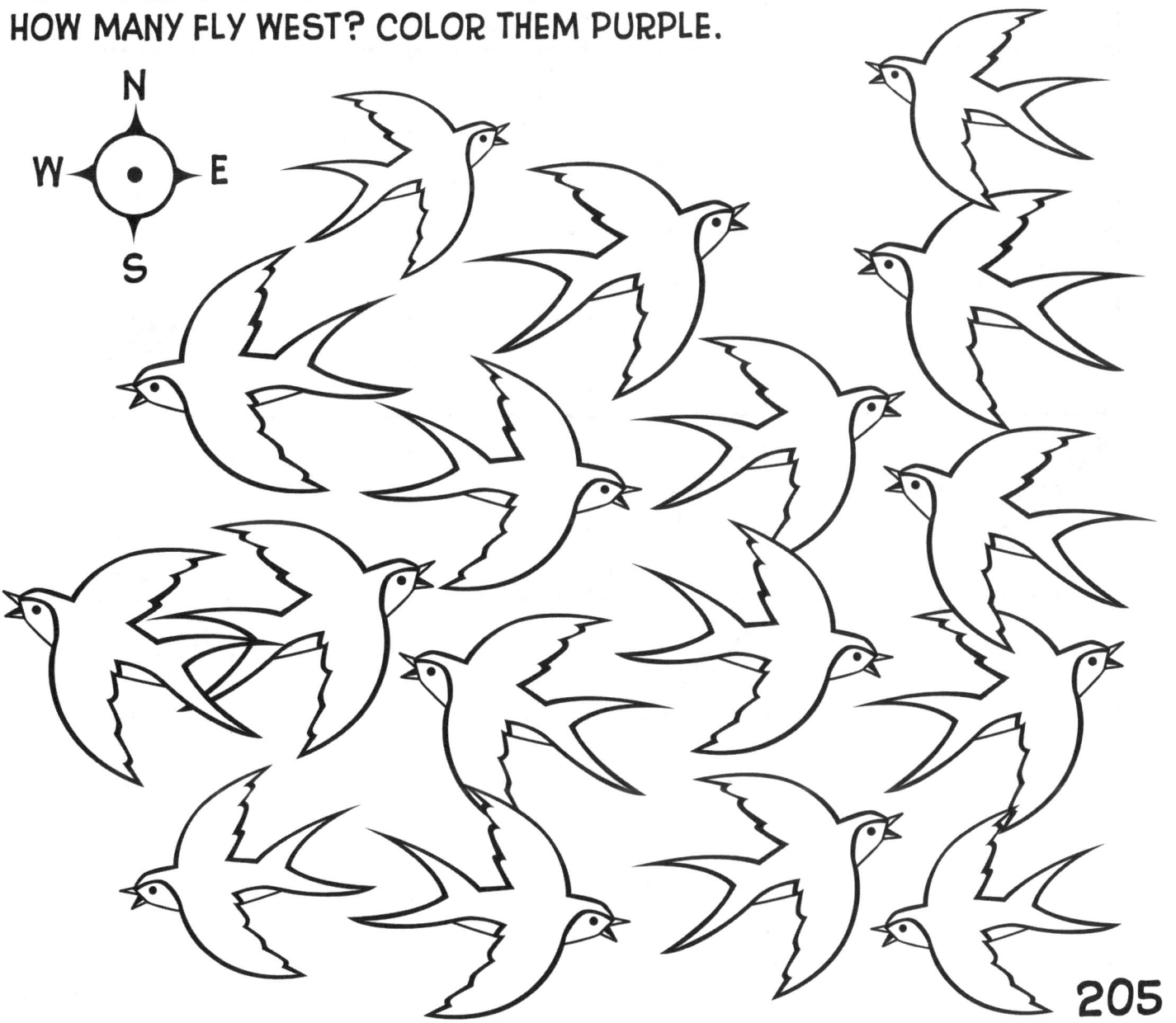

CAN YOU FIND THE SMALLER COMBINATIONS IN THE BIG GRID BELOW?
COLOR THEM WHEN YOU DO!

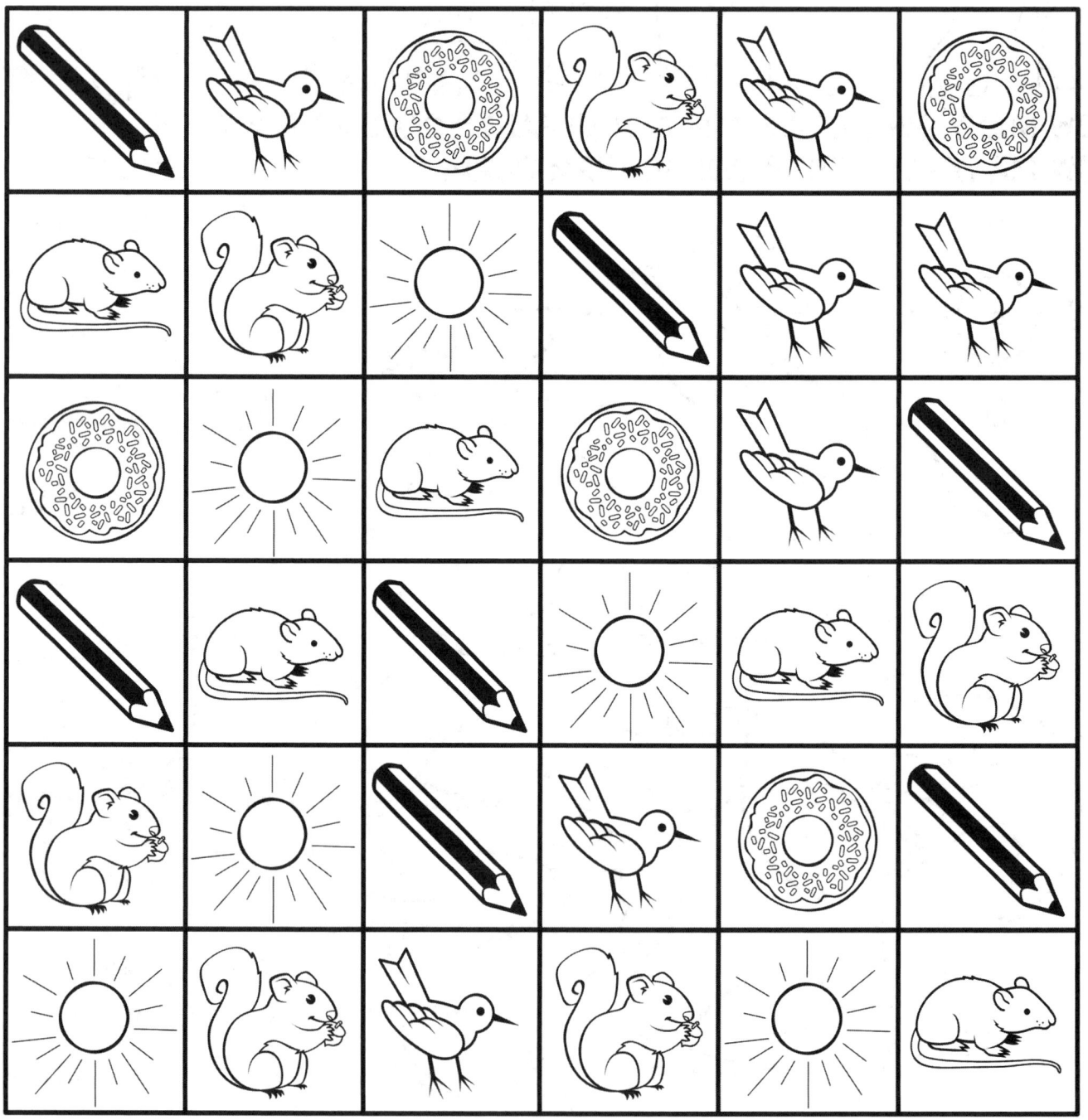

IF YOU CONTINUE THE PROGRESSION OF SYMBOLS FROM LEFT TO RIGHT, WHICH ONE WOULD SUBSTITUTE THE QUESTION MARK?

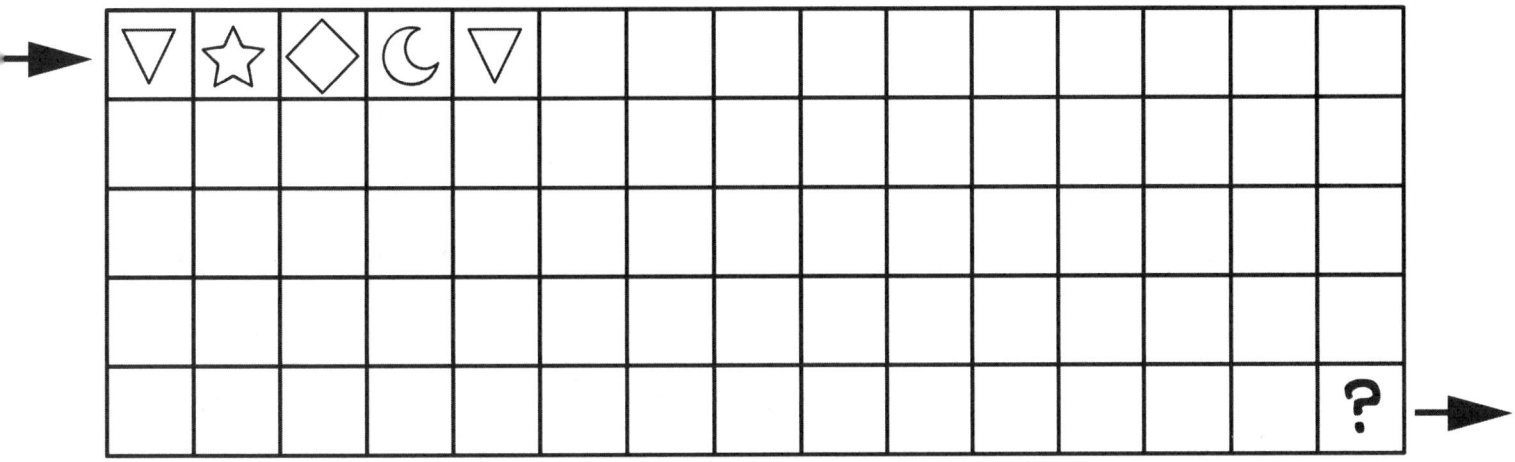

COLOR PLANE #1 RED, PLANE #2 BLUE, AND #3 YELLOW. THEN TRACE EACH PLANE'S AEROBATIC FLIGHT PATH USING THEIR COLORS.

IN WHAT ORDER SHOULD THESE PLANES TAKE FLIGHT IN ORDER TO AVOID CRASHING INTO EACH OTHER?

JUMPING ONLY FROM ONE WEBBING TO THE OTHER, WHILE AVOIDING THE DANGERS, HELP THE SPIDER REACH HER MEAL.

CAN YOU SEE THE TWO IDENTICAL DRAGONFLIES?

IT'S GETTING LATE, AND THE KIDS NEED TO BE BACK HOME BEFORE THE SUN SETS. TRACE THE DOTTED PATHS TO FIND OUT WHERE EACH ONE LIVES.

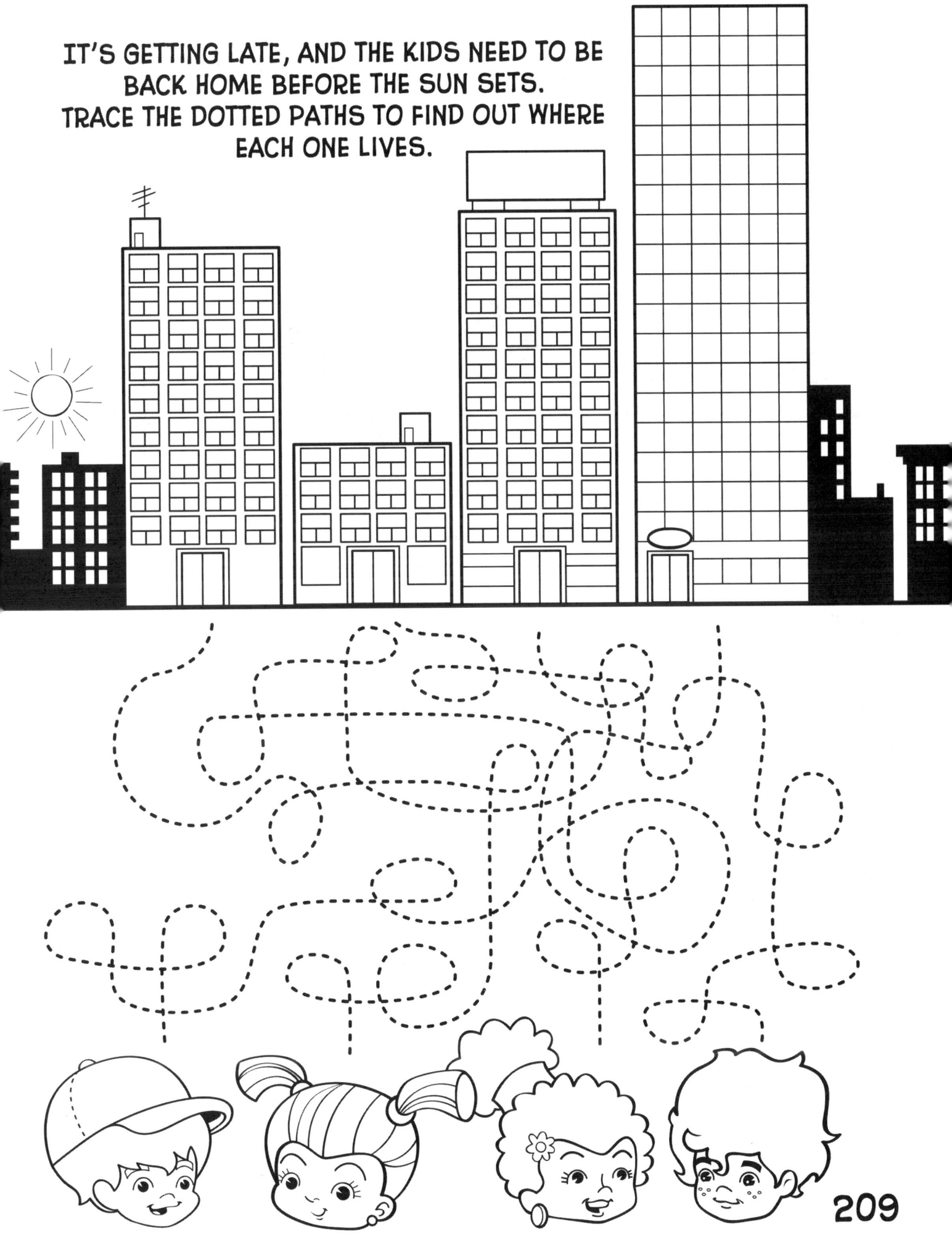

CONNECT EACH SHOE TO ITS APPROPIATE FOOTPRINT.

WRITE FOUR ANIMALS THAT START WITH THE LETTER "E" .

E

E

E

E

DRAW THE HANDS OF THE CLOCKS.

12:00

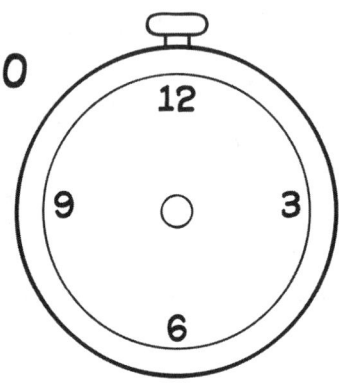

12:15

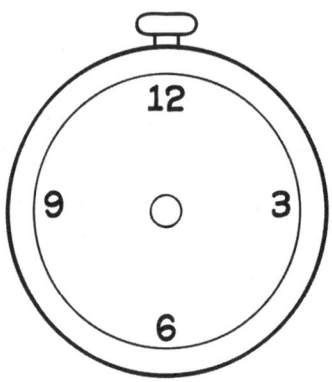

12:30

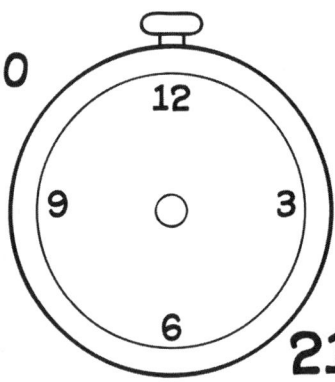

THE MORE LEAVES A CATERPILLAR EATS, THE MORE IT GROWS. COUNT THE LEAVES ON EACH PLANT AND DRAW AN EQUAL NUMBER OF CIRCLES FOR EACH CATERPILLAR.

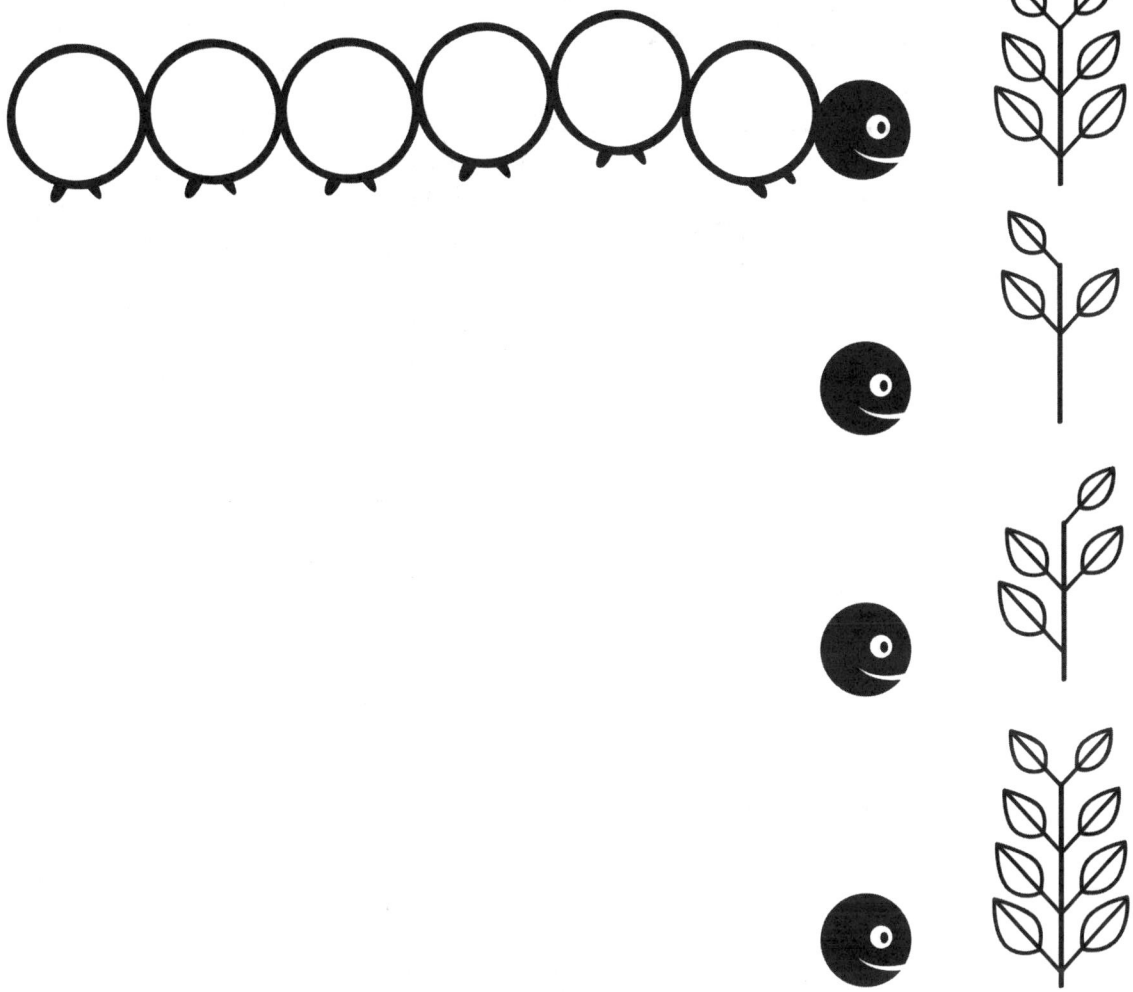

WHICH OF THE ANIMALS BELOW DO CATERPILLARS TURN INTO? COLOR IT. WHAT IS THE TRANSFORMATION CALLED?

M _ _ _ _ _ _ _ _ _ _ _ _

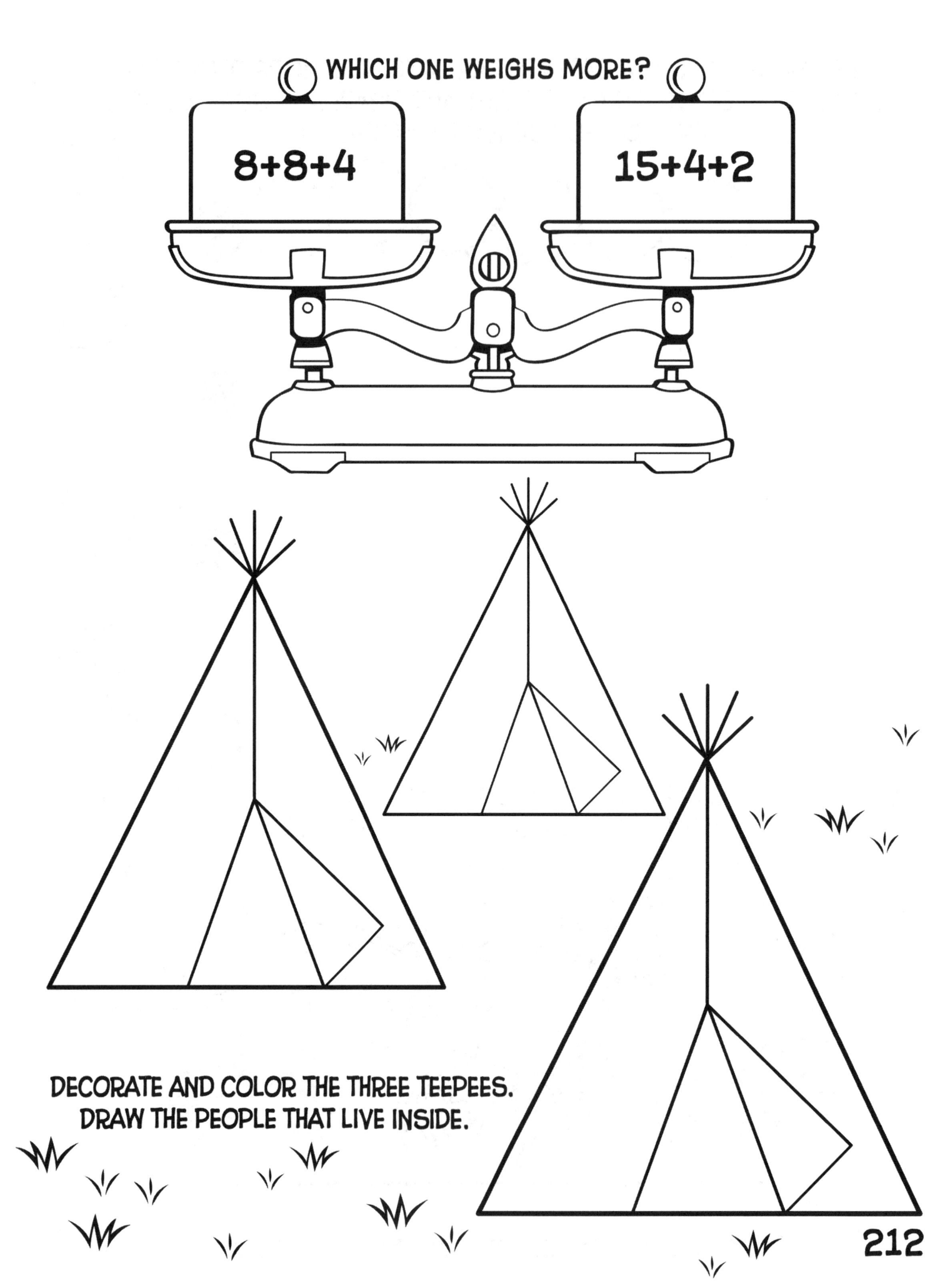
WHICH ONE WEIGHS MORE?
8+8+4
15+4+2
DECORATE AND COLOR THE THREE TEEPEES.
DRAW THE PEOPLE THAT LIVE INSIDE.

SOLVE THE ADDITIONS, AND WRITE YOUR RESULTS BELOW.

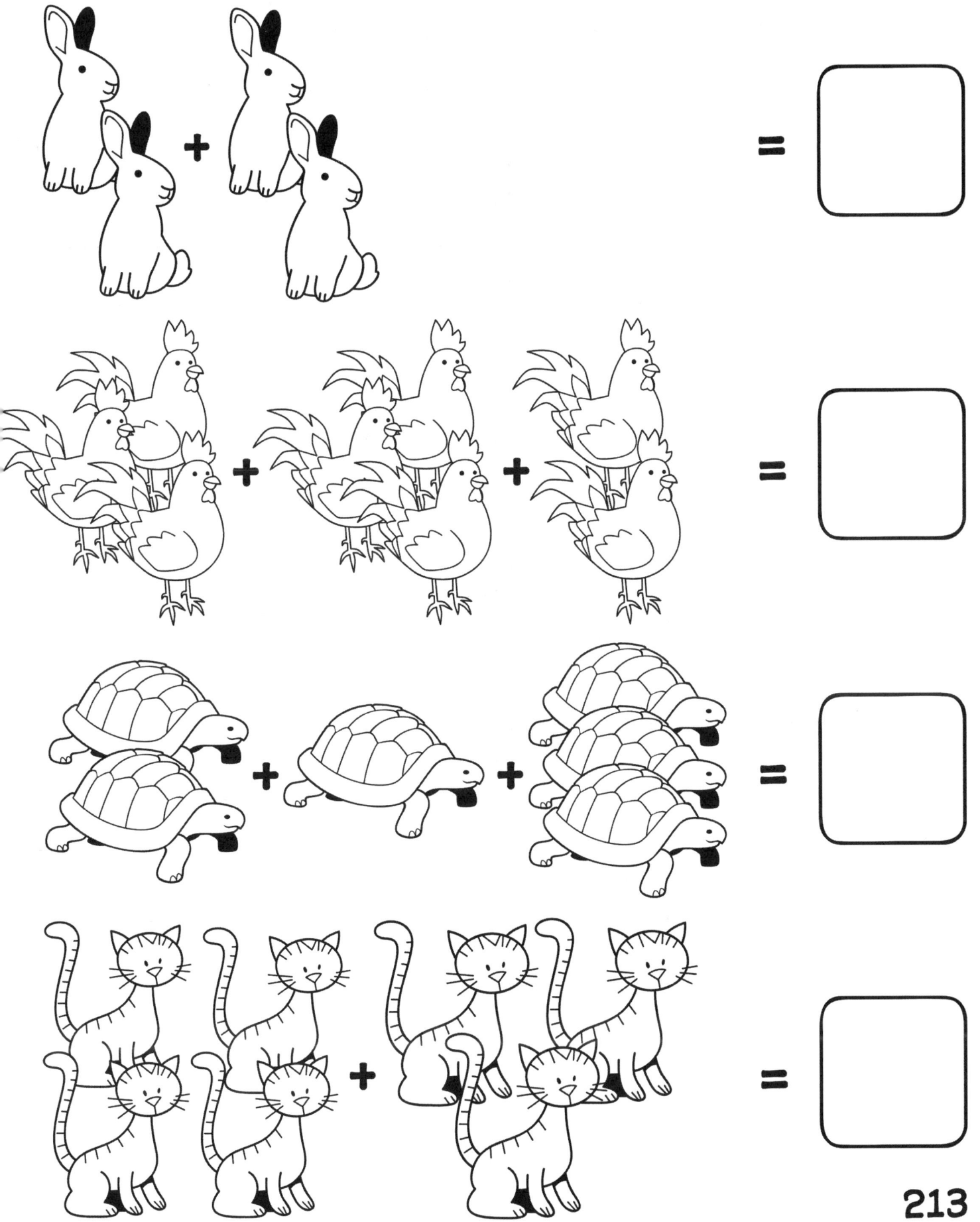

ALL THESE FLAGS ARE BLUE AND WHITE.
COLOR THEM ACCORDING TO THEIR COUNTRY.

ARGENTINA

ISRAEL

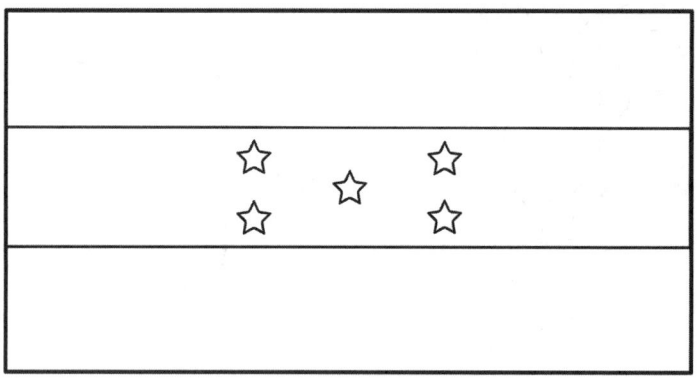

HONDURAS

GREECE

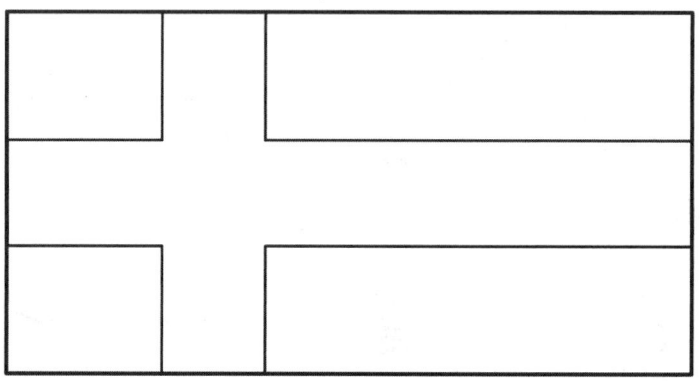

FINLAND

URUGUAY

SAN MARINO

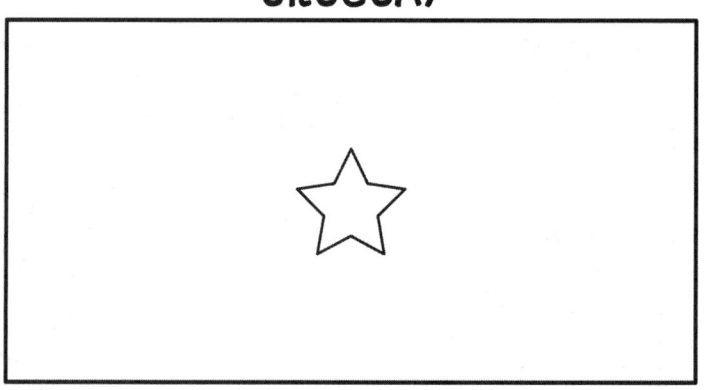

SOMALIA

FIND THE SILHOUETTE THAT DOESN'T BELONG TO THIS AIRPLANE.

DRAW THE HANDS OF THE CLOCKS.

5:35

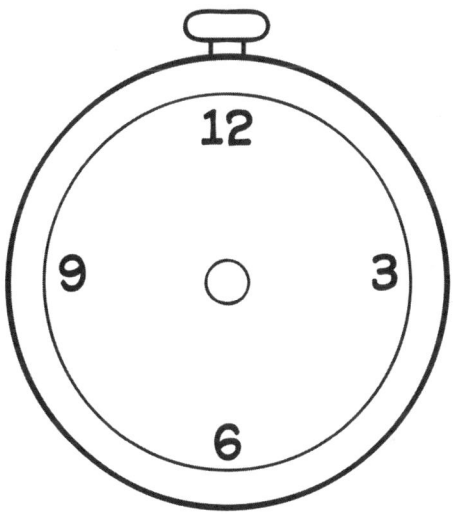

8:10

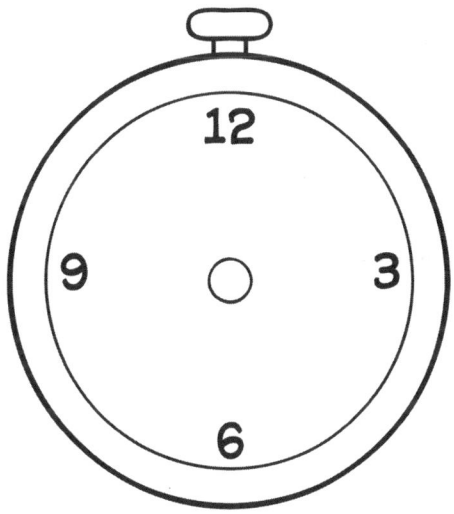

9:45

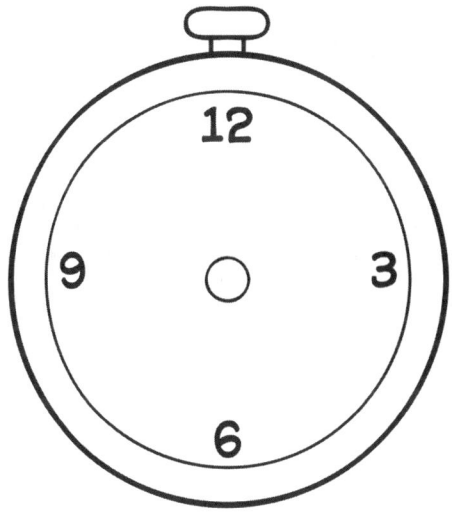

MULTIPLY THE NUMBERS ON EACH CAR BY 2.

YOU'RE FLYING ABOARD A ROCKET: DRAW STARS, SATELLITES, AND ANYTHING YOU CAN IMAGINE FLOATING IN SPACE, THEN COLOR IT ALL!

DECORATE THESE SKATEBOARDS WITH COLORFUL AND AMAZING DRAWINGS.

LOOK FOR THE DRAWINGS THAT APPEAR TWICE IN THE WHOLE GRID AND SURROUND THEM WITH A CIRCLE.

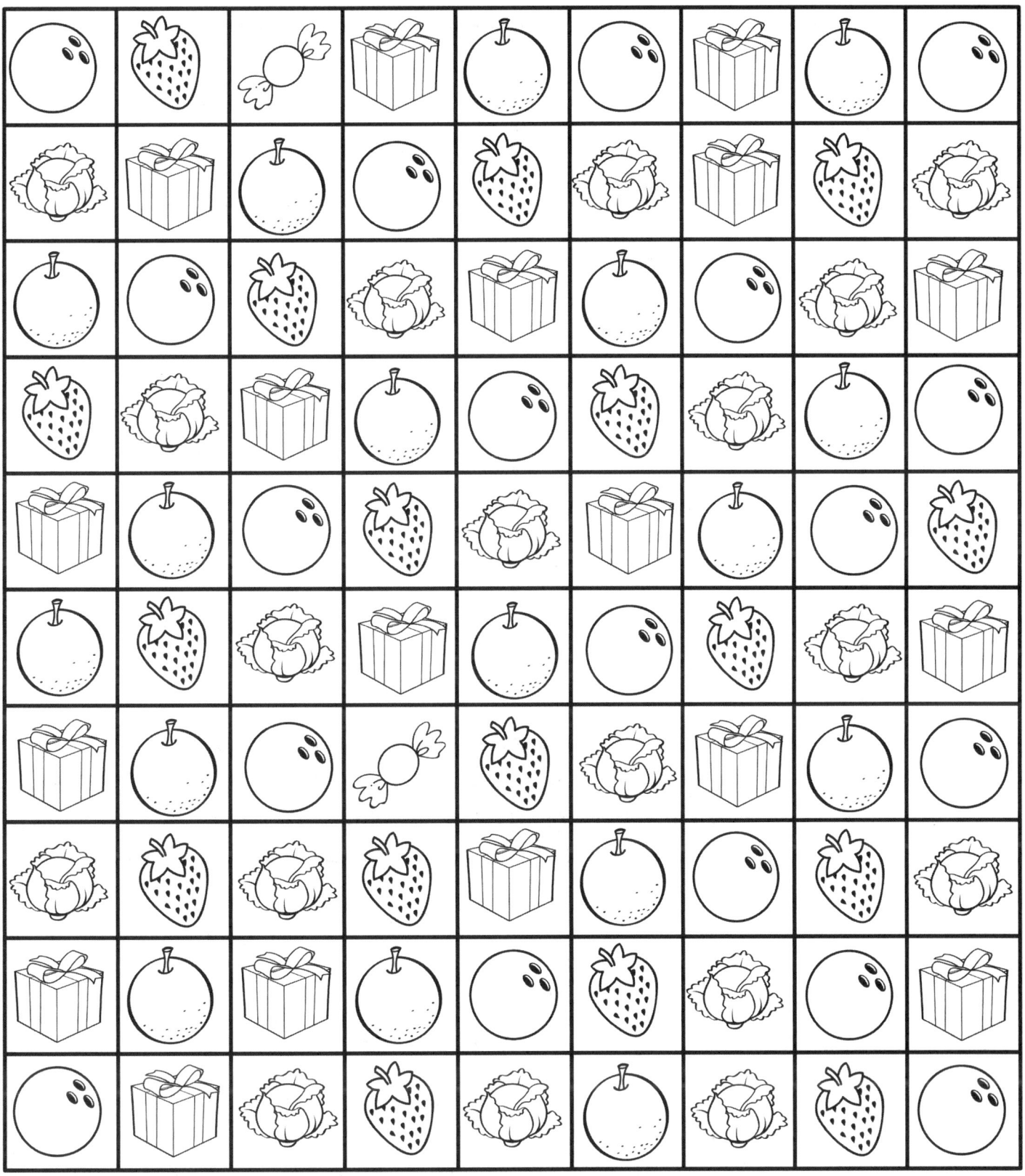

CRACK THE SUDOKU!
REMEMBER EACH SYMBOL CAN ONLY BE PLACED ONCE ON EACH LINE, ONCE ON EACH ROW, AND ONCE IN EACH FOUR CELL GRID.

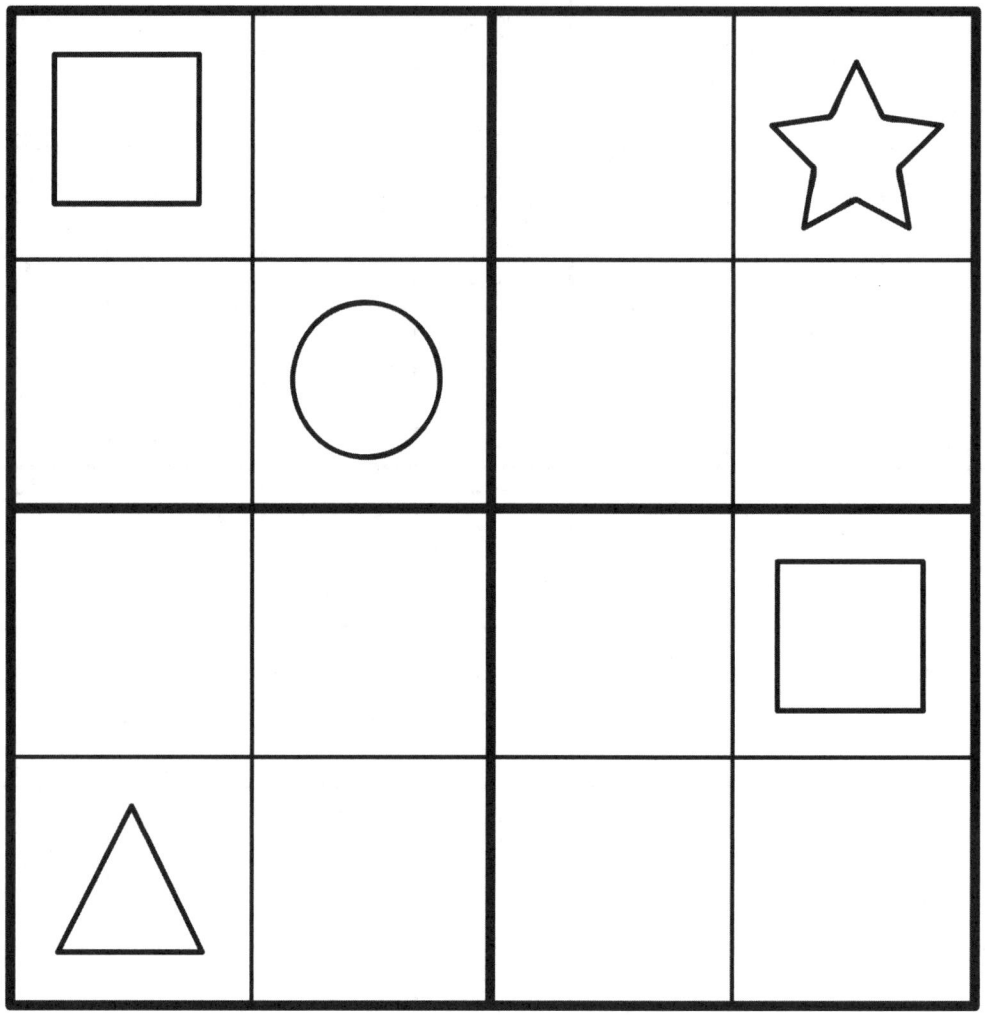

TO BEAT DAPHNE AT DOMINOES YOU NEED TO DRAW THE RIGHT AMOUNT OF MISSING DOTS ON EACH HEAD, OR WRITE THE TOTAL NUMBER ABOVE EACH TILE.

AND COLOR IT ALL!

WHICH ONE WEIGHS MORE?

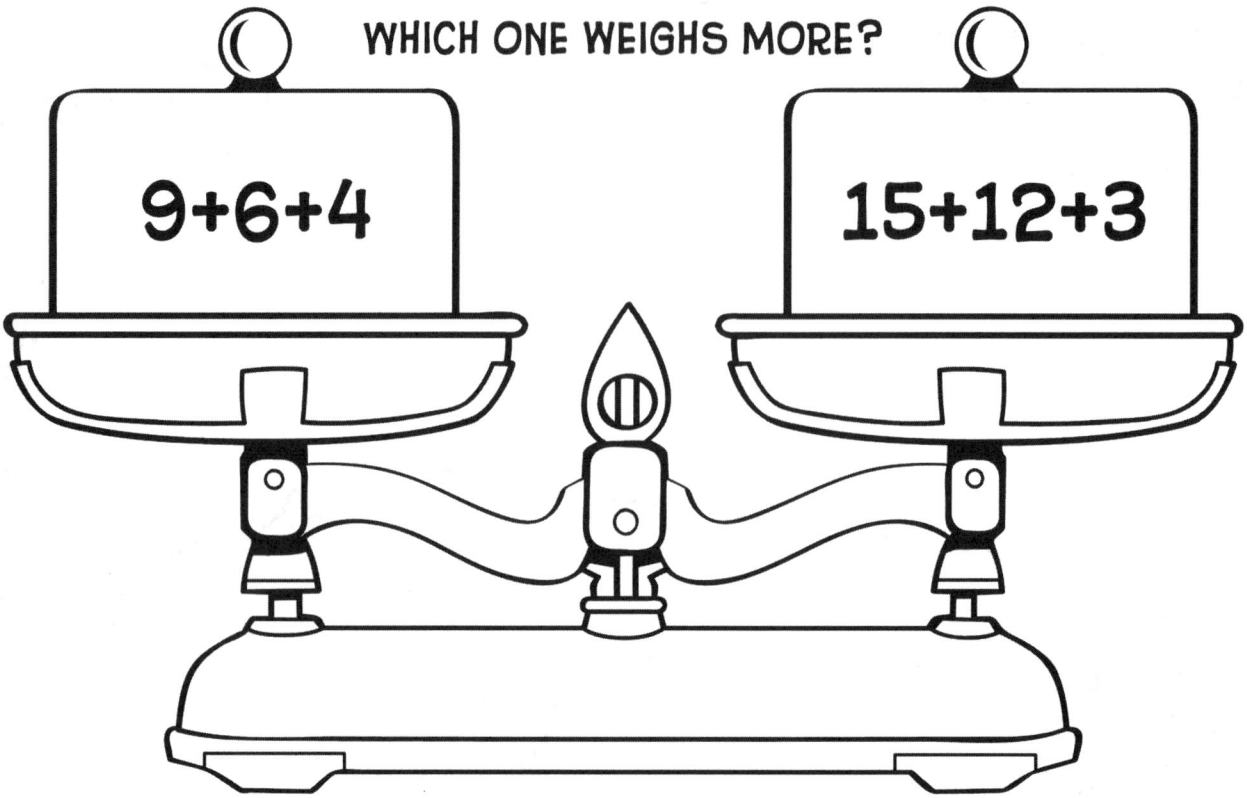

THERE'S AN INTRUDER AND THE ANTS ARE SLEEPING!
CAN YOU DRAW THE ONES MISSING FROM THE NEST AND WAKE THEM UP? CAN YOU COUNT THEM ALL? WHERE IS THE QUEEN?

THERE ARE TEN MAMMALS TO BE FOUND IN THIS WORDSEARCH.

CLUE: ONE OF THEM IS PICTURED BELOW!

G	D	O	L	P	H	I	N	H	S	E
E	O	G	D	S	P	P	T	O	A	W
B	A	R	B	E	A	V	E	R	Z	B
F	N	F	I	G	E	D	F	S	J	Z
R	T	N	I	L	R	T	W	E	I	F
M	E	P	B	I	L	Q	C	O	W	B
F	A	V	L	U	K	A	Z	Q	W	E
X	T	A	D	B	L	J	S	H	L	V
C	E	Q	M	A	E	L	G	A	L	I
B	R	E	H	I	U	A	H	E	A	O
V	J	I	W	V	H	W	R	P	B	M

WHAT'S ITS NAME?
WHERE DOES IT LIVE?
WHAT DOES IT EAT?

WRITE THE FIRST LETTER
OF EACH OBJECT.

DRAW THE CAT IN THREE EASY STEPS!

DIVIDE THIS PATCH OF LAND SO THAT EACH VEGGIE
WILL GET AN EQUAL SIZE AREA.

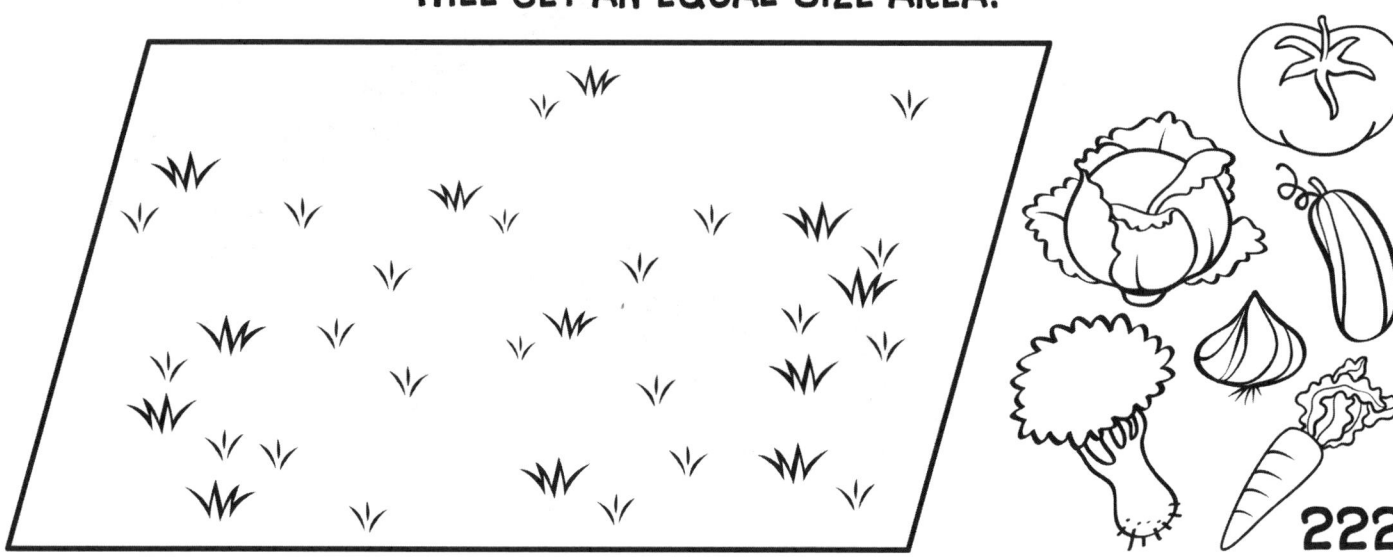

HAVE YOU EVER SEEN A PIG FLY?
GIVE EACH PIG ITS OWN PARACHUTE!

COLOR THE SKY BLUE AND
ADD MORE WHITE CLOUDS.

DRAW A CIRCLE AROUND
THE THINGS THAT FLY
AND A SQUARE AROUND
THE ONES THAT FLOAT.

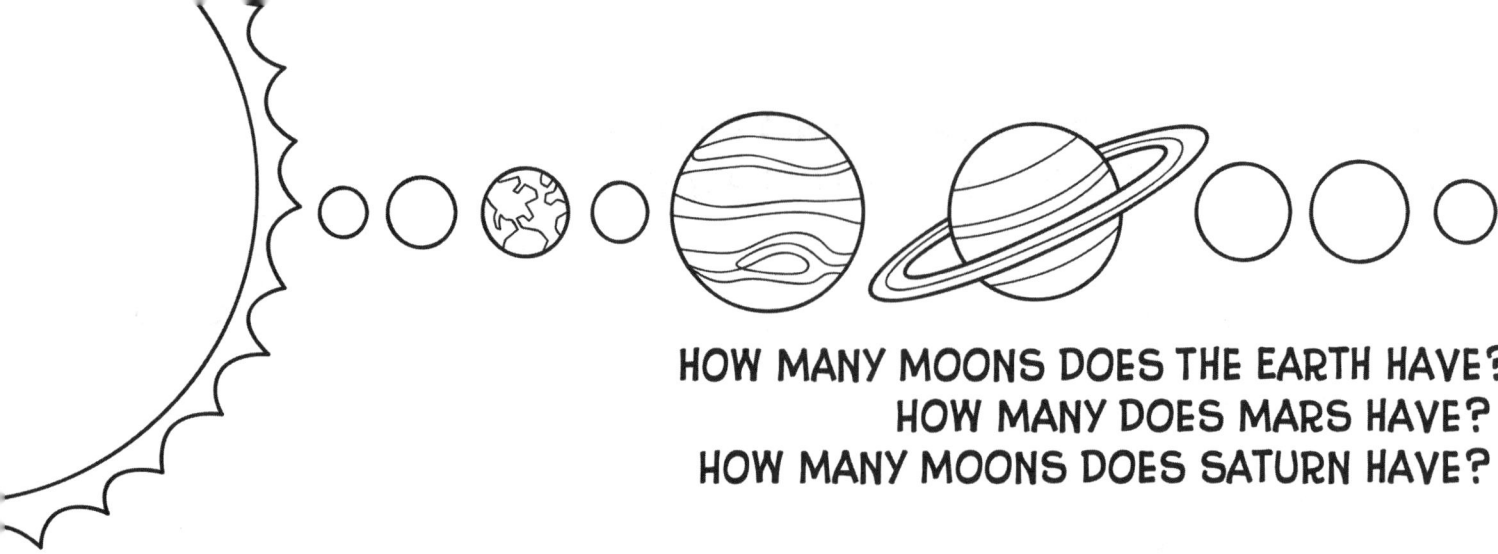

HOW MANY MOONS DOES THE EARTH HAVE?
HOW MANY DOES MARS HAVE?
HOW MANY MOONS DOES SATURN HAVE?

WHICH ONE DOES NOT BELONG IN THIS GROUP?

HOW MANY TIMES DOES THE BALL SPIN BEFORE HITTING THE FIRST PIN?
TRACE THE DOTTED LINE TO FIND OUT!

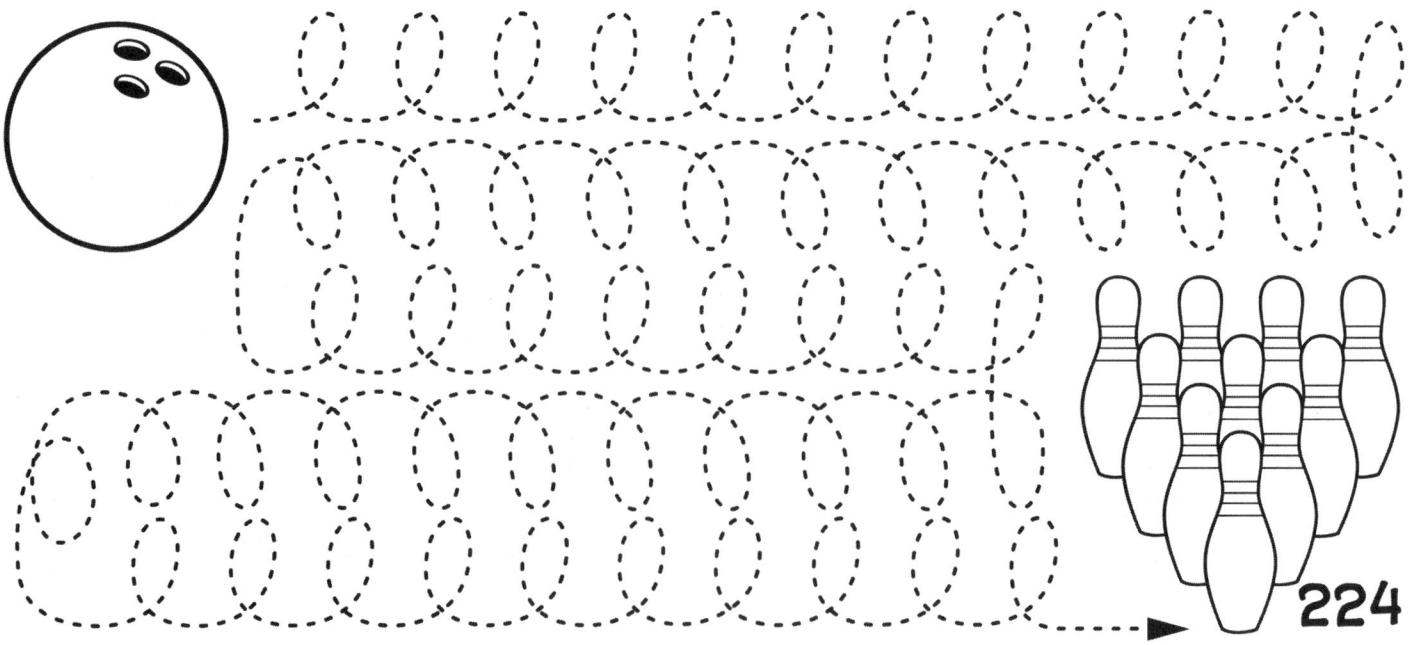

EACH CAR CONSUMES 1 GALLON PER BOX. CAR #1 HAS 12 GALLONS IN ITS TANK. CAR #2 HAS 38 GALLONS, AND #3 HAS 28 GALLONS, WHICH ONE GETS STOPPED BY TRAFFIC LIGHTS?

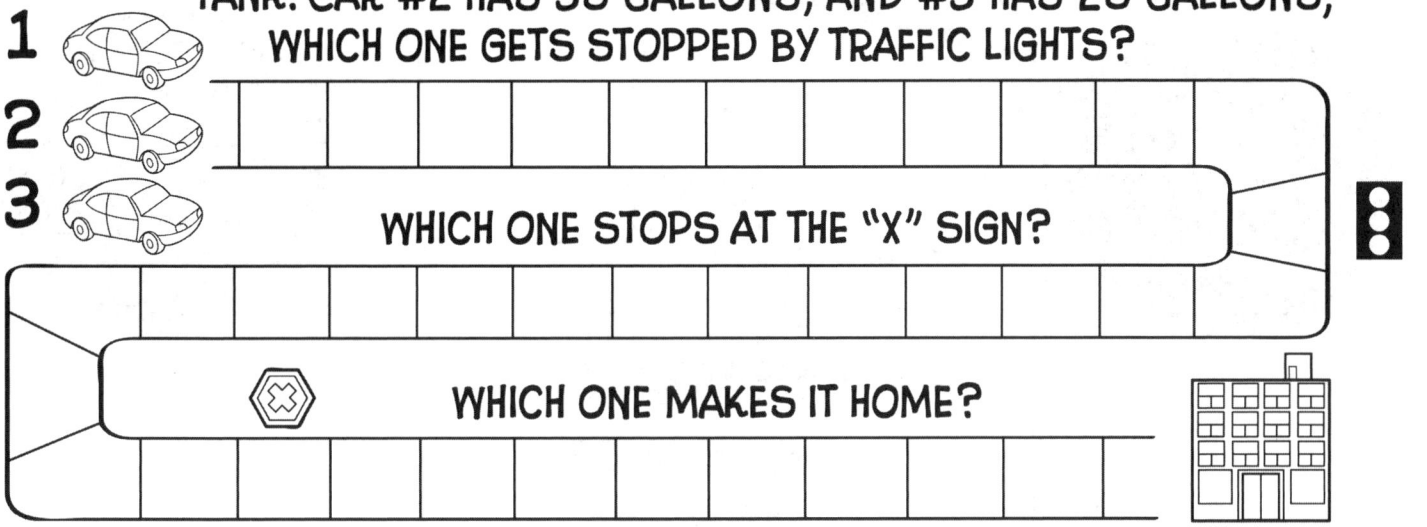

COMPLETE EACH COLUMN SO THE SUM OF THESE NUMBERS IS ALWAYS 27.

9	7	14	11	5	18	3	20	18	13	4	15
9											
5											
4											

C
C
C
C

WRITE FOUR COUNTRIES THAT START WITH THE LETTER "C".

ADD THE MISSING NUMBER TO LEVEL THE WEIGHT.

COLOR THE STRONGMAN'S LEOTARD!

COMPLETE AND COLOR THE FELINES TO TURN ONE INTO A TIGER AND THE OTHER A PANTHER.

COLOR THE BALL, ALTERNATING RED, WHITE, AND BLUE.

DRAW A CIRCLE AROUND THE FOOD THAT DOESN'T BELONG.

IF FOUR APPLES FROM THE TREE ON THE LEFT WILL FILL A BASKET,
HOW MANY BASKETS WILL YOU NEED?
KEEP IN MIND THE APPLES ON THE SECOND TREE
ARE TWICE AS BIG.

FILL THE CIRCLES TO MAKE LETTERS, SUCH AS THE "A" ABOVE.
CAN YOU WRITE YOUR NAME VERTICALLY OR HORIZONTALLY?

SALLY HAS SENT BILLY A CODED MESSAGE.
CAN YOU DECIPHER IT?

HOW MANY MOVES DOES THE HORSE NEED TO CHECK THE KING?

OLLIE LIVES IN A COUNTRY SURROUNDED BY SEA.
CAN YOU GUESS WHICH COUNTRY IT IS?

```
                E B X           V
              N V A H A         W
    X   I H T J E         Y R
  S T A S M A N I A       M G S
G U T I W S Y D N E Y     B P E R
S O R A C M K A U E A Y K Z T H H F
K X F E C V T U C C K B N Q J B Y W
  L C V C S E A H C A P M R I O Y O A R M U
H Y Q W O U Y B L T T S M E W O Q R L Z G P Z J
D K Y X O O L H L Q A B F E S O E C A I G N G K A
L I T B Z U N I X G B Y D A A E F L O O X G N A A G S
F B B D I T W U M M K J O W R H B K U F D A I U N K S
Q O K V B B X H O B Z I M T Z R V M V J R I H N G P F I
  S J F P A N W H F W T B E X Z I L H E C E L B A U F L
  M X S T C A J G V U P F I L W R E M W P Q F E R L R L
    X T B K F Z I Y M S F X R B B O R B K T M B O U F E
    M Z T H W L Z J O       E Z O X K R Q F X E O R X F
      X N J W U M             B H U B N E R V X X U F
      H U   S I               P   L R A U E J Y J U
                                L K N F O F M U U
                                  A B E M O D S
                                    B U G H Q
```

HIDDEN WITHIN ITS SHAPE, YOU WILL FIND FIFTEEN WORDS RELATED TO IT.
CLUE: ONE OF THEM IS AN OBJECT THAT RETURNS TO YOU AFTER YOU THROW IT AWAY!

COMPLETE EACH COLUMN SO THE SUM OF THESE NUMBERS IS ALWAYS 42.

↓	7	12	21	6	14	39	3	16	24	8	18	2
28												
4												
3												

DRAW THE NUMBER OF BALLS AND HATS AS INDICATED BY EACH TILE.

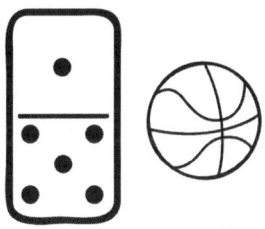

DRAW THE HANDS OF THE CLOCKS.

6:55

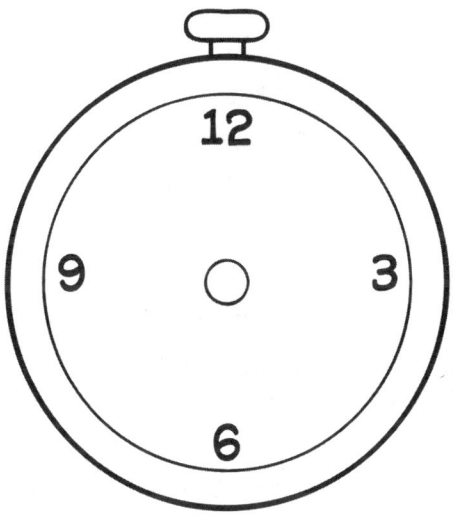

8:30

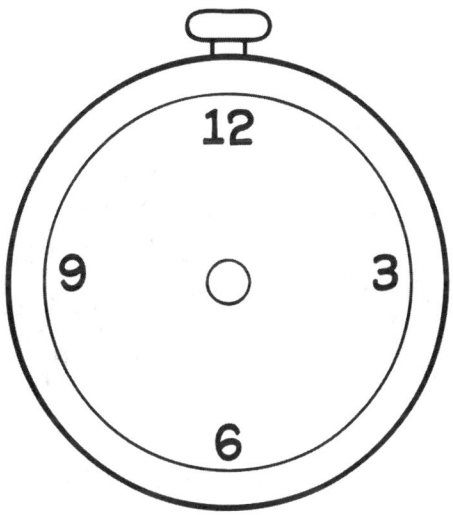

4:15

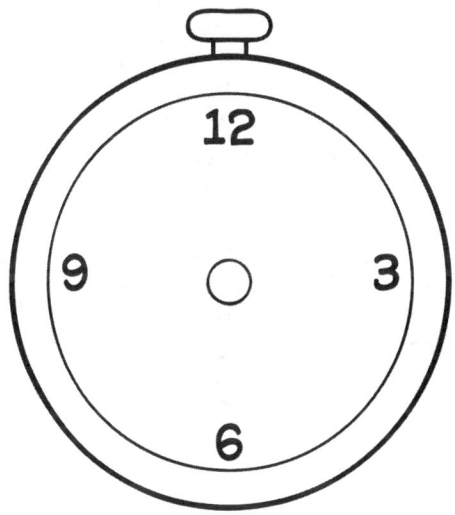

TO FIND THE WAY OUT, CONNECT THE NUMBERS DIVISIBLE BY TWO.

9	4	8	6	5	3	7	5	2	◀	
3	2	5	9	2	8	6	4	3		
6	5	3	1	7	5	3	9	5	4	7
6	3	1	4	6	8	2	4	7	5	3
8	2	4	2	3	4	1	4	6	8	▶

CONNECT EACH DOG TO ITS CORRESPONDING SHADOW.

DRAW WHAT'S MISSING FROM EACH TRAIN. THE TRAIN GOING LEFT HAS BLUE WHEELS AND THE TRAIN GOING RIGHT RED WHEELS.

CRACK THE SUDOKU!
EACH DRAWING CAN ONLY BE PLACED ONCE ON EACH LINE, ONCE ON EACH ROW, AND ONCE IN EACH FOUR CELL GRID.

THE ROOSTER AND THE HEN HAD MANY CHICKS.
FIGURE OUT HOW MANY BY COUNTING ALL THE BROKEN EGG SHELLS.
DRAW THE MISSING CHICKS.

SOLVE THE EQUATIONS AND WRITE YOUR RESULTS BELOW.

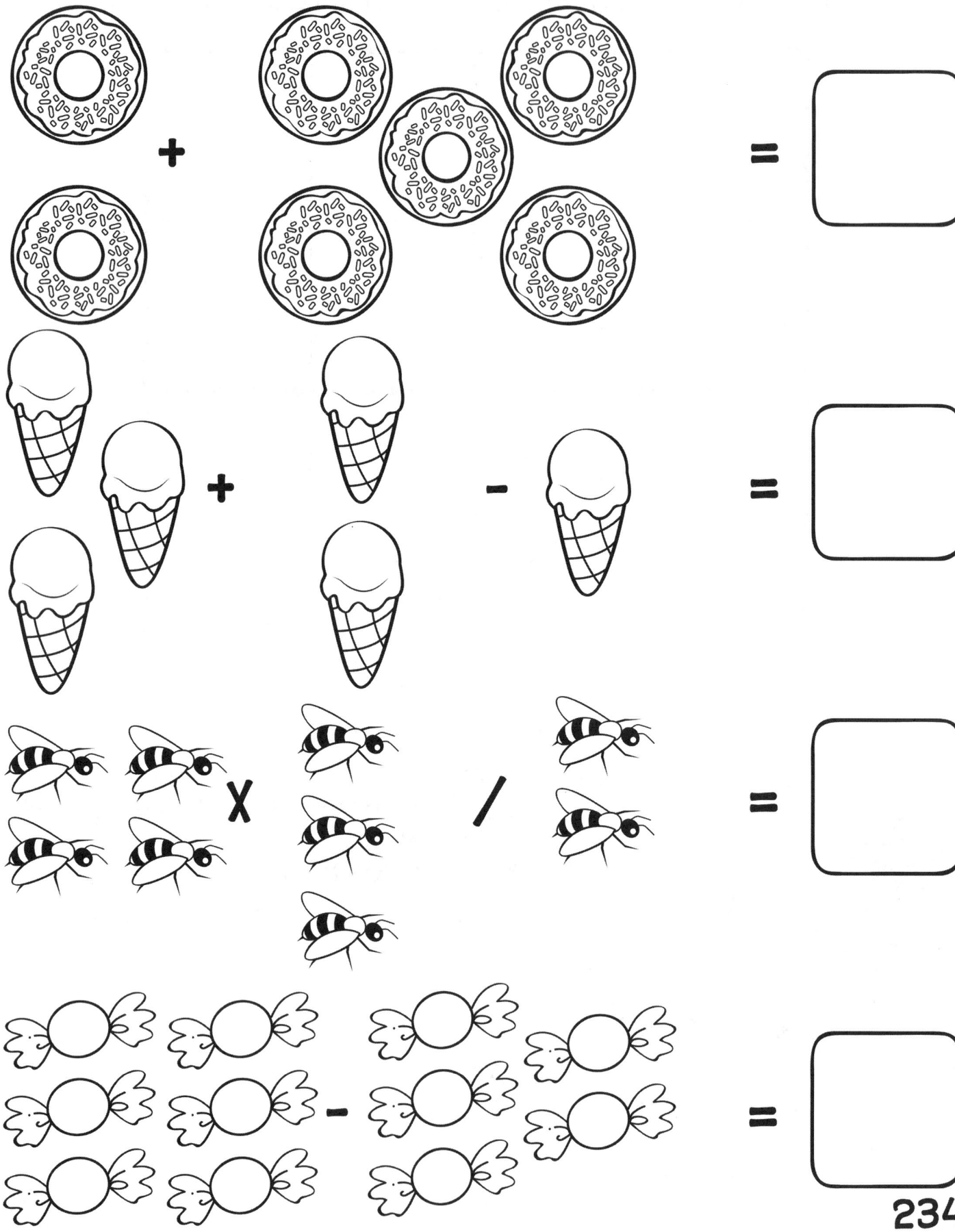

WHAT DO YOU GET WHEN YOU BLOW THROUGH THIS RING?

WRITE FOUR COUNTRIES THAT START WITH THE LETTER "A" .

A
A
A
A

WHICH ONE WEIGHS MORE?

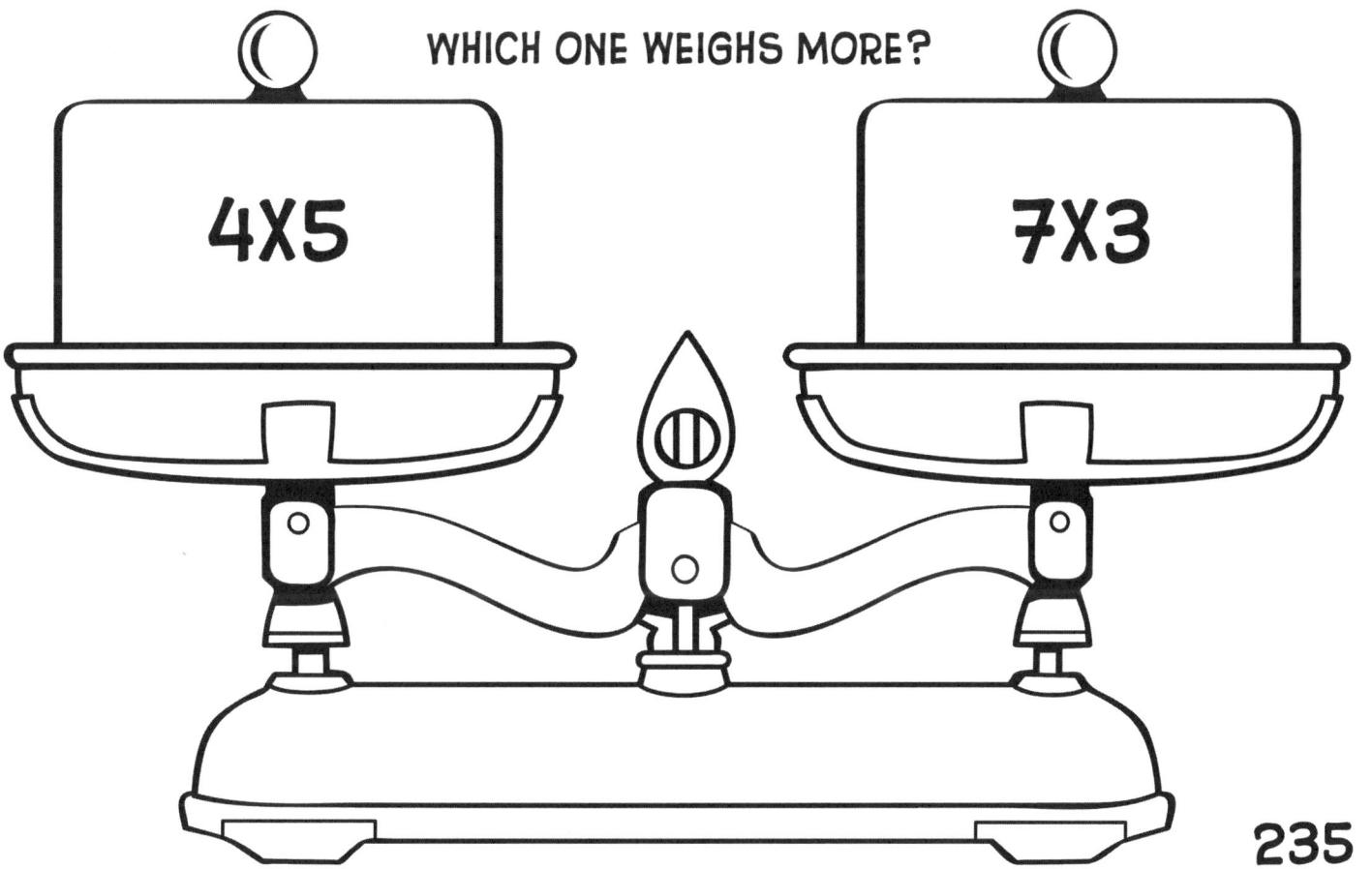

SOMETHING'S WRONG OR AMISS WITH THESE FLAGS.
CAN YOU FIX AND COLOR THEM ACCORDINGLY?
IT'S OK TO GO BACK TO PREVIOUS PAGES TO CHECK THEM OUT.

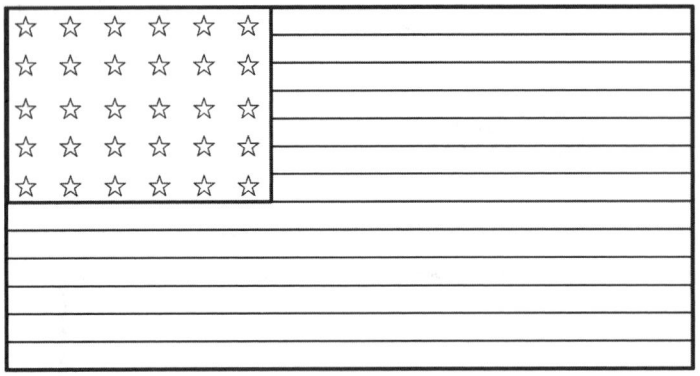

U.S.A

ISRAEL

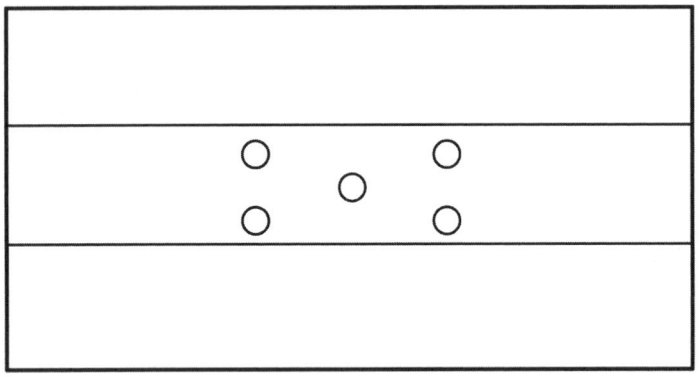

HONDURAS

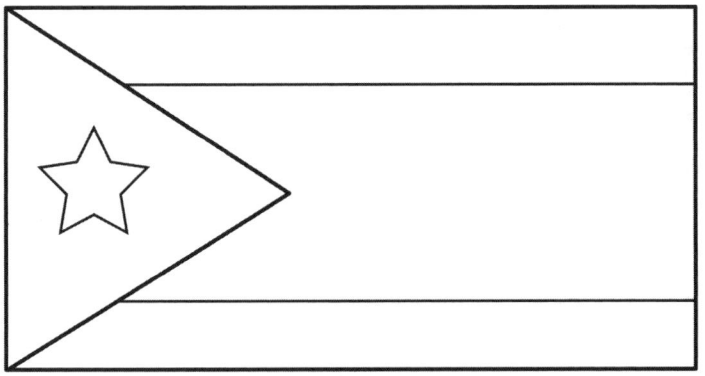

CUBA

FINLAND

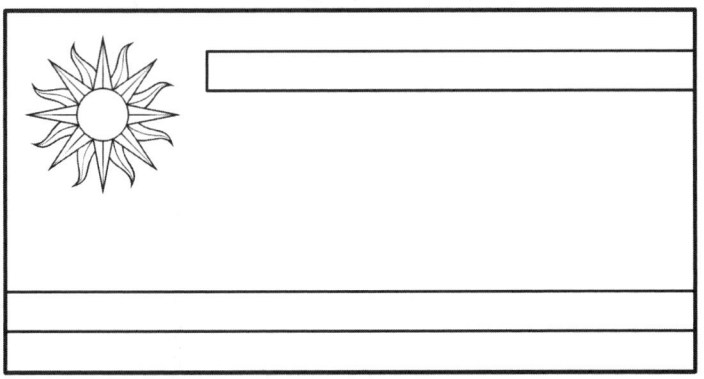

URUGUAY

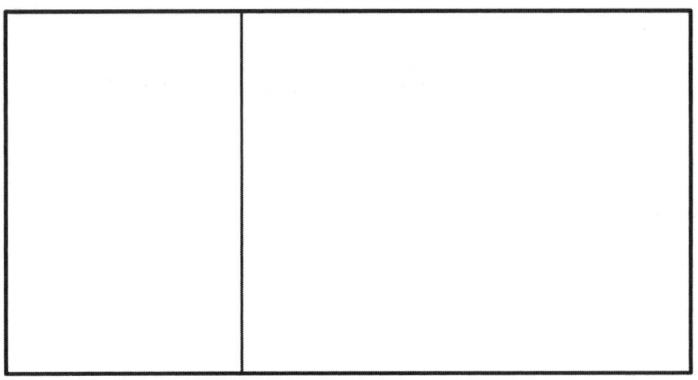

ITALY

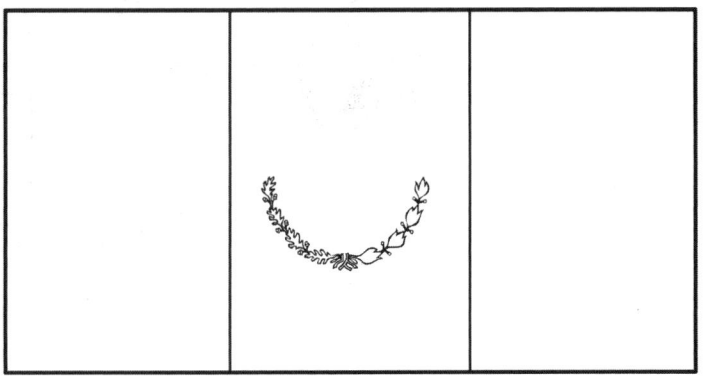

MEXICO

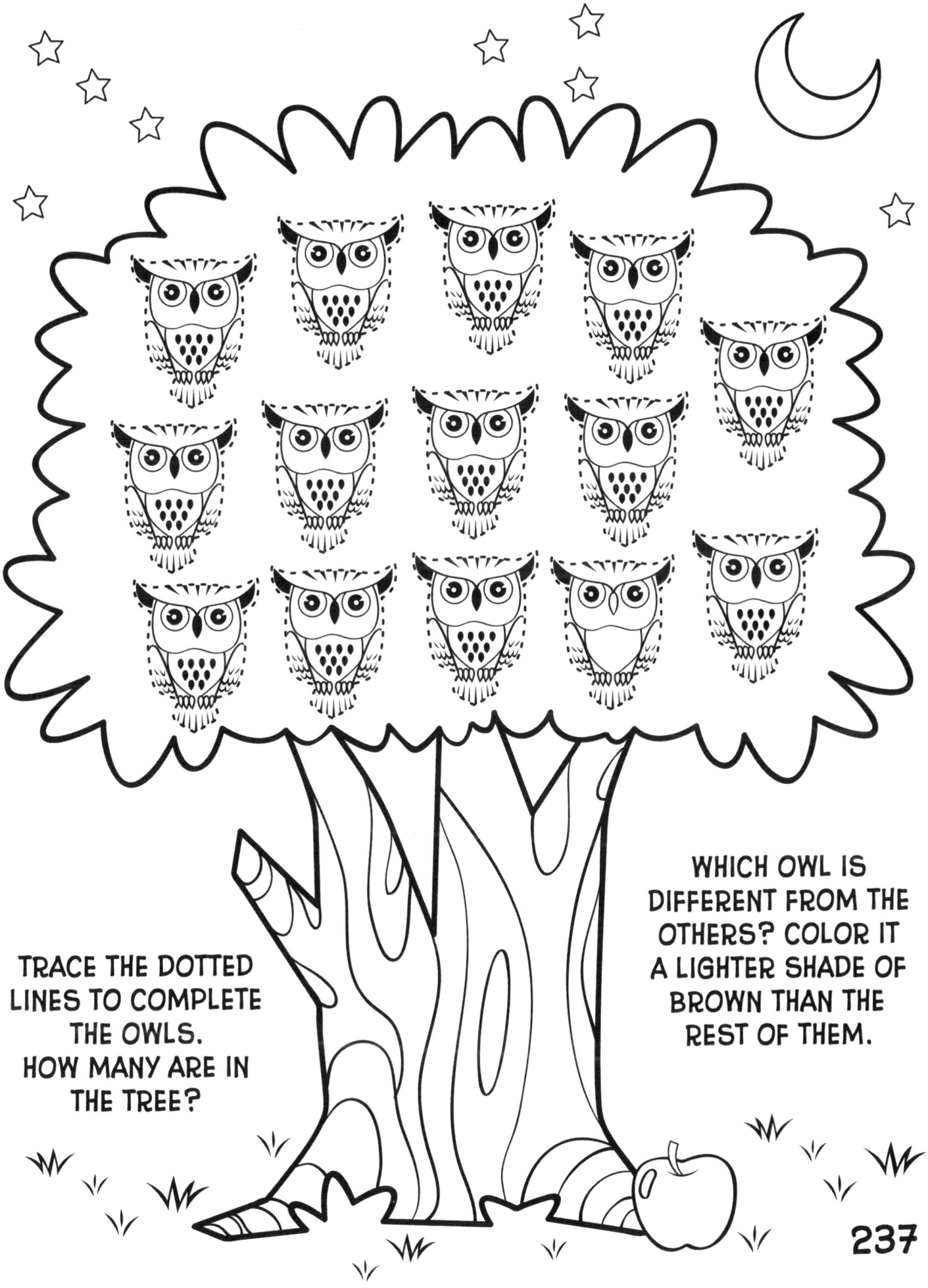

TRACE THE DOTTED LINES TO COMPLETE THE OWLS. HOW MANY ARE IN THE TREE?

WHICH OWL IS DIFFERENT FROM THE OTHERS? COLOR IT A LIGHTER SHADE OF BROWN THAN THE REST OF THEM.

COMPLETE EACH COLUMN SO THE SUM OF THESE NUMBERS WILL ALWAYS BE 36.

18	4	10	1	32	6	3	8	27	13	4	12
9											
5											
4											

HELP ICHA MAKE THREE NECKLACES BY DRAWING THE MISSING BEADS IN THE RIGHT SEQUENCE.

MULTIPLY THE NUMBER OF SPOTS ON EACH LADYBUG BY 5.
IF YOU ADD THE RESULTS, WHAT WILL THE TOTAL RESULT BE?

SUROUND THE DUCKIES WITH A LINE IN GROUPS OF THREE,
BUT BE CAREFUL NOT TO INCLUDE THE FROGS IN ANY OF THE GROUPS!

DRAW AS MANY PRESENTS AND ICE CREAM CONES
AS INDICATED BY EACH TILE.

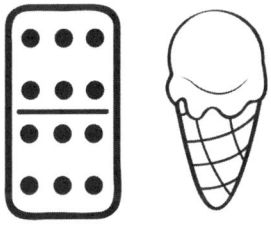

THESE SILHOUETTES CORRESPOND TO IMPORTANT MONUMENTS.
CAN YOU NAME THEM?

P _ _ _ _ _ _ _ _ O _ _ G _ _ _.

S _ _ _ _ _ O _ _ _ _ H _ _ _ _.

SPELL THE NAME OF EACH ANIMAL ALOUD, AND WRITE IT DOWN.

FIND THE NAMES OF TEN DIFFERENT COLORS,
AND FILL THE CIRCLES WITH EACH ONE AS YOU DO.

L	A	P	E	J	B	E	N	Y	V	K
D	Y	U	K	Q	H	B	J	D	T	E
X	L	R	S	X	Q	Y	K	W	G	F
B	L	P	O	L	Z	Q	K	N	S	A
C	S	L	D	B	Y	A	A	U	V	E
B	H	E	C	R	W	R	R	H	E	R
G	R	F	Z	O	O	D	O	R	O	V
D	L	O	L	I	V	E	P	P	E	P
Z	C	L	W	E	G	M	L	Y	W	D
D	E	T	N	N	P	I	N	K	B	S
Y	G	R	A	Y	G	R	E	E	N	L

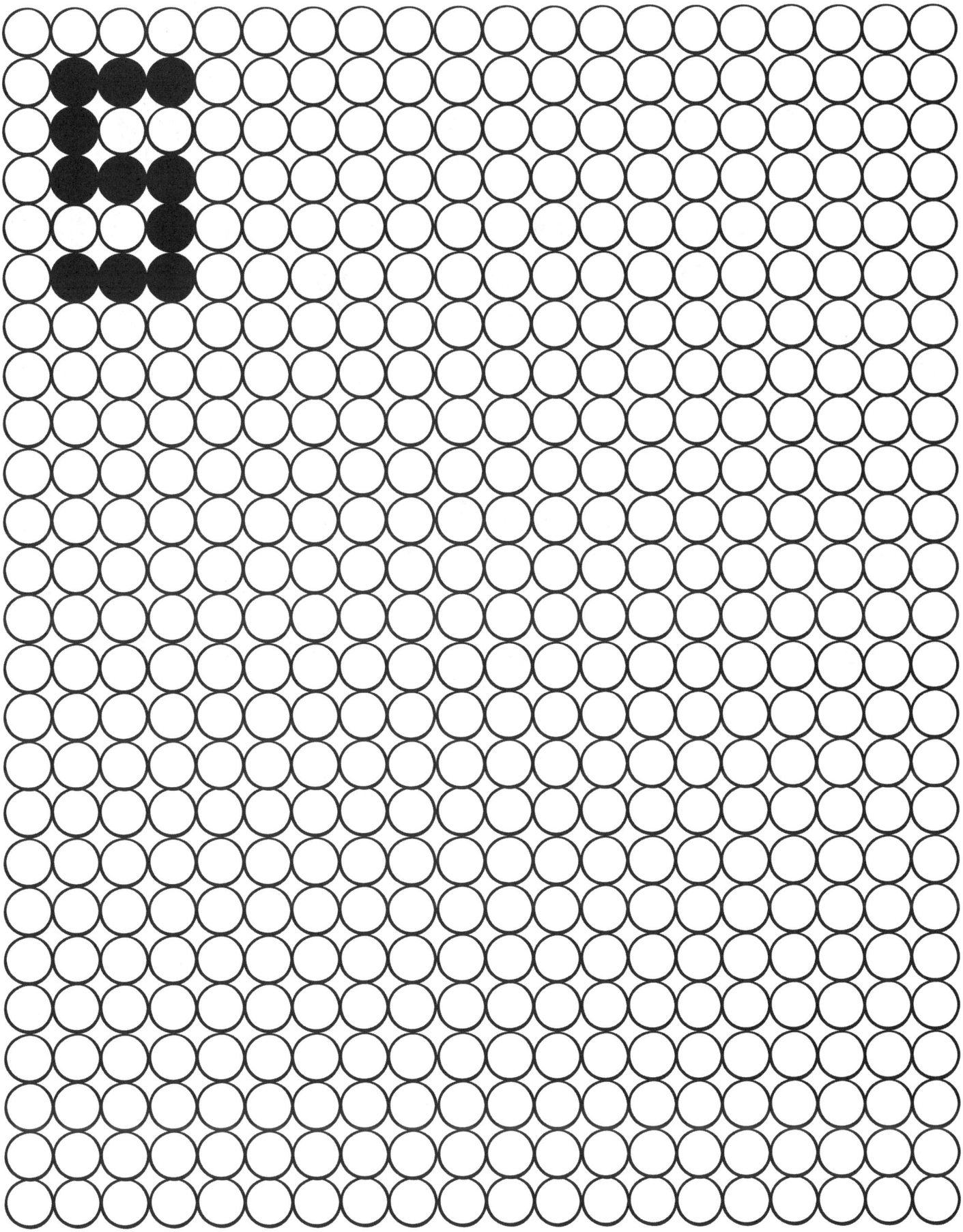

FILL THE CIRCLES TO MAKE LETTERS, SUCH AS THE "S" ABOVE.
CAN YOU WRITE THE NAME OF YOUR FAVORITE SUPERHERO?

HOW MANY MOVES DOES THE BISHOP NEED TO CHECK THE KING?

IDENTIFY THE FIGURE THAT LOOKS LIKE THE FIRST ON EACH ROW, AND COLOR BOTH THE SAME.

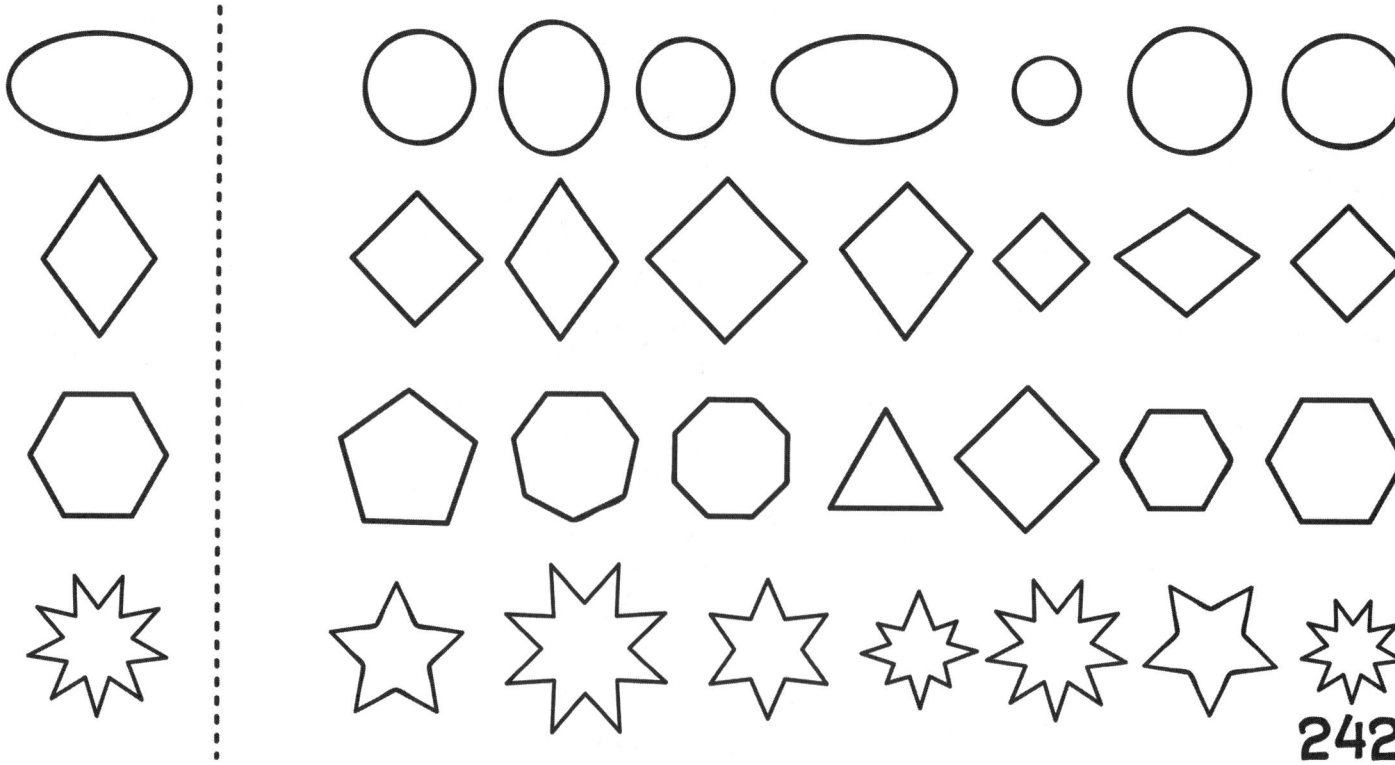

WHERE IS THE BUNGEE JUMPER? DRAW YOURSELF DANGLING FROM THE ROPE!

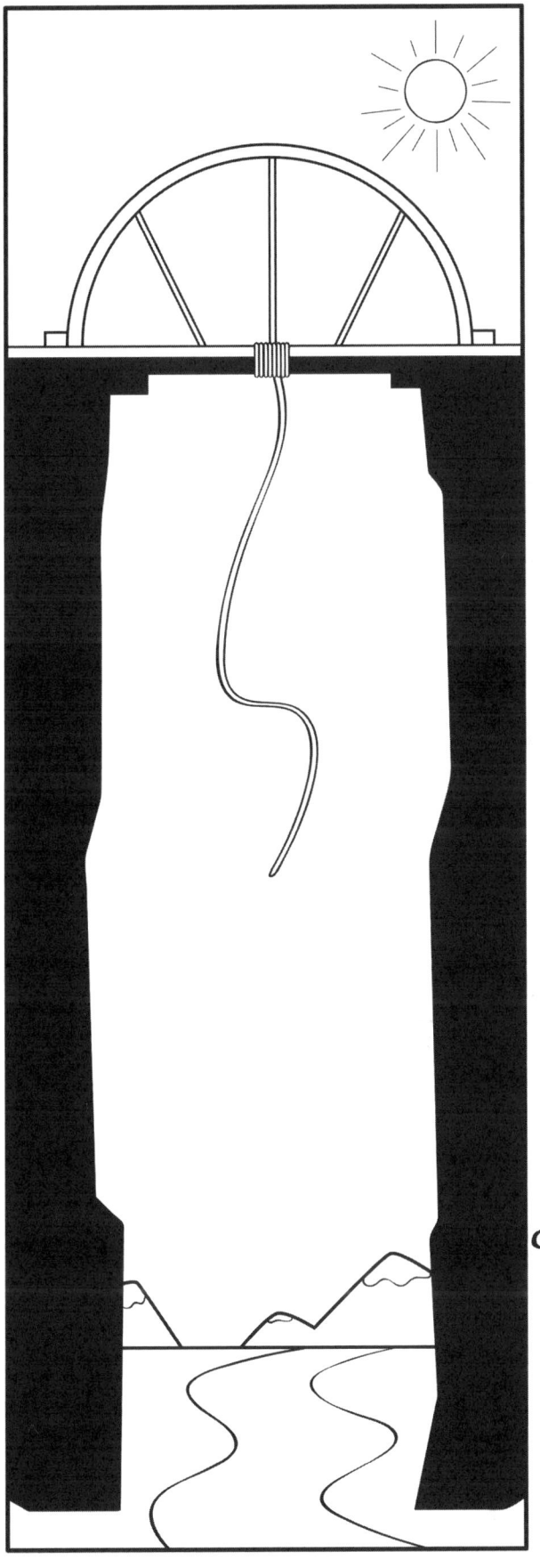

COLOR ONLY THE EVEN NUMBERS.

1 2 3 4 5
6 7 8 9 10
11 12 13 14
15 16 17 18

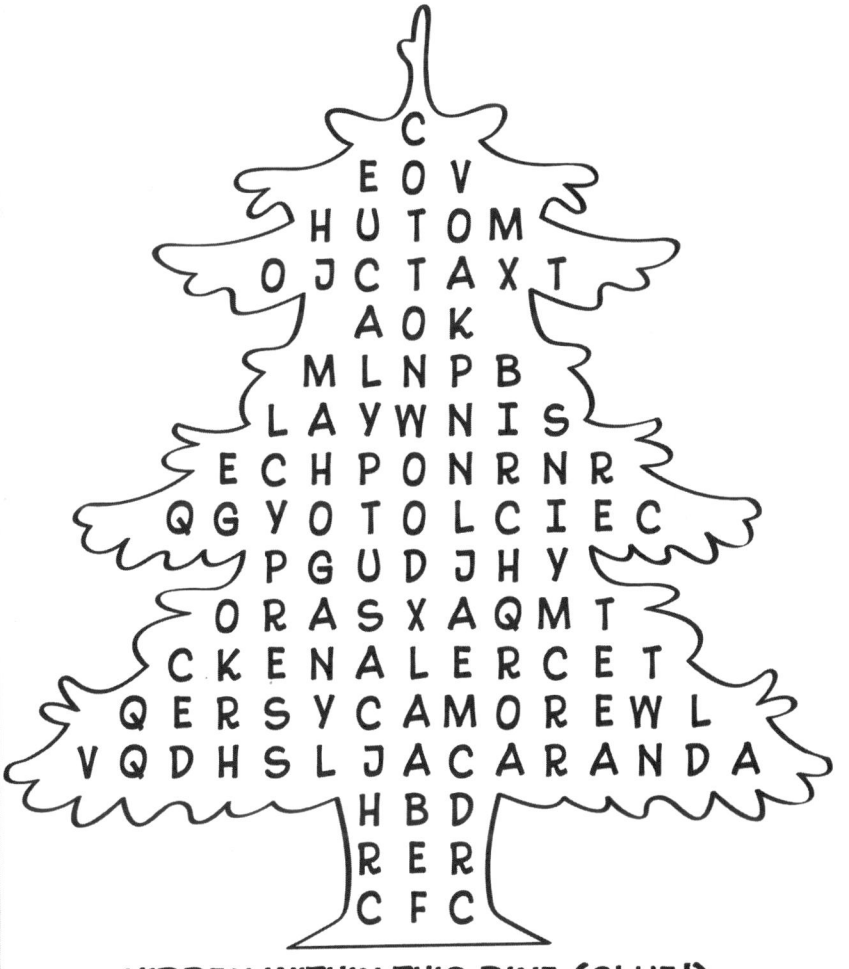

HIDDEN WITHIN THIS PINE (CLUE!) YOU WILL FIND ELEVEN OTHER TREE NAMES.

WRITE ANYTHING YOU LIKE ON THE BANNER.

WHICH ONE REQUIRES BATTERIES?

WHICH ONE IS NOT MAN-MADE?

COLOR THE MUSHROOMS RED, BUT LEAVE AS MANY WHITE SPOTS AS THE NUMBER ON EACH ONE INDICATES.

FIND THE TEN DIFFERENCES.

FILL THE OTHER COMPARTMENTS WITH OTHER ART SUPPLIES YOU USE!

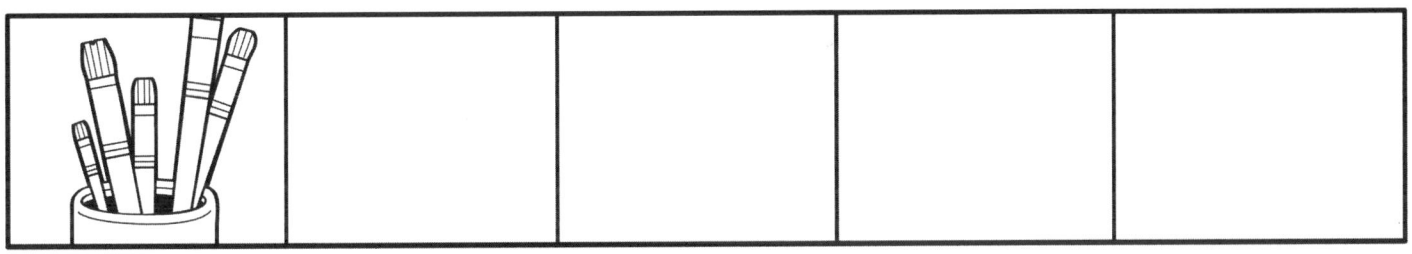

COLOR THE DOTTED SKIRT ONLY.

DECORATE THE ONE IN THE MIDDLE ANY WAY YOU LIKE!

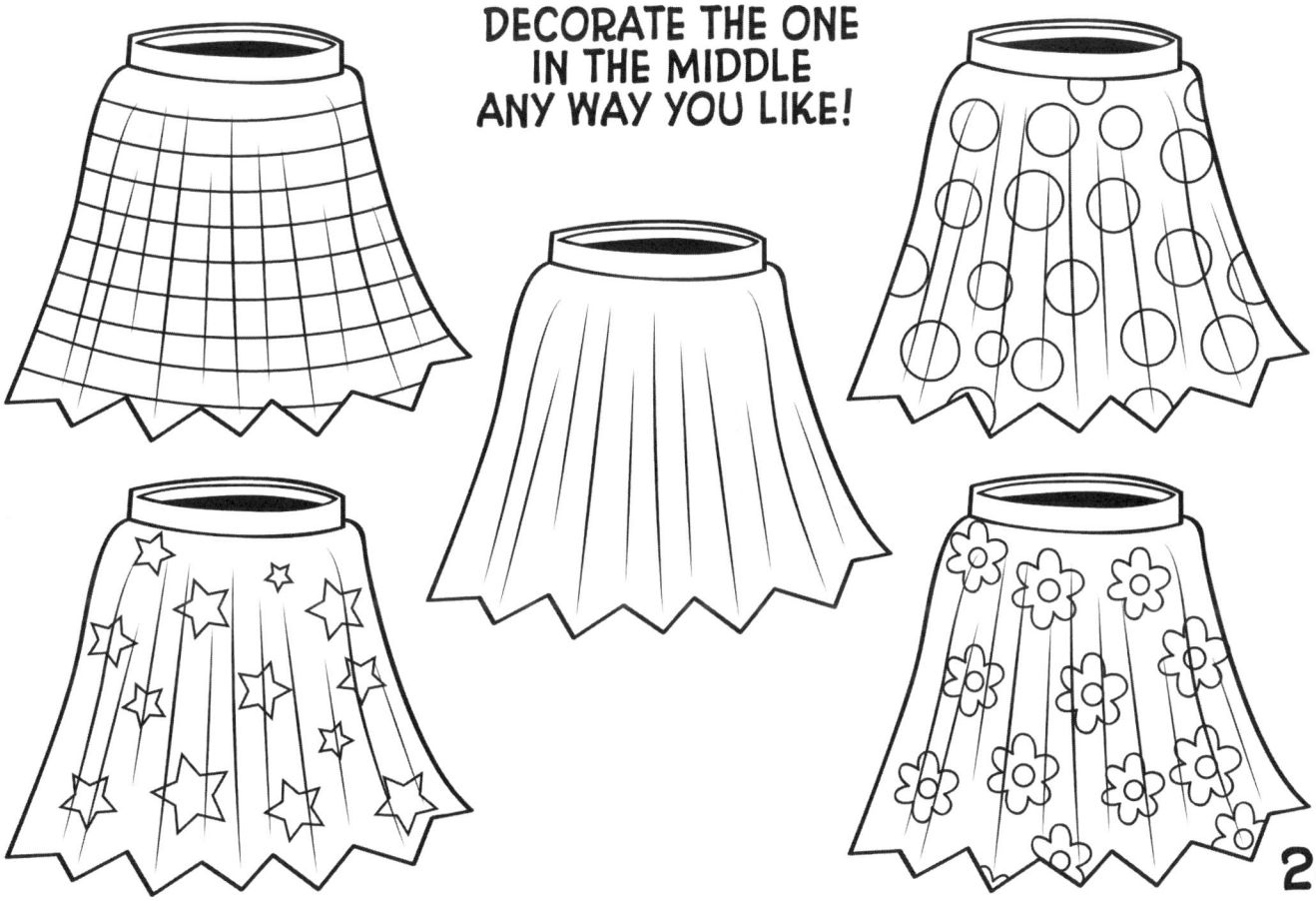

WHAT COUNTRY IS IT? WHERE IS IT LOCATED?
DO YOU REMEMBER THE COLOR OF ITS FLAG?
COLOR THE MAP THE SAME WAY.

THESE SILHOUETTES CORRESPOND
TO IMPORTANT MONUMENTS.
CAN YOU NAME THEM?

E_____T_____.

S_____O_L_____.

WRITE FOUR COUNTRIES THAT START WITH THE LETTER "U" .

U

U

U

U

IF EACH ICE CREAM COSTS FOUR DOLLARS, HOW MUCH DO THESE COST ALL TOGETHER?

DRAW AS MANY FRUITS ON EACH TREE AS INDICATED BY THE RESPECTIVE TILE.

HOW MANY CUPCAKES CAN YOU COUNT? COLOR THE RIGHT NUMBER.

1 2 3
4 5 6
7 8 9
10 11
12 13
14 15
16 17
18 19
20

HOW MANY HAVE SPRINKLED HEARTS? COLOR THE RIGHT NUMBER.

HOW MANY HAVE A CHERRY ON TOP? COLOR THE RIGHT NUMBER.

HOW MANY HAVE SPRINKLES? COLOR THE NUMBER.

COLOR ALL CUPCAKES IN DIFFERENT FLAVORS!

HELP THE DOG FIND THE FRISBEE!

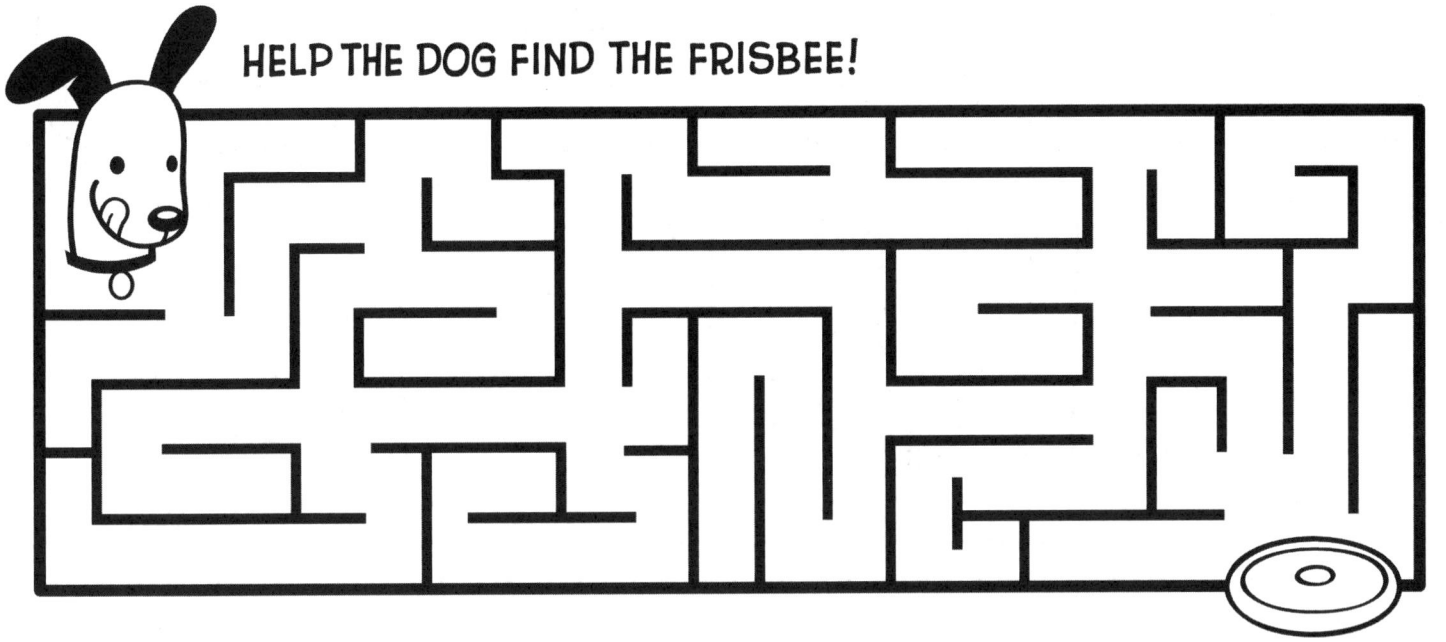

COMPLETE EACH COLUMN SO THE SUM OF THESE NUMBERS IS ALWAYS 57.

9	18	21	10	13	7	3	48	24	8	34	2
19											
19											
10											

WHAT IS THE NAME OF THIS ANIMAL?
WHERE DOES IT LIVE?

FILL THE EMPTY JARS WITH ALL THE ICKY, YUCKY, GOOEY,
AND HALLOWEENY STUFF YOU CAN IMAGINE!
THEN WRITE THEIR NAMES ON EACH LABEL, AND COLOR IT ALL.

CROSSWORDS.

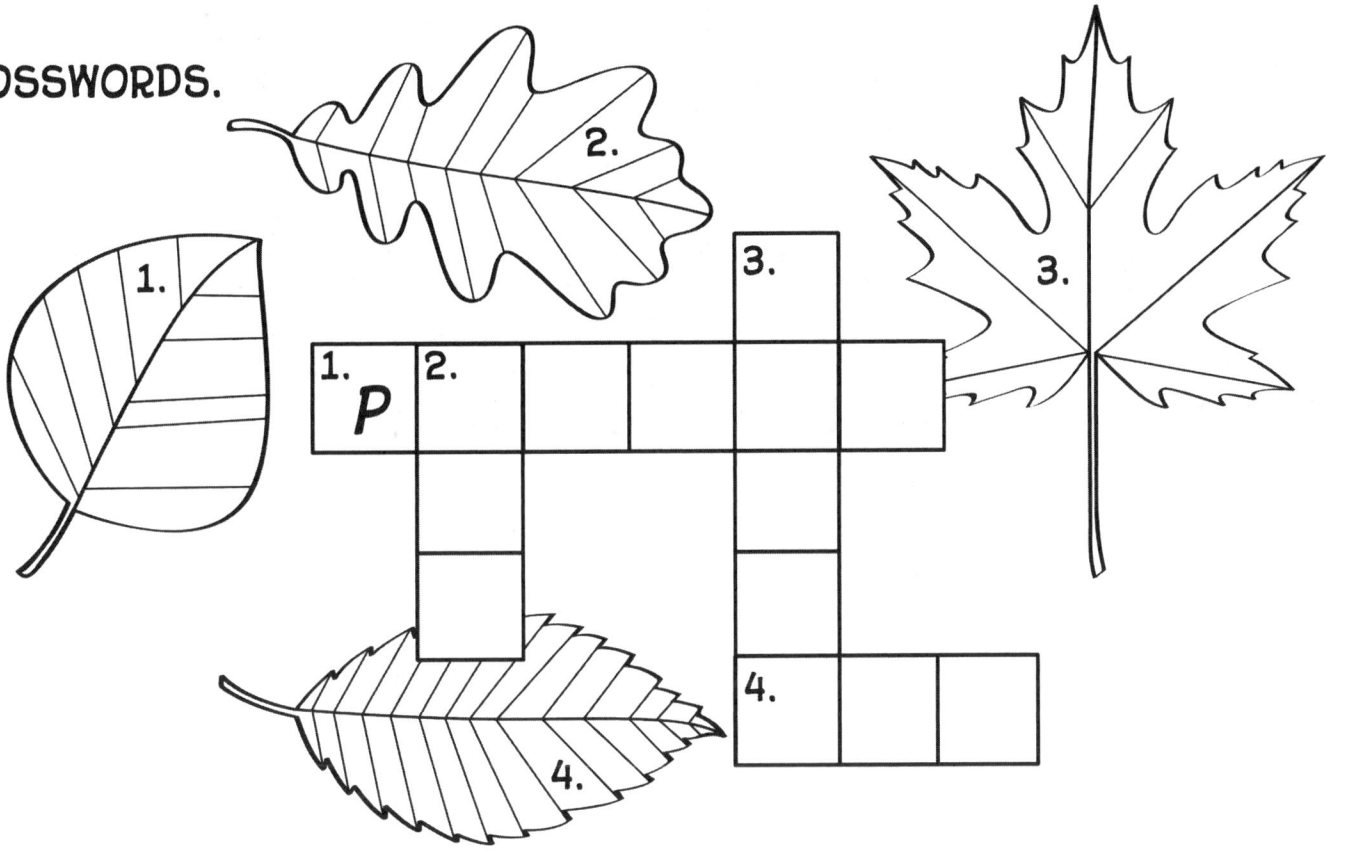

DRAW THE WATER AND THE GOLDFISH IN THE BOWL, THEN COLOR IT ALL!

WHAT ELSE CAN YOU DRAW TO MAKE IT NICER FOR THE FISH TO LIVE IN THERE?

JIMMY DREW HOPSCOTCH BOARDS FOR ALL HIS FRIENDS, BUT SOME NUMBERS ARE MISSING. CAN YOU HELP HIM FILL THE EMPTY BOXES?

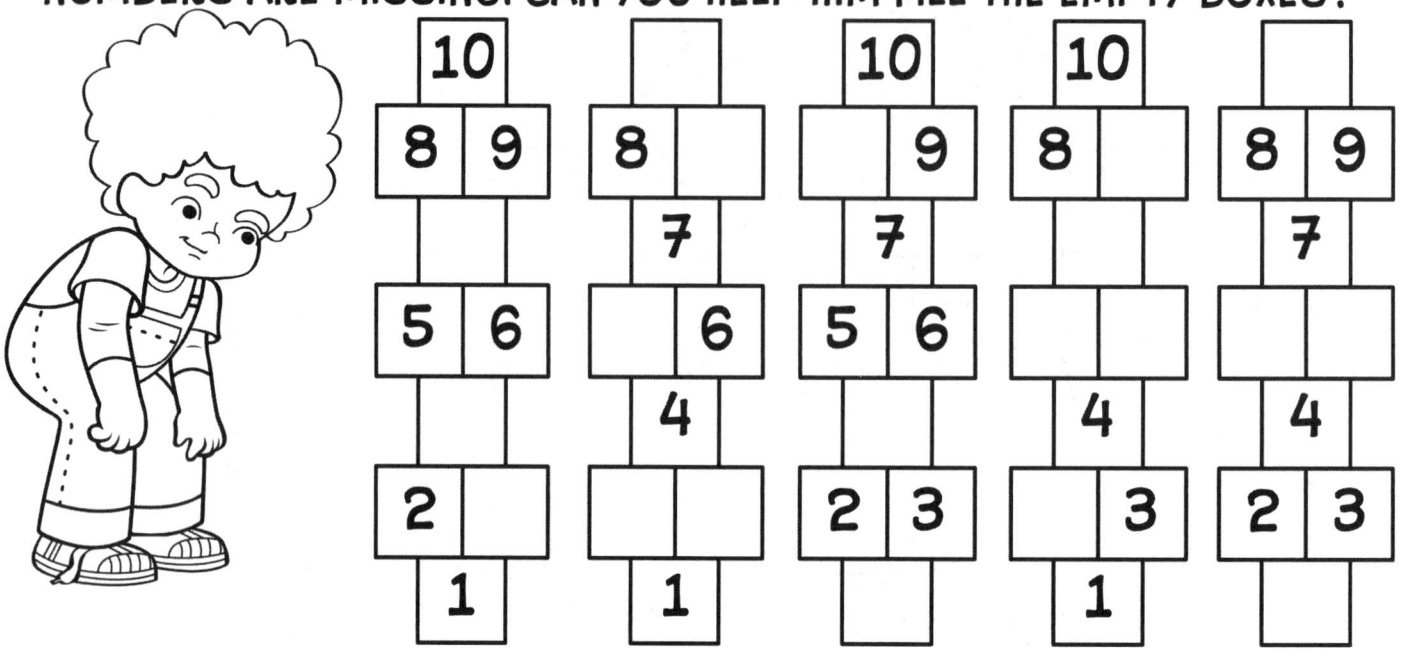

COUNT ONLY THE APPLES.

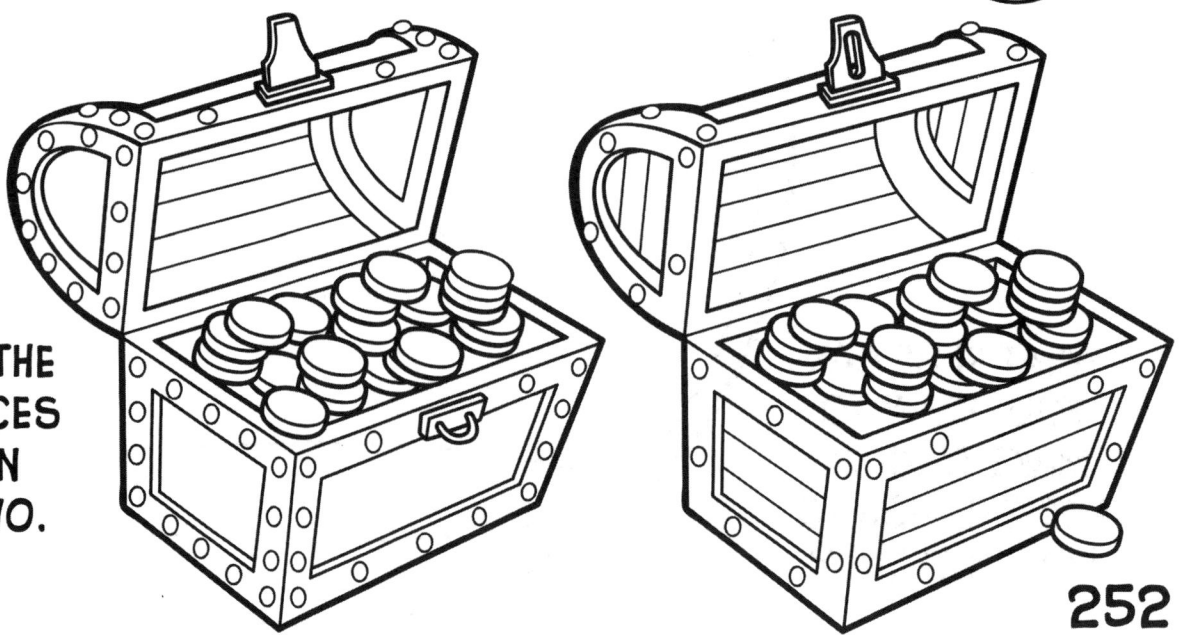

FIND ALL THE DIFFERENCES BETWEEN THESE TWO.

DESIGN YOUR OWN KITE,
ANYWAY YOU LIKE.

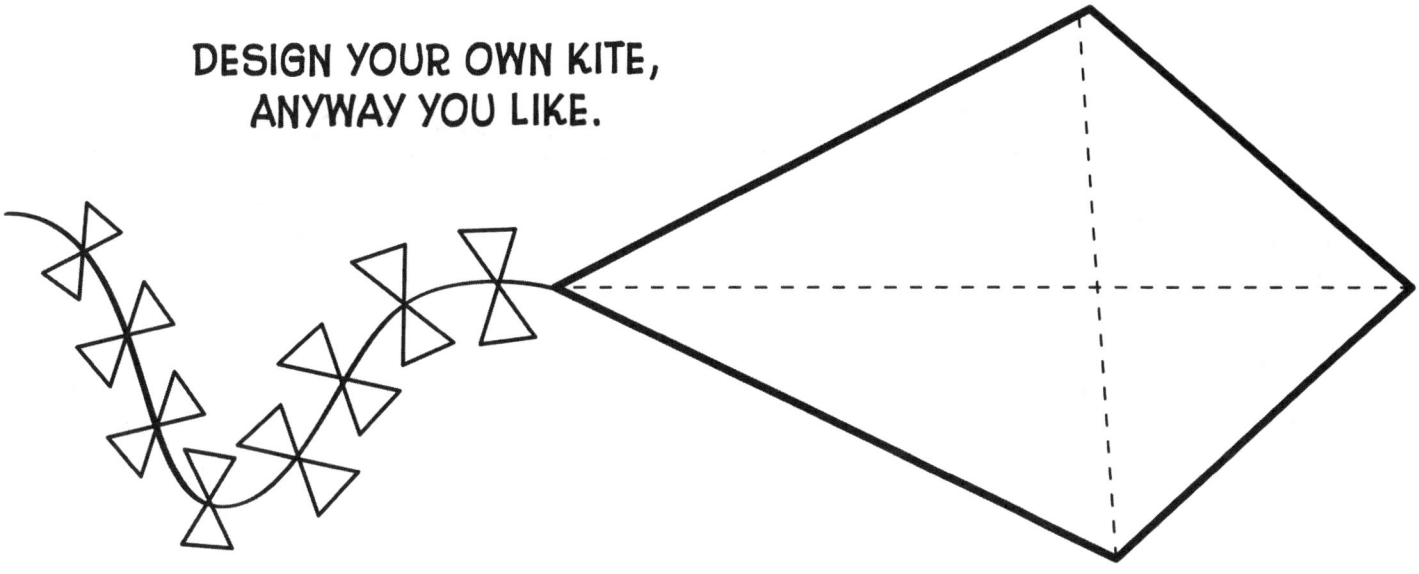

COMPLETE THIS BY CREATING YOUR OWN SYMBOLS MOVING FORWARD.

WRITE THE NAME OF EACH IMAGE AND DRAW A LINE TO CONNECT THE ONES THAT RHYME.

B

N

C

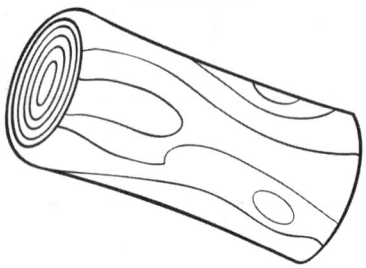

L

K

F

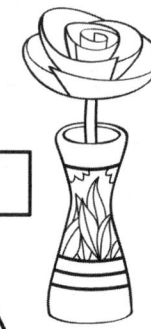

R

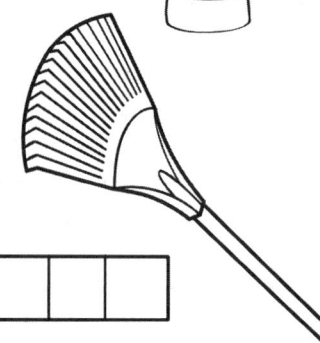

R

FIND THE MISSING PIECE.

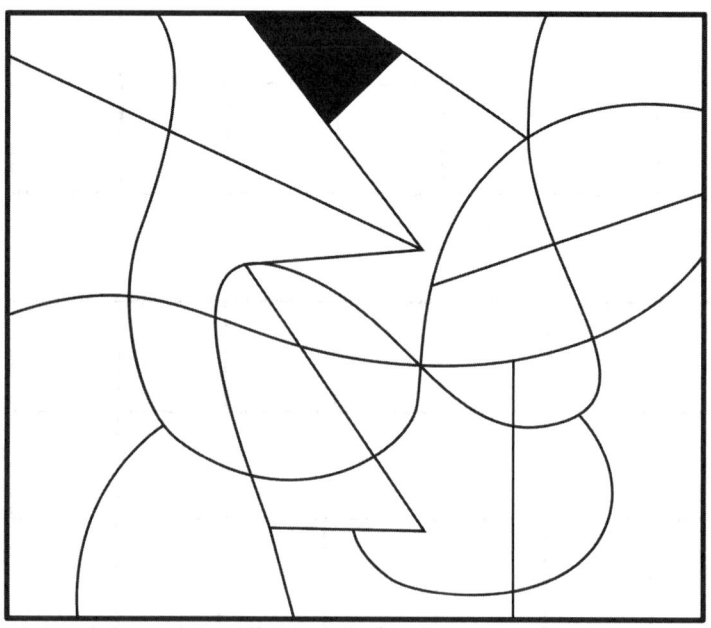

COLOR THE FIRST MASK, AND THEN
CREATE YOUR OWN CHARACTERS FOR HALLOWEEN!

PRINCESS

FAIRY

MERMAID

SORCERESS

SUPERHEROINE

PIRATE

FIND THE HAMMERHEAD SHARK'S NON-CORRESPONDING SHADOW.

WHAT COUNTRY IS IT? WHERE IS IT LOCATED? DO YOU REMEMBER THE SYMBOL ON ITS FLAG?

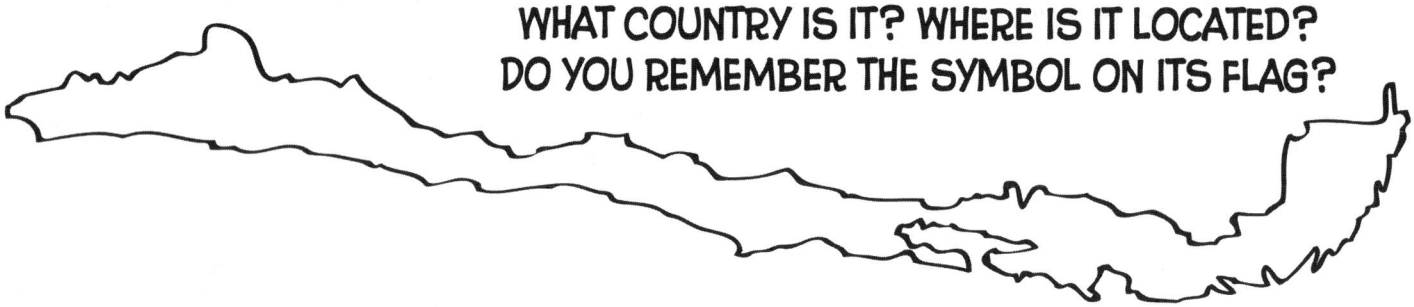

WHICH ONE WEIGHS MORE?

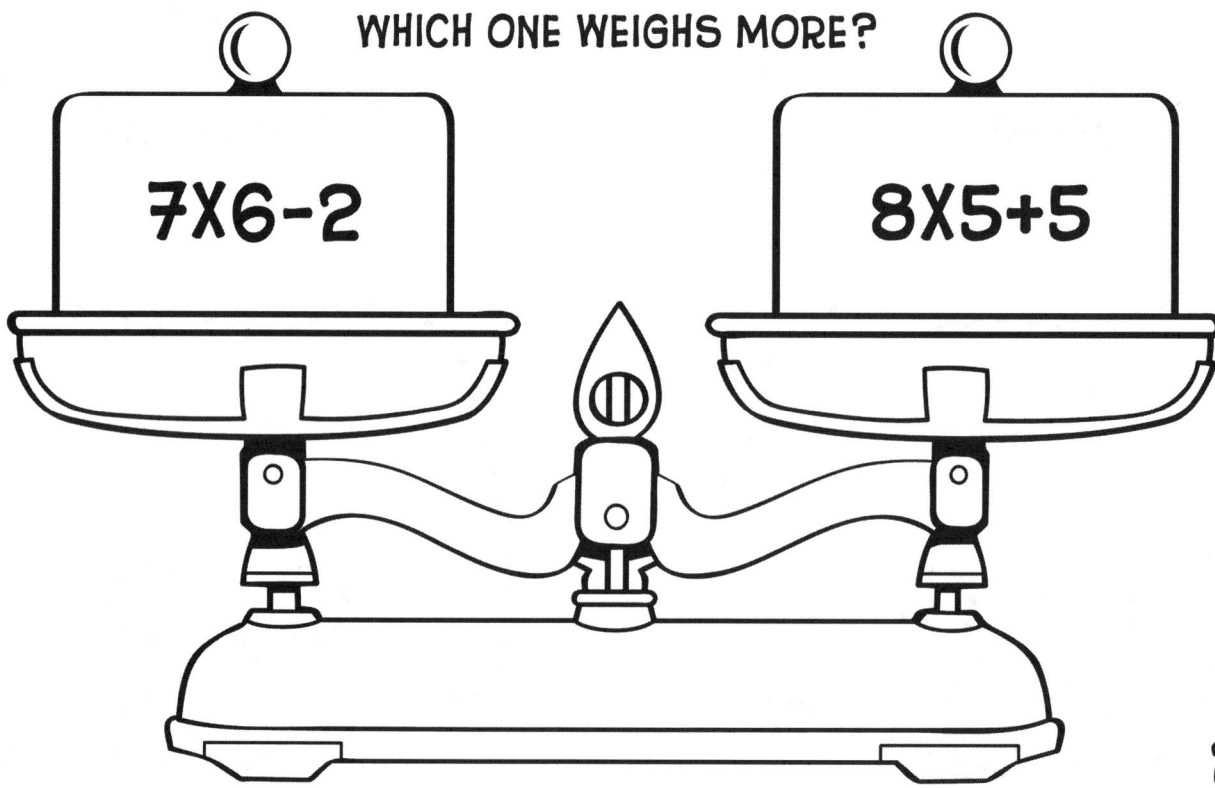

CAN YOU HELP THE SQUIRREL FIND HER TREE?

WHICH ONE DOESN'T BELONG? WHY?

DRAW THE DOVE IN THREE EASY STEPS!

COLOR THE GEOMETRICAL SHAPE EACH OBJECT IS MOSTLY BASED ON.

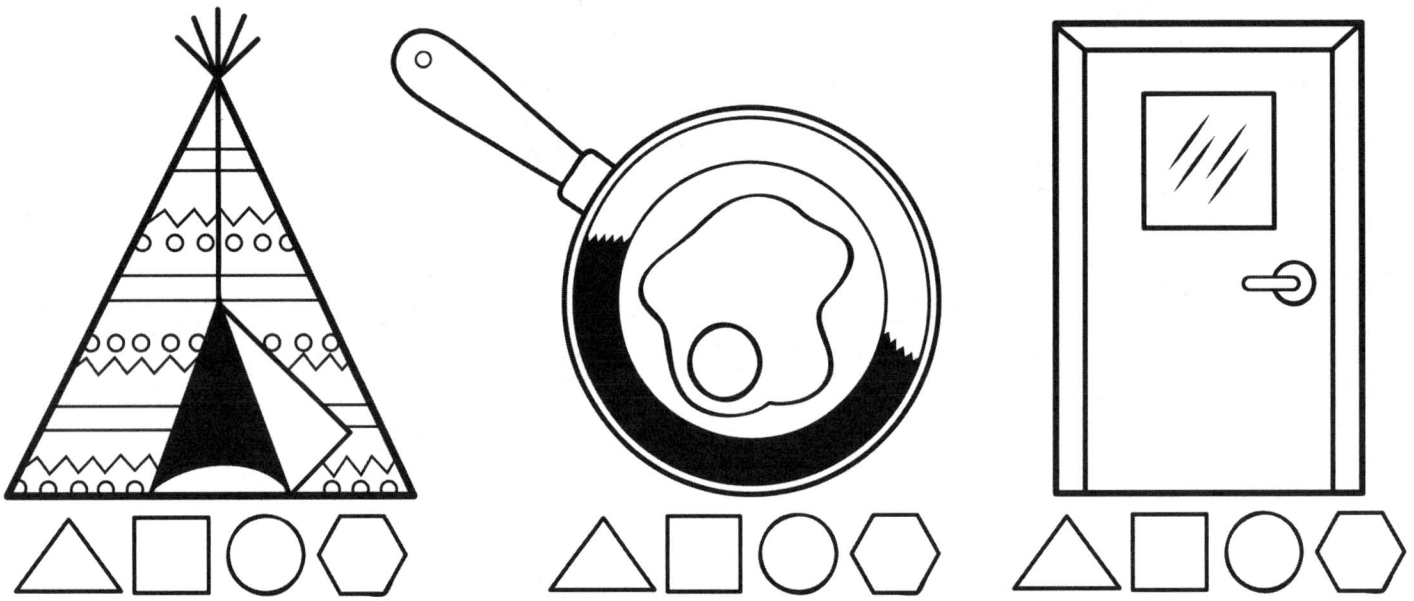

TURN EACH PIECE OF SCRAP METAL INTO THREE COOL ROBOTS!

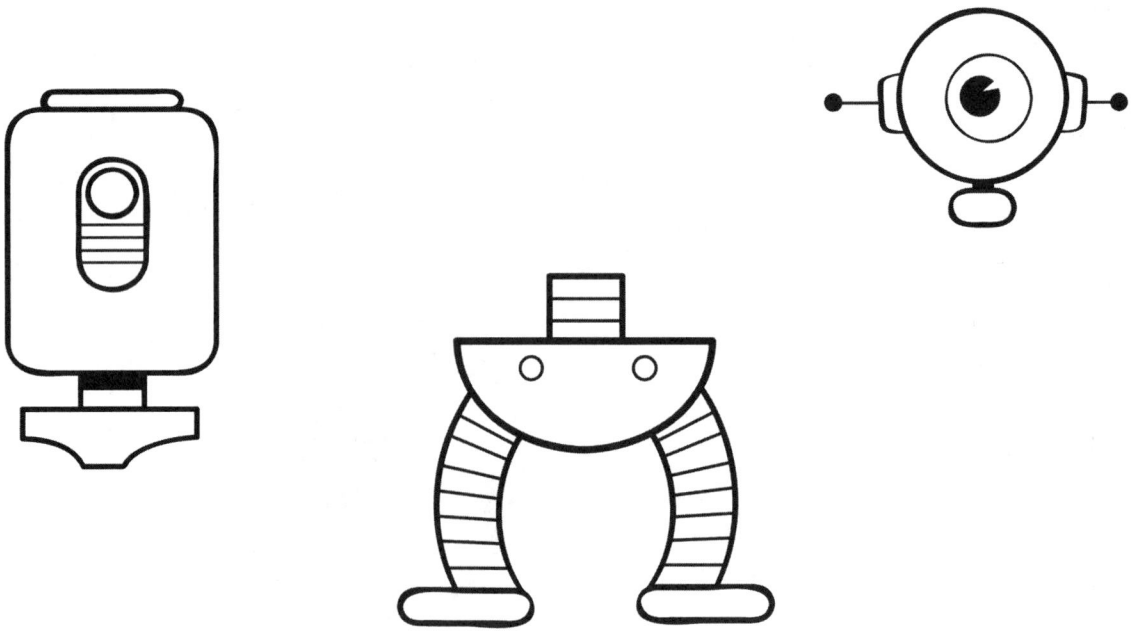

HELP OLLIE FIND THE TREASURE CHESTS
HIDDEN ON THE ISLAND!

N
W E
S

COLOR THE ISLAND'S MAP TO MAKE IT LOOK REAL,
AND GIVE NAMES TO ALL THE PLACES IN IT!

SALLY HAS SENT BILLY ANOTHER SECRET MESSAGE.
CAN YOU BREAK THE CODE?

A B C D E F G H I J K L M

N O P Q R S T U V W X Y Z

DRAW YOURSELF AND YOUR BEST FRIEND AS THE MEANEST
COWBOY OR COWGIRL OF THE OLD WEST!

WRITE BOTH YOUR NAMES BELOW THE PICTURES.

FIND THE BIRTHDAY CAKE
THAT DOESN'T MATCH ALL OTHERS,
AND COLOR THE REST.

THERE ARE TWENTY HOME-RELATED ITEMS TO BE FOUND IN THIS WORDSEARCH.

CLUE: START AT THE DOOR.

Z
L J J T G V
O I O A T V E J
I D G V C J R S C Z
P F S H K U W U E L T
B A T H T U B H E T O A
H P F I V S N M N D R S B
H D L N I Y C O F R I D G E L
D O O R S R O O M S A N I S Y T E
H F U A B E R C N H D M S W I X P
C F V H G G X E C S M R H I T N L
F A B A N W H I E W N C T K
E E R I A C N L L A D O O T
J A V P T K I I L S O U I E
G I P I E B D N A H W C L P
L X K Q N T B G R E S H E H
C U P B O A R D P R O U T Y

ILLUSTRATE YOUR OWN POSTAGE STAMPS!

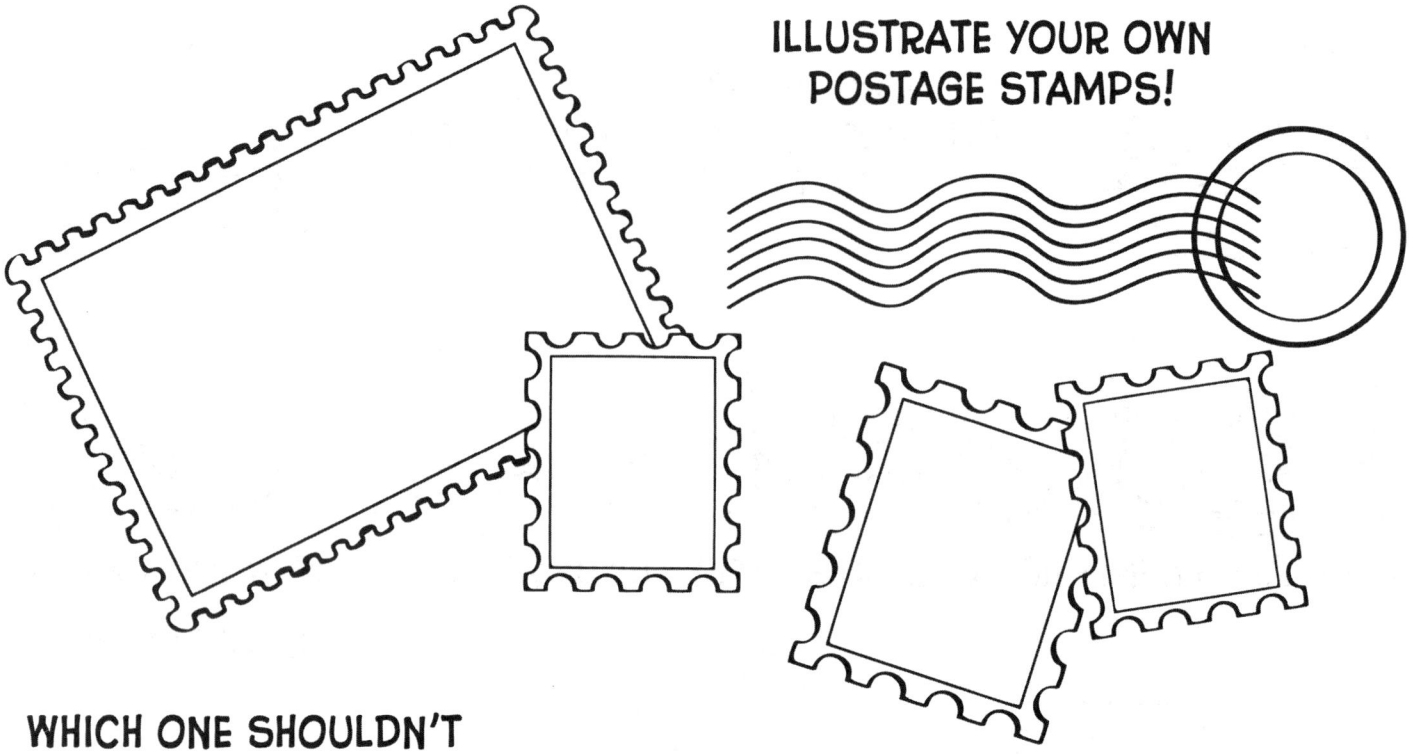

WHICH ONE SHOULDN'T BE HERE?

COMPLETE EACH COLUMN SO THE SUM OF THESE NUMBERS IS ALWAYS 74.

30	28	11	13	18	7	3	40	26	8	64	9
8											
6											
30											

FILL THE CIRCLES TO MAKE LETTERS, SUCH AS THE "U" ABOVE.
CAN YOU WRITE THE NAME OF YOUR TOWN AND COUNTRY?

DRAW MORE CUPCAKES, OR CROSS THEM OUT UNTIL THERE'S 15 ON EACH TRAY.

CAN YOU ALSO HELP HER FINISH BAKING HER COOKIES?

DRAW THE MISSING GINGERBREAD MEN IN EACH ROW.

COLOR THIS ENTIRE FLAG GREEN.

CAN YOU GUESS THE NAME OF THE COUNTRY IT BELONGS TO?

L

L

L

L

WRITE FOUR OTHER COUNTRIES THAT START WITH THE LETTER "L"!

IF THE SUN MEANS SUMMER, WHAT OTHER SYMBOLS CAN YOU DRAW TO REPRESENT THE OTHER SEASONS?

SUMMER

FALL

WINTER

SPRING

WHICH WAY TO THE ICE CREAM?

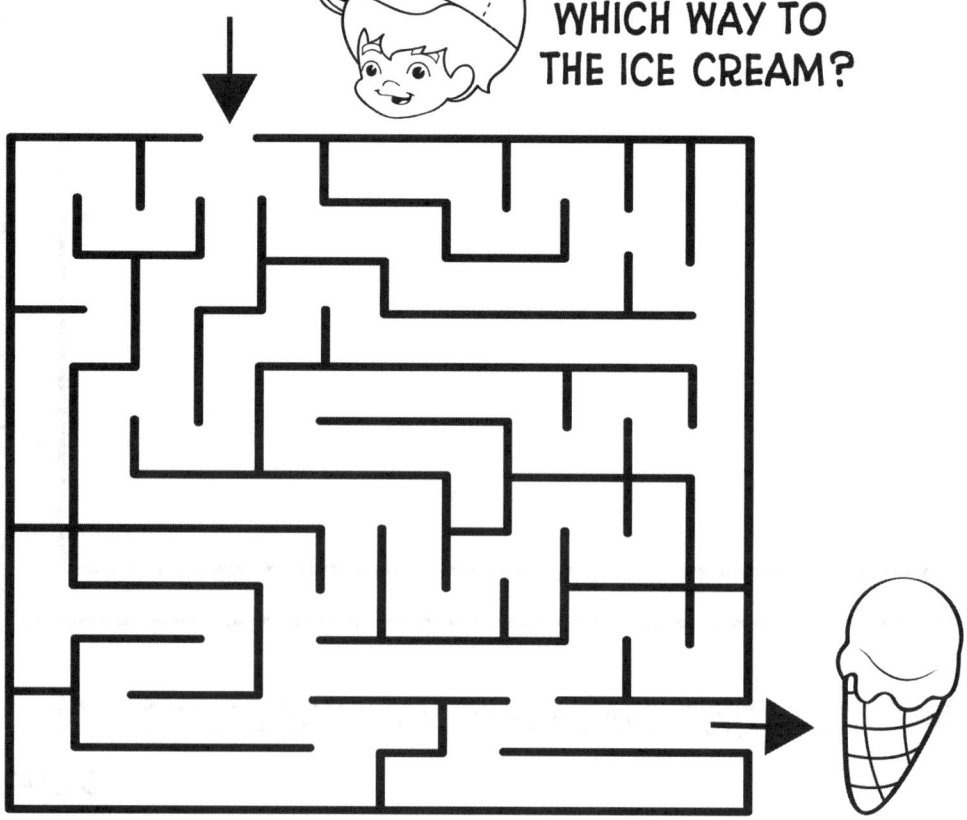

WHICH LEAF IS COMPLETELY DIFFERENT FROM THE REST?

WHAT ARE THE NAMES OF THESE TWO ANIMALS?

COLOR THEM BOTH GRAY AND WHITE.

WHAT MAKES THEM SIMILAR?

WHAT MAKES THEM DIFFERENT?

DRAW THE HANDS OF THE CLOCKS.

12:30

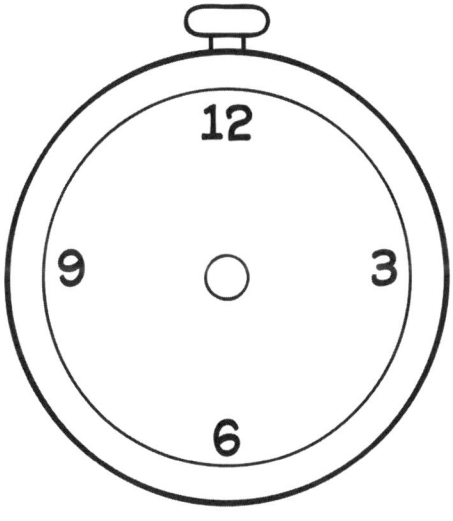

10:45

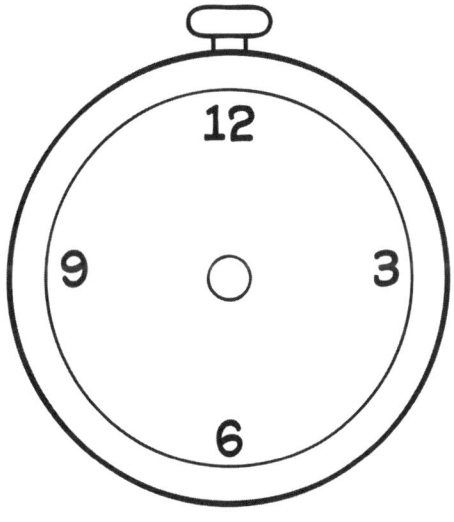

3:15

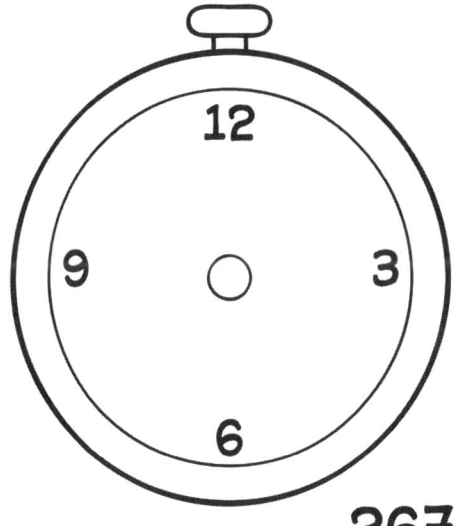

THAT IS ONE BIG SNAKE!
CAN YOU GUESS ITS NAME?

IF IT TAKES THE BEE A DAY TO POLLINATE THREE FLOWERS, HOW MANY DAYS WILL IT TAKE HER TO POLLINATE ALL THE ONES IN THIS FIELD?

CONNECT THE NUMBERS DIVISIBLE BY 2.

9	4	8	6	5	3	7	5	2
3	2	5	9	2	8	6	4	3
6	5	3	1	7	5	3	9	5	4	7
6	3	1	4	6	8	2	4	7	5	3
8	2	4	2	3	4	1	4	6	8	

FIND THE SIX DIFFERENCES.

THE FORTUNE COOKIE HAS A MESSAGE FOR YOU.
CAN YOU GUESS WHAT IT SAYS?

COMPLETE THE SERIES.

5 = ○ + ☆
2 = □ + □
? = □ + ○
4 = □ + ☆

FIND THE ONE SHADOW THAT DOESN'T MATCH THE SQUIRREL.

HOW MANY CHERRIES ARE HIDING IN THESE TWO TREES? DRAW THEM.
IF 16 FROM THE TREE ON THE LEFT WILL FILL A BASKET,
HOW MANY BASKETS WILL YOU NEED IF THE CHERRIES ON THE OTHER TREE ARE HALF AS BIG?

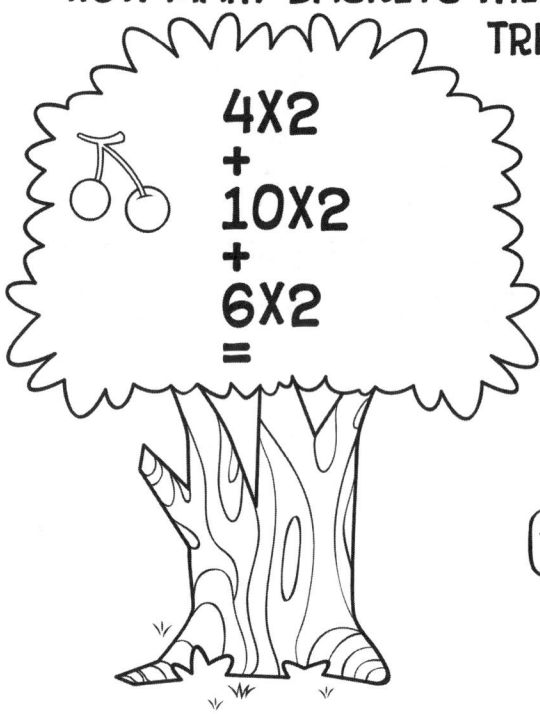

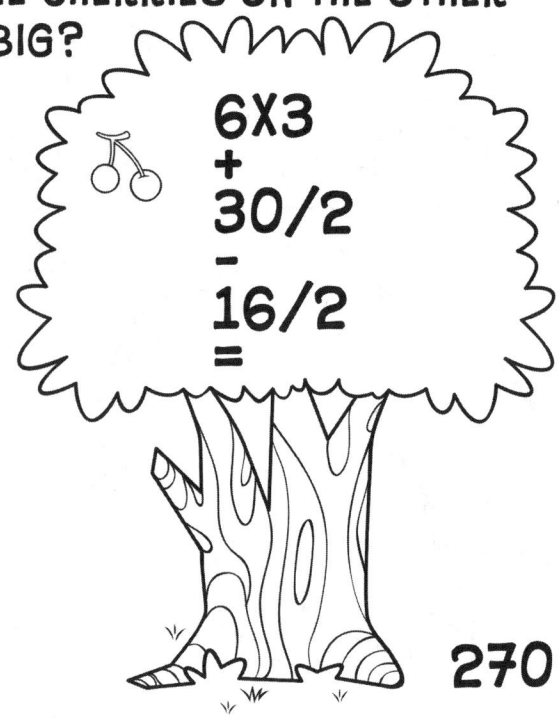

EACH ONE OF THESE TWO CAMELS IS CALLED BY A DIFFERENT NAME. DO YOU KNOW THEM?

TO PAINT A DOOR YOU NEED A WHOLE CAN OF PAINT.

TO PAINT A WINDOW FRAME YOU NEED TWO.

TO PAINT THE WALL ON EACH FLOOR THREE.

HOW MANY CANS WILL YOU NEED TO PAINT ALL THESE BUILDINGS?

R Y K M C
E W B E A C O B J
G R A Q N D A T M E O E L
I H I N T Y A M A Y O T T E
N L A T D T A G E N W A R H S R
E I N R A O Y A R Z P E N O I W
E B A E O G S S O A C G B G S O A
Z Y O A C O J C O N O Y E H O N P N
A L G E R I A N I N P N M O L S I A F
R O F R B A G T I I J S A K A M
Q U O U N M A L A W I
Z J R U I N C H A D
I E U A N A T Z
R M D N I E F C
O U B B D W A A
S O M A L I A N
N A M I B I A
G U G M E W X
U G A N D A E
Z B S L I
Z O X X
H N Q

THIS WORDSEARCH IS SHAPED LIKE A CONTINENT, AND CONTAINS THE NAMES OF SOME OF ITS MORE THAN FIFTY BEAUTIFUL COUNTRIES. CAN YOU GUESS WHICH ONE?

CLUE: ITS NAME STARTS WITH "A".

WHICH ONE OF THE FOLLOWING ANIMALS DOES NOT LIVE THERE?

DRAW AND COLOR YOUR FAVORITE FLAGS FROM SOME OF THE COUNTRIES ON THE PREVIOUS PAGE'S WORDSEARCH.

WRITE THE NAME OF EACH COUNTRY BELOW THE CORRESPONDING FLAG.

COMPLETE THE PATTERN AS BEST YOU CAN.

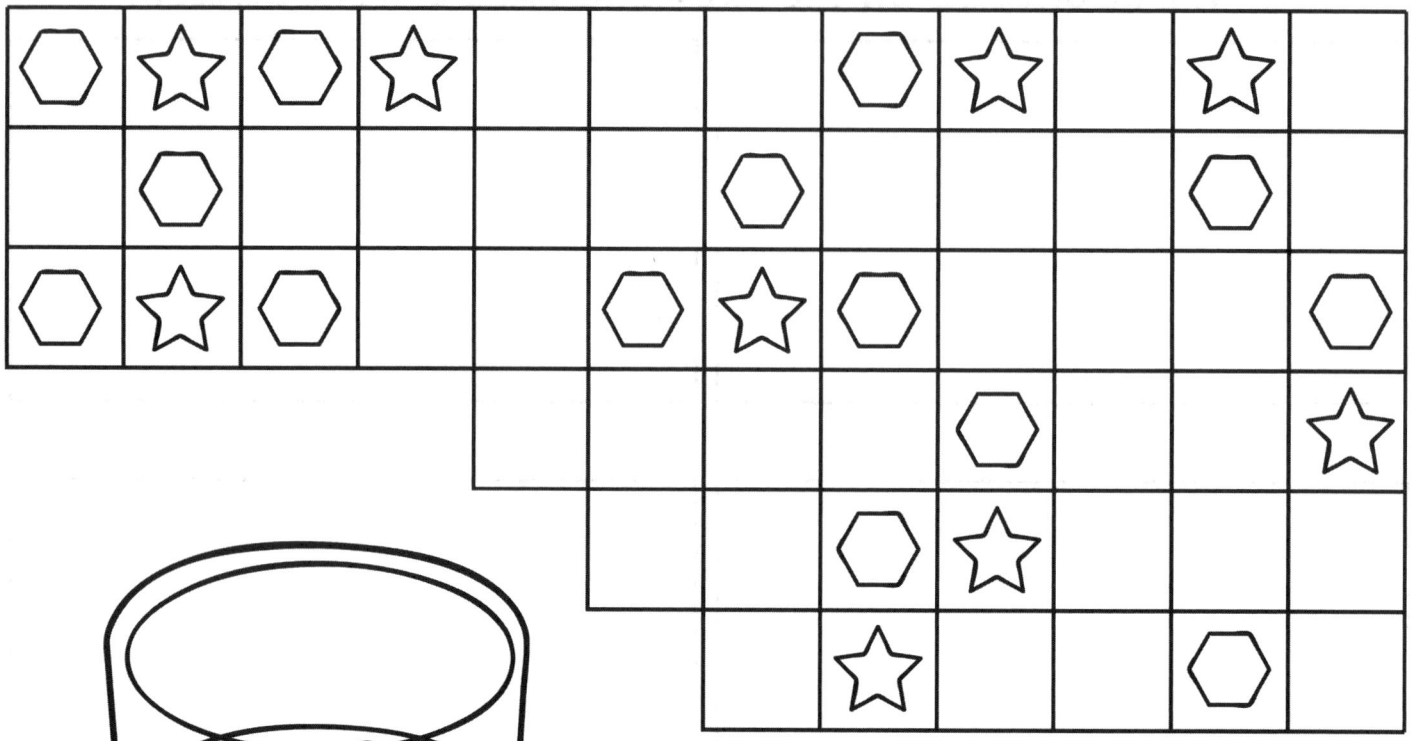

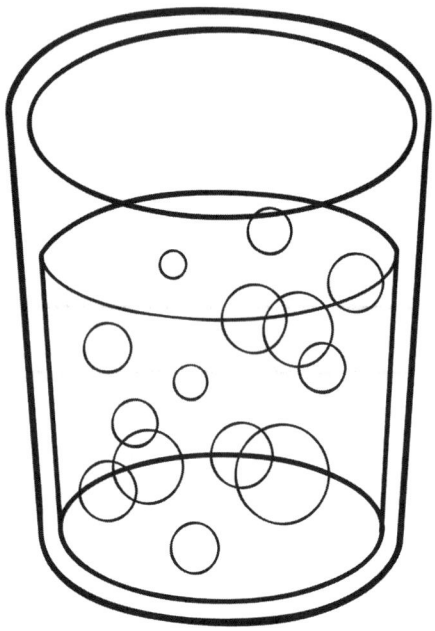

WHAT ARE SODA BUBBLES MADE OF?

HOW ARE THEY DIFFERENT FROM THE ONES WE MAKE WITH SOAP AND WATER?

WHY DO THEY FLOAT UPWARD?

ONLY ONE OF THESE IS WORN AROUND THE NECK. COLOR IT!

TURN EACH PIECE OF SCRAP METAL INTO THREE COOL ROBOTS!

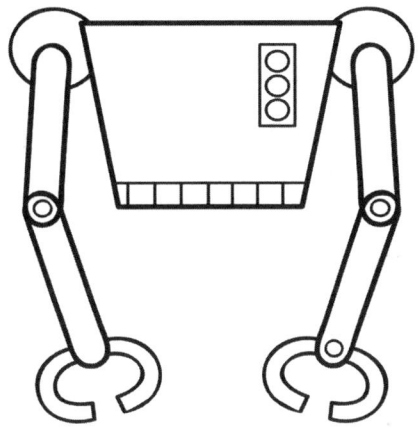

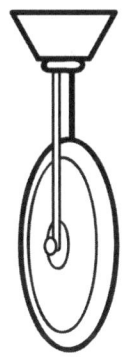

COMPLETE THE SERIES.

3 = ☆ + ☾

5 = ☾ + 🪐

? = ☆ + 🪐

4 = ☾ + ☾

COPY HER!

FILL IN THE BLANK SPACES TO GET THE GIVEN RESULTS.

10	+	75	-		+	18	-		=	100
	-	81	+	24	-	6	+		=	78
6	+	42	-		+		+		=	56
35	-	18	+	3	-	6	+		=	21

DRAW AND COLOR YOUR OWN COMIC-STRIP!

HELP THE DONKEY FIND ITS LUNCH!

ADD THE NUMBERS WRITTEN ON THE SAILS.
WHICH SAILBOAT CARRIES THE HEAVIER LOAD?

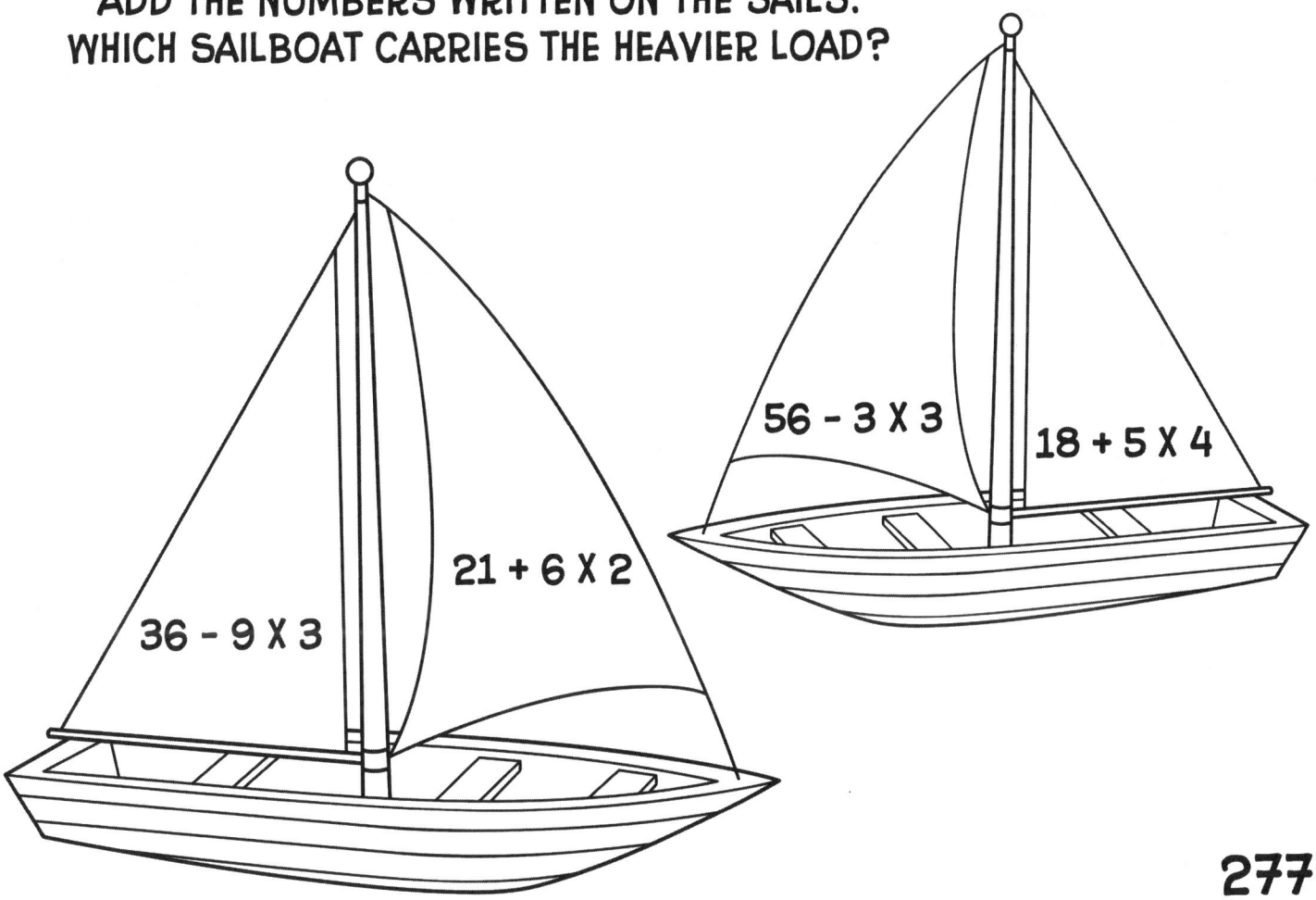

WHAT COUNTRY IS IT?
WHERE IS IT LOCATED?

DO YOU REMEMBER THE SYMBOL ON ITS FLAG?

CAN YOU FIND 14 FAMOUS PEOPLE IN THIS WORDSEARCH? CLUE: THEY COME FROM THE COUNTRY ABOVE!

C	H	E	S	P	I	R	I	T	O	P	W	N	L	Y
P	M	I	G	U	E	L	H	I	D	A	L	G	O	D
V	C	A	R	L	O	S	F	U	E	N	T	E	S	A
X	E	F	N	Z	V	P	I	W	I	C	Z	O	H	V
Z	V	L	M	R	V	L	J	U	S	H	P	F	J	I
L	U	I	S	B	U	N	U	E	L	O	A	F	O	D
T	Q	E	E	A	V	X	I	K	P	V	V	T	S	S
I	F	I	K	R	N	A	L	F	H	I	R	F	E	I
N	R	R	C	A	N	T	I	N	F	L	A	S	G	Q
X	S	X	Z	B	R	L	O	Y	F	L	S	O	P	U
F	R	I	D	A	K	A	H	L	O	A	Y	D	O	E
D	I	E	G	O	R	I	V	E	R	A	R	B	S	I
A	L	V	A	R	O	O	B	R	E	G	O	N	A	R
H	E	R	N	A	N	C	O	R	T	E	S	E	D	O
D	O	L	O	R	E	S	O	L	M	E	D	O	A	S

THIS IS A WORLD FAMOUS FRUIT FROM THE COUNTRY ABOVE.

COLOR ITS FLESH GREEN, AND ITS SEED BROWN. WHAT'S IT CALLED?

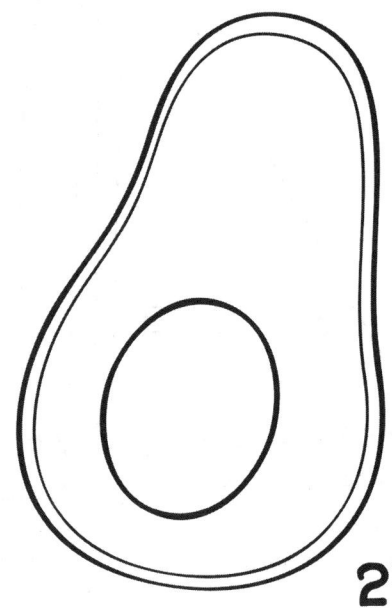

CRACK THE SUDOKU!
EACH DRAWING CAN ONLY BE PLACED ONCE ON EACH LINE, ONCE ON EACH ROW, AND ONCE IN EACH FOUR CELL GRID.

CAN YOU GUESS EACH DOUGHNUT'S FLAVOR? COLOR THEM ACCORDINGLY!

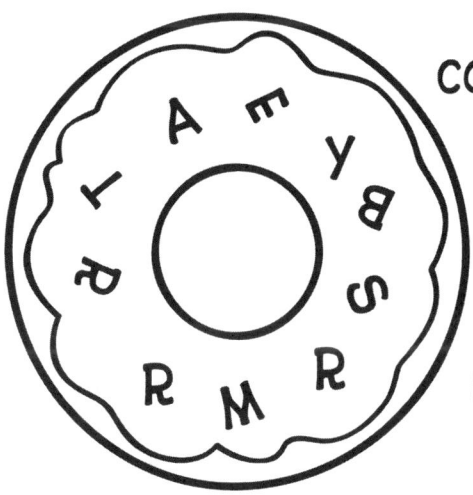

FILL THE PAGE WITH HEXAGONS UNTIL THE HONEYCOMB IS FINISHED.

THEN DRAW CUTE BEES LIVING IN IT. →

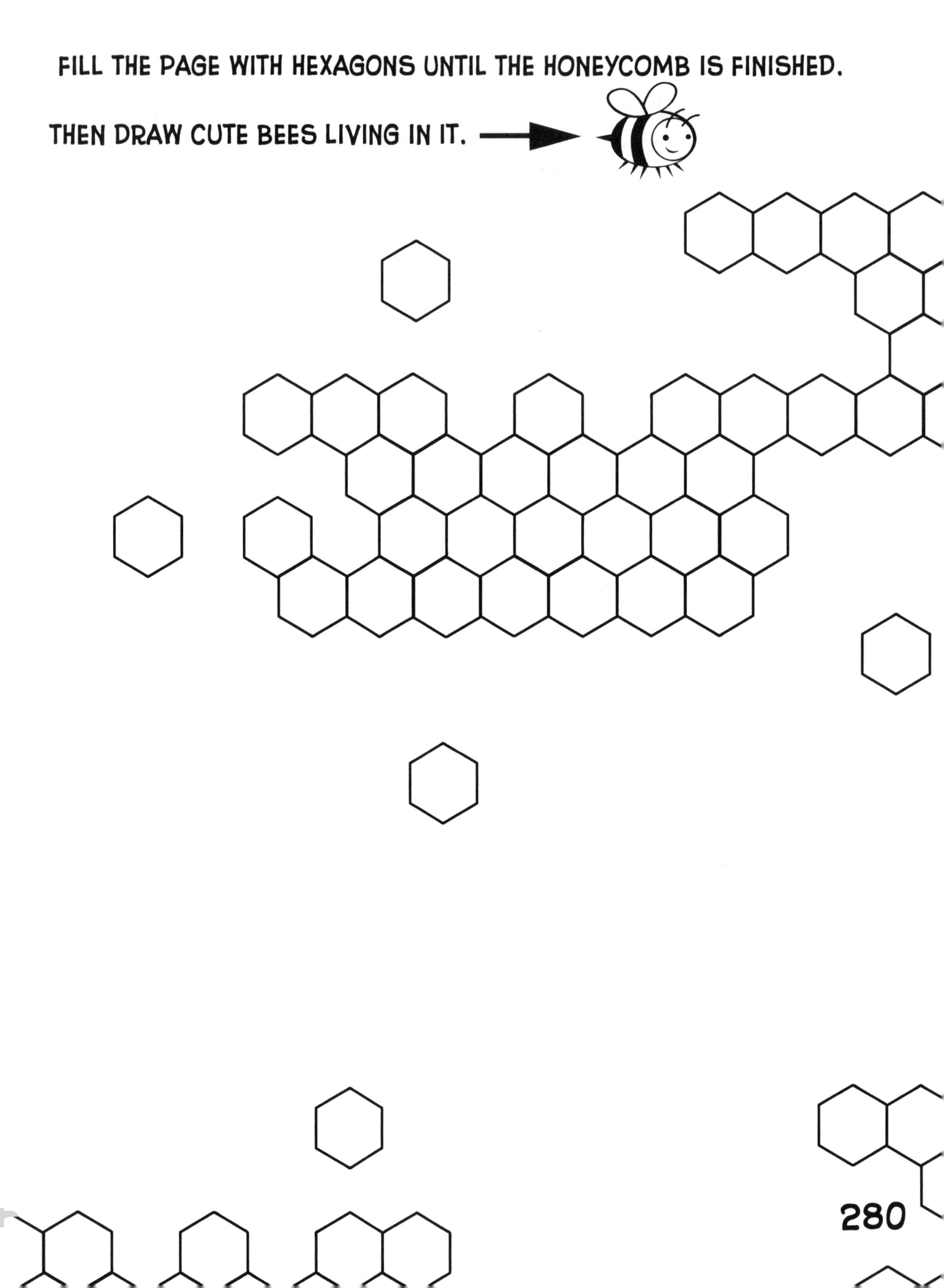

WHICH ONE WEIGHS MORE?

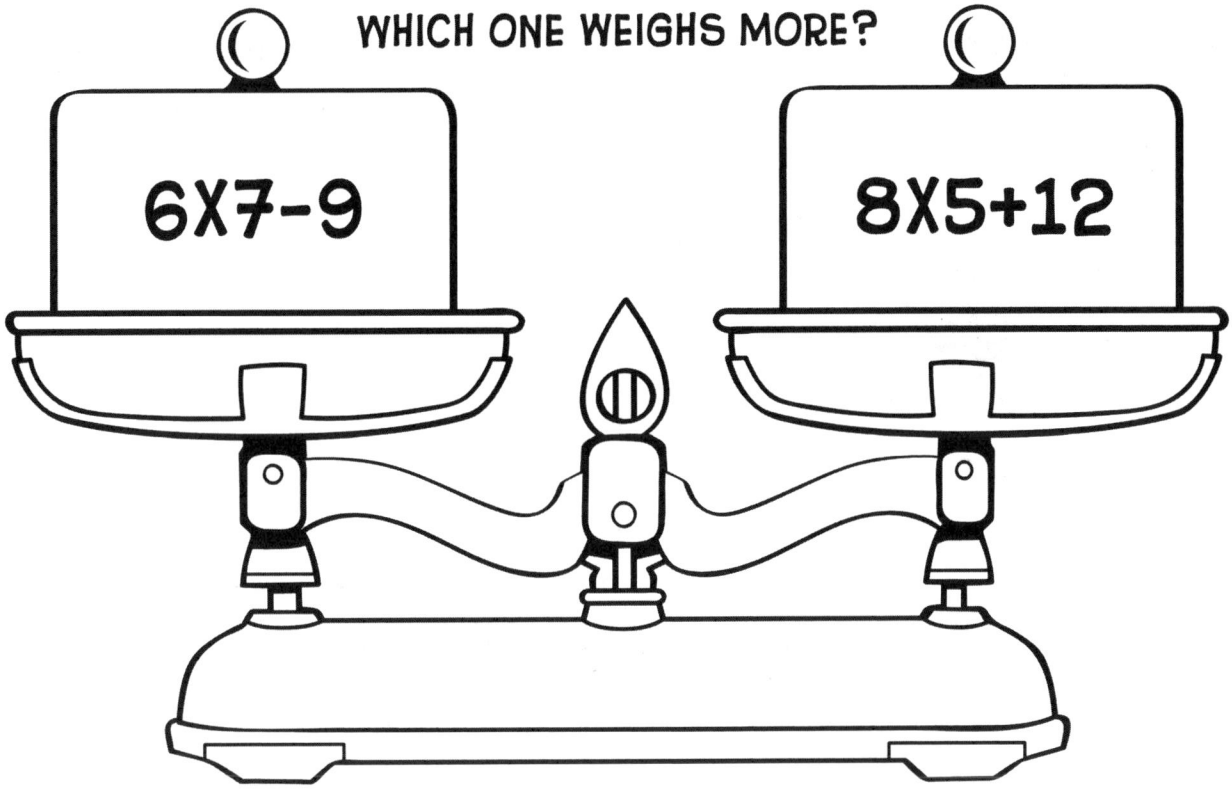

HOW LONG IS THE LADDER?

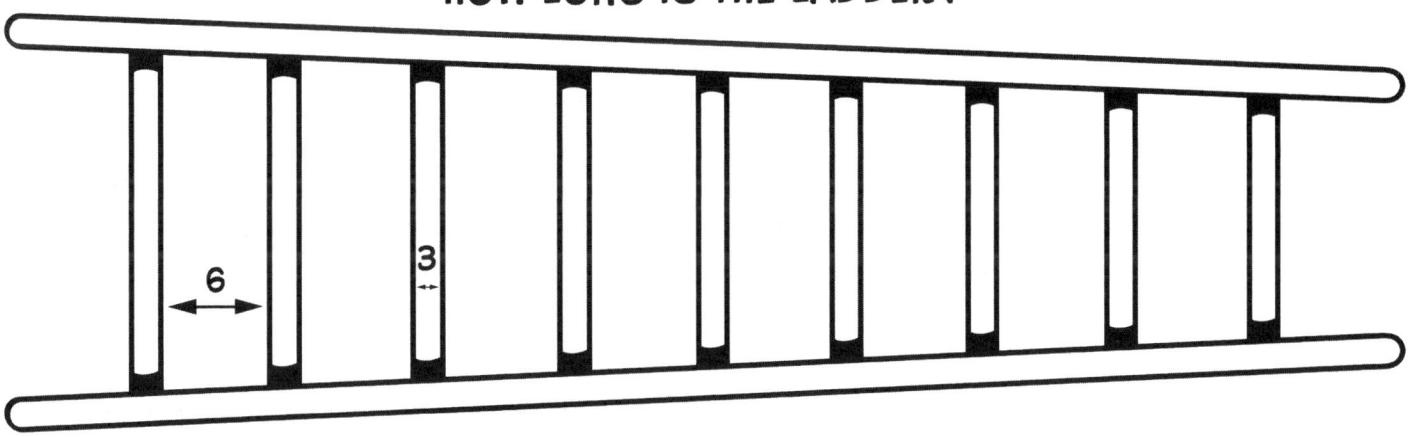

DRAW AS MANY BUTTERFLIES AND SNAILS
AS INDICATED BY EACH TILE.

WHAT IS THE NAME OF THIS BIRD?
WHAT DOES IT EAT?

DRAW ANOTHER ONE JUST LIKE IT.

FIND THE TWO IDENTICAL MUSHROOMS.

5	2		3	6		5	27
4		1	2	1	8	9	
9	3	4		7	11		

FILL THE BLANKS SO THE RESULTS OF ADDING THE NUMBERS MATCH HORIZONTALLY.

HOW MANY OF EACH TYPE OF ICE CREAM CAN YOU COUNT? WRITE THE CORRECT NUMBER.

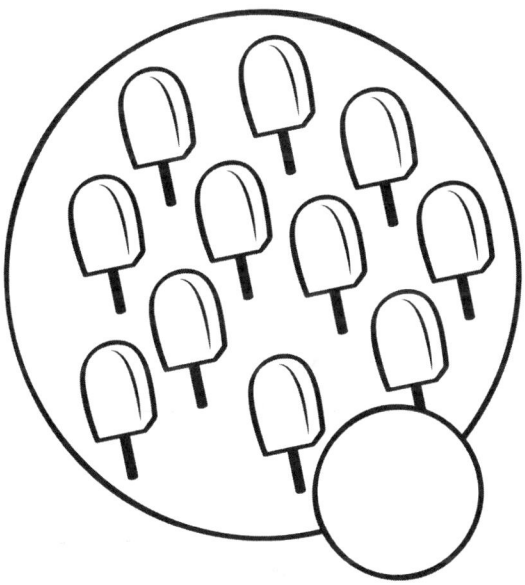

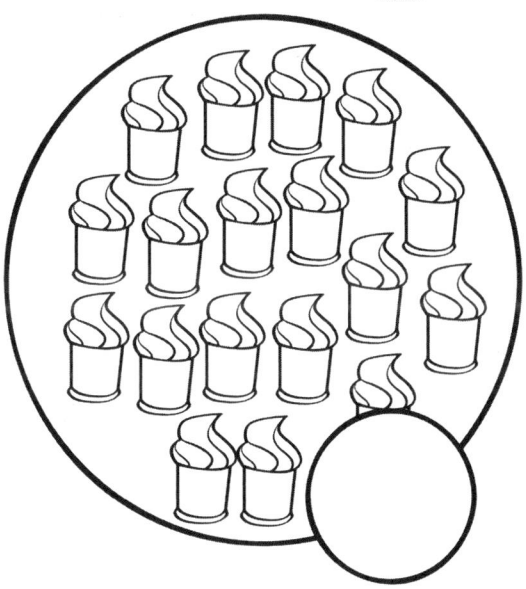

CAN YOU GUESS THE NAME OF THIS COUNTRY? WHAT IS IT FAMOUS FOR?

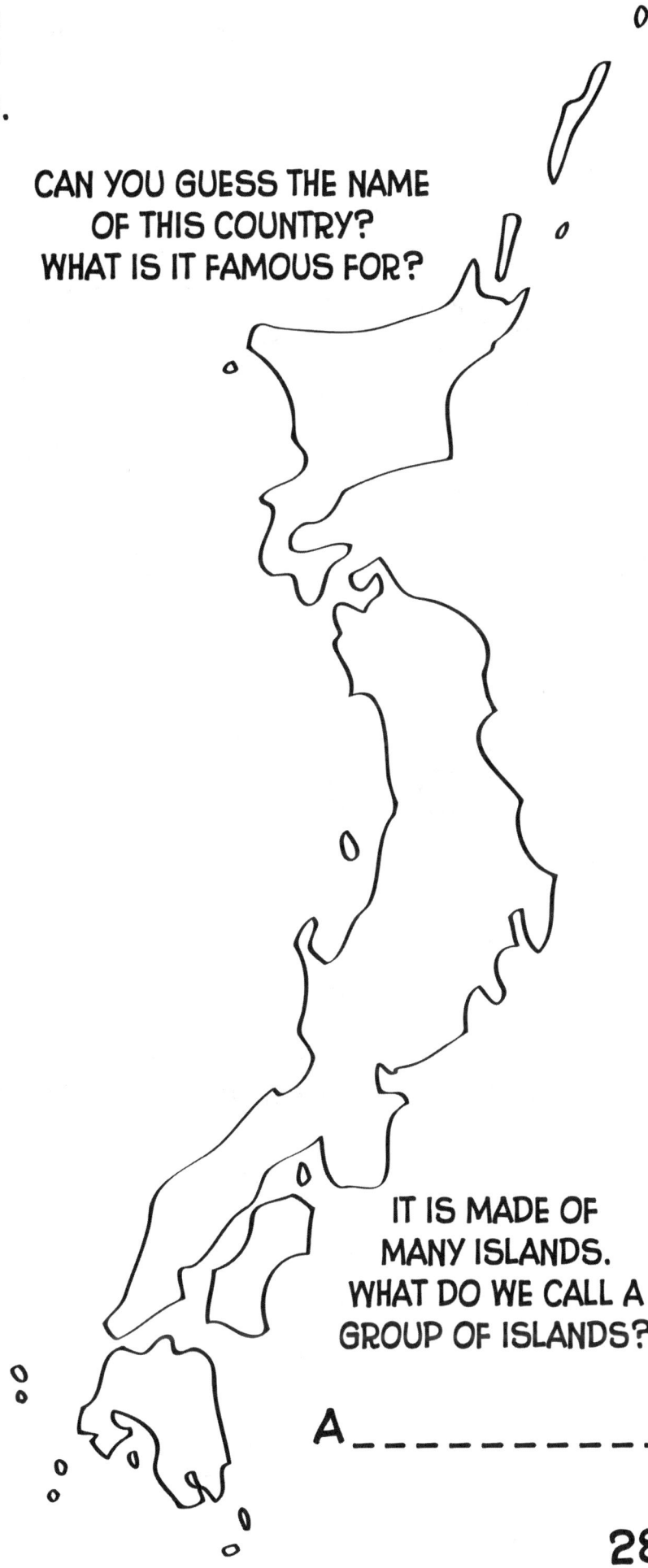

IT IS MADE OF MANY ISLANDS. WHAT DO WE CALL A GROUP OF ISLANDS?

A_____.

FIND THE MOON'S MISSING CHUNK.

TO WIN THIS GAME OF TIC-TAC-TOE,
MAKE AS MANY "OXO" COMBINATIONS AS YOU CAN.

O					O				X	O
	X						X		O	
		O	X	O						
O						O		X		
			X							

INSIDE EACH CIRCLE, DRAW AN ANIMAL MATCHING THE INITIALS BELOW.

G E A

THIS BEACH LOOKS EMPTY!
CAN YOU FILL IT WITH CHILDREN HAVING FUN?

SOME MAY BE SWIMMING.
SOME MAY BE PLAYING IN THE SAND.

CAN YOU DRAW MORE
BRIGHTLY COLORED
UMBRELLAS?

USING THESE ELEMENTS,
DRAW YOUR OWN SAND CASTLE.

WHICH ONE DOESN'T BELONG?

CAN YOU FIND THE NAMES OF TWENTY POPULAR BIRDS IN THIS WORDSEARCH? DRAW YOUR FAVORITE BELOW.

M	O	C	K	I	N	G	B	I	R	D	P	H	J	O
P	T	C	H	I	C	K	A	D	E	E	S	C	Z	R
I	J	U	E	C	T	Y	H	L	F	Q	K	E	B	F
G	W	E	R	D	R	U	U	V	P	T	F	O	L	C
E	O	T	K	K	Y	F	D	W	O	H	G	W	U	R
O	O	U	S	J	E	D	P	R	Q	N	V	L	E	O
N	D	U	E	R	D	Y	R	N	I	A	E	V	J	W
L	P	W	A	T	Q	A	B	M	I	F	G	J	A	V
R	E	Y	G	H	P	X	A	R	W	D	Q	U	Y	Q
C	C	Y	U	P	E	L	I	C	A	N	U	I	R	A
K	K	H	L	L	F	S	U	J	E	R	I	C	B	N
E	E	R	L	Y	L	R	H	O	A	O	G	V	K	Q
E	R	A	V	E	N	A	U	J	G	B	W	R	E	N
H	A	W	K	P	S	T	A	R	L	I	N	G	Z	K
V	U	L	T	U	R	E	F	M	E	N	S	X	P	U

WHAT SONG IS IT SINGING? WRITE IT DOWN.

⬡ ☆ □ △		

FILL WITH ALL POSSIBLE COMBINATIONS OF THE FOUR SYMBOLS.

COLOR THIS CATERPILLAR IN SEVEN COLORS AND CONTINUE THE SERIES. WHAT COLOR WILL THE LAST CIRCLE BE?

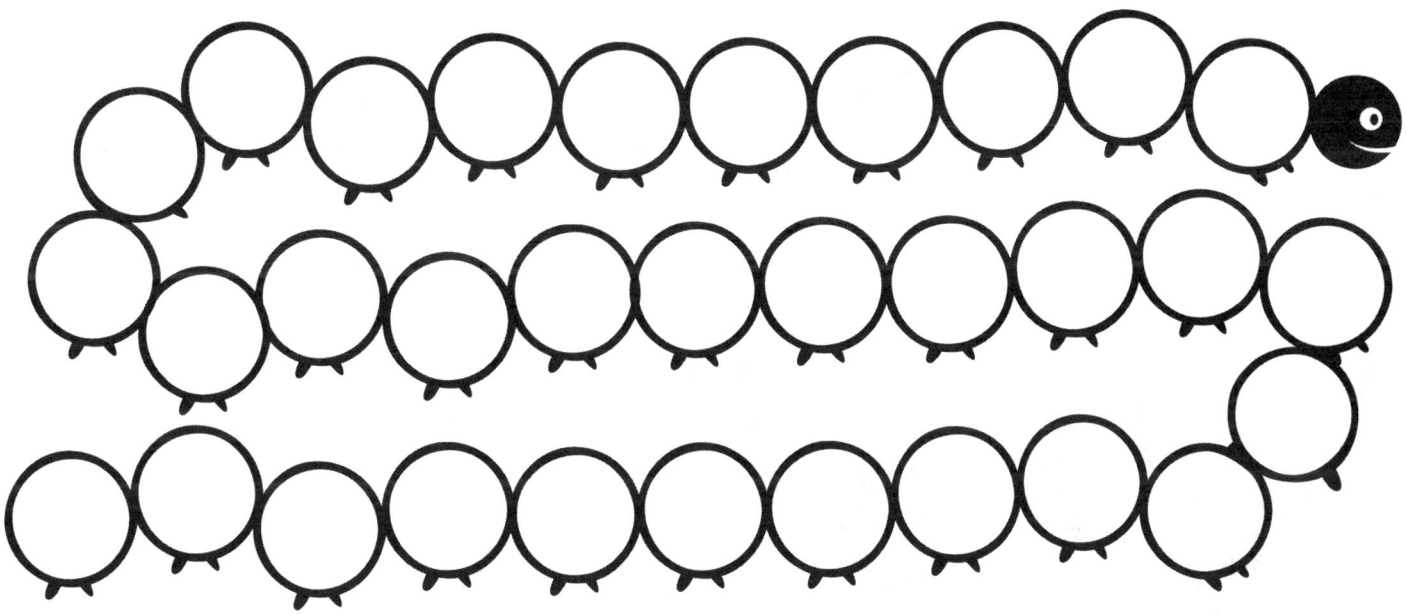

IF THE LITTLE FISH DOUBLES ITS CURRENT SIZE EVERY DAY, HOW LONG WILL IT TAKE IT TO BE BIGGER THAN IT'S MOM?

FILL THE SHELVES WITH AS MANY BOOKS AS YOU CAN.

CAN YOU ILLUSTRATE THE COVER OF HIS BOOK?

WHAT IS IT ABOUT?

HELP THE BEE GO FROM FLOWER #1 TO FLOWER #10, IN THE RIGHT ORDER.
THERE IS ONLY ONE CORRECT PATH, GOING THROUGH EACH NUMBER ONCE.

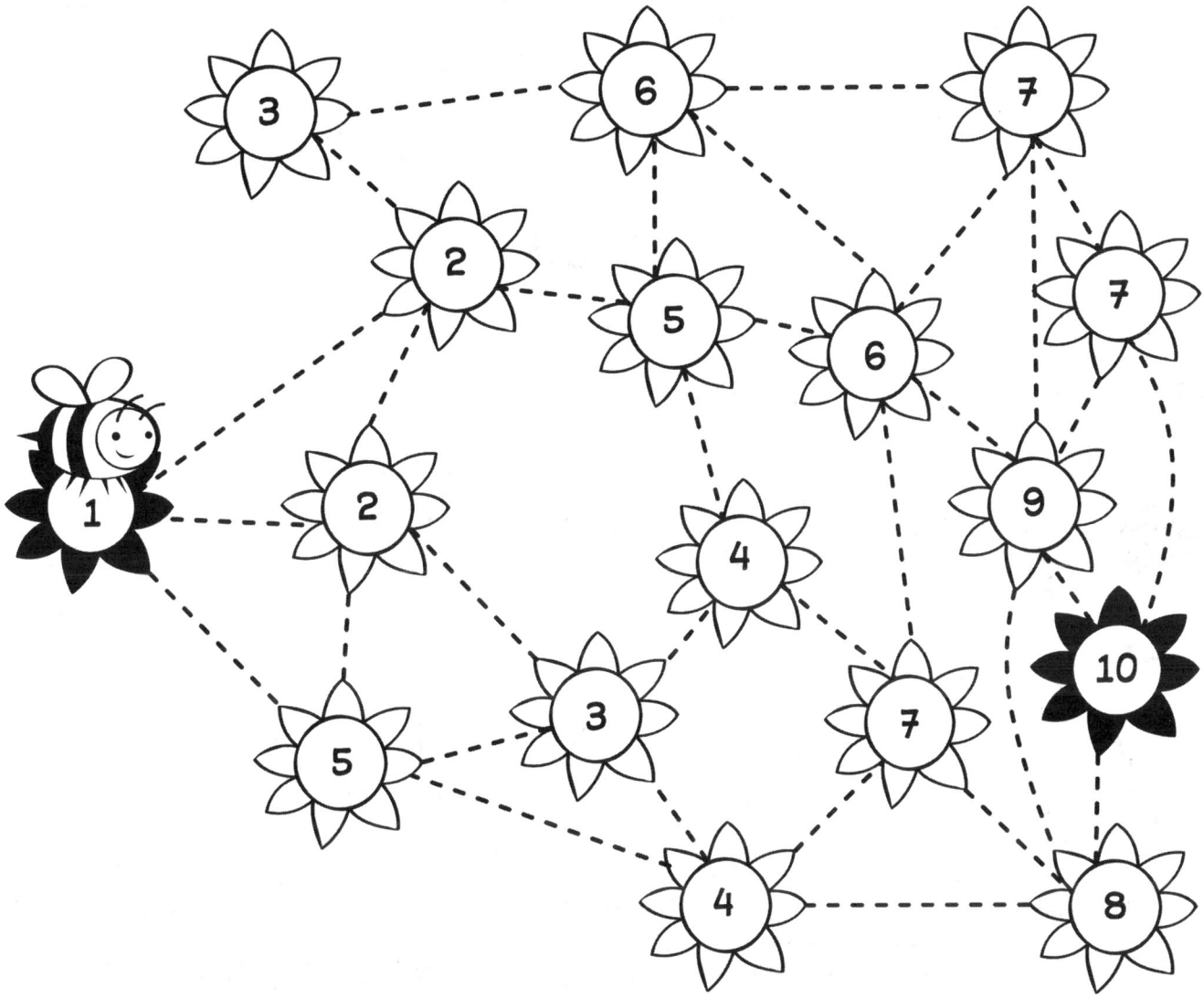

ANCIENT HUMANS USED TO MAKE HAND PRINTS ON CAVE WALLS.
CAN YOU DRAW THEIR HANDS ON THIS ONE TOO?

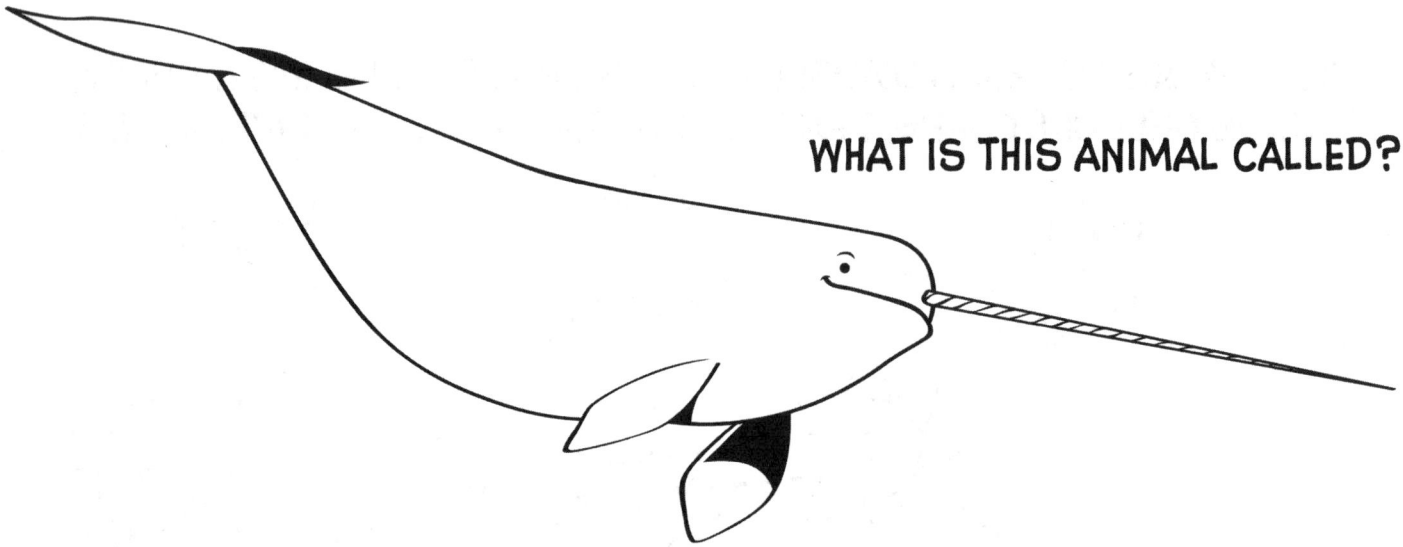

WHAT IS THIS ANIMAL CALLED?

ONE OF THESE DOES NOT BELONG. WHY?

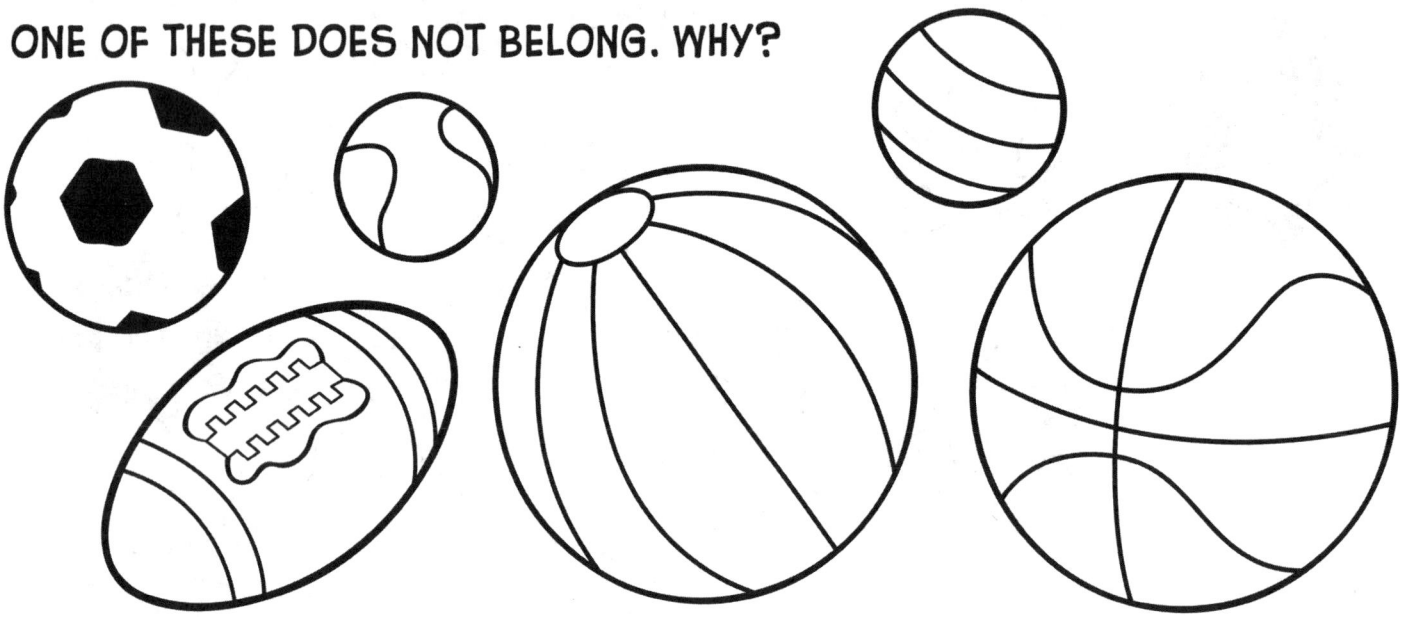

WHAT CAR BRANDS DO YOU KNOW THAT START WITH THESE INITIALS?

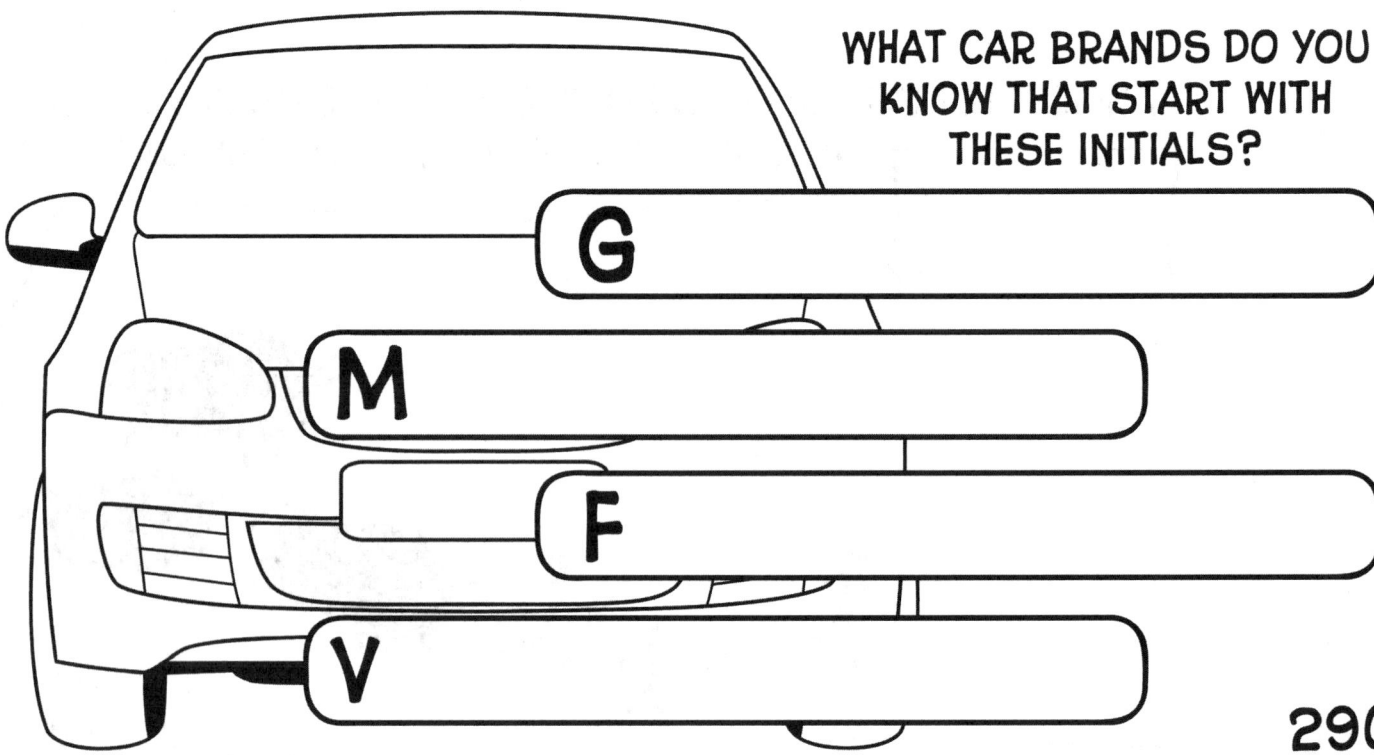

HOW LONG IS THE BRIDGE IF ALL ITS STONES ARE OF THE SAME LENGTH, AND THE TRAIN HAS COVERED SIXTY FEET ALREADY?

THIS WORDSEARCH IS SHAPED LIKE A COUNTRY. CAN YOU GUESS WHICH ONE? REMEMBER ITS FLAG COLORS?

```
            F M R S
        A N E M O M E T E R
    E   M O T O R W A Y C
  T T Q G R D V R A D I O S
  N I T R O G L Y C E R I N F
  E Y E G L A S S E S F
P A R A C H U T E T C P
  N E W S P A P E R N B
  H P J     P I Z Z A A
    G         V N O Y L H D
              I Q O L P Y X
              V O D E O B H
                X L T P Y A
                  P I A N O T
                    G N G B N T C B O
                      B O O K S E A
      J R                 X Y Q R K I
  Z U A V                 J B W O Y D X U
    J C U C                 A M D   H X
    E U O F                   E O
    A Z P U                   T R I
    N Z E Y                   E G J
    S I R                     R S
    M R A                     B P
                        P A S T A   L
                          B Z R L
                              X M
```

THIS WORDSEARCH IS SHAPED LIKE A COUNTRY. CAN YOU GUESS WHICH ONE? REMEMBER ITS FLAG COLORS?

IT IS FILLED WITH INVENTIONS THIS COUNTRY HAS GIFTED OUR WORLD WITH.

CLUE: 3 OF THOSE INVENTIONS BEGIN WITH THE LETTER "P".

HOW MANY PARTS FROM THE GLASS IN THE MIDDLE MUST WE POUR INTO THE LEFT AND RIGHT GLASSES TO EVENLY DISTRIBUTE ALL WATER?

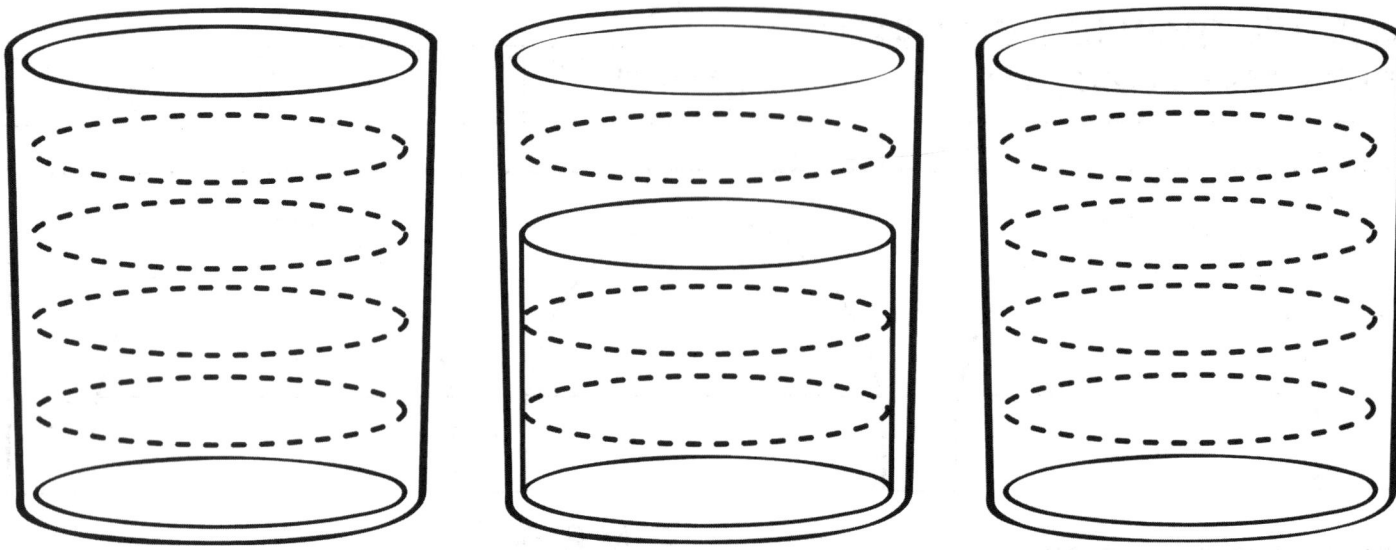

FIND THE ELEPHANT THAT'S DIFFERENT AND COLOR IT PINK.
COLOR ALL THE REST GRAY.

WHAT TIME IS IT?

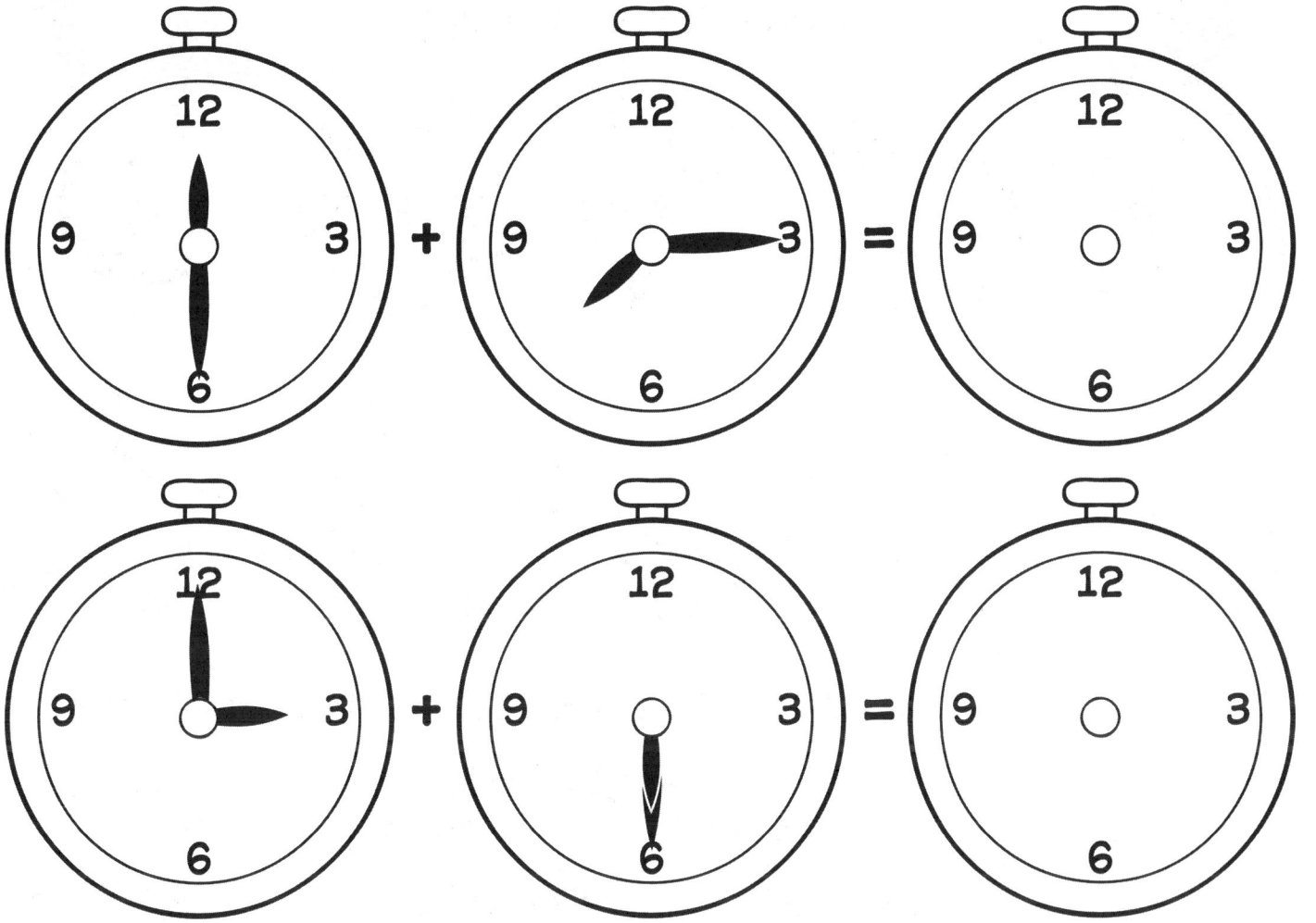

THIS STRANGE CREATURE IS MADE OF 3 ANIMALS. CAN YOU WRITE THEIR NAMES?

P

S

H

CONNECT THESE ANIMALS
TO THEIR FAVORITE FOOD!

WHICH ONE DOES NOT BELONG IN THIS SET OF TOOLS?

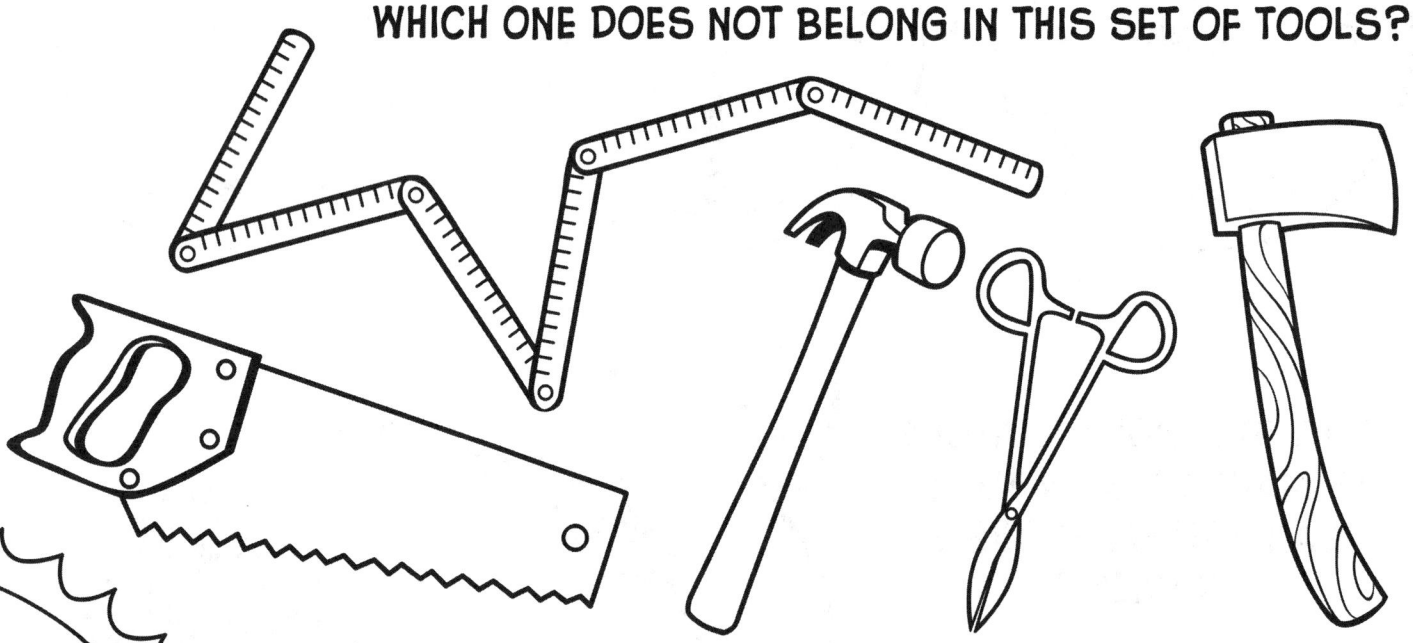

CAN YOU NAME ALL THE PLANETS? WHICH ONE IS CLOSEST AND
WHICH ONE IS FARTHEST FROM THE SUN?

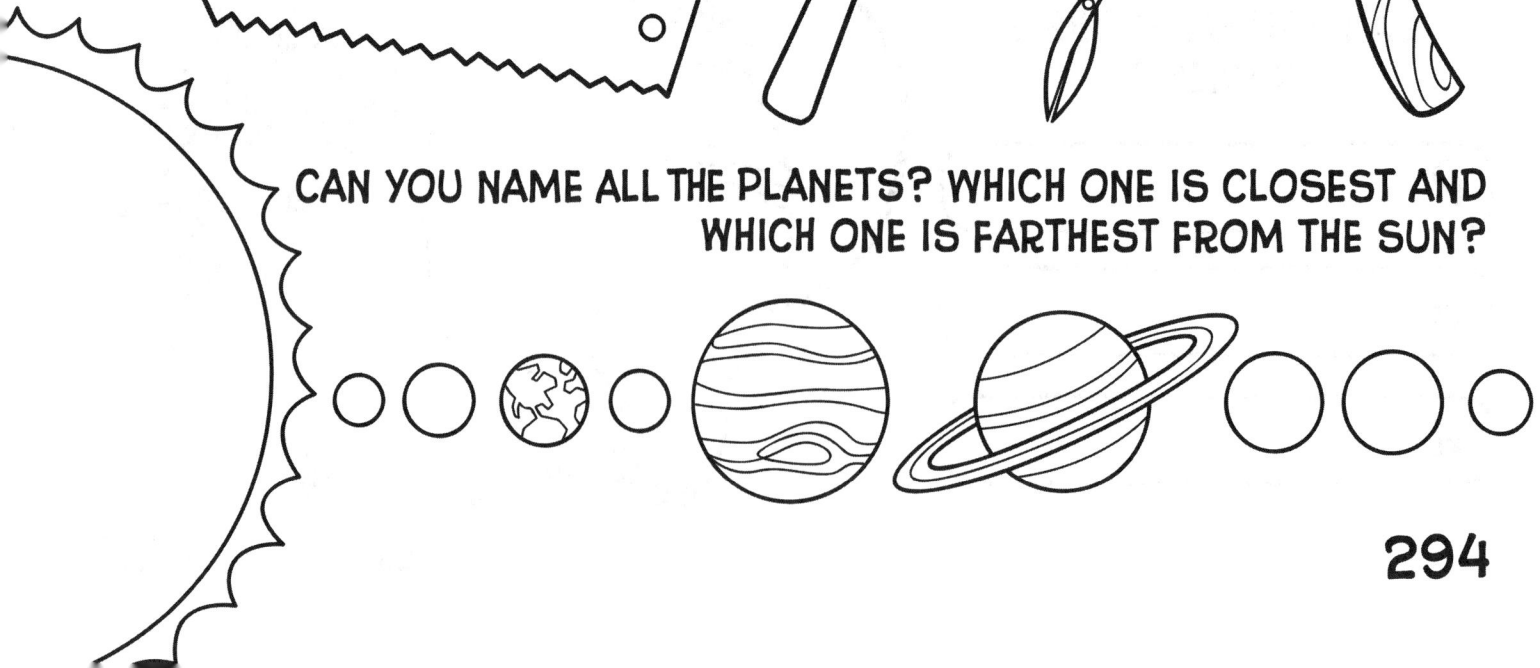

INSIDE EACH CIRCLE, DRAW AN INSECT MATCHING THE INITIALS BELOW.

S A B

FILL IN THE BLANK SPACES TO GET THE GIVEN RESULTS.

1	+	85	+		+	8	+		=	98
	-	27	+	44	-		+		=	128
7	+	62	-		+		+		=	86
10	-	5	+	8	-	4	+		=	49

WHICH DIRECTION WILL THE FIFTH WHEEL TURN ?

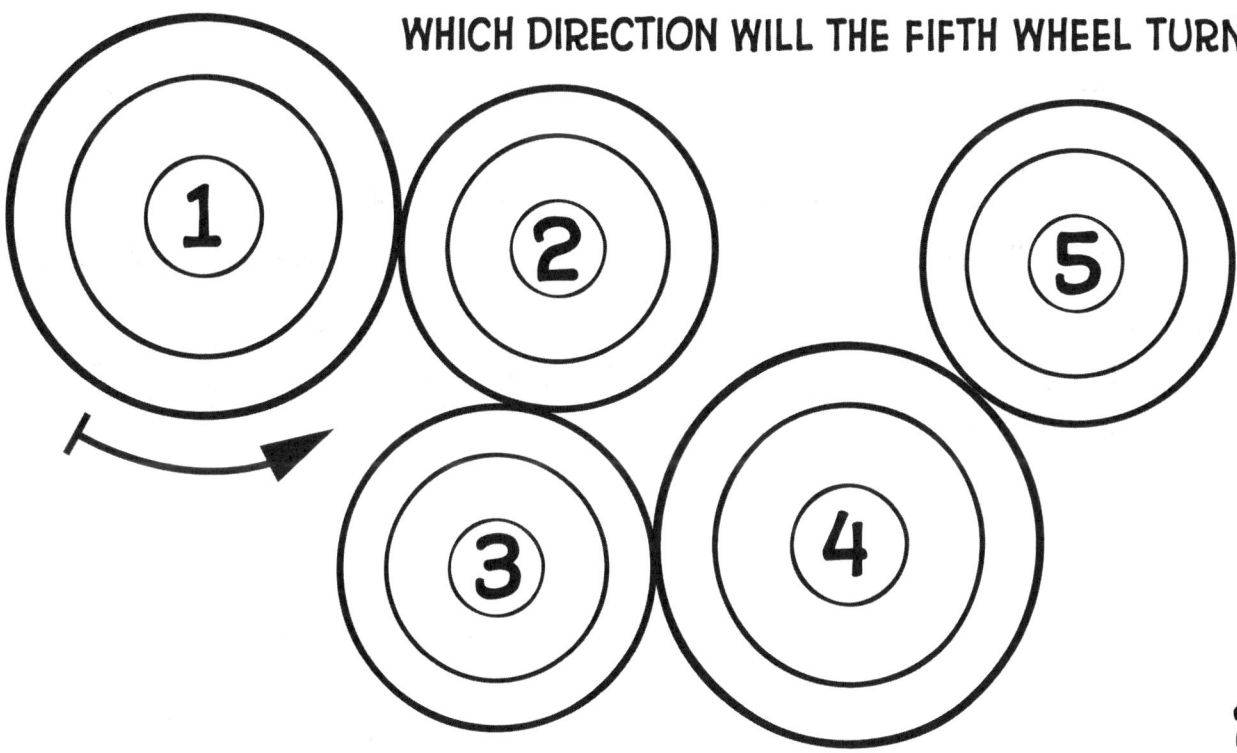

HOW WILL SHE FEEL WHEN SHE MAKES IT TO THE QUESTION MARK?

COMPLETE EACH COLUMN SO THE SUM OF THESE NUMBERS IS ALWAYS 68.

↓											
9	8	24	12	5	14	3	48	21	16	4	22
9											
45											
5											

SUBTRACT THE NUMBER OF BEES FROM THE TOTAL OF BUTTERFLIES YOU COUNT.

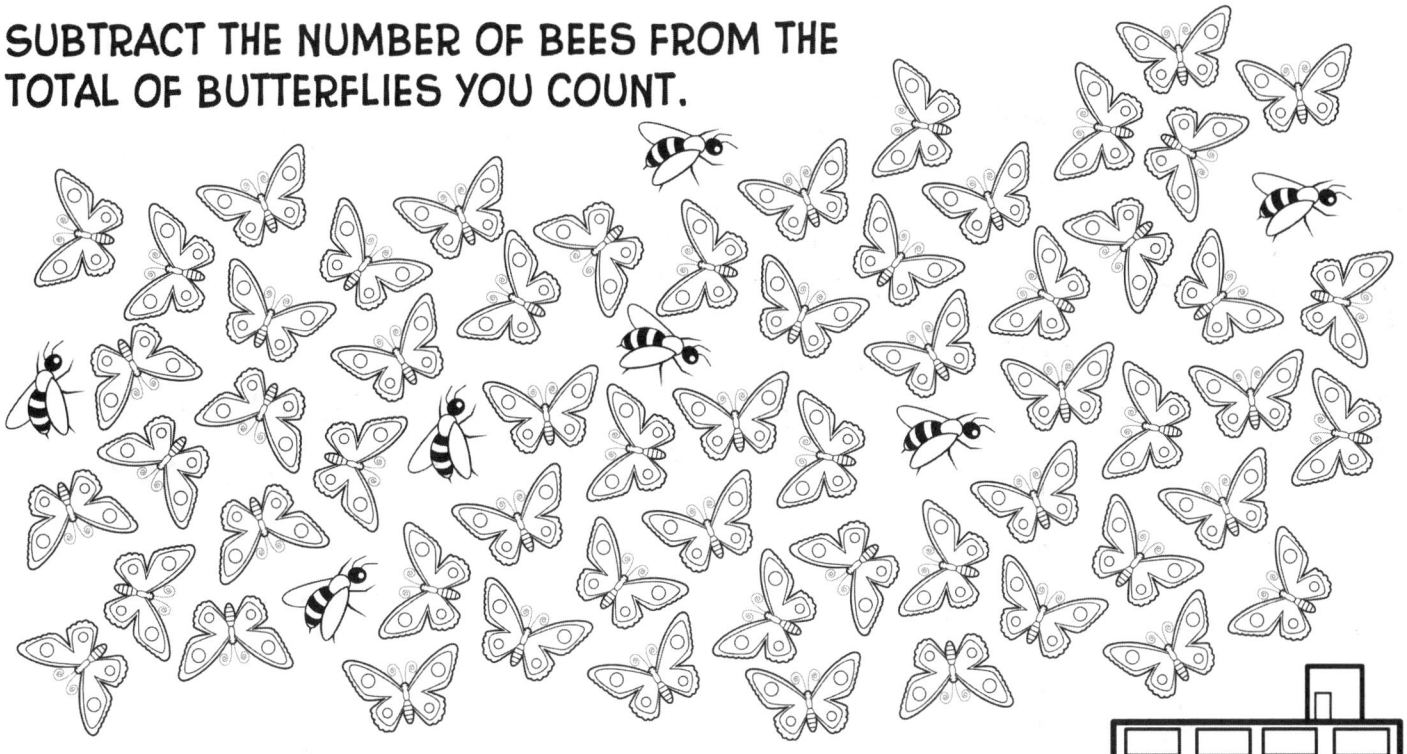

WHAT ROAD MUST THE CAR TAKE TO GET HOME IN EXACTLY 180 SECONDS?

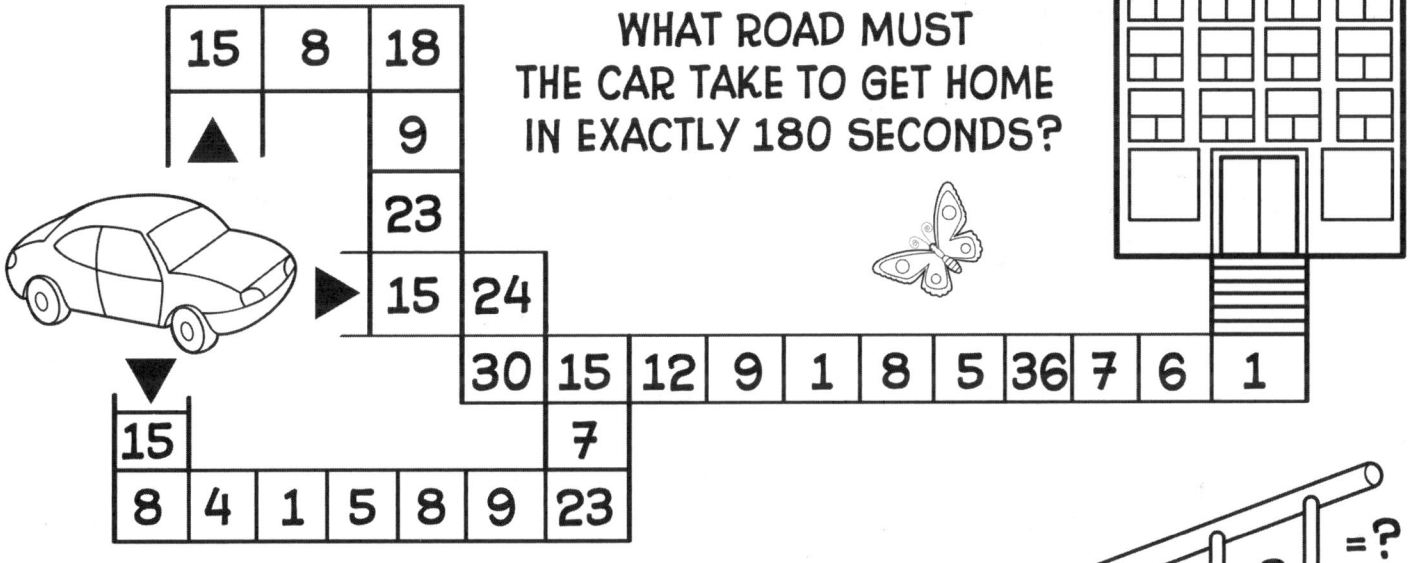

HOW TALL IS THE LADDER?

CIRCLE EVERY OTHER LETTER TO DECODE THE SECRET MESSAGE THAT CAME WITH THIS PRESENT.

XHPANPKPZY
FBTIPRCTWHEDKAGY
BTSO
QYFOKU!

WHAT TIME IS IT?

HELP THE ALIEN FIND
THE SHORTEST WAY
BACK TO ITS HOME PLANET,
PASSING THROUGH
ONLY TEN STARS.

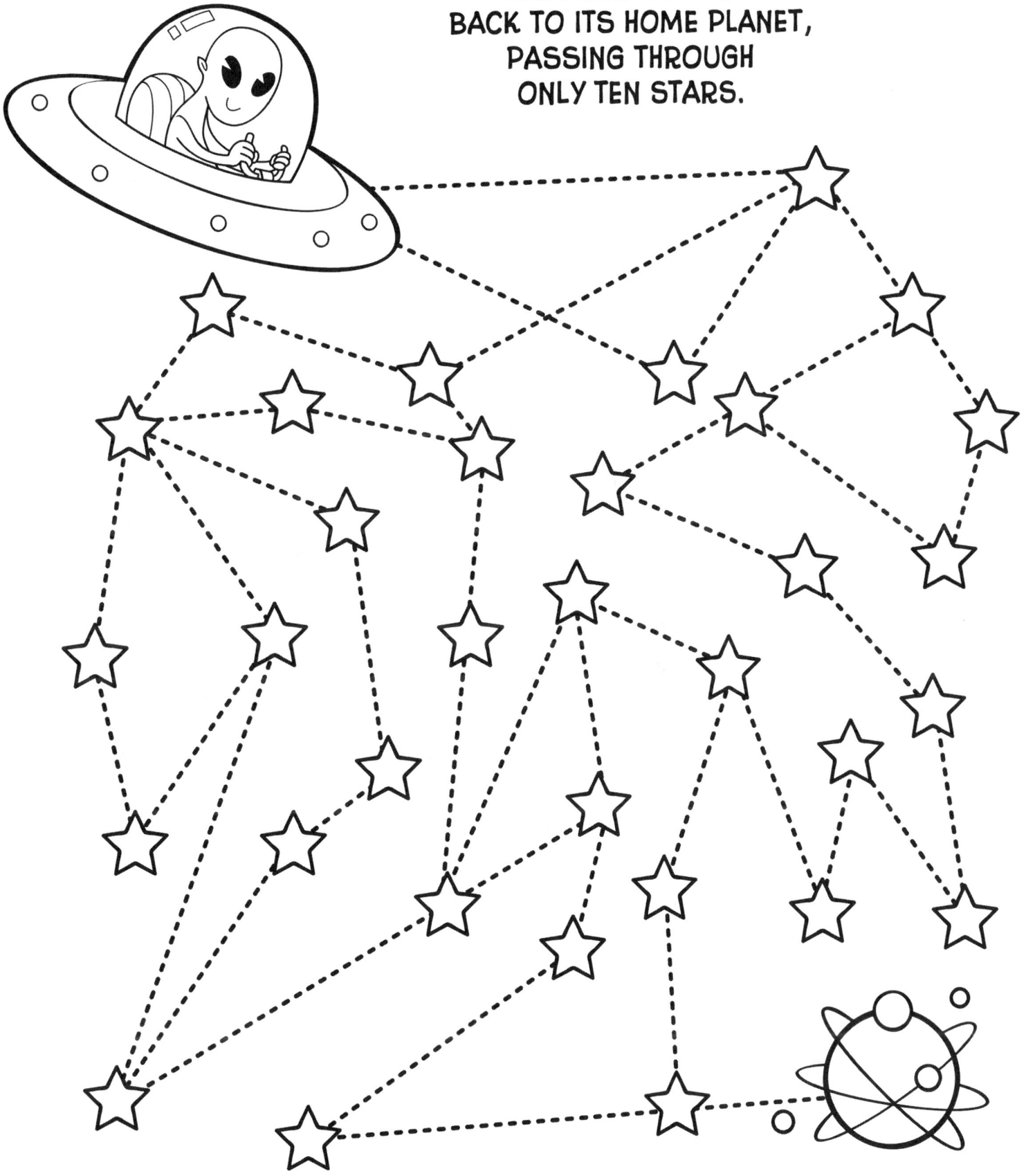

AMY IS ABOUT TO MAKE HER STAGE DEBUT. CAN YOU DRAW HER REFLECTION IN THE MIRROR?

C	U	R	T	A	I	N	S	C	O	M	E	D	Y	K	W
X	U	P	R	O	D	U	C	E	R	K	M	N	S	S	A
T	I	C	K	E	T	S	R	C	A	C	A	S	T	P	R
S	F	L	I	G	H	T	I	N	G	P	U	D	U	D	D
T	K	S	D	A	D	M	P	R	M	P	D	E	F	R	R
A	Y	D	I	R	E	C	T	O	R	U	K	D	Y	A	O
G	S	Q	Z	A	U	X	C	K	M	A	N	S	K	M	B
E	T	H	E	A	T	E	R	R	M	R	J	O	Q	A	E

FIND 15 TERMS RELATED TO THEATER (CLUE!) IN THIS WORDSEARCH!

LEVEL
4

HOW IS THE GANG GOING TO MAKE IT OUT OF THE MAZE?

TO WIN THIS GAME OF TIC-TAC-TOE,
MAKE AS MANY "OXO" COMBINATIONS AS YOU CAN.

O	X									O
									X	
X					X	O	X	O		
		X			O		O			

INSIDE EACH CIRCLE, DRAW A VEGGIE MATCHING THE INITIALS BELOW.

A E C

OMPLETE EACH COLUMN SO THE SUM OF THESE NUMBERS IS ALWAYS 124.

22	7	64	11	5	8	3	20	18	40	4	15
60											
2											
40											

SPELL THESE BIRTHDAY WORDS THE RIGHT WAY!

KEAC ----------

FTIG ----------

PYPAH ----------

LDSCANE ----------

USTSEG ----------

FIND THE DONKEY'S CORRESPONDING SILHOUETTE.

COMPLETE.

3	- 2	-	+ 5	+ 4	-	+ 6	-	+ 2	= 15

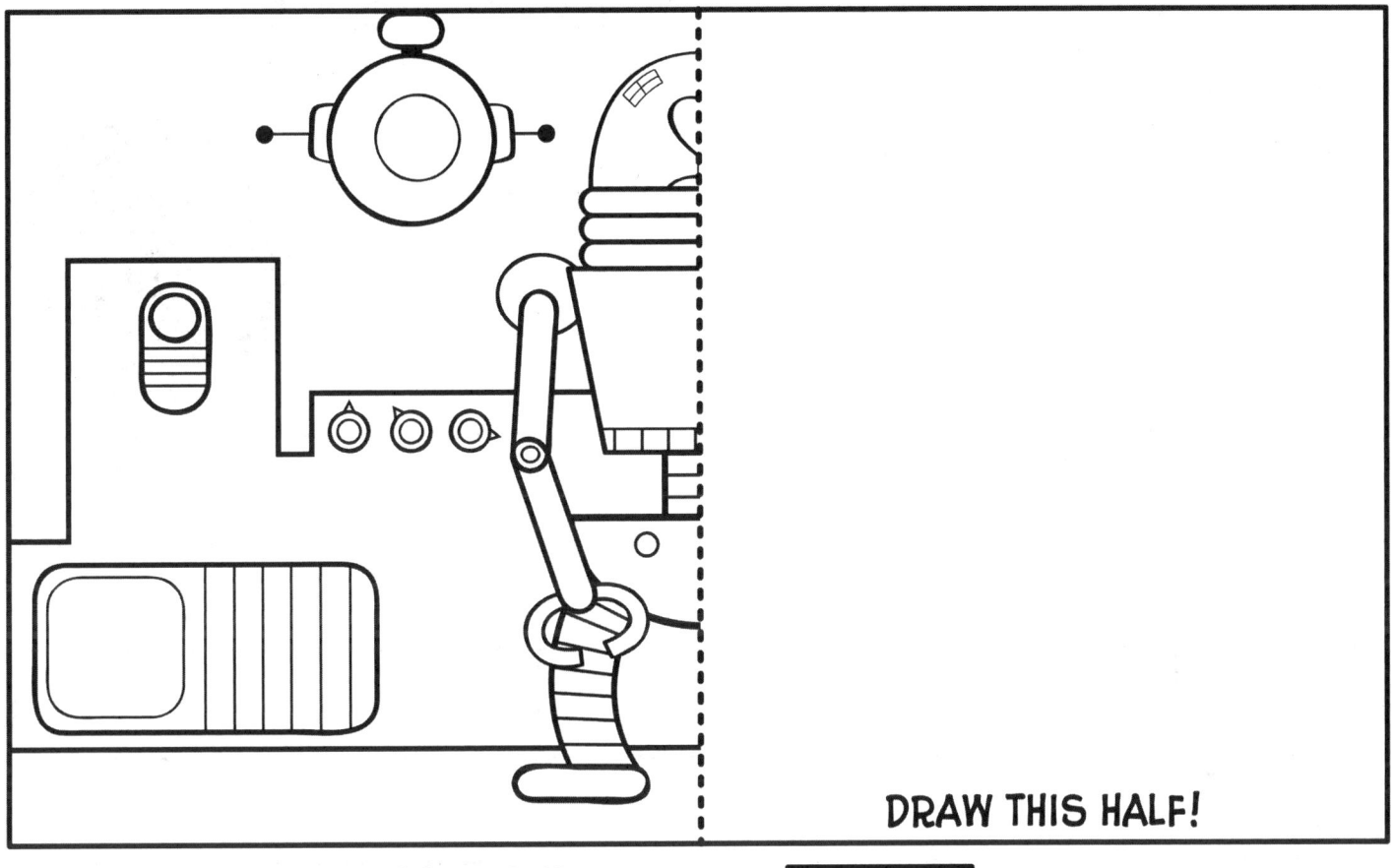

IN ORDER TO BUILD THE MAYAN PYRAMID, MAKE IT SO THE ADDITION OF EACH NUMBER ON THE LEFT TO THE NUMBER ON THE RIGHT EQUALS THE NUMBER OF THE BRICK ON TOP OF BOTH.

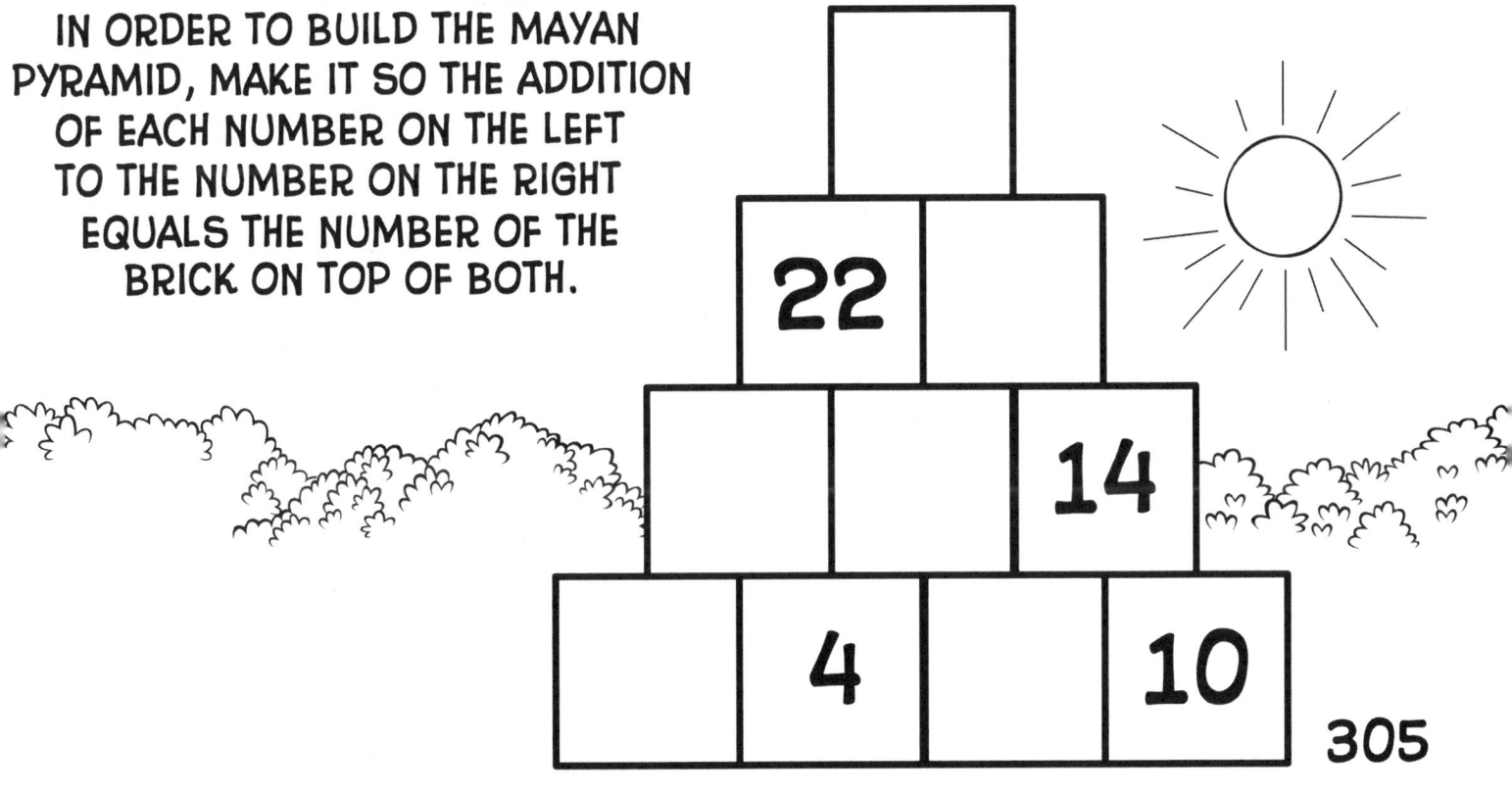

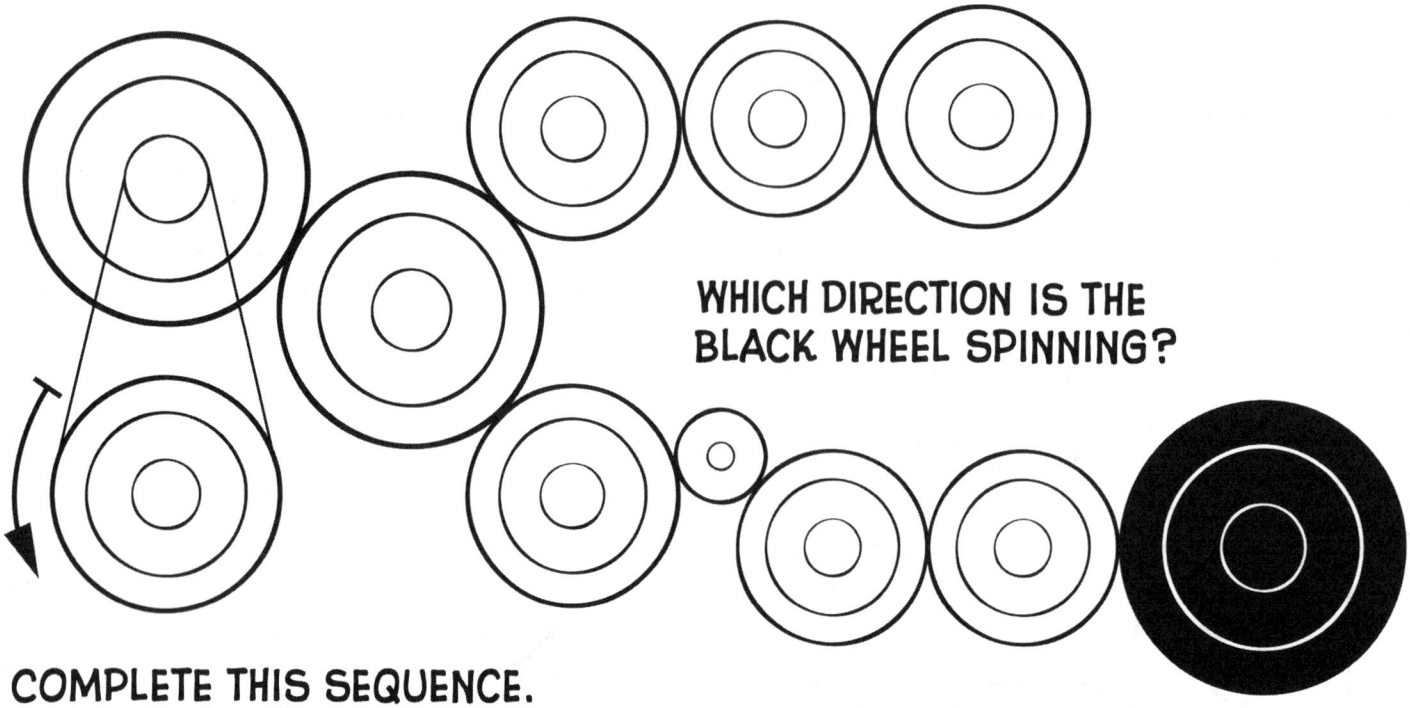

COMPLETE THIS SEQUENCE.

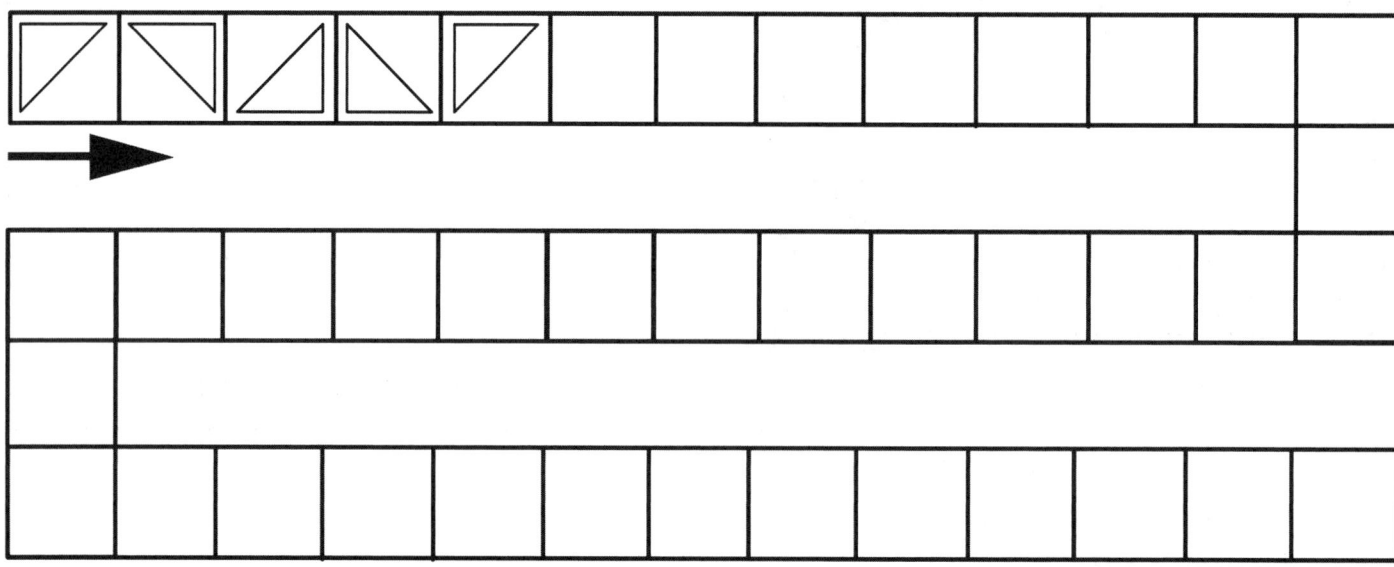

HELP MR. PIG FIND THE COB!

CAN YOU FIND THE FRUIT COMBINATIONS ON THE RIGHT WITHIN THE MAIN GRID?

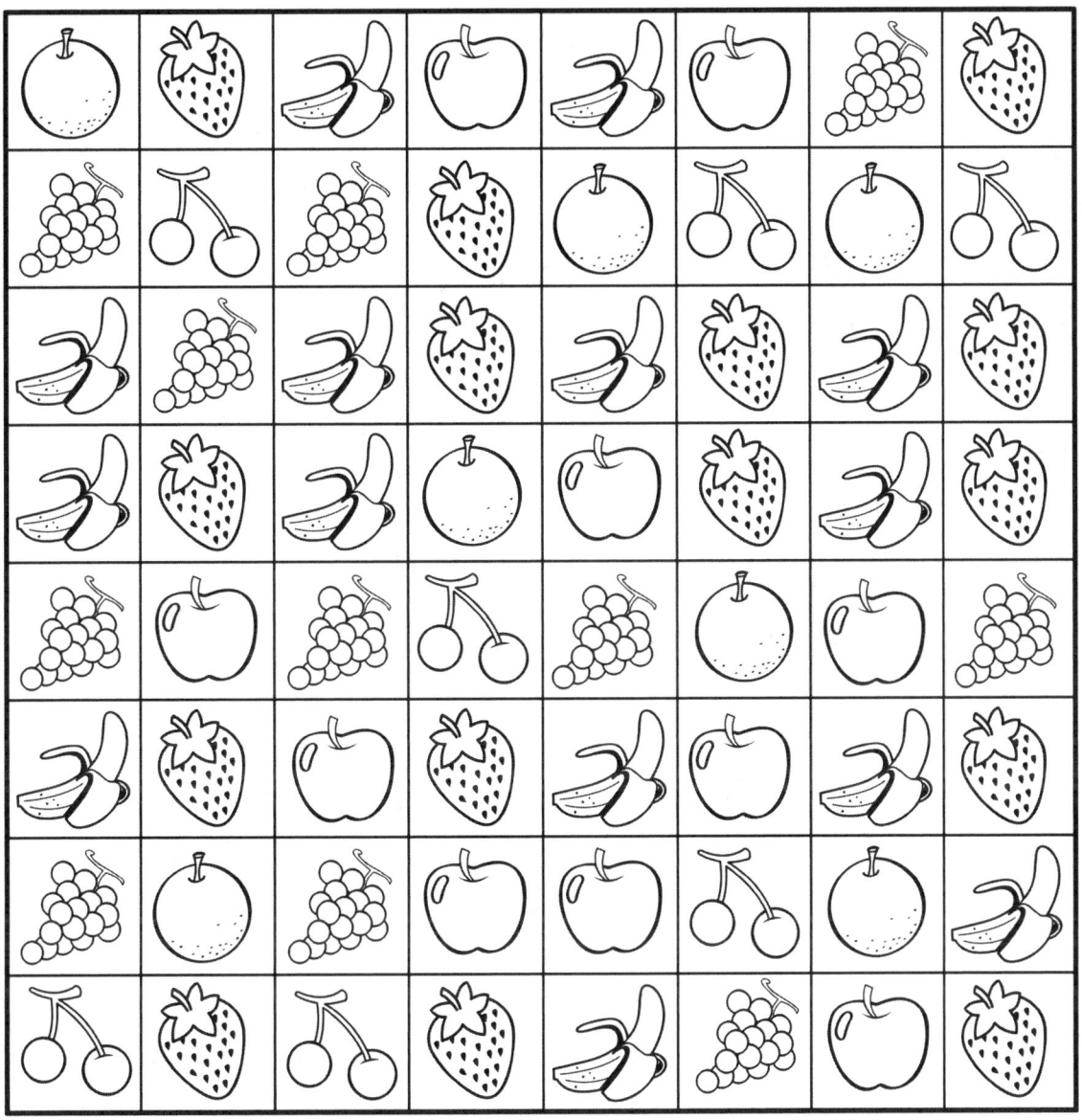

+5	+7	-2	+3	-4	-6	-9	-8	-2	+1	=
+9	+2	-3	-	-4	+5	-4	+6	-2	+4	= 11
+	+2	-1	+6	+2	+4	-5	-2	+9	-3	=
+6	+3	-2	+4	-1	+3	+5	-6	+5	-1	=
= 25	=	=	=	=	=	=	=	=	=	29

DO THE MATH BOTH VERTICALLY AND HORIZONTALLY!

HOW MUCH DO YOU KNOW ABOUT OUR PLANET? TEST YOUR KNOWLEDGE BY CRACKING THIS WORDSEARCH!

1. WHAT IS THE BIGGEST CONTINENT?
2. WHAT IS THE LARGEST OCEAN?
3. WHAT IS ITS LONGEST RIVER?
4. WHAT IS ITS BIGGEST DESERT?
5. WHAT IS ITS BIGGEST INLAND SEA?
6. WHAT IS THE COLDEST CONTINENT?
7. WHAT IS THE BIGGEST ISLAND?
8. WHAT IS ITS HIGHEST MOUNTAIN?
9. WHAT ABOUT THE SECOND HIGHEST?

T	P	C	N	G	E	V	E	R	E	S	T
K	I	D	E	F	Z	S	Y	I	M	H	N
W	J	J	U	B	K	Q	U	Z	E	O	P
Z	X	V	S	K	V	L	E	D	D	N	R
A	H	N	I	H	V	G	N	H	I	O	K
R	Z	N	U	P	I	A	J	A	T	W	K
T	O	I	G	H	L	A	O	C	E	R	M
R	D	Q	I	N	C	K	N	O	R	W	M
U	S	A	E	V	R	T	Z	N	R	V	W
I	U	E	X	E	C	B	O	C	A	I	I
I	R	J	H	U	Q	B	N	A	N	Q	X
G	Y	Z	W	R	B	D	C	G	E	F	V
Y	G	Z	R	A	F	I	J	U	A	Z	V
K	U	B	O	S	F	I	F	A	N	S	U
N	B	O	G	I	S	A	H	A	R	A	Z
N	Z	C	C	A	Z	N	B	D	M	O	Q
H	Y	A	J	V	O	N	K	Z	I	H	R
D	P	V	L	Z	U	X	I	N	V	D	U
A	N	T	A	R	C	T	I	C	A	I	B
M	H	M	A	G	W	J	F	Y	C	T	G
I	A	N	S	A	Z	J	Q	T	B	W	A

DESIGN AND COLOR YOUR OWN COAT OF ARMS.

THINK AND WRITE A GOOD MOTTO TOO!

DRAW PATHS CONNECTING NUMBERS 1 TO 9
TO FORM A CONSTELLATION.

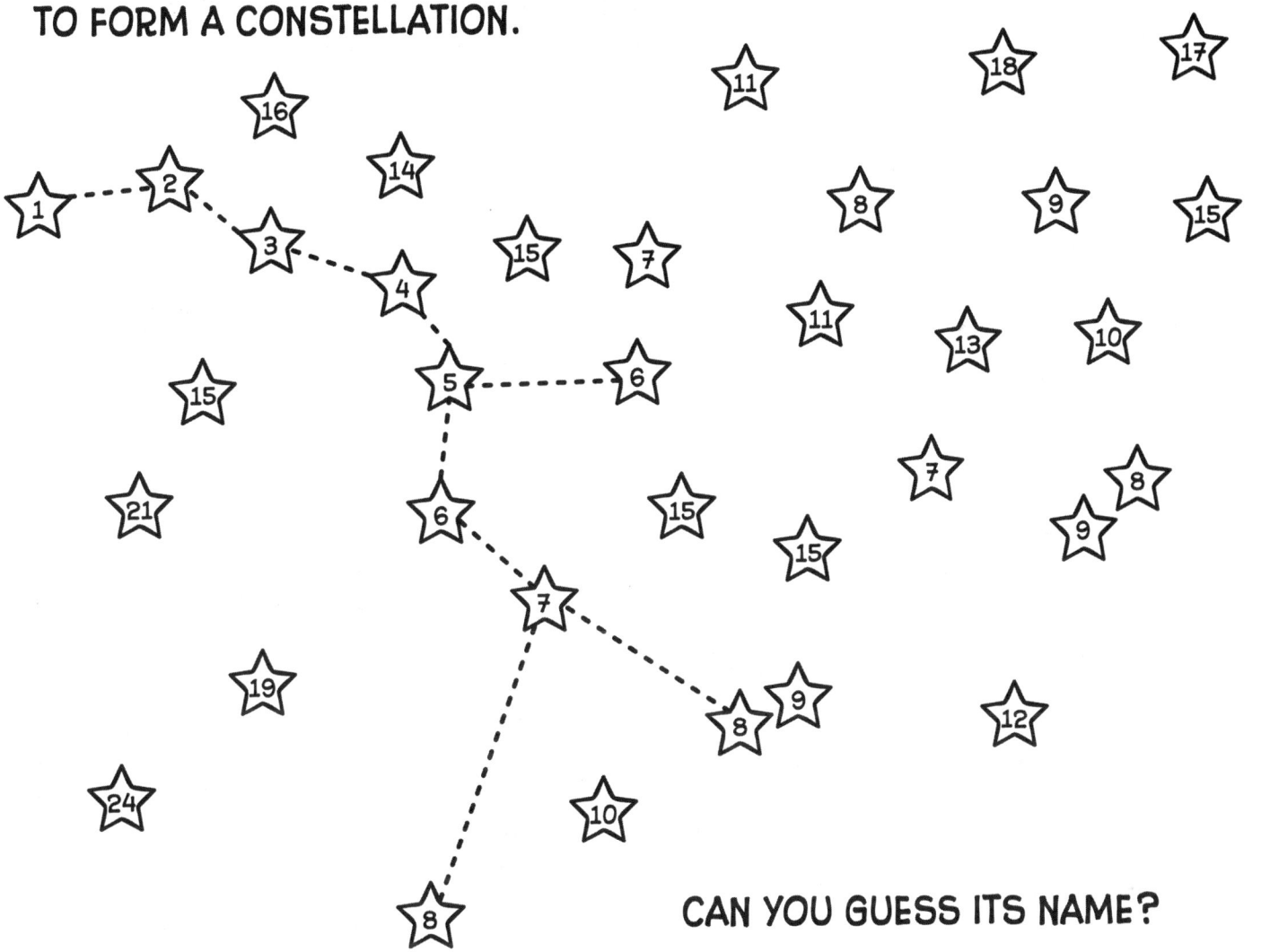

CAN YOU GUESS ITS NAME?

CONNECT ALL THE TOTALS THAT EQUAL 9!

8 + 1	6 + 3	11 - 2	7 + 3	4 + 5	6 + 3	2 + 7	8 + 7	3 + 6	1 X 9
6 + 5	4 + 5	3 X 3	2 X 5	3 X 3	5 - 2	7 + 2	5 + 6	4 + 5	5 + 5
9 - 3	12 + 5	5 X 2	3 X 6	13 - 4	1 + 3	9 X 1	12 - 6	9 X 1	1 + 5
4 + 8	7 + 2	13 + 4	8 + 1	9 - 0	4 X 3	14 + 6	13 - 4	16 - 7	8 - 2

9

DRAW MAYA'S PET.
IT CAN BE ANY ANIMAL YOU CHOOSE!
COLOR THE WHOLE PICTURE.

FILL THE MISSING NUMBERS FROM 1 TO 16, IN ORDER TO KEEP MOVING FROM LEFT TO RIGHT, UP OR DOWN, PANEL BY PANEL, WITHOUT REPEATING ANY NUMBERS, NOR SKIPPING ANY PANELS.

	11	16	
9			14
8			3
	6	5	

IF THE FIRST WHEEL OF CHEESE WEIGHS 12 POUNDS, WHAT IS THE SECOND WHEEL'S WEIGHT?

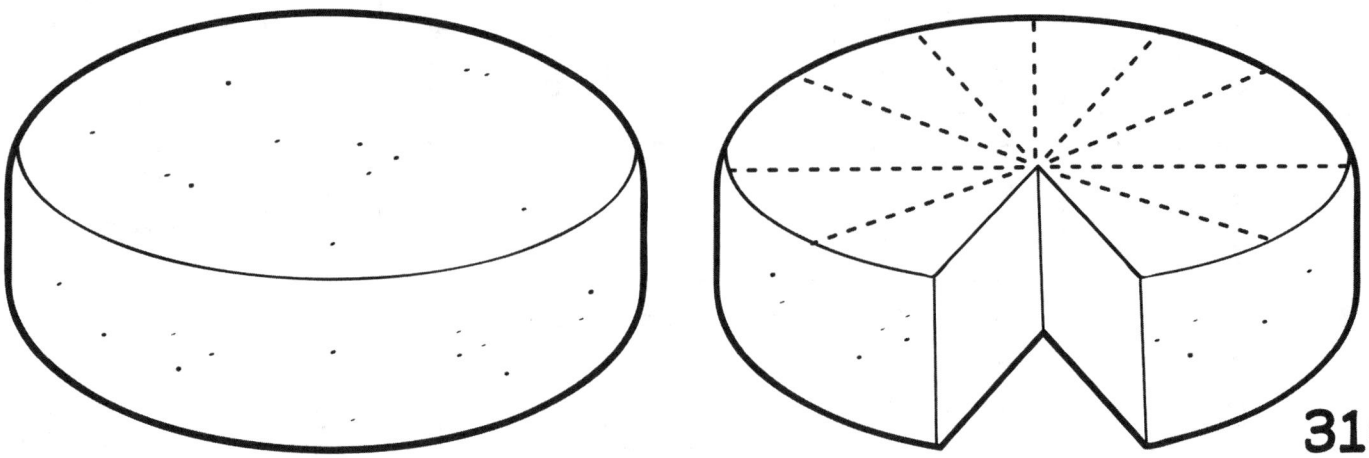

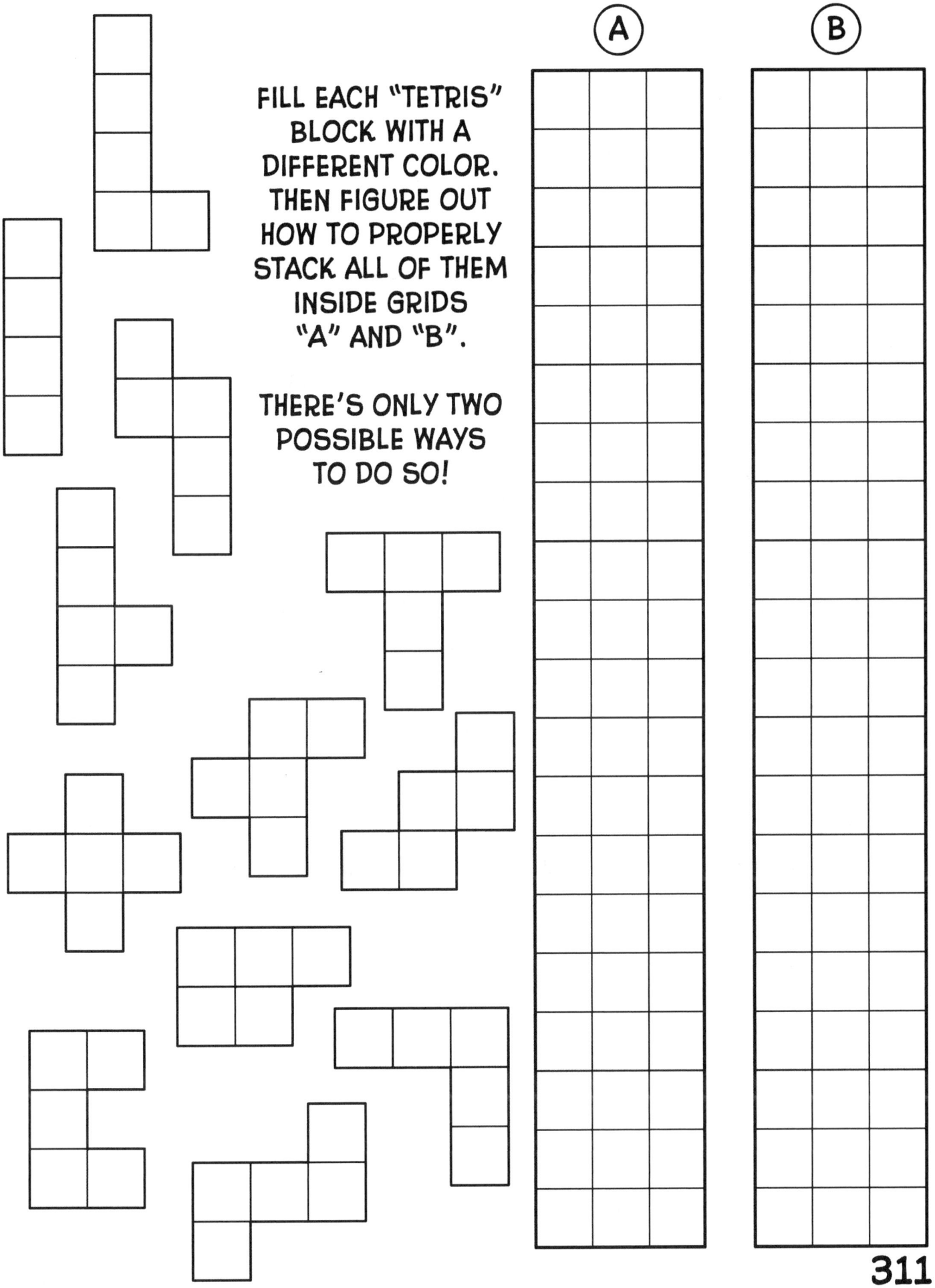
FILL EACH "TETRIS" BLOCK WITH A DIFFERENT COLOR. THEN FIGURE OUT HOW TO PROPERLY STACK ALL OF THEM INSIDE GRIDS "A" AND "B".
THERE'S ONLY TWO POSSIBLE WAYS TO DO SO!
A
B

HOW MANY THREADS WILL THE SPIDER NEED TO REPAIR HER WEB?

WHAT ANIMAL IS THIS? WHERE DOES IT LIVE?

CONNECT THE DOTS TO FIND OUT!

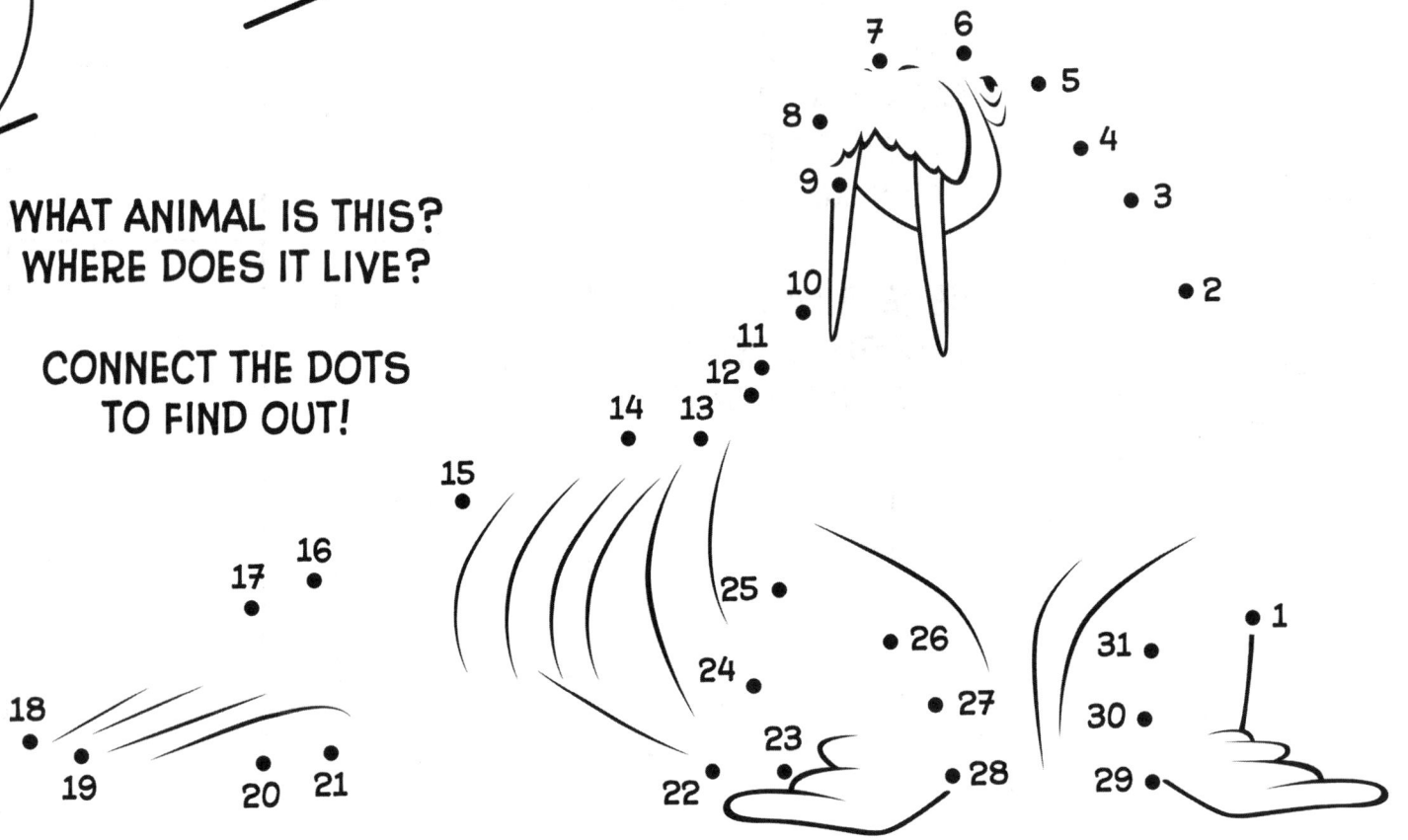

IMAGINE YOU'RE AN ANCIENT HUMAN, AND DRAW YOUR OWN CAVE WALL PAINTINGS.

COMPLETE THE HORIZOTAL SEQUENCES.

21		9		3	5		15	
	10	8		2		8	10	16
	6		2	0	2			8

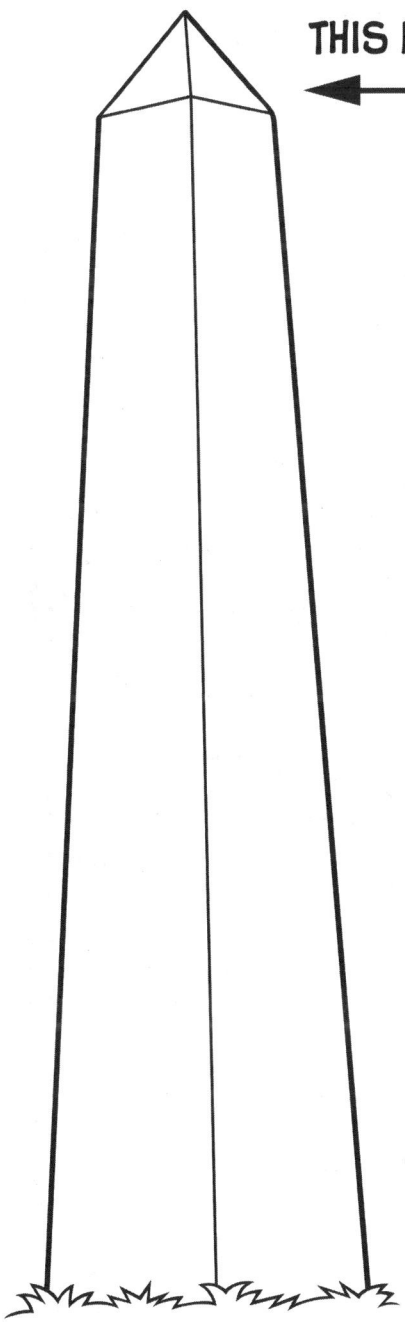

THIS MONUMENT IS A COMMON SIGHT AROUND THE WORLD.
WHAT IS IT CALLED?
WHERE WAS IT ORIGINALLY INVENTED?
NAME THREE CAPITAL CITIES WHERE YOU KNOW IT CAN BE FOUND.

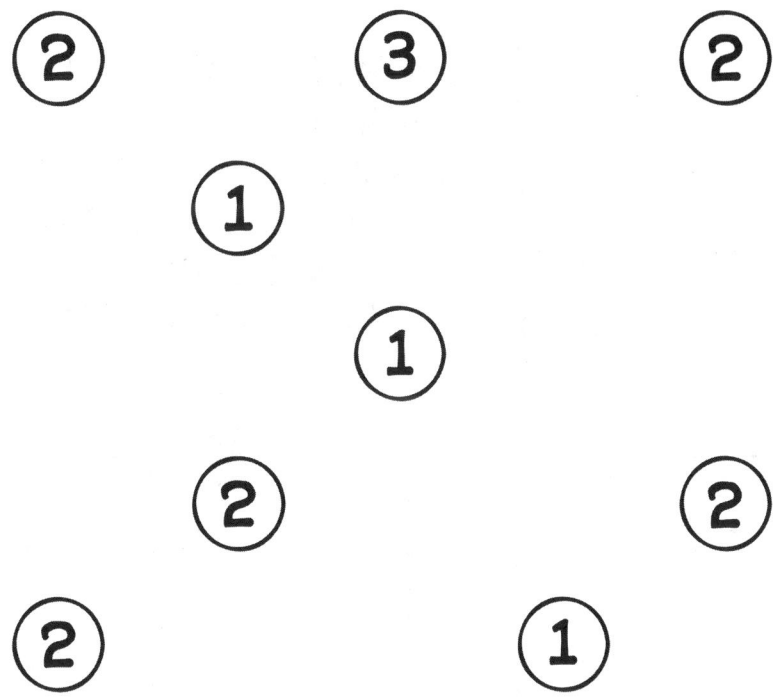

CONNECT EACH NUMBERED CIRCLE WITH ONLY VERTICAL OR HORIZONTAL, NON OVERLAPPING LINES. THE NUMBER ON EACH CIRCLE INDICATES THE NUMBER OF LINES EACH ONE IS ALLOWED.

HOW MANY PENCILS WOULD THE OCTOPUS NEED TO FINISH WRITING THE LETTER SOONER?

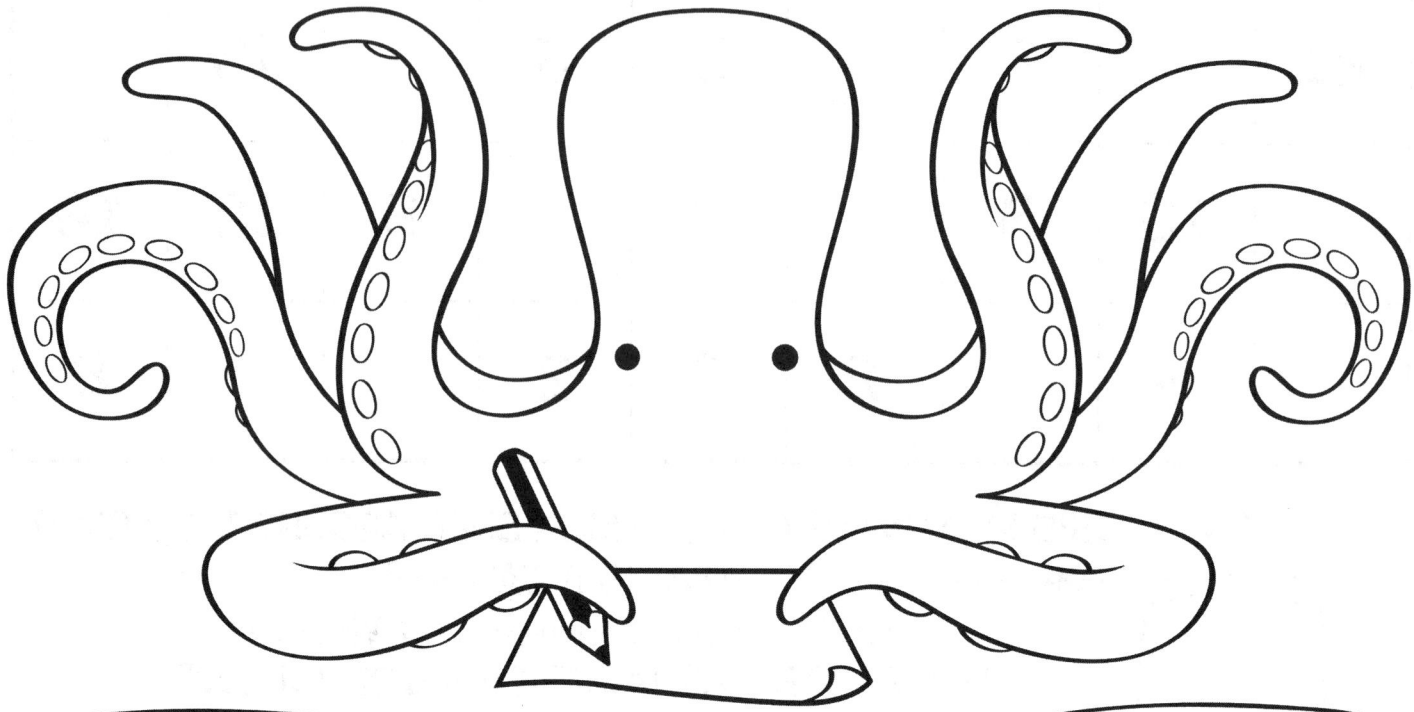

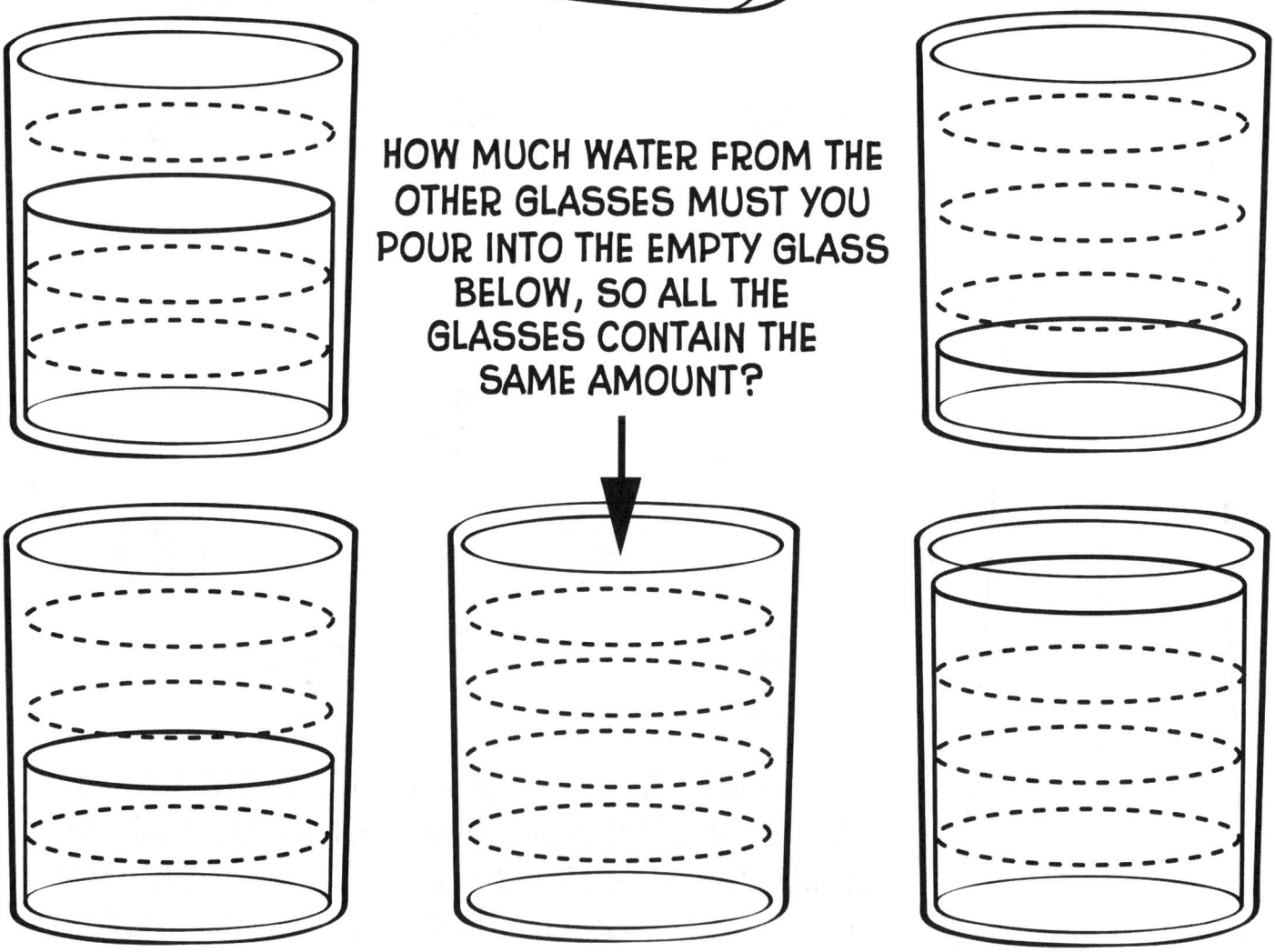

COMPLETE THIS SEQUENCE
TO FIND OUT WHICH INSECTS
WILL REPLACE THE QUESTION MARKS.

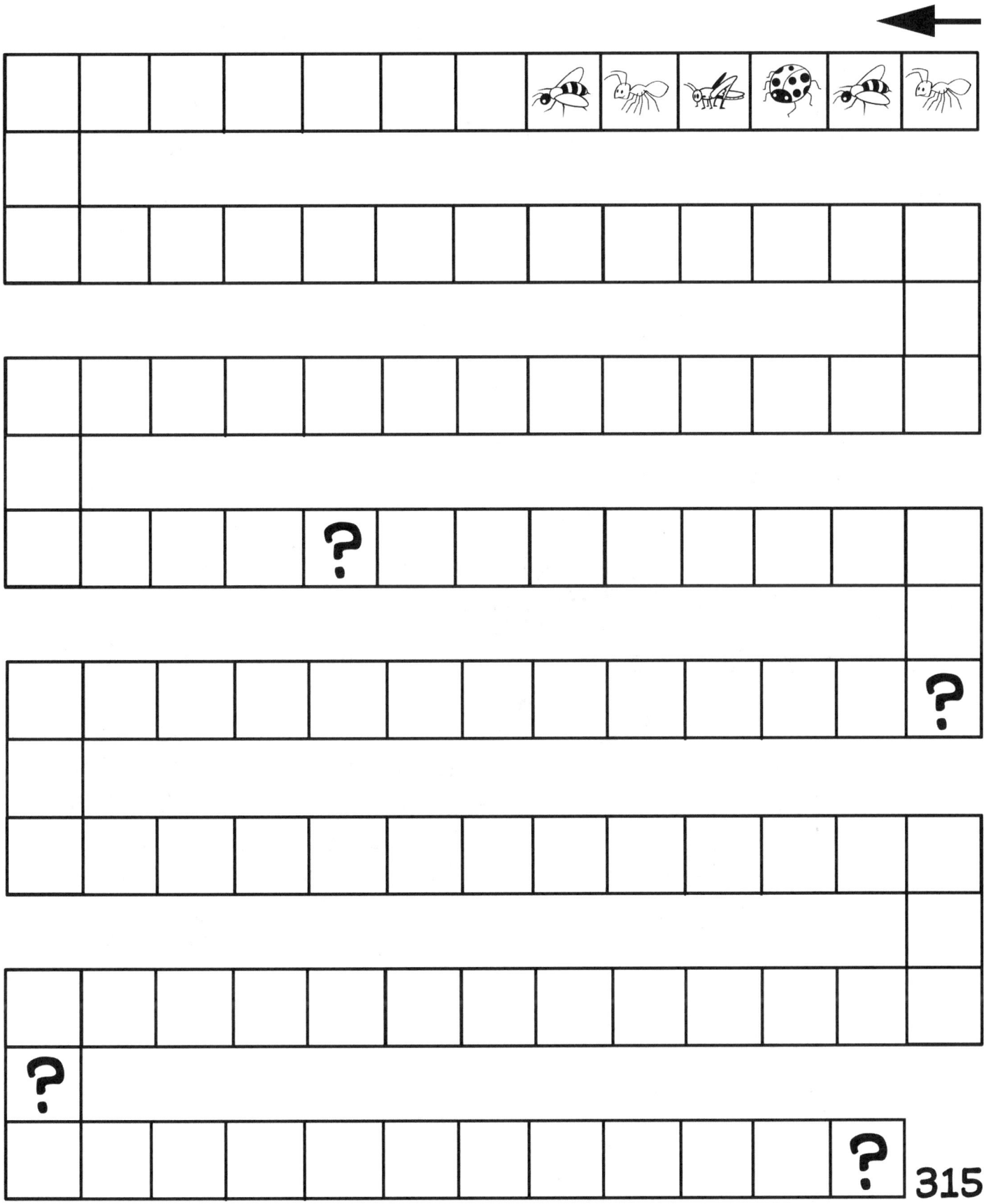

WHAT STRANGE ANIMAL IS THIS?
WHERE DOES IT LIVE?
WHAT DOES IT EAT?

DRAW A CIRCLE AROUND THE ANIMAL WE COMPARE IT TO.

COLOR BOTH THE SAME!

IN ORDER TO BUILD THE MAYAN PYRAMID, MAKE IT SO THE ADDITION OF EACH NUMBER ON THE LEFT TO THE NUMBER ON THE RIGHT EQUALS THE NUMBER OF THE BRICK ON TOP OF BOTH.

HELP AMY COLOR THIS PICTURE IN THE STYLE OF DUTCH PAINTER, PIET MONDRIAN! TO DO SO, FILL EACH PANEL USING ONLY PRIMARY COLORS, BUT NEVER PAINT JOINT PANELS USING THE SAME COLOR (YOU MAY CHEAT BY NOT COLORING A FEW).

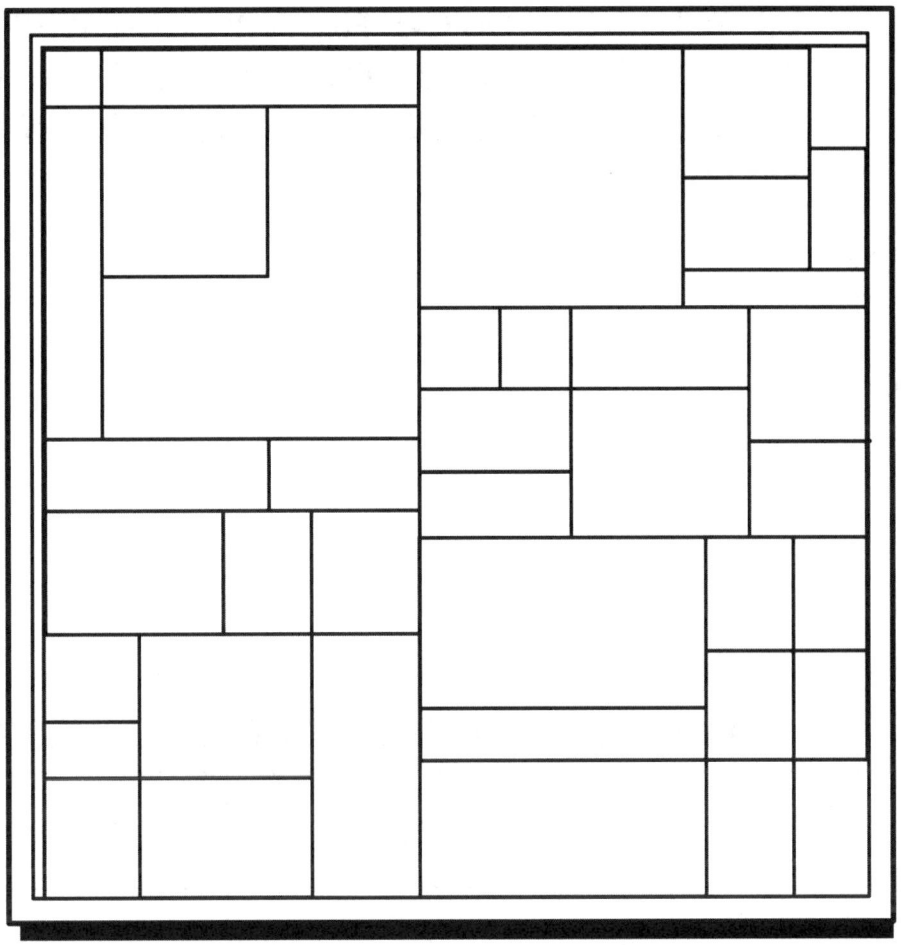

NOW DRAW AND PAINT YOUR OWN "MONDRIAN" USING ONLY STRAIGHT LINES AND THREE COLORS!

DID YOU KNOW YOU CAN FILL ANY SHAPE WITH AN INFINITE NUMBER OF CIRCLES? WHAT'S THE BIGGEST CIRCLE YOU CAN DRAW IN THIS RECTANGLE? GO AHEAD AN FILL EVERY AVAILABLE SPACE WITH SMALLER ONES!

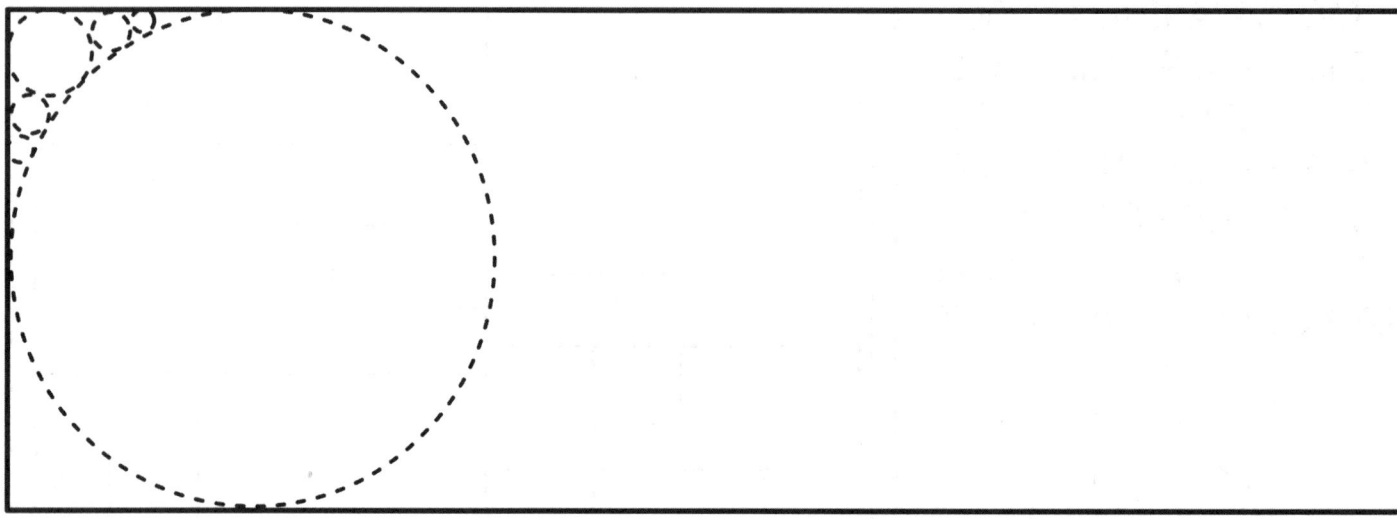

CAN YOU FIND THE NEW FOUR FRUIT COMBINATIONS AT THE RIGHT?

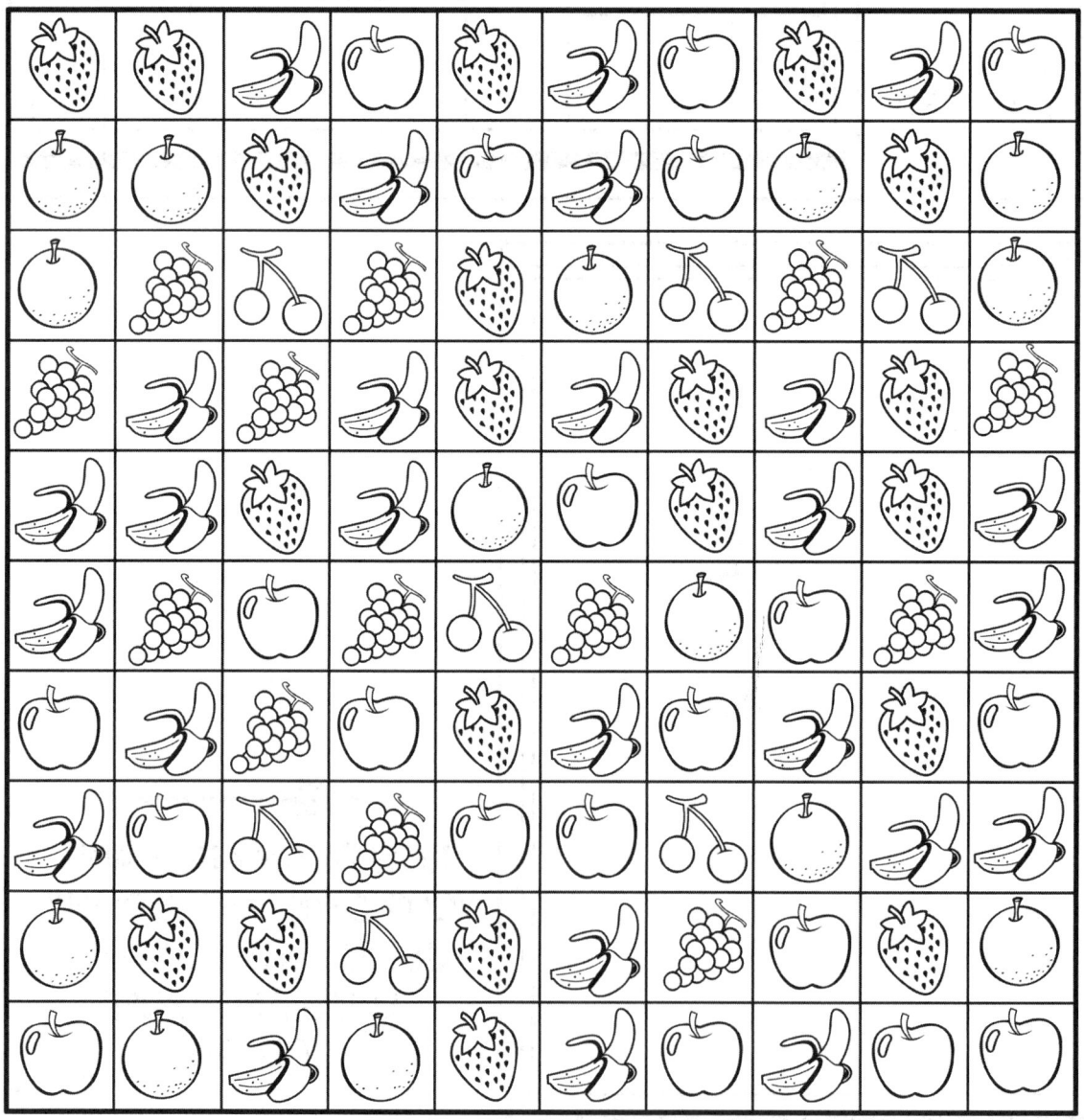

WHAT TIME IS IT?

SOLVE.

6+4	+ 3	-	+ 5	-2+8	X	- 6	X 2	+ 5	=

CAN YOU FIND ALL 14 FELINE SPECIES IN THIS WORDSEARCH?

T	H	L	A	D	O	M	E	S	T	I	C	C	A	T	F
P	P	Y	E	J	A	G	U	A	R	B	T	V	R	P	D
O	A	I	D	Y	O	L	Y	N	X	O	O	E	J	U	Z
B	E	N	C	A	R	A	C	A	L	T	G	B	Z	M	L
E	V	O	T	L	Y	M	F	E	W	I	L	D	C	A	T
Y	I	M	R	H	I	G	C	J	T	S	E	R	V	A	L
S	N	O	W	L	E	O	P	A	R	D	M	J	C	F	T
V	B	N	L	T	N	R	N	C	H	E	E	T	A	H	H

CLUE:
"FELINE" MEANS CAT!

THESE ANIMALS ARE RACING TO THE CITY OF MELBOURNE, IN AUSTRALIA. IF THE KANGAROO'S LEAPS ARE 10 FEET LONG, THE DOG'S 4 FEET LONG, THE RABBIT'S 6 FEET LONG, THE FROG'S 5 FEET, AND THE GRASSHOPPER'S 2, HOW MANY WILL IT TAKE EACH ONE TO ARRIVE?

ONLY ONE OF THEM IS ORIGINALLY FROM AUSTRALIA. CAN YOU GUESS WHICH ONE?

COUNT THE SNOWFLAKES!

IF SNOWMAN IS 5 FEET TALL, AND IT'S SNOWING 7 INCHES PER HOUR, HOW LONG WILL IT TAKE FOR IT TO COMPLETELY COVER HIM UP?

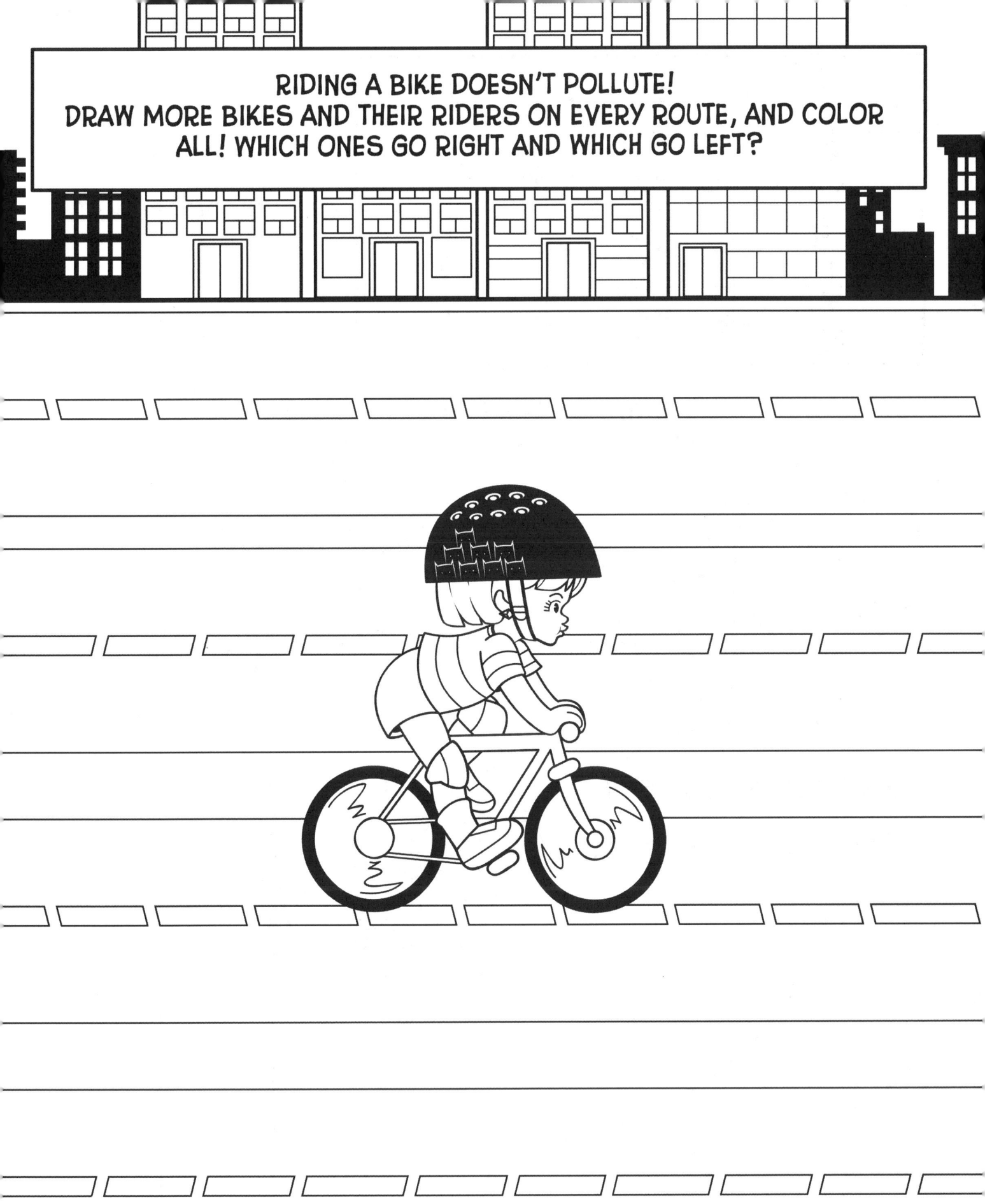
RIDING A BIKE DOESN'T POLLUTE!
DRAW MORE BIKES AND THEIR RIDERS ON EVERY ROUTE, AND COLOR ALL! WHICH ONES GO RIGHT AND WHICH GO LEFT?

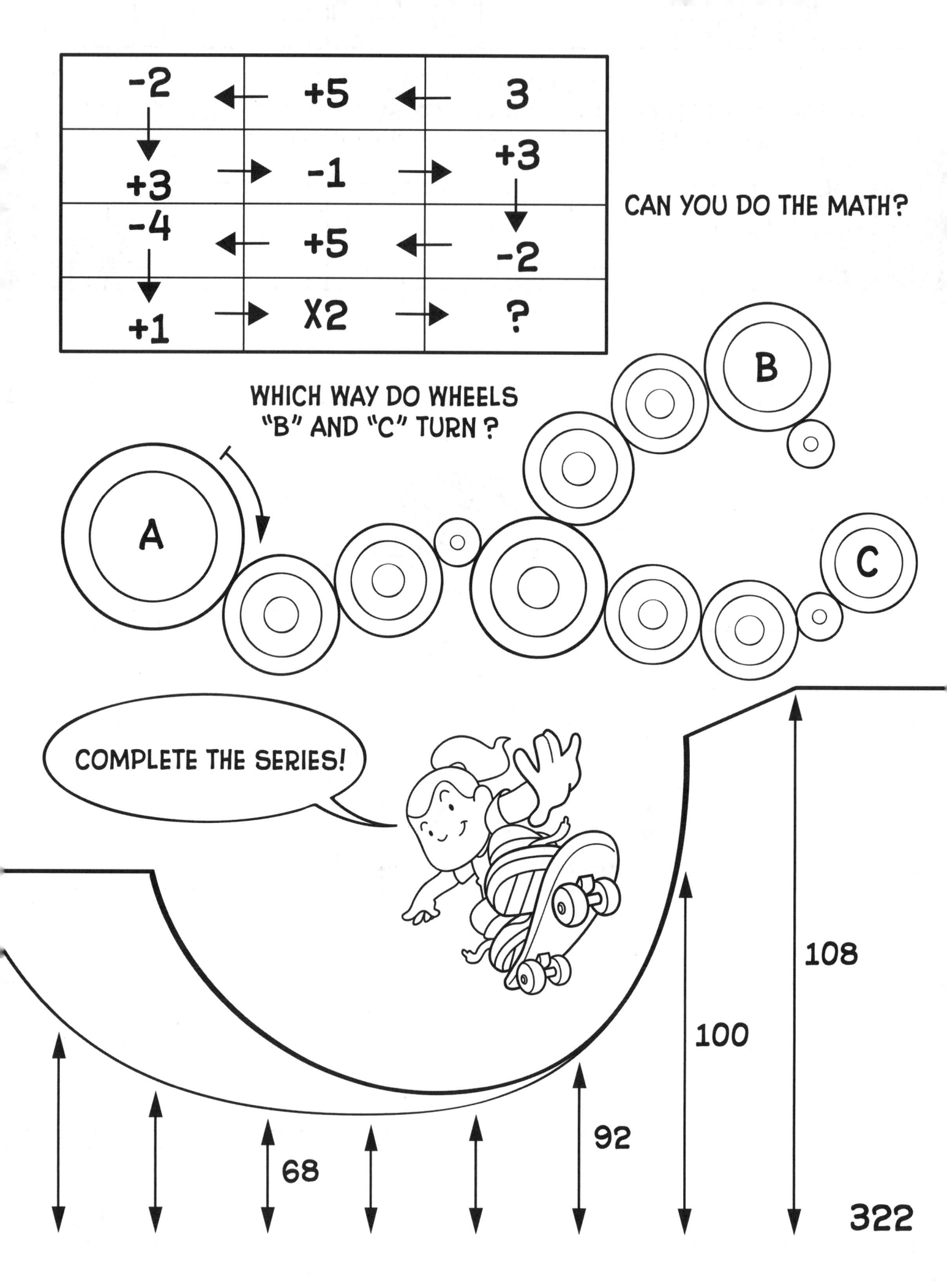
-2
+5
3
+3
-1
+3
-4
+5
-2
+1
X2
?
CAN YOU DO THE MATH?
WHICH WAY DO WHEELS "B" AND "C" TURN ?
A
B
C
COMPLETE THE SERIES!
68
92
100
108
322

CONNECT EACH NUMBERED CIRCLE WITH ONLY VERTICAL OR HORIZONTAL, NON OVERLAPPING LINES. THE NUMBER ON EACH CIRCLE INDICATES THE NUMBER OF LINES EACH ONE IS ALLOWED.

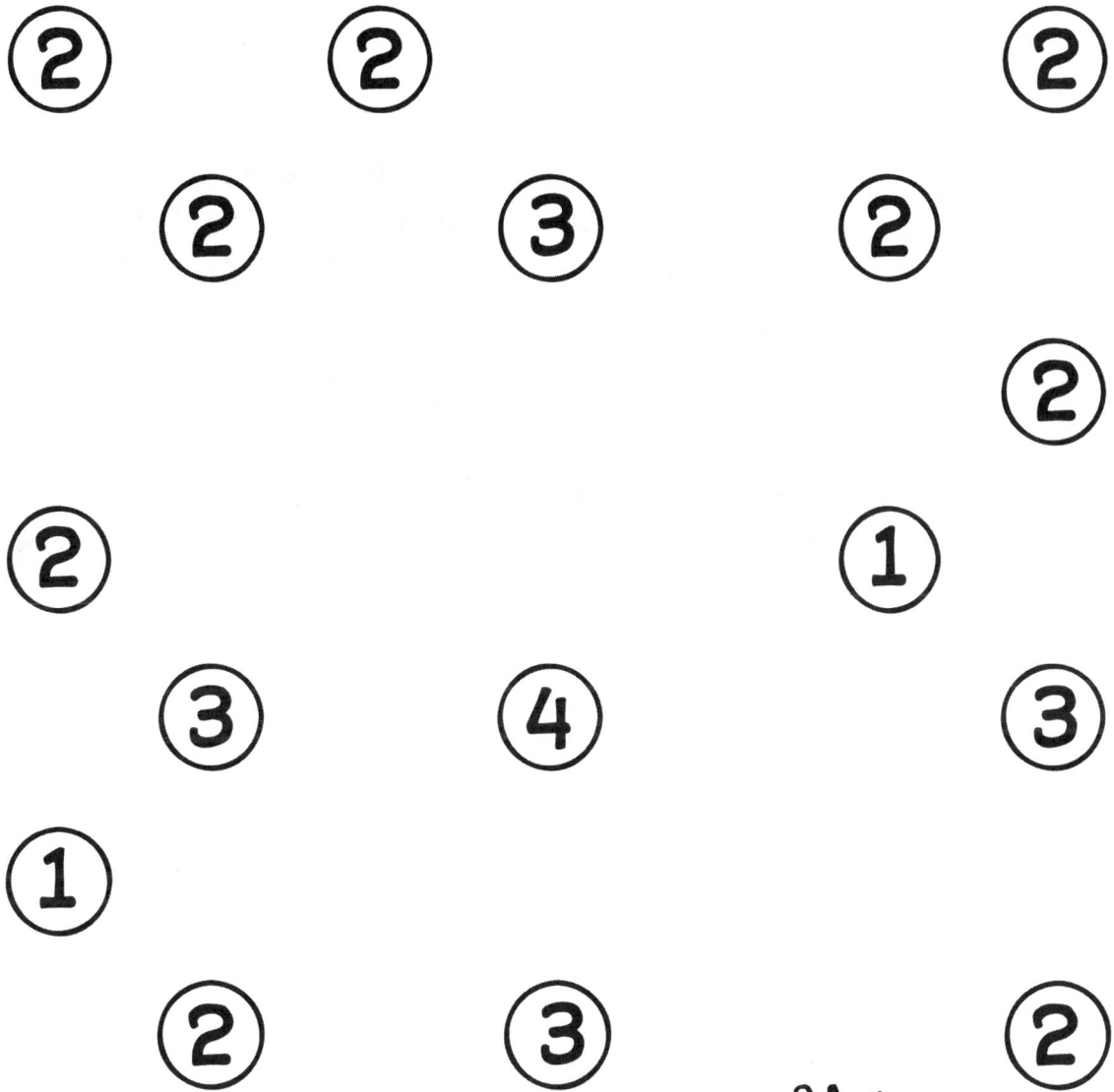

WHAT EUROPEAN COUNTRY IS THIS?

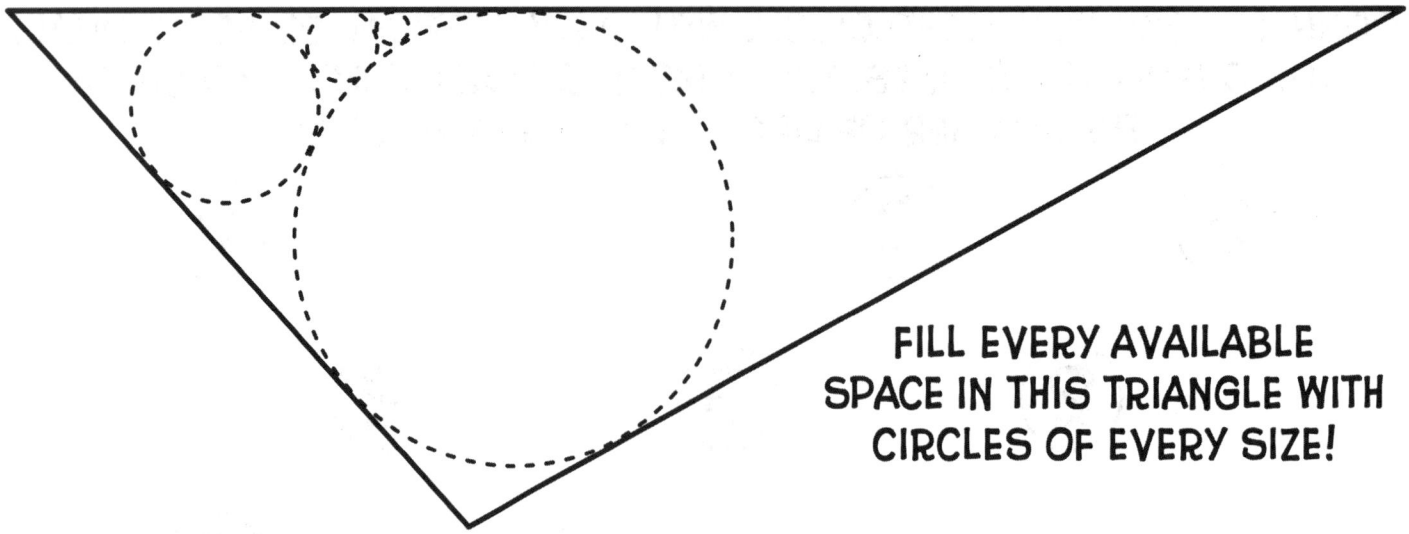

FILL EVERY AVAILABLE SPACE IN THIS TRIANGLE WITH CIRCLES OF EVERY SIZE!

CONNECT THE IDENTICAL DRAWINGS USING ONLY VERTICAL AND HORIZONTAL LINES. LINES CANNOT CROSS EACH OTHER, AND ONLY ONE LINE IS ALLOWED TO GO THROUGH EACH TILE.

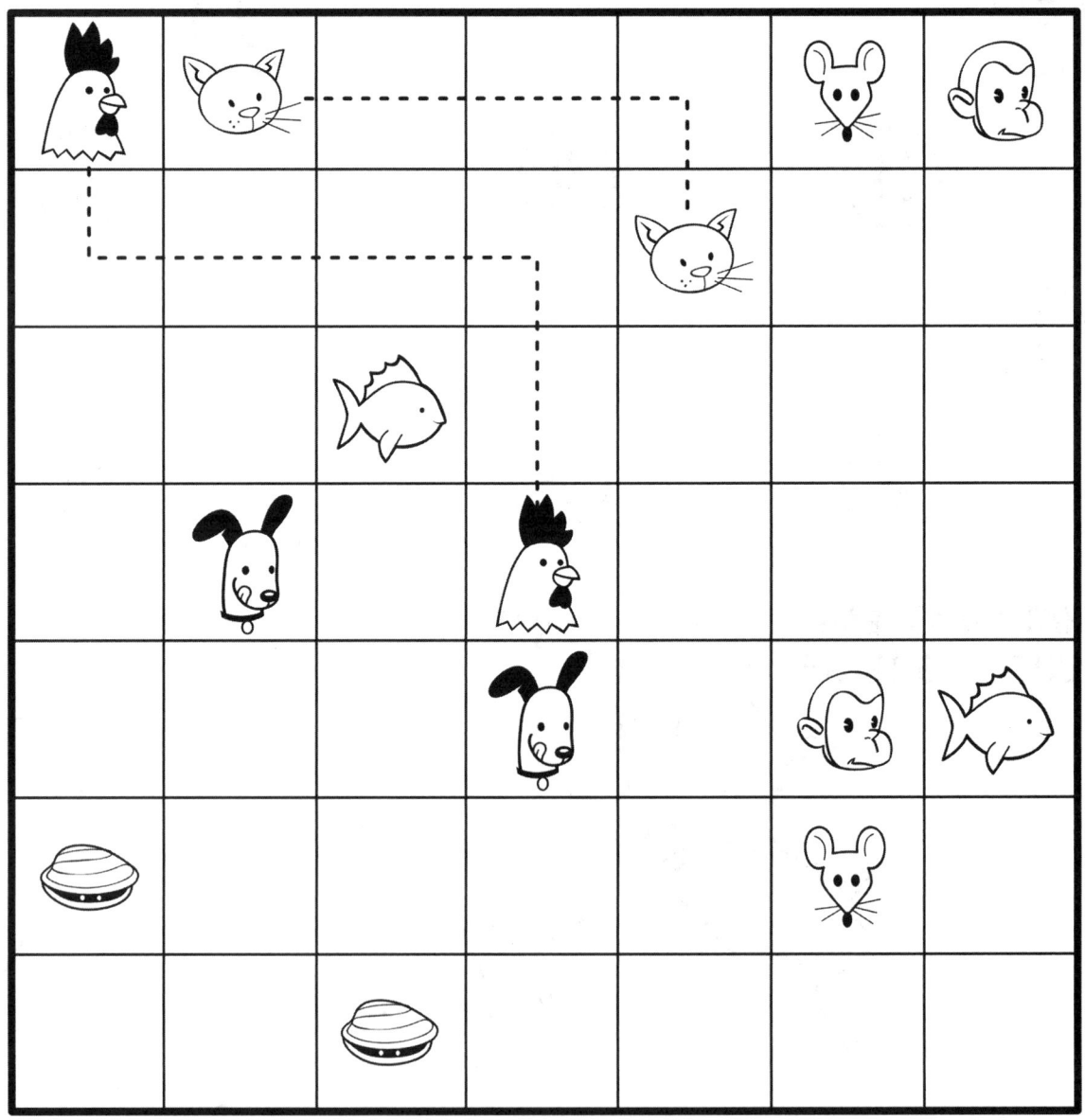

COMPLETE THIS TABLE WITH + AND − SIGNS.

3	5	2	5	6	9	= 30
8	3	6	5	2	1	= 3
4	5	9	6	8	7	= 25
6	3	5	9	8	2	= 7

FILL EACH EMPTY CIRCLE SO THE SUM OF EACH LINE IS ALWAYS 10.

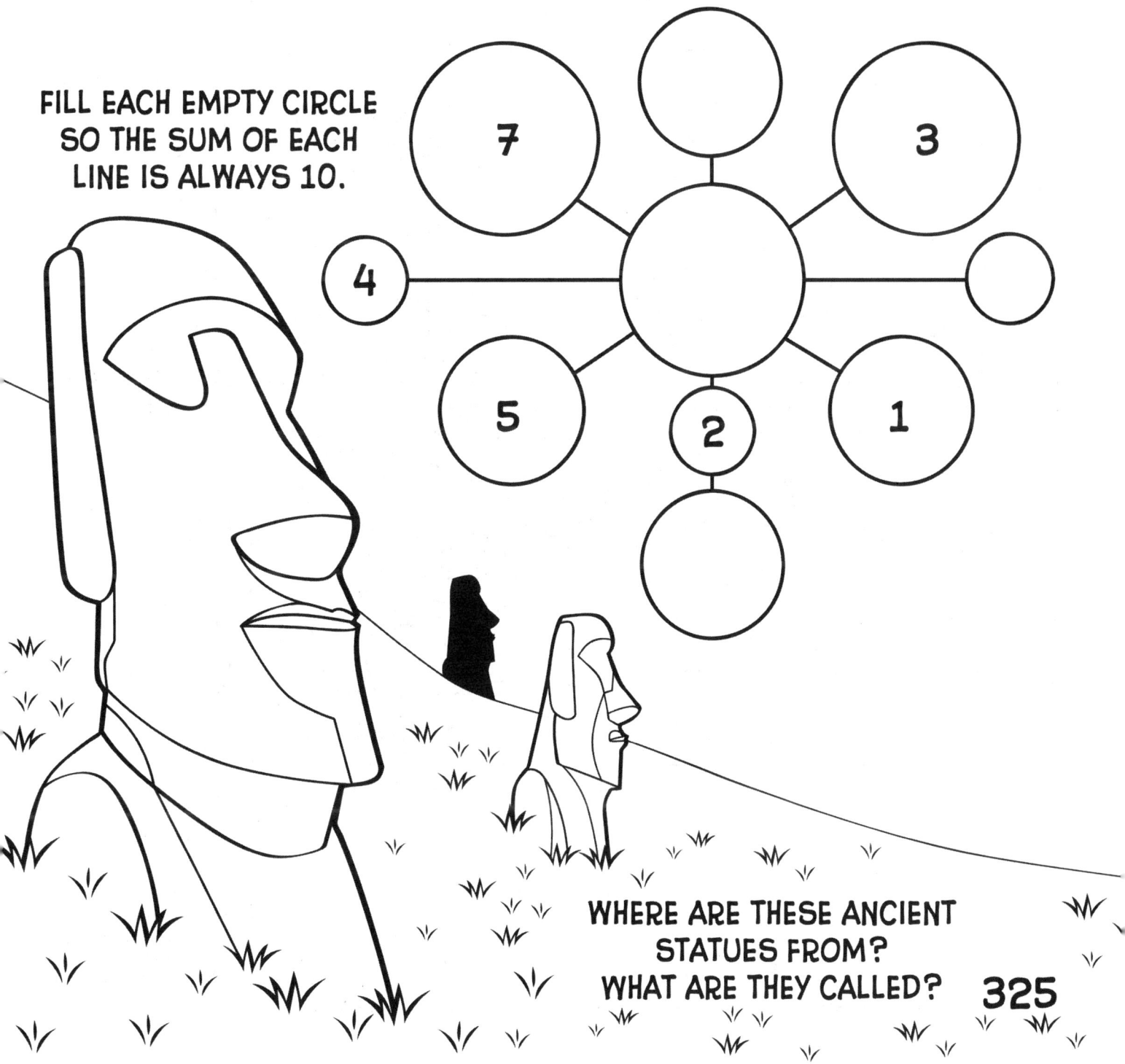

WHERE ARE THESE ANCIENT STATUES FROM? WHAT ARE THEY CALLED?

SOLVE.

8-3	+ 3	-	X 2	- 6	X	+ 12	/ 2	X 5	=

TO FIGURE OUT WHAT THE MYSTERY PICTURE IS,
FILL EACH NUMBERED AREA AS INSTRUCTED.

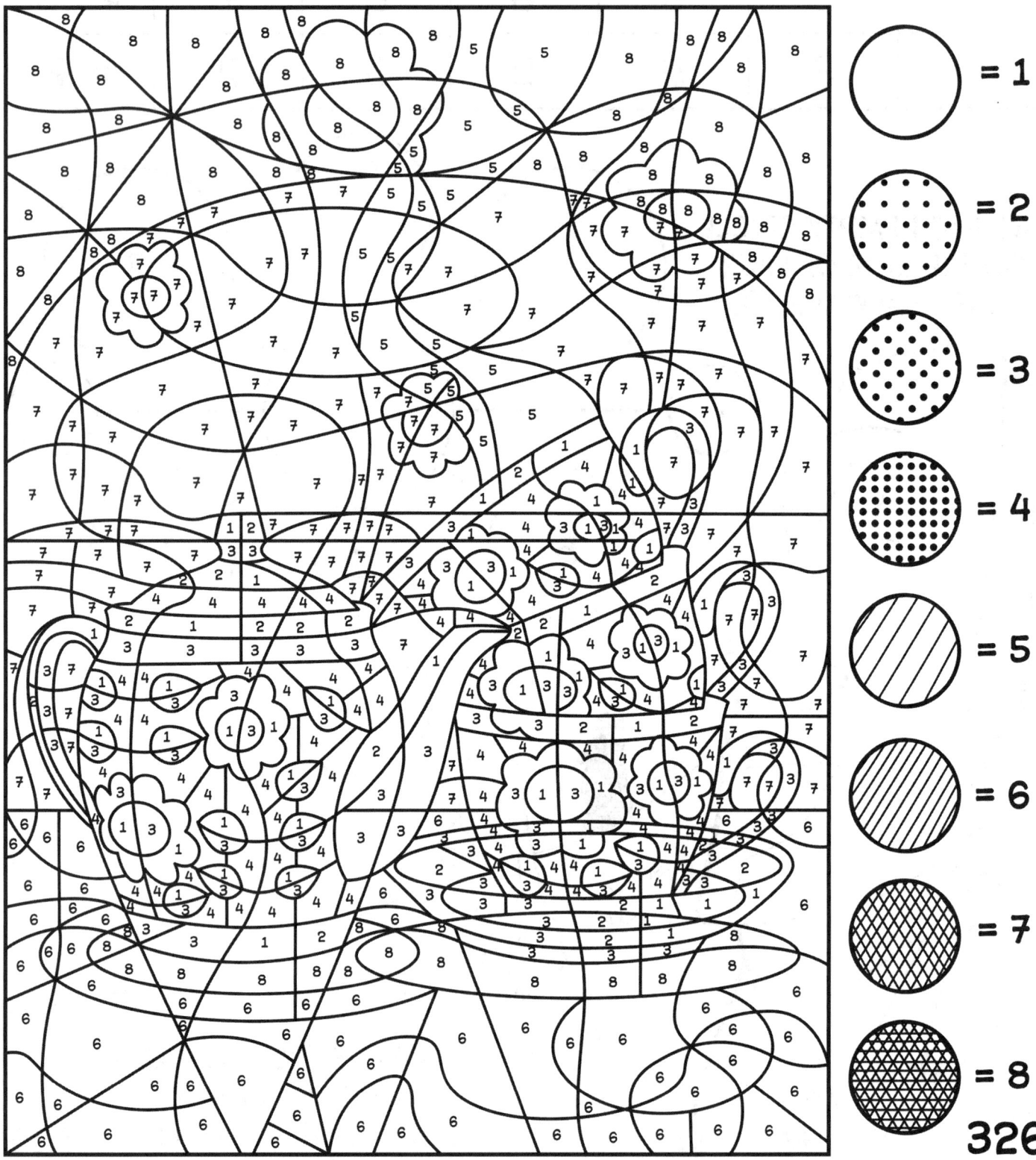

OLLIE IS A VEGETARIAN: DRAW A CIRCLE AROUND THE FOODS HE CAN EAT, AND COLOR IT.

WHAT IS THE NAME OF THIS ANIMAL?
IS IT A FISH?
WHERE DOES IT LIVE?
WHAT DOES IT EAT?

DRAW ANOTHER TYPE OF WHALE YOU LIKE!

CONTINUE THE PROGRESSION OF SYMBOLS FROM LEFT TO RIGHT, BUT AVOID THIS SIGN →

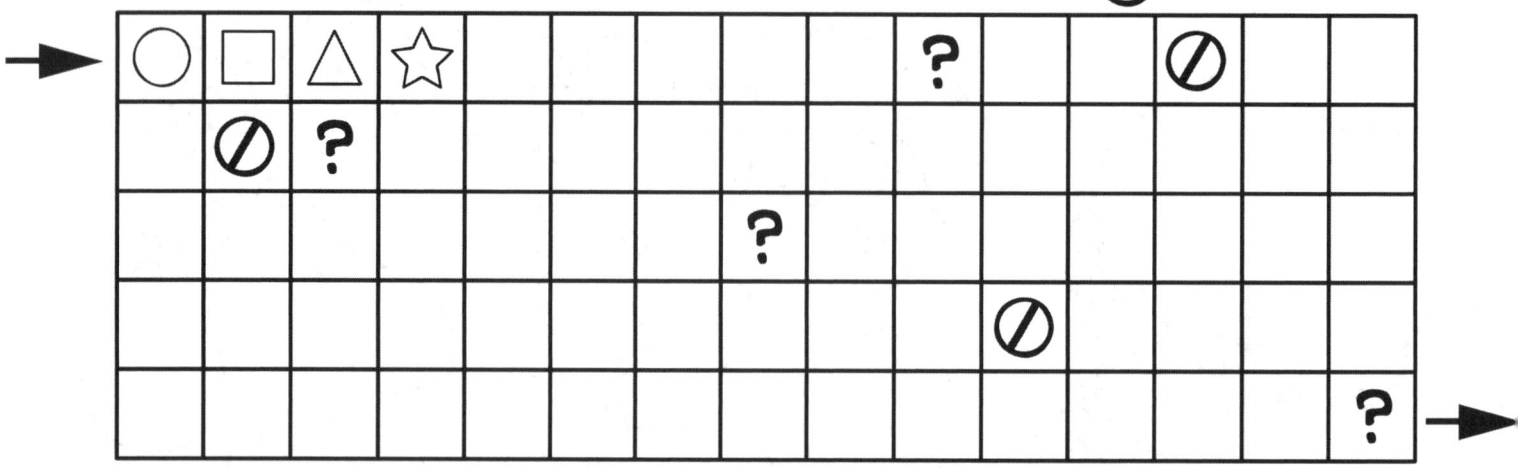

CAN YOU FIND ALL 14 MARINE MAMMALS IN THIS WORDSEARCH?

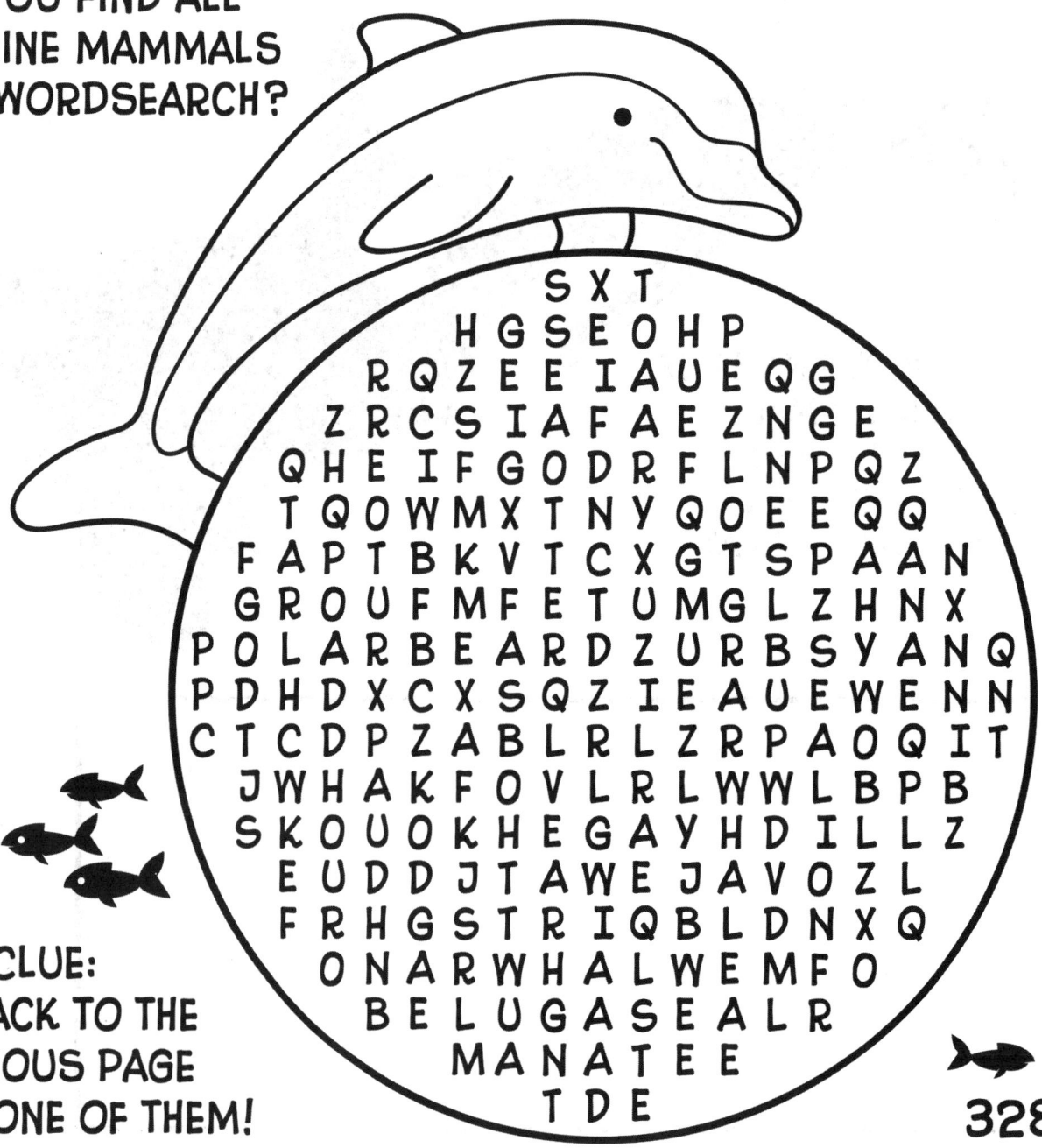

```
        S X T
      H G S E O H P
    R Q Z E E I A U E Q G
  Z R C S I A F A E Z N G E
Q H E I F G O D R F L N P Q Z
T Q O W M X T N Y Q O E E Q Q
F A P T B K V T C X G T S P A A N
G R O U F M F E T U M G L Z H N X
P O L A R B E A R D Z U R B S Y A N Q
P D H D X C X S Q Z I E A U E W E N N
C T C D P Z A B L R L Z R P A O Q I T
J W H A K F O V L R L W W L B P B
S K O U O K H E G A Y H D I L L Z
E U D D J T A W E J A V O Z L
F R H G S T R I Q B L D N X Q
O N A R W H A L W E M F O
B E L U G A S E A L R
M A N A T E E
T D E
```

CLUE:
GO BACK TO THE PREVIOUS PAGE TO FIND ONE OF THEM!

EARTH HAS ONE MOON, MARS HAS TWO.
DO YOU KNOW THEIR NAMES?

P_____ AND D_____.

WHICH ONE OF THESE INSECTS LIVES HERE?

8			3
9	6		
		14	
11		15	16

FILL THE MISSING NUMBERS FROM 1 TO 16, IN ORDER TO KEEP MOVING FROM LEFT TO RIGHT, UP OR DOWN, PANEL BY PANEL, WITHOUT REPEATING ANY NUMBERS, NOR SKIPPING ANY PANELS.

HELP MR. MOLE REACH THE SURFACE!

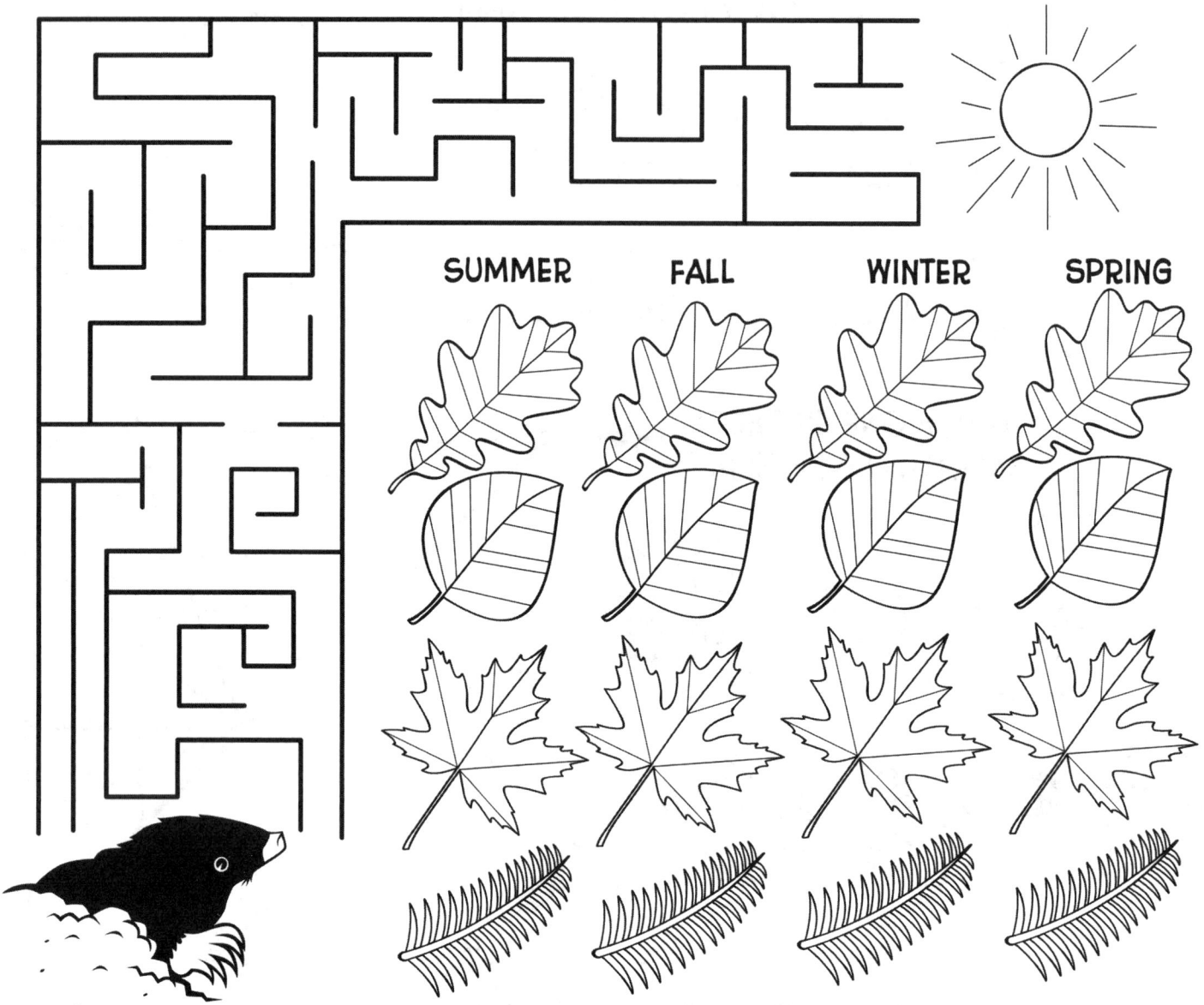

WHAT IS LIGHTNING MADE OF?

COLOR EACH OF THE LEAVES ACORDING TO THE SEASONS LISTED ABOVE THEM.

RIDDLE:

"RUNS OVER FIELDS AND WOODS ALL DAY. UNDER THE BED AT NIGHT, IT SITS NOT ALONE, WITH A LONG TONGUE HANGING OUT, WAITING FOR A BONE."

DESIGN BOTH SIDES OF YOUR OWN COIN!

REMEMBER: ONE SIDE MUST FEATURE YOUR PORTRAIT, AND THE OTHER, THE VALUE OF THE COIN.

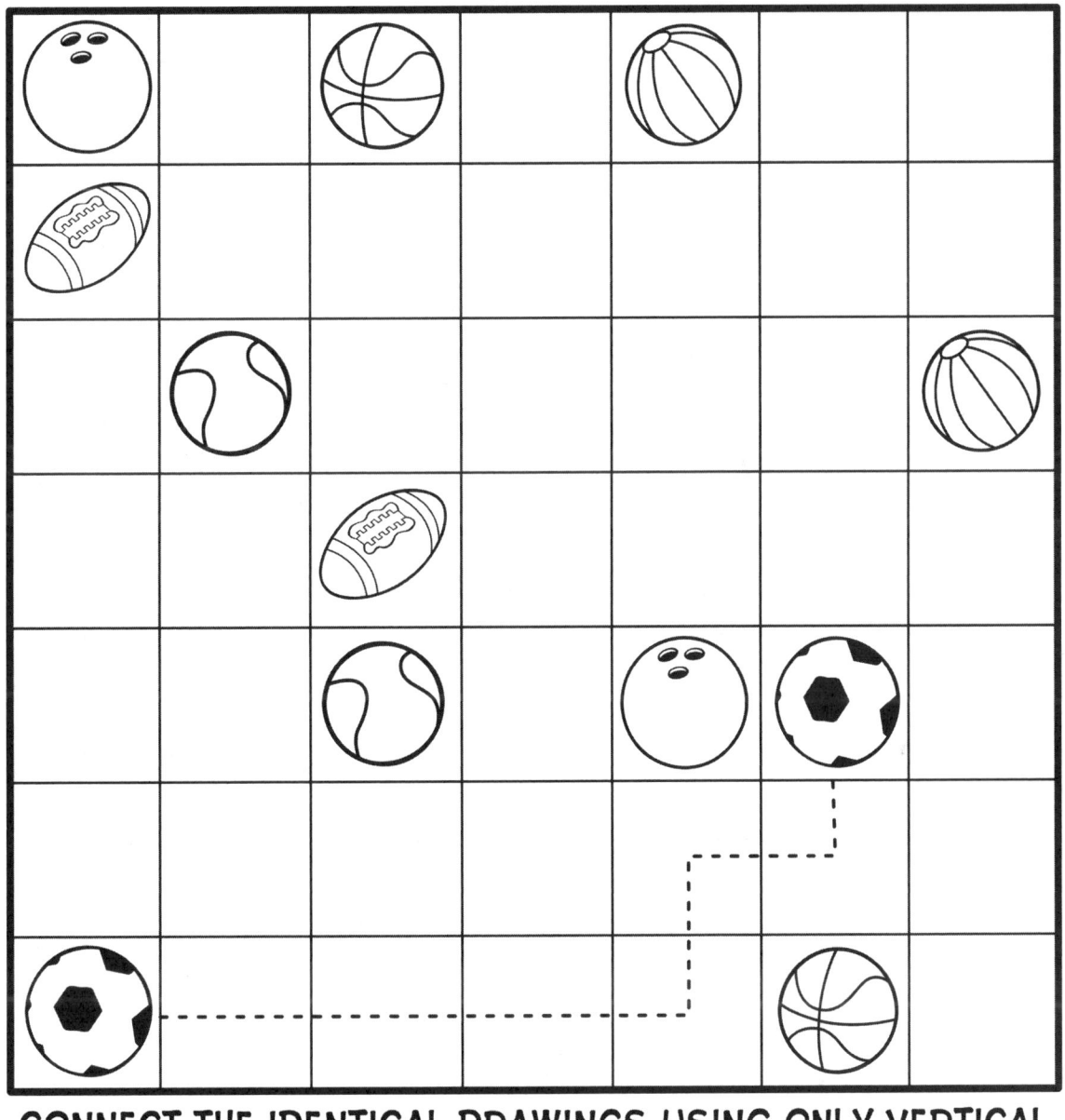

CONNECT THE IDENTICAL DRAWINGS USING ONLY VERTICAL AND HORIZONTAL LINES. LINES CANNOT CROSS EACH OTHER, AND ONLY ONE LINE IS ALLOWED TO GO THROUGH EACH TILE.

FIND THE TWO FRUIT COMBINATIONS THAT ARE ALIKE.

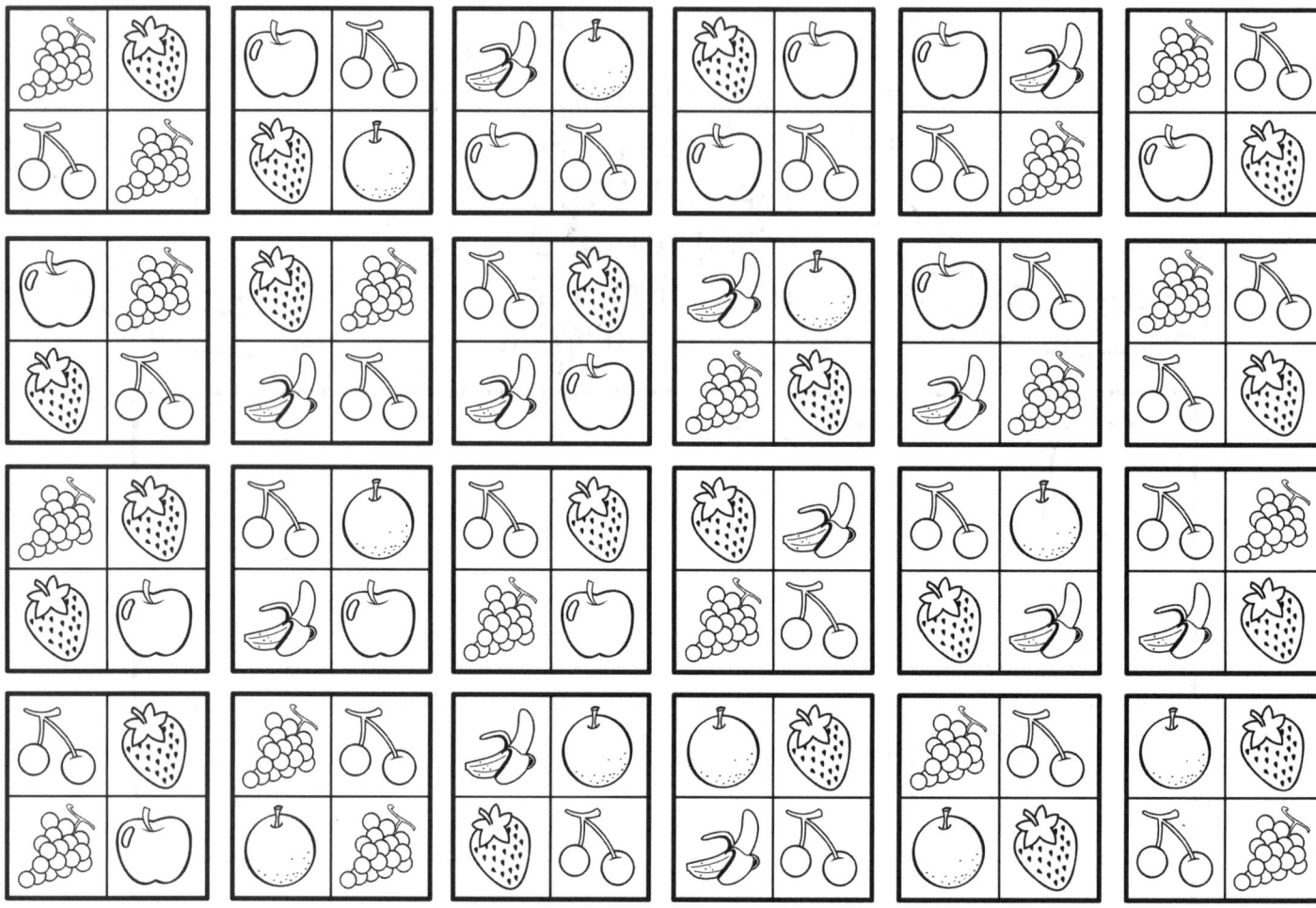

WHICH ONE WEIGHS MORE?

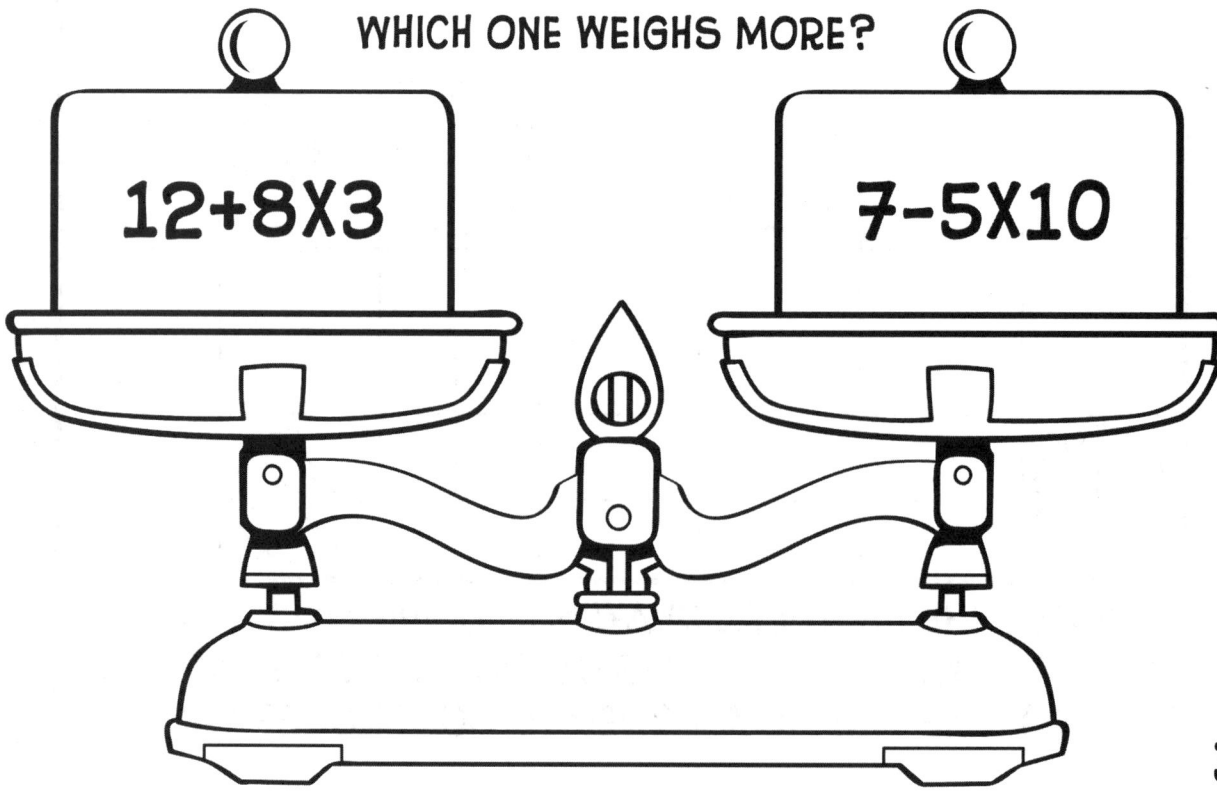

WOULD YOU HELP SALLY DESIGN HER BLANKET? BY DIVIDING A SQUARE DIAGONALLY, AND FILLING ONE HALF BLACK, YOU MAKE A TRIANGLE. IF YOU DO THAT TO OTHER SQUARES YOU CAN CREATE ANY PATTERN YOU CAN IMAGINE!

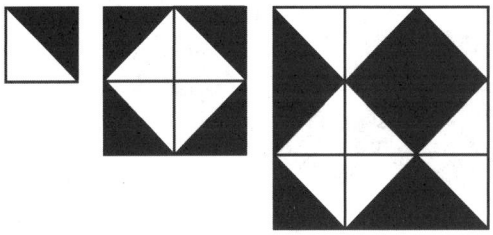

ONE OF THESE DOES NOT BELONG IN THIS GROUP.

CAN YOU THINK OF ANOTHER ANIMAL THAT'S BLACK AND WHITE? DRAW IT HERE! →

WHICH PATH DOES THE RABBIT NEED TO FOLLOW TO PICK ALL THE EGGS?

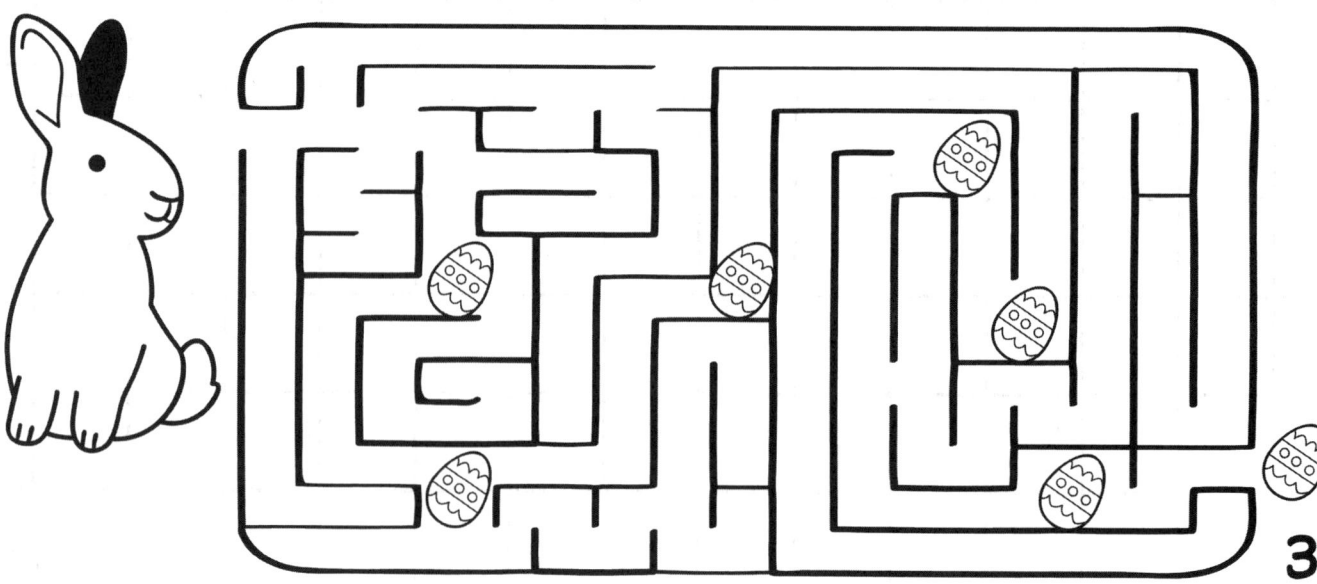

IDENTIFY AND COLOR ONLY THE TRIANGLES!

WHICH OF THE THREE BELLS IS SHE GOING TO RING?

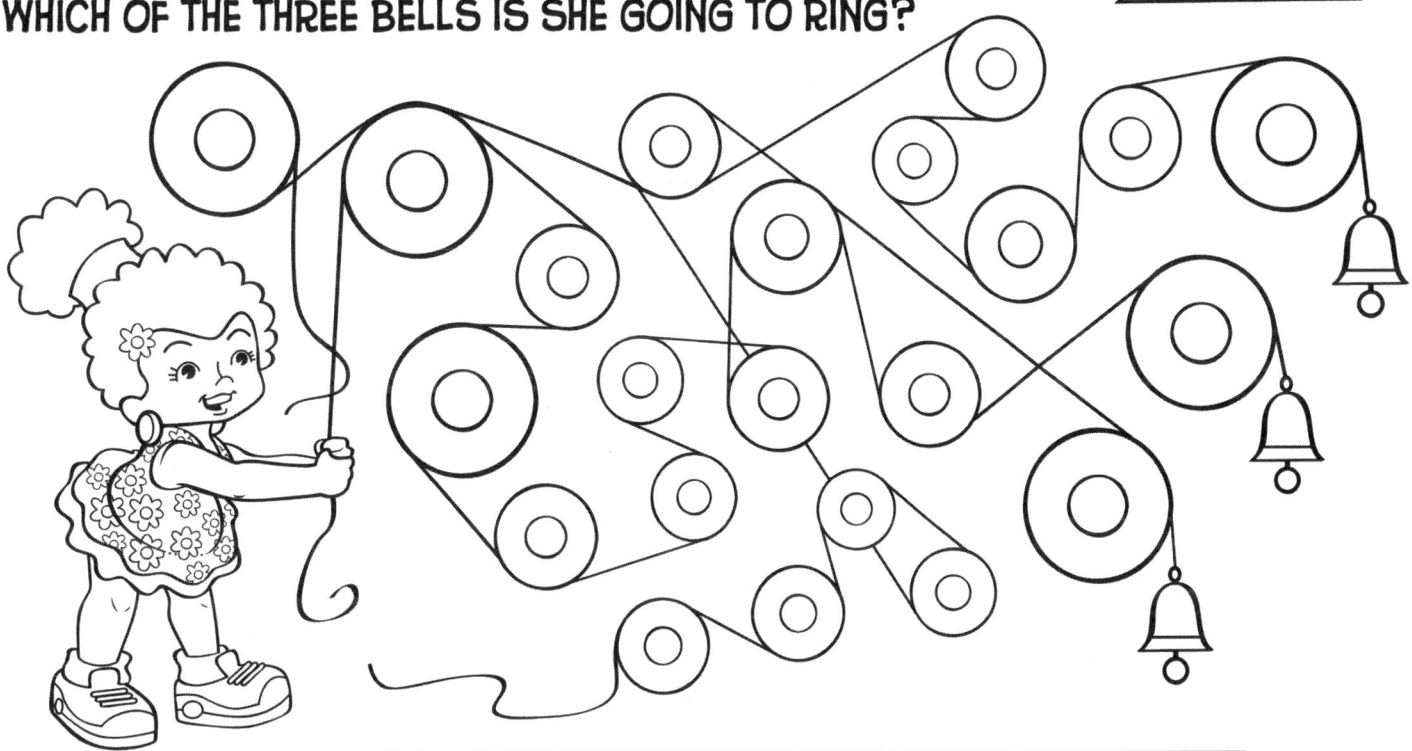

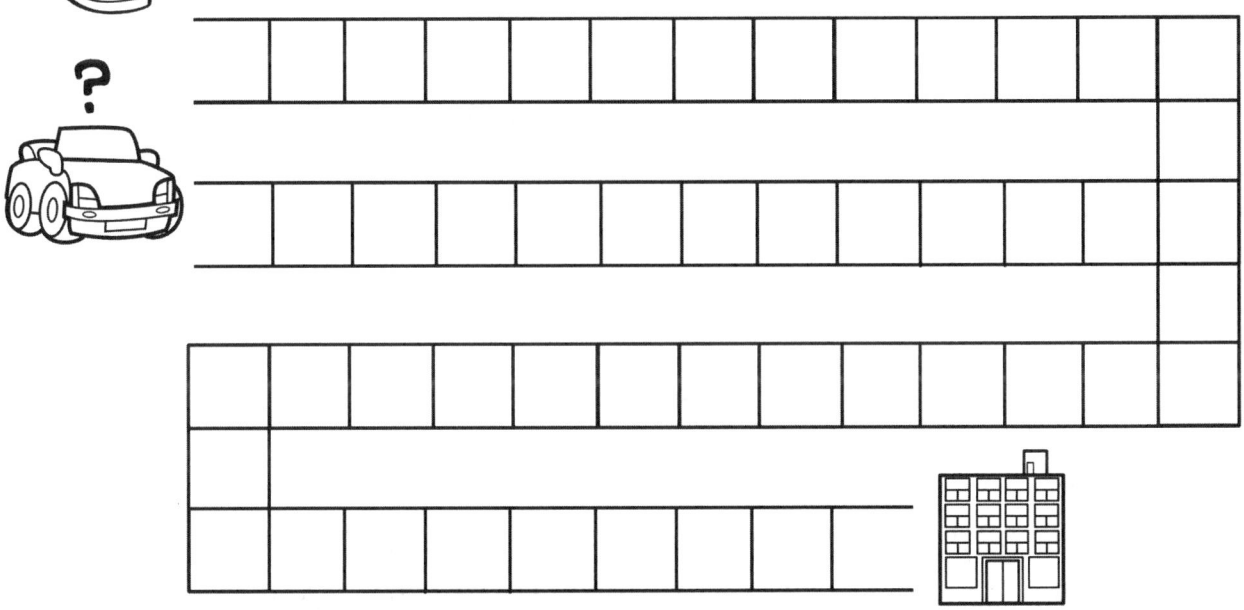

WHICH ROAD IS THE SHORTEST IF EACH TILE IS 10 FEET?

WHO WEARS THESE MODERN HELMETS?

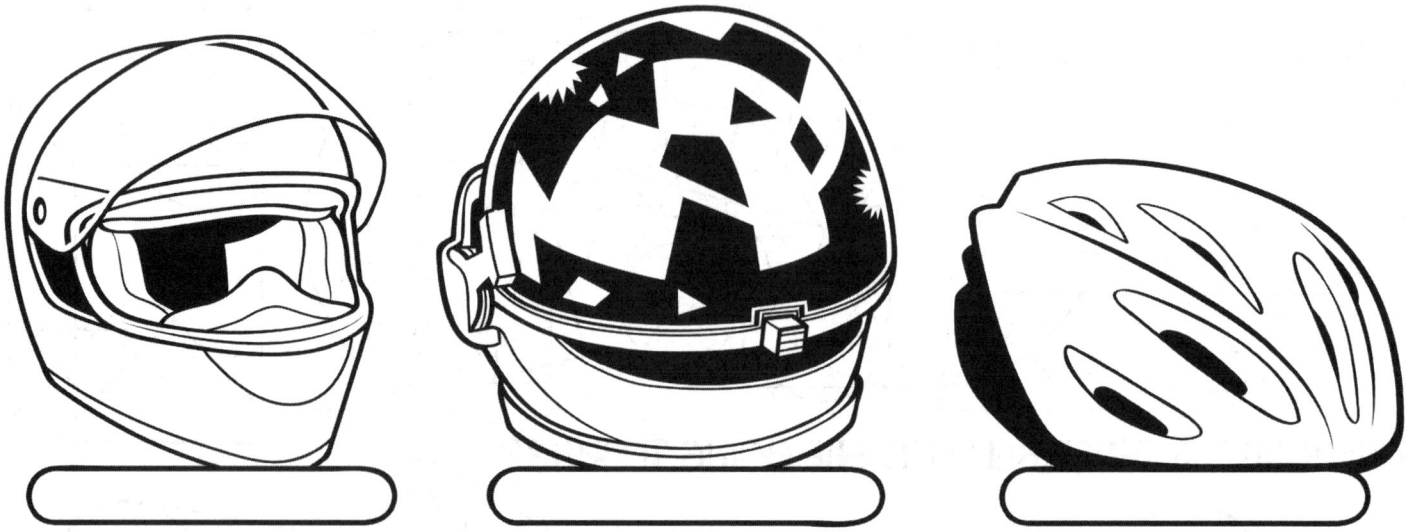

		17		
	25		23	
13		9		21
	11		7	
		3		

FILL THE MISSING NUMBERS FROM 1 TO 25, IN ORDER TO KEEP MOVING FROM LEFT TO RIGHT, UP OR DOWN, PANEL BY PANEL, WITHOUT REPEATING ANY NUMBERS, NOR SKIPPING ANY PANELS.

WHICH ONE OF THESE FOOTPRINTS BELONGS TO THE BOOT ON THE LEFT?

HOW TALL IS THIS BRIDGE, IF ITS LENGTH IS 4 TIMES ITS HEIGHT?

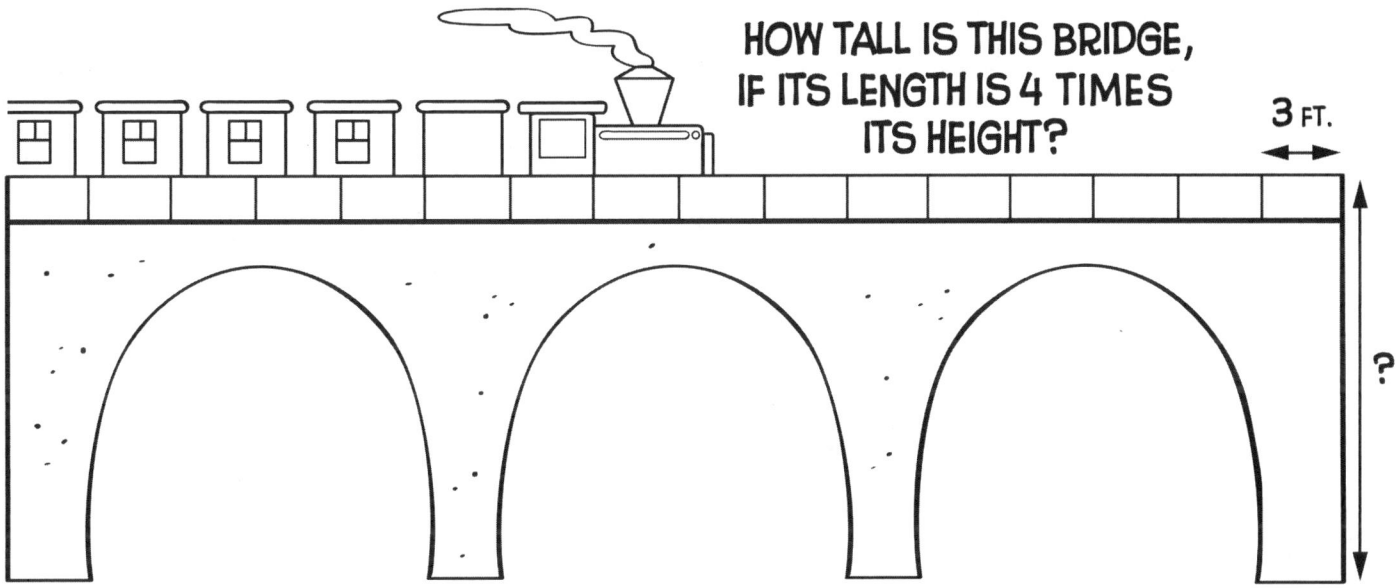

IN ORDER TO BUILD THE MAYAN PYRAMID, MAKE IT SO THE ADDITION OF EACH NUMBER ON THE LEFT TO THE NUMBER ON THE RIGHT EQUALS THE NUMBER OF THE BRICK ON TOP OF BOTH.

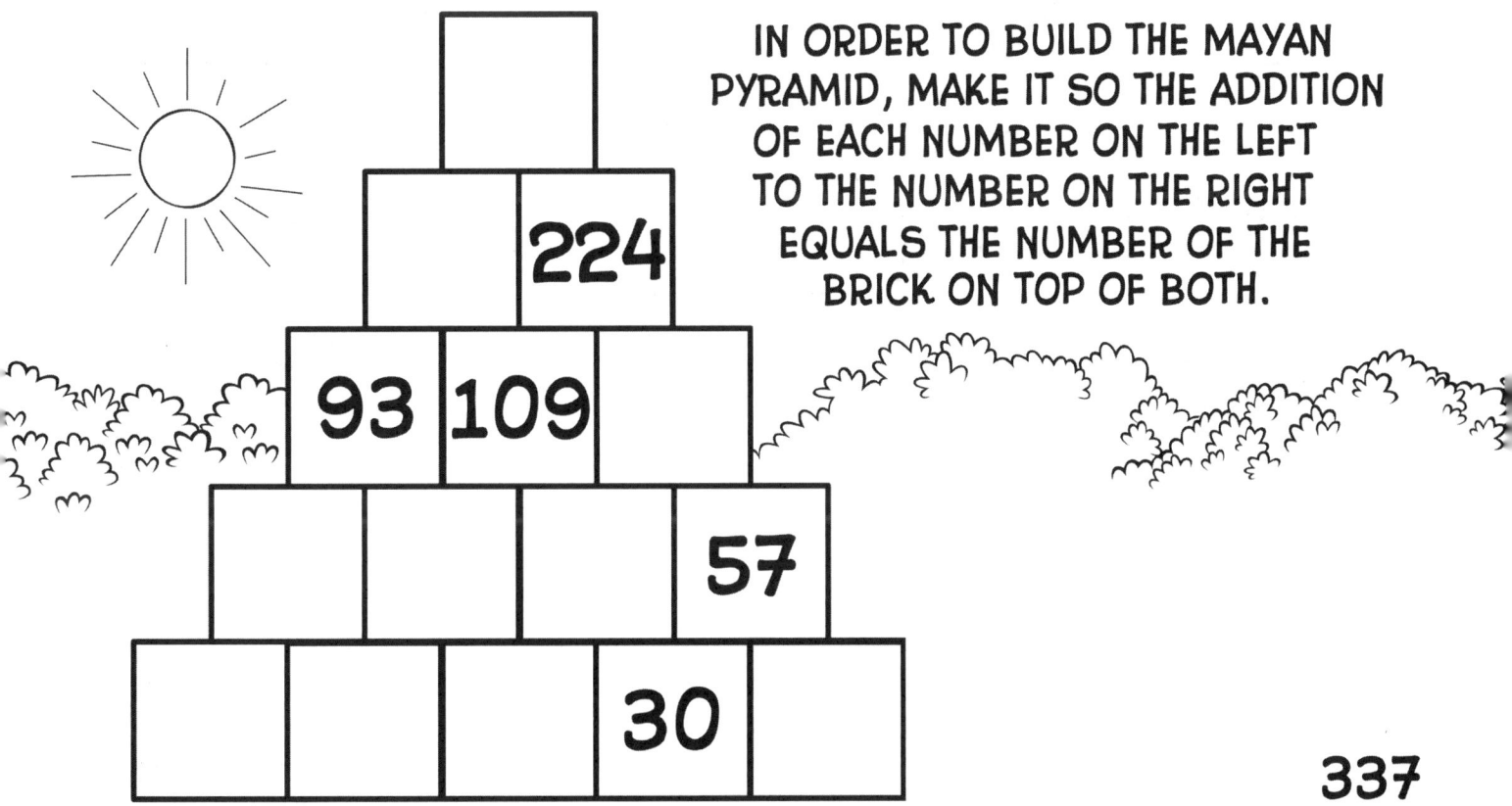

COMPLETE THE LOGICAL LEFT TO RIGHT PROGRESSION PER ROW.

1	2	4		8				16	18				
1	4			13			22						
2	6	10						34					
5			20	25				45		55			
1	3	5				13							

FIND THE OUTLINE MATCHING THIS MUSHROOM.

HOW LONG IS IT TILL...?

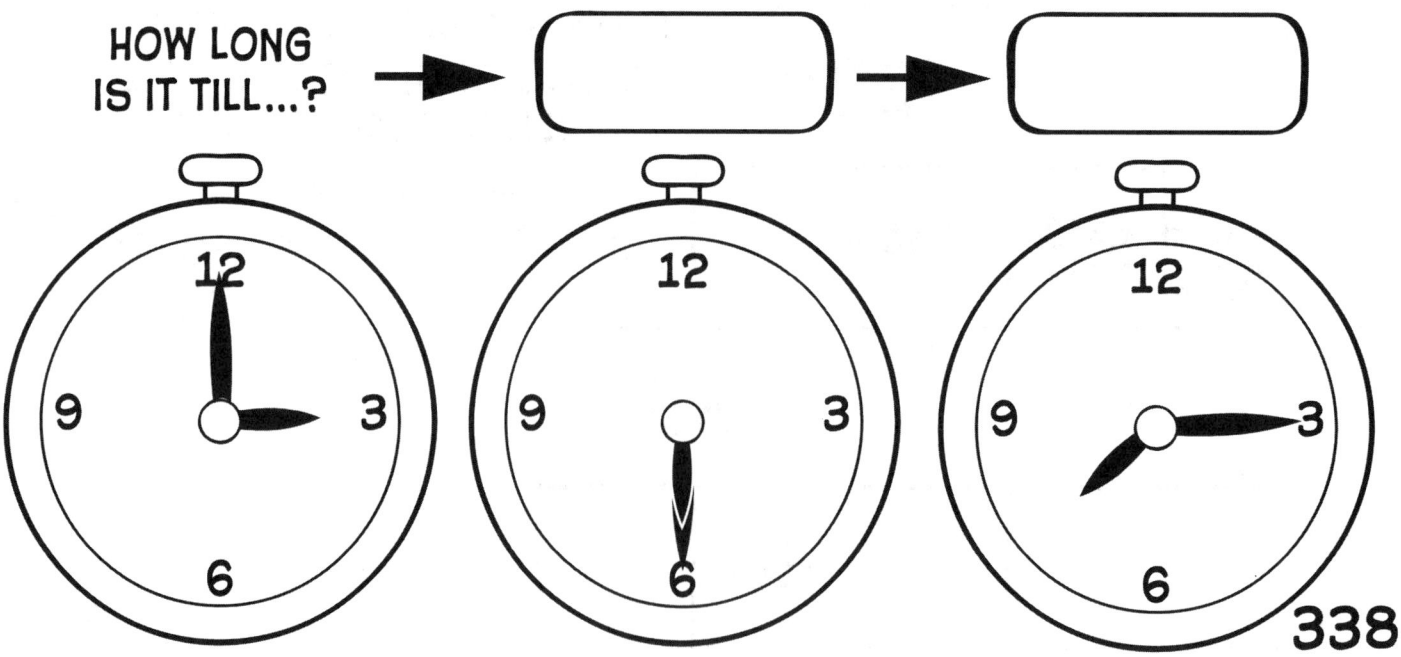

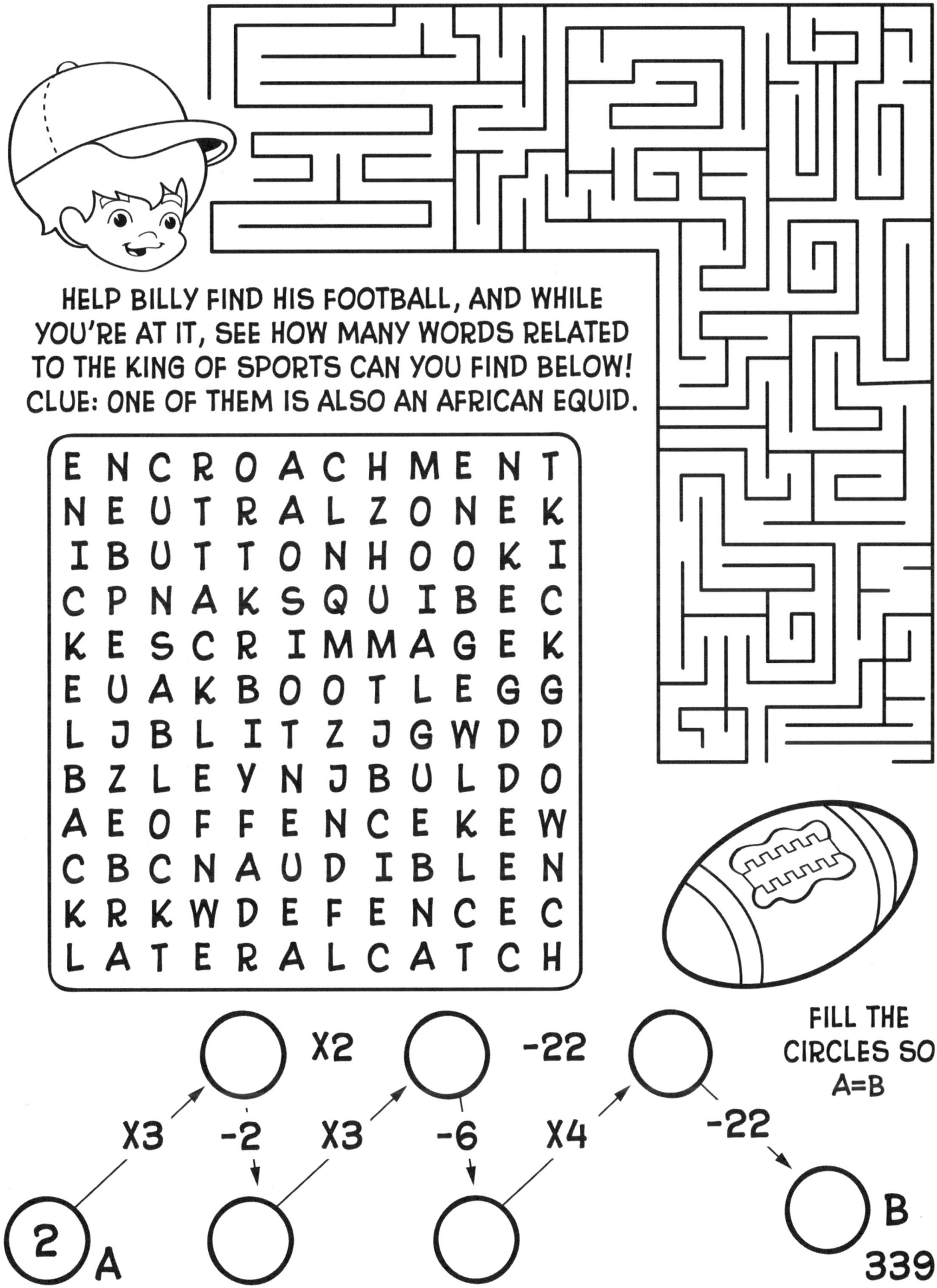
HELP BILLY FIND HIS FOOTBALL, AND WHILE YOU'RE AT IT, SEE HOW MANY WORDS RELATED TO THE KING OF SPORTS CAN YOU FIND BELOW! CLUE: ONE OF THEM IS ALSO AN AFRICAN EQUID.
E N C R O A C H M E N T
N E U T R A L Z O N E K
I B U T T O N H O O K I
C P N A K S Q U I B E C
K E S C R I M M A G E K
E U A K B O O T L E G G
L J B L I T Z J G W D D
B Z L E Y N J B U L D O
A E O F F E N C E K E W
C B C N A U D I B L E N
K R K W D E F E N C E C
L A T E R A L C A T C H
X2
-22
X3
-2
X3
-6
X4
-22
2
A
B
FILL THE CIRCLES SO A=B

WOULD YOU LIKE TO DESIGN AN EVEN MORE COMPLEX BLANKET PATTERN FOR SALLY?

CAN YOU GUESS WHAT THE PHOTOGRAPHER WAS SHOOTING AT?

HOW LONG IS IT TILL...?

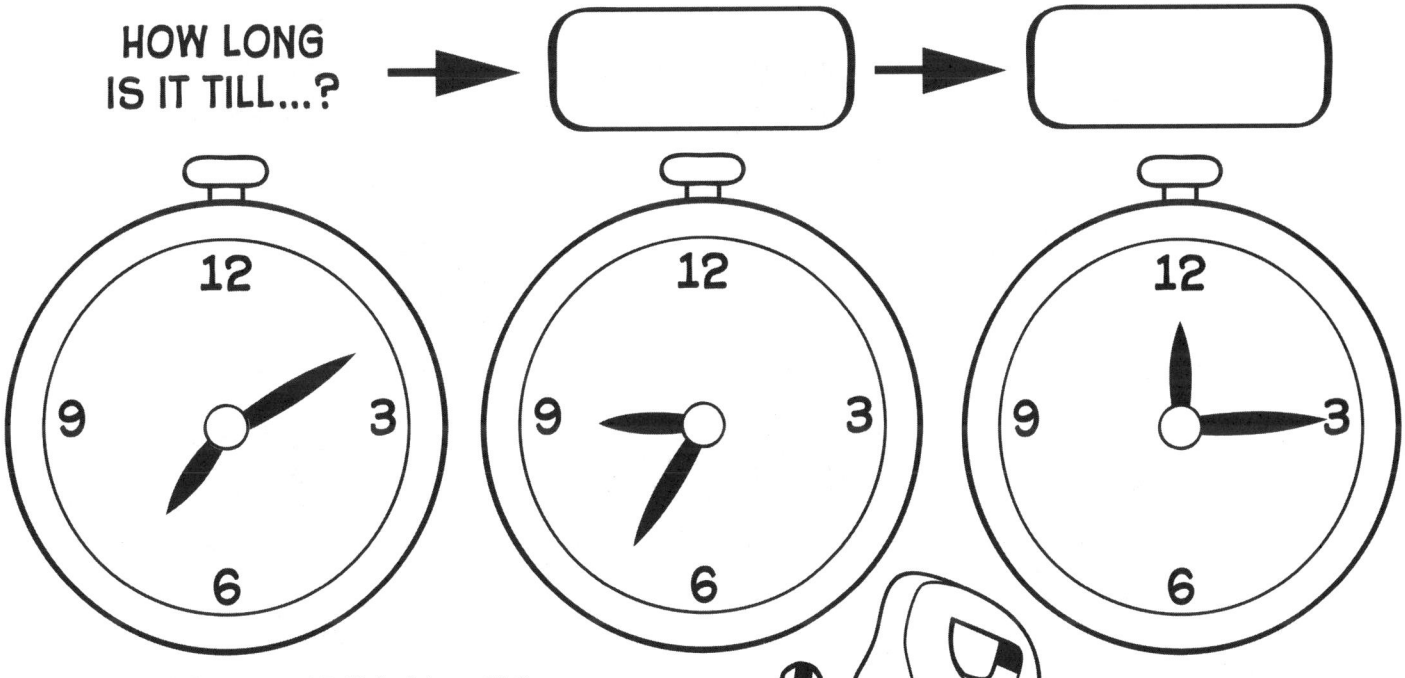

COLOR THE BEST TOOLS TO BUILD THIS BIRDHOUSE.

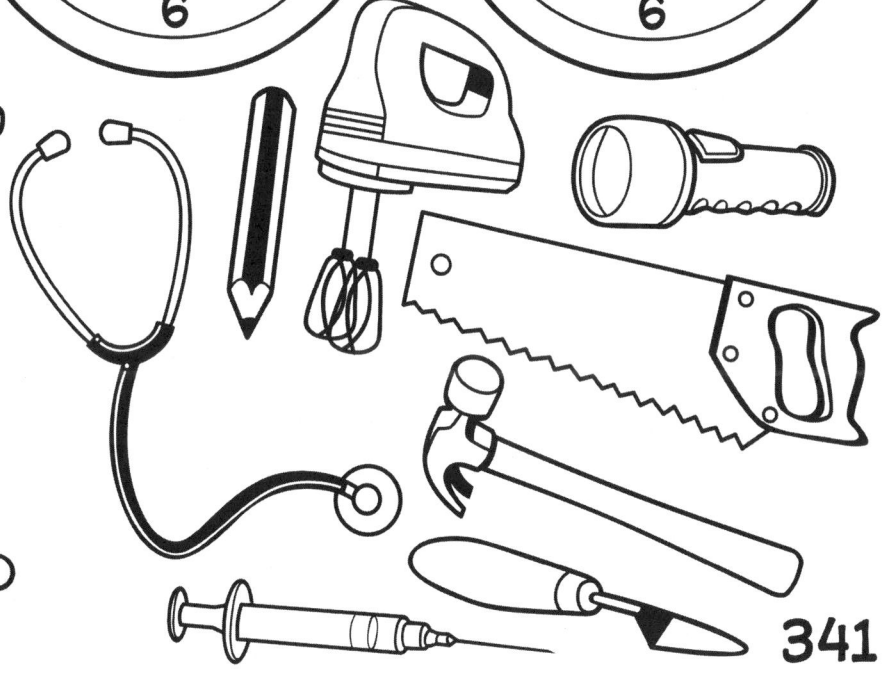

FILL THE MISSING NUMBERS FROM 1 TO 25, IN ORDER TO KEEP MOVING FROM LEFT TO RIGHT, UP OR DOWN, PANEL BY PANEL, WITHOUT REPEATING ANY NUMBERS, NOR SKIPPING ANY PANELS.

8		12	13		15
	10			17	
6		20	19		33
3		21	22		34
	25			30	
1		27	28		36

DRAW THEIR HEADS!

WHAT IS THE NAME OF THIS ANIMAL?

WHERE DOES IT LIVE?

COLOR THE BEST TOOLS TO BAKE THIS CAKE.

WHO USED TO WEAR THESE ANCIENT HELMETS?

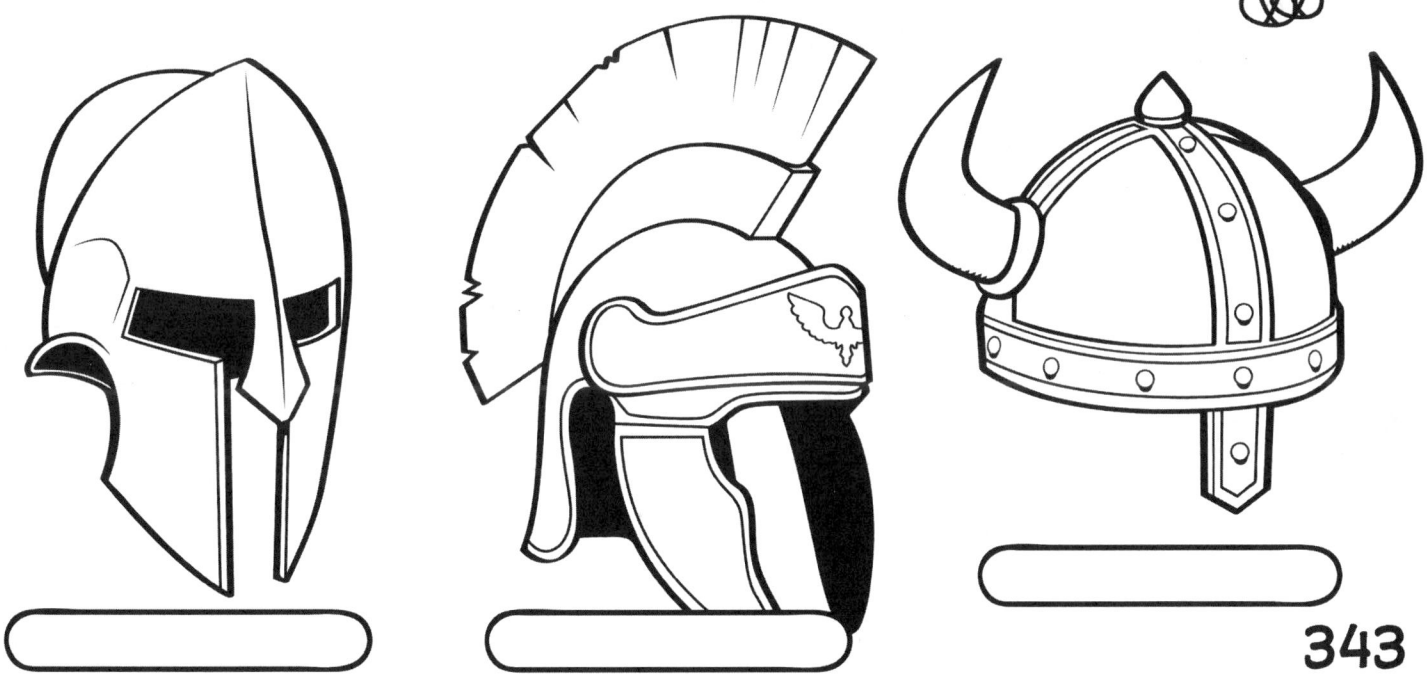

WHICH ONE WEIGHS LESS?

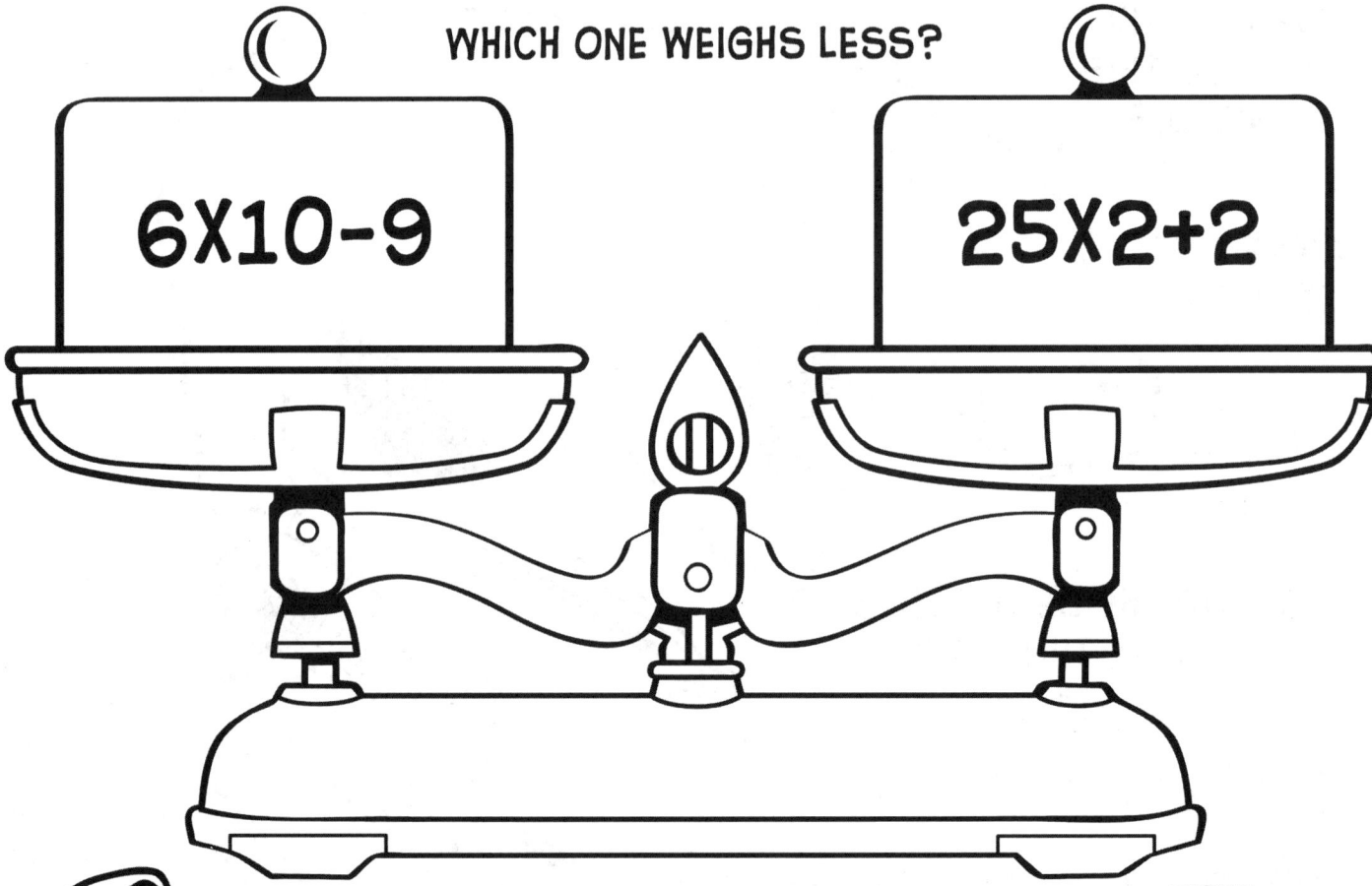

DRAW OR WRITE THE RESULT.

+

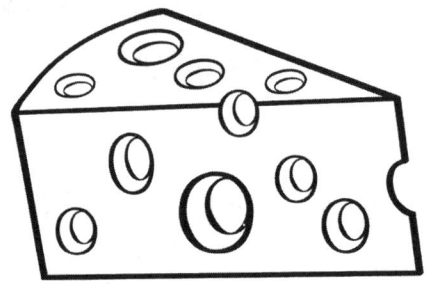

=

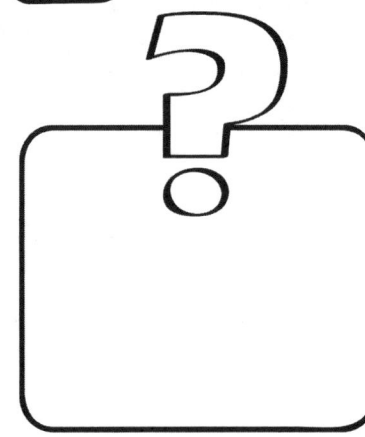

HELP THE BEE GET TO THE HONEY!

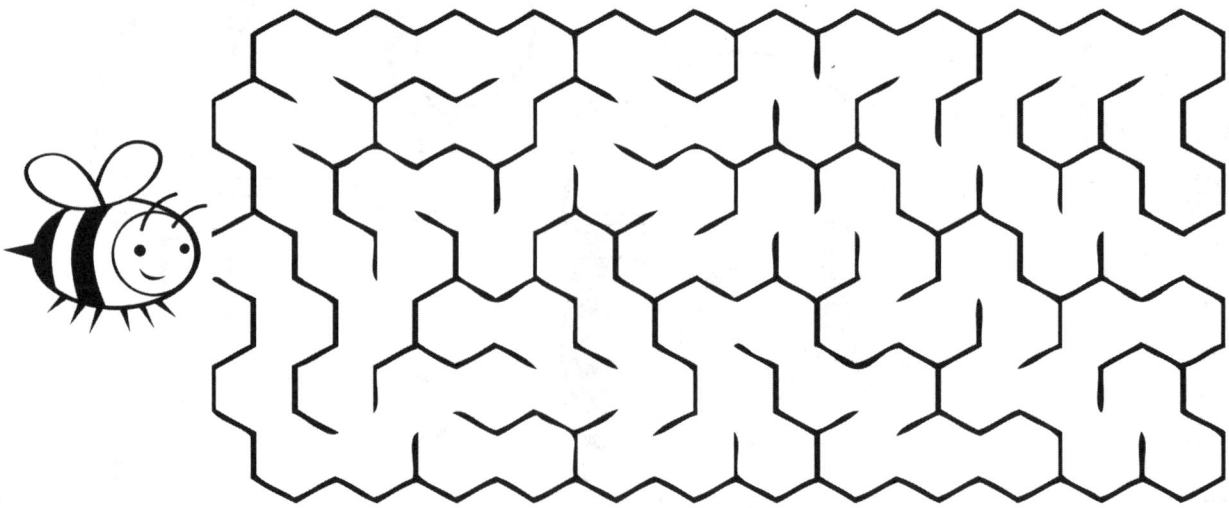

HELP THE LITTLE EXPLORER ESCAPE FROM THE CAVE!

INSIDE EACH CIRCLE, DRAW A FRUIT MATCHING THE INITIALS BELOW.

C B P

WHICH WAY IS THIS WHEEL TURNING?

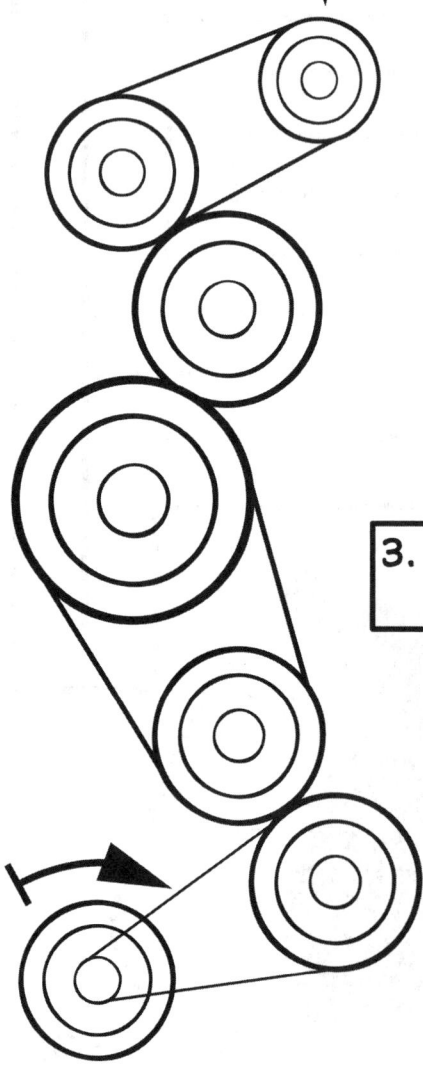

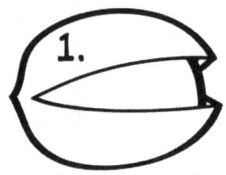

CROSSWORDS.

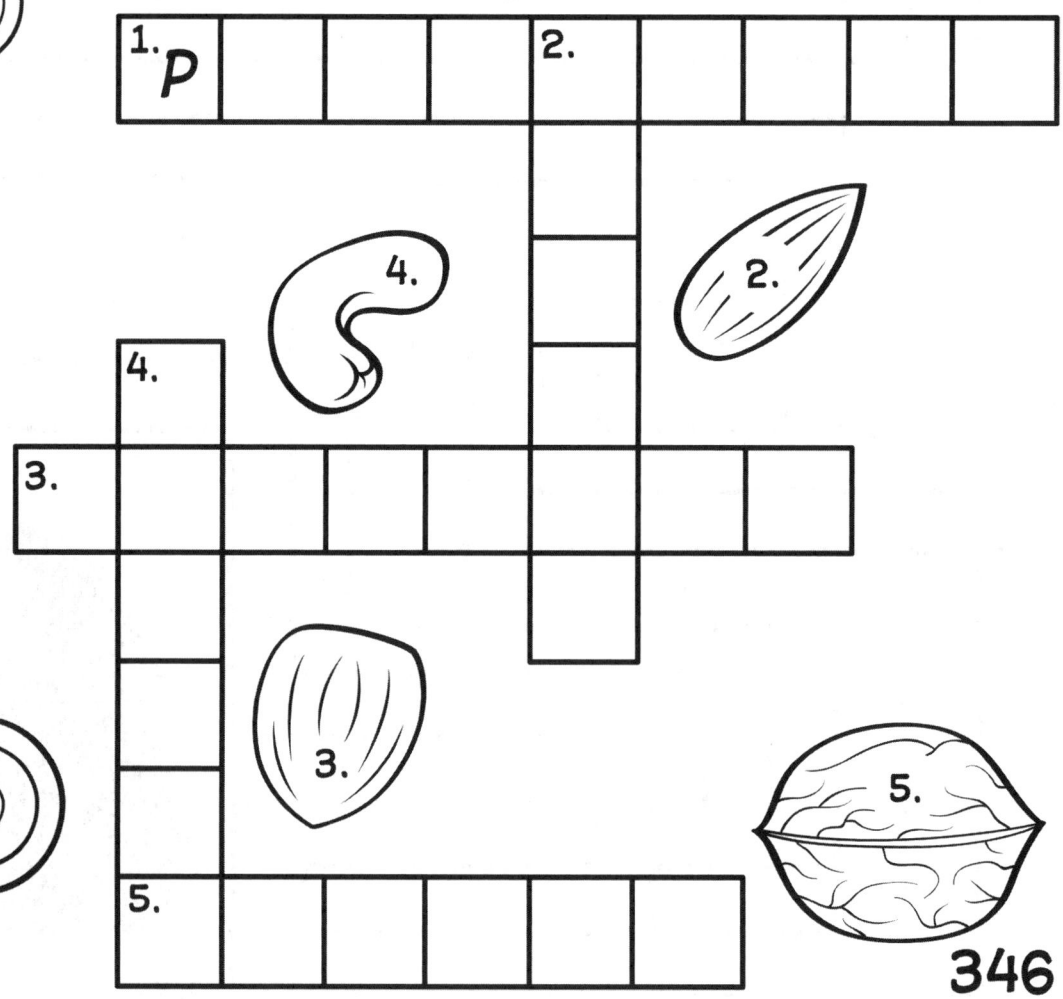

FIND THE TWO FRUIT COMBINATIONS THAT ARE ALIKE.

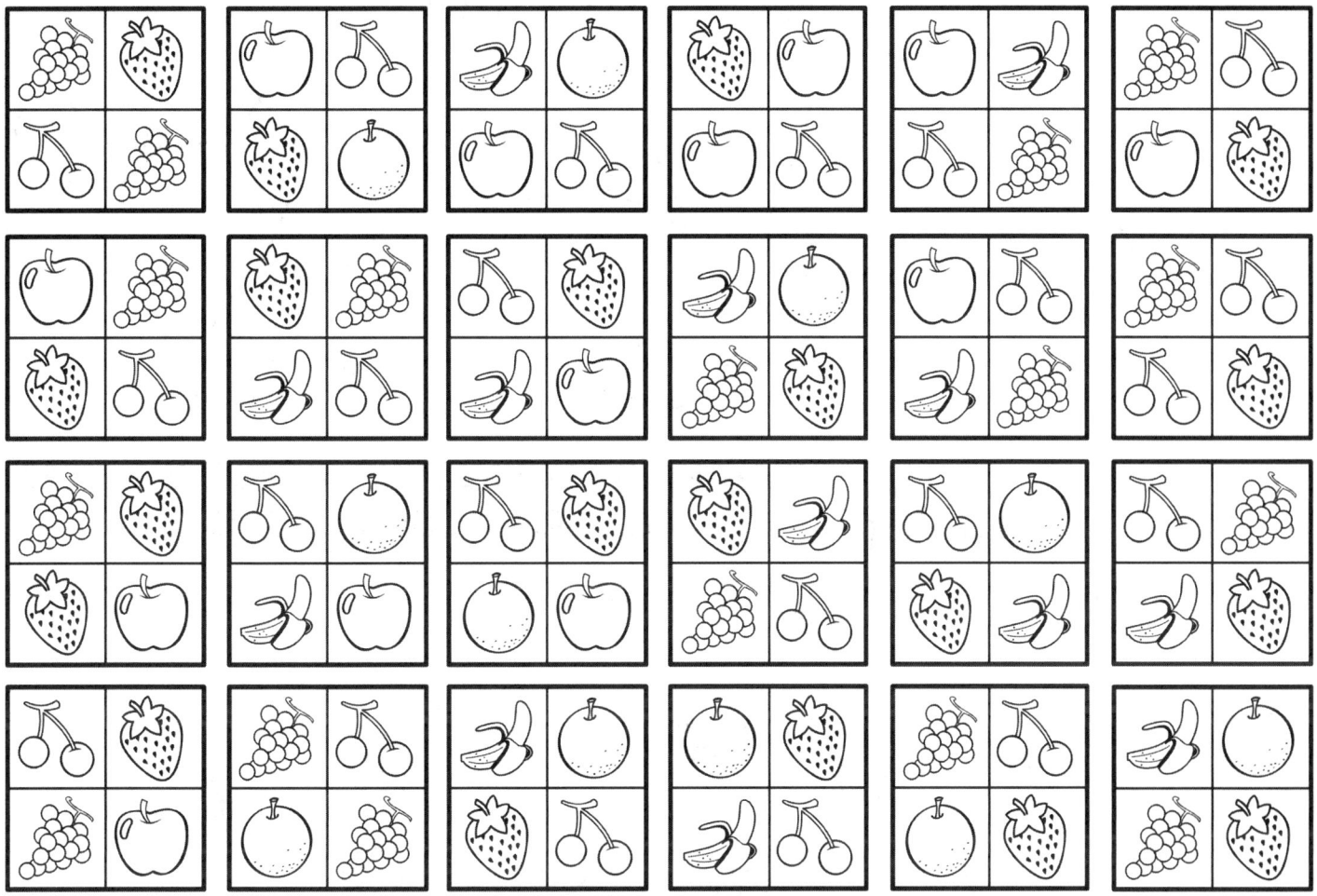

WHAT SHOULDN'T BE HERE?

WHAT ANIMALS IS THIS STRANGE CREATURE MADE OF?

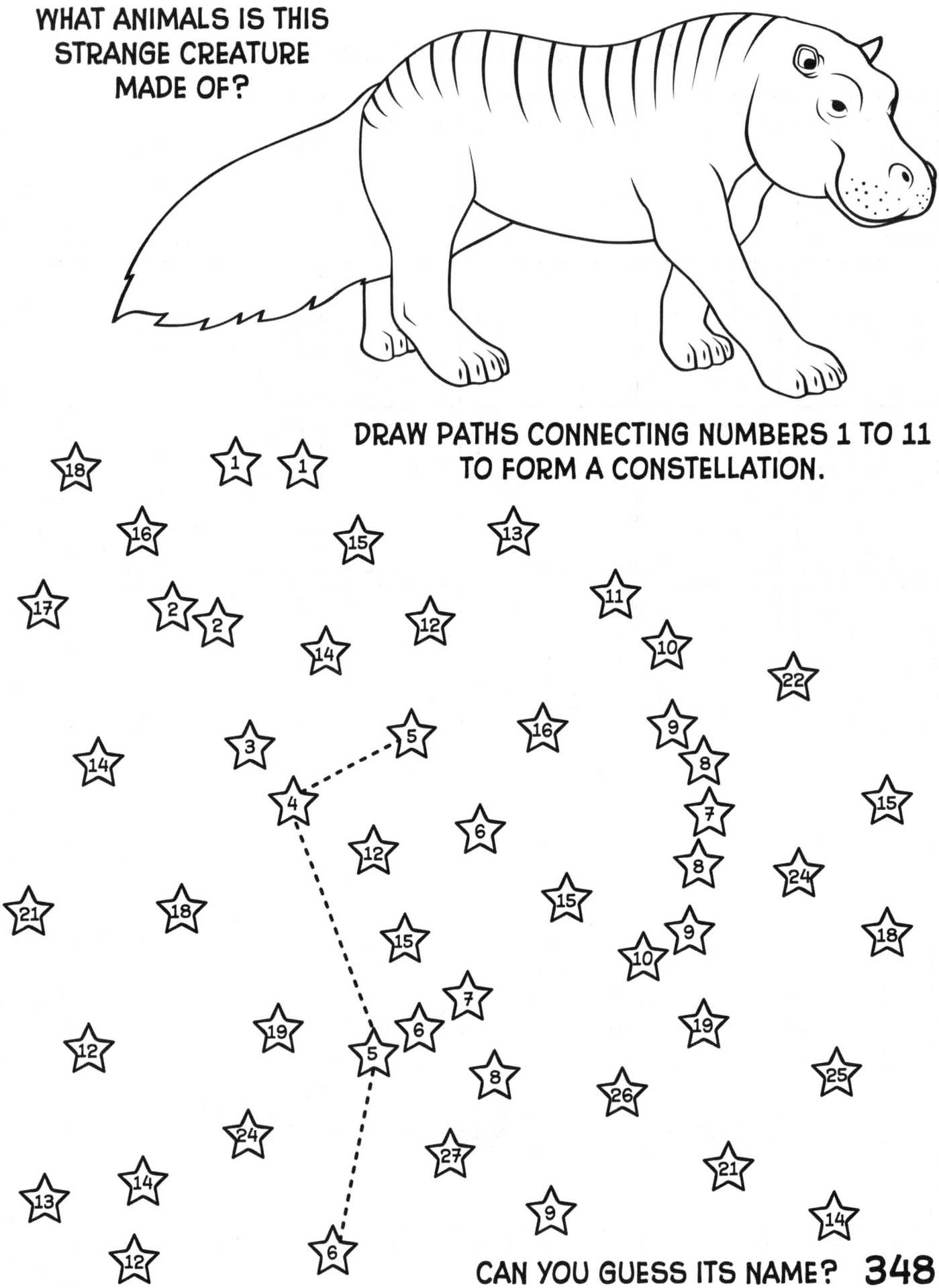

DRAW PATHS CONNECTING NUMBERS 1 TO 11 TO FORM A CONSTELLATION.

CAN YOU GUESS ITS NAME?

AT 20 MPH, THE BOAT HAS SAILED 1/4 OF THE DISTANCE TO THE TINY ISLAND IN 12 MINUTES. WHAT'S THE TOTAL DISTANCE?

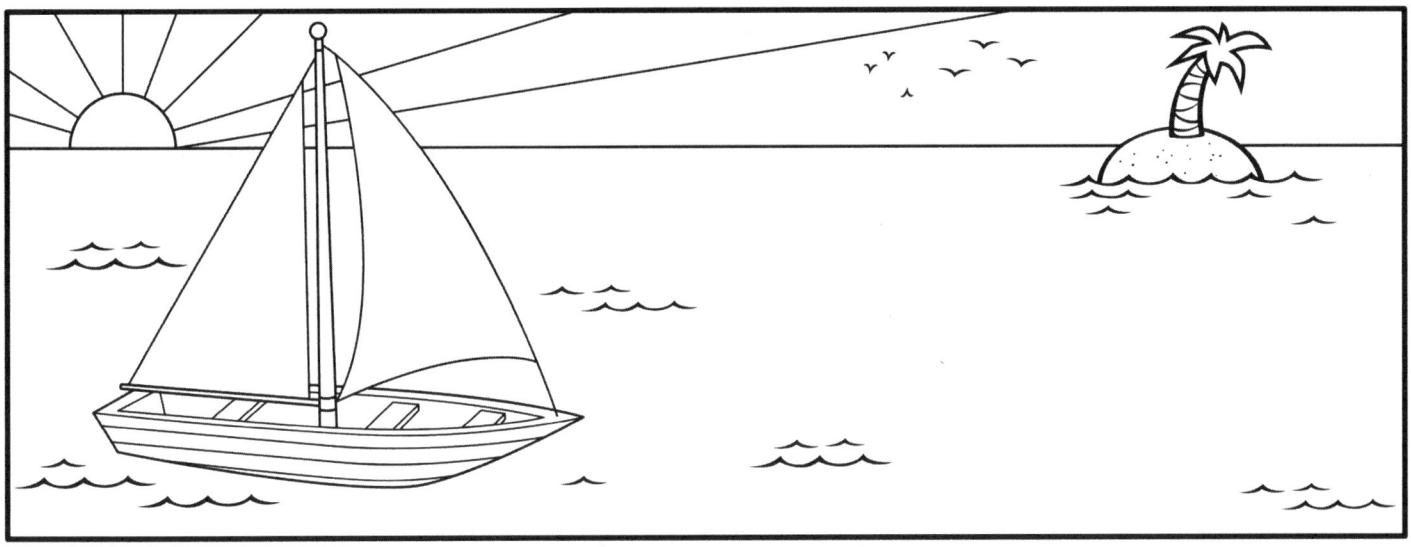

CONNECT EACH NUMBERED CIRCLE WITH ONLY VERTICAL OR HORIZONTAL, NON OVERLAPPING LINES. THE NUMBER ON EACH CIRCLE INDICATES THE NUMBER OF LINES EACH ONE IS ALLOWED.

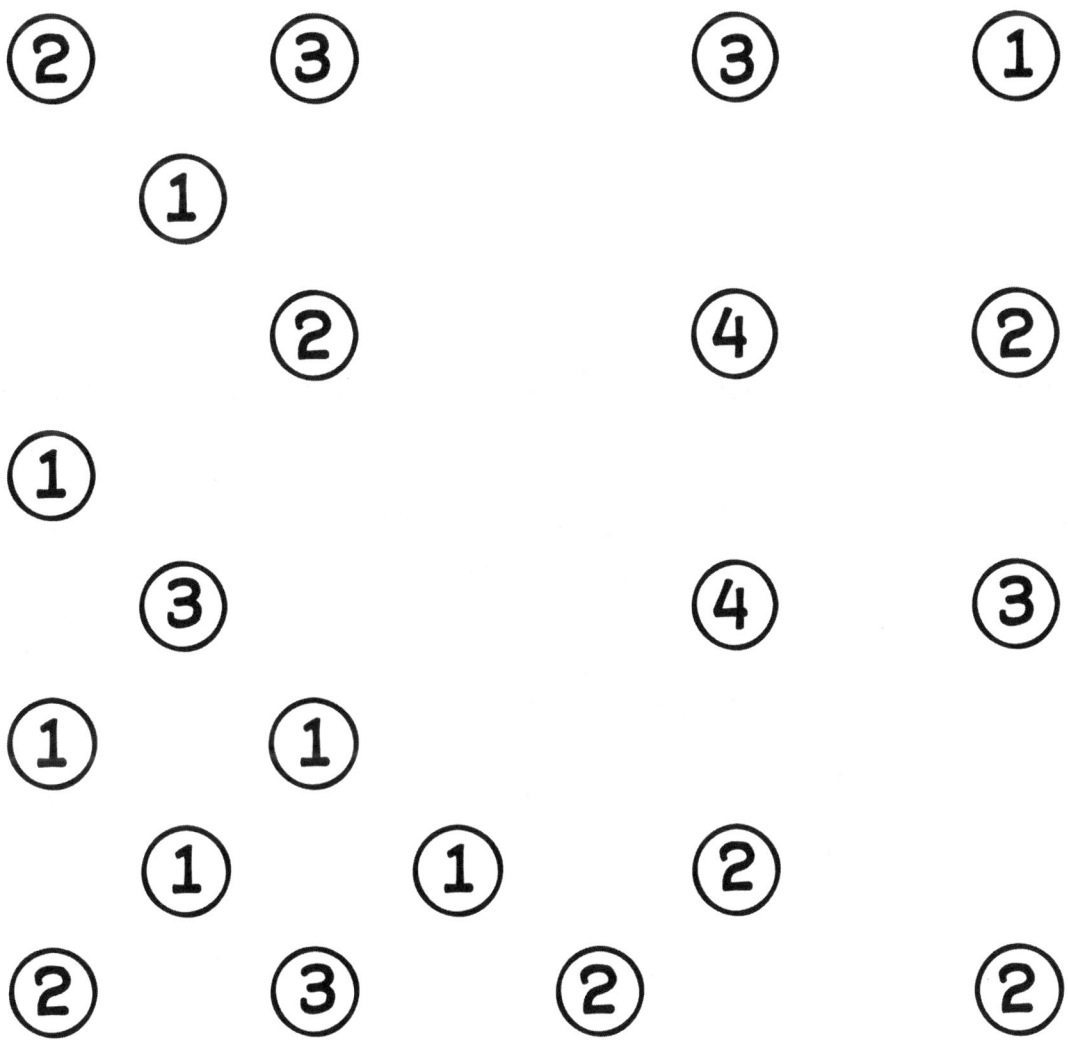

DRAW A VIKING, A COWBOY, AND A SPARTAN WARRIOR!

CAN YOU GUESS WHAT THE PHOTOGRAPHER TAKING A PICTURE OF?

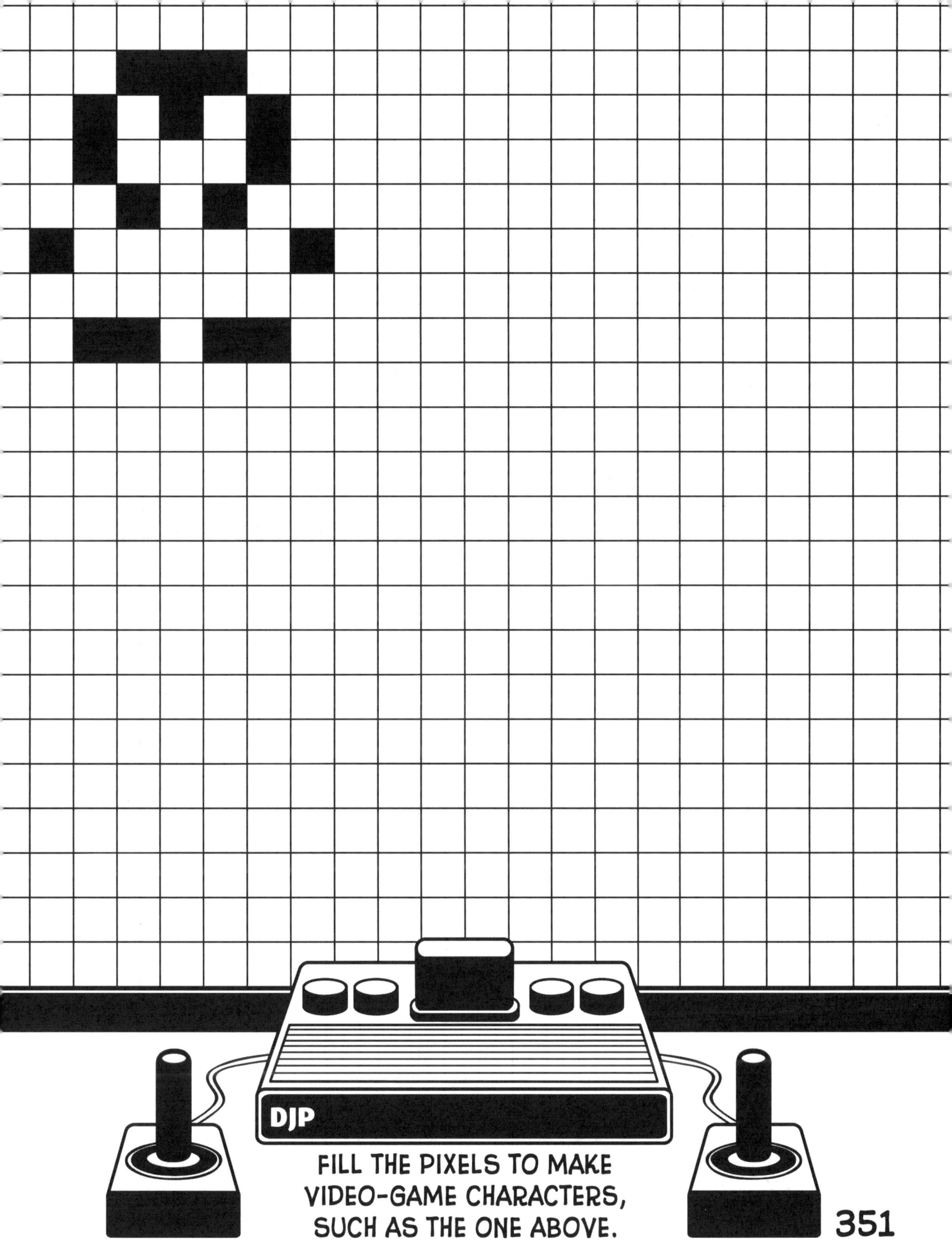

FILL THE PIXELS TO MAKE VIDEO-GAME CHARACTERS, SUCH AS THE ONE ABOVE.

WHICH TRIANGLE IS GOING TO WIN THE RACE TO THE END?

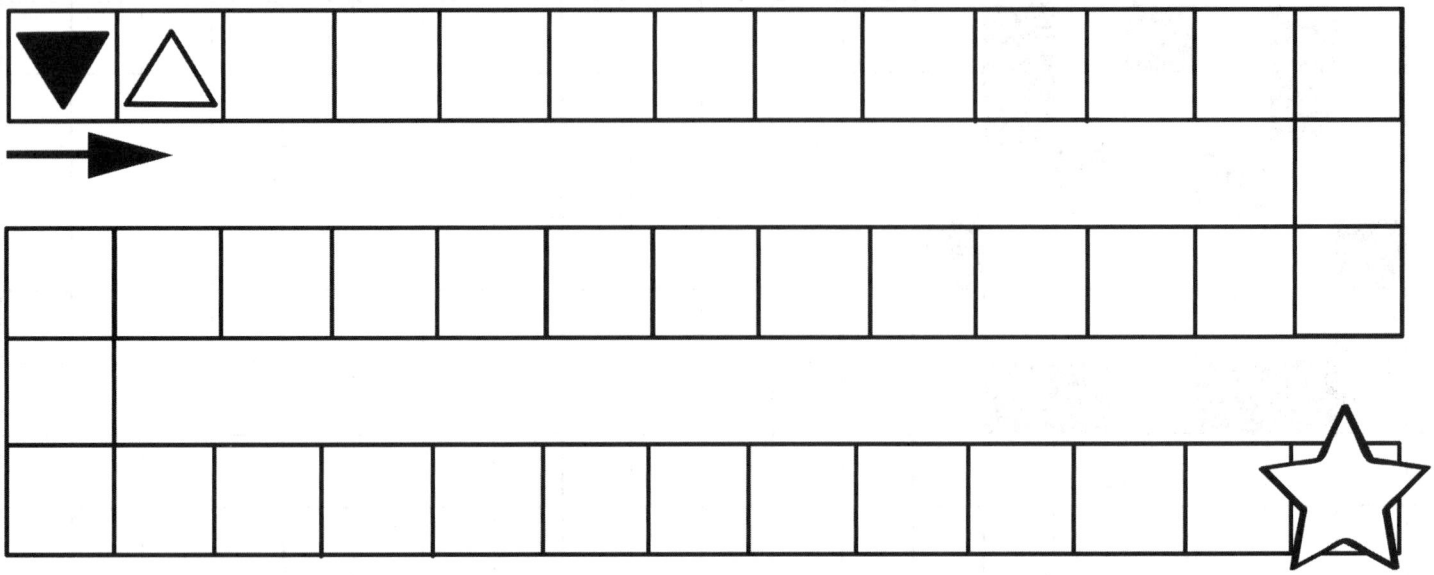

CONNECT THE IDENTICAL DRAWINGS USING ONLY VERTICAL AND HORIZONTAL LINES. LINES CANNOT CROSS EACH OTHER, AND ONLY ONE OF IT IS ALLOWED TO GO THROUGH EACH TILE.

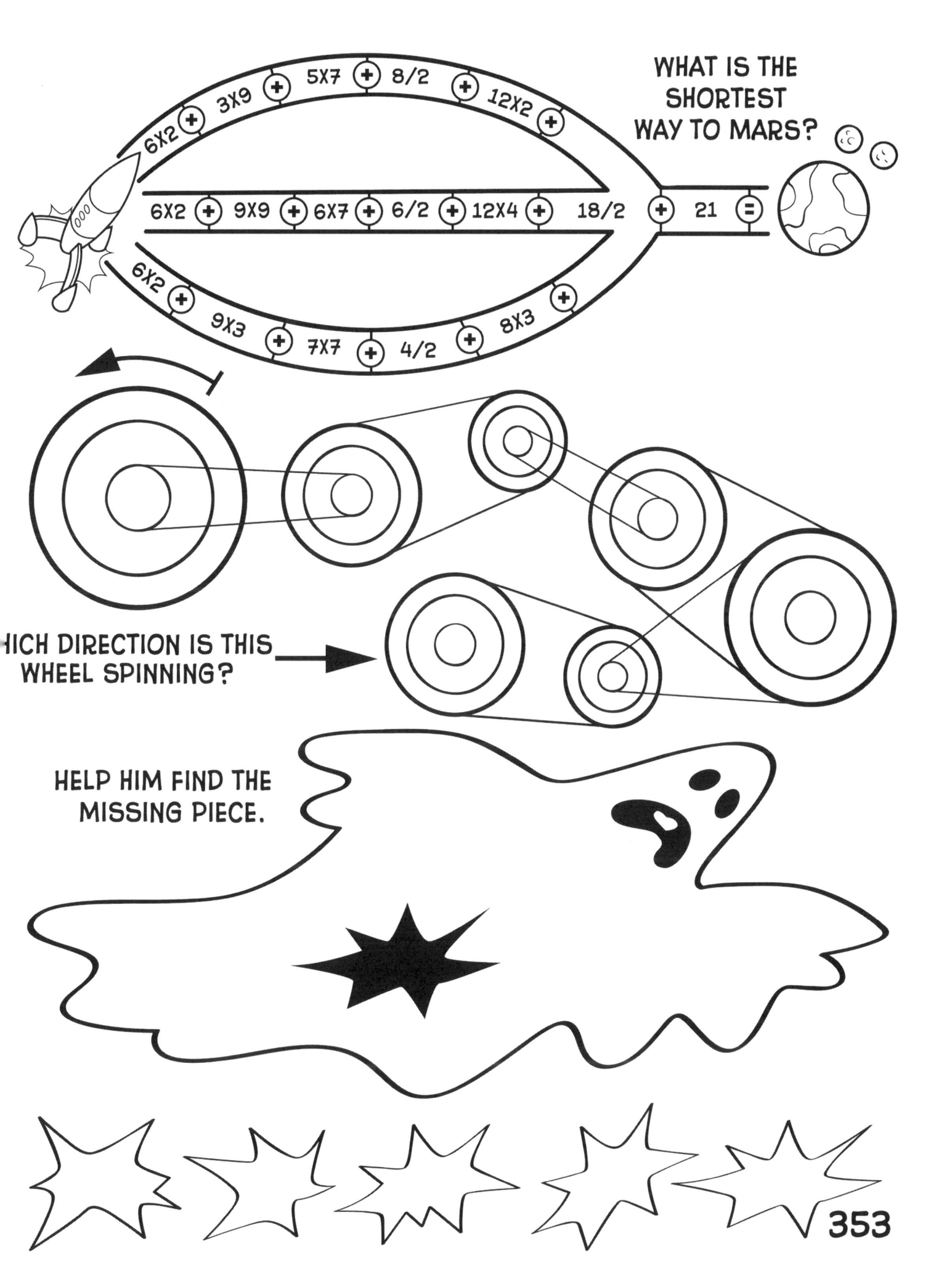
WHAT IS THE SHORTEST WAY TO MARS?
6X2 + 3X9 + 5X7 + 8/2 + 12X2 +
6X2 + 9X9 + 6X7 + 6/2 + 12X4 + 18/2 + 21 =
6X2 + 9X3 + 7X7 + 4/2 + 8X3 +
HICH DIRECTION IS THIS WHEEL SPINNING?
HELP HIM FIND THE MISSING PIECE.

NOW DRAW AN ASTRONAUT, A BIKER, AND A MAGICIAN!

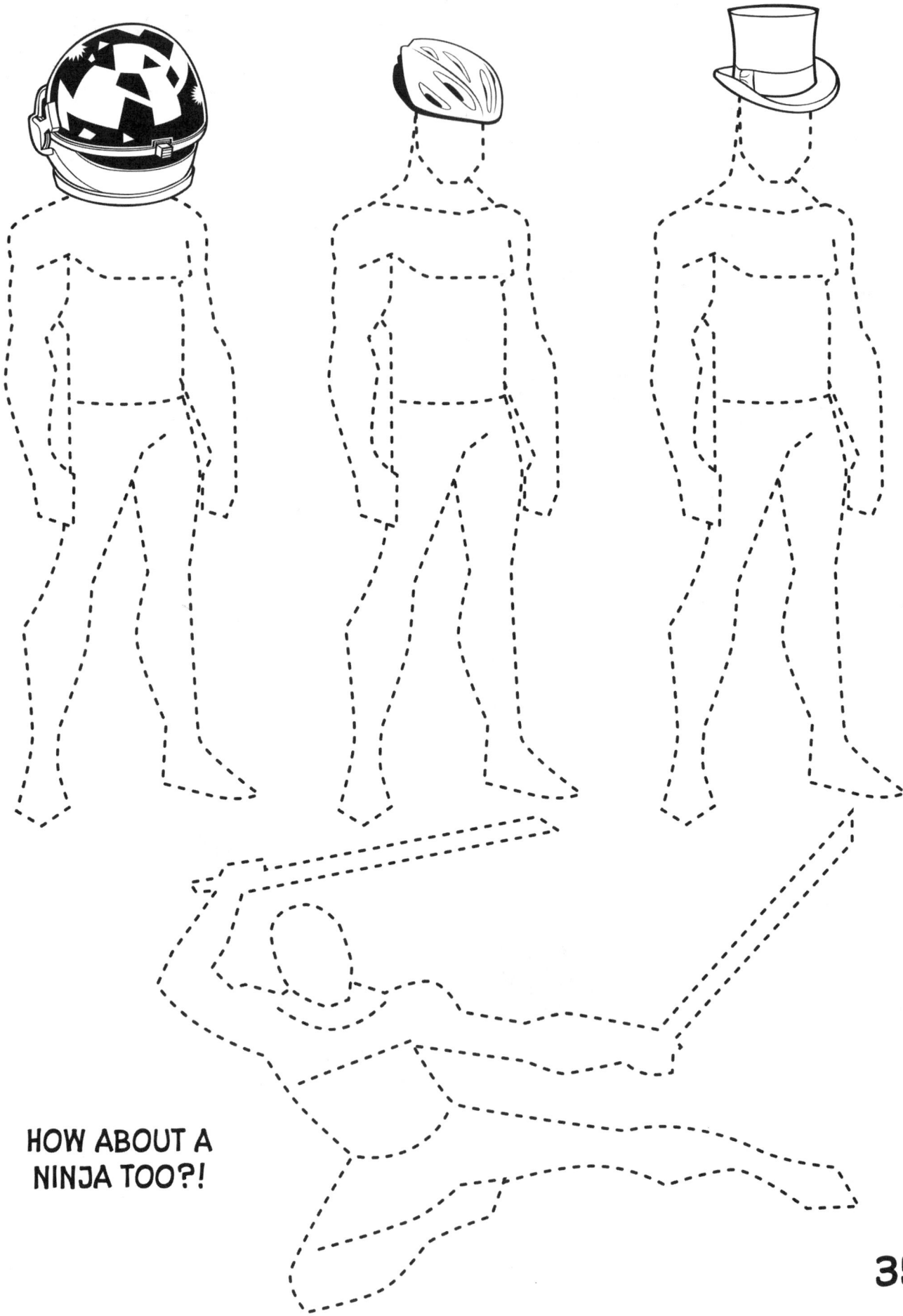

HOW ABOUT A NINJA TOO?!

SELECT AND COLOR ONLY
THE INGREDIENTS YOU NEED TO
MAKE A SALAD IN THIS BOWL.

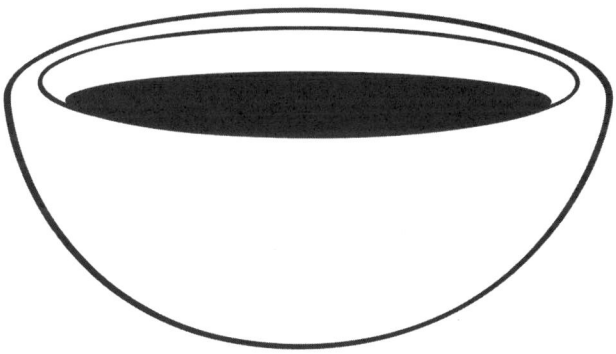

IN THIS NEW GAME OF TIC-TAC-TOE, THE GOAL IS TO AVOID VERTICAL, HORIZONTAL, OR DIAGONAL LINES OF UP TO FOUR CROSSES OR CIRCLES EACH.

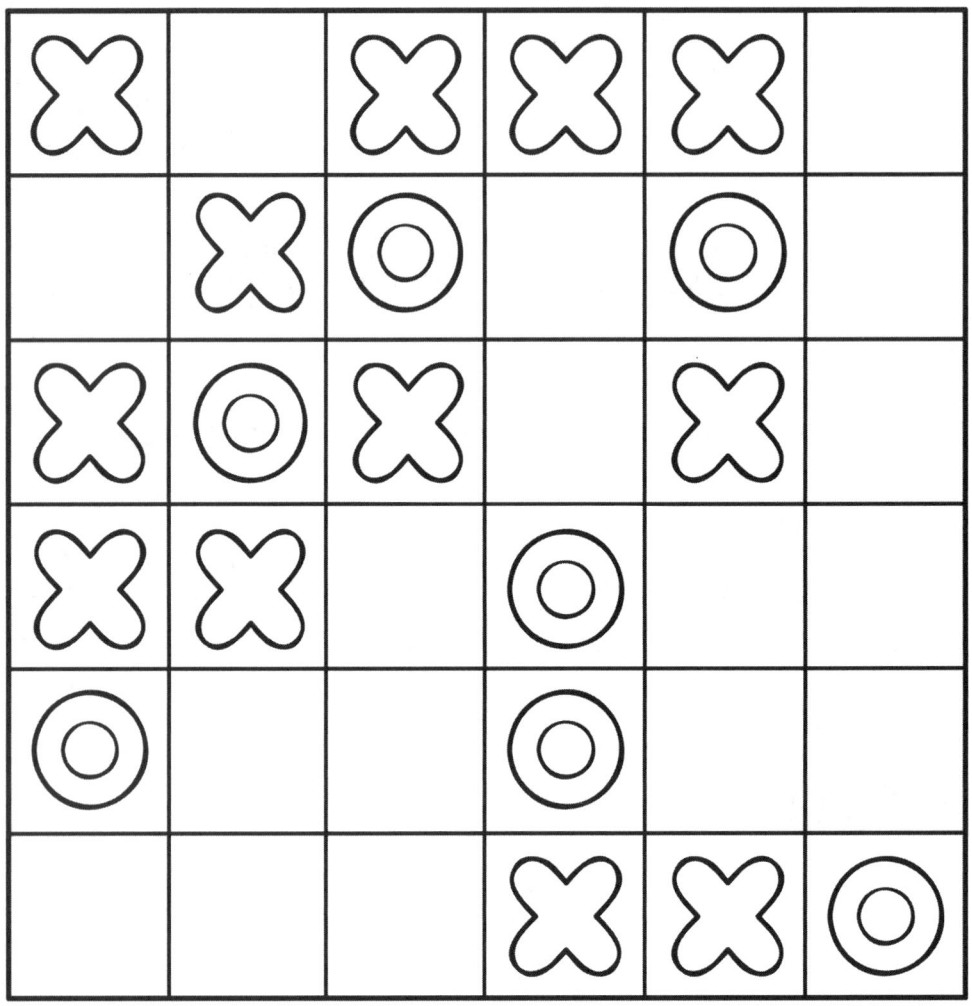

IF THIS BOAT CATCHES 2 BIG FISH EVERY HOUR, AND 10 SMALLER FISH EVERY 10 MINUTES, HOW MANY WILL IT HAVE WHEN THE DAY IS OVER?

DIVIDE THIS FLAG IN THREE EQUAL PARTS. COLOR EACH PART BLUE, WHITE, AND RED. WHAT COUNTRY IS IT FROM? WHAT IS FAMOUS FOR? FIND OUT IN THE WORDSEARCH BELOW!

CLUE: CHECK THE ACTIVITY AT THE BOTTOM OF THE PAGE.

R O L A N D G A R R O S S F C R O I S S A N T B C
L O U V R E M U S E U M R F C O Q A U V I N C A H
C Y D Z P S U H D I K O O S D A U N C Z A A A G O
C H A M P A G N E Q I P E L J V P D R Y D P M U C
I S F W H S N O I D A T L B I S Q N E V S O E E O
T O K E P C I L S P R W W I N E J R T M R L M T L
R W O C A N O R M A N D Y W G Y R O E O B E B T A
O L W T R U W T C A I N G R J I E E T N S O E E T
E D Y L I S Q S C B I Y L V F G W N H T A N R D E
N E B A S H E J O H X C G O U K S P M M S U T J B
N O T R E D A M E C A T H E D R A L E A T I L J R
Z M L T E B O C Y J D N P K C Z A N Q R E O J T E
R P L N P I Q T O U R D E F R A N C E T R A O S A
F S E I F F E L T O W E R L Y R P H W R I C X F D
E R J A C Q U E S L O U I S D A V I D E X S O R V

DRAW OR WRITE THE RESULT.

DRAW DIFFERENT FLOWERS ACCORDING TO THE NAMES ON EACH VASE.

IT TAKES THIS TRAIN 10 MINUTES TO COVER 200 FT.
HOW LONG WILL IT TAKE IT TO TRAVEL 160 MILES?

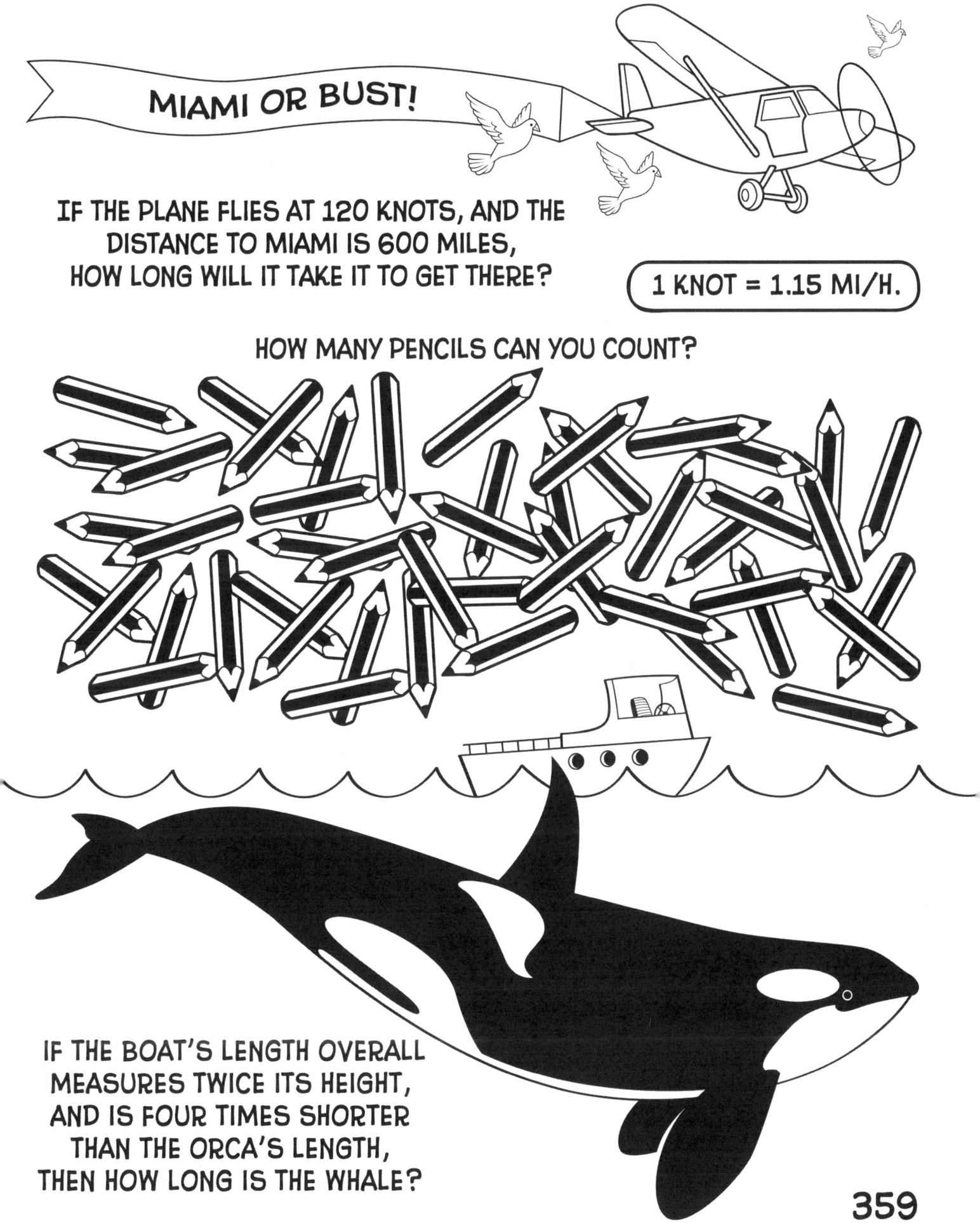

IF THE PLANE FLIES AT 120 KNOTS, AND THE DISTANCE TO MIAMI IS 600 MILES, HOW LONG WILL IT TAKE IT TO GET THERE?

1 KNOT = 1.15 MI/H.

HOW MANY PENCILS CAN YOU COUNT?

IF THE BOAT'S LENGTH OVERALL MEASURES TWICE ITS HEIGHT, AND IS FOUR TIMES SHORTER THAN THE ORCA'S LENGTH, THEN HOW LONG IS THE WHALE?

SOLVE.

12-3	+ 6	-	X 7	- 14	X	+ 5	/ 3	X 8	=

CONNECT EACH NUMBERED CIRCLE WITH ONLY VERTICAL OR HORIZONTAL, NON OVERLAPPING LINES. THE NUMBER ON EACH CIRCLE INDICATES THE NUMBER OF LINES EACH ONE IS ALLOWED.

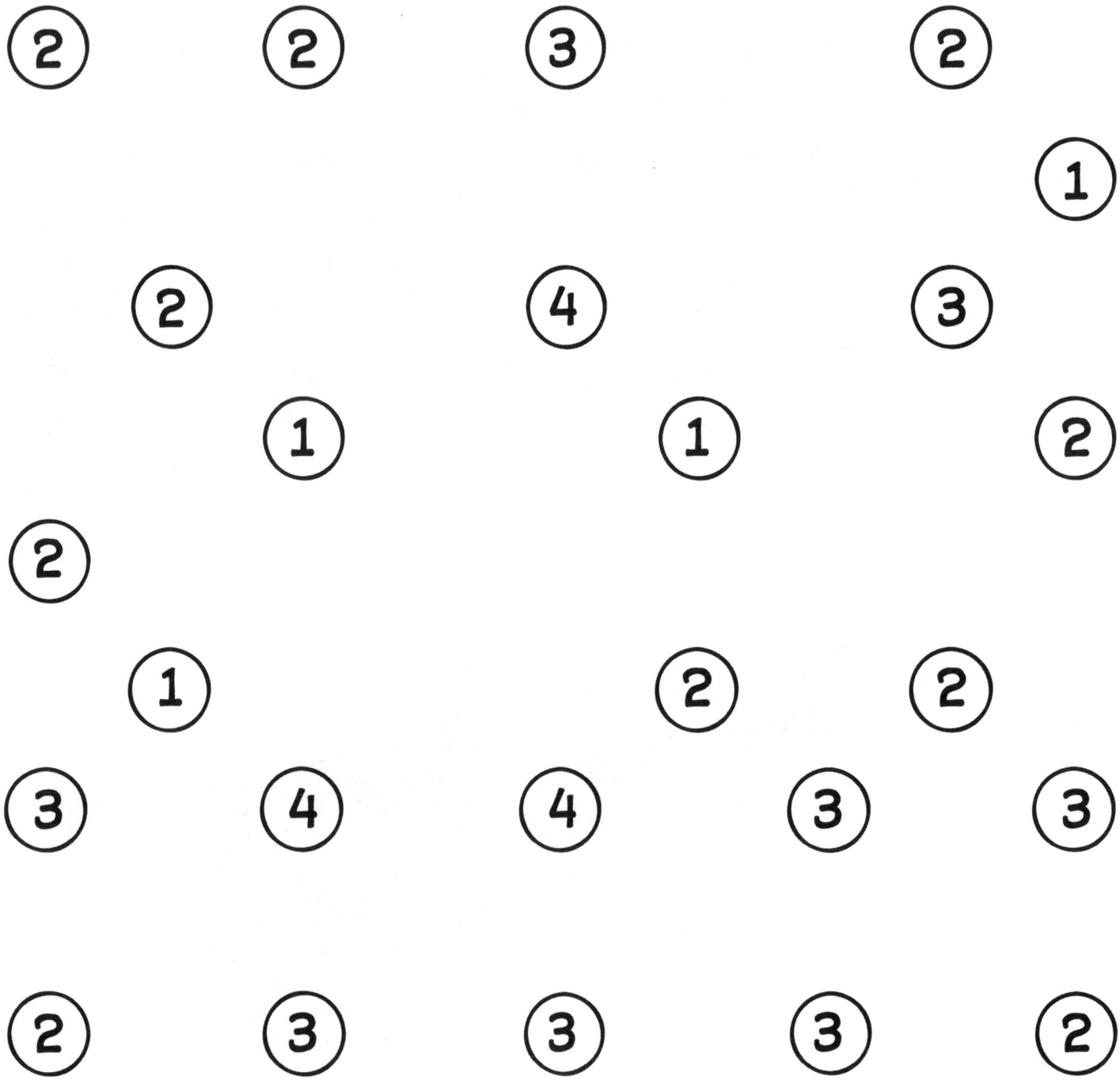

HOW MANY CIRCLES ARE IN THIS TABLE?
HOW MANY STARS? AND SQUARES?

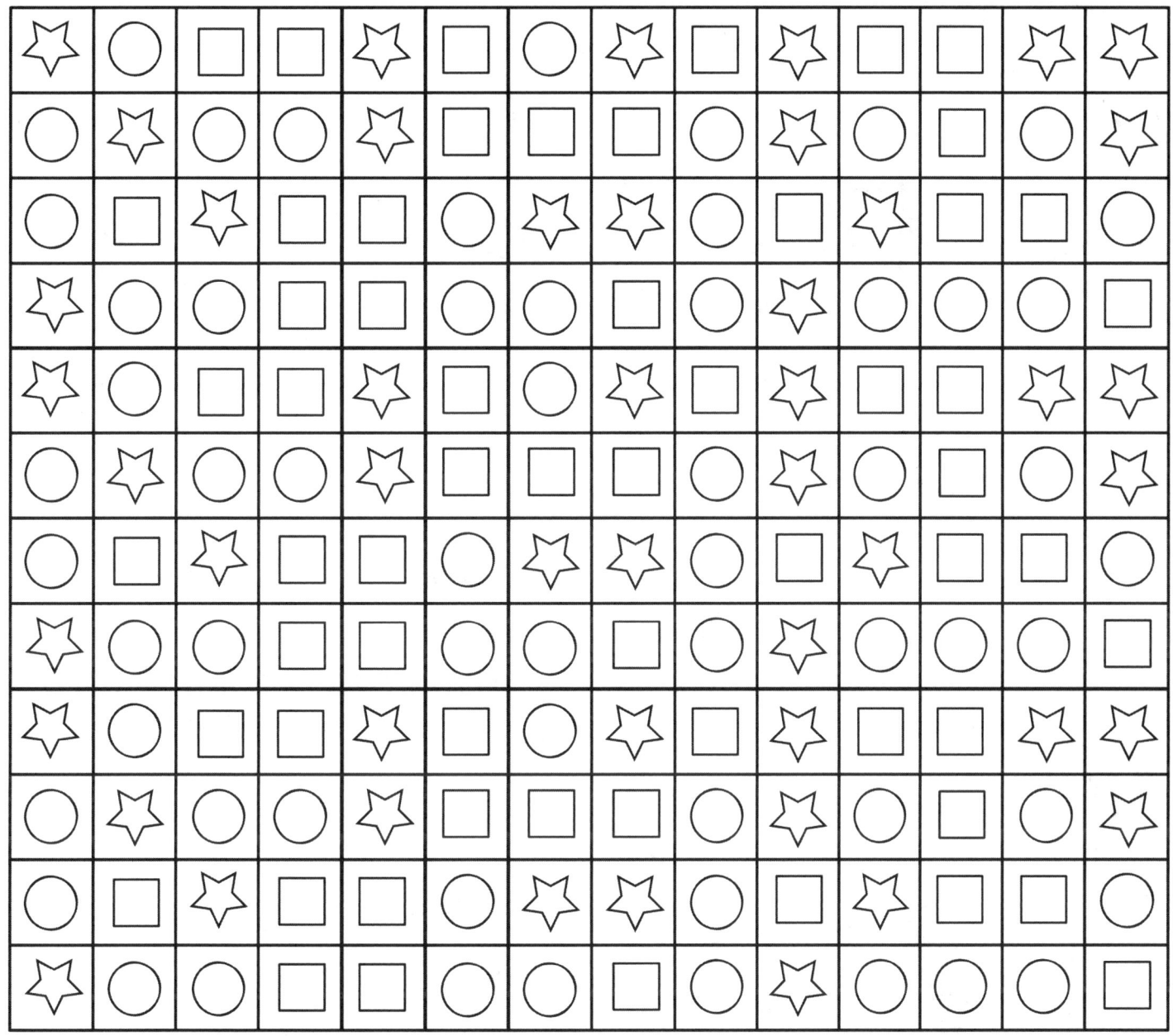

FILL EVERY AVAILABLE SPACE IN THIS SHAPE WITH CIRCLES OF EVERY SIZE!

WHAT DIRECTION IS 7 TURNING TOWARD?

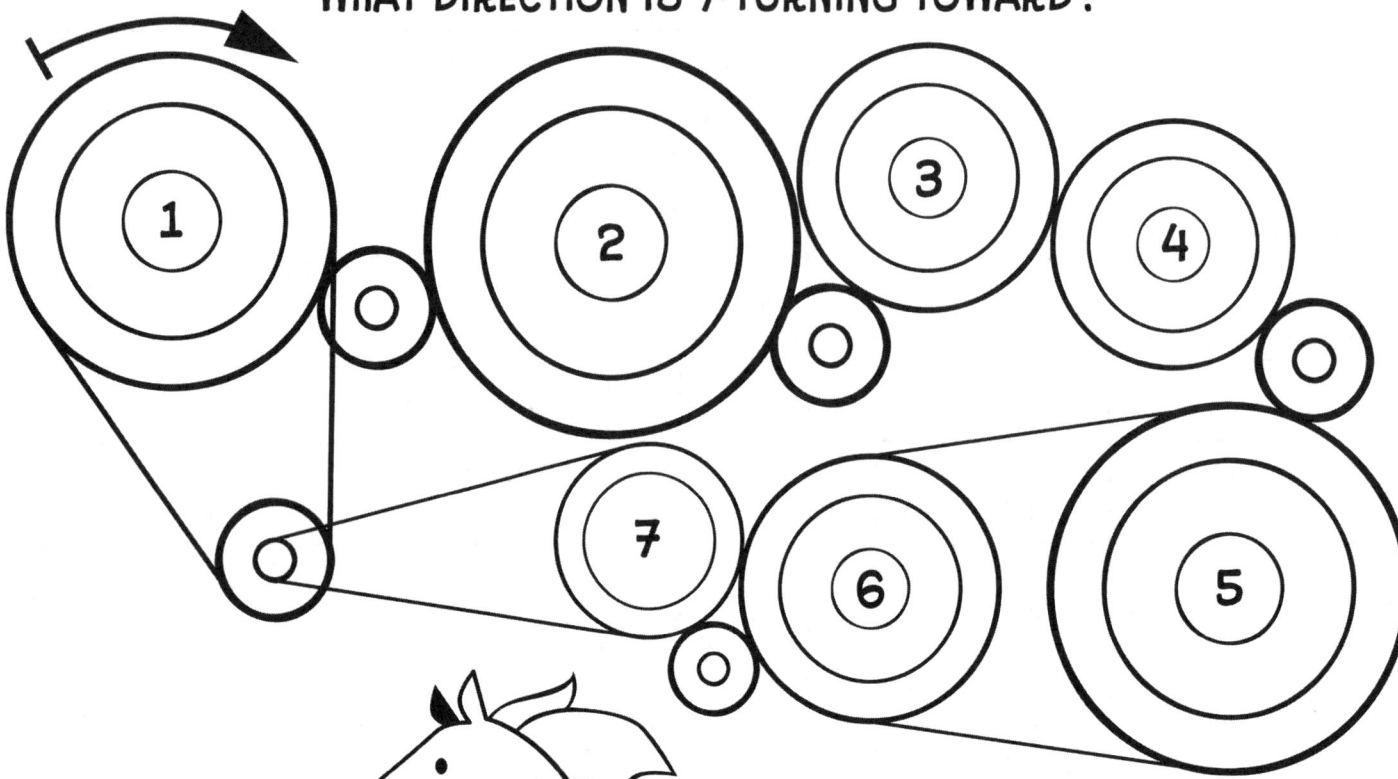

WHAT DOES THIS HORSE NEED TO BECOME A UNICORN?

CAN YOU TURN THIS ONE INTO A PEGASUS?

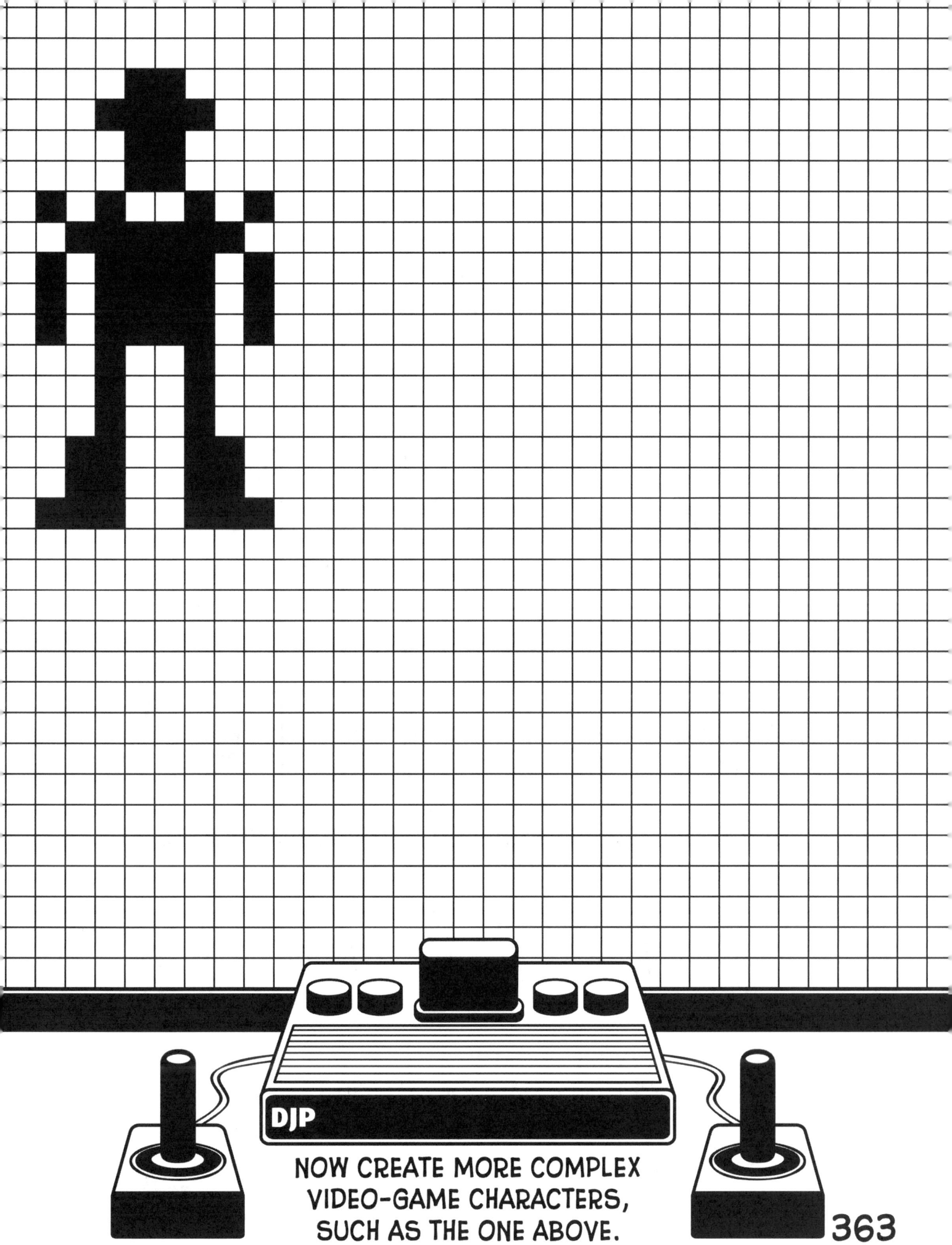

NOW CREATE MORE COMPLEX VIDEO-GAME CHARACTERS, SUCH AS THE ONE ABOVE.

CAN YOU FIND THE MISSING SYMBOL IN THIS ANCIENT EGYPTIAN PYRAMID?

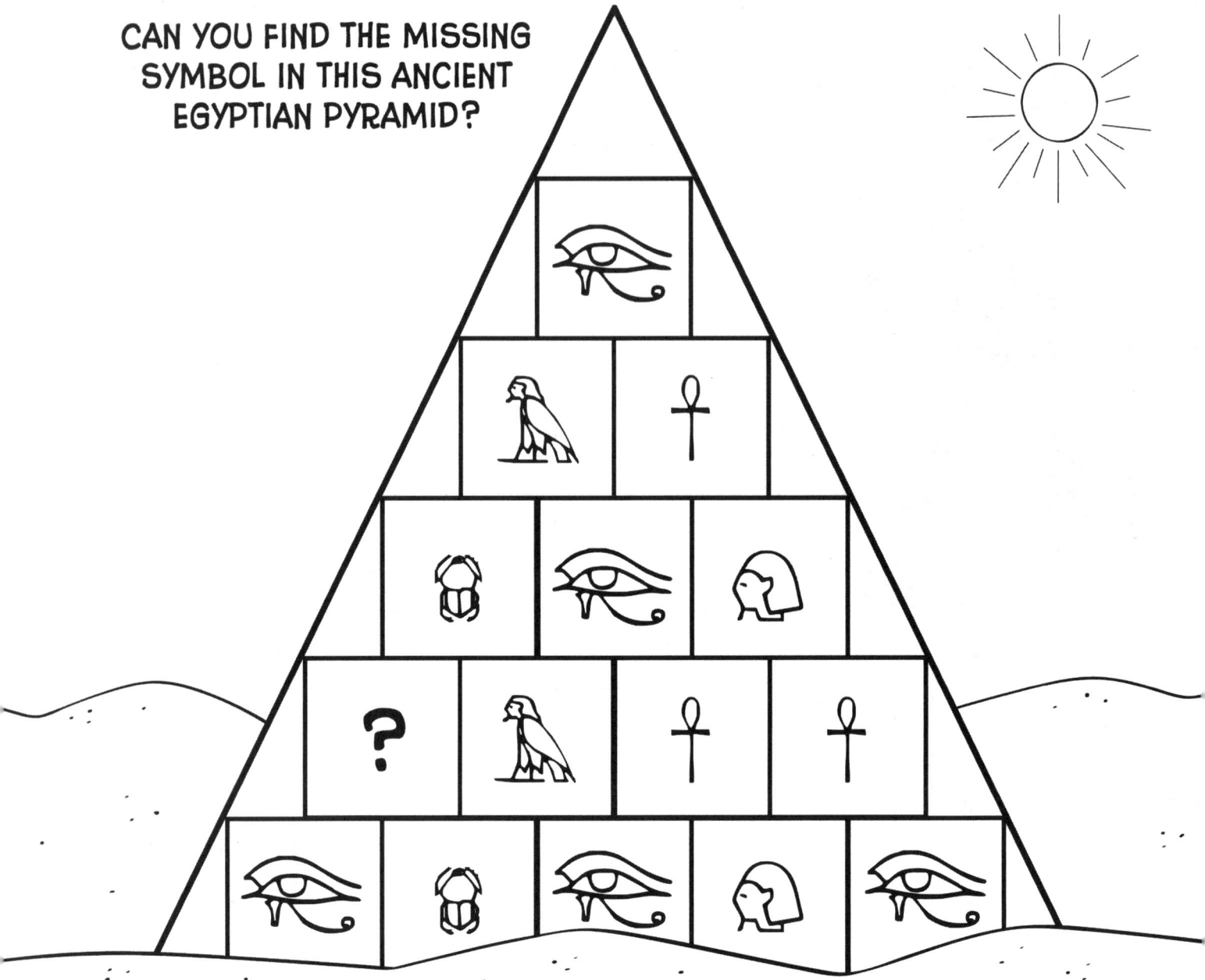

CAN YOU ALTERNATE FULL AND EMPTY SAND BUCKETS, BY ONLY MOVING ONE OF THEM?

WHERE DOES COTTON COME FROM?
NAME THREE CLOTHING ITEMS MADE OF COTTON.

HOW CAN THIS SHEET BE SPLIT, SO EACH OF THE KIDS GETS A PIECE OF THE SAME SIZE AND SHAPE?

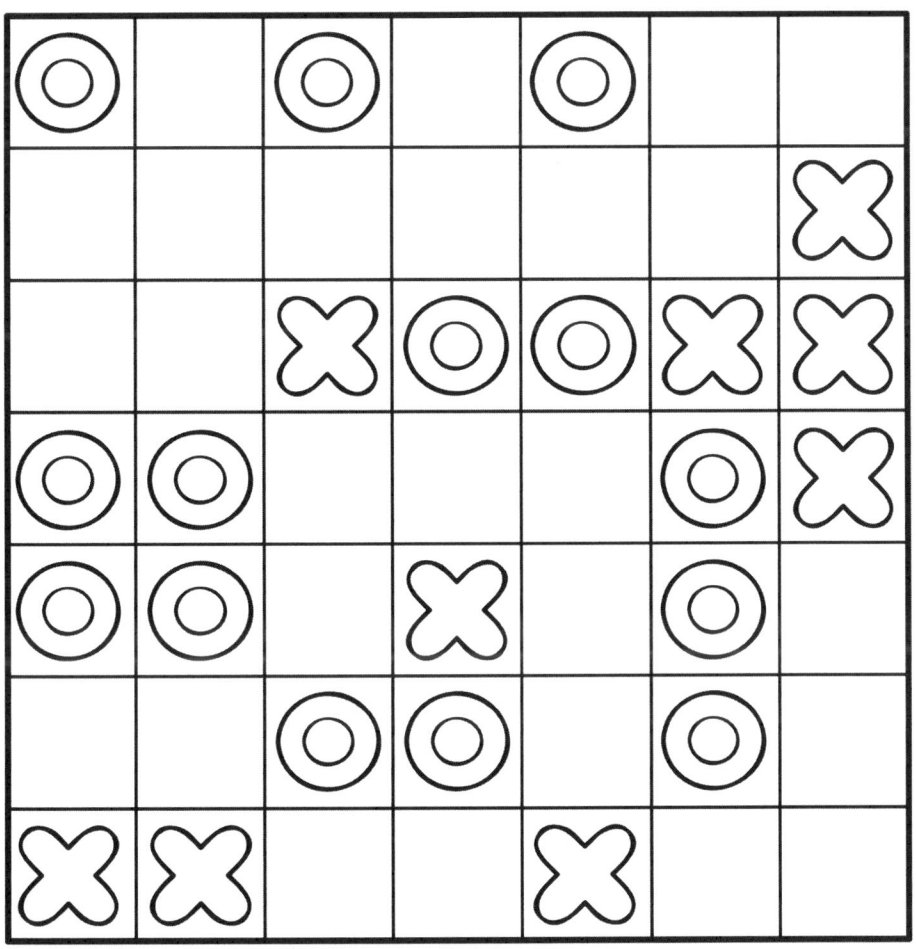

TO CRACK THIS GAME OF TIC-TAC-TOE, THE GOAL IS TO AVOID VERTICAL, HORIZONTAL, OR DIAGONAL LINES OF UP TO FOUR CROSSES OR CIRCLES.

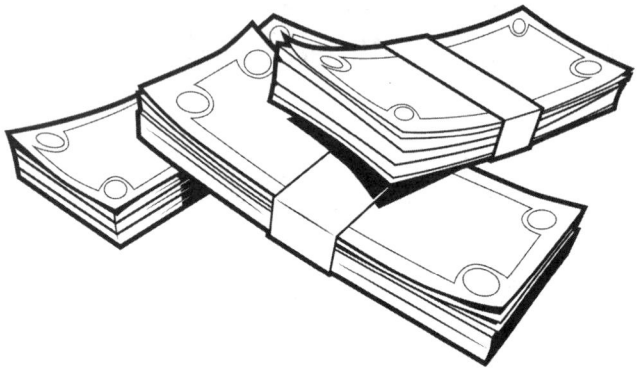

YOUR GRANDMOTHER GIVES YOU A 15 DOLLAR ALLOWANCE IN TWO BILLS.
ONE OF THE BILLS IS FIVE DOLLARS.
WHAT IS THE OTHER BILL?

IN WHICH BOX DO YOU END UP IF YOU FOLLOW THE ARROWS?

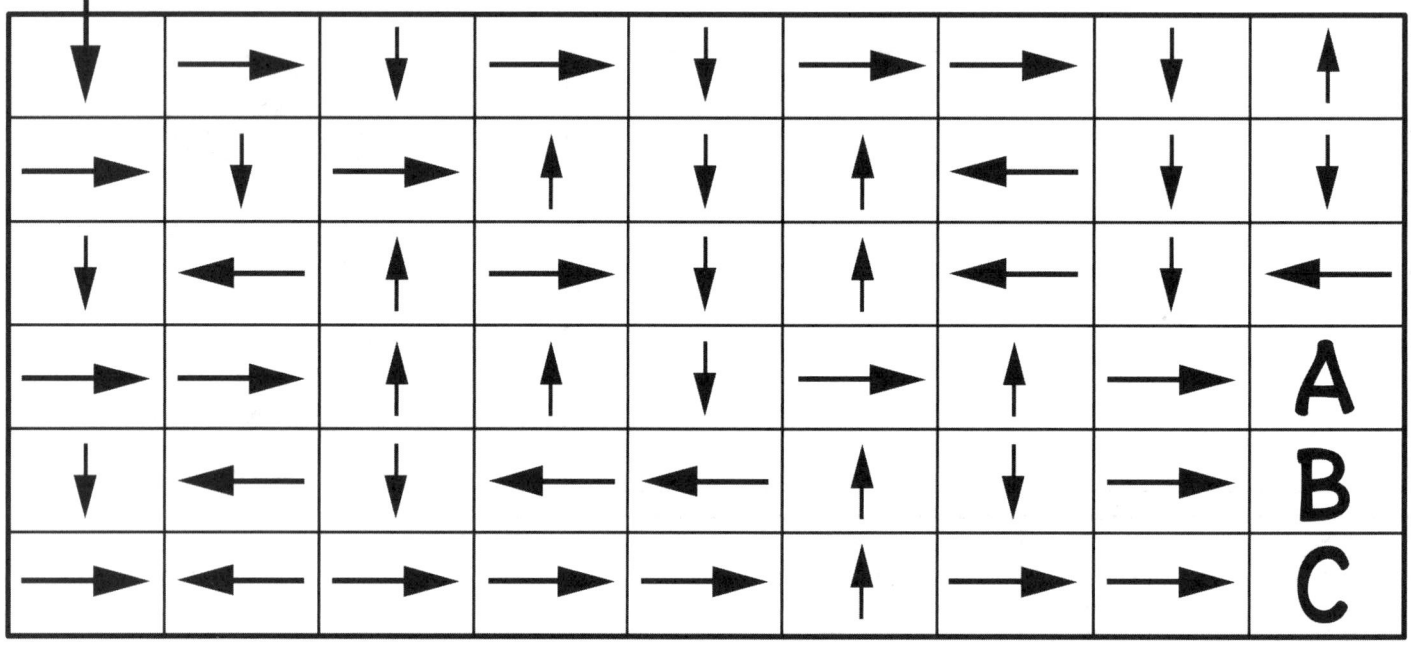

IN THIS CLASSIC GAME, CAN YOU MAKE THE "BULL" TURN ITS HEAD BY MOVING ONLY TWO MATCHES?

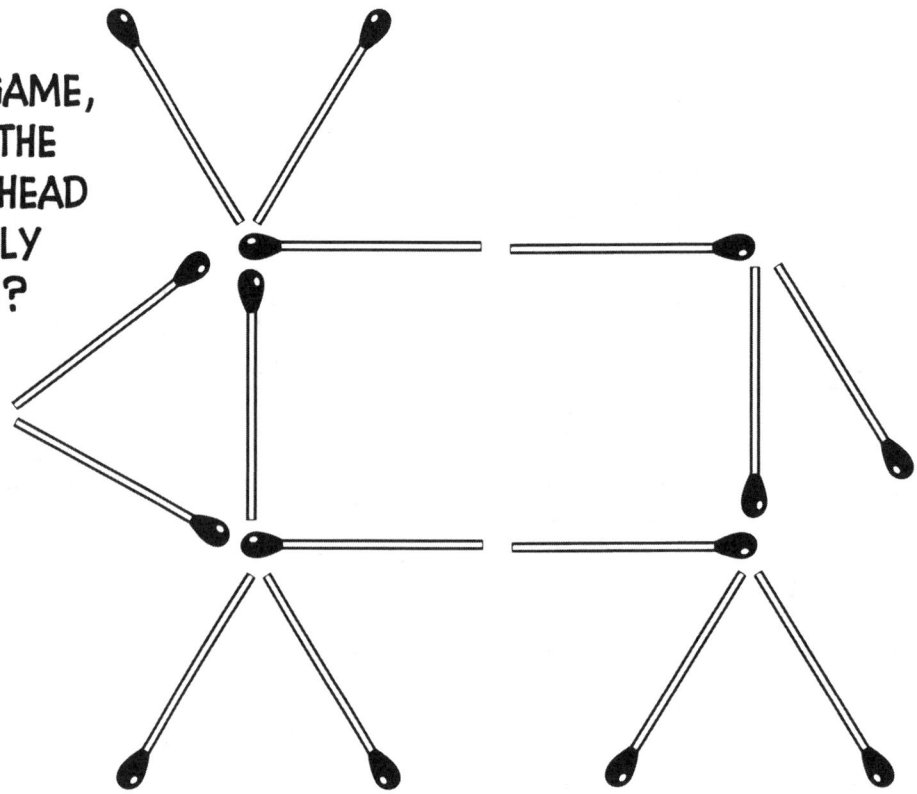

CONNECT THE IDENTICAL DRAWINGS USING ONLY VERTICAL AND HORIZONTAL LINES. LINES CANNOT CROSS EACH OTHER, AND ONLY ONE LINE IS ALLOWED TO GO THROUGH EACH TILE.

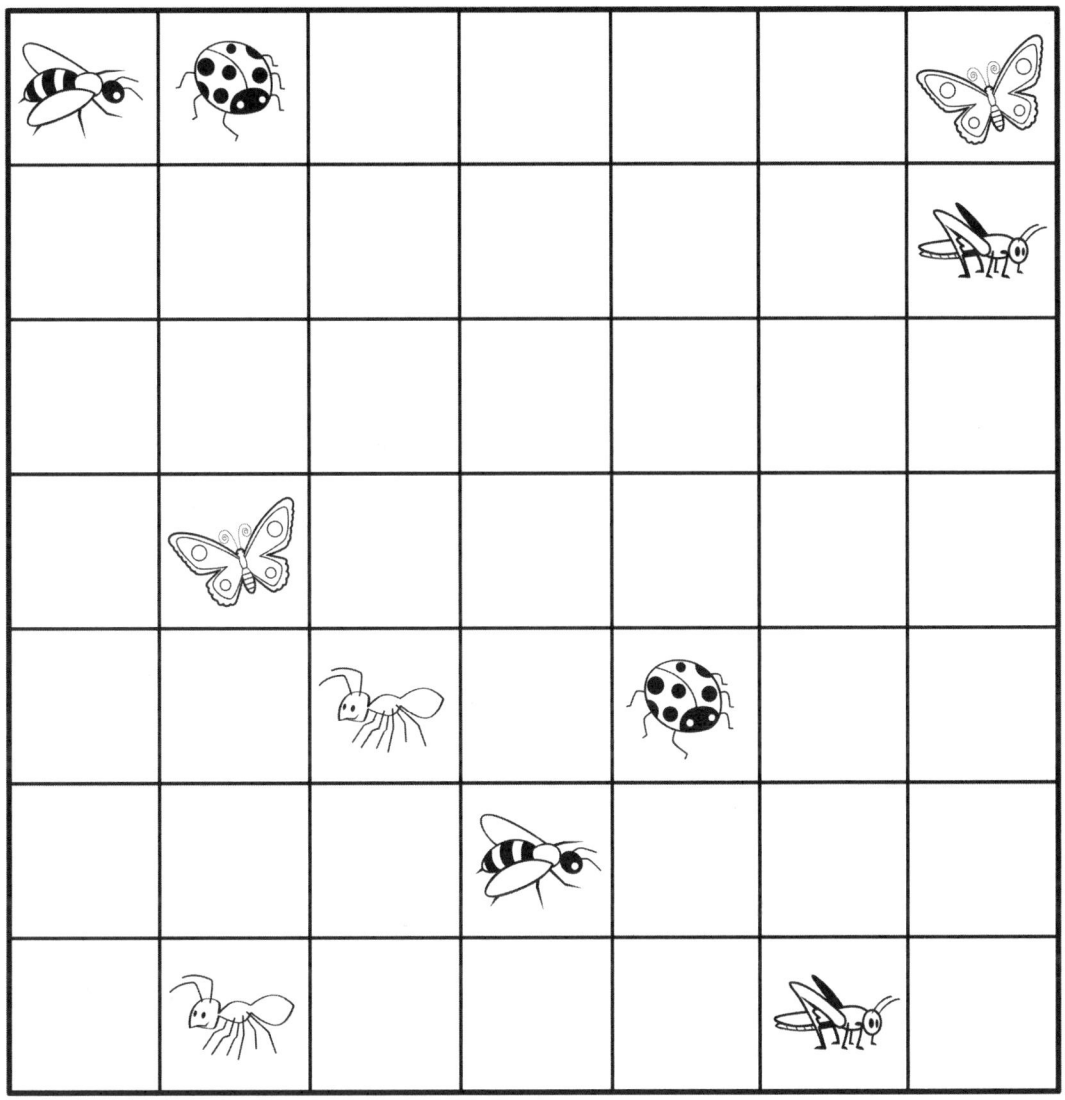

FIGURE OUT THE NUMERICAL VALUE OF EACH OBJECT.

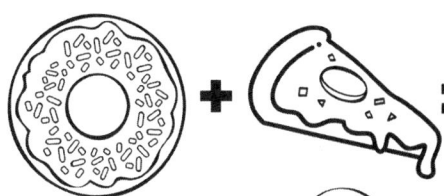

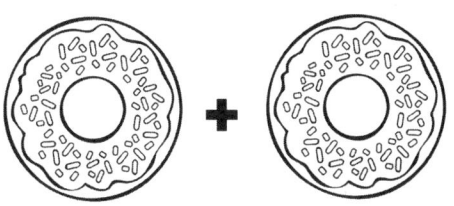

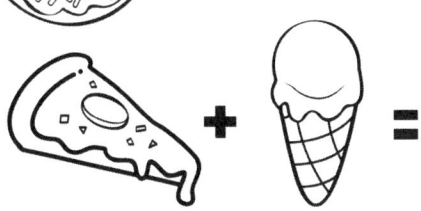

CONNECT EACH FISH TO ITS CORRESPONDING HOOK!

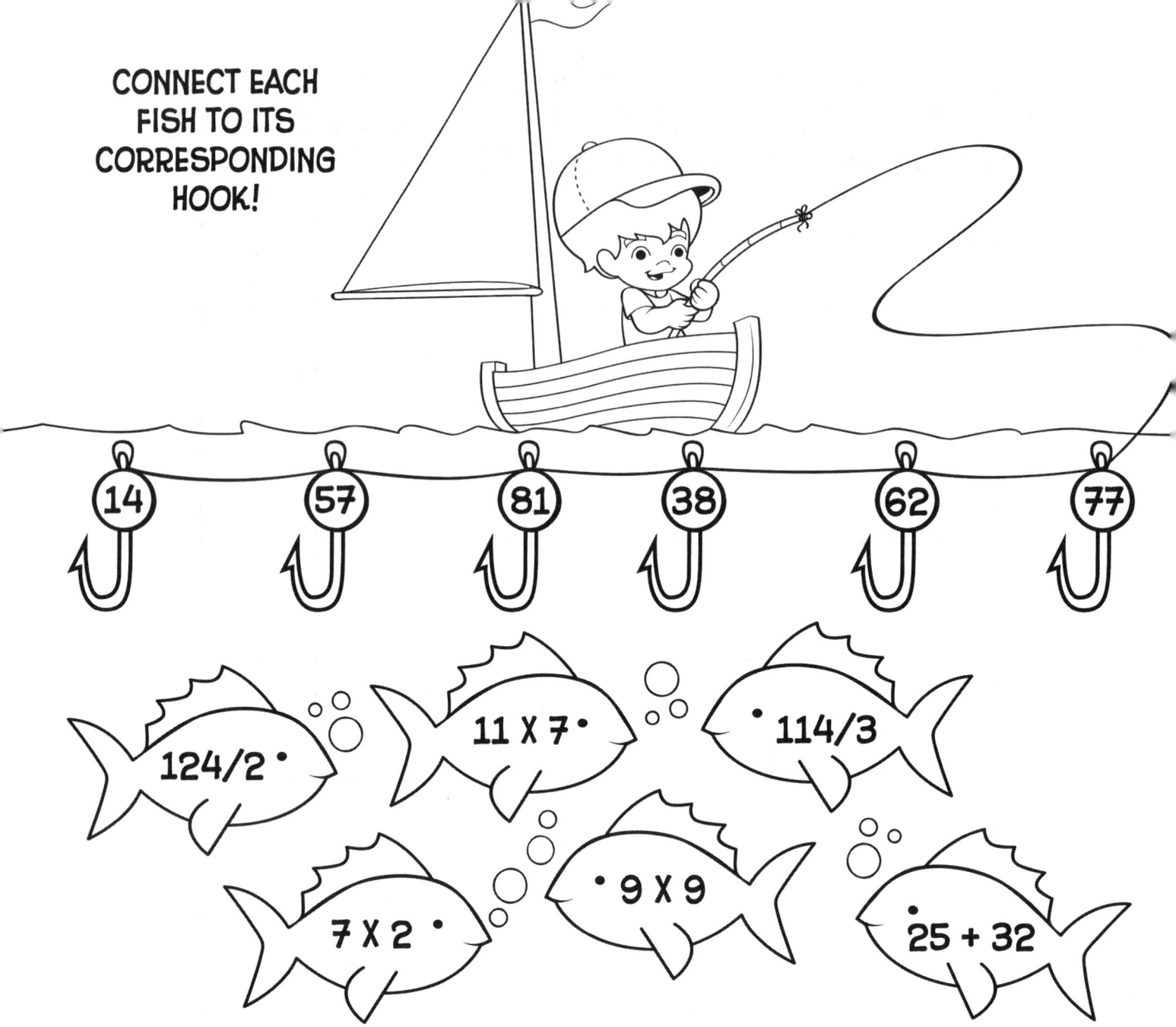

THE SPINNING TOP ON THE LEFT TURNS AROUND 20 TIMES PER SECOND, AND THE ONE ON THE RIGHT TURNS TWICE AS FAST.

HOW MANY TIMES DO THEY TURN IN ONE AND A HALF MINUTES?

CAN YOU GET RID OF THREE MATCHES, AND BE LEFT WITH THREE TRIANGLES?

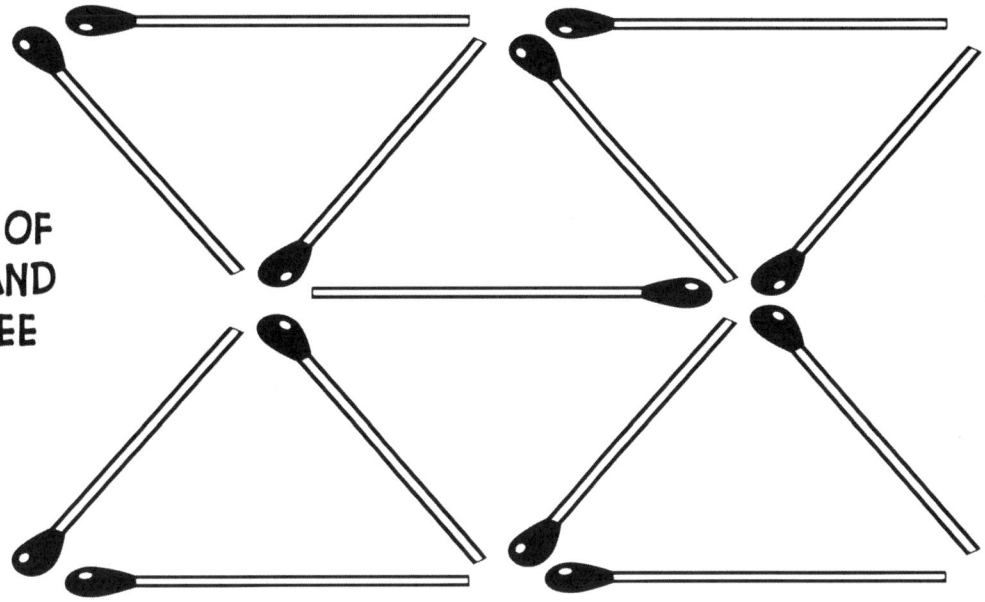

CRACK THE SUDOKU!
EACH ELEMENT CAN ONLY BE PLACED ONCE ON EACH LINE, ONCE ON EACH ROW, AND ONCE IN EACH 3 BY 2 CELLS GRID.

CAN YOU GUESS THE PASSWORD FOR THE REST OF THE KID'S PROFILES, BASED ON BILLY'S?

NAME:
BILLY BOB JAMES

PASSWORD:
50305

NAME:
OLIVER GREEN MONTGOMERY

PASSWORD:
?

NAME:
SOLEDAD ROBERTSON

PASSWORD:
?

NAME:
MAYA ANITA RODRIGUEZ

PASSWORD:
?

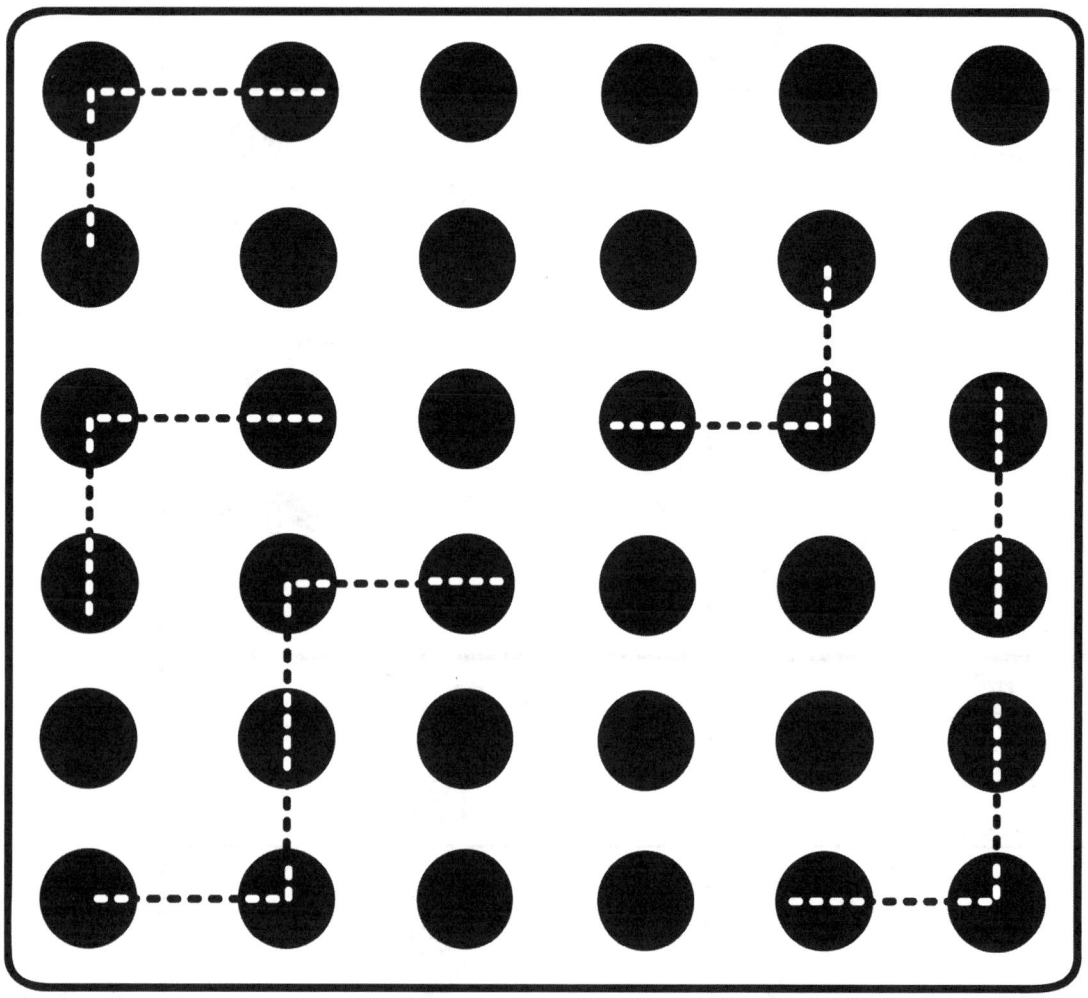

JOIN ALL DOTS USING A SINGLE LINE, WHICH GOES FROM ONE DOT TO THE NEXT, CROSSING EACH ONE ONLY ONCE!

WHERE DOES SILK COME FROM?
NAME THREE CLOTHING ITEMS
MADE OF SILK.

THIS IS THE FLAG OF
JAPAN. YOU ONLY NEED
TO COLOR ONE ELEMENT.
WHICH ONE IS IT?
WHAT COLOR DO YOU NEED?

WHAT DO THE JAPANESE
CALL THEIR COUNTRY?

N_ _ _ _ _.

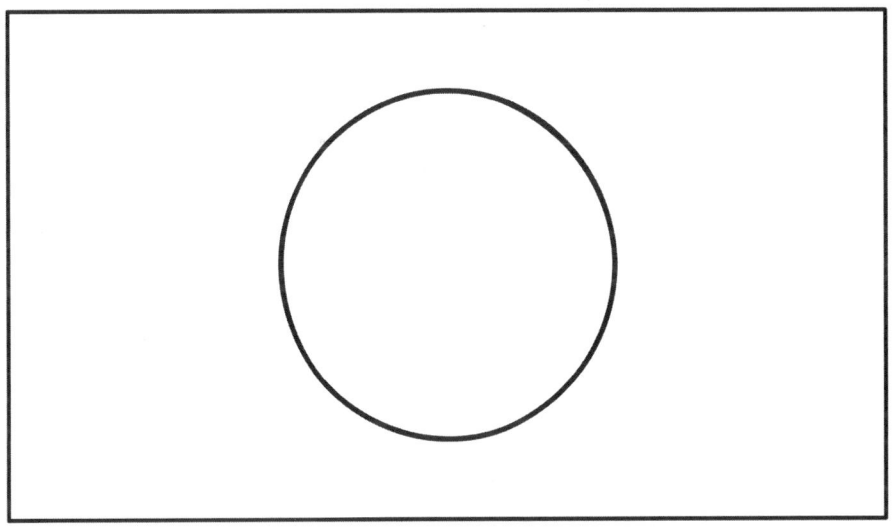

IF YOU JUST GOT 9
EQUAL VALUE COINS AS
AN ALLOWANCE AND WANT TO
SPLIT THEM BETWEEN 4
DIFFERENT PIGGY BANKS,
HOW DO YOU MAKE IT SO EACH
WILL GET A DIFFERENT
ODD NUMBER OF COINS?

BUNNY #4 ARRIVED RIGHT AFTER BUNNY #5, BUT BUNNY #3 MADE IT TO THE FINISH LINE RIGHT IN BETWEEN #1 AND #4.
WHO WON THE RACE?

THE GRID BELOW REPRESENTS THE NEIGHBORHOOD MAP.
EACH CELL IS A BLOCK AND EACH LINE IS A STREET.
THE STARS ARE THE LOCATIONS OF EVERY MEMBER OF THE KIDS' GANG.
HELP THEM FIND THE BEST CROSSING TO MEET AT.

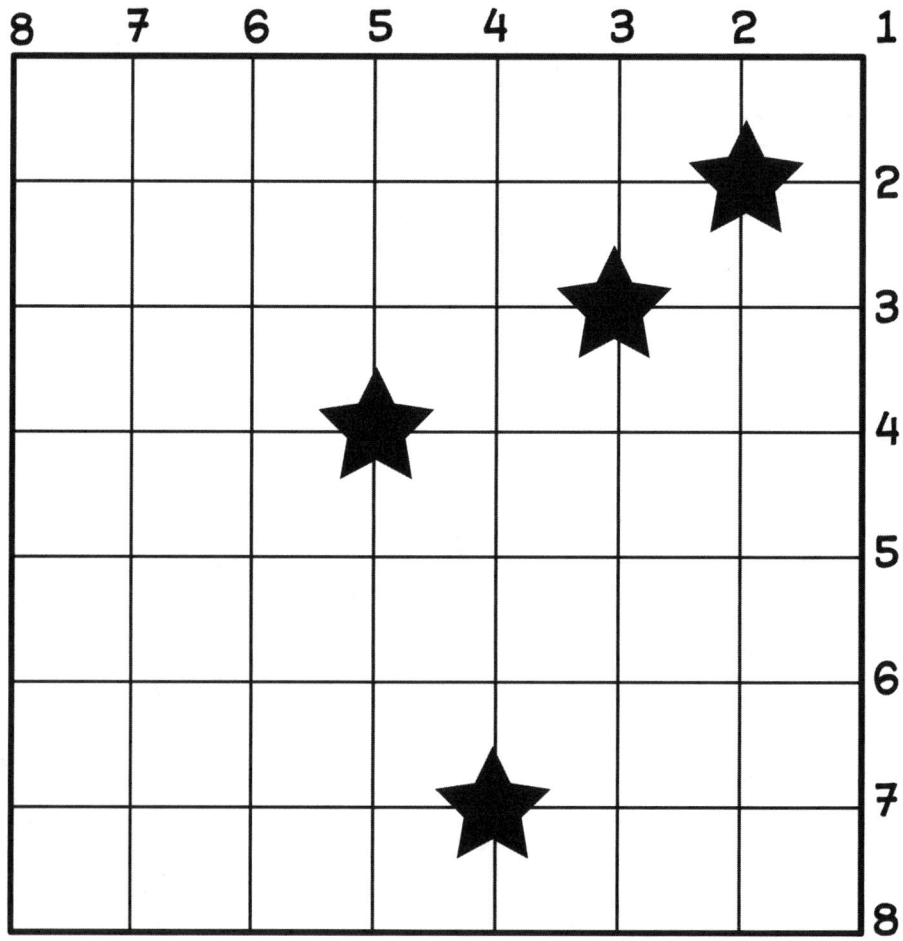

COLOR THE ONE THAT DOESN'T HIBERNATE.

ARRANGE THESE MATCHES SO ONLY TWO ARE LEFT AND NONE GOES MISSING.

THIS MOUSE HAS INVITED 8 MICE TO DINNER, BUT TO AVOID GETTING CAUGHT WITH THIS BIG WHEEL OF CHEESE, IT NEEDS TO SLICE IT IN ONLY 3 STROKES, TO TAKE ALL 8 SLICES AWAY FAST! HOW DOES IT DO IT?

JOIN ALL DOTS USING A SINGLE LINE, WHICH GOES FROM ONE DOT TO THE NEXT, CROSSING EACH ONE ONLY ONCE!

RIDDLE:
"A BOX WITHOUT HINGES, KEY, OR LID, YET GOLDEN TREASURE INSIDE IS HID."

JIMMY GETS 5 DOLLARS FROM HIS DAD EVERY WEEK, 10 FROM HIS MOM EVERY MONTH, AND 20 FROM GRANNY EVERY BIRTHDAY.

IF HE SAVES IT ALL, AND DOESN'T SPEND A PENNY, HOW MUCH MONEY WILL HE HAVE IN 10 YEARS?

CAN YOU DRAW THESE IN A DIFFERENT ORDER EACH TIME?.

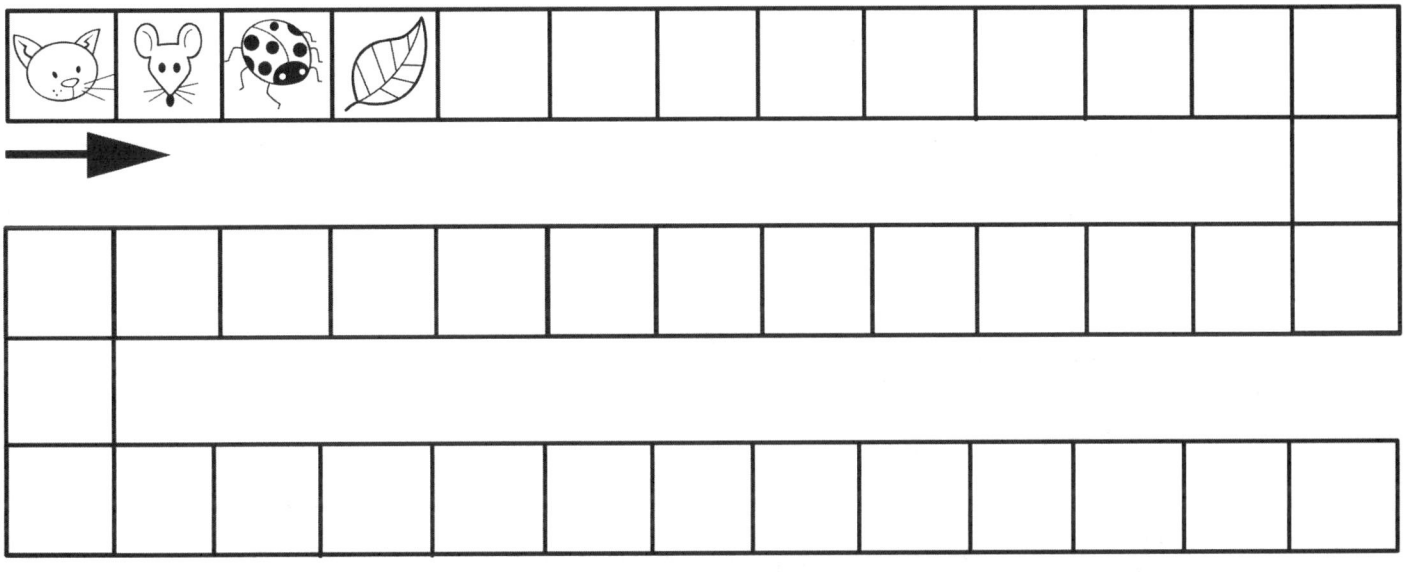

IF YOU TURN THE DIALS, HOW MANY POSSIBLE COMBINATIONS WILL YOU GET?

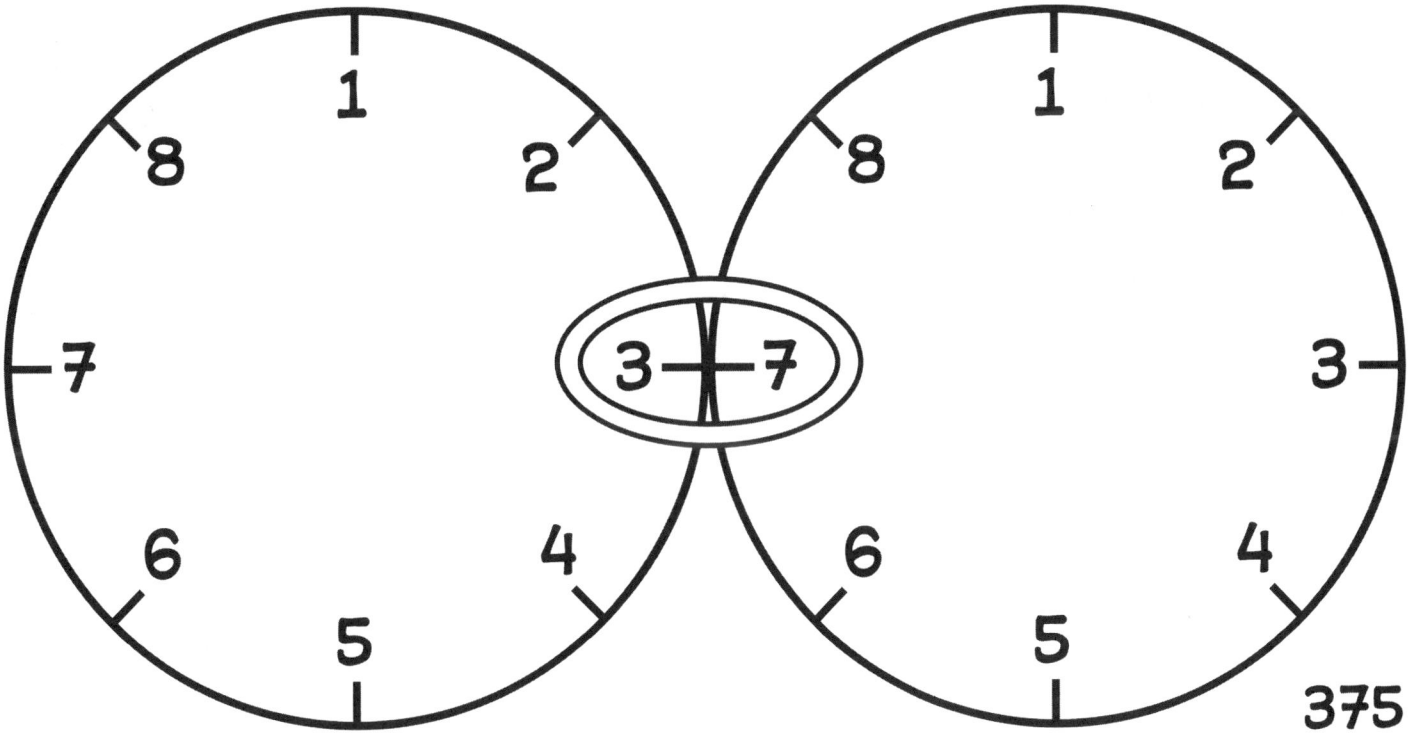

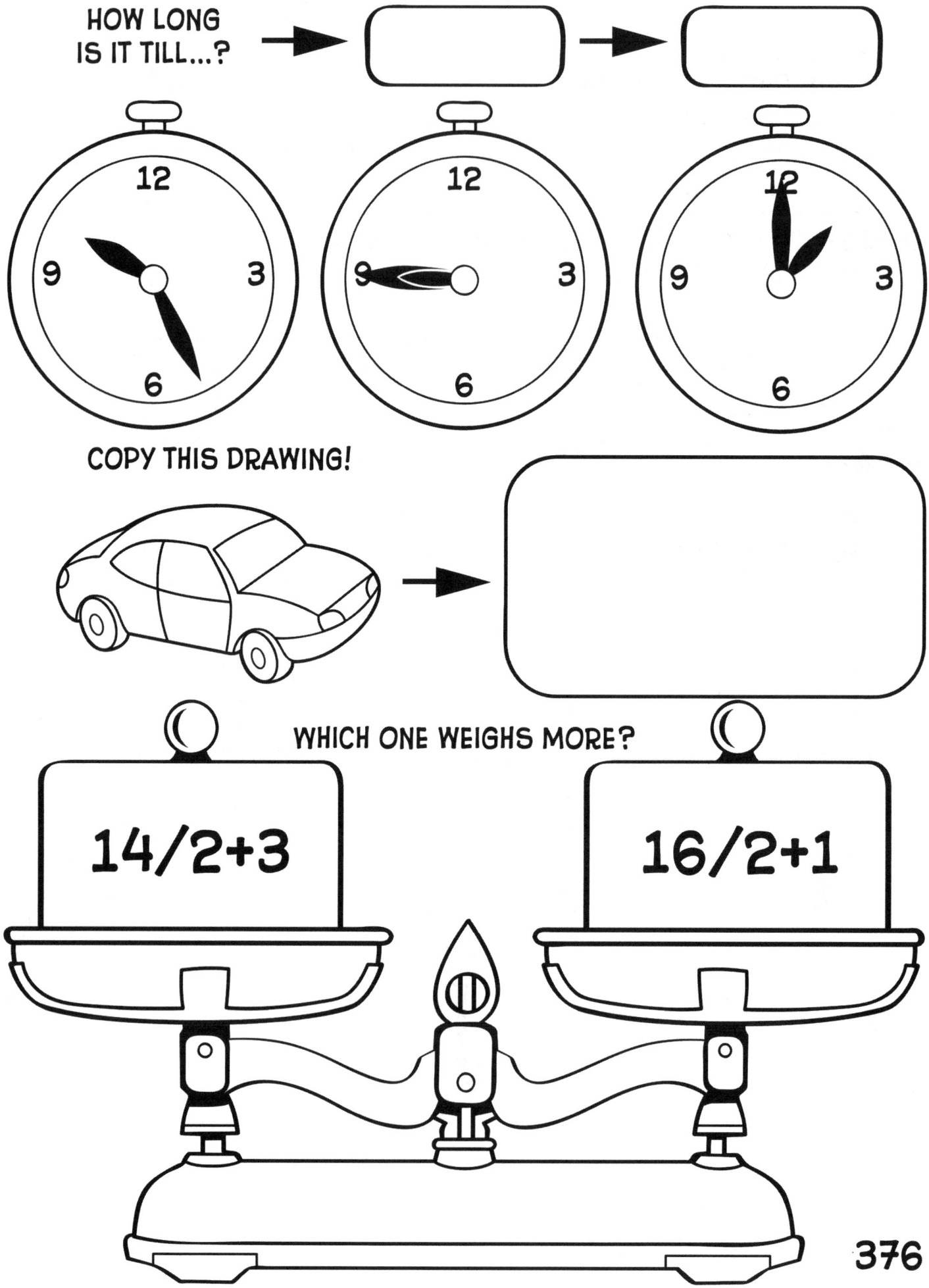
HOW LONG IS IT TILL...?
12
9
3
6
12
9
3
6
12
9
3
6
COPY THIS DRAWING!
WHICH ONE WEIGHS MORE?
14/2+3
16/2+1

WRITE A STORY ABOUT MR. BADGER.

THE END.

WILL THE WHEELS FALL LEFT OR RIGHT?

INSIDE THIS HEART, DRAW THE PERSON YOU LOVE THE MOST IN THE WHOLE, WIDE WORLD!

WHERE DOES WOOL COME FROM?

NAME THREE CLOTHING ITEMS MADE OF WOOL.

DECEPTIVELY SIMPLE! CAN YOU CHANGE THE "DONKEY" POSITION BY MOVING ONLY ONE MATCH?

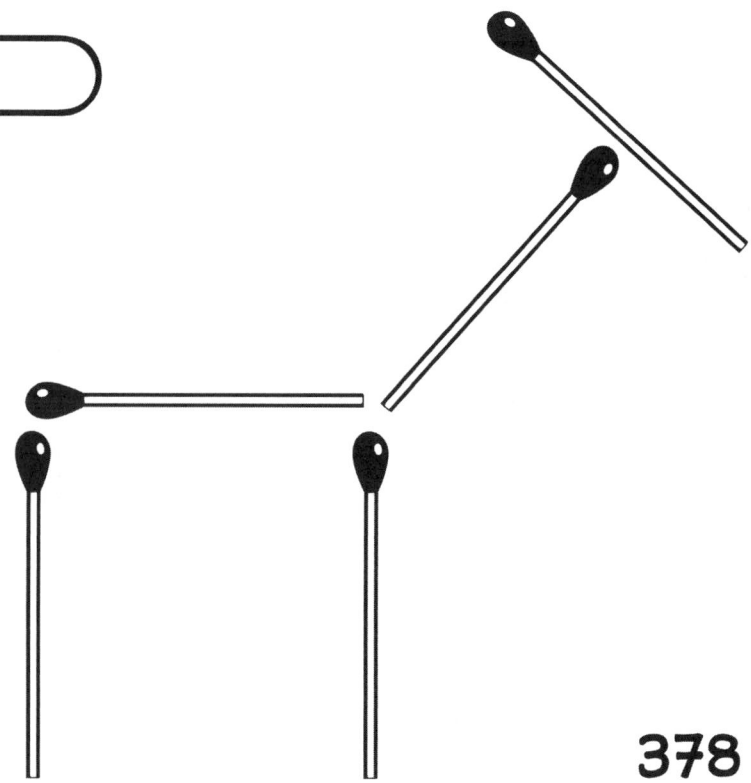

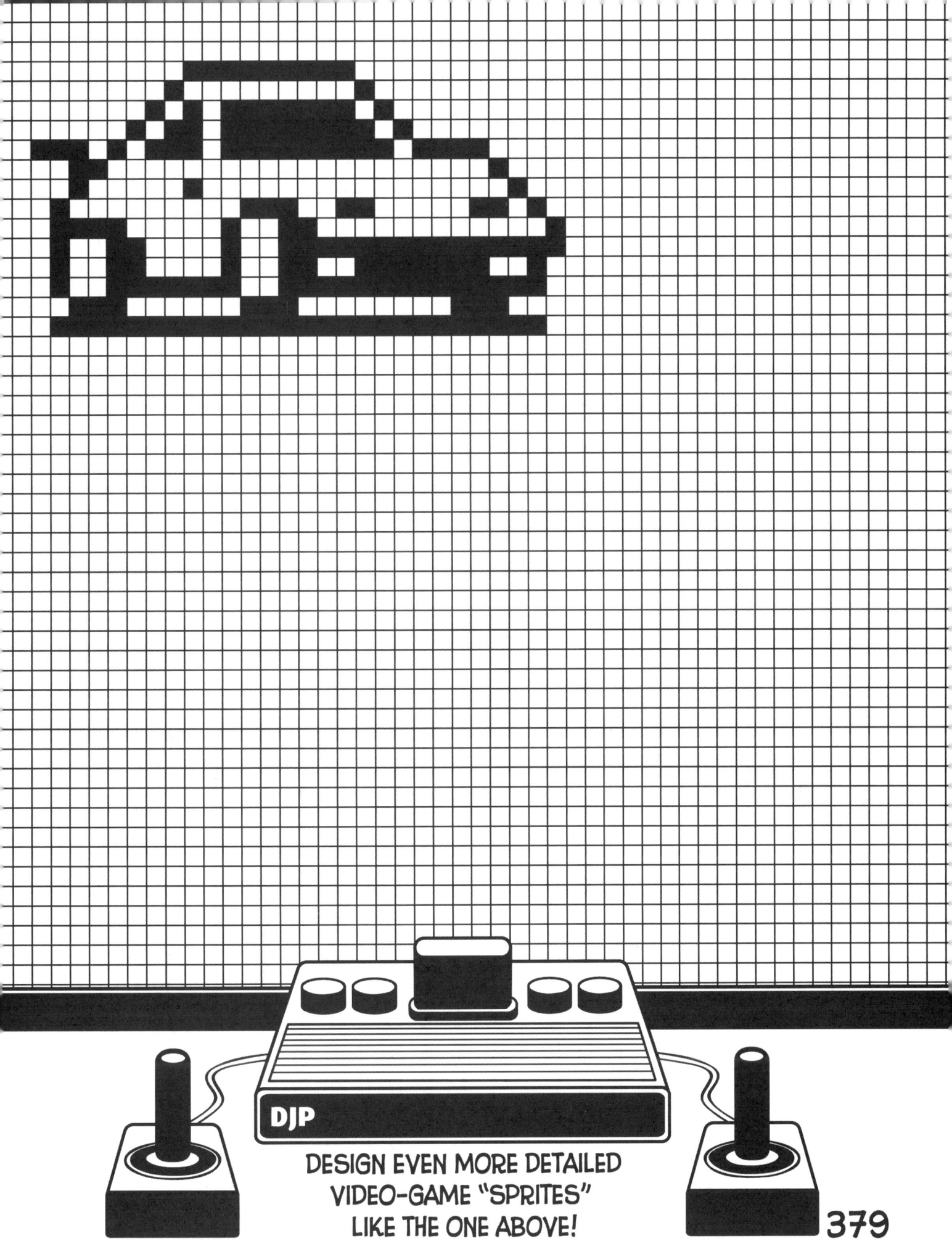

DESIGN EVEN MORE DETAILED
VIDEO-GAME "SPRITES"
LIKE THE ONE ABOVE!

COMPLETE EACH COLUMN SO THE SUM OF THESE NUMBERS IS ALWAYS 231.

1	38	54	21	5	18	96	42	27	16	30	210
30											
120											
80											

WHAT IS THE NAME OF THIS ANIMAL?

WHAT KIND OF MAMMAL IS IT?

CAN YOU FIND 15 GREAT AMERICAN PAINTERS IN THIS WORDSEARCH?
CLUE: ONE OF THEM WAS KNOWN TO SPLATTER PAINT ON THE CANVAS!

F R A N C I S L U I S M O R A K J P K F J
T H E L E N F R A N K E N T H A L E R Q A
M B Z J O H N S I N G E R S A R G E N T C
T L H V E E D W A R D H O P P E R D T E K
X Z D U E Q F H T Q G R F I O B F W L Y S
R O Y L I C H T E N S T E I N X Q O J C O
E D G A R P A Y N E Y P F W X C C H C C N
P K R A C D N Y G P R U E I L S X T Y Z P
M A R K R O T H K O K X B T A O V C B Z O
G E O R G I A O K E E F E M E O O G Q G L
J I R D W I N S L O W H O M E R L M F Z L
O Z Z L C T T P H B G H D G U B M U I Y O
L A N D R E W W Y E T H M J B E D A J S C
F R E D E R I C R E M I N G T O N A X B K

IF YOU TURN THE DIALS, HOW MANY POSSIBLE COMBINATIONS WILL YOU GET?

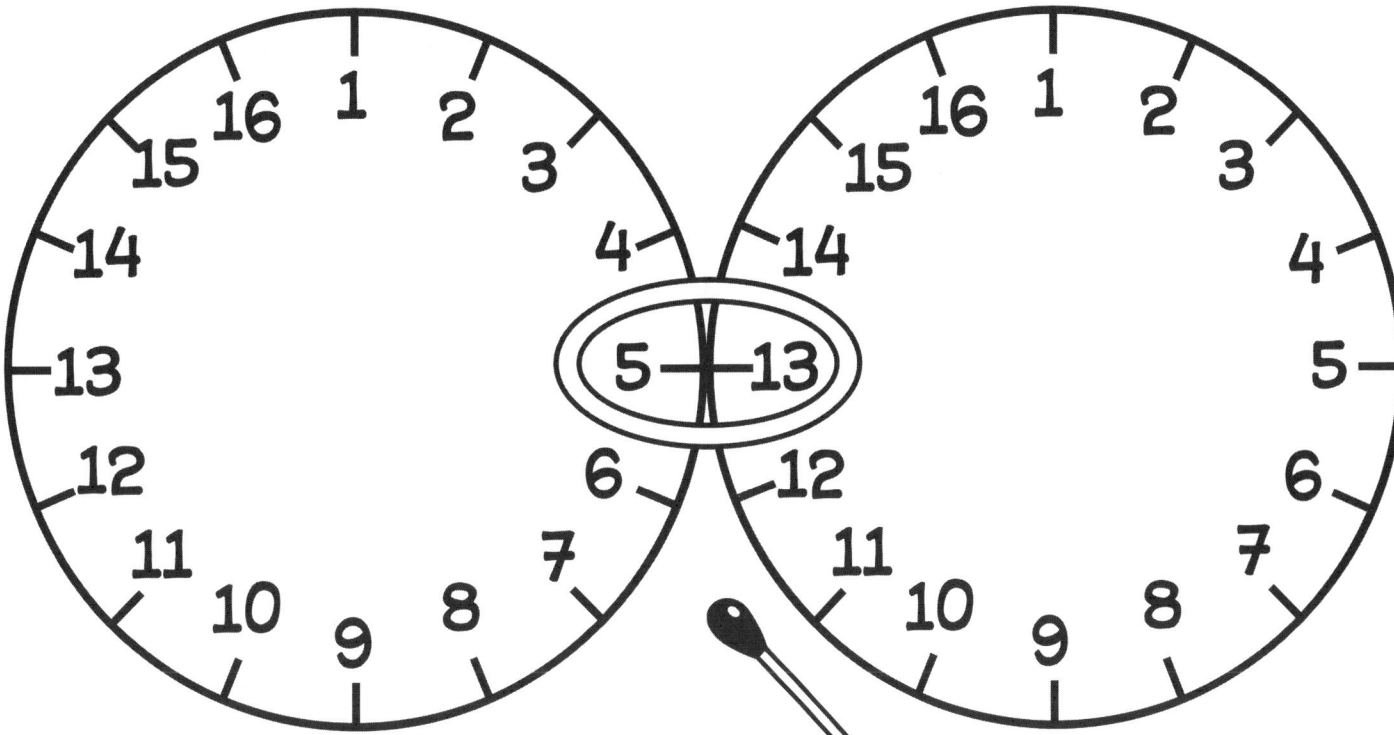

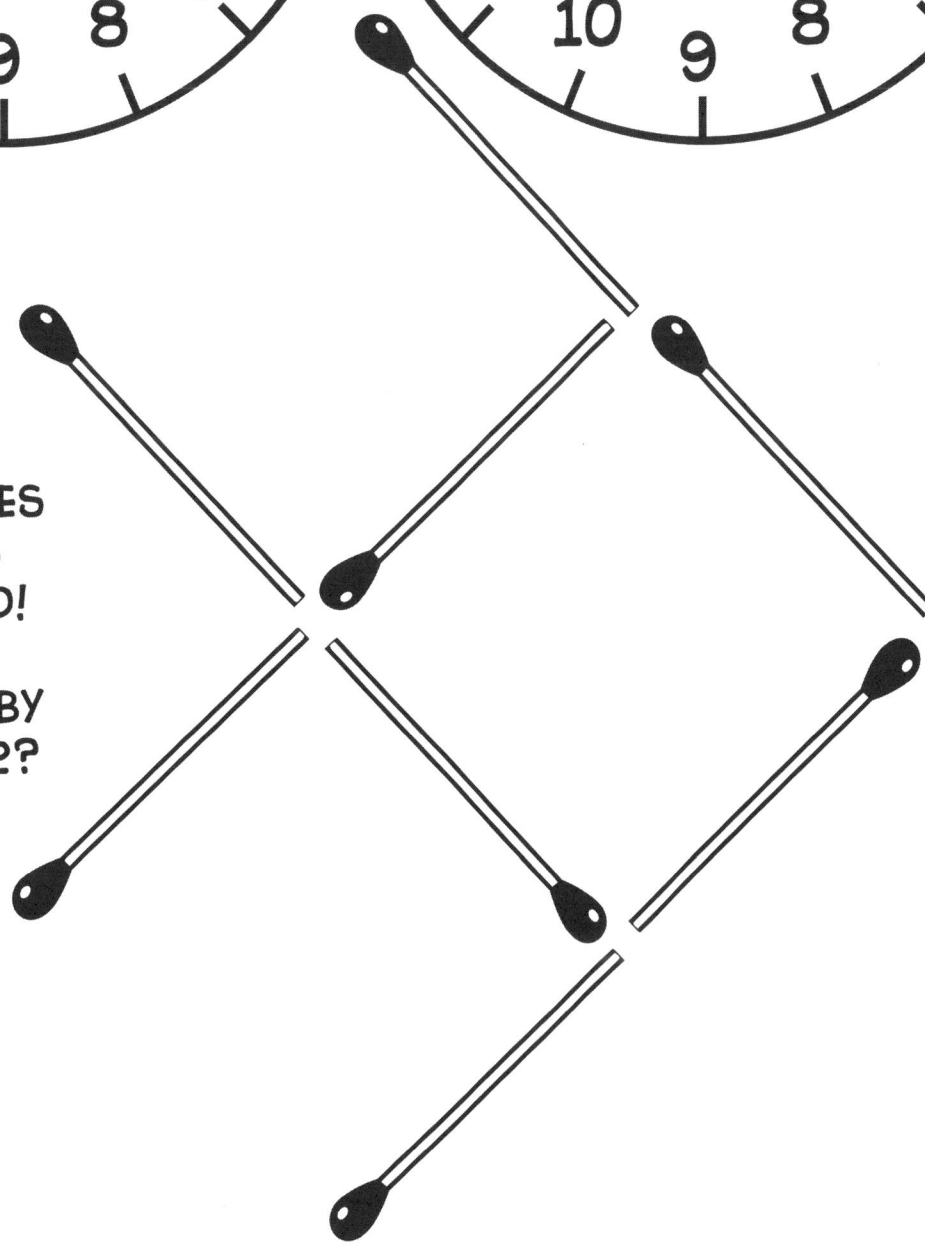

MOVE 3 MATCHES
TO TURN THIS
"FISH" AROUND!

CAN YOU DO IT BY
MOVING JUST 2?

CRACK THE SUDOKU!
EACH ELEMENT CAN ONLY BE PLACED ONCE ON EACH LINE, ONCE ON EACH ROW, AND ONCE IN EACH 3 BY 2 CELLS GRID.

TRACE THE DOTS TO DRAW THE INTERSECTING DIAMONDS IN A SINGLE STROKE.

FIND THE WAY OUT!

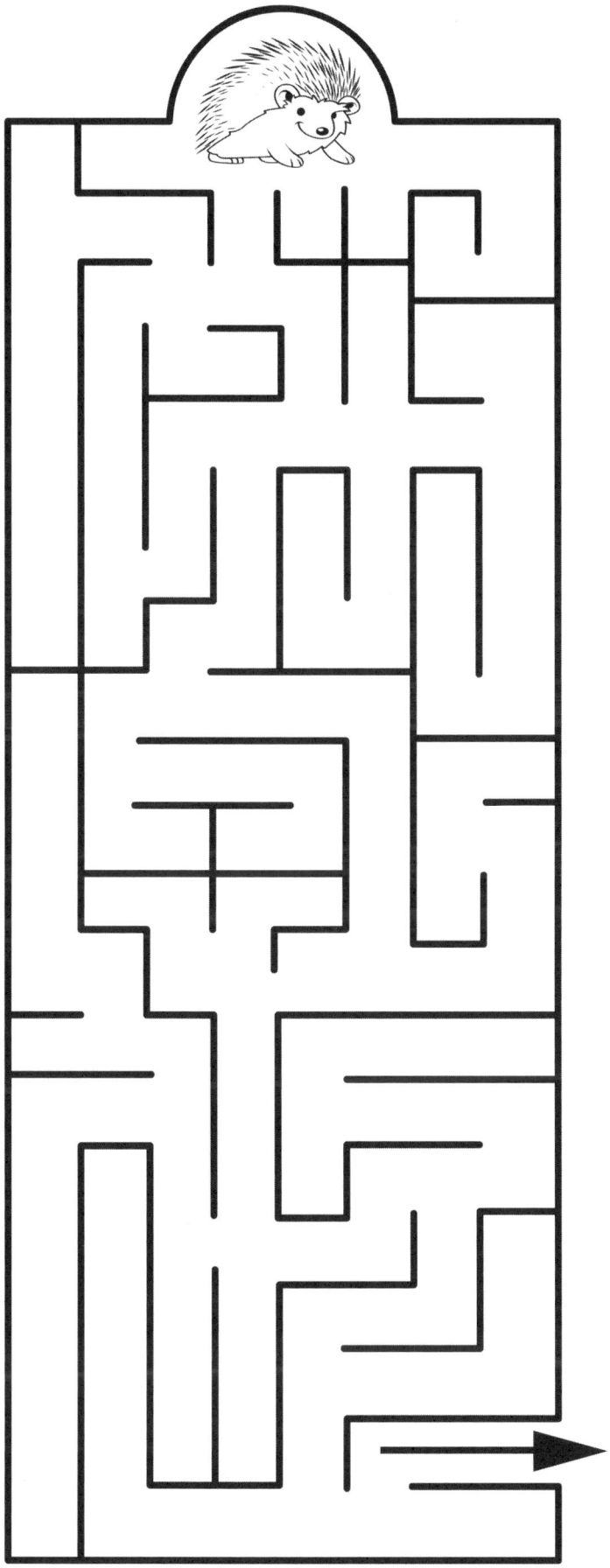

WRITE A STORY ABOUT MS. TORTOISE.

THE END.

RIDDLE:
"THERE ARE TWO MONKEYS ON A TREE AND ONE JUMPS OFF. WHY DOES THE OTHER MONKEY JUMP TOO?"

LOOK FOR THE SYMBOL THAT APPEARS TWICE IN THE WHOLE GRID, AND COLOR BOTH ALIKE.

ONLY THREE BLACK SHAPES WILL FIT THE DIAMOND.
WHICH ONES DO NOT?

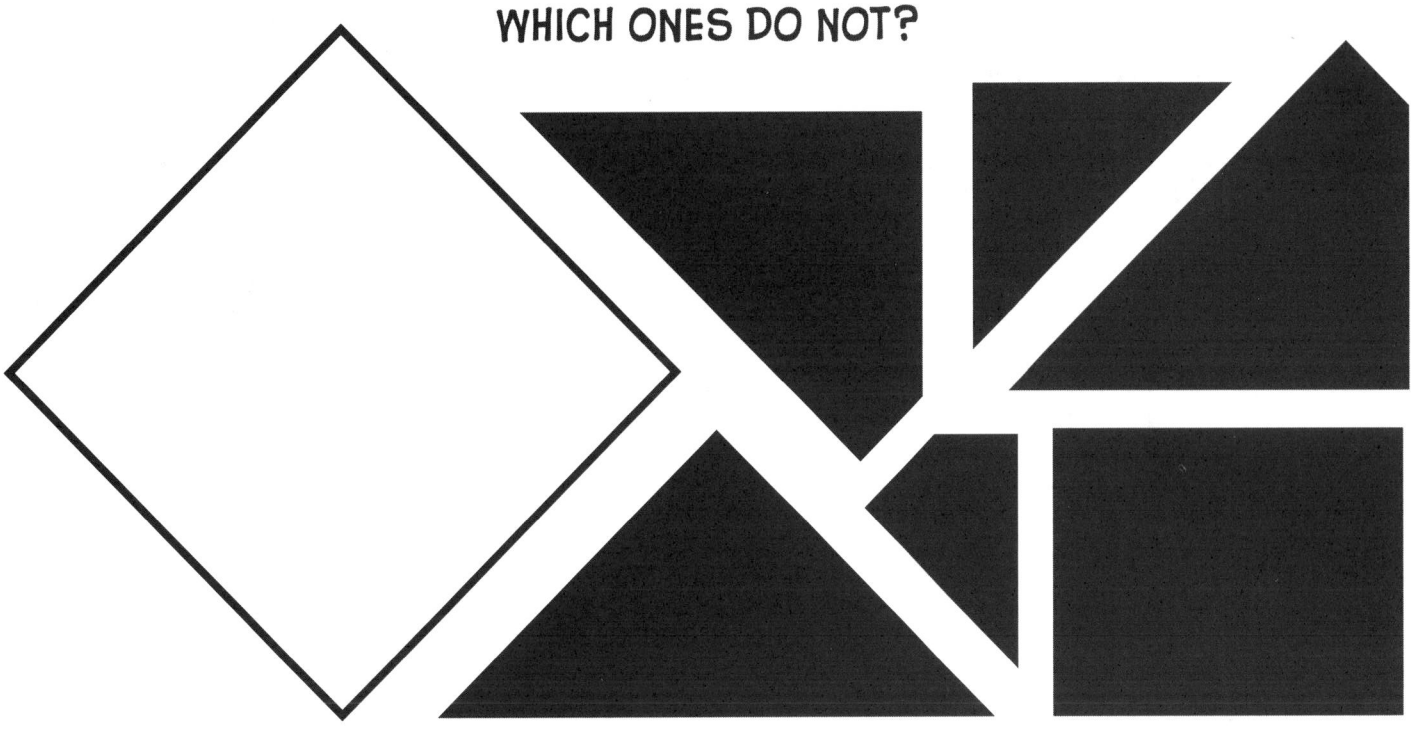

CAN YOU SET THIS TABLE RIGHT?
SEE THE RIGHT WAY TO DO IT ON THE NEXT PAGE!

SURPRISE YOUR PARENTS BY SETTING THE DINNER TABLE AT HOME!

NAME EACH NUMBERED ITEM BELOW.

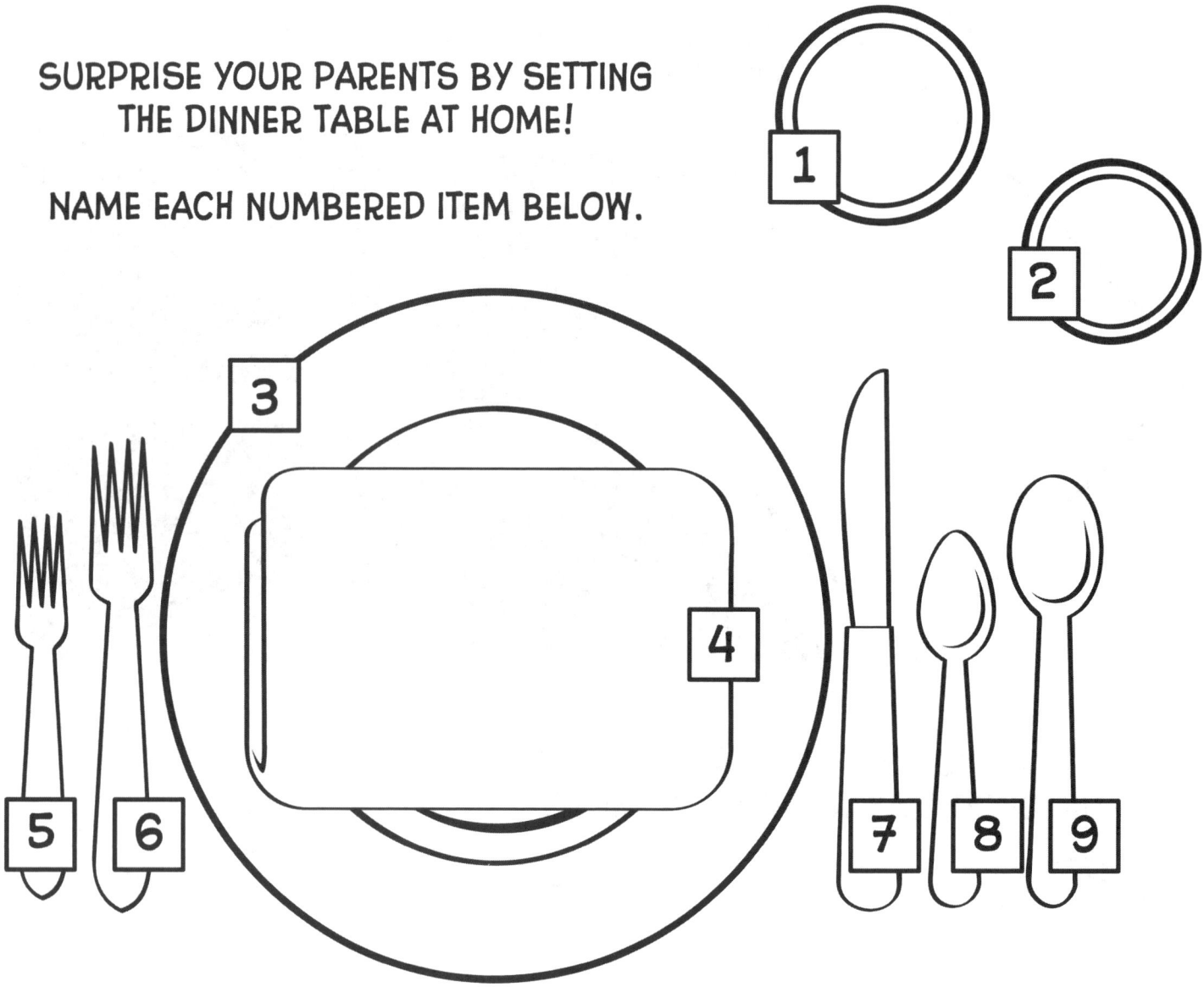

1 _____

2 _____

3 _____

4 _____

5 _____

6 _____

7 _____

8 _____

9 _____

TRACE THE DOTS TO DRAW IT ALL IN A SINGLE STROKE, WITHOUT ONCE LIFTING YOUR PENCIL OR PEN FROM THE PAGE!

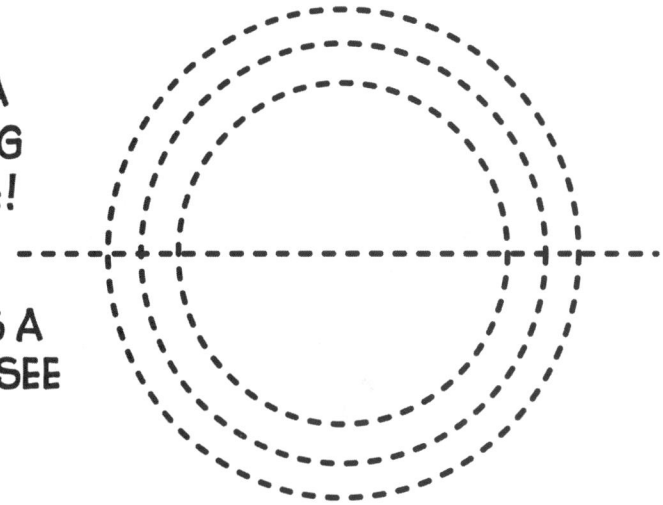

RIDDLE:
"FLAT AS A LEAF, ROUND AS A RING; HAS TWO EYES, CAN'T SEE A THING." WHAT IS IT?

IN THIS NEW GAME OF TIC-TAC-TOE, THE GOAL IS TO AVOID VERTICAL, HORIZONTAL, OR DIAGONAL LINES OF UP TO FOUR CROSSES OR CIRCLES.

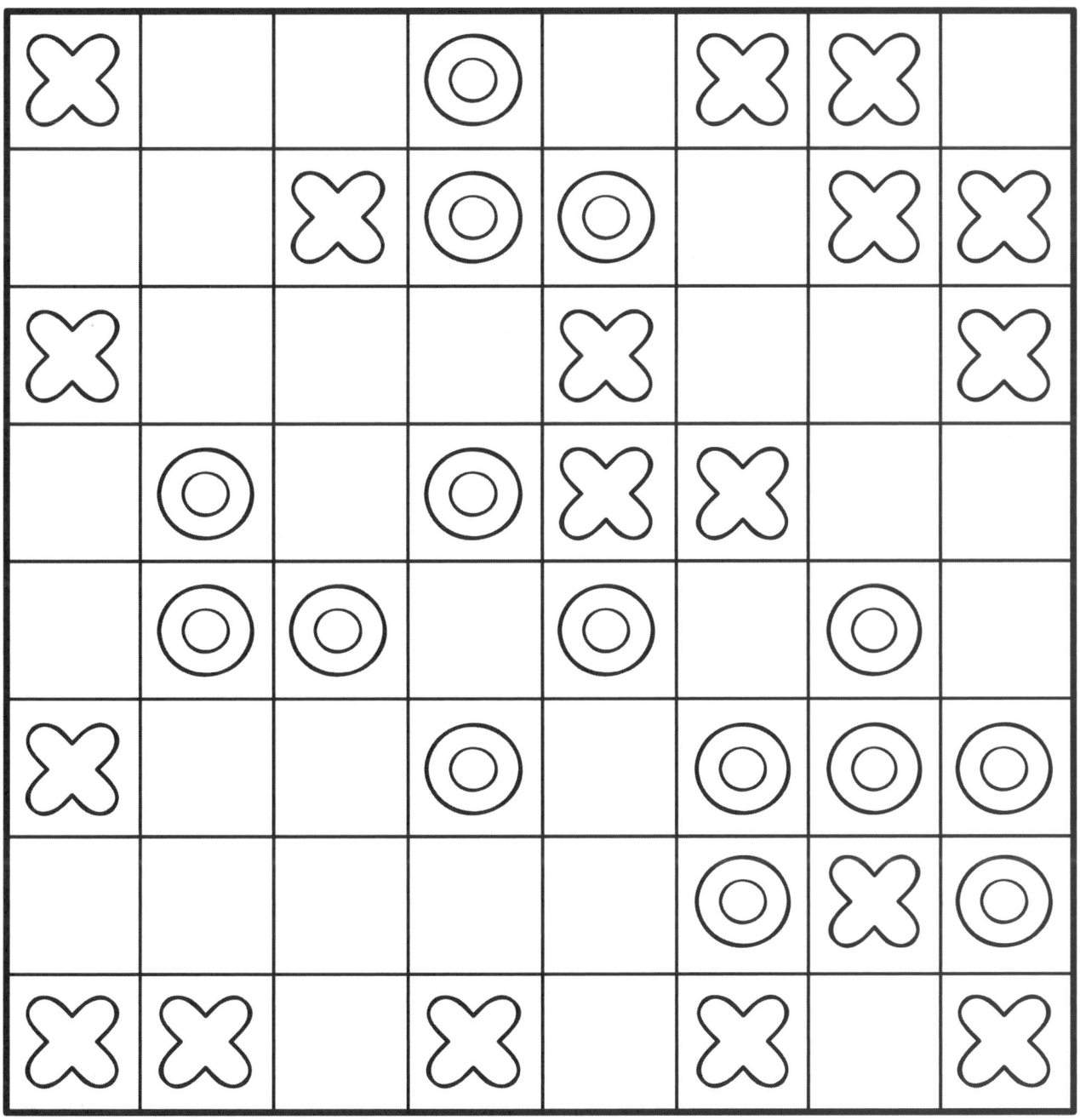

WHICH MOAI DOES NOT LOOK LIKE THE OTHERS?

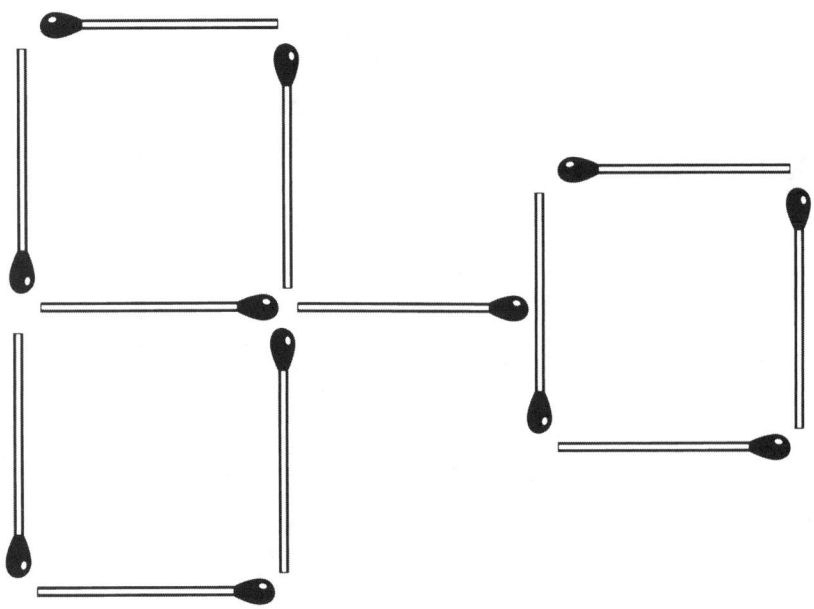

MOVE 6 MATCHES
TO FORM
5 SQUARES!

FOLLOW EACH PATH TO FIND OUT WHICH TAPES ACTUALLY BELONG TO THIS MUSIC CASSETTE!

EVERY GOOD STORY HAS THREE PARTS. CAN YOU GUESS WHAT IS EACH ONE IS CALLED?

1.

2.

3.

USE THEM IN THE FOLLOWING ACTIVITY!

THE END.

WHY IS SHE WALKING IN THE RAIN? WRITE HER STORY!

CRACK THE SUDOKU! EACH ELEMENT CAN ONLY BE PLACED ONCE ON EACH LINE, ONCE ON EACH ROW, AND ONCE IN EACH 3 BY 2 CELLS GRID.

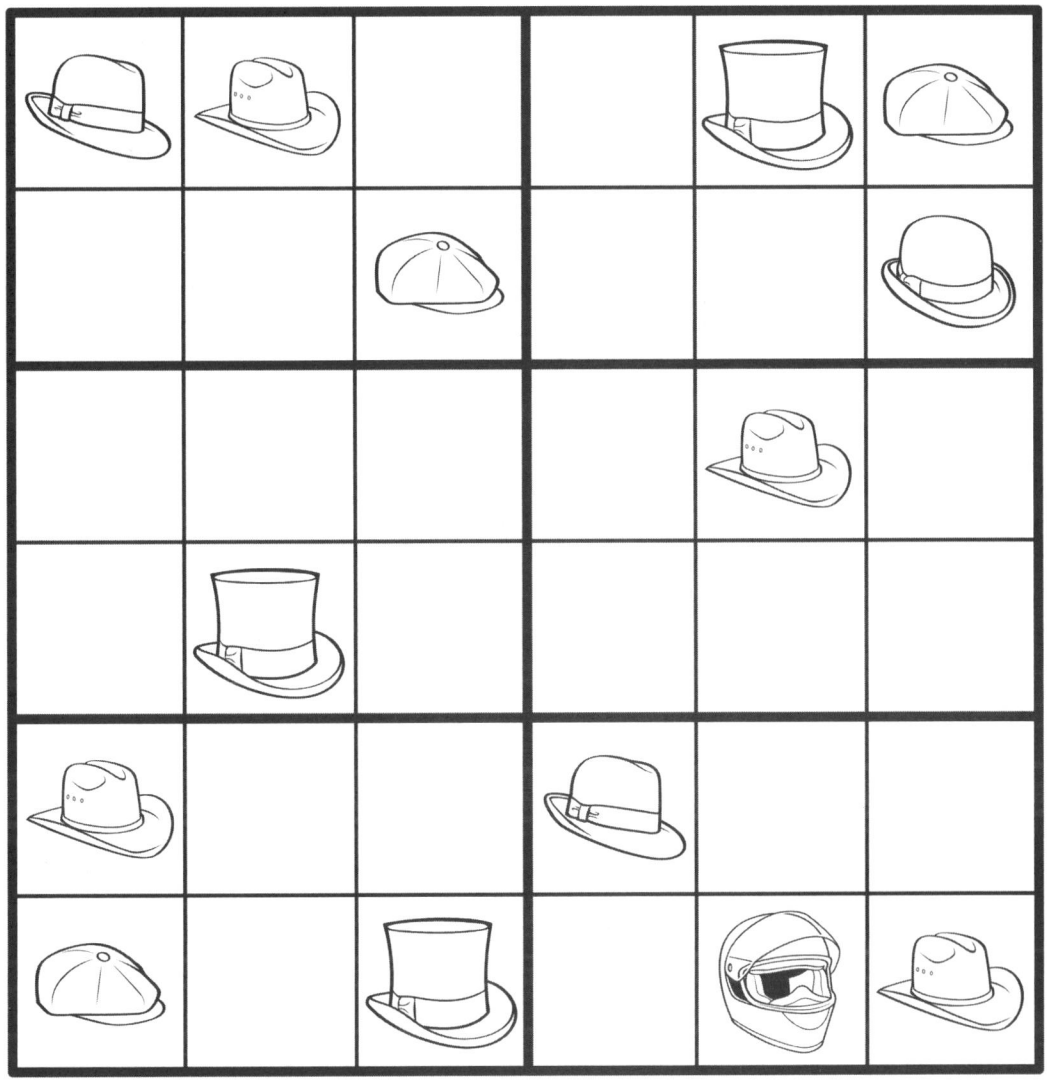

K	H	W	D	E	N	N	I	S	T	H	E	M	E	N	A	C	E	I	S
A	L	I	T	T	L	E	O	R	P	H	A	N	A	N	N	I	E	C	T
T	U	E	C	T	O	Q	Z	B	K	W	J	G	Y	B	D	A	P	A	E
Z	C	M	Q	H	K	P	P	O	P	E	Y	E	A	A	E	F	R	L	V
E	H	L	M	A	N	D	R	A	K	E	L	Y	N	R	Y	F	I	V	E
N	A	E	I	S	R	Z	T	R	G	I	C	A	P	N	X	F	N	I	C
J	R	D	O	F	J	A	Q	A	A	A	G	P	C	E	A	V	C	N	A
A	L	V	W	D	K	F	P	B	R	R	A	L	L	Y	C	M	E	A	N
M	I	O	F	Y	D	F	E	T	O	C	B	O	F	G	H	A	V	N	Y
M	E	K	Z	U	P	L	K	M	Y	W	T	T	T	O	Q	R	A	D	O
E	B	A	N	T	T	C	X	D	F	W	R	N	C	O	P	Y	L	H	N
R	R	E	T	E	I	E	N	A	J	E	X	D	H	G	Z	W	I	O	P
K	O	K	E	D	R	A	J	N	B	Y	L	Z	Z	L	I	O	A	B	M
I	W	B	F	W	J	M	R	L	A	Z	A	I	O	E	P	R	N	B	T
D	N	Z	L	F	D	D	I	M	A	R	V	I	N	G	P	T	T	E	Q
S	Z	Z	T	X	Z	D	D	N	L	B	O	M	X	T	Y	H	O	S	P

HOW MUCH DO YOU KNOW ABOUT COMICS? THIS WORDSEARCH CONTAINS THE NAMES OF 20 CLASSIC CHARACTERS FROM THE FUNNIES FOR YOU TO FIND.

CLUE:
NONE OF THEM IS A SUPERHERO!

HELP SALLY FIND BILLY ON THE NEXT PAGE!

DRAW THE MISSING ASTEROID BELT!

OR PLAY WITH A FRIEND TO SEE WHO FINDS THE OTHER ONE FIRST!

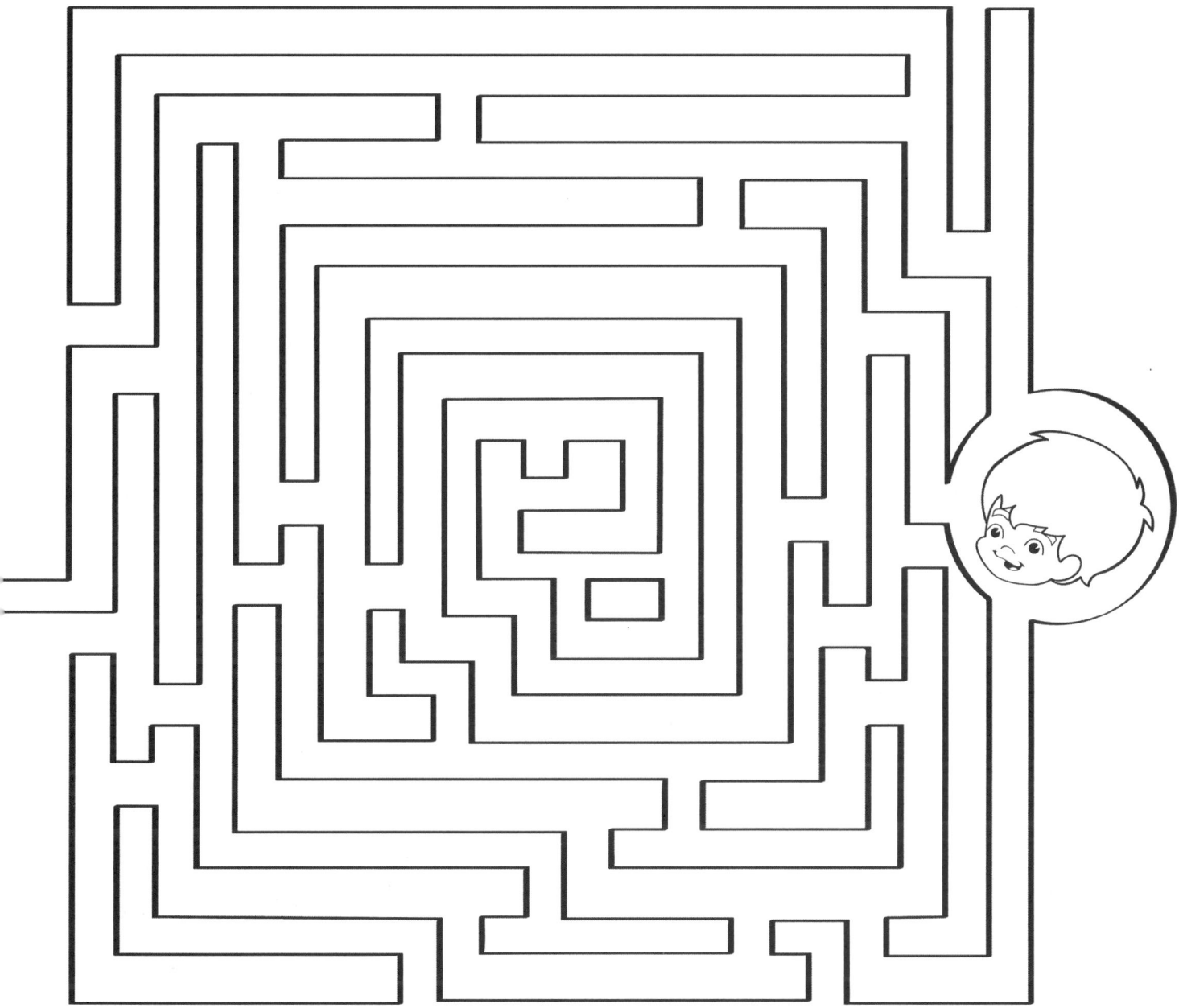

WHERE WERE THESE TOYS FIRST INVENTED?

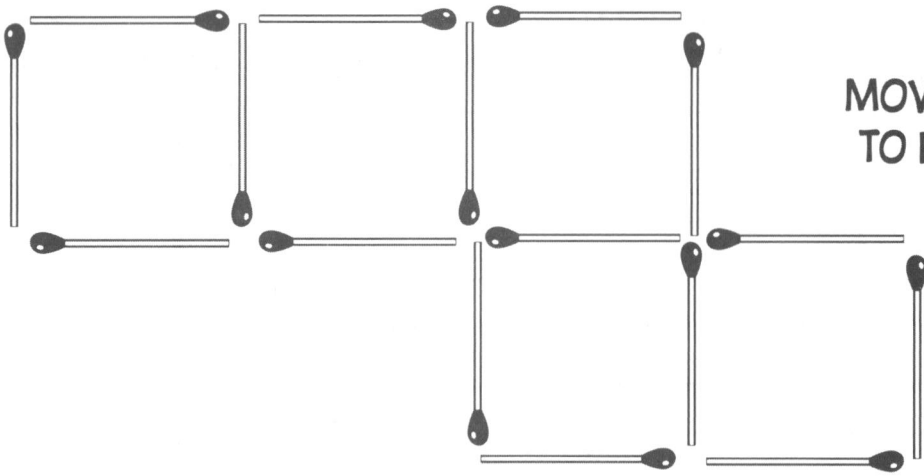

MOVE ONLY 2 MATCHES
TO FORM 4 SQUARES!

JOIN ALL DOTS USING A SINGLE LINE, WHICH GOES FROM ONE DOT
TO THE NEXT, CROSSING EACH ONE ONLY ONCE!

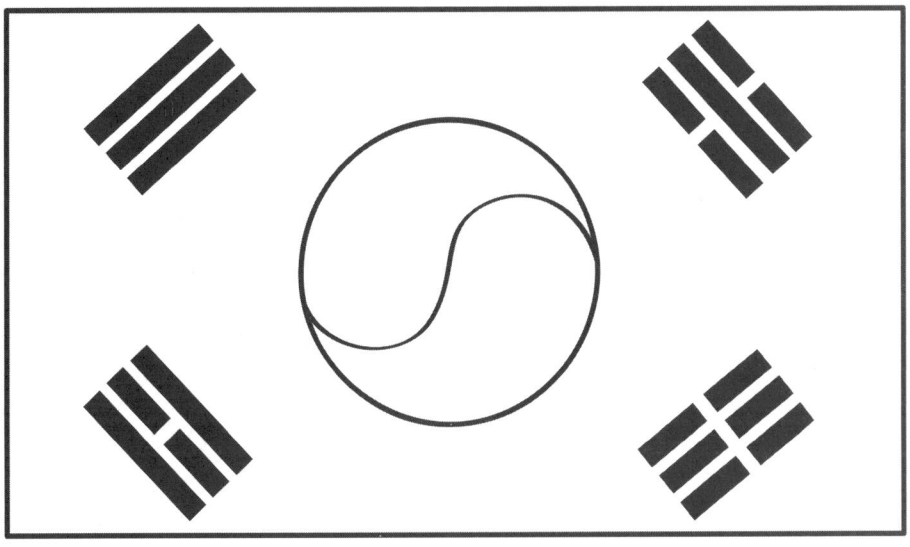

THESE FLAGS BELONG TO NORTH KOREA AND SOUTH KOREA.

WHAT DO YOU KNOW ABOUT THESE TWO COUNTRIES?

THEIR FLAGS ARE BOTH RED, WHITE, AND BLUE.

COLOR THEM!

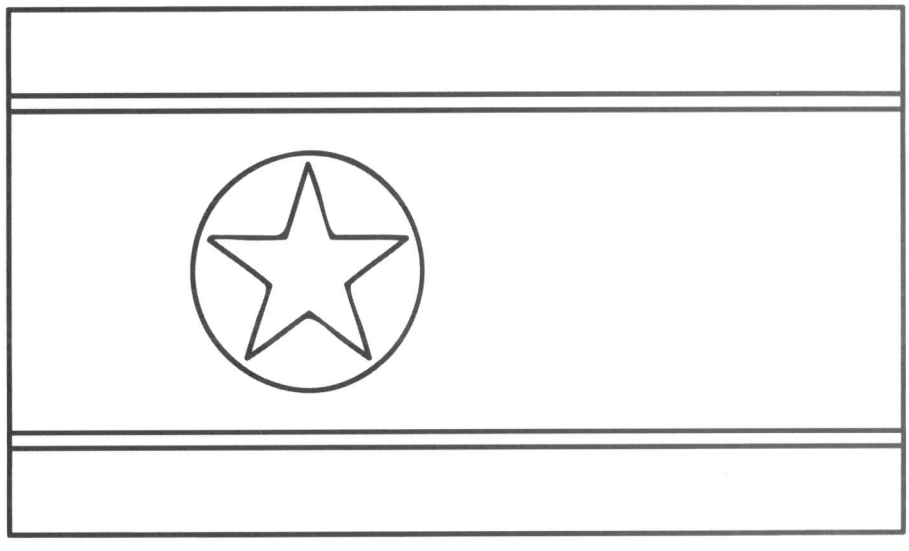

FIND THE HIPPO'S MATCHING SILHOUETTE.

WHAT CONTINENT IS THIS?

CAN YOU NAME ITS OCEANS?

FIND ALL ITS COUNTRIES IN THE WORDSEARCH BELOW!

X	M	S	Q	P	C	T	U	O	N	P	H	I	L	I	P	P	I	N	E	S	C	I	S
P	A	K	I	S	T	A	N	A	A	B	A	N	G	L	A	D	E	S	H	V	H	T	H
P	P	C	Q	E	A	J	R	N	N	O	A	K	C	A	F	W	H	D	I	R	A	Q	X
E	R	I	P	W	R	I	F	K	U	W	A	I	T	A	O	K	A	I	N	D	I	A	D
G	H	U	S	B	M	K	U	N	I	T	E	D	A	R	A	B	E	M	I	R	A	T	E
N	B	Y	S	Q	E	I	C	A	M	B	O	D	I	A	T	C	F	Z	M	Y	A	N	M
W	A	L	N	S	N	S	T	F	Y	W	S	L	A	O	S	U	V	I	E	T	N	A	M
C	H	I	N	A	I	T	A	Z	E	R	B	A	I	J	A	N	R	M	A	L	D	I	V
D	R	J	O	V	A	A	N	O	R	T	H	K	O	R	E	A	Z	K	M	I	O	F	N
B	A	O	B	I	I	N	D	O	N	E	S	I	A	D	K	Y	H	K	M	A	U	U	Q
U	I	M	S	A	U	D	I	A	R	A	B	I	A	N	W	A	O	G	O	E	R	A	E
J	N	A	L	A	F	G	H	A	N	I	S	T	A	N	E	H	J	E	N	B	N	B	N
B	O	N	Y	L	H	U	E	K	Y	L	P	L	X	Q	N	J	N	O	G	I	Z	I	B
G	Q	R	L	H	A	Q	B	M	J	Q	I	S	R	A	E	L	X	R	O	U	S	Q	S
Q	P	W	D	Q	Y	Z	H	K	Y	R	G	Y	Z	S	T	A	N	G	L	L	P	R	L
L	P	Y	K	A	Z	A	K	H	S	T	A	N	Z	J	E	C	L	I	I	C	R	A	U
Z	L	E	B	A	N	O	N	S	O	U	T	H	K	O	R	E	A	A	A	X	M	H	C
P	A	L	E	S	T	I	N	I	A	N	T	E	R	R	I	T	O	R	Y	S	B	X	Y

R	I	A	U	A							
H	A	I	L	A	N	D					
Q	X	M	A	C	A	O	N				
A	D	P	R	D	L	D	V				
E	S	S	J	F	T	N					
A	R	D	I	A	E						
A	I	X	T	R	H						
E	S	S	O	T	Y						
F	N	P	I	P	D	E	A				
A	P	K	A	Z							
G	M	R	I	T	F						
Z	U	S	E	B	Q						
I	B	T	Y	N	J	H	A				
A	A	C	A	L	T						
P	R	L	T	D	H	P	A	A			
I	C	R	A	U	N	A	V	A	H	R	
M	H	C	Q	O	N	N	Q	F			
E	M	E	N	Y	K						

CLUE: SEE TWO OF THESE COUNTRIES IN THE PREVIOUS PAGE!

JIMMY LOST HIS PIGGY BANK! HELP HIM FIND IT, WHILE GRABBING THE MOST COINS ON HIS WAY!

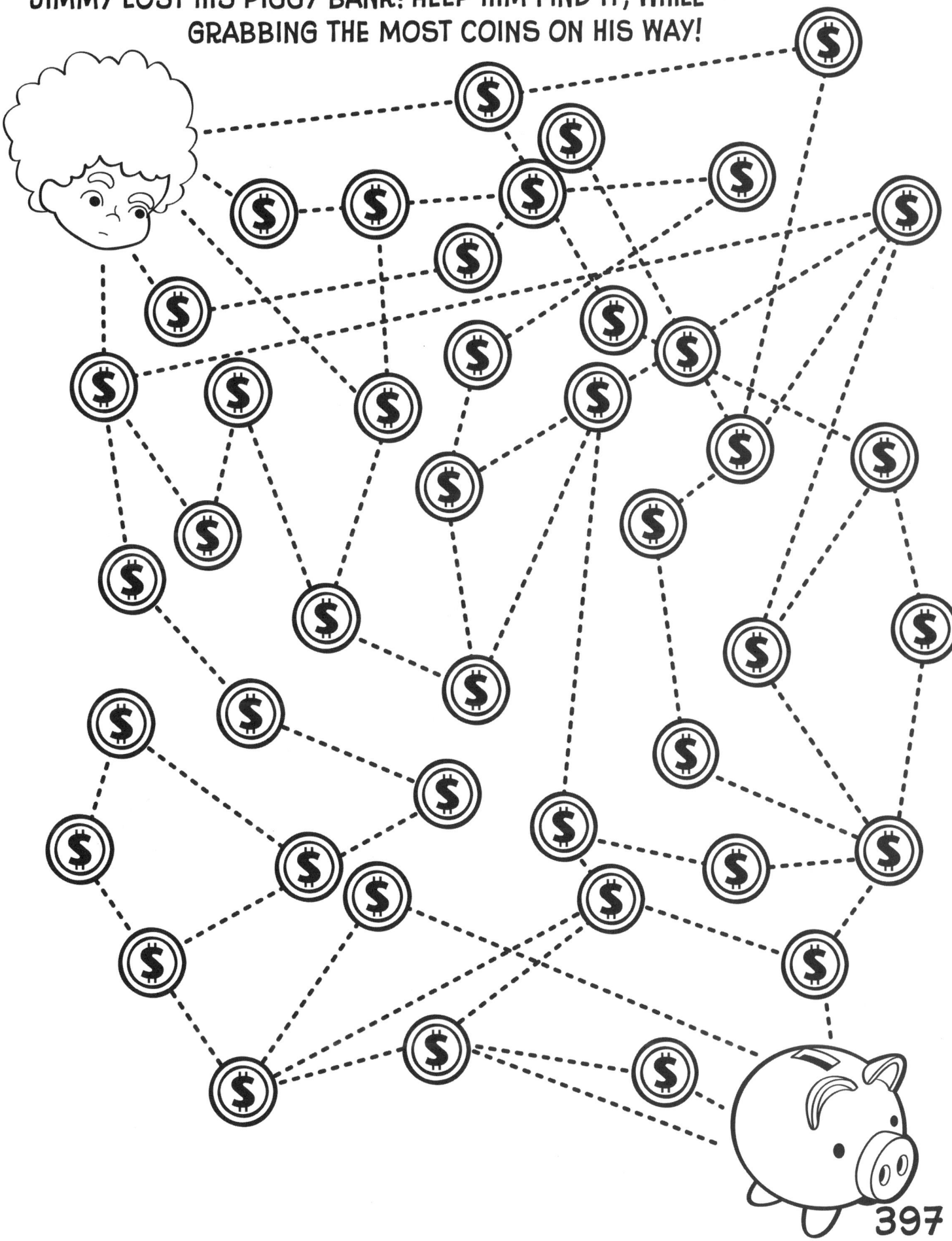

TO FIGURE OUT WHAT THE MYSTERY PICTURE IS, FILL EACH NUMBERED AREA AS INSTRUCTED.

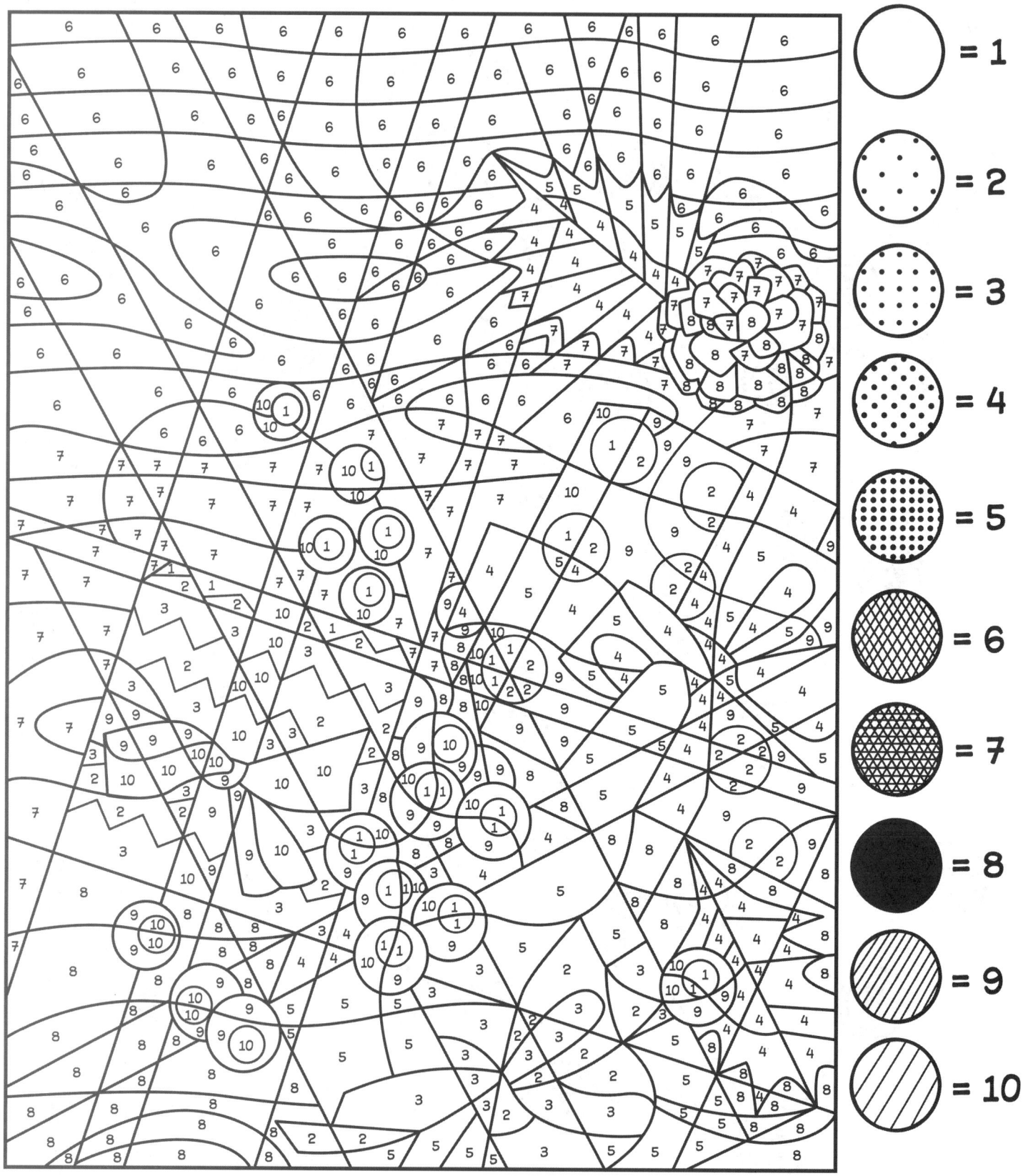

HOW MANY CANDY CANES AND BAUBLES CAN YOU COUNT?
COLOR THE CANES RED AND WHITE, THE BALLS BLUE,
AND A VERY MERRY CHRISTMAS TO ALL OF YOU!

THIS BOOK WAS COMPLETED BY:

DIEGO JOURDAN PEREIRA IS A LEADING PUZZLE DESIGNER AND NONFICTION WRITER WITH A BACKGROUND IN ILLUSTRATION, COMIC-BOOKS, AND GRAPHIC DESIGN. IN ADDITION TO HIS OWN BOOKS FOR CHILDREN AND ADULTS, HE HAS WORKED ON LICENSED PROPERTIES SUCH AS TEENAGE MUTANT NINJA TURTLES, TRANSFORMERS, DONALD DUCK, GRUMPY CAT, LEGO, MARS ATTACKS!, REGULAR SHOW, SESAME STREET, STAR WARS, TOY STORY, AND WWE, FOR AN INTERNATIONAL CLIENTELE INCLUDING DC COMICS, DC THOMSON MEDIA, DOVER PUBLICATIONS, IDW PUBLISHING, SKYHORSE PUBLISHING, AND THE TOPPS COMPANY.

ANSWER
KEYS

6

THE POOR ZEBRA GOT SCARED AND LOST HER STRIPES!
CAN YOU DRAW THEM?

BE CREATIVE!

WHAT ABOUT THE TIGER'S?

COLOR THEM BOTH!

YOU CAN DO IT!

6

7

COLOR THE CUTE CATERPILLAR.

REPEAT THE THREE PATTERNS.

YOU CAN DO IT!

AND FINISH DRAWING HER BODY!

7

8

1 = GREEN AND 2 = BLUE

WHAT ANIMAL IS IT? FROG

HOW MANY WATERLILIES DO YOU COUNT? 5

HOW MANY LEAPS DOES THE FROG NEED TO CATCH THE FLY?

4

8

9

FILL EACH FISH WITH A DIFFERENT PATTERN.

HOW MANY FISH DO YOU COUNT? 4

BE CREATIVE!

DECORATE AND COLOR THE SEASHELLS TOO!

9

10

COLOR THE INSECTS ON EACH GROUP.
THEN COUNT THEM, AND COLOR THE RIGHT NUMBER.

HOW MANY ANTS DO YOU COUNT?

1 **2** 3 4

HOW MANY LADYBUGS?

1 2 **3** 4

HOW MANY BEES?

1 2 3 **4**

10

11

COLOR THE FOOD YOU HAVE EATEN.

YOU CAN DO IT!

WHICH TEDDY BEAR DOES NOT LOOK LIKE THE OTHERS?

WHAT IS IT? SNAIL

WHERE DOES IT LIVE?

GARDEN

COLOR IT!

11

12

TURN THESE CIRCLES INTO FUN STUFF, AND COLOR THEM ALL!

DOUGHNUT.

PIZZA.

BE CREATIVE!

BASKETBALL.

TIRE.

PUMPKIN.

PLANET.

12

13

IF THE CABBAGE IS ALL GREEN, WHAT COLORS IS THE CARROT?

ORANGE & GREEN

DECORATE THE GHOST'S SHEET TO MAKE HIM HAPPY!

BE CREATIVE!

COUNT AND COLOR THE STARS YOU SEE 11

13

14

TRACE THE DOTS TO DRAW THE WATER
THE ELEPHANT IS SPRAYING.

COLOR THIS RUBBER DUCK YELLOW!

YOU CAN DO IT!

CONNECT EACH ANIMAL TO THE NOISE IT MAKES.

MEOW! CHIRP! BARK! CLICK!

14

15

16

17

18

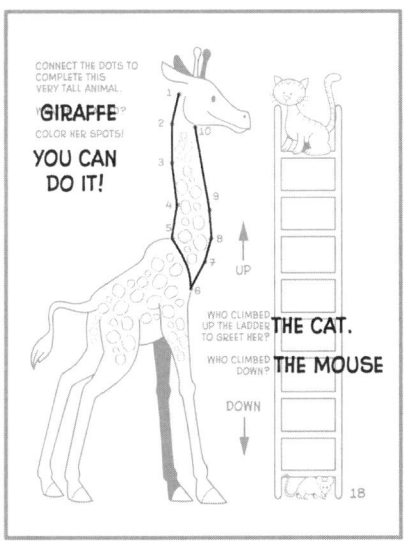

19

20

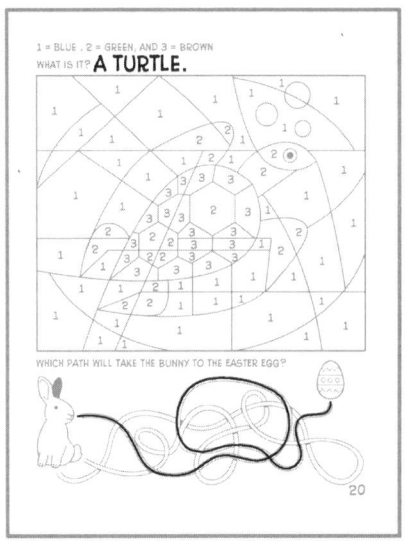

21

22

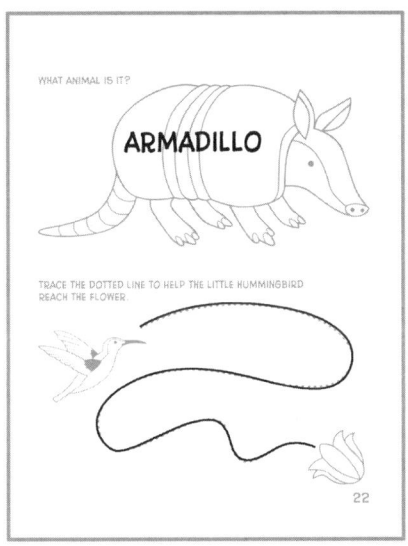

23

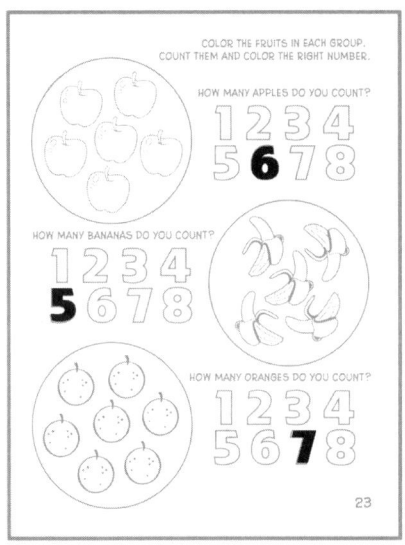

24

25

26

27

28

29

30

31

32

33

34

35

36

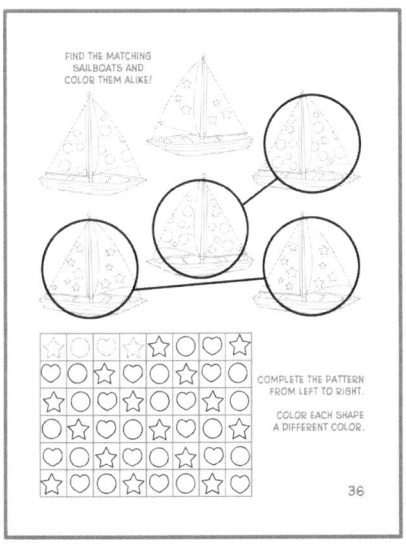

37

38

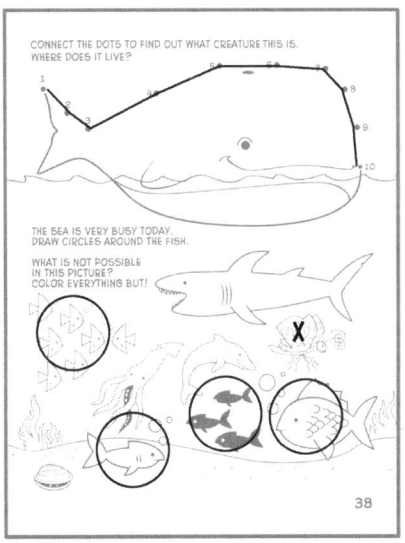

39

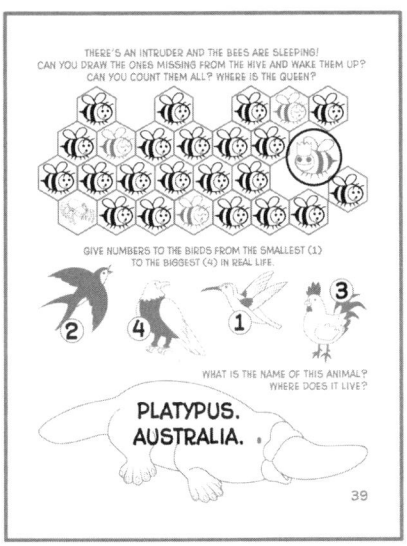

40

41

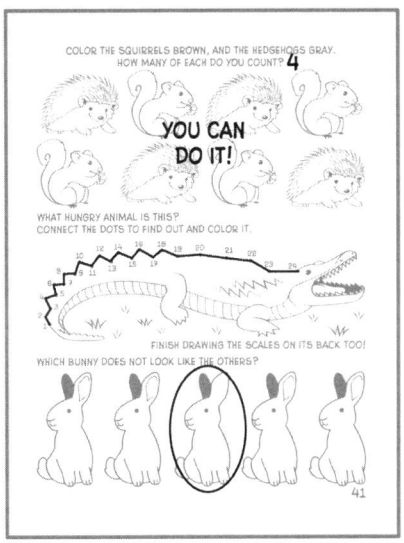

42

43

44

45

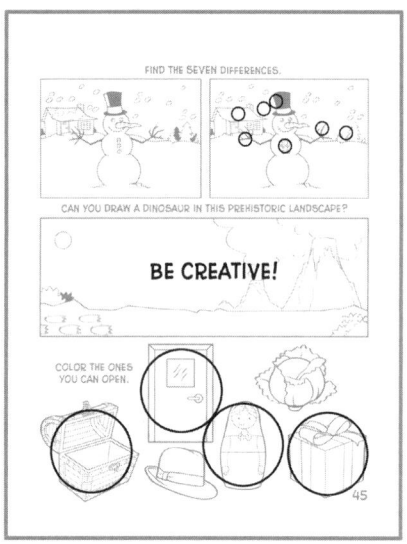

46

47

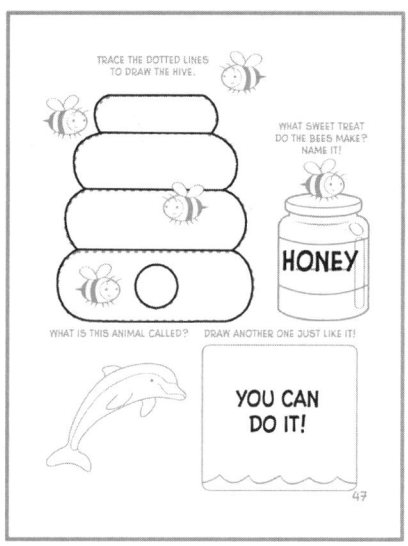

48

49

50

51

COLOR THE BENT WANDS ORANGE AND THE STRAIGHT ONES YELLOW.

Y Y O Y O O Y

DRAW THE RAYS OF SUNSHINE THROUGH THE CLOUDS.

YOU CAN DO IT!

WHAT ANIMAL IS THIS? A SHARK.
WHERE DOES IT LIVE? IN THE OCEAN.

51

52

TRACE THE FIRST FLOWER, AND THEN FOLLOW THE BEE'S FLIGHT PATH TO THE NEXT FLOWER.

GIVE NUMBERS TO EACH FRUIT FROM THE SMALLEST (1) TO THE BIGGEST (4) IN REAL LIFE.

2 1 3 4

COLOR THE GRAPES PURPLE, THE BANANA YELLOW, AND THE STRAWBERRY RED. WHAT COLOR IS THE ORANGE?

WHICH ONE IS NOT A VEHICLE?

52

53

TURN THESE SQUARES INTO FUN STUFF, AND COLOR IT ALL!

TV SET. BUILDING.

BE CREATIVE!

ENVELOPE. TABLET.

PRESENT. BOOK.

53

54

COLOR THE SWALLOWS BLUE AND THE BUTTERFLIES PINK!

YOU CAN DO IT!

CROW! SQUEAK! MOO! CHATTER!

CONNECT EACH ANIMAL TO THE NOISE IT MAKES.

54

55

DRAW THE KITTY'S LONG TAIL, AND THEN COLOR HIM ORANGE.

DO YOU HAVE A PET? DRAW IT HERE.

YOU CAN DO IT!

FILL THE JAR WITH CANDY. COLOR HALF OF THEM RED, AND THE REST BLUE.

COUNT THEM ALL.

YOU CAN DO IT!

55

56

WHOOPS! HOW MANY DOUGHNUTS DID SALLY DROP?

WHICH ONE OF THESE DOES NOT BELONG IN THE KITCHEN?

15

56

57

DRAW THE SHEEP'S COAT OF WOOL— ONE WAVY AND THE OTHER CURLY.

YOU CAN DO IT!

DRAW TWO MORE SHEEP WITH DIFFERENT COATS.

BE CREATIVE!

57

58

WHAT IS NOT POSSIBLE IN THIS PICTURE? WHY?

DOLPHINS LIVE IN THE OCEAN.
THE HALF MOON CAN'T BE SEEN NEXT TO THE SUN.

1 = GRAY
2 = PINK
3 = WHITE
4 = YELLOW
5 = ORANGE

A CAT.

DRAW A CIRCLE AROUND ITS FAVORITE FOOD BELOW.

58

59

ONE OF THESE ANIMALS CAN'T SWIM. CAN YOU GUESS WHICH ONE?

WHAT IS THIS ANIMAL CALLED? DRAW ANOTHER ONE JUST LIKE IT!

YOU CAN DO IT!

FINISH THIS DRAWING.

59

60

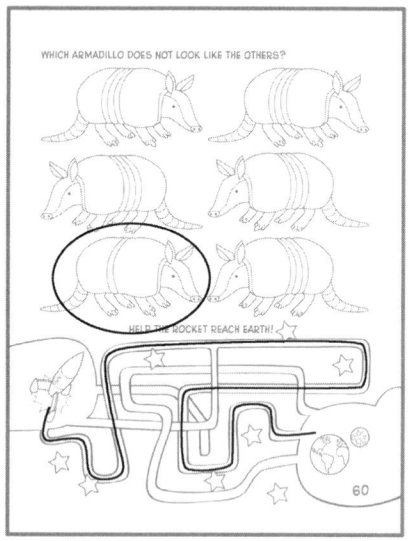

61

62

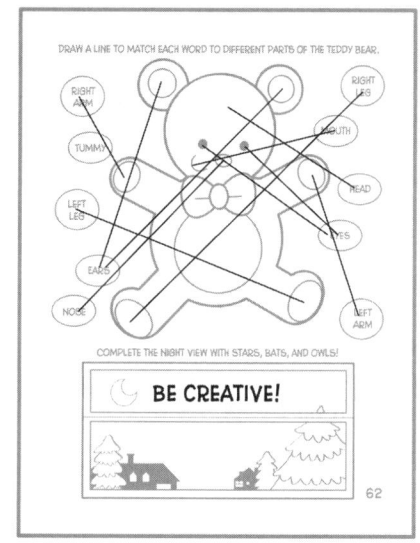

63

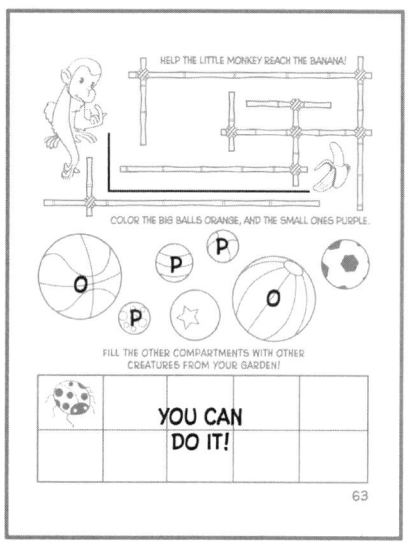

64

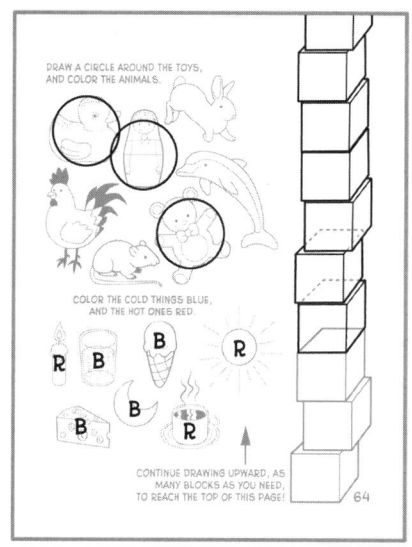

65

66

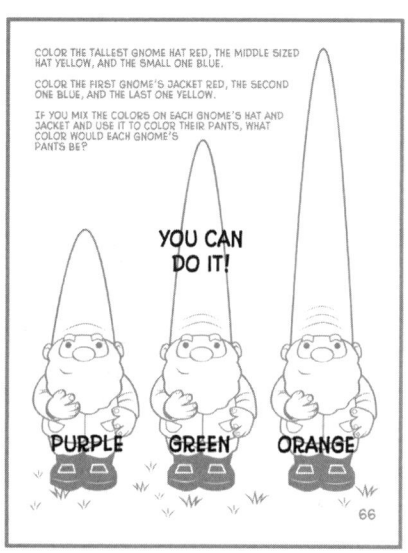

67

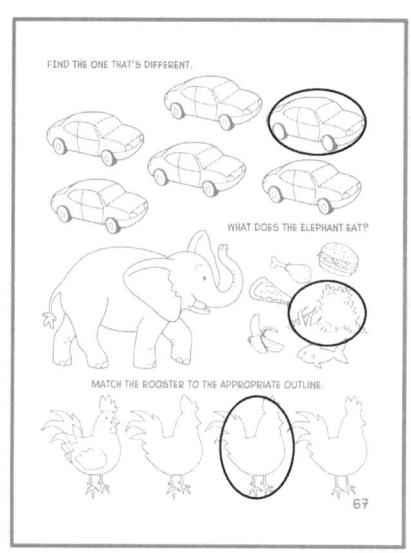

68

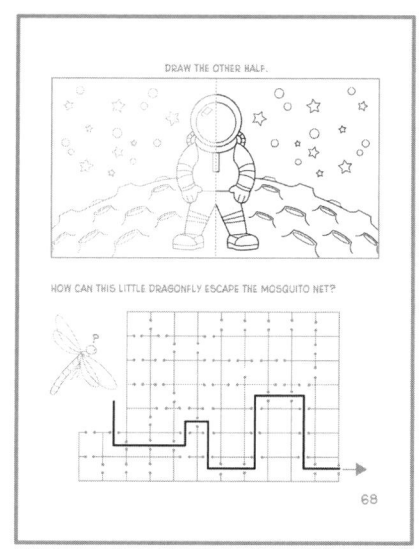

69

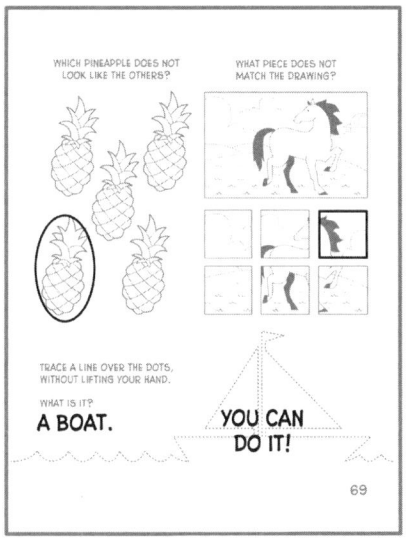

70

71

72

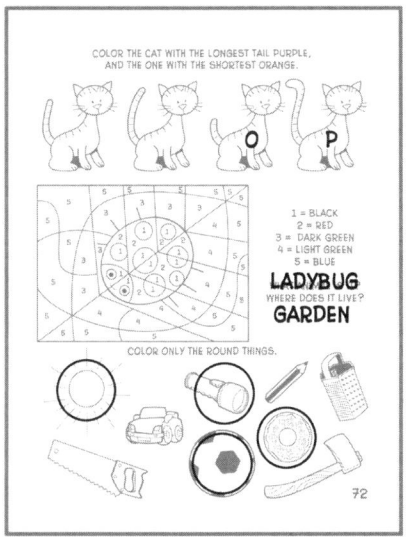

73

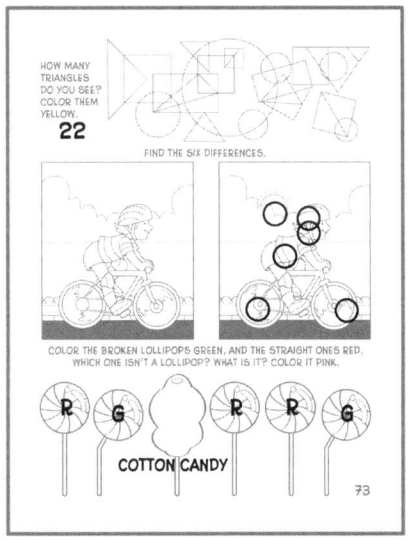

74

75

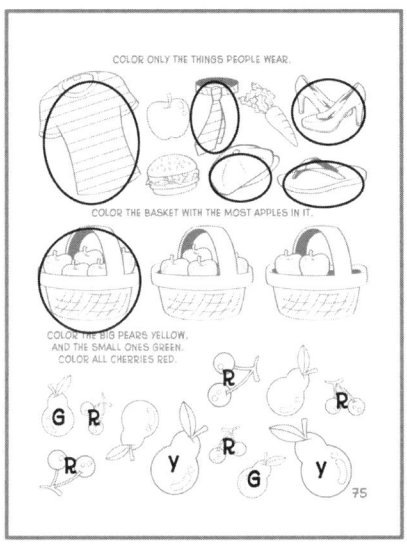

76

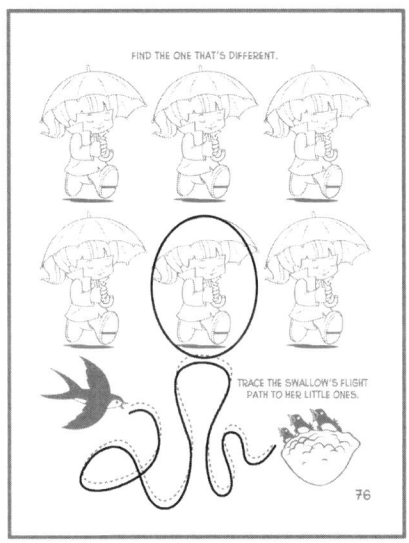

77

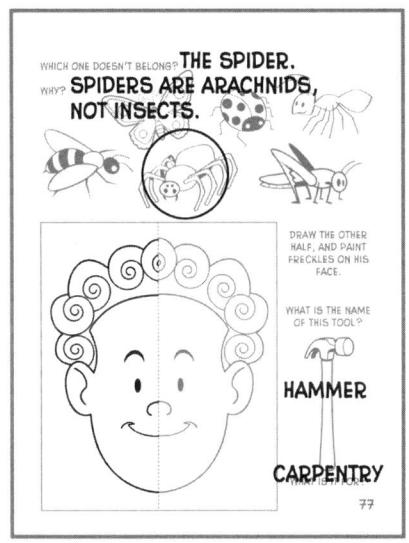

78

79

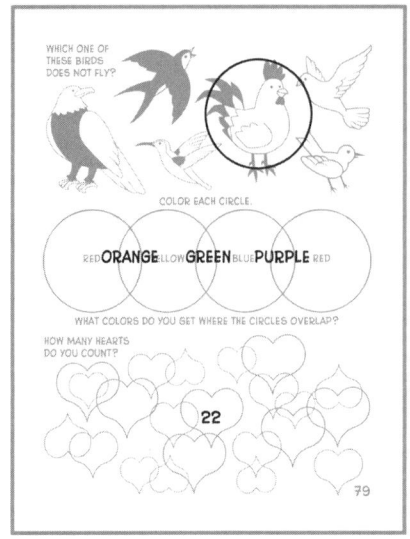

80

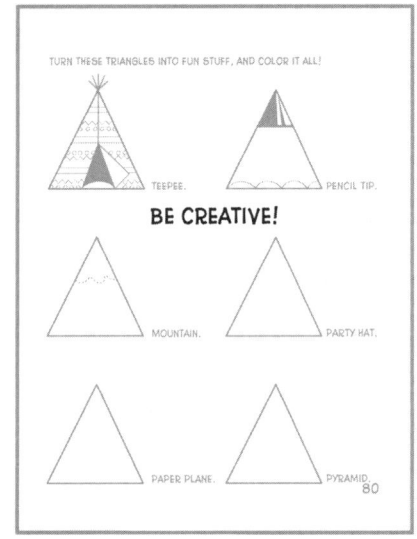

81

82

83

84

85

86

87

88

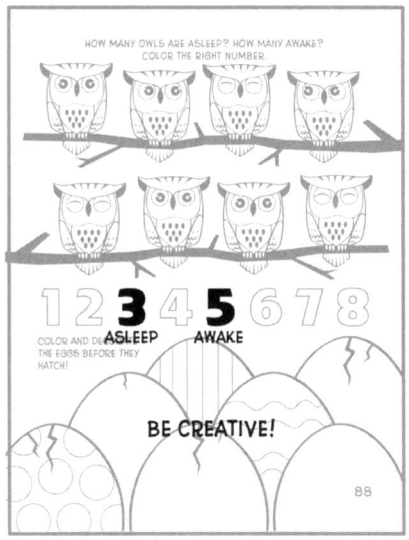

89

90

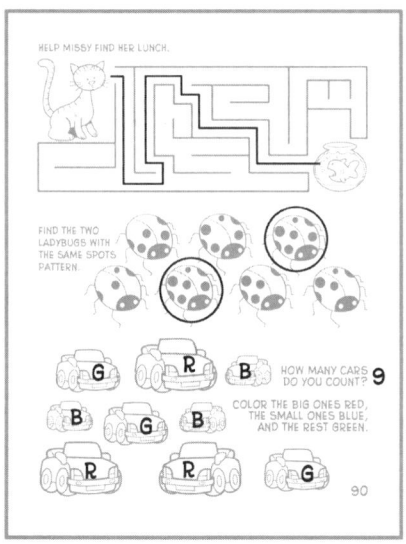

91

92

93

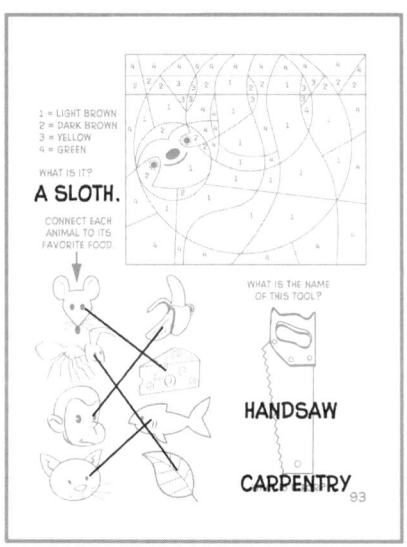

94

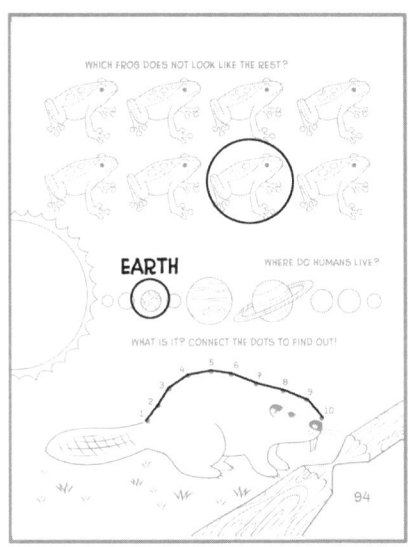

95

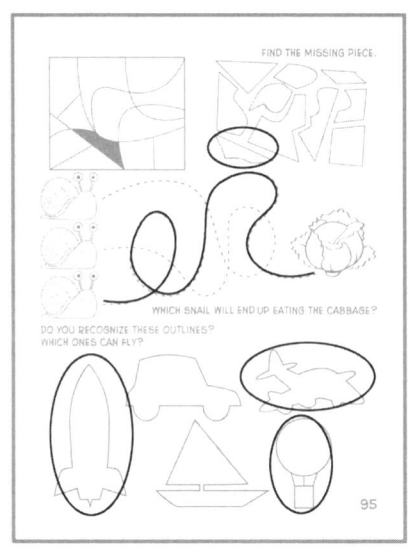

96

97

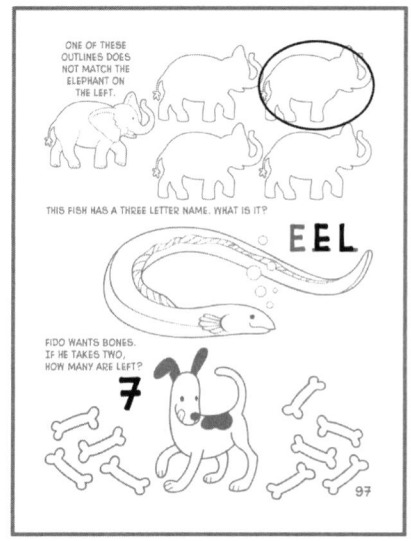

98

99

100

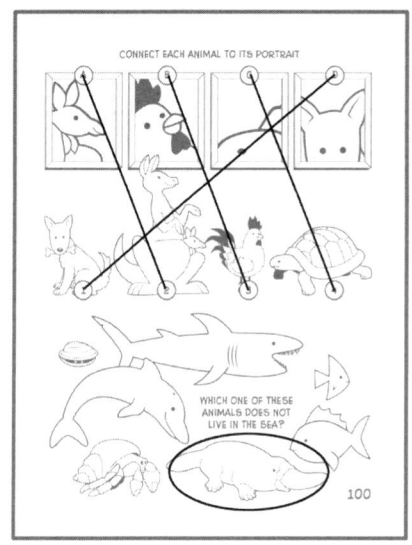

102

103

104

105

106

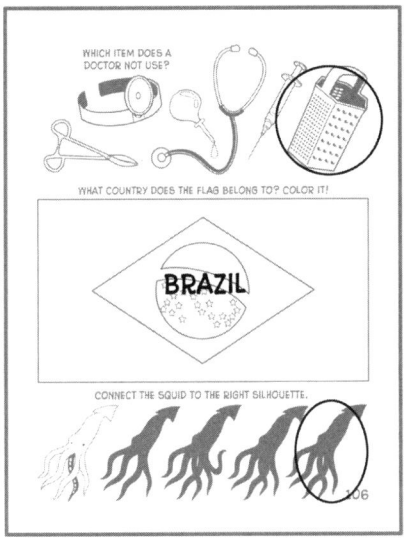

107

108

109

110

111

112

113

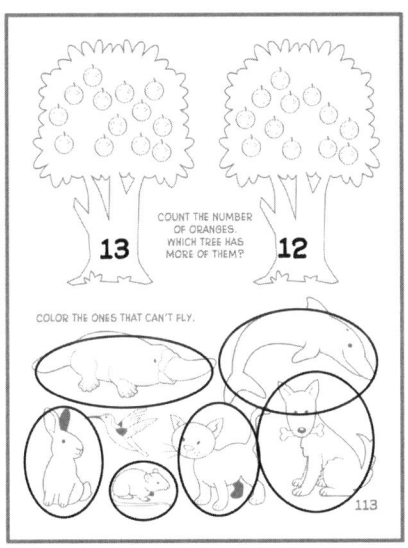

114

115

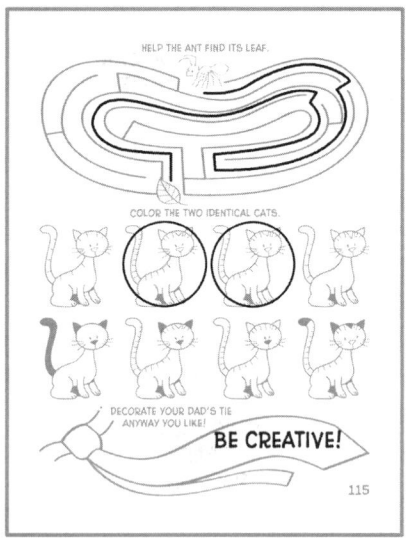

116

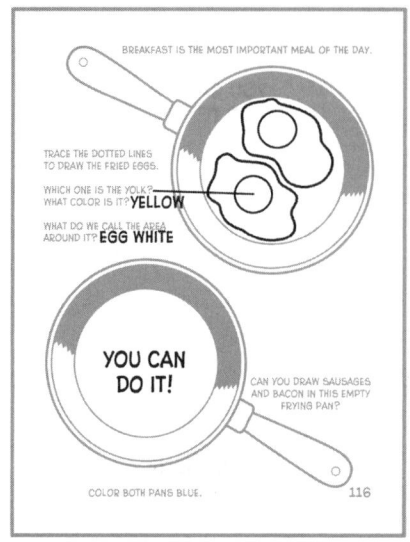

117

118

119

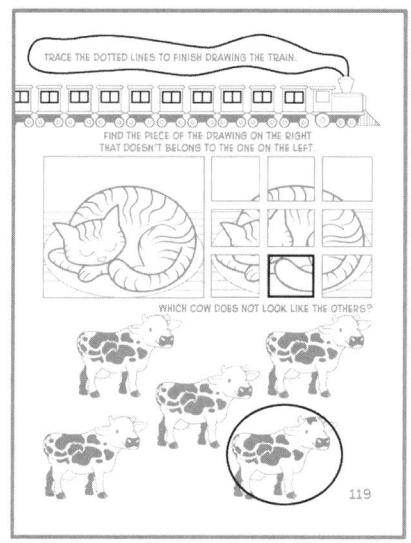

120

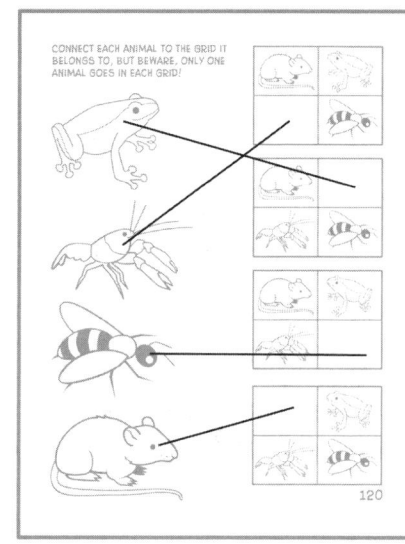

121

122

123

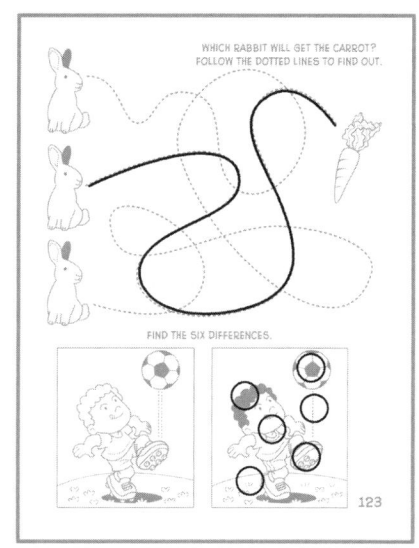

124

125

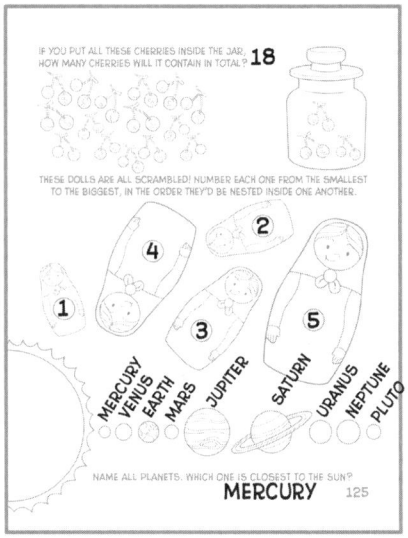

126

127

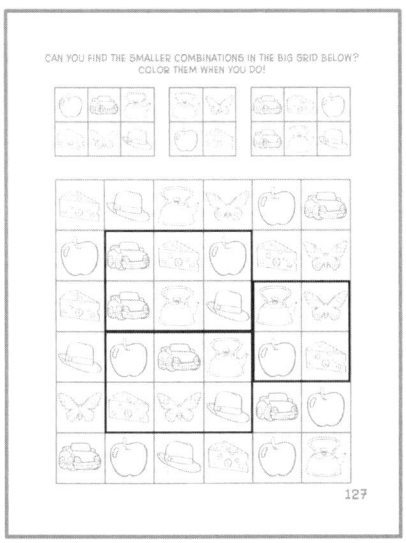

128

129

130

131

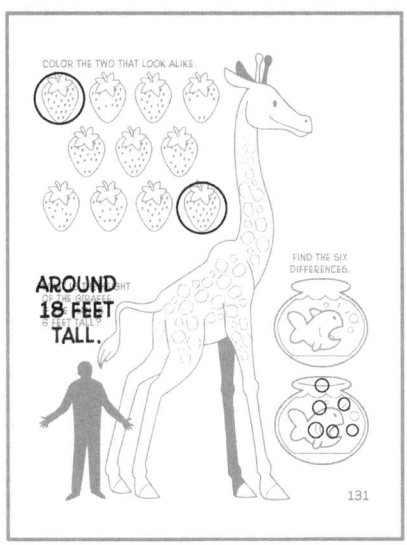

132

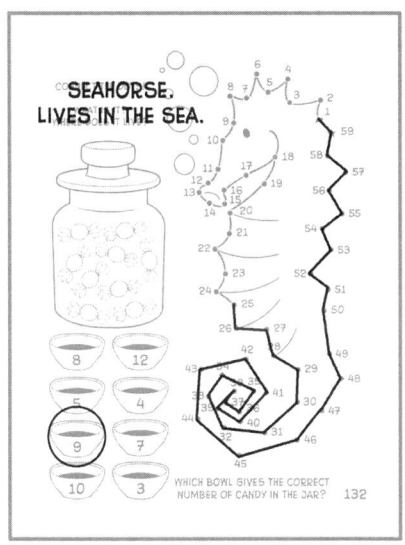

133

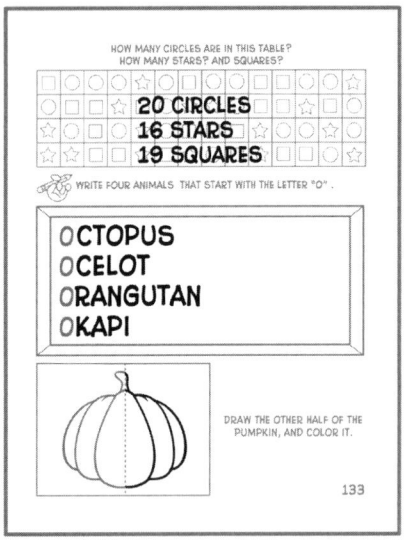

134

135

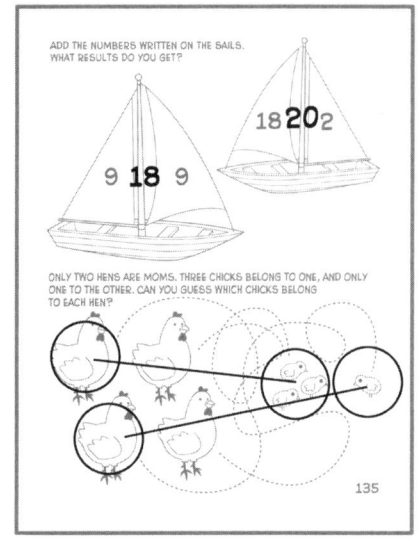

136

137

138

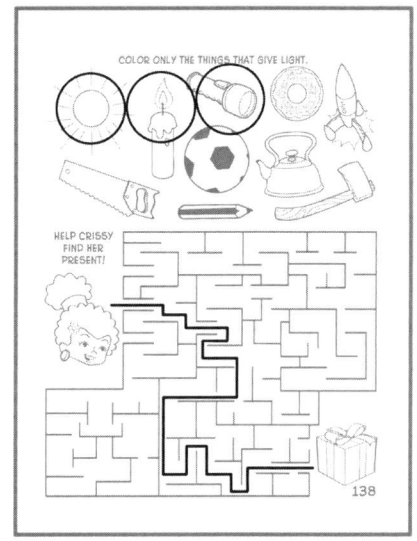

139

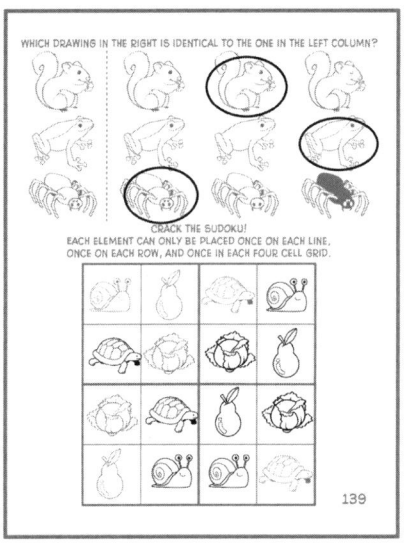

140

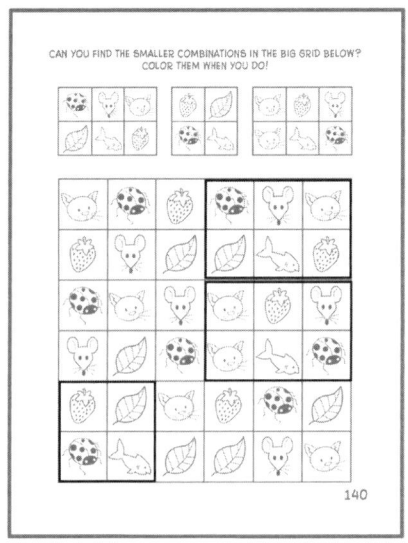

141

142

143

144

145

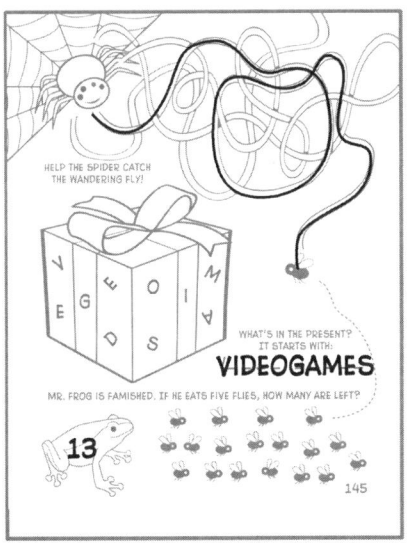

146

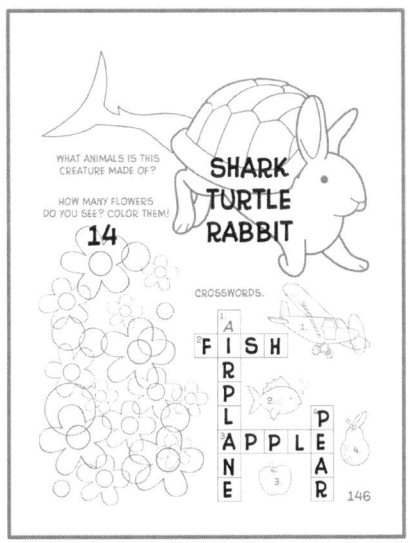

147

148

149

150

151

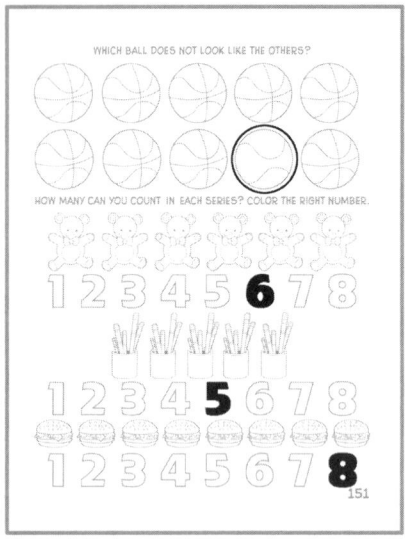

152

153

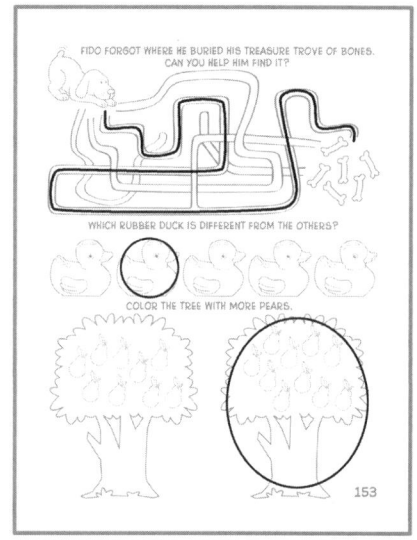

154

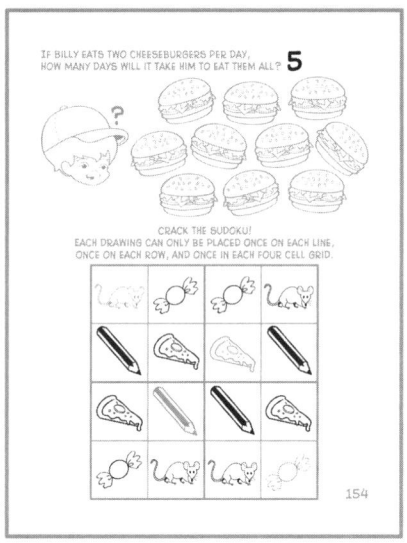

155

156

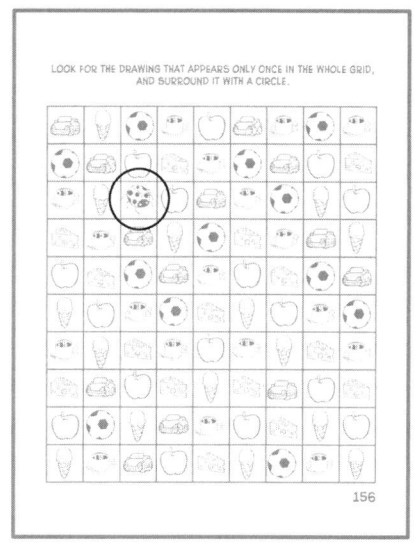

157

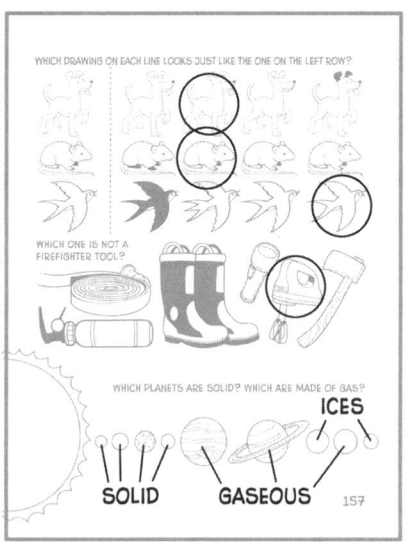

158

159

160

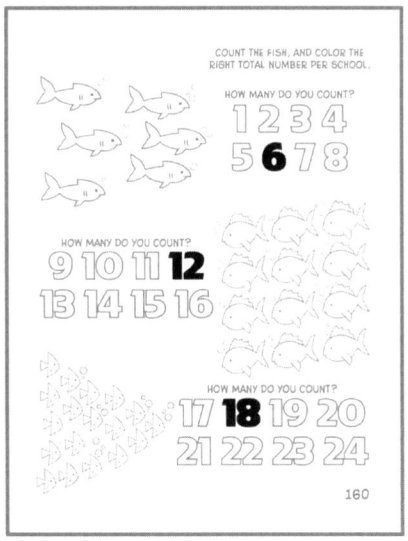

161

162

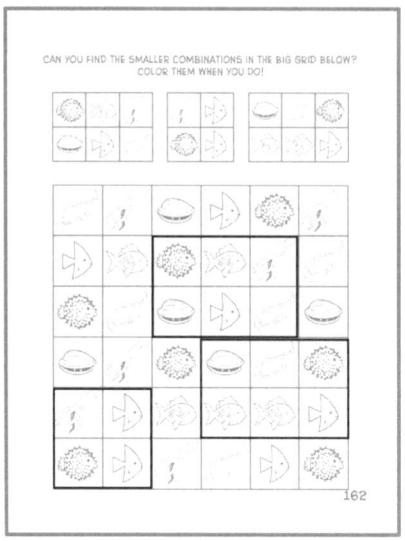

163

164

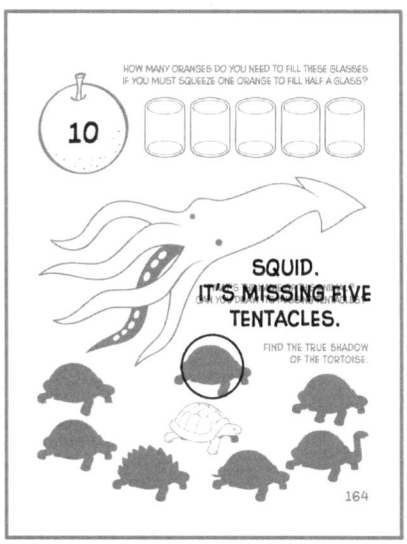

165

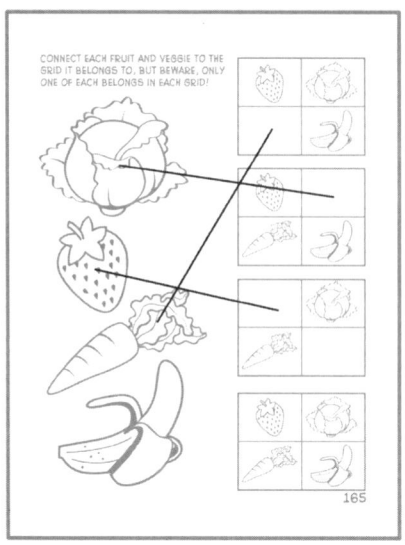

166

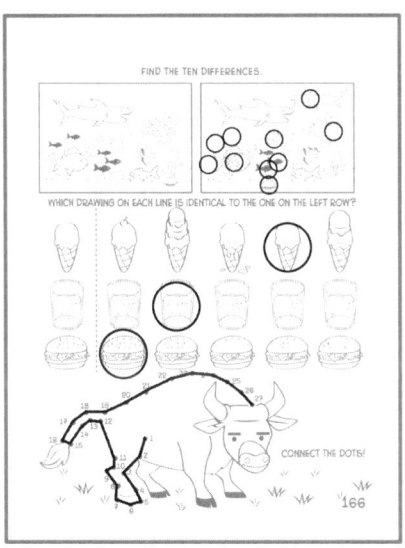

167

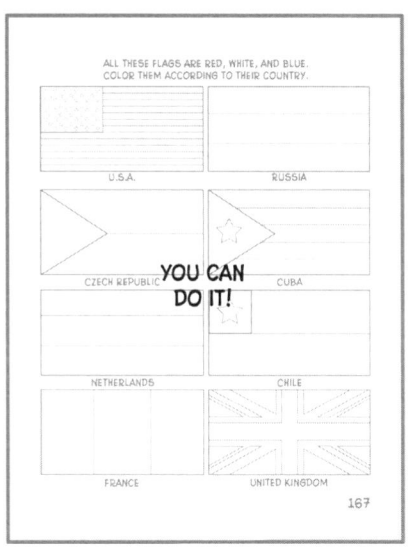

168

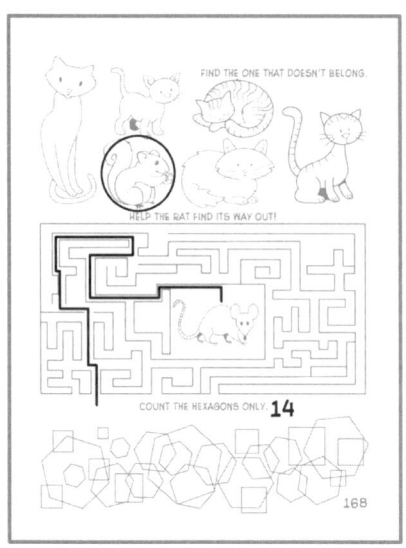

169

170

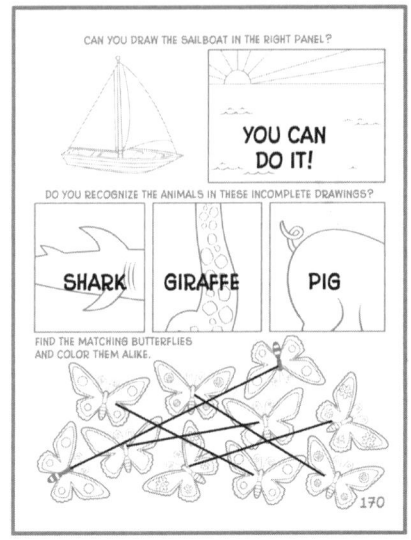

171

172

173

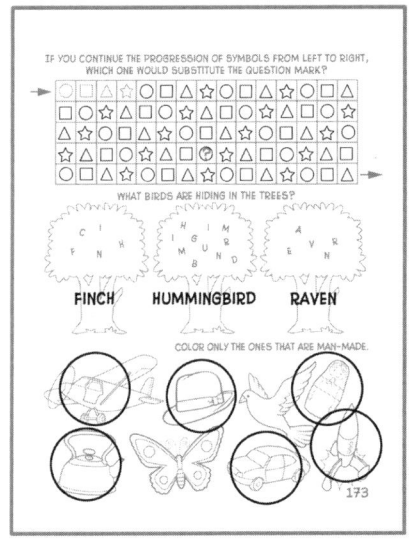

174

175

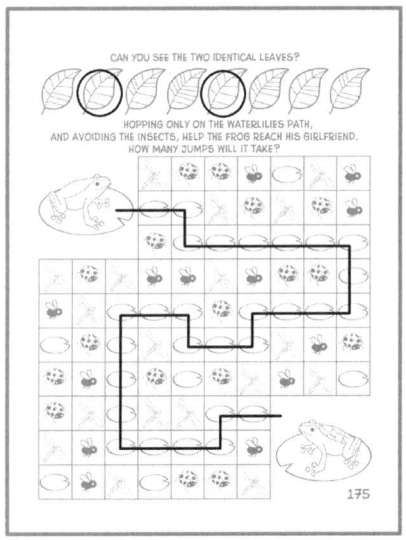

176

177

178

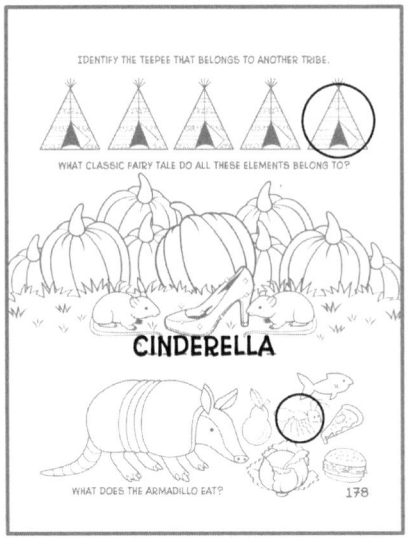

179

180

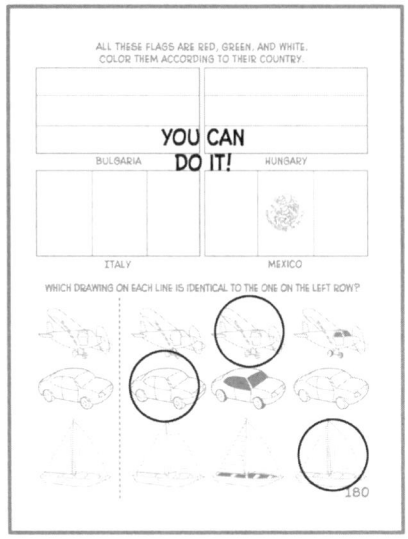

181

182

183

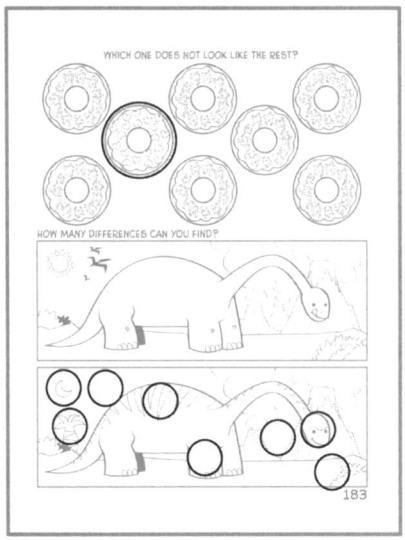

184

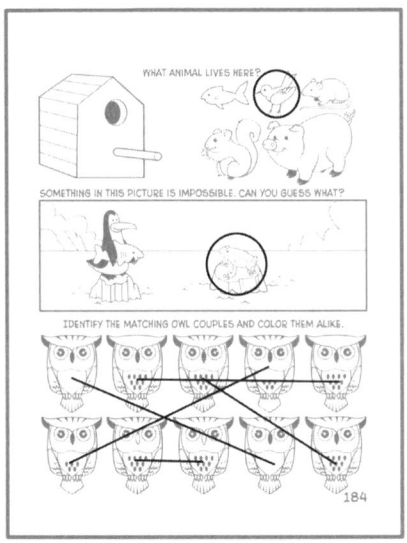

185

186

187

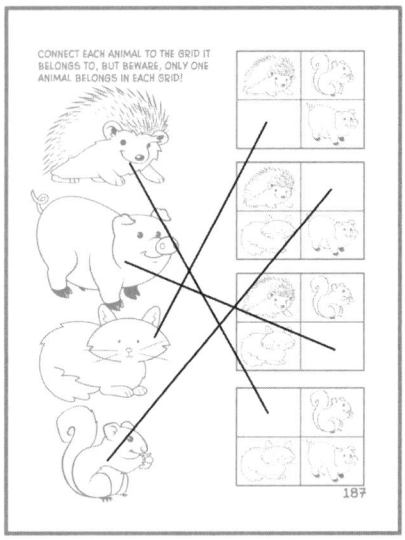

188

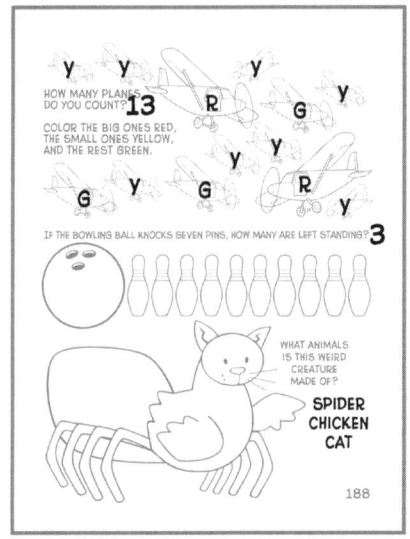

189

190

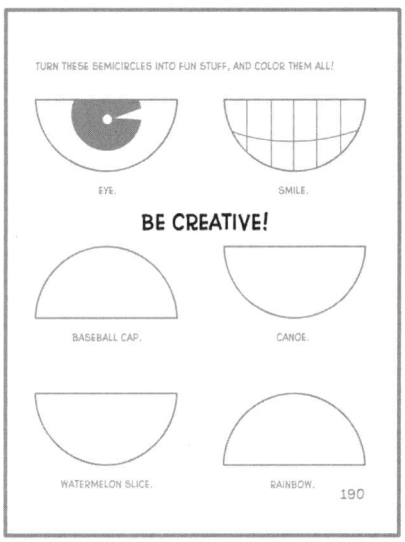

191

192

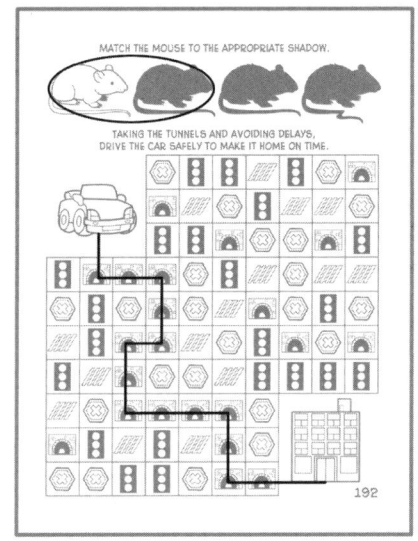

193

194

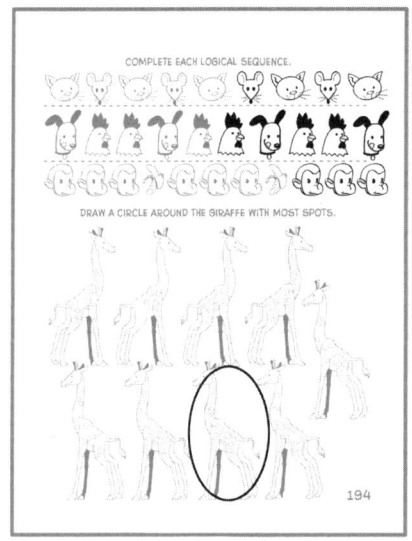

195

196

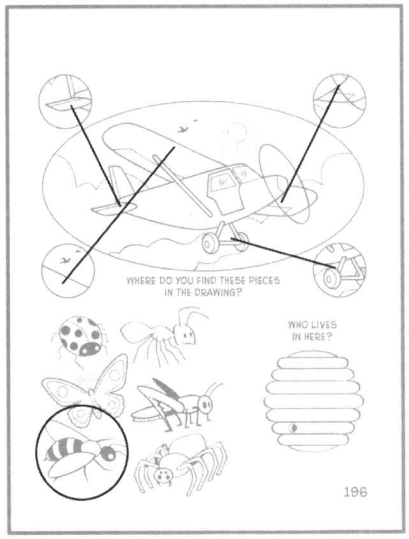

197

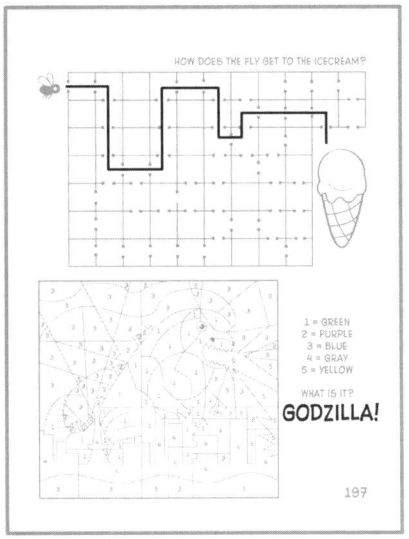

198

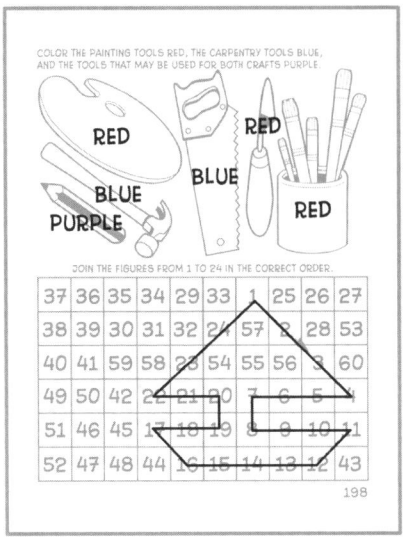

199

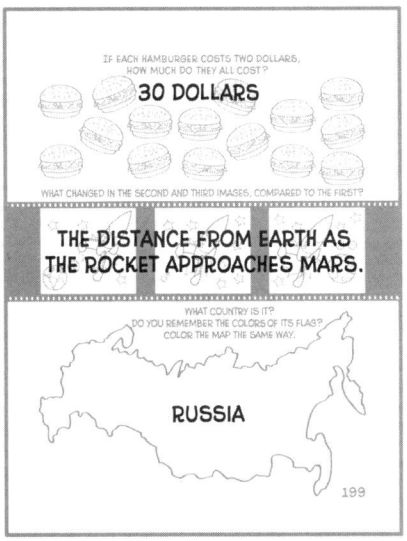

200

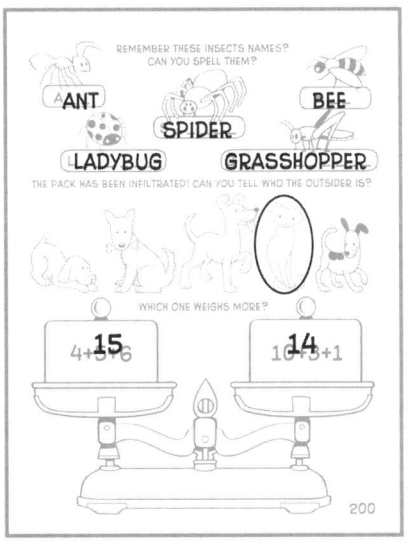

202

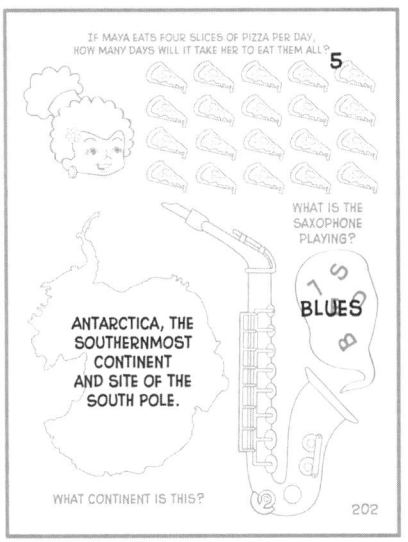

203

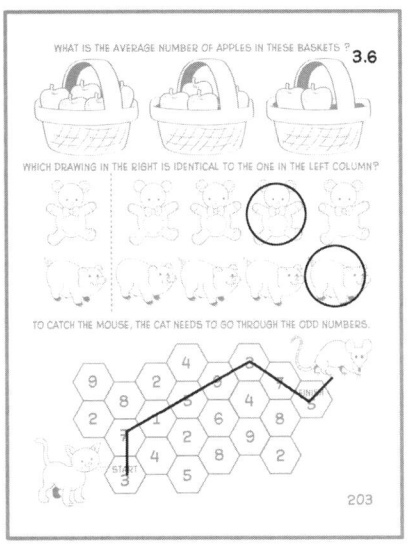

204

205

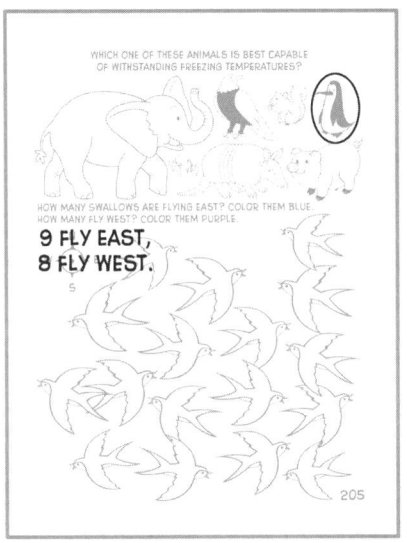

206

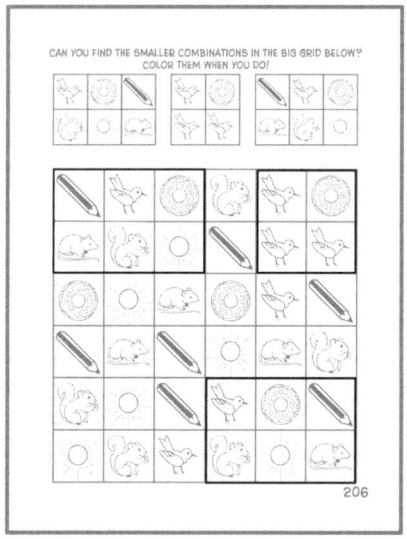

207

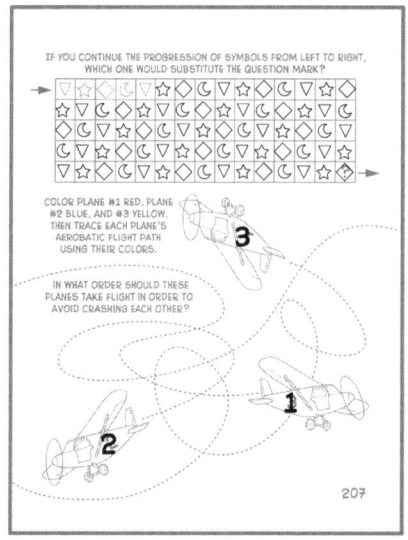

208

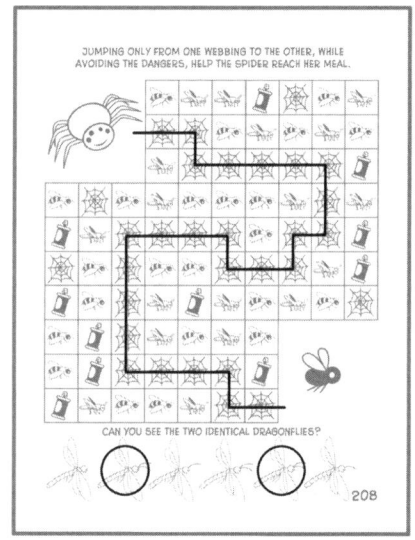

209

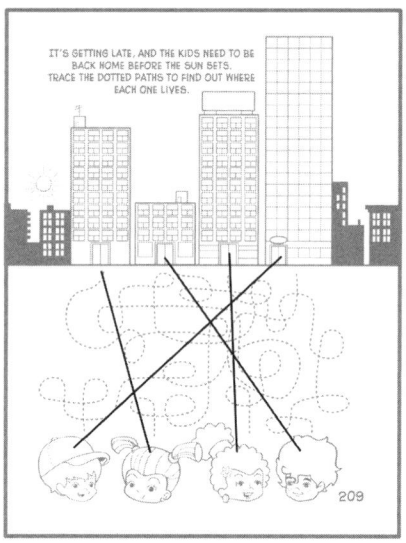

210

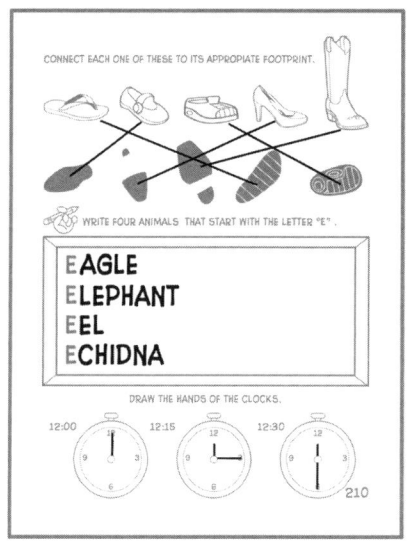

211

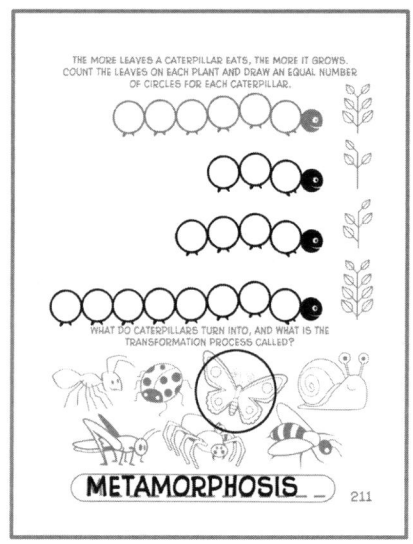

212

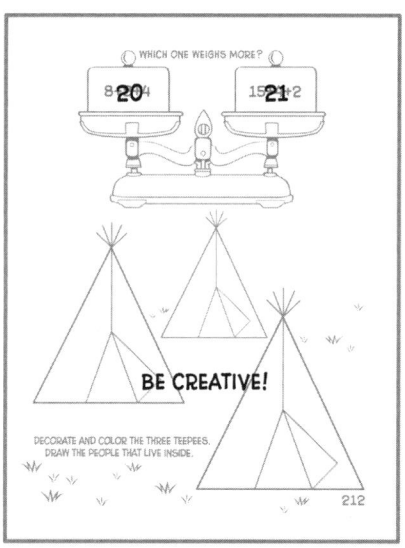

213

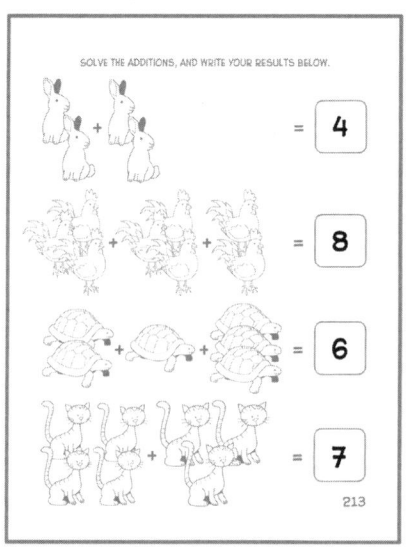

214

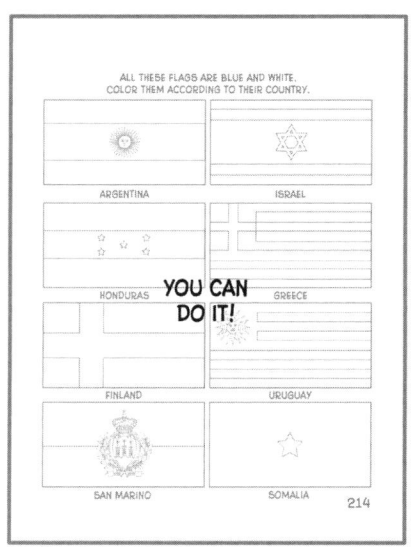

215

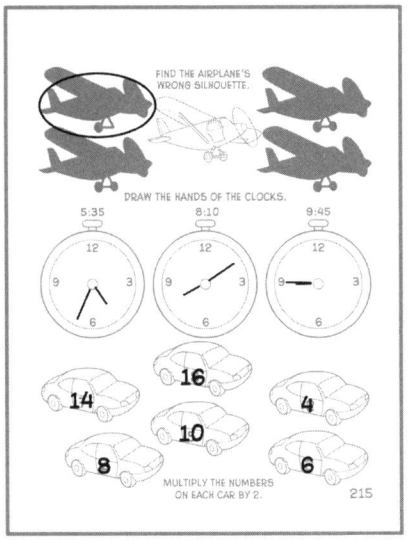

216

217

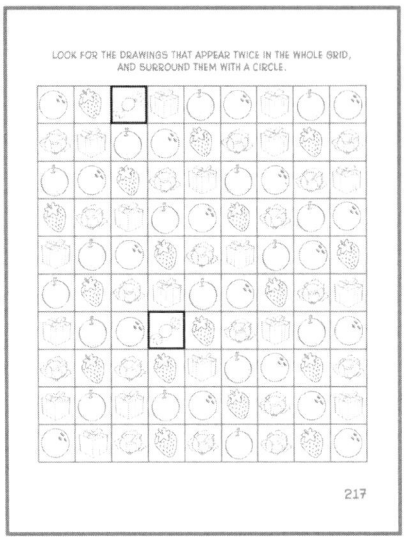

218

219

220

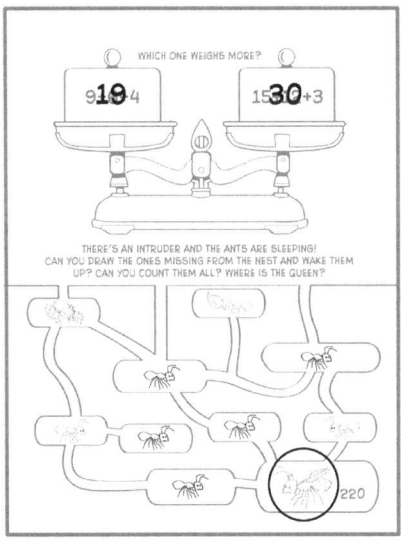

221

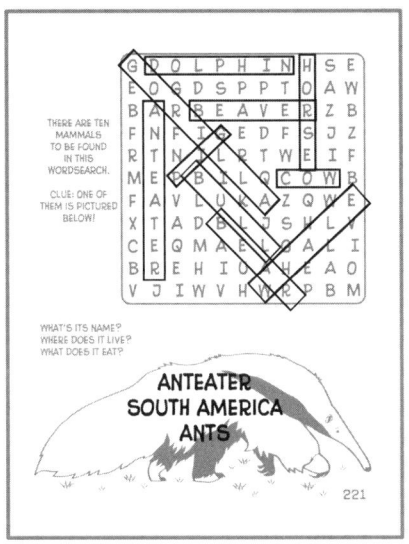

222

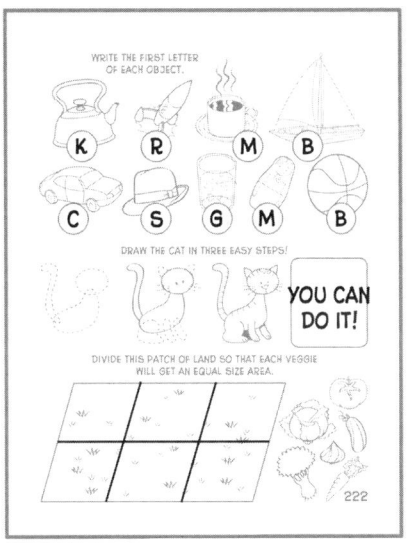

223

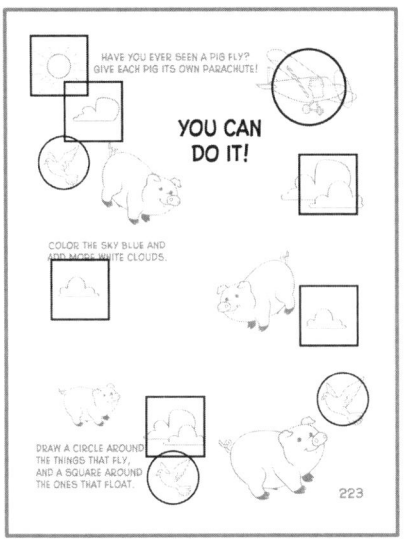

224

1 2 62

HOW MANY MOONS DOES HE EARTH HAVE?
HOW MANY DOES MARS HAVE?
HOW MANY MOONS DOES SATURN HAVE?

WHICH ONE DOES NOT BELONG IN THIS GROUP?

HOW MANY TIMES DOES THE BALL SPIN BEFORE HITTING THE FIRST PIN?
TRACE THE DOTTED LINE TO FIND OUT!

53

224

225

EACH CAR CONSUMES 1 GALLON PER BOX. CAR #1 HAS 12 GALLONS IN ITS TANK. CAR #2 HAS 38 GALLONS, AND #3 HAS 28 GALLONS.
WHICH ONE GETS STOPPED BY TRAFFIC LIGHTS? #1
WHICH ONE STOPS AT THE "X" SIGN? #3
WHICH ONE MAKES IT HOME? #2

COMPLETE EACH ROW SO THE SUM OF THESE NUMBERS IS ALWAYS 27.

↓	9	7	14	11	5	18	3	20	18	13	4	15
9	5	5	5	10	2	10	3	3	5	10	6
5	5	5	5	10	2	10	2	3	5	10	3
4	10	3	6	2	5	4	2	3	4	3	3

CANADA
CAMBODIA
CAMEROON
COSTA RICA

WRITE FOUR COUNTRIES THAT START WITH THE LETTER "C".

225

226

ADD THE MISSING NUMBER TO LEVEL THE WEIGHT.

80 35 + 45

COLOR THE STRONGMAN'S LEOTARD!

COMPLETE AND COLOR THE FELINES TO TURN ONE INTO A TIGER, AND THE OTHER A PANTHER.

YOU CAN DO IT!

COLOR THE BALL, ALTERNATING RED, WHITE, AND BLUE.

226

227

DRAW A CIRCLE AROUND THE FOOD THAT DOESN'T BELONG.

IF FOUR APPLES FROM THE TREE ON THE LEFT WILL FILL A BASKET, HOW MANY BASKETS WILL YOU NEED?
KEEP IN MIND THE APPLES ON THE SECOND TREE ARE TWICE AS BIG.

2 3

5 BASKETS

227

228

YOU CAN DO IT!

FILL THE CIRCLES TO MAKE LETTERS, SUCH AS THE "A" ABOVE.
CAN YOU WRITE YOUR NAME VERTICALLY OR HORIZONTALLY?

228

229

SALLY HAS SENT BILLY A CODED MESSAGE.
CAN YOU DECIPHER IT?

A B C D E F G H I J K L M
N O P Q R S T U V W X Y Z

I LOVE YOU

HOW MANY MOVES DOES THE HORSE NEED TO CHECK THE KING? 5

229

230

OLLIE LIVES IN A COUNTRY SURROUNDED BY SEA.
CAN YOU GUESS WHICH COUNTRY IT IS?

HIDDEN WITHIN ITS SHAPE, YOU WILL FIND FIFTEEN WORDS RELATED TO IT.
CLUE: ONE OF THEM IS AN OBJECT THAT RETURNS TO YOU AFTER YOU THROW IT AWAY!

COMPLETE EACH COLUMN SO THE SUM OF THESE NUMBERS IS ALWAYS 42.

↓	7	12	21	6	14	39	3	16	24	8	18	2
28	15	10	15	10	1	15	10	9	15	10	15
4	10	10	15	10	1	15	10	1	15	10	15
3	5	1	6	8	1	9	6	8	4	4	10

230

231

DRAW THE NUMBER OF BALLS AND HATS AS INDICATED BY EACH TILE.

DRAW THE HANDS OF THE CLOCKS.

18:55 20:30 16:15

TO FIND THE WAY OUT, CONNECT THE NUMBERS DIVISIBLE BY TWO.

9	4	8	6	5	3	7	5	2
3	2	5	9	2	8	6	4	3
6	5	3	1	7	5	3	9	5	4	7
6	3	1	4	6	8	2	4	7	5	3
8	2	4	2	3	4	1	4	6	8

231

232

CONNECT EACH DOG TO ITS CORRESPONDING SHADOW.

DRAW WHAT'S MISSING FROM EACH TRAIN.
THE TRAIN GOING LEFT HAS BLUE WHEELS, AND THE TRAIN GOING RIGHT RED WHEELS.

YOU CAN DO IT!

232

233

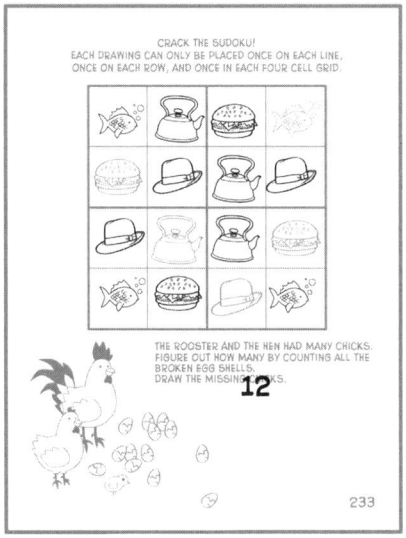

234

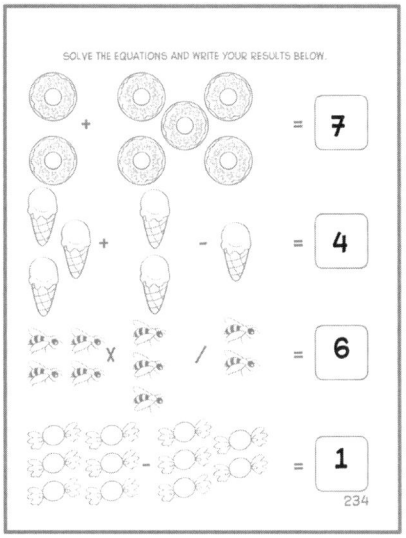

235

236

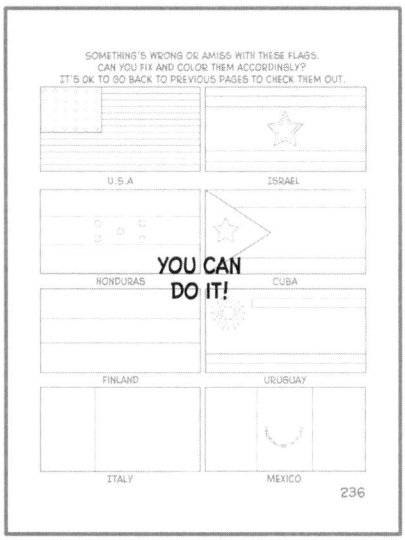

237

238

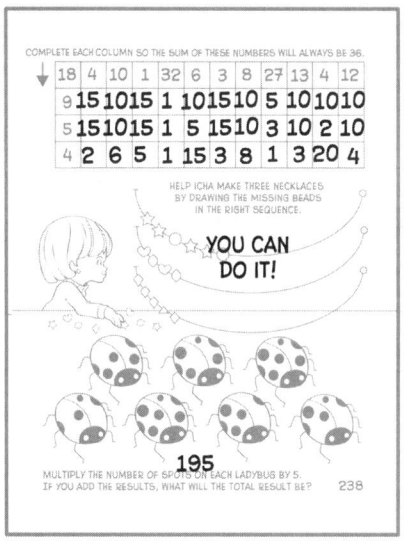

239

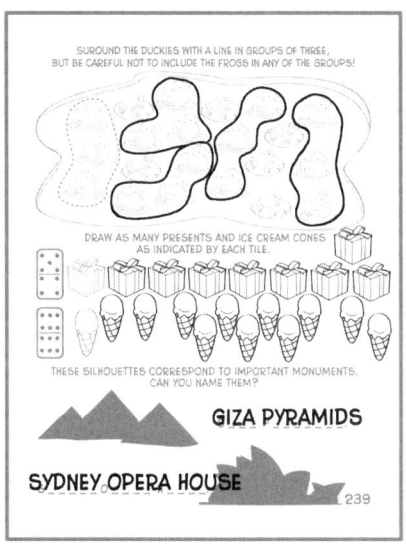

240

241

242

HOW MANY MOVES DOES THE BISHOP NEED TO CHECK THE KING? 2

IDENTIFY THE FIGURE THAT LOOKS LIKE THE FIRST ON EACH ROW, AND COLOR BOTH THE SAME.

242

243

WHERE IS THE BUNGEE JUMPER? DRAW YOURSELF DANGLING FROM THE ROPE!

COLOR ONLY THE EVEN NUMBERS.

BE CREATIVE!

HIDDEN WITHIN THIS PINE (CLUE!) YOU WILL FIND ELEVEN OTHER TREE NAMES.

243

244

WRITE ANYTHING YOU LIKE ON THE BANNER.

BE CREATIVE!

WHICH ONE REQUIRES BATTERIES?

WHICH ONE IS NOT MAN-MADE?

COLOR THE MUSHROOMS RED, BUT LEAVE AS MANY WHITE SPOTS AS THE NUMBER ON EACH ONE INDICATES.

YOU CAN DO IT!

244

245

FIND THE TEN DIFFERENCES.

FILL THE OTHER COMPARTMENTS WITH OTHER ART SUPPLIES YOU USE!

YOU CAN DO IT!

COLOR THE DOTTED SKIRT ONLY.

DECORATE THE ONE IN THE MIDDLE ANYWAY YOU LIKE!

BE CREATIVE!

245

246

WHAT COUNTRY IS IT? WHERE IS IT LOCATED? DO YOU REMEMBER THE COLOR OF ITS FLAG? COLOR THE MAP THE SAME WAY.

ARGENTINA

THESE SILHOUETTES CORRESPOND TO IMPORTANT MONUMENTS. CAN YOU NAME THEM?

EIFFEL TOWER

STATUE OF LIBERTY

246

247

WRITE FOUR COUNTRIES THAT START WITH THE LETTER "U".

URUGUAY
UGANDA
UKRAINE
UNITED KINGDOM

IF EACH ICE CREAM COSTS FOUR DOLLARS, HOW MUCH DO THESE COST ALL TOGETHER?

64 DOLLARS

DRAW AS MANY FRUITS ON EACH TREE AS INDICATED BY THE RESPECTIVE TILE.

247

248

HOW MANY CUPCAKES CAN YOU COUNT? COLOR THE RIGHT NUMBER.

HOW MANY HAVE SPRINKLED HEARTS? COLOR THE RIGHT NUMBER.

3

HOW MANY HAVE A CHERRY ON TOP? COLOR THE RIGHT NUMBER.

4

HOW MANY HAVE SPRINKLES? COLOR THE NUMBER.

ALSO 4

YOU CAN DO IT!

248

249

HELP HIM FIND THE FRISBEE!

COMPLETE EACH COLUMN SO THE SUM OF THESE NUMBERS IS ALWAYS 57.

9	18	21	10	13	7	3	48	24	8	34	2
19	15	15	20	20	20	25	4	15	20	10	25
19	15	15	20	20	20	25	4	15	20	10	25
10	9	6	7	4	10	4	1	3	9	3	5

WHAT IS THE NAME OF THIS ANIMAL? WHERE DOES IT LIVE?

BADGER
NORTH AMERICA AND EURASIA

249

250

EYES

BE CREATIVE!

FILL THE EMPTY JARS WITH ALL THE ICKY, YUCKY, GOOEY, AND HALLOWEENY STUFF YOU CAN IMAGINE! THEN WRITE THEIR NAMES ON EACH LABEL, AND COLOR IT ALL. 250

251

252

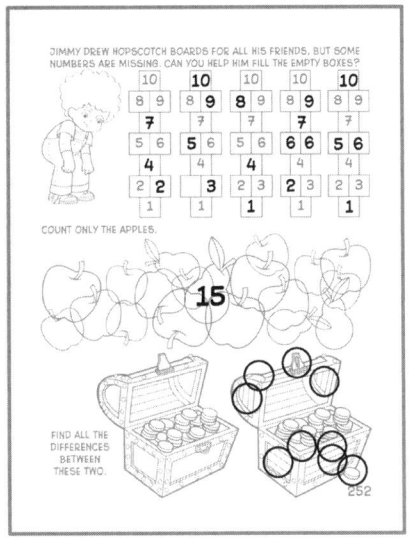

253

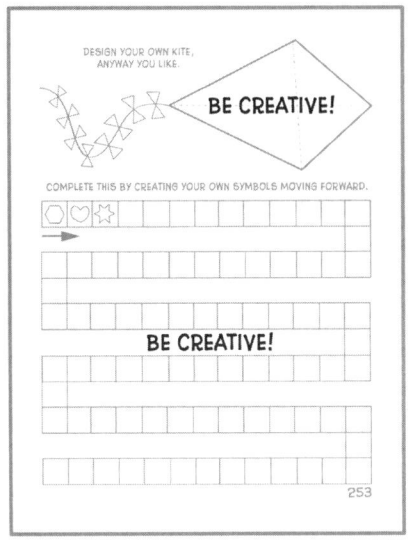

254

255

256

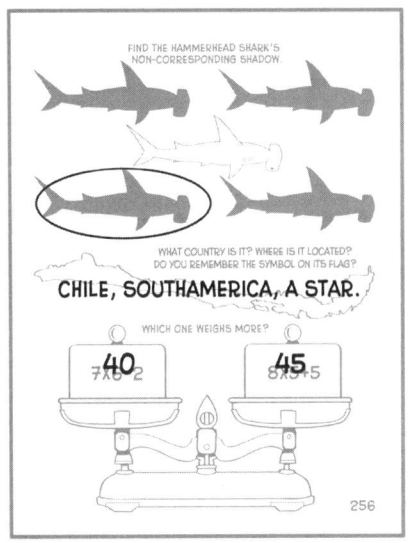

257

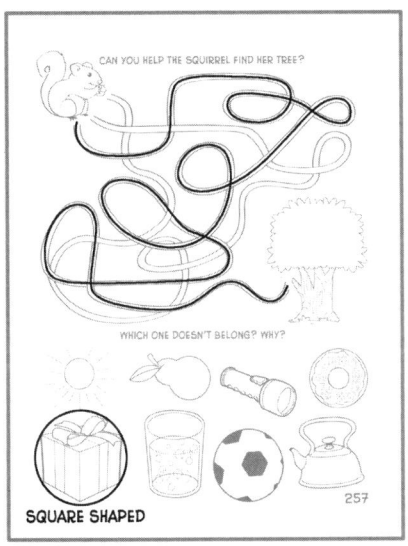

258

259

260

SALLY HAS SENT BILLY ANOTHER SECRET MESSAGE. CAN YOU BREAK THE CODE?

A B C D E F G H I J K L M

N O P Q R S T U V W X Y Z

LET'S GO TO THE MOVIES.

DRAW YOURSELF AND YOUR BEST FRIEND AS THE MEANEST COWBOY OR COWGIRL OF THE OLD WEST!

WANTED WANTED

BE CREATIVE!

WRITE BOTH YOUR NAMES BELOW THE PICTURES.

260

261

FIND THE BIRTHDAY CAKE THAT DOESN'T MATCH ALL OTHERS, AND COLOR THE REST.

THERE ARE TWENTY HOME-RELATED ITEMS TO BE FOUND IN THIS WORDSEARCH.

CLUE: START AT THE DOOR.

261

262

ILLUSTRATE YOUR OWN POSTAGE STAMPS!

BE CREATIVE!

WHICH ONE SHOULDN'T BE HERE?

COMPLETE EACH COLUMN SO THE SUM OF THESE NUMBERS IS ALWAYS 74.

30	28	11	13	18	7	3	40	26	8	64	9
8	20	30	30	25	20	40	15	20	30	3	30
6	20	30	30	25	40	30	15	20	30	3	30
30	6	3	1	6	7	1	4	8	6	4	5

262

263

YOU CAN DO IT!

FILL THE CIRCLES TO MAKE LETTERS, SUCH AS THE "U" ABOVE. CAN YOU WRITE THE NAME OF YOUR TOWN AND COUNTRY?

263

264

DRAW MORE CUPCAKES, OR CROSS THEM OUT UNTIL THERE'S 15 ON EACH TRAY.

CAN YOU ALSO HELP HER FINISH BAKING HER COOKIES?

DRAW THE MISSING GINGERBREAD MEN IN EACH ROW.

264

265

COLOR THIS ENTIRE FLAG GREEN.

LIBYA

CAN YOU GUESS THE NAME OF THE COUNTRY IT BELONGS TO?

LAOS
LITHUANIA
LEBANON
LIECHTENSTEIN

WRITE FOUR OTHER COUNTRIES THAT START WITH THE LETTER "L"!

265

266

IF THE SUN MEANS SUMMER, WHAT OTHER SYMBOLS CAN YOU DRAW TO REPRESENT THE OTHER SEASONS?

SUMMER

FALLING LEAVES

FALL

SNOWMAN

WINTER

FLOWERS

SPRING

WHICH WAY TO THE ICECREAM?

WHICH LEAF IS COMPLETELY DIFFERENT FROM THE REST?

266

267

WHAT ARE THE NAMES OF THESE TWO ANIMALS?

COLOR THEM BOTH GRAY AND WHITE.

DONKEY

BOTH ARE MAMMALS, BUT WHILE THE DONKEY WORKS VERY HARD, THE SLOTH SLEEPS ALL DAY LONG.

SLOTH

WHAT MAKES THEM DIFFERENT?

DRAW THE HANDS OF THE CLOCKS.

00:30 22:45 15:15

267

268

THAT IS ONE BIG SNAKE! CAN YOU GUESS ITS NAME? ANACONDA

IF IT TAKES THE BEE A DAY TO POLLINATE THREE FLOWERS, HOW MANY DAYS WILL IT TAKE HER TO POLLINATE ALL THE ONES IN THIS FIELD?

9

CONNECT THE NUMBERS DIVISIBLE BY 2.

268

269

FIND THE SIX DIFFERENCES.

1 2 3 4 5 6

THE FORTUNE COOKIE HAS A MESSAGE FOR YOU. CAN YOU GUESS WHAT IT SAYS?

"YOU ARE LUCKY" 269

270

COMPLETE THE SERIES.

5 = ○ + ☆
2 = □ + □
3 = □ + ○
4 = □ + ☆

FIND THE ONE SHADOW THAT DOESN'T MATCH THE SQUIRREL.

HOW MANY CHERRIES ARE HIDING IN THESE TWO TREES? DRAW THEM. IF 16 FROM THE TREE ON THE LEFT WILL FILL A BASKET, HOW MANY BASKETS WILL YOU NEED IF THE CHERRIES ON THE OTHER TREE ARE HALF AS BIG?

4X2 + 10X2 + 6X2 = 40

6X3 + 30/2 - 16/2 = 16

4.5 BASKETS

270

271

DROMEDARY — BACTRIAN

EACH ONE OF THESE TWO CAMELS IS CALLED BY A DIFFERENT NAME. DO YOU KNOW THEM?

TO PAINT A DOOR YOU NEED A WHOLE CAN OF PAINT.

TO PAINT A WINDOW FRAME YOU NEED TWO.

TO PAINT THE WALL ON EACH FLOOR THREE.

HOW MANY CANS WILL YOU NEED TO PAINT ALL THESE BUILDINGS?

3 DOORS = 3 CANS
88 WINDOWS = 176 CANS
25 FLOORS = 75 CANS

TOTAL: 254 CANS

271

272

THIS WORDSEARCH IS SHAPED LIKE A CONTINENT, AND CONTAINS THE NAMES OF SOME OF ITS MORE THAN FIFTY BEAUTIFUL COUNTRIES. CAN YOU GUESS WHICH ONE?

CLUE: ITS NAME STARTS WITH "A".

WHICH ONE OF THE FOLLOWINS ANIMALS DOES NOT LIVE THERE?

272

273

DRAW AND COLOR YOUR FAVORITE FLAGS FROM SOME OF THE COUNTRIES ON THE PREVIOUS PAGE'S WORDSEARCH.

YOU CAN DO IT!

WRITE THE NAME OF EACH COUNTRY BELOW THE CORRESPONDING FLAG. 273

274

COMPLETE THE PATTERN AS BEST YOU CAN.

WHAT ARE SODA BUBBLES MADE OF?
CARBON DIOXIDE (CO_2).

HOW ARE THEY DIFFERENT FROM THE ONES WE MAKE WITH SOAP AND WATER?
SOAP BUBBLES ARE JUST AIR.

WHY DO THEY FLOAT UPWARD?
THEY ARE LIGHTER THAN WATER.

ONLY ONE OF THESE IS WORN AROUND THE NECK. COLOR IT!

274

275

TURN EACH PIECE OF SCRAP METAL INTO THREE COOL ROBOTS!

BE CREATIVE!

COMPLETE THE SERIES.

3 = ☆ + ☾
5 = ☾ + ☾
4 = ☆ + ☾
4 = ☾ + ☾

COPY HER!

YOU CAN DO IT!

275

276

FILL IN THE BLANK SPACES TO GET THE GIVEN RESULTS.

10	+	75	-	1	+	18	-	2	=	100
88	-	81	+	24	-	6	+	53	=	78
6	+	42	-	48	+	48	+	8	=	56
35	-	18	+	3	-	6	+	7	=	21

DRAW AND COLOR YOUR OWN COMIC-STRIP!

YOU CAN DO IT!

276

277

HELP THE DONKEY FIND ITS LUNCH!

ADD THE NUMBERS WRITTEN ON THE SAILS. WHICH SAILBOAT CARRIES THE HEAVIER LOAD?

85 — 56 - 3 X 3 — 18 + 5 X 4

42 — 21 + 6 X 2 — 36 - 9 X 3

277

278

WHAT COUNTRY IS IT?
WHERE IS IT LOCATED?

DO YOU REMEMBER THE SYMBOL ON ITS FLAG?

MEXICO
NORTH AMERICA
AN EAGLE LANDING ON A CACTUS, WITH AN EAGLE CAUGHT IN ITS TALONS.

CAN YOU FIND 14 FAMOUS PEOPLE IN THIS WORDSEARCH? CLUE: THEY COME FROM THE COUNTRY ABOVE!

C	H	E	S	P	I	R	I	T	O	P	W	N	L	Y
P	M	I	G	U	E	L	H	I	D	A	L	G	O	P
V	C	A	R	L	O	S	F	U	E	N	T	E	S	A
X	C	E	N	Z	Y	P	I	W	I	C	Z	O	H	Y
Z	Y	L	M	R	Y	L	J	U	S	H	P	F	D	I
L	U	I	S	B	U	N	U	E	L	O	A	E	D	D
T	Q	E	E	A	Y	X	I	K	P	V	V	T	E	S
I	F	I	K	E	N	A	L	F	H	I	R	F	S	I
N	R	R	C	A	M	E	R	O	N	I	L	A	S	Q
X	S	Y	Z	B	R	D	Y	F	L	S	Q	P	U	E
F	R	I	D	A	K	A	H	L	O	A	Y	D	E	T
D	I	E	G	O	R	I	V	E	R	A	R	B	S	K
A	L	V	A	R	O	U	B	R	E	G	O	N	A	O
H	E	R	N	A	N	C	O	R	T	E	S	E	P	O
D	O	L	O	R	E	S	O	L	M	E	D	O	A	O

THIS IS A WORLD FAMOUS FRUIT FROM THE COUNTRY ABOVE.

COLOR ITS FLESH GREEN, AND ITS SEED BROWN. WHAT'S IT CALLED?

AVOCADO

278

279

CRACK THE SUDOKU!
EACH DRAWING CAN ONLY BE PLACED ONCE ON EACH LINE, ONCE ON EACH ROW, AND ONCE IN EACH FOUR CELL GRID.

CAN YOU GUESS EACH DOUGHNUT'S FLAVOR? COLOR THEM ACCORDINGLY!

STRAWBERRY

CHOCOLATE

MAPLE

279

280

FILL THE PAGE WITH HEXAGONS, UNTIL THE HONEYCOMB IS FINISHED.

THEN DRAW CUTE BEES LIVING IN IT. →

YOU CAN DO IT!

280

281

WHICH ONE WEIGHS MORE?

6 **33** 9

8 X **52** 12

HOW LONG IS THE LADDER? **87**

DRAW AS MANY BUTTERFLIES AND SNAILS AS INDICATED BY EACH TILE.

281

282

WHAT IS THE NAME OF THIS BIRD? WHAT DOES IT EAT?

DRAW ANOTHER ONE JUST LIKE IT.

YOU CAN DO IT!

FIND THE TWO IDENTICAL MUSHROOMS.

5	2	3	3	6	3	5	27
4	1	1	2	1	8	9	26
9	3	4	5	7	11	14	53

FILL THE BLANKS SO THE RESULTS OF ADDING THE NUMBERS MATCH BOTH VERTICALLY AND HORIZONTALLY.

282

283

HOW MANY OF EACH TYPE OF ICECREAM CAN YOU COUNT? WRITE THE CORRECT NUMBER.

7

11

18

CAN YOU GUESS THE NAME OF THIS COUNTRY? WHAT IS IT FAMOUS FOR?

JAPAN

BEAUTIFUL LANDSCAPE

RICH HISTORY

INSPIRING ART

GREAT MANNERS

CUTTING EDGE TECHNOLOGY

GIANT MONSTERS

IT IS MADE OF MANY ISLANDS. WHAT DO WE CALL A GROUP OF ISLANDS?

ARCHIPELAGO

283

284

FIND THE MOON'S MISSING CHUNK.

TO WIN THIS GAME OF TIC-TAC-TOE, MAKE AS MANY "OXO" COMBINATIONS AS YOU CAN.

O	■	X	O	X	O	X	O	X	X	O
O	X	O	X	O	X	O	X	O	O	X
O	X	O	X	O	X	O	X	O	X	O
O	X	O	X	O	X	O	X	X	O	X
X	O	X	X	O	X	O	X	O	X	O

INSIDE EACH CIRCLE, DRAW AN ANIMAL MATCHING THE INITIALS BELOW.

YOU CAN DO IT!

G E A 284

285

THIS BEACH LOOKS EMPTY!
CAN YOU FILL IT WITH CHILDREN HAVING FUN?

SOME MAY BE SWIMMING.
SOME MAY BE PLAYING IN THE SAND.

CAN YOU DRAW MORE BRIGHTLY COLORED UMBRELLAS?

BE CREATIVE!

YOU CAN DO IT!

USING THESE ELEMENTS, DRAW YOUR OWN SAND CASTLE.

285

286

WHICH ONE DOESN'T BELONG?

CAN YOU FIND THE NAMES OF TWENTY POPULAR BIRDS IN THIS WORDSEARCH? DRAW YOUR FAVORITE BELOW.

M	O	C	K	I	N	G	B	I	R	D	P	H	J	D
C	H	I	C	K	A	D	E	E	S	C	Z	R		
I	N	E	C	T	Y	H	L	F	O	K	E		F	
G	E	E	P	R	O	U	V	E	R					
E	C	T		Y	F	D	W	O						
O	O	U	S	O	P	O	R	O	W				E	
N	S	U	E	R	O	M	A	E	W				J	
L	R	W	A	T	O	M	M	E	G	D	A		A	Y
R	E	Y	G	L	O	K	W	O	U	D			Q	
C	C	Y	B				C	A			V		R	A
K	K	H	L			S	U	J			N		B	N
E	E	R	L	Y	L	R	H	O	A	D	G		N	P
E		A	Y	N		A	U	J	S	B	Y	K	E	N
H	A	W	K		P		L	A	R	K		N	G	Z	K
Y	U	L	U	R	E	F	M		N		S	X	P	U

YOU CAN DO IT!

BE CREATIVE!

WHAT SONG IS IT SINGING? WRITE IT DOWN.

286

287

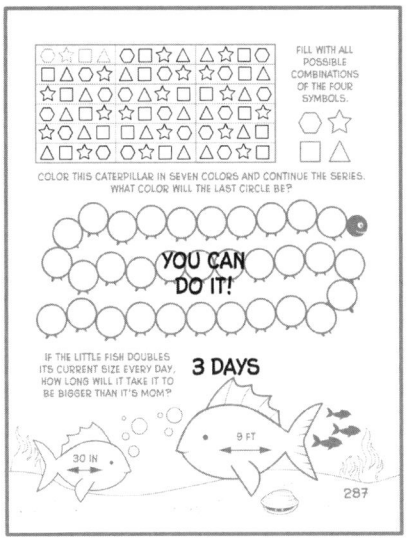

288

289

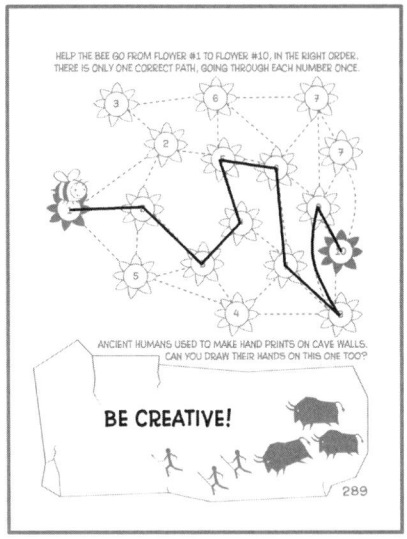

290

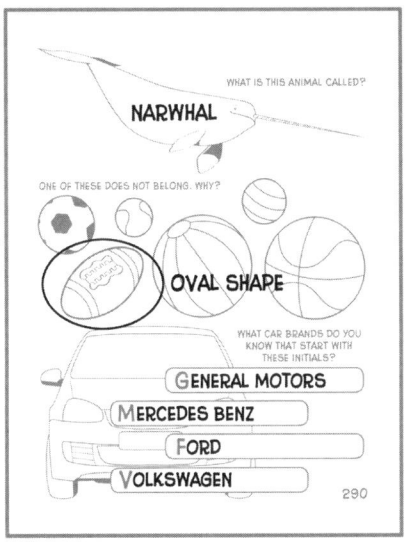

291

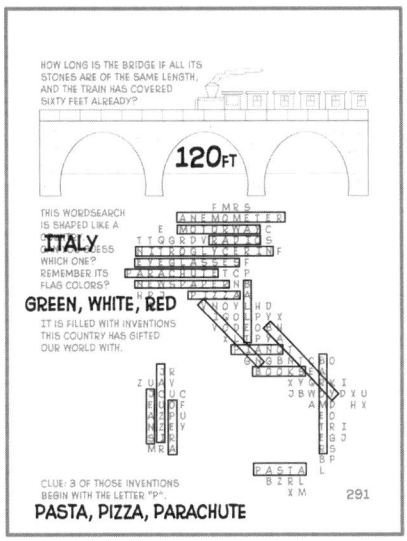

292

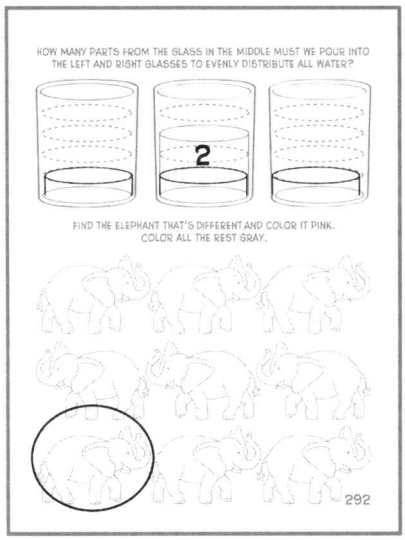

293

294

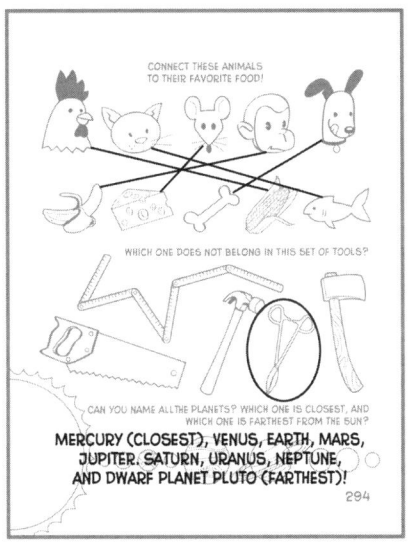

295

296

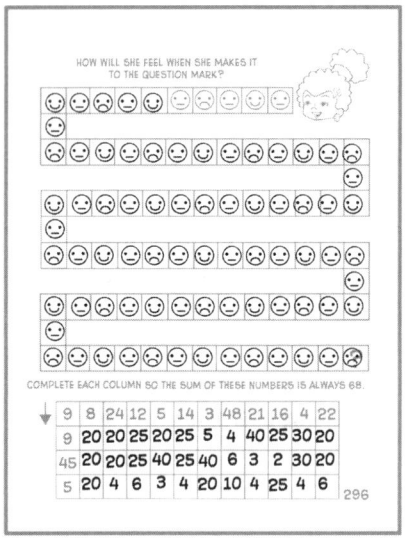

297

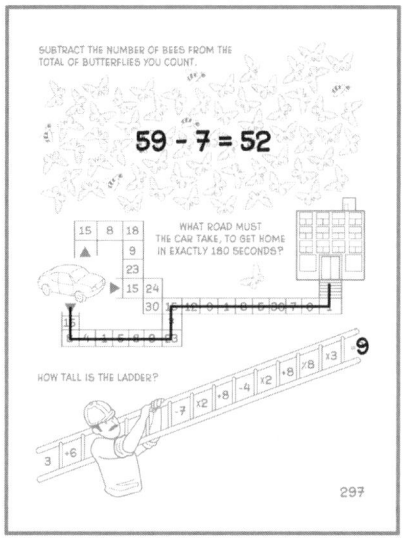

298

299

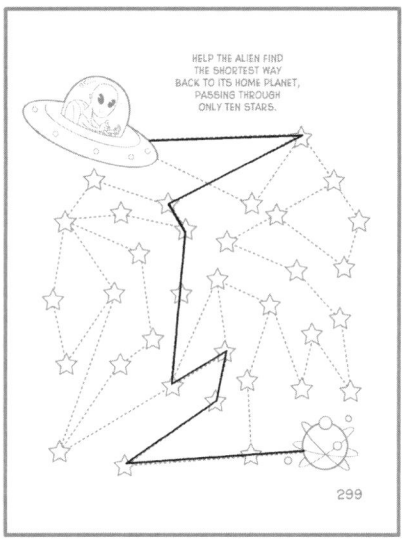

300

302

303

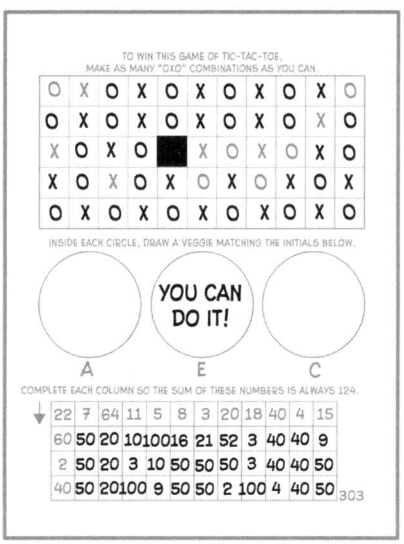

304

305

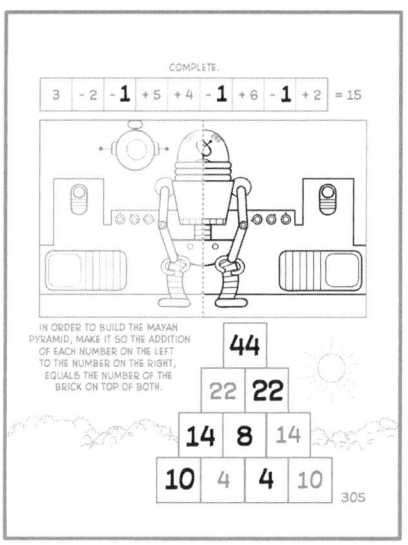

306

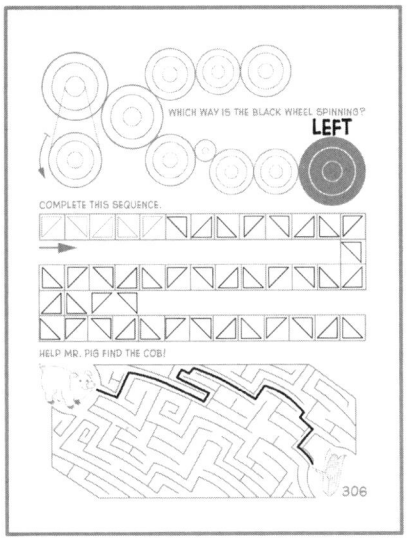

307

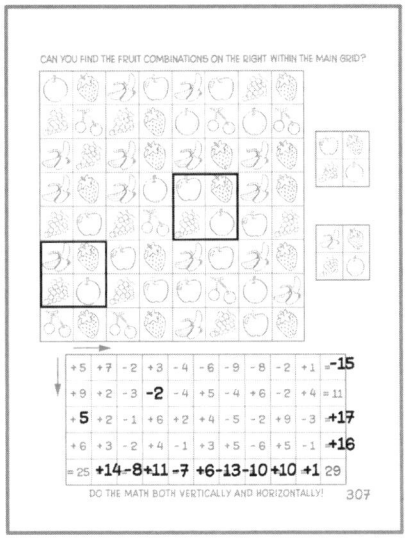

308

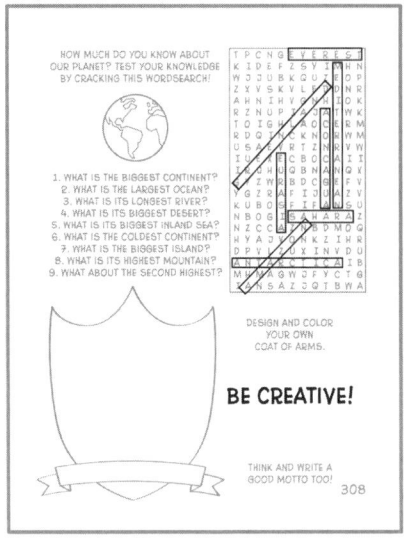

309

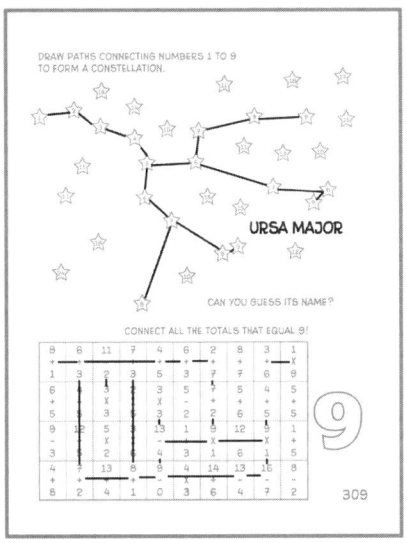

310

311

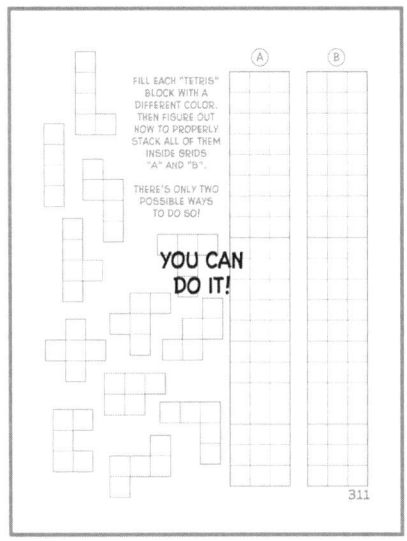

312

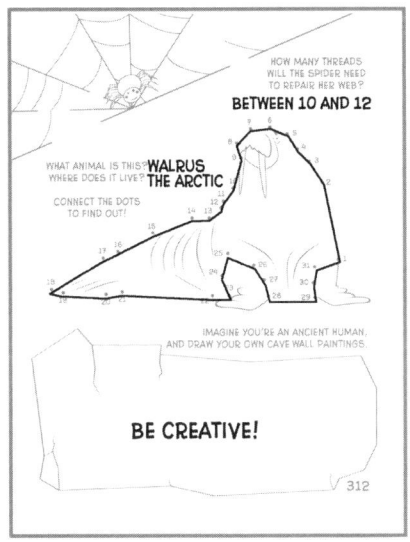

313

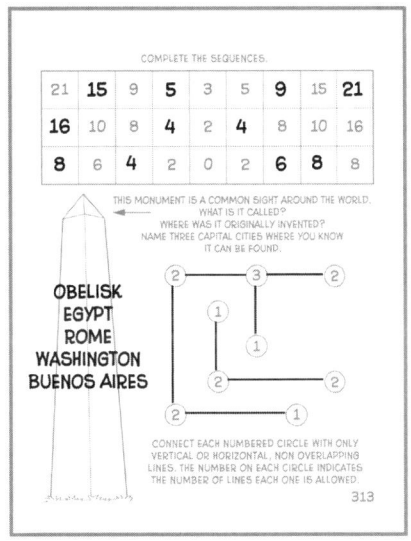

314

315

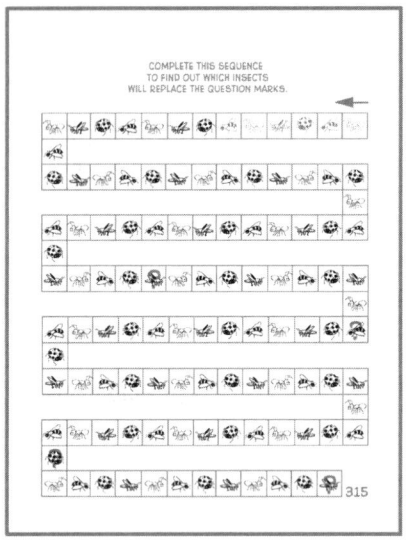

316

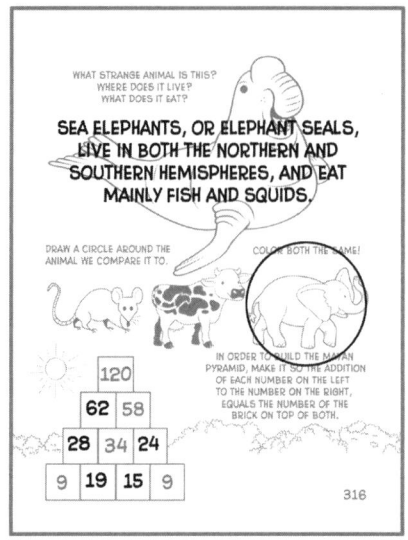

317

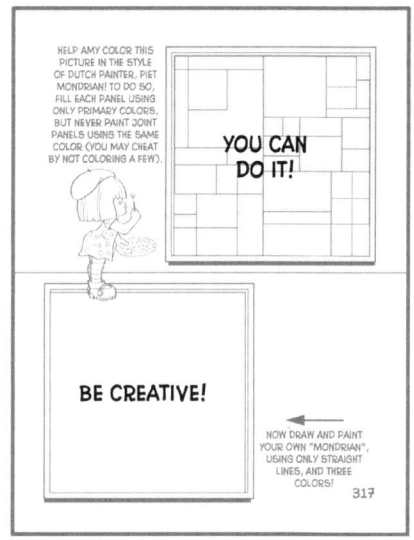

318

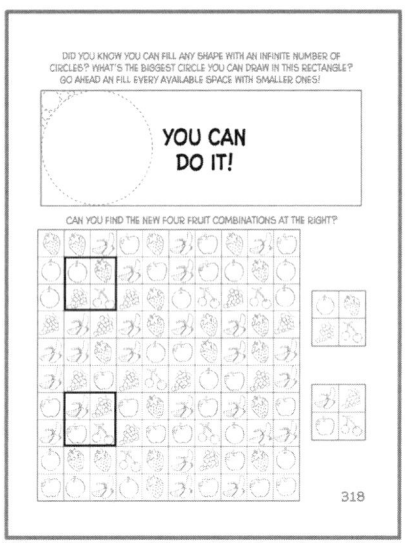

319

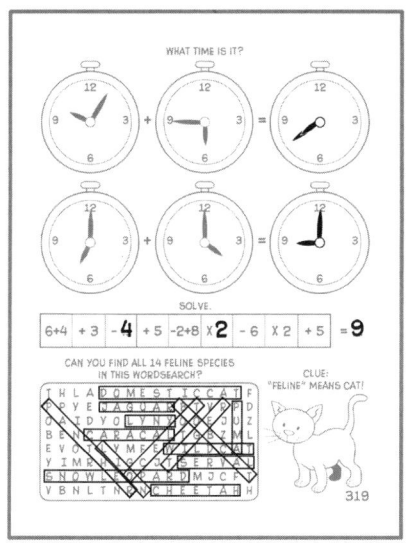

320

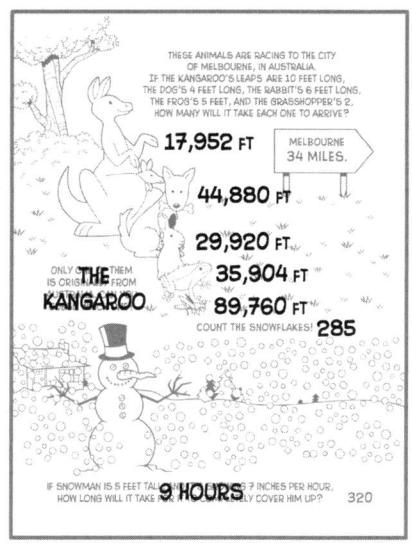

321

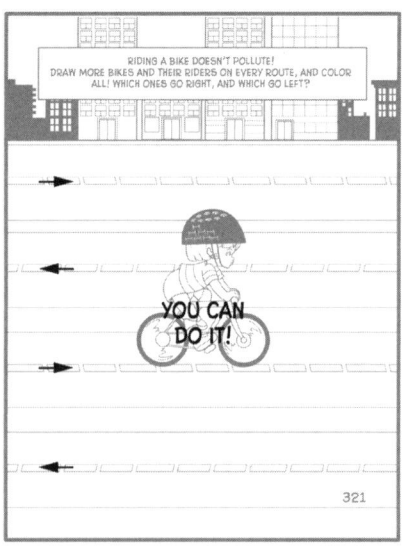

322

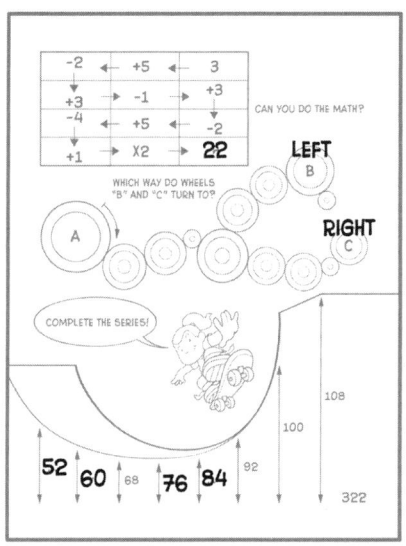

323

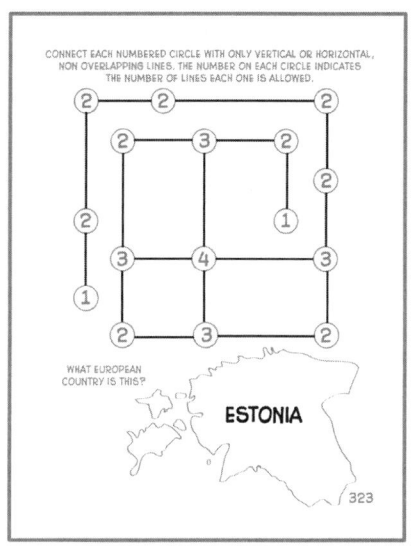

324

YOU CAN DO IT!

FILL EVERY AVAILABLE ROOM IN THIS TRIANGLE WITH CIRCLES OF EVERY SIZE!

CONNECT THE IDENTICAL DRAWINGS USING ONLY VERTICAL AND HORIZONTAL LINES. LINES CANNOT CROSS EACH OTHER, AND ONLY ONE LINE IS ALLOWED TO GO THROUGH EACH TILE.

324

325

COMPLETE THIS TABLE WITH + AND − SIGNS.

3	+	5	+	2	+	5	+	6	+	9	=	30
8	+	3	−	6	−	5	+	2	+	1	=	3
4	+	5	+	9	+	6	+	8	−	7	=	25
6	+	3	−	5	+	9	−	8	+	2	=	7

FILL EACH EMPTY CIRCLE SO THE SUM OF EACH LINE IS ALWAYS 10.

THESE ARE CALLED "MOAI". THEY COME FROM EASTER ISLAND OR "RAPA NUI".

WHERE ARE THESE ANCIENT STATUES FROM? WHAT ARE THEY CALLED?

325

326

SOLVE.

8-3	+	3	−	2	X	2	−	6	X	2	+	12	/	2	X	5	=	60

TO FIGURE OUT WHAT THE MYSTERY PICTURE IS, FILL EACH NUMBERED AREA AS INSTRUCTED.

1 KETTLE AND 3 TEACUPS

= 1
= 2
= 3
= 4
= 5
= 6
= 7
= 8

326

327

OLLIE IS A VEGETARIAN: DRAW A CIRCLE AROUND THE FOOD HE CAN EAT, AND COLOR IT.

WHAT IS THE NAME OF THIS ANIMAL? IS IT A FISH? WHERE DOES IT LIVE? WHAT DOES IT EAT?

AN ORCA. MAMMAL. LIVES IN THE SEA. EATS MEAT.

YOU CAN DO IT!

DRAW ANOTHER TYPE OF WHALE YOU LIKE!

327

328

CONTINUE THE PROGRESSION OF SYMBOLS FROM LEFT TO RIGHT, BUT AVOID THIS SIGN →

CAN YOU FIND ALL 14 MARINE MAMMALS IN THIS WORDSEARCH?

CLUE: GO BACK TO THE PREVIOUS PAGE TO FIND ONE OF THEM!

328

329

EARTH HAS ONE MOON, MARS HAS TWO. DO YOU KNOW THEIR NAMES?

PHOBOS AND DEIMOS.

WHICH ONE OF THESE LIVES HERE? →

8	7	4	3
9	6	5	2
10	13	14	1
11	12	15	16

FILL THE MISSING NUMBERS FROM 1 TO 16, IN ORDER TO KEEP MOVING FROM LEFT TO RIGHT, UP OR DOWN, PANEL BY PANEL, WITHOUT REPEATING ANY NUMBERS, NOR SKIPPING ANY PANELS.

329

330

HELP MR. MOLE REACH THE SURFACE!

SUMMER FALL WINTER SPRING

YOU CAN DO IT!

WHAT IS LIGHTNING MADE OF?

ELECTRICITY

COLOR EACH OF THE LEAVES ACCORDING TO THE SEASONS LISTED ABOVE THEM.

RIDDLE:

A SHOE.

"RUNS OVER FIELDS AND WOODS ALL DAY. UNDER THE BED AT NIGHT, IT SITS NOT ALONE, WITH A LONG TONGUE HANGING OUT, WAITING FOR A BONE."

330

331

DESIGN BOTH SIDES

BE CREATIVE!

REMEMBER: ONE SIDE MUST FEATURE YOUR PORTRAIT, AND THE OTHER, THE VALUE OF THE COIN.

CONNECT THE IDENTICAL DRAWINGS USING ONLY VERTICAL AND HORIZONTAL LINES. LINES CANNOT CROSS EACH OTHER, AND ONLY ONE LINE IS ALLOWED TO GO THROUGH EACH TILE.

331

332

FIND THE TWO FRUIT COMBINATIONS THAT ARE ALIKE.

WHICH ONE WEIGHS MORE?

12 60 X 3

7 - 20 0

332

333

334

335

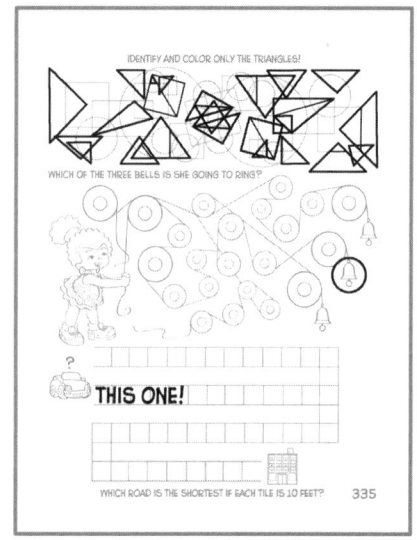

336

337

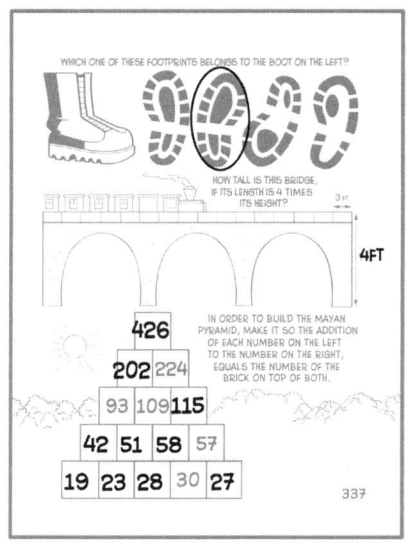

338

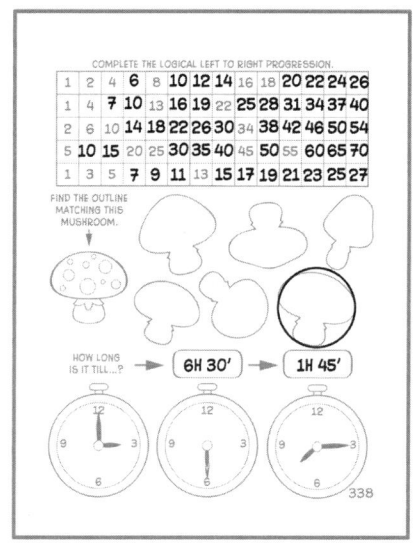

339

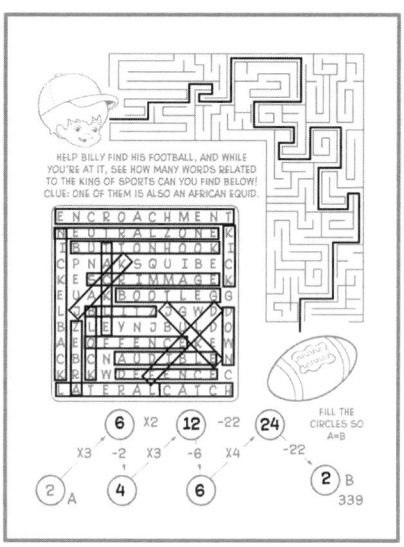

340

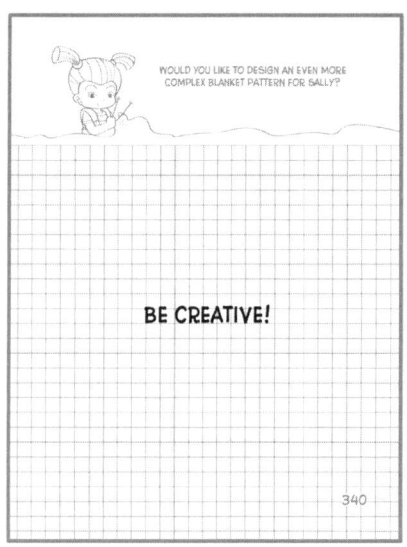

341

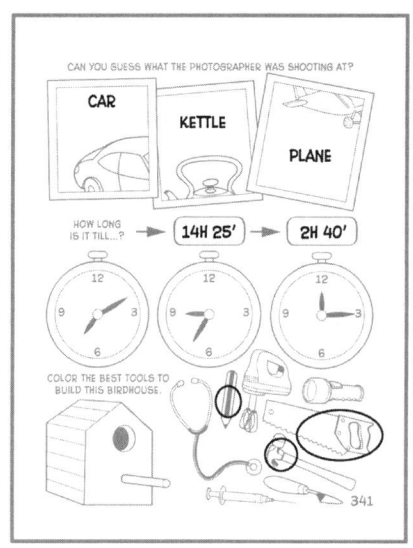

342

FILL THE MISSING NUMBERS FROM 1 TO 25, IN ORDER TO KEEP MOVING FROM LEFT TO RIGHT, UP OR DOWN, PANEL BY PANEL, WITHOUT REPEATING ANY NUMBERS, NOR SKIPPING ANY PANELS.

8	9	12	13	14	15
7	10	11	18	17	16
6	5	20	19	32	33
3	4	21	22	31	34
2	25	24	23	30	35
1	26	27	28	29	36

DRAW THEIR HEADS!

YOU CAN DO THIS!

342

343

WHAT IS THE NAME OF THIS ANIMAL?

HIPPOPOTAMUS

WHERE DOES IT LIVE?

AFRICA

COLOR THE BEST TOOLS TO BAKE THIS CAKE.

WHO USED TO WEAR THESE ANCIENT HELMETS?

SPARTAN

ROMAN

VIKING

343

344

WHICH ONE WEIGHS LESS?

6X51-9

25+52+2

DRAW OR WRITE THE RESULT.

GRATED CHEESE

HELP THE BEE GET TO THE HONEY!

HONEY

344

345

HELP THE LITTLE EXPLORER ESCAPE FROM THE CAVE!

345

346

INSIDE EACH CIRCLE, DRAW A FRUIT MATCHING THE INITIALS BELOW.

YOU CAN DO THIS!

C B P

WHICH WAY IS THIS WHEEL TURNING?

LEFT

CROSSWORDS.

1 P I S T A C H I O

2 A L M O N D

3 H A Z E L N U T

4 C A S H E W

5 W A L N U T

346

347

FIND THE TWO FRUIT COMBINATIONS THAT ARE ALIKE.

WHAT SHOULDN'T BE HERE?

347

348

WHAT ANIMALS IS THIS STRANGE CREATURE MADE OF?

TIGER
ANTEATER
HIPPOPOTAMUS

DRAW PATHS CONNECTING NUMBERS 1 TO 11 TO FORM A CONSTELLATION.

ORION

CAN YOU GUESS ITS NAME? 348

349

AT 20 MPH, THE BOAT HAS SAILED 1/4 OF THE DISTANCE TO THE TINY ISLAND IN 12 MINUTES. WHAT'S THE TOTAL DISTANCE?

16MI

CONNECT EACH NUMBERED CIRCLE WITH ONLY VERTICAL OR HORIZONTAL, NON OVERLAPPING LINES. THE NUMBER ON EACH CIRCLE INDICATES THE NUMBER OF LINES EACH ONE IS ALLOWED.

349

350

DRAW A VIKING, A COWBOY, AND A SPARTAN WARRIOR!

BE CREATIVE!

CAN YOU GUESS WHAT THE PHOTOGRAPHER WAS SHOOTING AT?

BICYCLE

OCTOPUS

SKATEBOARD

350

351

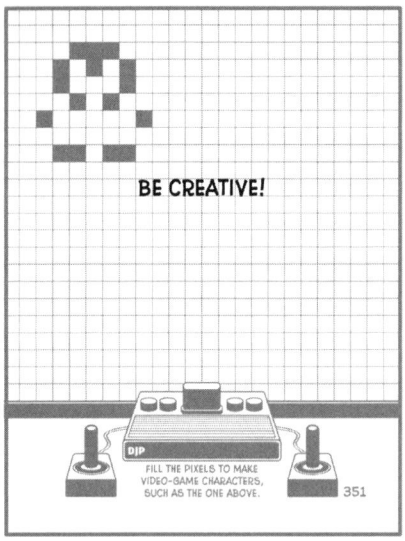

352

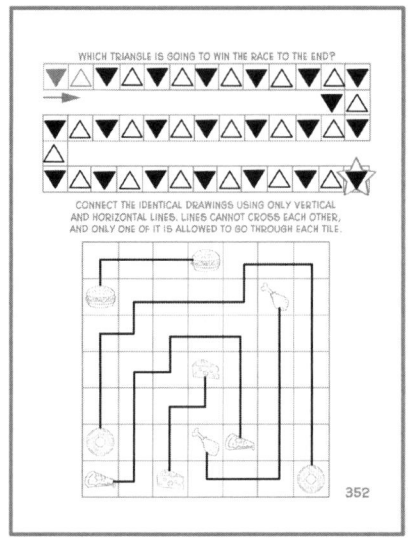

353

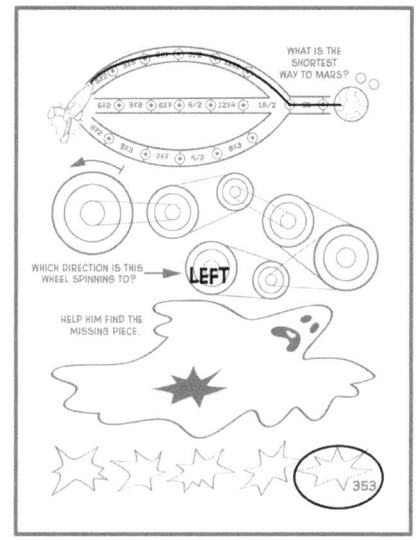

354

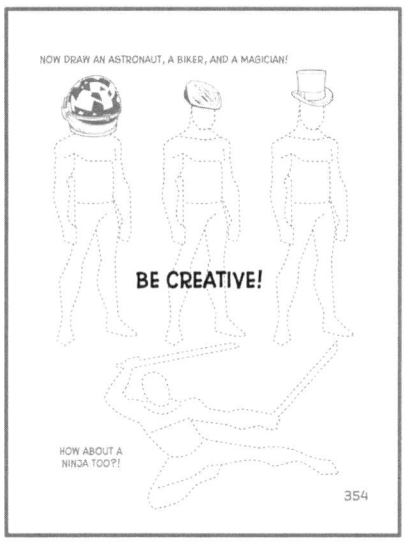

355

356

357

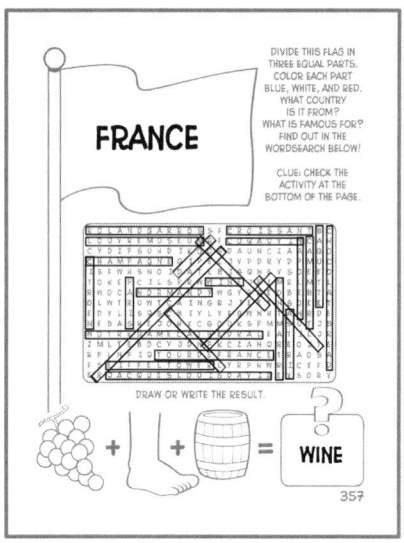

358

359

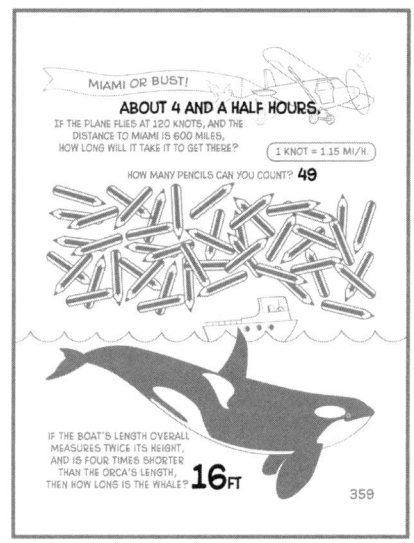

360

SOLVE.

12-3	+ 6	- 5	X 7	- 14	X 5	+ 5	/ 3	X 8	= 760

CONNECT EACH NUMBERED CIRCLE WITH ONLY VERTICAL OR HORIZONTAL, NON OVERLAPPING LINES. THE NUMBER ON EACH CIRCLE INDICATES THE NUMBER OF LINES EACH ONE IS ALLOWED.

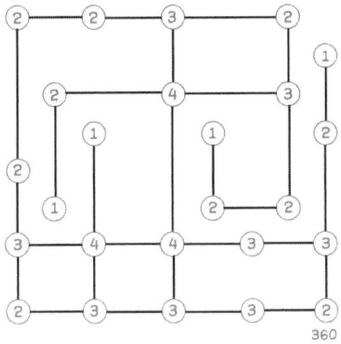

360

361

HOW MANY CIRCLES ARE IN THIS TABLE?
HOW MANY STARS? AND SQUARES?

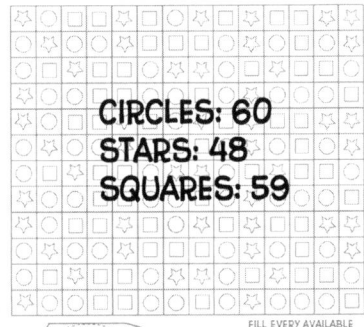

CIRCLES: 60
STARS: 48
SQUARES: 59

FILL EVERY AVAILABLE SPACE IN THIS SHAPE WITH CIRCLES OF EVERY SIZE!

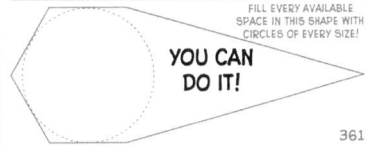

YOU CAN DO IT!

361

362

WHAT DIRECTION IS 7 TURNING TOWARD?

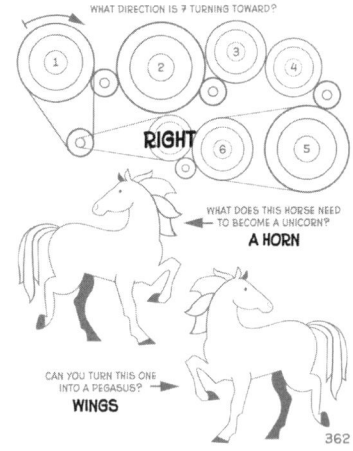

RIGHT

WHAT DOES THIS HORSE NEED TO BECOME A UNICORN?

A HORN

CAN YOU TURN THIS ONE INTO A PEGASUS?

WINGS

362

363

BE CREATIVE!

NOW CREATE MORE COMPLEX VIDEO-GAME CHARACTERS, SUCH AS THE ONE ABOVE.

363

364

CAN YOU FIND THE MISSING SYMBOL IN THIS ANCIENT EGYPTIAN PYRAMID? .

CAN YOU ALTERNATE FULL AND EMPTY SAND BUCKETS, [illegible]

ALL YOU NEED TO DO IS POUR THE SAND FROM BUCKET #2 INSIDE BUCKET #5.

WHERE DOES COTTON COME FROM? A PLANT

NAME THREE CLOTHING ITEMS MADE OF COTTON.

JEANS

TSHIRTS

SOCKS

364

365

HOW CAN THIS SHEET BE SPLIT, SO EACH OF THE KIDS GETS A PIECE OF THE SAME SIZE AND SHAPE?

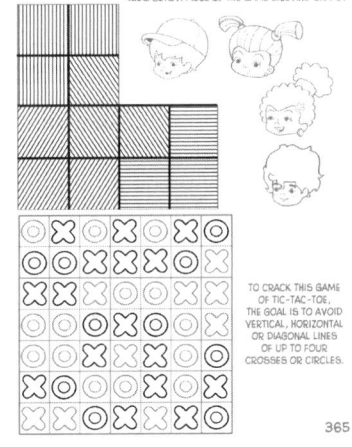

TO CRACK THIS GAME OF TIC-TAC-TOE, THE GOAL IS TO AVOID VERTICAL, HORIZONTAL OR DIAGONAL LINES OF UP TO FOUR CROSSES OR CIRCLES.

365

366

YOUR GRANDMOTHER GIVES YOU [illegible] CHANCE IN TWO [illegible] ONE OF THE BILLS IS FIVE DOLLARS. [illegible] OTHER BILL?

THE OTHER BILL IS A 10 DOLLAR BILL.

IN WHICH BOX DO YOU END UP IF YOU FOLLOW THE ARROWS?

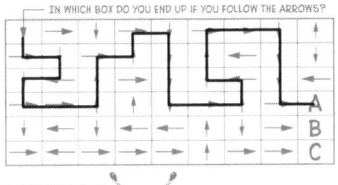

A
B
C

IN THIS CLASSIC GAME, CAN YOU MAKE THE "BULL" TURN ITS HEAD BY MOVING ONLY TWO MATCHES?

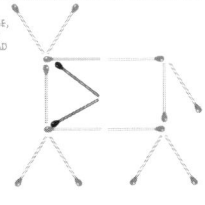

366

367

CONNECT THE IDENTICAL DRAWINGS USING ONLY VERTICAL AND HORIZONTAL LINES. LINES CANNOT CROSS EACH OTHER, AND ONLY ONE LINE IS ALLOWED TO GO THROUGH EACH TILE.

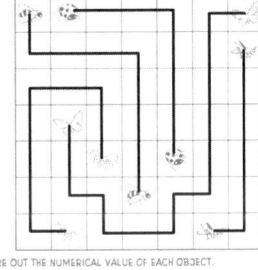

FIGURE OUT THE NUMERICAL VALUE OF EACH OBJECT.

1 + 1 = 2
2 + 3 = 5
2 + 1 = 3
2 + 4 = 6
2 + 2 = 4
3 + 4 = 7

367

368

CONNECT EACH FISH TO ITS CORRESPONDING HOOK!

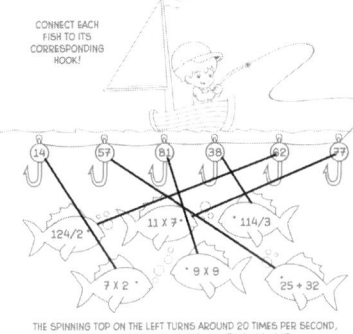

THE SPINNING TOP ON THE LEFT TURNS AROUND 20 TIMES PER SECOND, AND THE ONE ON THE RIGHT TURNS TWICE AS FAST.

HOW MANY TIMES DO THEY TURN IN ONE AND A HALF MINUTES?

368

369

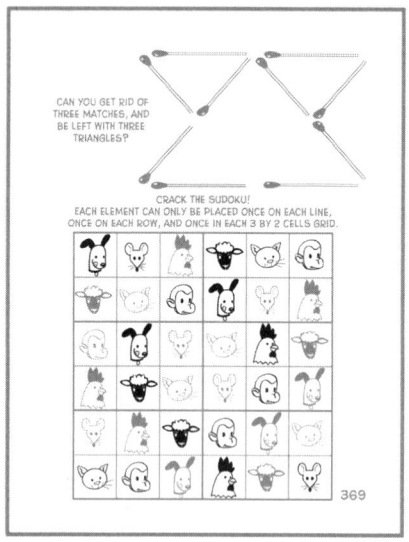

370

371

372

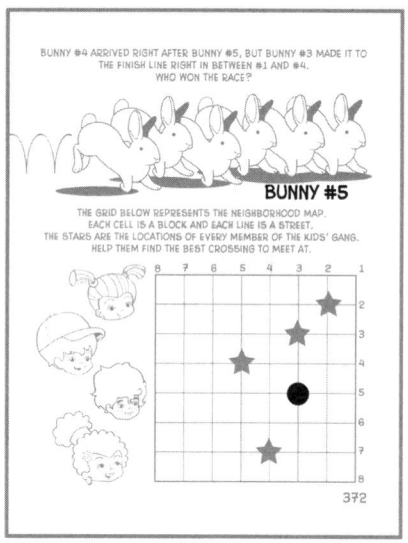

373

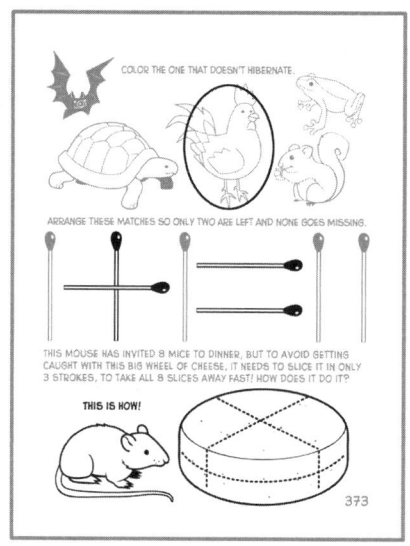

374

375

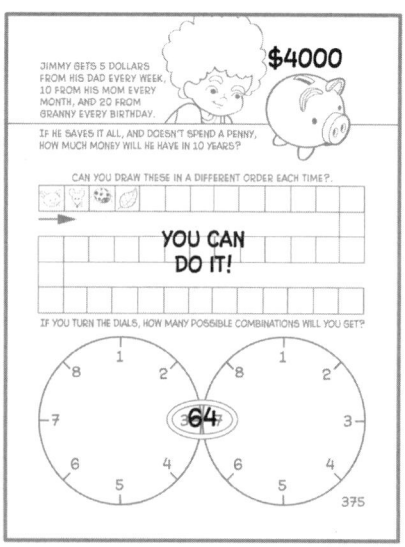

376

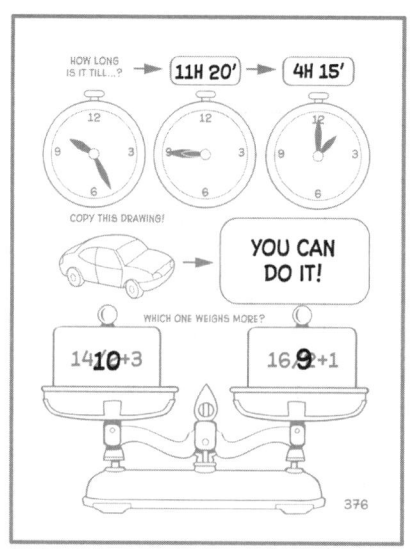

377

378

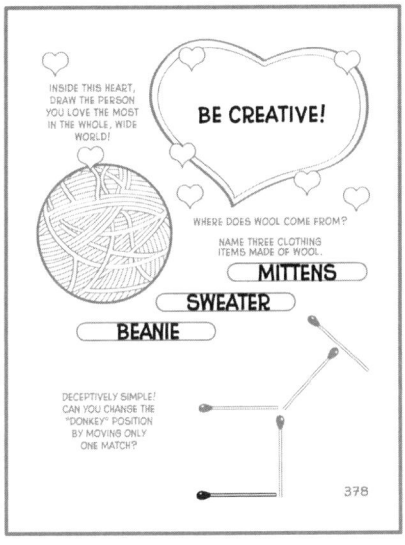

379

380

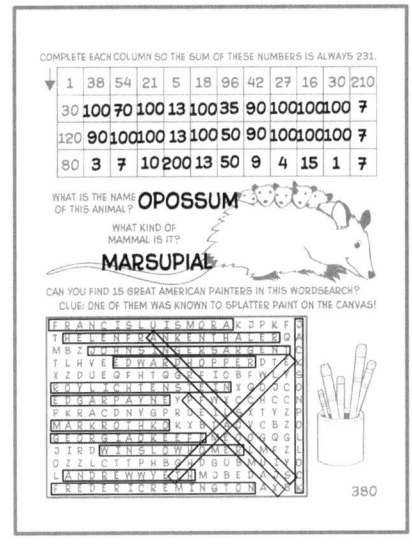

381

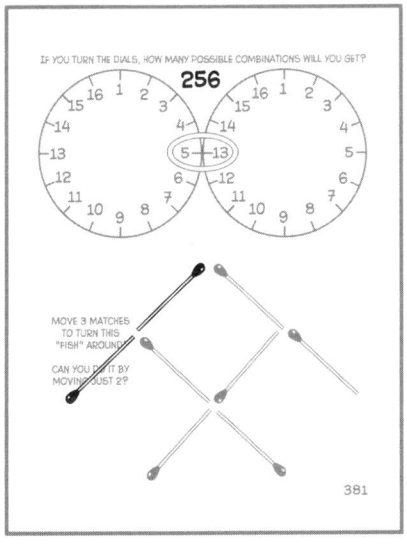

382

383

384

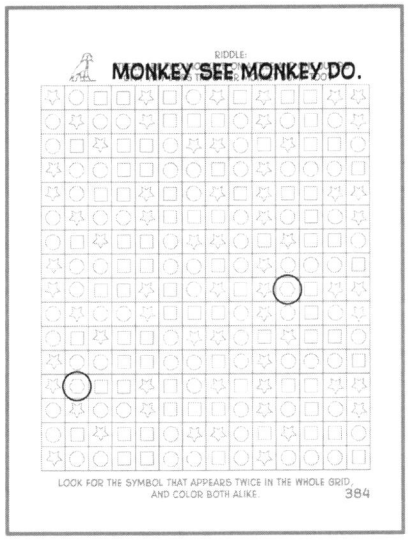

385

386

387

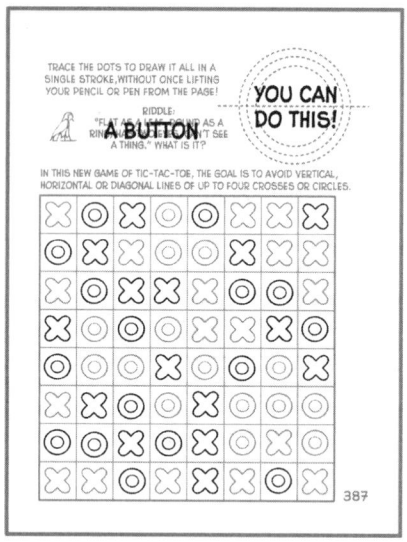

388

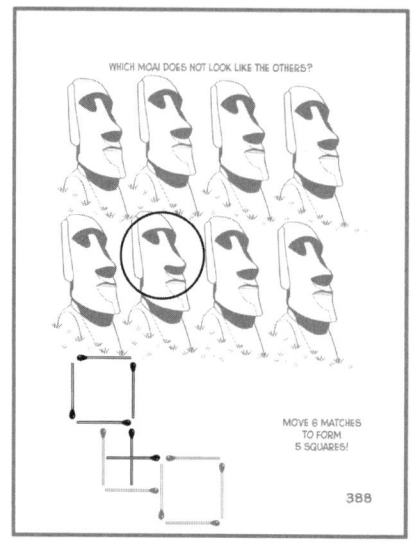

389

390

391

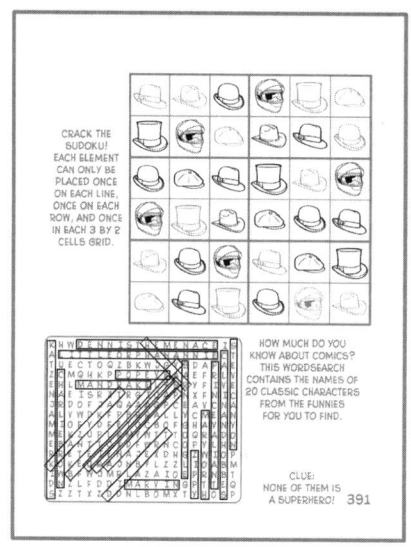

392

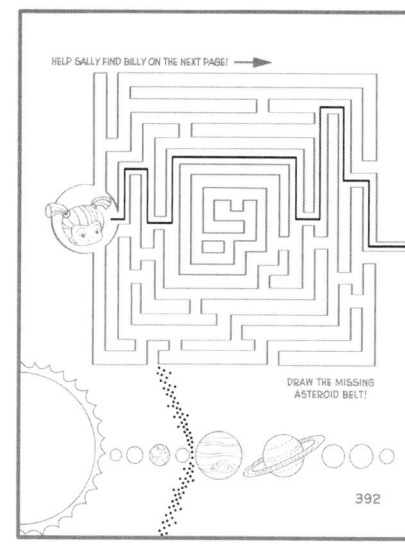

393

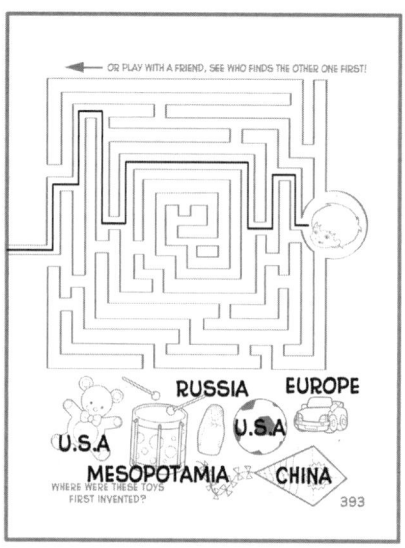

394

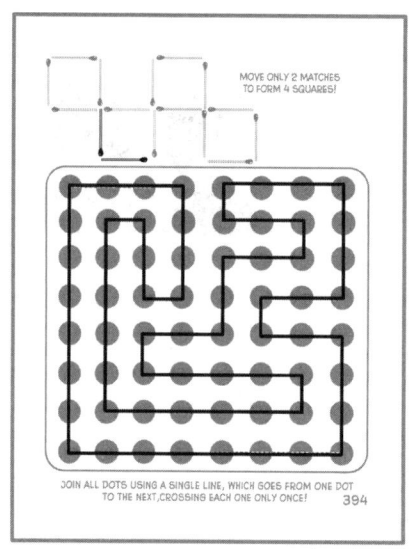

395

396

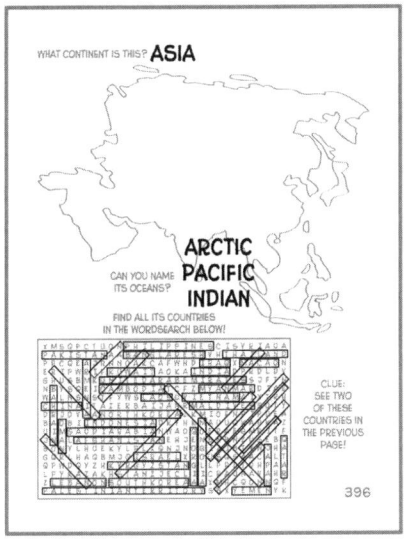

397

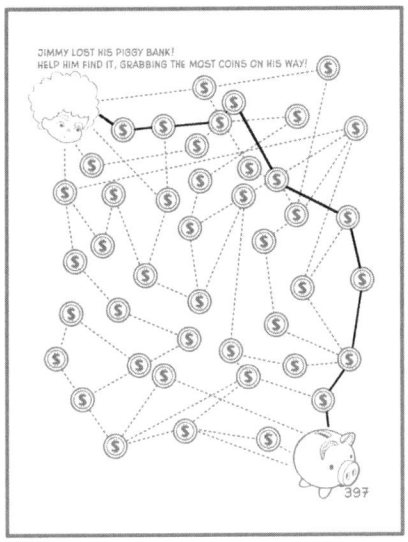

398

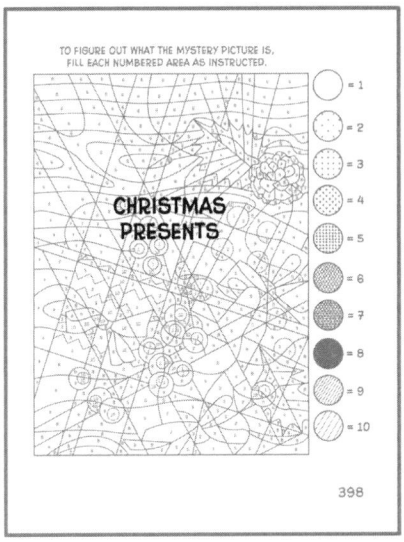

399